Did You Know?

JUMPSTART IS RECRUITING COLLEGE STUDENTS

Jumpstart is a national organization that offers college students serving as AmeriCorps members the opportunity to work one-to-one with children in Head Start or other early learning centers to build the literacy, language, and social skills they need to succeed in school.

THE NEXT STEP FOR JUMPSTART ALUMNI - THE PEARSON TEACHER FELLOWSHIP

Each year, Pearson and Jumpstart select up to 50 Jumpstart Alumni to participate in the **Pearson Teacher Fellowship** program. This fellowship provides the opportunity for Jumpstart Alumni to become full-time teachers in Head Start and other preschools following graduation.

BENEFITS
- A $5,000 stipend per year (in addition to salary)
- Partial or full cancellation of Federal Perkins and Stafford loans
- A professional mentor from the ranks of Pearson's employees
- Assistance with gaining early childhood credentials
- Pre-service training and resource materials
- Opportunity to become a paid Team Leader of Jumpstart Corps members

REQUIREMENTS
- Jumpstart Alumnus who has completed, or is completing, a term of service
- A bachelor's or associate's degree
- Ability to commit to teaching full-time for two years

"Building America's Future
...one child at a time!"

Literacy
for the 21st Century

Teaching Reading and Writing in Pre-Kindergarten Through Grade 4

Gail E. Tompkins
California State University, Fresno

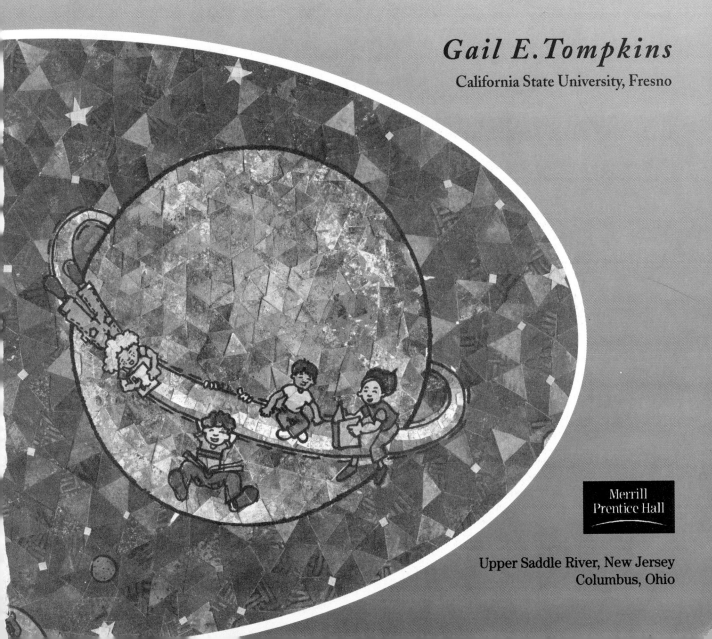

Merrill
Prentice Hall

Upper Saddle River, New Jersey
Columbus, Ohio

Library of Congress Cataloging-in-Publication Data

Tompkins, Gail E.
  Literacy for the 21st century : teaching reading and writing in pre-kindergarten through grade 4 / Gail E. Tompkins.
    p. cm.
  Includes bibliographical references and index.
  ISBN 0-13-098719-0
  1. Language arts (Preschool) 2. Language arts (Elementary) I. Title: Literacy for the twenty-first century. II. Title.

LB1140.5.L3 T66 2003
372.6—dc21   2002033808

Vice President and Publisher: Jeffery W. Johnston
Editor: Linda Ashe Montgomery
Development Editor: Hope Madden
Production Editor: Mary M. Irvin
Design Coordinator: Diane C. Lorenzo
Photo Coordinators: Sandy Schaefer, Cynthia Cassidy
Text Design: Grannan Art and Design
Cover Designer: Linda Sorrells-Smith
Cover Art: Christy Terry
Production Manager: Pamela D. Bennett
Director of Marketing: Ann Castel Davis
Marketing Manager: Krista Groshong
Marketing Services Manager: Tyra Cooper

This book was set in Galliard by Carlisle Communications, Ltd., and was printed and bound by Courier Kendallville, Inc. The cover was printed by The Lehigh Press, Inc.

Photo Credits: Scott Cunningham/Merrill, p. 2; Tony Freeman/PhotoEdit, p. 124; Anthony Magnacca/Merrill, pp. 82, 90, 151, 198; Julie Peters/Merrill, p. 354; David J. Sams/Getty Images Inc., p. 356; Barbara Schwartz/Merrill, p. 162; Gail E. Tompkins, pp. 10, 32, 45, 50, 52, 58, 62, 73, 104, 109, 116, 142, 172, 192, 228, 241, 255, 264, 279, 300, 311, 323, 330; Anne Vega/Merrill, pp. 19, 178, 210, 283, 338, 350; Tom Watson/Merrill, p. 135. **Color insert:** Corbis Digital Stock, 1; Scott Cunningham/Merrill, 3.

Pearson Education Ltd., *London*
Pearson Education Australia Pty. Limited, *Sydney*
Pearson Education Singapore Pte. Ltd.
Pearson Education North Asia Ltd., *Hong Kong*
Pearson Education Canada, Ltd., *Toronto*
Pearson Educación de Mexico, S.A. de C.V.
Pearson Education—Japan, *Tokyo*
Pearson Education Malaysia Pte. Ltd.
Pearson Education, *Upper Saddle River, New Jersey*

10 9 8 7 6 5 4 3
ISBN 0-13-098719-0

With love to my grandson, Jordan

About the Author

Gail E. Tompkins is a Professor at California State University, Fresno, in the Department of Literacy and Early Education, where she teaches courses in reading, language arts, and writing for preservice teachers and students in the reading/language arts master's degree program. She directs the San Joaquin Valley Writing Project and works regularly with teachers, both by teaching model lessons in classrooms and by leading staff development programs. Recently Dr. Tompkins was inducted into the California Reading Association's Reading Hall of Fame in recognition of her publications and other accomplishments in the field of reading. She has also been awarded the prestigious Provost's Award for Excellence in Teaching at California State University, Fresno.

Previously, Dr. Tompkins taught at Miami University in Ohio and at the University of Oklahoma in Norman where she received the prestigious Regents' Award for Superior Teaching. She was also an elementary teacher in Virginia for eight years.

Dr. Tompkins is the author of three books published by Merrill/Prentice Hall: *Teaching Writing: Balancing Process and Product*, 3rd ed. (2000), *50 Literacy Strategies* (1998), and *Language Arts: Content and Teaching Strategies*, 5th ed. (2002). She has written numerous articles related to reading and language arts that have appeared in *The Reading Teacher, Language Arts,* and other professional journals.

Preface

Helping children become literate is one of the greatest challenges facing teachers today. As some teachers and researchers tout and defend one approach after another, parents are frightened that the new instructional methods aren't getting the job done. The media fuels the controversy with reports lamenting low test scores and criticism that many schools are failing to produce literate citizens who can function competently.

I have written this textbook to blaze a pathway toward implementing a thoughtful, balanced approach to teaching reading and writing in the early grades, a pathway that incorporates the most effective teaching approaches and strategies.

Literacy for the 21st Century: Teaching Reading and Writing in Pre-Kindergarten Through Grade 4 builds on the research-based approaches to literacy instruction outlined in *Literacy for the 21st Century*, the most popular reading methods text in the market, but focuses squarely on the issues, concerns, and opportunities involved in teaching children in pre-kindergarten through grade 4.

I created this text for core literacy courses that have been split to meet a growing demand for credentialing teachers with more in-depth knowledge of early literacy strategies, aiming to provide a solid foundation for teaching phonemic awareness, phonics, fluency, vocabulary, and comprehension. This comprehensive text presents sound approaches to literacy instruction and guides teachers toward best practice in teaching skills as well as strategies. The principles of effective reading instruction outlined in Chapter 1 provide a strong, easily understood foundation for the entire book. I have culled and created minilessons and assessment tools geared specifically toward assessing and teaching PreK–4 skills; the authentic classroom activities and student artifacts include spotlights on primary teachers who illustrate how they plan for and engage their students in literacy activities; and PreK margin notes address the specific concerns of this audience of learners.

DRIVING PRINCIPLES

My goal in this text is to show beginning teachers how to teach reading and writing effectively in the early grades, how to create a classroom climate where literacy flourishes, and how to empower the diverse array of young children in today's classrooms to function competently as literate adults in the twenty-first century. To that end, I have based the text on four contemporary theories of literacy learning: constructivist, interactive, socio-linguistic, and reader response theories.

Readers will learn how to implement a reading program with skills and strategies taught in context using a whole-part-whole organizational approach. The approach I take can, I believe, best be described as balanced and comprehensive. You will learn how to teach vital skills and strategies within the context of authentic reading and writing experiences. I have carefully selected the principles, skills, strategies, and examples of literature that will empower the beginning teachers to get up to speed quickly with their young readers. In creating this textbook, I used knowledge I gleaned from a host of teachers who have been students in my beginning reading course over the years, and I also sifted through the array of practices and procedures proven effective in today's classrooms and with today's diverse student populations. Although there are many other useful ideas and strategies that can accomplish the goal of producing literate students, I have deliberately and painstakingly chosen research-based, classroom-tested ideas—the best of the best—as the focus of this textbook.

SPECIAL FEATURES

These special features increase the effectiveness of the text and address the most current resources in the field of literacy.

Instructional Procedures

The easily accessible Compendium of Instructional Procedures following Chapter 12 offers clearly articulated instructional methods, an invaluable resource and quick reference.

Real Classrooms

My texts have always been grounded in real classroom teaching and learning. I want readers to feel as at home in their own classrooms as possible, so I provide as many examples from real classrooms as I can, to model best practice and teacher decision-making.

- **Spotlights** look closely at individual students and teachers, including student artifacts and an analysis of each student's strengths and weaknesses, highlighting individual attention, assessment and evaluation, and the best teaching practices while emphasizing a focus on struggling readers and English language learners.
- Starting with Chapter 2, I begin each chapter with a **vignette** in which you will see how a real teacher teaches the topic addressed in the chapter. These vignettes are rich and detailed, with chapter-opening photos, dialogue, student writing samples, and illustrations. Readers will be drawn into the story of literacy instruction in a real classroom as they build background and activate prior knowledge about the chapter's topic. Throughout the chapter, I refer readers to the vignette so that they can apply the concepts they are reading about and make connections to the world of practice.
- The CD-ROM, the CD margin notes, and the CD insert all provide concrete illustrations of real classroom teaching and connections between chapter content and teaching.

Technology

I have taken an integrated approach to technology in this text, highlighting resources and applications within the text and including technological resources as part of the text package.

CD-ROM: A free CD comes with my text. The CD, *Primary Grades Literacy: A K–3 Integrated Unit on Insects,* contains footage of a master teacher in her early grades reading and writing classroom. You will have the opportunity to observe the classroom footage, hear from the teacher and students involved, listen to my feedback, and consider the research behind the teacher's decisions.

- Margin notes throughout the text serve to link specific chapter content with that of the CD.
- A full-color insert walks you through using the CD to the fullest.

Technology Links: Readers will learn about innovative uses of technology in teaching reading and writing through the **Technology Links.** Among the topics I present in these special features are screen reading using captioned text on television to develop reading fluency and interactive electronic books on CD-ROM to teach high-frequency words and phonics skills.

Companion Website: Providing more ways to use technology effectively as a teaching tool, the Companion Website, available at www.prenhall.com/tompkins, offers opportunities for self-assessment; analysis, synthesis and application of concepts; regularly updated links to web addresses; and special information for teachers required to pass state tests in teaching reading in order to obtain credentials.

- Margin notes throughout the text highlight Internet websites that provide resources that readers might use to extend their learning and read the most up-to-date information about phonics, phonemic awareness, guided reading, interactive writing, fluency, comprehension, literature circles, and other literacy topics. Links to these sites are found on the Companion Website.

English Language Learners

Throughout the text are ELL margin notes specifying which strategies and methods are most appropriate for English language learners and how to adapt teaching to benefit all students.

Pre-kindergarten Learners

PreK margin notes make clear the most appropriate strategies and adaptations for that age range.

Mini-lessons

This feature presents clear information showing how to teach skills and strategies within the PreK–4 reading and writing classrooms.

Assessment

Assessment Resources: These features in Chapter 3 list tests and other assessments that can be used to gauge students' reading level and their progress in learning to read and write.

Assessment Tools: These figures in most chapters provide samples of tools used in classrooms to assess student understanding and learning.

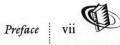

Supplements

Companion Website: This text-specific website featuring chapter overviews, self-assessments, links to sites highlighted in the text, and a threaded message board to promote student dialogue with a national audience, is available at www.prenhall.com/tompkins.

CD–ROM: Containing classroom footage, this free supplement allows users to view, examine, and manipulate clips of PreK–4 literacy classroom teaching, ideal for reflection and developing a deep, lasting understanding of text content.

Video: Free to adopters, the video *Guidelines for Reading Comprehension Instruction* contains footage of Gail Tompkins providing guidance for preservice and inservice literacy teachers.

Instructor's Manual: This useful tool provides additional support for instructors, including test questions and online integration.

ACKNOWLEDGMENTS

Many people helped and encouraged me during the development of this text. My heartfelt thanks go to each of them. First, I want to thank my students at California State University, Fresno, who taught me as I taught them, and to the Teacher Consultants of the San Joaquin Valley Writing Project, who shared their expertise with me. Their insightful questions challenged and broadened my thinking.

Thanks, too, go to the teachers who welcomed me into their classrooms, showed me how they taught reading and writing effectively, and allowed me to learn from them and their students. In particular, I want to express my appreciation to Susan McCloskey, a primary grade teacher at Greenberg Elementary School, Fresno, CA, who appears in the CD-ROM, and to these teachers who are featured in the vignettes: Roberta Dillon, Armona Elementary School, Armona, CA; Whitney Donnelly, Williams Ranch School, Penn Valley, CA; Judy Hoddy, Hennessey School, Grass Valley, CA; Sally Mast, Thomas Elementary School, Fresno, CA; Susan McCloskey, Greenberg Elementary School, Fresno, CA; Kristi McNeal, Copper Hills Elementary School, Clovis, CA; Gay Ockey, Hildago Elementary School, Fresno, CA: Kristi Ohashi, Terry Elementary School, Selma, CA, Judy Roberts, Lincoln Elementary School, Madera, CA;, Darcy Williams, Aynesworth Elementary School, Fresno, CA, and Susan Zumwalt, Jackson Elementary School, Selma, CA.

I appreciate so many other teachers who shared children's writing samples with me and allowed me to take photos in their classrooms, including: Sonja Wiens, Leavenworth Elementary School, Fresno, CA; Kimberly Clark, Aynesworth Elementary School, Fresno, CA, Stephanie Collom, Hildago Elementary School, Fresno, CA; Bob Dickinson, Williams Ranch School, Penn Valley, CA; Carol Ochs, Jackson Elementary School, Norman, OK, Pam Papaleo, Greenberg Elementary School, Fresno, CA; and Judy Reeves and Jenny Reno, Western Hills Elementary School, Lawton, OK.

Thanks to R. Carl Harris, Brigham Young University, for creating such an innovative CD-ROM design and successfully showcasing Susan McCloskey and her expert teaching techniques in the CD-ROM that accompanies this text, and to Helen Hoffner for preparing the Instructor's Manual that supports this text. I want also to thank the reviewers of my manuscript for their comments and insight: Judy A. Abbott, West Virginia University; Sister Regina Alfonso, Notre Dame College, Cleveland, Ohio; Joanne E. Bernstein, Brooklyn College; Jean M. Casey, California State University, Long

Beach; Hollis Lowery-Moore, Sam Houston State University; Carolyn L. Piazza, Florida State University; Thomas C. Potter, California State University, Northridge; Cheryl Rosaen, Michigan State University; Sam Sebesta, University of Washington (retired); and Sharyn Walker, Bowling Green State University.

Finally, I am indebted to Jeff Johnston and his team at Merrill/Prentice Hall in Columbus, Ohio, who produce so many high-quality publications. I am honored to be a Merrill author. Linda Montgomery is the guiding force behind my work, and Hope Madden is my cheerleader, encouraging me every step of the way and spurring me toward impossible deadlines. I want to express my sincere appreciation to Mary Irvin, who has again done a fine job supervising the production of this book, to Melissa Gruzs, who has so expertly copy edited the manuscript, and to Carol Sykes, whose careful attention to detail makes the text look so good. Thank you all.

Discover the Companion Website Accompanying This Book

THE PRENTICE HALL COMPANION WEBSITE: A VIRTUAL LEARNING ENVIRONMENT

Technology is a constantly growing and changing aspect of our field that is creating a need for content and resources. To address this need I have developed an online learning environment for students and professors alike—a Companion Website—to support this textbook.

In creating this Companion Website, my goal was to build on and enhance what the textbook already offers. For this reason, the content for this user-friendly website is organized by chapter and provides the professor and student with a variety of meaningful resources. The features for my Companion Website include:

For the Professor

Every Companion Website integrates **Syllabus Manager**™, an online syllabus creation and management utility.

- **Syllabus Manager**™ provides you, the instructor, with an easy, step-by-step process to create and revise syllabi, with direct links into Companion Website and other online content without having to learn HTML.

- Students may log on to your syllabus during any study session. All they need to know is the web address for the Companion Website and the password you've assigned to your syllabus.

- After you have created a syllabus using **Syllabus Manager**™, students may enter the syllabus for their course section from any point in the Companion Website.

- Clicking on a date, the student is shown the list of activities for the assignment. The activities for each assignment are linked directly to actual content, saving time for students.

- Adding assignments consists of clicking on the desired due date, then filling in the details of the assignment—name of the assignment, instructions, and whether or not it is a one-time or repeating assignment.

- In addition, links to other activities can be created easily. If the activity is online, a URL can be entered in the space provided, and it will be linked automatically in the final syllabus.

- Your completed syllabus is hosted on our servers, allowing convenient updates from any computer on the Internet. Changes you make to your syllabus are immediately available to your students at their next logon.

For the Student

- **Chapter Outlines**—outline key concepts from the text.
- **Interactive Self-Quizzes**—multiple choice and essay quizzes, complete with hints and automatic grading that provide immediate feedback for students. After students submit their answers for the interactive self-quizzes, the Companion Website **Results Reporter** computes a percentage grade, provides a graphic representation of how many questions were answered correctly and incorrectly, and gives a question-by-question analysis of the quiz. Students are given the option to send their quiz to up to four email addresses (professor, teaching assistant, study partner, etc.).
- **Web Destinations**—links to all Internet sites mentioned in my chapters, as well as other meaningful literacy-related sites.
- **Message Board**—serves as a virtual bulletin board to post—or respond to—questions or comments to/from a national audience.
- **Chat**—real-time chat with anyone who is using the text anywhere in the country—ideal for discussion and study groups, class projects, etc.

To take advantage of these and other resources, please visit the LITERACY IN THE 21ST CENTURY Companion Website at

www.prenhall.com/tompkins

Contents

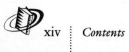

5   *Learning to Spell*   116

6   *Developing Fluent Readers and Writers*   142

10   *Scaffolding Children's Reading Development*   264

11   *Scaffolding Children's Writing Development*   300

12 Integrating Reading and Writing Into Thematic Units

330

Compendium of Instructional Procedures 360

SPECIAL FEATURES

Spotlight on . . .

How Effective Teachers . . .

Technology Link

Assessment Resources

Minilessons

Literacy
for the 21st Century

chapter 1

Becoming an Effective Teacher of Reading

- How do effective teachers teach reading and writing?

- Which instructional practices are most effective for teaching reading and writing?

- How are instruction and assessment linked?

- What is a balanced approach to literacy?

The children of the 21st century will face many challenges that require them to use reading and writing in different forms. As we begin the new millennium, teachers are learning research-based approaches to teach reading and writing that will prepare their children for the future. Teachers make a significant difference in children's lives, and this book is designed to help you become an effective reading teacher. Researchers have examined many teaching practices and have drawn some important conclusions about the most effective ones: We must teach children the processes of reading and writing, as well as how to use reading and writing as learning tools. Bill Teale (1995) challenges us to teach children to think with and through reading and writing, to use reading and writing to get a wide variety of things done in their lives, and to use reading and writing for pleasure and insight.

Let's start with some definitions. "Literacy" used to mean knowing how to read, but the term has been broadened to encompass both reading and writing. Now literacy means the competence "to carry out the complex tasks using reading and writing related to the world of work and to life outside the school" (*Cases in Literacy,* 1989, p. 36). Educators are also identifying other literacies that they believe will be needed in the 21st century (Harris & Hodges, 1995). Our reliance on radio and television for conveying ideas has awakened us to the importance of "oracy," the ability to express and understand spoken language. Visual literacy, the ability to create meaning from illustrations, is also receiving a great deal of attention.

The term "literacy" is being used in other ways as well. For example, teachers are introducing even very young children to computers and developing their "computer literacy." Similarly, math and science educators speak of mathematical and scientific literacies. Hirsch (1987) called for another type of literacy, "cultural literacy," as a way to introduce children "to the major ideas and ideals from past cultures that have defined and shaped today's society" (p. 10). Literacy, however, is not a prescription of certain books to read or concepts to define. Rather, according to Rafferty (1999), literacy is a tool, a way to learn about the world and a means to participate more fully in the technological society of the 21st century.

In this chapter I introduce the eight principles of an effective literacy program in prekindergarten through fourth grade. Each principle is stated in terms of what effective teachers do. Ernest Boyer, in his book *The Basic School* (1995), explains that we really do know what works in elementary schools. From the research that has been conducted in the last 25 years and the effective practices used in good schools today, we can identify the characteristics of a quality literacy program and incorporate them in our own teaching.

PRINCIPLE 1: EFFECTIVE TEACHERS UNDERSTAND HOW CHILDREN LEARN

Understanding how children learn, and particularly how they learn to read, influences the instructional approaches that effective teachers use. A generation ago, behaviorists influenced how teachers taught reading. According to behavioral theory, children learn to read by learning a series of discrete, sequenced skills (Skinner, 1968), and teachers applied this theory by drilling children on skills and having them complete skills worksheets.

Figure 1-1   The Four Learning Theories

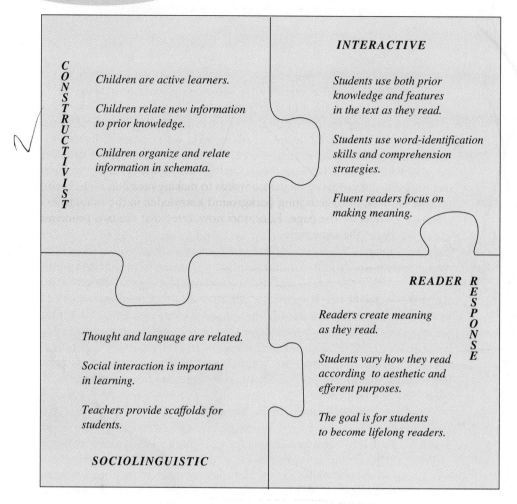

Reading instruction has changed considerably in the past 25 years, thanks to four intertwining theories of learning, language, and literacy: the constructivist, interactive, sociolinguistic, and reader response theories. Figure 1-1 presents an overview of these theories. In the figure, the theories are drawn as though they were parts of a jigsaw puzzle in order to show that they are linked.

Constructivist Learning Theories

Jean Piaget's (1969) theoretical framework differed substantially from behaviorist theories. Piaget described learning as the modification of children's cognitive structures, or schemata, as they interact with and adapt to their environment. Schemata are like mental filing cabinets, and new information is organized with prior knowledge in the filing system. Piaget also posited that children are active and motivated thinkers and learners. This definition of learning and children's role in learning requires a reexamination of the teacher's role: Instead of being simply dispensers of knowledge, teachers engage children with experiences so that they modify their schemata and construct their own knowledge. The key concepts are:

Young children construct their own knowledge about reading as parents and teachers read books to them, they observe parents reading for a variety of purposes, and they have opportunities to explore books.

1. Children are active learners.
2. Children relate new information to prior knowledge.
3. Children organize and integrate information in schemata.

Interactive Learning Theories

The interactive theories describe what readers do as they read. They emphasize that readers focus on comprehension, or making meaning, as they read (Rumelhart, 1977; Stanovich, 1980). Readers construct meaning using a combination of text-based information (information from the text) and reader-based information (information from readers' backgrounds of knowledge, or schemata). These theories echo the importance of schemata described in the constructivist theories. In the past, educators have argued over whether children's attention during reading moves from noticing the letters on the page and grouping them into words to making meaning in the brain, or the other way around, from activating background knowledge in the brain to examining letters and words on the page. Educators now agree that the two processes take place interactively, at the same time.

The interactive model of reading includes an executive function, or decision maker. Fluent readers identify words automatically and use word-identification skills when they come across unfamiliar words so that they can focus their attention on comprehension. The decision maker monitors the reading process and the skills and strategies that readers use. Teachers focus on reading as a comprehension process and teach both word-identification skills and comprehension strategies. The key concepts are:

1. Children use both their prior knowledge and features in the text as they read.
2. Children use word-identification skills and comprehension strategies to understand what they read.
3. Teachers help children become fluent readers.

Sociolinguistic Learning Theories

The sociolinguists contribute a cultural dimension to our consideration of how children learn. They view reading and writing as social activities that reflect the culture and community in which children live (Heath, 1983; Vygotsky, 1978, 1986). According to Lev Vygotsky, language helps to organize thought, and children use language to learn as well as to communicate and share experiences with others. Understanding that children use language for social purposes allows teachers to plan instructional activities that incorporate a social component, such as having children talk about books they are reading or share their writing with classmates. And, because children's language and concepts of literacy reflect their cultures and home communities, teachers must respect children's language and appreciate cultural differences in their attitudes toward learning and becoming literate.

Social interaction enhances learning in two other ways: scaffolding and the zone of proximal development (Dixon-Krauss, 1996). Scaffolding is a support mechanism that teachers and parents use to assist children. Vygotsky suggests that children can accomplish more difficult tasks in collaboration with adults than they can on their own. For example, when teachers assist children in reading a book they could not read independently or help children revise a piece of writing, they are scaffolding. Vygotsky also suggests that children learn very little when they perform tasks that they can already do independently. He recommends the zone of proximal development, the range of tasks between children's actual developmental level and their potential development. More challenging tasks done with the teacher's scaffolding are more conducive to learning. As children learn, teachers gradually withdraw their support so that eventually children perform the task independently. Then the cycle begins again. The key concepts are:

1. Thought and language are interrelated.
2. Social interaction is important in learning.
3. Teachers provide scaffolds for children.
4. Teachers plan instruction based on children's zone of proximal development.

Reader Response Learning Theories

Louise Rosenblatt (1978, 1983) and other reader response theorists consider how children create meaning as they read. Their theories extend the constructivist theories about schemata and making meaning in the brain, not the eyes. According to reader response theorists, children do not try to figure out the author's meaning as they read. Instead, they negotiate or create a meaning that makes sense based on the words they are reading and their own background knowledge. Reader response theorists agree with Piaget that readers are active and responsible for their learning.

Rosenblatt (1991) explains that there are two stances or purposes for reading. When readers read for enjoyment or pleasure, they assume an aesthetic stance, and when they read to locate and remember information, they read efferently. Rosenblatt suggests that these two stances represent the ends of a continuum and that readers often use a combination of the two stances when they read, whether they are reading stories or informational books. For example, when children read *Nature's Green Umbrella* (Gibbons, 1994), an informational book about tropical rain forests, they may read efferently to locate information about the animals that live in rain forests. Or they may read aesthetically, carried off—in their minds, at least—on an expedition to the Amazon River. When children read a novel such as *Sarah, Plain and Tall* (MacLachlan, 1985), a story about a mail-order bride, they usually read aesthetically as they relive life on the prairie a century ago. Children are encouraged to step into the story and become a character and to "live" the story. This conflicts with more traditional approaches in which teachers ask children to recall specific information from the story, thus forcing children to read efferently, to take away information. Reader response theory suggests that when children read efferently rather than aesthetically, they do not learn to love reading and may not become lifelong readers. The key concepts are:

1. Readers create meaning as they read.
2. Children vary how they read depending on whether they are reading for aesthetic or efferent purposes.
3. The goal of literacy instruction is for children to become lifelong readers.

PRINCIPLE 2: EFFECTIVE TEACHERS SUPPORT CHILDREN'S USE OF THE FOUR CUEING SYSTEMS

Language is a complex system for creating meaning through socially shared conventions (Halliday, 1978). English, like other languages, involves four cueing systems:

- the phonological or sound system
- the syntactic or structural system

- the semantic or meaning system
- the pragmatic or social and cultural use system

Together these four systems make communication possible, and children and adults use all four systems simultaneously as they read, write, listen, and talk. The priority people place on each cueing system can vary; however, the phonological system is especially important for beginning readers and writers as they apply phonics skills to decode and spell words. Information about the four cueing systems is summarized in Figure 1-2.

The Phonological System

There are approximately 44 speech sounds in English. Children learn to pronounce these sounds as they learn to talk, and they learn to associate the sounds with letters as they learn to read and write. Sounds are called phonemes, and they are represented in print with diagonal lines to differentiate them from graphemes (letters or letter combinations). Thus, the first grapheme in *mother* is *m,* and the phoneme is /m/. The phoneme in *soap* that is represented by the grapheme *oa* is called "long o" and is written /ō/.

The phonological system is important for both oral and written language. Regional and cultural differences exist in the way people pronounce phonemes. For example, people from Massachusetts pronounce sounds differently from people from Georgia. Similarly, the English spoken in Australia is different from American English. Children who are learning English as a second language must learn to pronounce English sounds, and sounds that are different from those in their native language are particularly difficult to learn. For example, Spanish does not have /th/, and children who have immigrated to the United States from Mexico and other Spanish-speaking countries have difficulty pronouncing this sound. They often substitute /d/ for /th/ because the sounds are articulated in similar ways (Nathenson-Mejia, 1989). Younger children usually learn to pronounce the difficult sounds more easily than older children and adults.

The phonological system plays a crucial role in reading instruction during the primary grades (and it is often referred to as the *visual* system in early literacy programs). Children use their knowledge of phonics as they learn to read and write. In a purely phonetic language, there would be a one-to-one correspondence between letters and sounds, and teaching children to sound out words would be a simple process. But English is not a purely phonetic language because there are 26 letters and 44 sounds and many ways to combine the letters to spell some of the sounds, especially vowels. Consider these ways to spell long *e: sea, green, Pete, me,* and *people.* And sometimes the patterns used to spell long *e* don't work, as in *head* and *great.* Phonics, which describes the phoneme-grapheme correspondences and related spelling rules, is an important part of reading instruction. Children use phonics information to decode words, but phonics instruction is not a complete reading program because many common words cannot be decoded easily and because good readers do much more than just decode words when they read.

Children in the primary grades also use their understanding of the phonological system to create invented spellings. First graders, for example, might spell *home* as *hom,* and second graders might spell *school* as *skule,* based on their knowledge of phoneme-grapheme relationships and the English spelling patterns. As children learn more phonics and gain more experience reading and writing, their spellings become more conventional. For children who are learning English as a second language, their spellings often reflect their pronunciations of words (Nathenson-Mejia, 1989).

Figure 1-2   Relationships Among the Four Cueing Systems

Type	Terms	Uses in the Primary Grades
Phonological System The sound system of English with approximately 44 sounds and more than 500 ways to spell the 44 sounds	• Phoneme (the smallest unit of sound) • Grapheme (the written representation of a phoneme using one or more letters) • Phonemic awareness (understanding that speech is composed of individual sounds) • Phonics (teaching sound-symbol correspondences and spelling rules)	• Pronouncing words • Decoding words when reading • Using invented spelling • Reading and writing alliterations and onomatopoeia • Noticing rhyming words • Dividing words into syllables
Syntactic System The structural system of English that governs how words are combined into sentences	• Syntax (the structure or grammar of a sentence) • Morpheme (the smallest meaningful unit of language) • Free morpheme (a morpheme that can stand alone as a word) • Bound morpheme (a morpheme that must be attached to a free morpheme)	• Adding inflectional endings to words • Combining words to form compound words • Adding prefixes and suffixes to root words • Using capitalization and punctuation to indicate beginnings and ends of sentences • Writing simple, compound, and complex sentences • Combining sentences
Semantic System The meaning system of English that focuses on vocabulary	• Semantics (meaning)	• Learning the meanings of words • Discovering that some words have multiple meanings • Using context clues to figure out an unfamiliar word • Studying synonyms, antonyms, and homonyms • Using a dictionary and thesaurus • Reading and writing comparisons (metaphors and similes)
Pragmatic System The system of English that varies language according to social and cultural uses	• Function (the purpose for which a person uses language) • Standard English (the form of English used in textbooks and by television newscasters) • Nonstandard English (other forms of English)	• Varying language to fit specific purposes • Reading and writing dialogue in dialects • Comparing standard and nonstandard forms of English

The Syntactic System

The syntactic system is the structural organization of English. This system is the grammar that regulates how words are combined into sentences. The word *grammar* here means the rules governing how words are combined in sentences, not parts of speech. Children use the syntactic system as they combine words to form sentences. Word order is important in English, and English speakers must arrange words into a sequence that makes sense. Young Spanish-speaking children who are learning English as a second language, for example, learn to say "This is my red sweater," not "This is my sweater red," which is the literal translation from Spanish.

Children use their knowledge of the syntactic system as they read. They expect that the words they are reading have been strung together into sentences. When they come to an unfamiliar word, they recognize its role in the sentence even if they don't know the terms for parts of speech. In the sentence "The horses galloped through the gate and out into the field," children may not be able to decode the word *through,* but they can easily substitute a reasonable word or phrase, such as *out of* or *past.*

Many of the capitalization and punctuation rules that elementary children learn reflect the syntactic system of language. Similarly, when children learn about simple, compound, and complex sentences, they are learning about the syntactic system.

Another component of syntax is word forms. Words such as *dog* and *play* are morphemes, the smallest meaningful units in language. Word parts that change the meaning of a word are also morphemes. When the plural marker *-s* is added to *dog* to make *dogs,* for instance, or the past-tense marker *-ed* is added to *play* to make *played,* these words now have two morphemes because the inflectional endings change the meaning of the words. The words *dog* and *play* are free morphemes because they convey meaning while standing alone. The endings *-s* and *-ed* are bound morphemes because they must be attached to free morphemes to convey meaning. Compound words are two or more morphemes combined to create a new word: *Birthday,* for example, is a compound word made up of two free morphemes.

During the primary grades, children learn to add prefixes to the beginning of words, and suffixes to the end of words. Both kinds of affixes are bound morphemes. The prefix *un-* in *unhappy* is a bound morpheme, and *happy* is a free morpheme because it can stand alone as a word. Similarly, the inflectional suffix *-ed* in *wanted* is a bound morpheme, and *want* is a free morpheme.

The Semantic System

The third language system is the semantic or meaning system. Vocabulary is the key component of this system. As children learn to talk, they acquire a vocabulary that is continually increasing. Researchers estimate that children have a vocabulary of 5,000 words by the time they enter school, and they continue to acquire 3,000 to 4,000 words each year during the elementary grades (Lindfors, 1987; Nagy, 1988). Considering how many words children learn each year, it is unreasonable to assume that they learn words only through formal instruction. They learn many, many words informally through reading and through social studies and science lessons.

Children learn approximately 8 to 10 words a day. A remarkable achievement! As children learn a word, they move from a general understanding of the meaning of the word to a better-developed understanding, and they learn these words through real reading, not by copying definitions from a dictionary. Researchers have estimated that children need to read a word 4 to 14 times to make it their own, and this is possible only when children read and reread books and write about what they are reading.

The Pragmatic System

The fourth language system is pragmatics, which deals with the social aspects of language use. People use language for many purposes, and how they talk or write varies according to their purpose and audience. Language use also varies among social classes, ethnic groups, and geographic regions; these varieties are known as dialects. School is one cultural community, and the language of school is Standard English.

Children use all four cueing systems as they write and present a puppet show.

This dialect is formal—the one used in textbooks, newspapers, and magazines and by television newscasters. Other forms, including those spoken in urban ghettos, in Appalachia, and by Mexican Americans in the Southwest, are generally classified as nonstandard English. These nonstandard forms of English are alternatives in which the phonology, syntax, and semantics differ from those of Standard English. These forms are neither inferior nor substandard. They reflect the communities of speakers, and the speakers communicate as effectively as those who use Standard English. The goal is for children to add Standard English to their repertoire of language registers, not to replace their home dialect with Standard English.

As children who speak nonstandard English read texts written in Standard English, they often translate what they read into their dialect. Sometimes this occurs when children are reading aloud. For example, a sentence written "They are going to school" might be read aloud as "They be goin' to school." Beginning readers are not usually corrected when they translate words into nonstandard dialects as long as they don't change the meaning, but older, more fluent readers should be directed to read the words as they are printed in the book.

Effective teachers understand that children use all four cueing systems as they read and write. For example, when children read the sentence "Jimmy is playing ball with his father" correctly, they are probably using information from all four systems. When a child substitutes *dad* for *father* and reads "Jimmy is playing ball with his dad," he might be focusing on the semantic or pragmatic system rather than on the phonological system. When a child substitutes *basketball* for *ball* and reads "Jimmy is playing basketball with his father," he might be relying on an illustration or his own experience playing basketball. Because both *basketball* and *ball* begin with *b*, he might have used the beginning sound as an aid in decoding, but he apparently did not consider how long the word *basketball* is compared with the word *ball*. When the child changes the syntax, as in "Jimmy, he play ball with his father," he may speak a nonstandard dialect. Sometimes a child reads the sentence as "Jump is play boat with his father," so that it doesn't make sense. The child chooses words with the correct beginning sound and uses appropriate parts of speech for at least some of the words, but there is no comprehension. This is a serious problem because the child doesn't seem to understand that what he reads must make sense.

You will learn ways to apply this information on the cueing systems in upcoming chapters. The information on the phonological system is applied to phonics in Chapter 4, "Breaking the Alphabetic Code," and to spelling in Chapter 5, "Learning to Spell," and the information on the syntactic system is applied to words in Chapter 6, "Developing Fluent Readers and Writers." The information on the semantic and pragmatic systems is applied to comprehension in Chapter 8, "Guiding Children's Comprehension."

PRINCIPLE 3: EFFECTIVE TEACHERS CREATE A COMMUNITY OF LEARNERS

Elementary classrooms are social settings in which children read, discuss, and write about literature. Together, children and their teachers create the classroom community, and the type of community they create strongly influences children's learning. Effective teachers establish a community of learners in which children are motivated to learn and are actively involved in reading and writing activities. Teachers and children work collaboratively and purposefully. Perhaps the most striking quality of classroom communities is the partnership that the teacher and children create. Children are a "family" in which all the members respect one another and support each other's learning. Children value culturally and linguistically diverse classmates and recognize that all children make important contributions to the classroom (Wells & Chang-Wells, 1992).

Children and teachers work together for the common good of the community. Consider the differences between renting and owning a home. In a classroom community, children and the teacher are joint "owners" of the classroom. Children assume responsibility for their own learning and behavior, work collaboratively with classmates, complete assignments, and care for the classroom. In traditional classrooms, in contrast, the classroom is the teacher's and children are simply "renters" for the school year. This doesn't mean that in a classroom community, teachers abdicate their responsibility to the children. On the contrary, teachers retain all of their roles as guide, instructor, monitor, coach, mentor, and grader. Sometimes these roles are shared with children, but the ultimate responsibility remains with the teacher.

Preschool classrooms should reflect the reading and writing experiences that occur in many homes and provide opportunities for children to continue to develop their literacy.

Ten Characteristics of Classroom Communities

Classroom communities have specific characteristics that are conducive to learning and that support children's interactions with literature. Ten of the characteristics are:

1. ***Responsibility.*** Children are responsible for their learning, their behavior, and the contributions they make in the classroom. They see themselves as valued and contributing members of the classroom community.

See the Compendium of Instructional Procedures, which follows Chapter 12, to read more about the terms marked with the symbol [C].

2. ***Opportunities.*** Children have opportunities to read and write for genuine and meaningful purposes. They read real books and write for real audiences—their classmates, their parents, and members of their community. They rarely use workbooks or drill-and-practice sheets.

3. ***Engagement.*** Children are motivated to learn and actively involved in reading and writing activities. Children sometimes choose which books to read, how they will respond to a book, and which reading and writing projects they will pursue.

4. ***Demonstration.*** Teachers provide demonstrations of literacy skills and strategies, and children observe in order to learn what more capable readers and writers do.

5. ***Risk taking.*** Children are encouraged to explore topics, make guesses, and take risks.

6. ***Instruction.*** Teachers are expert readers and writers, and they provide instruction through minilessons[C] on procedures, skills, and strategies related to reading and writing.

7. ***Response.*** Children share personal connections to stories, make predictions, ask questions, and deepen their comprehension as they write in reading logs[C] and participate in grand conversations[C]. When they write, children share their rough drafts in writing groups[C] to get feedback on how well they are communicating, and they celebrate their published books by sharing them with classmates.

8. ***Choice.*** Children often make choices about the books they read and the writing they do within the parameters set by the teacher. When given opportunities to make choices, children are often more highly motivated to read and write, and they value their learning experience more because it is meaningful to them.

9. ***Time.*** Children need large chunks of time to pursue reading and writing activities; it doesn't work well for teachers to break the classroom schedule into many small time blocks. Two to three hours of uninterrupted time each day for reading and writing instruction is recommended. It is important to minimize disruptions during the time set aside for literacy instruction, and administrators should schedule computer, music, art, and other pull-out programs so that they do not interfere. This is especially important in the primary grades.

10. ***Assessment.*** Teachers and children work together to establish guidelines for assessment so that children can monitor their own work and participate in the evaluation.

These 10 characteristics are reviewed in Figure 1-3.

How to Create a Classroom Community

Teachers are more successful when they take the first 2 weeks of the school year to establish the classroom environment (Sumara & Walker, 1991). Teachers can't assume that children will be familiar with the procedures and routines or that they will instinctively be cooperative, responsible, and respectful of classmates. Teachers explicitly explain classroom routines, such as how to get supplies out and put them away and how to work with classmates in a cooperative group, and set the expectation that children will adhere to the routines. Next, they demonstrate literacy procedures, including how to choose a book from the classroom library to read, how to provide feedback about a classmate's writing, and how to participate in a grand conversation about a

Figure 1-3   Ten Characteristics of a Community of Learners

Characteristic	Teacher's Role	Children's Role
Responsibility	Teachers set guidelines and have the expectation that children will be responsible. Teachers also model responsible behavior.	Children are responsible for fully participating in the classroom, including completing assignments, participating in groups, and cooperating with classmates.
Opportunities	Teachers provide opportunities for children to read and write in genuine and meaningful activities, not contrived practice activities.	Children take advantage of learning opportunities provided in class. They read independently during reading workshop, and they share their writing during sharing time.
Engagement	Teachers make it possible for children to be engaged by the literature and activities they provide for children. Also, by planning units with children and allowing them to make choices, they motivate children to complete assignments.	Children are actively involved in reading and writing activities. They are motivated and industrious because they are reading real literature and are involved in activities they find meaningful.
Demonstration	Teachers demonstrate what readers and writers do and use think-alouds to explain their thinking during the demonstrations.	Children observe the teacher's demonstrations of skills and strategies that readers and writers use.
Risk taking	Teachers encourage children to take risks, make guesses, and explore their thinking. They deemphasize children's need to get things "right."	Children explore what they are learning, take risks as they ask questions, and make guesses. They expect not to be laughed at or made fun of. They view learning as a process of exploration.
Instruction	Teachers provide instruction through minilessons. During minilessons, teachers provide information and make connections to the reading and writing in which children are involved.	Children look to the teacher to provide instruction on procedures, concepts, strategies, and skills related to reading and writing. Children participate in minilessons and then apply what they have learned in their own reading and writing.
Response	Teachers provide opportunities for children to share and respond to reading and writing activities. Children are a supportive audience for classmates.	Children respond to books they are reading in reading logs and grand conversations. They share their writing in writing groups and get feedback from classmates.
Choice	Teachers encourage children to choose some of the books they read and some of the writing activities and projects they develop.	Children make choices about some books they read, some writing activities, and some projects they develop within parameters set by the teacher.
Time	Teachers organize the class schedule with large chunks of time for reading and writing activities. They plan units and set deadlines with children.	Children have large chunks of time for reading and writing activities. They work on projects over days and weeks and understand when assignments are due.
Assessment	Teachers set grading plans with children before beginning each unit, and meet with children in assessment conferences.	Children understand how they will be assessed and graded, and they participate in their assessment. They collect their work in progress in folders.

book. Third, teachers model ways of interacting with children, responding to literature, respecting classmates, and assisting classmates with reading and writing projects.

Teachers are the classroom managers. They set expectations and clearly explain to children what is expected of them and what is valued in the classroom. The classroom rules are specific and consistent, and teachers also set limits. For example, children might be allowed to talk quietly with classmates when they are working, but they are not allowed to shout across the classroom or talk when the teacher is talking or when children are making a presentation to the class. Teachers also model classroom rules themselves as they interact with children. According to Sumara and Walker (1991), the process of socialization at the beginning of the school year is planned, deliberate, and crucial to the success of the literacy program.

Not everything can be accomplished during the first 2 weeks, however; teachers continue to reinforce classroom routines and literacy procedures. One way is to have student leaders model the desired routines and behaviors. When this is done, other children are likely to follow their lead. Teachers also continue to teach additional literacy procedures as children are involved in new types of activities. The classroom community evolves during the school year, but the foundation is laid during the first 2 weeks.

Teachers develop a predictable classroom environment with familiar routines and literacy procedures. Children feel comfortable, safe, and more willing to take risks and experiment in a predictable classroom environment. This is especially true for children from varied cultures, children learning English as a second language, and less capable readers and writers.

The classroom community also extends beyond the walls of the classroom to include the entire school and the wider community. Within the school, children become "buddies" with children in other classes and get together to read and write in pairs (Morrice & Simmons, 1991). When parents and other community members come into the school, they demonstrate the value they place on education by working as tutors and aides, sharing their cultures, and demonstrating other types of expertise (Graves, 1995).

PRINCIPLE 4: EFFECTIVE TEACHERS ADOPT A BALANCED APPROACH TO LITERACY INSTRUCTION

In recent years, we have witnessed a great deal of controversy about the best way to teach reading. On one side are the proponents of a skills-based or phonics approach; on the other side are advocates of a literature-based approach. Teachers favoring each side cite research to support their views, and state legislatures are joining the debate by mandating systematic, intensive phonics instruction in the primary grades. Today many teachers agree with Richard Allington that there is "no quick fix" and no one program to meet the needs of all children (Allington & Walmsley, 1995). Many teachers recognize value in both points of view and recommend a "balance" or combination of holistic and skills approaches (Baumann, Hoffman, Moon, & Duffy-Hester, 1998). That is the perspective taken in this text.

A balanced approach to literacy, according to Spiegel (1998), is a decision-making approach through which teachers make thoughtful and purposeful decisions about how to help children become better readers and writers. A balanced approach "is built on research, views the teacher as an informed decision maker who develops a flexible program, and is constructed around a comprehensive view of literacy" (Spiegel, 1998, p. 117).

In a classroom community, social interaction and small-group activities are rich learning opportunities for children who are second language learners.

Fitzgerald (1999) identified three principles of a balanced literacy approach. First, teachers develop children's skills knowledge, including decoding skills, their strategy knowledge for comprehension and responding to literature, and their affective knowledge, including nurturing children's love of reading. Second, instructional approaches that are sometimes viewed as opposites are used to meet children's learning needs. Phonics instruction and reading workshop, for instance, are two very different instructional programs that are used in a balanced literacy approach. Third, children read a variety of reading materials, ranging from trade books to leveled books with controlled vocabulary and basal reading textbooks.

Even though balanced programs vary, they usually embody these characteristics:

1. Literacy is viewed comprehensively, as involving both reading and writing.
2. Literature is at the heart of the program.
3. Skills and strategies are taught both directly and indirectly.
4. Reading instruction involves learning word recognition and identification, vocabulary, and comprehension.
5. Writing instruction involves learning to express meaningful ideas and to use conventional spelling, grammar, and punctuation to express those ideas.
6. Children use reading and writing as tools for learning in the content areas.
7. The goal of a balanced literacy program is to develop lifelong readers and writers. (Baumann & Ivey, 1997; McIntyre & Pressley, 1996; Spiegel, 1998; Strickland, 1994/1995; Weaver, 1998)

No longer do teachers need to choose a side—either whole language or phonics—because a balanced approach recognizes the contributions of many different approaches and perspectives. Reutzel (1998/1999) urges teachers to incorporate the contributions of the many approaches that have been proven effective.

PRINCIPLE 5: EFFECTIVE TEACHERS SCAFFOLD CHILDREN'S READING AND WRITING EXPERIENCES

Teachers scaffold or support children's reading and writing as they demonstrate, guide, and teach, and they vary the amount of support they provide according to their instructional purpose and the children's needs. Sometimes teachers model how experienced readers read, or they record children's dictation when the writing is too difficult for children to do on their own. At other times, they carefully guide children as they read a leveled book or proofread their writing. Teachers also provide plenty of time for children to read and write independently and to practice skills they have learned. Teachers use five levels of support, moving from the greatest amount to the least as children assume more and more of the responsibility for themselves (Fountas & Pinnell, 1996). Figure 1-4 summarizes these five levels—modeled, shared, interactive, guided, and independent—of reading and writing.

Teachers working with prekindergartners through fourth graders use all five levels. For instance, when teachers introduce a new writing form or teach a reading strategy or skill, they use demonstrations or modeling. Or, when teachers want children to practice a strategy or skill they have already taught, they might use a guided or independent literacy activity. The purpose of the activity, not the activity itself, determines which level

A balanced approach is effective for English learners because they receive direct instruction on skills and strategies and have opportunities to participate in authentic reading and writing activities.

To link to *Every Child Reading,* an action paper adopted by 12 educational organizations to ensure that all children learn to read well, visit our Companion Website at **www.prenhall.com/tompkins**

Figure 1-4   A Continuum of Literacy Instruction

	Reading	**Writing**
Modeled	Teacher reads aloud, modeling how good readers read fluently and with expression. Books too difficult for children to read themselves are used. Examples: reading aloud and listening centers.	Teacher writes in front of children, creating the text, doing the writing, and thinking aloud about writing strategies and skills. Example: demonstrations.
Shared	Teacher and children read books together, with the children following as the teacher reads and then repeating familiar refrains. Books children can't read by themselves are used. Examples: big books, buddy reading.	Teacher and children create the text together; then the teacher does the actual writing. Children may assist by spelling familiar or high-frequency words. Example: language experience approach.
Interactive	Teacher and children read together and take turns doing the reading. The teacher helps children read fluently and with expression. Instructional-level books are used. Examples: choral reading and readers theatre.	Teacher and children create the text and share the pen to do the writing. Teacher and children talk about writing conventions. Examples: interactive writing and daily news.
Guided	Teacher plans and teaches small, homogeneous group reading lessons using instructional-level books. Focus is on supporting and observing children's use of strategies. Example: guided reading groups.	Teacher plans and teaches lesson on a writing procedure, strategy, or skill, and children participate in supervised practice activities. Examples: class collaborations and sentence frames.
Independent	Children choose and read self-selected books independently. Teachers conference with children to monitor their progress. Examples: reading workshop and reading center.	Children use the writing process to write stories, informational books, and other compositions. Teacher monitors children's progress. Examples: writing workshop and writing center.

of support is used. Teachers are less actively involved in directing independent reading and writing, but the quality of instruction that children have received is clearest when children work independently because they are applying what they have learned.

Modeled Reading and Writing

Teachers provide the greatest amount of support when they demonstrate or model how expert readers read and expert writers write while children observe. When teachers read aloud to children, they are modeling. They read fluently and with expression, and they talk about the strategies they use while they are reading. When they model writing, teachers write a composition on chart paper or using an overhead projector so that all children can see what the teacher does and what is being written. Teachers use this level to demonstrate how to make small books and how to do new writing forms and formats, such as poems and letters. Often teachers talk about or reflect on their reading and writing processes as they read and write to show children the types of decisions they make and the strategies they use.

Four purposes of modeling are:

1. To demonstrate fluent reading and writing.
2. To demonstrate how to use reading and writing strategies, such as predicting, monitoring, and revising.

ELL

Modeling is especially important for children who have difficulty understanding oral directions given in English.

3. To demonstrate the procedure for a new reading or writing activity.
4. To demonstrate how reading and writing conventions and other skills work.

Shared Reading and Writing

Children and the teacher often "share" responsibilities in reading and writing tasks. Teachers use shared reading[C] to read big books with primary-grade children. The teacher does most of the reading, but children join in the reading of familiar and repeated words and phrases. Even fourth-grade teachers use shared reading techniques, but they use the approach differently—to read difficult chapter books with their students. When a book is too difficult for children to read independently, teachers often read aloud while the children follow along, reading aloud softly or silently.

Primary-grade teachers often use the language experience approach[C] to write children's dictation on paintings and other artwork. They also used shared writing to brainstorm lists of words on the chalkboard, when they make K-W-L charts[C], draw story maps[C] and clusters[C], and write group poems.

The most important way that sharing differs from modeling is that children actually participate in the activity rather than simply observe the teacher. In the shared reading activity, children follow along as the teacher reads, and in shared writing, they suggest the words and sentences that the teacher writes. Three purposes for shared reading and writing are:

1. To involve children in reading and writing activities that they could not do independently.
2. To provide opportunities for children to experience success in reading and writing.
3. To provide practice before children read and write independently.

Interactive Reading and Writing

Children assume an increasingly important role in interactive reading and writing activities. At this level, children no longer observe the teacher read or write, repeat familiar words, or suggest what the teacher will write. Instead, children are more actively involved in reading and writing. They support their classmates by sharing the reading and writing responsibilities, and their teacher provides assistance when needed. Choral reading[C] and readers theatre[C] are two examples of interactive reading. In choral reading, children take turns reading lines of a poem, and in readers theatre, they assume the roles of characters and read lines in a script. In both of these interactive reading activities, the children support each other by actively participating and sharing the work. Teachers provide support by helping children with unfamiliar words or reading a sentence with more expression.

Interactive writing[C] is a recently developed writing activity in which children and the teacher create a text and "share the pen" to write the text on chart paper (Button, Johnson, & Furgerson, 1996; Collom, 1998). The text is composed by the group, and the teacher assists children as they write the text word by word on chart paper. Children take turns writing known letters and familiar words, adding punctuation marks, and marking spaces between words. The teacher helps children to spell all words correctly and use written language conventions so that the text can be easily read. All children participate in creating and writing the text on chart paper, and they also write the text on small white boards. After writing, children read and reread the text using shared and independent reading.

Figure 1-5 shows a piece of interactive writing done by a group of kindergartners after reading Eric Carle's repetitive book *Does a Kangaroo Have a Mother, Too?*

Figure 1-5 A Kindergarten Interactive Writing Chart

Does a Kangaroo Have a Mother, Too?
by Eric Carle
Animals have mothers just like me and you.

(2000). The teacher wrote the title and the author's name and the kindergartners created the sentence *Animals have mothers just like me and you*. The children took turns writing the letters they knew and the teacher wrote the unfamiliar letters indicated by dotted lines in the figure. The boxes around four of the letters represent correction tape that was placed over an incorrectly formed letter before the child tried again to form the letter correctly.

Four purposes of interactive reading and writing are:

1. To practice reading and writing high-frequency words.
2. To teach and practice phonics and spelling skills.
3. To successfully read and write texts that children could not do independently.
4. To have children share their reading and writing expertise with classmates.

Guided Reading and Writing

Teachers continue to support children's reading and writing during guided literacy activities, but the children do the actual reading and writing themselves. In guided reading[C], small, homogeneous groups of children meet with the teacher to read a book at their instructional level. The teacher introduces the book and guides children as they begin reading. Then children continue reading on their own while the teacher monitors their reading. After reading, children and the teacher discuss the book, and children often reread the book.

To view a shared reading activity, an interactive writing lesson, and a guided reading group, play the CD-ROM entitled *Primary Grades Literacy: A K–3 Unit on Insects* that accompanies this text.

Teachers plan structured writing activities in guided writing and then supervise as children do the writing. For example, when children make pages for a class alphabet book[C] or write formula poems, they are doing guided writing because the teacher has set up the writing activity. Teachers also guide children's writing when they conference with children as they write, participate in writing groups to help children revise their writing, and proofread with children.

Teachers use guided reading and writing to provide instruction and assistance as children are actually reading and writing. Four purposes of guided reading and writing activities are:

1. To support children's reading in instructional-level materials.
2. To teach literacy procedures, concepts, skills, and strategies during minilessons.
3. To introduce different types of writing activities.
4. To teach children to use the writing process—in particular, how to revise and edit.

Independent Reading and Writing

Children do the reading and writing themselves during independent reading and writing activities. They apply and practice the procedures, concepts, strategies, and skills they have learned. Children may be involved in reading workshop or literature circles. During independent reading, they usually choose the books they read and work at their own pace. Similarly, during independent writing, children may be involved in writing workshop or work at a writing center. They usually choose their own topics for writing and move at their own pace through the steps of the writing process as they develop and refine their writing.

Through independent reading experiences, children learn the joy of reading and, teachers hope, become lifelong readers. And, through independent writing experiences,

Young children enjoy rereading favorite books during independent reading time.

children come to view themselves as authors. Three purposes of independent reading and writing activities are:

1. To create opportunities for children to practice reading and writing procedures, concepts, strategies, and skills that have been taught.
2. To provide authentic literacy experiences in which children choose their own topics, purposes, and materials.
3. To develop lifelong readers and writers.

PRINCIPLE 6: EFFECTIVE TEACHERS ORGANIZE LITERACY INSTRUCTION IN FOUR WAYS

Effective teachers put literature at the center of their instructional programs, and they combine opportunities for children to read and write with lessons on literacy skills and strategies. Teachers choose among four instructional approaches for their reading programs:

1. *Literature focus units.* All children in the class read and respond to the same book, and the teacher supports children's learning through a variety of related activities. Books chosen for literature focus units should be of high quality; teachers often choose books for literature focus units from a district- or state-approved list of books that all children are expected to read at that grade level.

2. *Literature circles.* Teachers select five or six books for a text set. These books range in difficulty level to meet the needs of all children in the classroom, and they are often related in theme or written by the same author. Teachers collect five or six copies of each book and give a book talk to introduce the books. Then children choose a book to read from the text set and form a group to read and respond to the book they have chosen.

3. *Reading and writing workshop.* Children individually select books to read and then read independently and conference with the teacher about their reading. Similarly, in writing workshop, children write books on topics that they choose and the teacher conferences with them about their writing. Usually teachers set aside a time for reading and writing workshop, and all children read and write while the teacher conferences with small groups of children. Sometimes, however, when the teacher is working with guided reading groups, the remainder of the class works in reading and writing workshop.

4. *Basal reading programs.* Commercially developed reading programs are known as basal readers. These programs consist of a textbook or anthology of stories and other reading selections and accompanying skill sheets, books, and related instructional materials at each grade level. Instructional manuals and testing materials are also included. Teachers usually divide children into small, homogeneous groups, and then teachers meet with groups to read selections and teach skills. They use guided reading to scaffold children's reading and monitor their progress. The publishers tout these books as complete reading programs, but effective teachers integrate basal reading programs with other instructional approaches.

These four approaches are used at all grade levels, and effective teachers generally use a combination of them. Children need a variety of reading opportunities, and some books that children read are more difficult than others and require more support from the teacher. Some teachers alternate literature focus units or literature circles with reading and writing workshop and basal readers, whereas others use some components from each approach throughout the school year. Figure 1-6 presents a comparison of the four approaches.

As you continue reading, you'll often see the terms *literature focus units, literature circles, reading and writing workshop,* and *basal reading programs* used because they are the instructional approaches advocated in this text, and you'll learn how primary-grade teachers use these approaches in their classrooms.

PRINCIPLE 7: EFFECTIVE TEACHERS CONNECT INSTRUCTION AND ASSESSMENT

Teachers understand that children learn to read and write by doing lots of reading and writing and applying skills and strategies in real reading and writing, not by doing exercises on isolated literacy skills. This understanding affects the way they assess children's learning. No longer does it seem enough to grade children's phonics exercises or ask them to answer multiple-choice comprehension questions on reading passages that have no point beyond the exercise. Similarly, it no longer seems appropriate to measure success in writing by means of spelling tests. Instead, teachers need assessment information that tells about the complex achievements that children are making in reading and writing.

Teachers use assessment procedures that they develop and others that are commercially available to:

- monitor children's progress
- identify children's instructional levels
- determine children's knowledge of phonics
- check children's reading fluency
- monitor children's comprehension
- diagnose children's reading problems
- identify strengths and weaknesses in children's writing
- analyze children's spelling development
- document children's learning
- assign grades

And, teachers use the results of standardized achievement tests as indicators of children's literacy levels and their strengths and weaknesses, as well as to assess the effect of their instruction.

Assessment is more than testing; it is an integral and ongoing part of teaching and learning (Glazer, 1998). Serafini (2000/2001) describes assessment as an inquiry process that teachers use in order to make informed instructional decisions. Figure 1-7 (on page 24) shows the teach-assess cycle. Effective teachers identify their goals and plan their instruction at the same time as they develop their assessment plan. The assessment plan involves three components: preassessing, monitoring, and assessing.

Preassessing

Teachers assess children's background knowledge before reading in order to determine whether children are familiar with the topic they will read about. They also check

Figure 1-6   Four Instructional Approaches

Features	Literature Focus Units	Literature Circles
Description	Teacher and children read and respond to one text together as a class or in small groups. The teacher chooses texts that are high-quality literature, either trade books or from a basal reader textbook. After reading, children explore the text and apply their learning by creating projects.	The teacher chooses five or six books and collects multiple copies of each book. Children each choose the book they want to read and form groups or "book clubs" to read and respond to the book. They develop a reading and discussion schedule, and the teacher often participates in the discussions.
Strengths	• Teachers develop units using the reading process. • Teachers select picture books, chapter books, or use selections from basal reader textbooks for units. • Teachers scaffold reading instruction as they read with the whole class or small groups. • Teachers teach minilessons on reading skills and strategies. • Children explore vocabulary and literary language. • Children develop projects to extend their reading.	• Books are available at a variety of reading levels. • Children are more strongly motivated because they choose the books they read. • Children have opportunities to work with their classmates. • Children participate in authentic literacy experiences. • Activities are child-directed, and children work at their own pace. • Teachers may participate in discussions to help children clarify misunderstandings and think more deeply about the book.
Drawbacks	• Children all read the same book whether or not they like it and whether or not it is at their reading level. • Many of the activities are teacher-directed.	• Teachers often feel a loss of control because children are reading different books. • Children must learn to be task-oriented and use time wisely in order to be successful. • Sometimes children choose books that are too difficult or too easy for them.

to see that children are familiar with the genre, vocabulary, skills, and strategies. Then, based on the results of the assessment, teachers either help children develop more background knowledge or move on to the next step of their instructional plan. Some preassessment tools are:

- creating a K-W-L chart
- quickwriting[C] about a topic
- discussing a topic with children
- brainstorming a list of characteristics about a topic

Monitoring

Teachers often monitor children's progress in reading and writing as they observe children participating in literacy activities. Children might participate in conferences with the teacher, for example, and talk about what they are reading and writing, the strategies and skills they are learning to use, and problem areas. They reflect on what they do well as readers and writers and on what they need to learn next. Here are some monitoring tools:

Reading and Writing Workshop	Basal Reading Programs
Children choose books and read and respond to them independently during reading workshop and write books on self-selected topics during writing workshop. The teacher monitors children's work through conferences. Children share the books they read and the books they write with classmates during a sharing period.	The teacher groups children into small, homogeneous groups for reading instruction and uses commercially developed basal readers that are graded according to difficulty so that children can read selections at their instructional level. The teacher uses guided reading to scaffold children so they can be successful. Children read independently and the teacher provides assistance as needed. The teacher also uses running records to monitor children's reading.
• Children read books appropriate for their reading levels. • Children are more strongly motivated because they choose the books they read. • Children work through the stages of the writing process during writing workshop. • Teachers teach minilessons on reading skills and strategies. • Activities are child-directed and children work at their own pace. • Teachers have opportunities to work individually with children during conferences.	• Children read selections at their instructional level. • Teachers teach word-identification skills and vocabulary words. • Teachers teach strategies and skills and provide structured practice opportunities. • Teachers monitor children's reading. • Teachers are available to reteach strategies as needed. • The instructor's guide provides detailed instructions for teachers.
• Teachers often feel a loss of control because children are reading different books and working at different stages of the writing process. • Children must learn to be task-oriented and use time wisely in order to be successful.	• Children do not select the books they read and thus may not be interested in them. • The reading lesson is very structured. • Programs include many skill workbooks and worksheets.

- listening to children read aloud
- making running records[C] of children's oral reading "miscues" or errors
- conferencing with children during reading and writing workshop
- listening to comments children make during grand conversations and other book discussions
- reading children's reading log entries and rough drafts of other compositions
- examining children's work in progress

Figure 1-8 presents two pages from MacKenzie's reading log. This second grader is reading at grade level, and she wrote the entry after reading the first chapter of *Horrible Harry and the Green Slime* (Kline, 1989), an easy-to-read chapter book about a second grader named Harry who is full of horrible surprises during the class's Secret Pal week. During a reading conference, MacKenzie's teacher talks to her about the book she is reading, helps her decode the difficult vocabulary words, and reviews her reading log. She notes that MacKenzie has addressed all four questions and concludes that the second grader understands what she has read, but she is concerned that MacKenzie is writing brief entries without thinking deeply about the story. The

Figure 1-7 The Teach-Assess Cycle

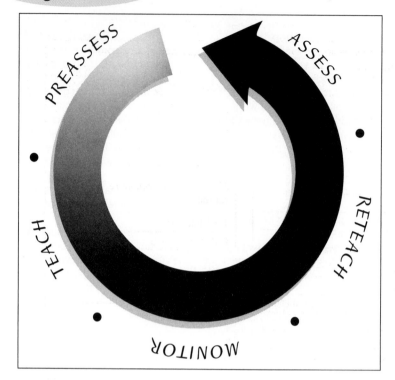

teacher encourages MacKenzie to talk more about the chapter she is currently read-ing; as they talk, she pushes MacKenzie to think more deeply about the story. Then she asks the child to continue to think deeply and show her deeper thinking through her writing.

Assessing

Teachers assess and grade children's learning at the end of a unit. Besides grading children's written assignments, teachers collect other assessment information through the following activities:

- observing children's presentation of oral language projects, such as puppet shows, oral reports, and story retellings
- examining children's art and other visual projects
- analyzing children's comprehension through charts, dioramas, murals, Venn diagrams, and other story maps they have made
- examining all drafts of children's writing to document their use of the writing process
- analyzing children's spelling in their compositions

Teachers also have children keep track of their progress using checklists that list as-signments and other requirements. Then at the end of the unit, teachers collect and grade children's assignments. Figure 1-9 shows a checklist from a third-grade litera-ture focus unit on fables, featuring Arnold Lobel's award-winning book *Fables* (1980), a collection of 20 brief stories with a moral at the end, written in Aesop's style. Dur-

Figure 1-8   A Second Grader's Reading Log Entry

Title of book: Horrible Harry and the Green Slime - Ch. 1.

What did you like or didn't you like about the story?

I like when Harry and Song Lee Were writeing letters.

My questions about the story:

What color was Song Lee's salamander?

This story reminded me of:

When I was in kindergarden I would write my friend notes.

A list of words that were "tricky" for me:

1. aluminun
2. apologizes
3. _____
4. _____
5. _____

ing the unit, children read Lobel's book and fables in their basal reading textbooks and other trade books in the classroom. They also participate in a variety of literacy activities, some of which are included on the checklist. Children check off items on the checklist as they complete them, and at the end, they assess their own work before submitting it to the teacher.

You will learn more about how to monitor, document, and grade children's literacy learning in Chapter 3, "Assessing Young Children's Literacy Development."

PRINCIPLE 8: EFFECTIVE TEACHERS BECOME PARTNERS WITH PARENTS

Effective teachers communicate the importance of parent involvement to parents, view parents as teaching partners, and understand that even parents with limited education or those who do not speak English are valuable resources. They recognize that families from various cultures use literacy in different ways, but that parents from all sociocultural groups value literacy and want their children to succeed in school (Shockley, 1993).

Parents are the most powerful influence on children's literacy development, and when parents are involved in their children's literacy development, children become better readers and writers. Three ways that parents can become involved are as teaching partners in the classroom, as resource people, and as teachers at home (Tinajero & Nagel, 1995).

Teachers are also learning that working with parents of preschoolers and kindergartners can help prevent children's reading problems later on (France & Hager,

Fables

Name _____   Date _____

Student's   Teacher's
Check _____   Check

- ☐ 1. Read these fables: ☐
     ___ *Fables*
     ___ "The Ant and the Grasshopper"
     ___ "The Lion and the Mouse"
     ___ "The Tortoise and the Hare"

- ☐ 2. Write about the fables in your reading log.   ☐

- ☐ 3. Write information about fables in your log.   ☐

- ☐ 4. Draw and write about the opposites in a fable.   ☐

- ☐ 5. Make a chart to show the moral of one fable.   ☐

- ☐ 6. Do a group oral or written retelling of a fable.   ☐

Assessment Tools

1993). Through parent programs, low-income and minority parents can learn how to create a home environment that fosters literacy and how to read aloud to their young children. Parents with limited literacy skills benefit in other ways, too: They develop their own reading and writing abilities through family literacy programs.

Providing Literacy Information to Parents

Today children are learning to read in new ways, and these instructional methods are often unfamiliar to parents. Not surprisingly, these changes have made many parents anxious about how their children are learning to read and write. Parent information programs are crucial in helping parents to understand why children use trade books as well as textbooks, why children explore meanings of stories they have read through grand conversations, how skills and strategies are taught in minilessons, how writing supports children's reading development, and what invented spelling is. Teachers provide literacy information to parents in a variety of ways:

- back to school nights
- newsletters
- conferences with parents
- workshops on strategies for working with young readers and writers
- homework telephone hot lines
- telephone calls and notes conveying good news

In parent workshops and other information-sharing sessions, teachers use videotapes, demonstrations, and guest speakers to provide information about literacy development and the programs in their classrooms. Teachers share some of the books children are reading, especially books representing the cultures of the children in the classroom.

Parents can write small books during a writing workshop session, use the computer for literacy activities, and learn how to examine the work their children bring home. Teachers also show parents how to work with their children at home. Without sharing these types of information, parents often feel isolated from the school and are unsure of how to help their children at home.

Patricia Edwards (1995) developed a literacy program for low-income parents in Louisiana, and she reports that parents want to know how to work with their children. Parents told her that they didn't know reading books aloud to their young children was so important and wished they had known sooner how to support their children's literacy development. In her study, parents were grateful that someone explained and demonstrated to them exactly what teachers expect them to do at home.

Parent Volunteers

Schools need lots of adults to read with children and to conference with them about books they are reading and compositions they are writing. Parents, grandparents, older students, and other community volunteers can be extremely useful.

Volunteer experiences can be beneficial for parents, too, and they learn about the school and the literacy program. Come and Fredericks (1995) report that parents need to be involved in planning the program, and that parents are more likely to become involved if they believe the school has their needs and those of their children at heart. Rasinski and Fredericks (1988) recommend five steps for establishing a quality volunteer program:

1. *Recruitment.* Teachers invite parents and others to volunteer to assist in the classroom. Sometimes telephone calls and home visits are necessary to let parents know they are truly welcome and needed.
2. *Training.* Volunteers need to be trained so that they know how to work with children, where things are located in the school, and how to assist teachers.
3. *Variety.* Teachers need to offer parents a variety of ways to be involved in schools. Volunteers may feel more comfortable helping in one way than in another, or they may have a special talent to share.
4. *Recognition.* For a volunteer program to be successful, the volunteers need to know they are appreciated. Often schools plan recognition receptions each spring to publicly thank the volunteers for their dedication and service.
5. *Evaluation.* Teachers evaluate their volunteer programs and make changes based on the feedback they get from the volunteers and students.

In bilingual schools with children from many cultural backgrounds, parents play a key role in their children's education. Monolingual English-speaking teachers rely on parents to develop an environment that is linguistically and culturally relevant for the children. Minority parents also provide a feeling of security and belonging for culturally and linguistically diverse students. Some parents from other cultures feel inadequate to help in schools, either because they speak another language or because they have limited education themselves, so it is the teacher's responsibility to let parents know they are valued (Tinajero & Nagel, 1995).

Supporting Literacy at Home

Parents are children's first and best teachers, and parents can do many things to support their children's literacy development at home. In addition to reading to their children and listening to their children read to them, parents can build children's self-esteem and spend quality time with them.

Families use literacy in many ways. Some read the Bible and other religious publications, and others read the newspaper or novels as entertainment. In some homes, the main reading experience is reading *TV Guide,* and in other homes, families write letters and sign greeting cards. Some parents read to their children each evening, and in other homes, parents are busy catching up on work from the office while children do homework in the evening. Some children and parents communicate with friends and relatives over the Internet. In many homes, parents demonstrate daily living routines, such as making shopping lists, paying bills, and leaving messages for family members that involve reading and writing. Figure 1-10 identifies some of the many ways parents can support children's literacy development.

Many teachers assume that children from families with low socioeconomic status have few, if any, literacy events in their homes, but other teachers argue that such children live in homes where people use print for many and varied functions, even though some of those purposes might be different from those of middle-class families. In an interesting study, researchers uncovered great variation in the number and types of uses of reading and writing in low-income families (Purcell-Gates, L'Allier, & Smith, 1995). Included in the study were white, African American, Hispanic American, and Asian American low-income families, and all children spoke English as their primary language. The findings confirm that teachers cannot make generalizations and must look at each child as an individual from a unique family setting. It is not enough to use demographic characteristics such as family income level to make assumptions about a child's literacy environment.

Figure 1-10 **Ways Parents Support Children's Literacy Development**

Visit children's classrooms and get acquainted with their teachers

Talk to children about school activities

Display children's schoolwork at home

Place books in children's bedrooms and in living rooms

Keep pens and paper available in the home

Get a library card and take children to the library on a regular basis to check out books

Model reading and writing for children

Read to or with children every day

Subscribe to newspapers and magazines and read them

Write in family journals

Write letters and cards to extended family members and friends

Share family histories and memories with children

Set an area of the home aside for children to do their homework

Supervise children as they do homework and work on school projects

Watch literacy-related television programs such as *Sesame Street* and *Reading Rainbow* with children

Point out environmental signs and labels to young children

Volunteer to help in children's classrooms

Demonstrate that reading and writing are valued

Audiotape and videotape children reading

Have high expectations for children

Encourage children to have hobbies and outside interests

Give children books as gifts

Family Literacy

Schools are designing family literacy programs for minority parents, parents who are not fluent readers and writers, and parents who are learning English as a second language. These programs are intergenerational and are designed to improve the literacy development of both children and their parents. Adults learn to improve their literacy skills as well as how to work with their children to foster their literacy development (Morrow, Tracey, & Maxwell, 1995). Family literacy programs have four components:

1. *Parent literacy education.* Parents participate in activities to develop their own reading and writing competencies.
2. *Information about how young children become literate.* Parents learn how they can support their young children as they emerge into reading and writing and how they can work with their elementary-grade children at home.
3. *Support groups for parents.* Parents get acquainted with other parents and share ways of working with their children.
4. *Planned interactions between parents and children.* Parents and their children participate together in reading and writing activities.

Now family literacy programs are based on the "wealth model," which stresses that all families have literacy patterns within their homes and that family literacy programs should build on these patterns rather than impose mainstream, school-like activities on parents (Morrow et al., 1995). Cultural differences in reading and writing development and literacy use are now regarded as strengths, not weaknesses. The wealth model has replaced the older deficit model, which assumed that children from minority groups and low-income families lacked the preschool literacy activities necessary for success in school (Auerback, 1989).

Organizations dedicated to family literacy include The National Center for Family Literacy (NCFL), Reading Is Fundamental (RIF), and the Barbara Bush Foundation for Family Literacy. These organizations have been instrumental in promoting family literacy initiatives at the national level. The NCFL, which began in 1989, disseminates information about family literacy and works to implement family literacy programs across the country. The NCFL has trained staff for almost 1,000 family literacy programs and sponsors an annual Family Literacy Conference. RIF was formed in 1966 to promote children's reading, and the organization originally provided assistance to local groups in obtaining and distributing low-cost books for children and sponsoring reading-related events. Since 1982, RIF has developed other programs to support parents as children's first teachers. Former First Lady Barbara Bush organized the Barbara Bush Foundation in 1989 to promote family literacy. This foundation provides grants for family literacy programs and published a book describing 10 model family literacy programs in the United States (Barbara Bush Foundation for Family Literacy, 1989).

A variety of local programs have been developed. Some programs are collaborations among local agencies, whereas others are run by adult literacy groups. Businesses in many communities, too, are forming partnerships to promote family literacy. Also, schools in multicultural communities are creating literacy programs for parents who are not yet proficient in English so that they can support their children's literacy learning. Shanahan, Mulhern, and Rodriguez-Brown (1995) developed a literacy project in a Chicago Latino neighborhood. Through this program, parents learned to speak and read English and became actively involved in their children's education.

Schools also organize writing programs for parents. Susan Akroyd (1995), a principal of a multicultural program in Virginia, developed a 1-week program for her school. She advertised the program in the school's newsletter for parents, and approximately 15 parents from different cultures speaking languages ranging from Korean and

Vietnamese to Urdu attended. Many parents spoke very little English, but they came together to write and to learn more about writing. They wrote about memories, their experiences immigrating to America, and hopes and dreams for their children. Some parents wrote in English, and others wrote in their native languages. Akroyd brought in translators so that the parents' writing could be shared with the group. At each class meeting, parents wrote, shared their writing in small groups, and then shared selected compositions with the class. At the end of the program, Akroyd published an anthology of the parents' writing. This sort of program can work in diverse communities, even when parents read and write in different languages.

Review

This chapter set out eight principles of effective teaching of reading:

1. Effective teachers understand how children learn.
2. Effective teachers support children's use of the four cueing systems.
3. Effective teachers of reading create a community of learners in their classrooms.
4. Effective teachers adopt a balanced approach to literacy instruction.
5. Effective teachers scaffold children's reading and writing experiences.
6. Effective teachers organize literacy instruction in literature focus units, literature circles, reading and writing workshop, and basal reading programs.
7. Effective teachers connect instruction and assessment.
8. Effective teachers become partners with parents.

These principles were drawn from research over the past 30 years about how children learn to read and the "best teaching practices" used in successful elementary schools. These principles suggest a balanced reading program. In the chapters that follow, you will learn how to develop and implement a balanced reading program for prekindergarten through fourth grade.

Professional References

Akroyd, S. (1995). Forming a parent reading-writing class: Connecting cultures, one pen at a time. *The Reading Teacher, 48,* 580–584.

Allington, R., & Walmsley, S. (Eds.). (1995). *No quick fix: Rethinking literacy programs in America's elementary schools.* New York: Teachers College Press.

Auerbach, E. R. (1989). Toward a social-contextual approach to family literacy. *Harvard Educational Review, 59,* 165–181.

Barbara Bush Foundation for Family Literacy. (1989). *First teachers.* Washington, DC: Author.

Baumann, J. F., Hoffman, J. V., Moon, J., & Duffy-Hester, A. M. (1998). Where are teachers' voices in the phonics/whole language debate? Results from a survey of U.S. elementary teachers. *The Reading Teacher, 51,* 636–650.

Baumann, J. F., & Ivey, G. (1997). Delicate balances: Striving for curricular and instructional equilibrium in a second-grade, literature/strategy-based classroom. *Reading Research Quarterly, 23,* 244–275.

Boyer, E. (1995). *The basic school: A community for learning.* Princeton, NJ: Carnegie Foundation for the Advancement of Teaching.

Button, K., Johnson, M. J., & Furgerson, P. (1996). Interactive writing in a primary classroom. *The Reading Teacher, 49,* 446–454.

Cases in literacy: An agenda for discussion. (1989). Newark, DE: International Reading Association and the National Council of Teachers of English.

Collom, S. (1998). *Sharing the pen: Interactive writing with young children.* Fresno: California State University, Fresno, and San Joaquin Valley Writing Project.

Come, B., & Fredericks, A. D. (1995). Family literacy in urban schools: Meeting the needs of at-risk children. *The Reading Teacher, 48,* 556–570.

Dixon-Krauss, L. (1996). *Vygotsky in the classroom.* White Plains, NY: Longman.

Edwards, P. A. (1995). Empowering low-income mothers and fathers to share books with young children. *The Reading Teacher, 48,* 558–564.

Fitzgerald, J. (1999). What is this thing called "balance"? *The Reading Teacher, 53,* 100–107.

Fountas, I. C., & Pinnell, G. S. (1996). *Guided reading: Good first teaching for all children.* Portsmouth, NH: Heinemann.

France, M. G., & Hager, J. M. (1993). Recruit, respect, respond: A model for working with low-income families and their preschoolers. *The Reading Teacher, 46*, 568–572.

Glazer, S. M. (1998). *Assessment is instruction: Reading, writing, spelling, and phonics for all learners.* Norwood, MA: Christopher-Gordon.

Graves, D. H. (1995). A tour of Segovia School in the year 2005. *Language Arts, 72*, 12–18.

Halliday, M. A. K. (1978). *Language as social semiotic: The social interpretation of language and meaning.* Baltimore: University Park Press.

Harris, T. L., & Hodges, R. E. (Eds.). (1995). *The literacy dictionary: The vocabulary of reading and writing.* Newark, DE: International Reading Association.

Heath, S. B. (1983). Research currents: A lot of talk about nothing. *Language Arts, 60*, 999–1007.

Hirsch, E. D., Jr. (1987). *Cultural literacy: What every American needs to know.* Boston: Houghton Mifflin.

Lindfors, J. W. (1987). *Children's language and learning* (2nd ed.). Englewood Cliffs, NJ: Prentice Hall.

McIntyre, E. & Pressley, M. (Eds.). (1996). *Balanced instruction: Strategies and skills in whole language.* Norwood, MA: Christopher-Gordon.

Morrice, C., & Simmons, M. (1991). Beyond reading buddies: A whole language cross-age program. *The Reading Teacher, 44*, 572–578.

Morrow, L. M., Tracey, D. H., & Maxwell, C. M. (1995). *A survey of family literacy in the United States.* Newark, DE: International Reading Association.

Nagy, W. E. (1988). *Teaching vocabulary to improve reading comprehension.* Urbana, IL: ERIC Clearinghouse on Reading and Communication Skills and the National Council of Teachers of English and the International Reading Association.

Nathenson-Mejia, S. (1989). Writing in a second language: Negotiating meaning through invented spelling. *Language Arts, 66*, 516–526.

Piaget, J. (1969). *The psychology of intelligence.* Paterson, NJ: Littlefield, Adams.

Purcell-Gates, V., L'Allier, S., & Smith, D. (1995). Literacy as the Harts' and Larsons': Diversity among poor, inner city families. *The Reading Teacher, 48*, 572–579.

Rafferty, C. D. (1999). Literacy in the information age. *Educational Leadership, 57*, 22–25.

Rasinski, T. V., & Fredericks, A. D. (1988). Sharing literacy: Guiding principles and practices for parent involvement. *The Reading Teacher, 41*, 508–512.

Reutzel, D. R. (1998/1999). On balanced reading. *The Reading Teacher, 52*, 322–324.

Rosenblatt, L. (1978). *The reader, the text, the poem: The transactional theory of the literary work.* Carbondale, IL: Southern Illinois University Press.

Rosenblatt, L. (1983). *Literature as exploration* (4th ed.). New York: Modern Language Association.

Rosenblatt, L. (1991). Literature–S.O.S.! *Language Arts, 68*, 444–448.

Rumelhart, D. E. (1977). Toward an interactive model of reading. In S. Dornic (Ed.), *Attention and performance* (Vol. 6). Hillsdale, NJ: Erlbaum.

Serafini, F. (2000/2001). Three paradigms of assessment: Measurement, procedure, and inquiry. *The Reading Teacher, 54*, 384–393.

Shanahan, T., Mulhern, M., & Rodriguez-Brown, F. (1995). Project FLAME: Lessons learned from a family literacy program for linguistic minority families. *The Reading Teacher, 48*, 586–593.

Shockley, B. (1993). Extending the literate community: Reading and writing with families. *The New Advocate, 6*, 11–24.

Skinner, B. F. (1968). *The technology of teaching.* New York: Appleton-Century-Crofts.

Spiegel, D. L. (1998). Silver bullets, babies, and bath water: Literature response groups in a balanced literacy program. *The Reading Teacher, 52*, 114–124.

Stanovich, K. (1980). Toward an interactive-compensatory model of individual differences in the development of reading fluency. *Reading Research Quarterly, 16*, 32–71.

Strickland, D. S. (1994/1995). Reinventing our literacy programs: Books, basics, and balance. *The Reading Teacher, 48*, 294–306.

Sumara, D., & Walker, L. (1991). The teacher's role in whole language. *Language Arts, 68*, 276–285.

Teale, B. (1995). Dear readers. *Language Arts, 72*, 8–9.

Tinajero, J. V., & Nagel, G. (1995). "I never knew I was needed until you called!": Promoting parent involvement in schools. *The Reading Teacher, 48*, 614–617.

Vygotsky, L. S. (1978). *Mind in society.* Cambridge, MA: Harvard University Press.

Vygotsky, L. S. (1986). *Thought and language.* Cambridge, MA: MIT Press.

Weaver, C. (Ed.). (1998). *Reconsidering a balanced approach to reading.* Urbana, IL: National Council of Teachers of English.

Wells, G., & Chang-Wells, G. L. (1992). *Constructing knowledge together: Classrooms as centers of inquiry and literacy.* Portsmouth, NH: Heinemann.

Children's Book References

Carle, E. (2000). *Does a kangaroo have a mother, too?* New York: HarperCollins.

Gibbons, G. (1994). *Nature's green umbrella: Tropical rain forests.* New York: Morrow.

Kline, S. (1989). *Horrible Harry and the green slime.* New York: Scholastic.

Lobel, A. (1980). *Fables.* New York: HarperCollins.

MacLachlan, P. (1985). *Sarah, plain and tall.* New York: Harper & Row.

chapter 2

Examining Children's Literacy Development

- How does emergent literacy differ from traditional reading readiness?

- What are the three stages of early literacy development?

- What do children learn as they develop as readers and writers?

- How do teachers facilitate children's literacy learning?

Ms. McCloskey's Students Become Readers and Writers

Kindergarten through third-grade children sit together on the carpet in an open area in the classroom for a shared reading[C] lesson. They watch and listen intently as Ms. McCloskey prepares to read aloud *Make Way for Ducklings* (McCloskey, 1969), the big-book version of an award-winning story about the dangers facing a family of ducks living in the city of Boston. She reads the title and the author's name, and some children recognize that the author's last name is the same as hers, but she points out that they are not related. She reads the first page of the text and asks the children to make predictions about the story. During this first reading of the book, Ms. McCloskey reads each page expressively and tracks the text, word by word, with a pointer

See the Compendium of Instructional Procedures, which follows Chapter 12, for more information on terms marked with the symbol [C].

as she reads. She clarifies the meaning as she talks about the illustrations on each page. A child helps balance the book on the easel and turn the pages for her. After she finishes reading the book, the children participate in a grand conversation[C] and talk about the story. Some of the children learning English as a second language are hesitant at first, but others are eager to relate their own experiences to the story and ask questions to clarify misunderstandings and learn more about the story.

The next day, Ms. McCloskey prepares to reread *Make Way for Ducklings.* She begins by asking for volunteers to retell the story. Children take turns retelling each page, using the illustrations as clues. Ms. McCloskey includes this oral language activity because many of her students are English language learners. The class is multilingual and multicultural; approximately 45% of the children are Asian Americans who speak Hmong, Khmer, or Lao, 45% are Hispanics who speak Spanish or English at home, and the remaining 10% are African Americans and whites who speak English.

After the children retell the story, Ms. McCloskey rereads it, stopping several times to ask children to think about the characters, make inferences, and reflect on the theme. Her questions include: Why did the police officer help the ducks? What would have happened to the ducks if the police officer didn't help? Do you think that animals should live in cities? What was Robert McCloskey trying to say to us in this story?

On the third day, Ms. McCloskey reads the story again and the children take turns using the pointer to track the text and join in reading familiar words. After they finish reading the story, the children clap. They're proud of their reading, and rereading the now familiar story provides a sense of accomplishment.

Ms. McCloskey understands that her students are moving through three developmental stages—emergent, beginning, and fluent—as they learn to read and write. She monitors each child's stage of development to provide instruction that meets his or her needs. As she reads the big book aloud, she uses a pointer to show the direction of print, from left to right and top to bottom on the page. She also moves the pointer across the lines of text, word by word, to demonstrate the relationship between the words on the page and the words she is reading aloud. These are concepts that many of the younger, emergent-stage readers are learning.

Other children are beginning readers who are learning to recognize high-frequency words and decode phonetically regular words. One day after rereading the story, Ms. McCloskey turns to one of the pages and asks the children to identify familiar high-frequency words (e.g., *don't, make*) and decode other CVC words (e.g., *run, big*). She also asks children to isolate individual sentences on the page and note the capital letter at the beginning and the punctuation that marks the end of the sentence.

The third group of children are fluent readers, and Ms. McCloskey addresses their needs, too, as she rereads a page from the story. She asks several children to identify the words that are adjectives and to notice inflectional endings on verbs. She also rereads the last sentence on the page and asks a child to explain why commas are used in that sentence.

Ms. McCloskey draws the children's attention to the text as a natural part of shared reading. She demonstrates concepts, points out letters, words, and punctuation marks, models strategies, and asks questions. All of the children are usually present for these lessons no matter what their stage of development, and as they think about the words and sentences, watch Ms. McCloskey, and listen to their classmates, they are learning more about literacy.

Ms. McCloskey and her teaching partner, Mrs. Papaleo, share a large classroom and the 38 students, and despite the number of children in the classroom, it feels spacious. Children's desks are arranged in clusters around the large, open area in the middle of the classroom where children meet for whole-class activities. An easel to display big books is placed next to the teacher's chair. Several chart racks stand nearby; one rack holds morning messages and other interactive writings that children have written, a second one holds charts with poems that the children have used for choral reading, and a third rack holds a pocket chart with word cards and sentence strips.

On one side of the classroom is a large classroom library with books arranged by topic in crates. One crate has frog books, and others have books about the ocean, plants, and the five senses. Other crates contain books by authors who have been featured in author studies, including Eric Carle, Norman Bridwell, Paul Galdone, and Paula Danziger. Picture books and chapter books are neatly arranged in the crates; children take turns keeping the area neat. Sets of leveled books are arranged above the children's reach for the teachers to use in guided reading instruction. A child-size sofa, a table and chairs, pillows, and rugs make the library area cozy and inviting to children. A listening center is set up at a nearby table with a tape player and headphones that can accommodate up to six children at a time.

A word wall[C] with high-frequency words fills a divider separating sections of the classroom. The word wall is divided into small sections, one for each letter of the alphabet. Arranged on the word wall are nearly 100 words written on small cards cut into the shape of the words. The teachers introduce new words each week and post them on the word wall. The children often practice reading and writing the words as a center activity, and they refer to the word wall to spell words when they are writing.

On another side of the classroom is a bank of computers and a printer. All of the children, even the youngest ones, use the computers. Children who have stronger computer skills help their classmates. They use word processing and publishing software to publish their writing during writing workshop. They monitor their independent reading practice on the computer using the Accelerated Reader program. At other times during the day, they use the Internet to find information related to topics they are studying in science and social studies and use other computer software to learn typing skills.

Literacy, math, and science center materials are stored in another area. Clear plastic boxes hold sets of magnetic letters, puppets and story box objects, white boards and dry-erase pens, puzzles and games, flash cards, and other manipulatives. The teachers choose materials from the boxes to use during minilessons[C] and guided reading[C] lessons, and they also set carefully prepared boxes of materials out on the children's desks for them to use during the centers time.

Ms. McCloskey spends the morning teaching reading and writing using a variety of teacher-directed and student-choice activities. Her daily schedule is

Figure 2-1 Ms. McCloskey's Schedule

Time	Activity	Explanation
8:10–8:20	Class Meeting	Children participate in opening activities, including saying the Pledge of Allegiance, marking the calendar, and reading the morning message.
8:20–8:45	Shared Reading	Ms. McCloskey reads and rereads big books and poems written on charts with children. She often uses this activity as a lead-in to the minilesson.
8:45–9:00	Minilesson	Ms. McCloskey teaches a minilesson to a small group or to the whole class on a literacy procedure, concept, strategy, or skill, depending on children's needs.
9:00–9:45	Writing Workshop	Children write stories, books, letters, and other compositions independently while Ms. McCloskey confers with individual children and small groups. She also does interactive writing activities with emergent and beginning writers.
9:45–10:00	Recess	
10:00–11:15	Reading Workshop	Children read self-selected books and reread leveled books independently while Ms. McCloskey does guided reading with small groups of children reading at the same level.
11:15–11:30	Class Meeting	Children meet together to review the morning's activities and children share their writing from the author's chair.
11:30–12:10	Lunch	
12:10–12:30	Read Aloud	Ms. McCloskey reads aloud picture books and chapter books, and children discuss the books in grand conversations.

shown in Figure 2-1. After shared reading and a minilesson, the children participate in reading and writing workshop.

Children write books and other compositions during writing workshop. The children pick up their writing folders and write independently at their desks. While most of the children are working, Ms. McCloskey brings together a small group of children for a special activity. She conducts interactive writing lessons with emergent writers and teaches the writing process and revision strategies to more fluent writers. Today she is conferencing with a group of six children who are beginning writers. They are writing longer compositions, and Ms. McCloskey has decided to introduce revising. Each child reads his or her composition aloud to the group, classmates ask questions and offer compliments, and Ms. McCloskey encourages them to make a change in their writing so that their readers will understand it better. Anthony reads aloud a story about his soccer game and after a classmate asks a question, he realizes that he needs to add more about how he scored a goal. He moves back to his desk to revise. The group continues with children sharing their writing and beginning to make revisions. At the end of the writing workshop, the teachers bring the children together for author's chair. Each day, three children take turns sitting in a special chair called "the author's chair" to read their writing aloud to their classmates. Classmates clap after each child reads and they offer compliments.

During reading workshop, children read and reread books independently while Ms. McCloskey and her teaching partner conduct guided reading lessons. The children have access to a wide variety of books in the classroom library, including predictable books for emergent readers, decodable books for beginning readers, and easy-to-read chapter books for fluent readers. Ms. McCloskey has taught them how to choose books that they can read successfully so they are able to spend their time reading, either independently or with a buddy. They read library books, reread books they have recently read in guided reading, and read books in the Accelerated Reader program and take the computer-generated comprehension tests. The children keep lists of the books they read and reread in their workshop folders so that Ms. McCloskey can monitor their progress.

Ms. McCloskey is working with a group of four emergent readers. They will read *Playing* (Prince, 1999), a seven-page predictable book with one line of text on each page that uses the pattern "I like to _____ ." She begins by asking children what they like to do when they are playing. Der says, "I like to play with my brother," and Ms. McCloskey writes the sentence on a strip of paper. Some of the children say only a word or two, and she expands the words into a sentence for the child to repeat. Then she writes the expanded sentence and reads it with the child. After this introduction, she introduces the book and reads the title and the author's name. Next, Ms. McCloskey does a picture walk with the children, talking about the picture on each page and naming the activity the child is doing—running, jumping, sliding, and so on. She reviews the "I like to _____" pattern and then the children read the book independently while Ms. McCloskey supervises and provides assistance as needed. The children eagerly reread the book several times, becoming more confident and excited with each reading.

Ms. McCloskey reviews the high-frequency words *I, like,* and *to,* and the children point them out on the classroom word wall. They use magnetic letters to form the words and then write sentences that begin with *I like to . . .* on white boards. Then Ms. McCloskey cuts apart their sentence strips for them to sequence and the children each put their sentences into an envelope to practice another day. At the end of the group session, Ms. McCloskey suggests that the children might want to write "I like to _____" books during writing workshop the next day.

During the last 30 minutes before lunch, the children work at literacy centers. Ms. McCloskey and Mrs. Papaleo have set out 12 centers in the classroom, and the children are free to work at any centers they choose. They practice phonics at the games center, for example, and reread texts at the interactive chart center and the library center. The children are familiar with the routine and know what is expected of them at each center. The two teachers circulate around the classroom, monitoring children's work and taking advantage of teachable moments to clarify misunderstandings, reinforce previous lessons, and extend children's learning. A list of the literacy centers is presented in Figure 2-2.

After lunch, Ms. McCloskey finishes her literacy block by reading aloud picture books and easy-to-read chapter books. Sometimes she reads aloud books

Figure 2-2 The Literacy Centers in Ms. McCloskey's Classroom

Center	Activities
Bag a Story	The teacher places seven objects in a lunch bag. Children use the objects to create a story. They divide a sheet of paper into eight sections, and they introduce the character in the first section and focus on one object in each of the remaining boxes.
Clip Boards	Children search the classroom for words beginning with a particular letter or featuring a particular characteristic. They read books, charts, and signs and consult dictionaries.
Games	Children play alphabet, phonics, opposites, and other literacy card games and board games.
Interactive Chart	The teacher introduces a poetry frame and children create a poem together as a class. They brainstorm words for each category and the teacher writes the words on cards. The children arrange the cards in a pocket chart to make the poem. Then the materials are placed in the center, and children arrange the word cards to create poems.
Library	Children read books related to a thematic unit. Then they write a sentence or two about the book and draw an illustration in their reading logs.
Listening	Children listen to a tape of a story or informational book while they follow along in copies of the book.
Making Words	The teacher chooses a secret word related to a story children are reading or to a thematic unit and sets magnetic letters spelling the word in a metal pan for children to use to make words. Children use the letters to spell two-, three-, and four-letter words. Then they arrange all of the letters to discover the secret word.
Messages	Children write messages to classmates and to Ms. McCloskey and post them on a special bulletin board titled "Message Center."
Pocket Chart	Children use the high-frequency and thematic word cards displayed in the pocket chart for word sorts.
Reading the Room	Children use pointers to point to and reread big books, charts, signs, and other texts in the classroom.
Research	Children use the Internet, informational books, photos, and realia to learn about the social studies or science topics as part of thematic units.
Story Reenactment	Children use small props, finger puppets, or flannel board figures to reenact stories they have read or listened to the teacher read aloud.

by a particular author, such as Marc Brown, Lois Ehlert, and Paula Danziger, but at other times she reads books related to a social studies or science unit. She uses these read-alouds to teach comprehension strategies, such as predicting, visualizing, and making connections. This week, she is reading award-winning books, and today she reads aloud *The Stray Dog* (Simont, 2001), the story of a homeless dog that is taken in by a loving family. After she reads the book aloud, the children talk about it in a grand conversation, and Ms. McCloskey asks them to make text-to-self, text-to-world, and text-to-text connections. As the children share their connections, the teachers record them on a chart divided into three sections. Most of their comments are text-to-self connections, but several children make other types of connections: Rosario says, "I am thinking of a movie. It was 101 Dalmations. It was about dogs, too." Angelo offers, "You got to stay away from stray dogs. They can bite you, and they might have this bad disease that can kill you. I know that you have to get shots if a dog bites you."

Ms. McCloskey knows her students well. She knows about their families, their language backgrounds, their interests, and their academic abilities. She knows how to monitor progress, facilitate their development, and what to do if they are not progressing. She knows the level of achievement that is expected by the end of the school year according to school district guidelines and state-mandated standards. Ms. McCloskey's literacy program facilitates her instruction and assessment.

L iteracy is a process that begins well before children begin school and continues into adulthood, if not throughout life. It used to be that 5-year-old children came to kindergarten to be "readied" for reading and writing instruction, which would formally begin in first grade. The implication was that there was a point in children's development when it was time to begin teaching them to read and write. For those not ready, a variety of "readiness" activities would prepare them for reading and writing. Since the 1970s, this view has been discredited by the observations of both teachers and researchers (Clay, 1989). The children themselves demonstrated that they could recognize signs and other environmental print, retell stories, scribble letters, invent printlike writing, and listen to stories read aloud. Some children even taught themselves to read.

This new perspective on how children become literate—that is, how they learn to read and write—is known as *emergent literacy,* a term that New Zealand educator Marie Clay is credited with coining. Studies from 1966 on have shaped the current outlook (Clay, 1967; Durkin, 1966; Holdaway, 1979; Snow, Burns & Griffin, 1998; Taylor, 1983; Teale & Sulzby, 1989). Now, researchers look at literacy learning from the child's point of view. The age range has been extended to include children as young as 1 or 2 who listen to stories being read aloud, notice labels and signs in their environment, and experiment with pencils. The concept of literacy has been broadened to incorporate the cultural and social aspects of language learning, and children's experiences with and understandings about written language—both reading and writing—are included as part of emergent literacy.

Teale and Sulzby (1989) paint a portrait of young children as literacy learners with these characteristics:

- Children begin to learn to read and write very early in life.
- Young children learn the functions of literacy through observing and participating in real-life settings in which reading and writing are used.
- Young children's reading and writing abilities develop concurrently and interrelatedly through experiences in reading and writing.
- Through active involvement with literacy materials, young children construct their understanding of reading and writing.

To link to the *Clearinghouse on Elementary and Early Childhood Education* for reports on special topics related to emergent literacy, listserv discussion groups, and Internet links, visit our Companion Website at www.prenhall.com/tompkins

In the vignette at the beginning of this chapter, Ms. McCloskey's students exemplified many of these characteristics.

Teale and Sulzby describe young children as active learners who construct their own knowledge about reading and writing with the assistance of parents and other literate people. These caregivers help by demonstrating literacy as they read and write, by supplying materials, and by structuring opportunities for children to be involved in reading and writing. The environment is positive, with children experiencing reading and writing in many facets of their everyday lives and observing others who are engaged in literacy activities.

FOSTERING YOUNG CHILDREN'S INTEREST IN LITERACY

Children's introduction to written language begins before they come to school. Parents and other caregivers read to young children, and children observe adults reading. They learn to read signs and other environmental print in their community. Children experiment with writing and have their parents write for them. They also observe adults writing. When 4- and 5-year-olds come to school, their knowledge about written language expands quickly as they participate in meaningful, functional, and genuine experiences with reading and writing.

Concepts About Print

Through experiences in their homes and school-based early childhood programs, children learn that print carries meaning and that reading and writing are used for a variety of purposes. They read restaurant menus to know what foods are being served, write and receive cards and letters to communicate with friends and relatives, and read and listen to stories for enjoyment. Children also learn about language purposes as they observe parents and teachers using written language in many different ways.

Children's understanding about the purposes of reading and writing reflects how written language is used in their community. Although reading and writing are part of daily life for almost every family, families use written language for different purposes in different communities (Heath, 1983). Young children have a wide range of literacy experiences in both middle-class and working-class families, even though those experiences might be different (Taylor, 1983; Taylor & Dorsey-Gaines, 1987). In some communities, written language is used mainly as a tool for practical purposes such as paying bills, whereas in other communities, reading and writing are also used for leisure-time activities. In still other communities, written language serves even wider functions, such as debating social and political issues.

PreK and kindergarten teachers demonstrate the purposes of written language and provide opportunities for children to experiment with reading and writing in many ways:

- posting signs in the classroom
- making a list of classroom rules
- using reading and writing materials in literacy play centers
- writing notes to students in the class
- exchanging messages with classmates
- reading and writing stories
- making posters about favorite books

- labeling classroom items
- drawing and writing in journals
- writing morning messages
- recording questions and information on charts
- writing notes to parents
- reading and writing letters to pen pals
- singing and reading songs and poems on charts
- writing charts and maps

Young children learn concepts about print as they observe print in their environment, listen to parents and teachers read books aloud, and experiment with reading and writing themselves. They learn basic concepts about letters, words, writing, and reading, concepts about combining letters to create words and combining words to compose sentences, and terms for positions in words and text such as *beginning, middle,* and *end* (Clay, 1991, 1993). Three types of concepts about print are:

1. ***Book-orientation concepts.*** Children learn how to hold books and turn pages, and they learn that the text, not the illustrations, carries the message.
2. ***Directionality concepts.*** Children learn that print is written and read from left to right and from top to bottom on a page, and they match voice to print, pointing word by word to text as it is read aloud. Children also notice punctuation marks and learn their names and purposes.
3. ***Letter and word concepts.*** Children learn to identify letter names and match upper- and lowercase letters. They also learn that words are composed of letters, that sentences are composed of words, that a capital letter highlights the first word in a sentence, and that spaces mark boundaries between words and between sentences (Clay, 1991).

Children develop these three concepts about print as they learn to read and write, and during the primary grades, they refine their concepts about print through increasingly sophisticated reading and writing experiences. It is important that children understand the terms that teachers use in literacy instruction, such as *letter, word,* and *sentence.*

Concept of a Word. Children's understanding of the concept of a "word" is an important part of becoming literate. Young children have only vague notions of language terms, such as *word, letter, sound,* and *sentence,* that teachers use in talking about reading and writing (Downing, 1970, 1971–1972). Researchers have found that young children move through several levels of awareness and understanding about this terminology during the primary grades (Downing & Oliver, 1973–1974).

Preschoolers equate words with the objects they represent. As they are introduced to reading and writing experiences, children begin to differentiate between objects and words, and finally they come to appreciate that words have meanings of their own. Templeton (1980) explains children's development with these two examples:

> When asked if "dog" were a word, a four-year-old acquaintance of mine jumped up from the floor, began barking ferociously, and charged through the house, alternately panting and woofing. Confronted with the same question, an eight-year-old friend responded "of course 'dog' is a word," and went on to explain how the spelling

represented spoken sounds and how the word *dog* stood for a particular type of
animal. (p. 454)

Several researchers have investigated children's understanding of a word as a unit
of language. Papandropoulou and Sinclair (1974) identified four stages of word con-
sciousness. At the first level, young children do not differentiate between words and
things. At the second level, children describe words as labels for things. They consider
words that stand for objects as words, but they do not classify articles and prepositions
as words because words such as *the* and *with* cannot be represented with objects. At
the third level, children understand that words carry meaning and that stories are built
from words. At the fourth level, more fluent readers and writers describe words as au-
tonomous elements having meanings of their own with definite semantic and syntactic relationships. Children might say, "You make words with letters." Also at this level,
children understand that words have different appearances: They can be spoken, listened to, read, and written.

Environmental Print. Words and logos that children see in the world around
them—the sign *WalMart* above the door to the store, the label *Crest* on the tooth-
paste tube, and the words *Fruity Pebbles* on the cereal package—are environmental
print. Children move from recognizing environmental print to reading decontextual-
ized words in books. Young children begin reading by recognizing logos for fast-food
restaurants, department stores, grocery stores, and commonly used household items
within familiar contexts (Harste, Woodward, & Burke, 1984). They recognize the
golden arches of McDonald's and say "McDonald's," but when they are shown the
word *McDonald's* written on a sheet of paper without the familiar sign and restaurant
setting, they cannot read the word. Researchers have found that young emergent readers depend on context to read familiar words and memorized texts (Dyson, 1984;
Sulzby, 1985). Slowly, children develop relationships linking form and meaning as
they learn concepts about written language and gain more experience reading and
writing.

Literacy Play Centers. Young children learn about the purposes of reading and writing as they use written language in their play. As they construct block buildings, children write signs and tape them on the buildings. As they play doctor, children write
prescriptions on slips of paper. And as they play teacher, children read stories aloud to
classmates who are pretending to be students or to doll and stuffed animal "students."
Young children use these activities to reenact familiar, everyday activities and to pretend to be someone or something else. Through these literacy play activities, children
use reading and writing for a variety of purposes.

PreK and kindergarten teachers adapt play centers and add literacy materials to enhance the value of the centers for literacy learning. Housekeeping centers are probably the most common play centers, but these centers can be transformed into a grocery
store, a post office, or a medical center by changing the props. They become literacy
play centers when materials for reading and writing are included: Food packages, price
stickers, and play money are props in grocery store centers; letters, stamps, and mail-
boxes are props in post office centers; and appointment books, prescription pads, and
folders for patient records are props in medical centers. A variety of literacy play centers can be set up in classrooms, and they can often be coordinated with literature focus units and themes. Ideas for nine literacy play centers are offered in Figure 2-3.
Each center includes authentic literacy materials that children can experiment with and
use to learn more about the purposes of written language.

As 4-year-olds ex-
periment with liter-
acy materials in
play centers, they
develop an understanding of
what literacy is and how it can
be used.

Figure 2-3   Literacy Play Centers

Post Office Center

mailboxes	pens	packages	address labels
envelopes	wrapping paper	scale	cash register
stamps (stickers)	tape	package seals	money

Hairdresser Center

hair rollers	empty shampoo bottle	wig and wig stand	ribbons, barrettes, clips
brush and comb	towel	hairdryer (remove cord)	appointment book
mirror	posters of hair styles	curling iron (remove cord)	open/closed sign

Office Center

typewriter/computer	stapler	pens and pencils	message pad
calculator	hole punch	envelopes	rubber stamps
paper	file folders	stamps	stamp pad
notepads	in/out boxes	telephone	

Restaurant Center

tablecloth	silverware	tray	vest for waiter
dishes	napkins	order pad and pencil	hat and apron for chef
glasses	menus	apron for waitress	

Travel Agency Center

travel posters	maps	wallet with money and	cash register
travel brochures	airplane, train tickets	credit cards	suitcases

Medical Center

appointment books	hypodermic syringe (play)	bandages	prescription bottles
white shirt/jacket	thermometer	prescription pad	and labels
medical bag	tweezers	folders (for patient	walkie-talkie (for
stethoscope		records)	paramedics)

Grocery Store Center

food packages	grocery cart	money	cents-off coupons
plastic fruit and	price stickers	grocery bags	advertisements
artificial foods	cash register	marking pen	

Veterinarian Center

stuffed animals	white shirt/jacket	medicine bottles	popsicle stick splints
cages (cardboard boxes)	medical bag	prescription labels	hypodermic syringe (play)
	stethoscope	bandages	

Bank Center

teller window	play money	deposit slips	signs
checks	roll papers for coins	money bags	receipts

Concepts About the Alphabet

Young children also develop concepts about the alphabet and how letters are used to represent phonemes. Pinnell and Fountas (1998) have identified these eight components of letter knowledge:

1. The letter's name
2. The formation of the letter in the upper- and lowercase manuscript handwriting

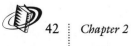

3. The features of the letter that distinguish it from other letters
4. The direction the letter must be turned to distinguish it from other letters (e.g., *b* and *d*)
5. The use of the letter in known words (e.g., names and common words)
6. The sound the letter represents in isolation
7. The sound the letter represents in combination with others (e.g., *ch, th*)
8. The sound the letter represents in the context of a word

The vignette at the beginning of this chapter about Ms. McCloskey and Mrs. Papaleo's multigrade primary class illustrated a variety of ways that young children develop letter knowledge.

The most basic information that young children learn about the alphabet is how to identify and form the letters in handwriting. They notice letters in environmental print, and they often learn to sing the ABC song. By the time children enter kindergarten, they can usually recognize some letters, especially those in their own names, in names of family members and pets, and in common words in their homes and communities. Children can also write some of these familiar letters.

Young children associate letters with meaningful contexts—names, signs, T-shirts, and cereal boxes. Baghban (1984) notes that the letter *M* was the first letter her daughter noticed. She pointed to the *M* in the word *K Mart* and called it "McDonald's." Even though the child confused a store and a restaurant, this account demonstrates how young children make associations with letters. Research suggests that children do not learn alphabet letter names in any particular order or by isolating letters from meaningful written language. McGee and Richgels (2001) conclude that learning letters of the alphabet requires many, many experiences with meaningful written language. They recommend that teachers take three steps to encourage children's alphabet learning:

1. *Capitalize on children's interests.* Teachers provide letter activities that children enjoy and talk about letters when children are interested in talking about them. Teachers know what features to comment on because they observe children during reading and writing activities to find out which letters or features of letters children are exploring. Children's questions also provide insights into what they are curious about.
2. *Talk about the role of letters in reading and writing.* Teachers talk about how letters represent sounds and how letters combine to spell words, and they point out capital letters and lowercase letters. Teachers often talk about the role of letters as they write with children.
3. *Teach routines and provide a variety of opportunities for alphabet learning.* Teachers use children's names and environmental print in literacy activities, do interactive writing[C], encourage children to use invented spellings, share alphabet books, and play letter games.

Teachers begin teaching letters of the alphabet using two sources of words—children's own names and environmental print. Teachers also provide routines, activities, and games for talking about and manipulating letters. During these familiar, predictable activities, teachers and children say letter names, manipulate magnetic letters, and write letters on the white boards. At first the teacher structures and guides the activities, but with experience, the children internalize the routine and do it independently, often at a literacy center. Figure 2-4 presents 10 routines or activities to teach the letters of the alphabet.

Being able to name the letters of the alphabet is a good predictor of beginning reading achievement, even though knowing the names of the letters does not directly

Figure 2-4 Routines to Teach the Letters of the Alphabet

1. Environmental Print
Teachers collect food labels, toy traffic signs, and other environmental print for children to use in identifying letters. Children sort labels and other materials to find examples of a letter being studied.

2. Alphabet Books
Teachers read aloud alphabet books to build vocabulary and teach students the names of words that represent each letter. Then children reread the books and consult them to think of words when making books about a letter.

3. Magnetic Letters
Children pick all examples of one letter from a collection of magnetic letters or match upper- and lowercase letter forms of magnetic letters. They also arrange the letters in alphabetical order and use the letters to spell their names and other familiar words.

4. Letter Stamps
Students use letter stamps and ink pads to stamp letters on paper or in booklets. They also use letter-shaped sponges to paint letters and letter-shaped cookie cutters to make cookies and to cut out clay letters.

5. Key Words
Teachers use alphabet charts with a picture of a familiar object for each letter. It is crucial that children be familiar with the objects or they won't remember the key words. Teachers recite the alphabet with children, pointing to each letter and saying, "A—apple, B—bear, C—cat," and so on.

6. Letter Containers
Teachers collect coffee cans or shoe boxes, one for each letter of the alphabet. They write upper- and lowercase letters on the outside of the container and place several familiar objects that represent the letter in each container. Teachers use these containers to introduce the letters, and children use them at a center for sorting and matching activities.

7. Letter Frames
Teachers make circle-shaped letter frames from tagboard, collect large plastic bracelets, or shape pipe cleaners or Wikki-Stix (pipe cleaners covered in wax) into circles for students to use to highlight particular letters on charts or in big books.

8. Letter Books and Posters
Children make letter books with pictures of objects beginning with a particular letter on each page. They add letter stamps, stickers, or pictures cut from magazines. For posters, the teacher draws a large letter form on a chart and children add pictures, stickers, and letter stamps.

9. Letter Sorts
Teachers collect objects and pictures representing two or more letters. Then children sort the objects and place them in containers marked with the specific letters.

10. White Boards
Children practice writing upper- and lowercase forms of a letter and familiar words on white boards.

Virtual Field Experience
How to Use the Accompanying CD-ROM

*F*ollowing examples of good teaching is one means of becoming an effective teacher. Simply reading and researching, however, is not enough. Witnessing meaningful teaching firsthand; observing master teachers; and reflecting on actions, decisions, and artistry behind good teaching can bring you further along on your journey toward becoming a better teacher. The CD-ROM included in this edition allows you to observe, reflect on, and learn from master teachers.

Introducing the CD

This CD contains video clips, grouped by theme, that will lead you through a full day of classroom decisions in a multi-age primary grades classroom working through a unit on insects. Margin notes throughout the text lead you to connections between chapter content and the CD. Take this time to look closely at what you'll find as you open the CD.

Study Buttons
The CD illustrates a teacher and students engaged in various aspects of literacy learning. Each teaching topic has its own button on the navigation bar on the left of the screen. By clicking on the topic of your choice, you move into the specific video clips and discussions of that topic.

Video Clips
Each topic includes nine video clips. Individual clips are labeled according to the topics illustrated. Simply click on the thumbnail of one clip to watch the video segment. Across the bottom of the video screen you'll find buttons that allow you to pause, fast forward, and rewind the clip.

Text Button
The commentators' text for the CD is provided in this area and is available for copying and pasting to your own study.

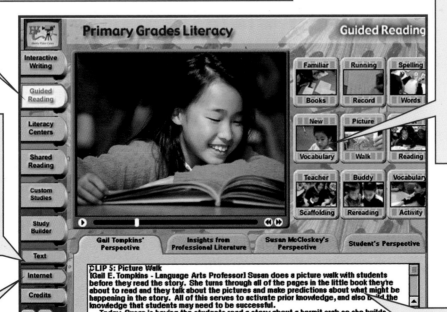

Internet Button
Clicking on the Internet button will allow you to select and launch an Internet browser such as Netscape Communicator or Microsoft Explorer. Once an Internet browser is running, you can visit the links provided or insert an Internet address and go to literature sources, discussion groups, e-mail, or other relevant sites.

Reflection Comments
As soon as a specific video clip is highlighted, comments concerning that clip also become available.

The Purpose of the CD

The CD provides immediate access to living classroom examples of teaching and learning principles. The examples provide context and anchor thinking in the realities of an authentic classroom.

The *Reflection Comments* allow you to understand a variety of reasons why selected video clips are interpreted as being examples of certain teaching or learning principles. The perspectives reveal the richness of meaning embedded in the living classroom when seen from the viewpoint of various stakeholders, including Gail Tompkins, the teacher being observed, students involved, and the professional literature that provides the research base behind the teacher's decisions. Be sure to click on the arrow at the bottom that begins the audio.

Click on a topic in the Help Topics Menu for a multimedia guide through each element in the CD, clarifying its navigation, purposes, and uses.

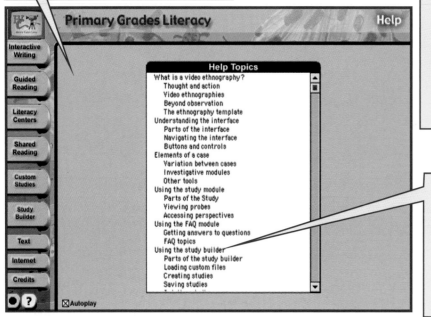

Help Topics
The ? button provides a wealth of clear, step-by-step information. Clicking on the ? button in the lower left corner will open up the help file, where you will find explanations and directions for every button and a guided tour through using the CD and building your own study.

Click on Using the Study Builder, then Using Custom Studies for a complete guide through perhaps the most innovative and meaningful piece on the CD, the opportunity to build your own video cases, perfect for an electronic teaching portfolio. We will cover this more fully over the next two pages.

Study Builder

To create your own study, begin by clicking the *Study Builder* button on the left-hand navigation bar.

Begin with your own question, then look for answers in the numerous video clips provided. For example, consider how you would teach struggling readers, or how you would manage the rest of the class during small-group instruction. Compare and contrast teaching and learning principles as they are applied with students at different levels of intellectual, emotional, and physical development. Focus on these or any other question by isolating clips in which Susan McCloskey's teaching supplies answers.

A total of 8 clips can be used in each of your personal ethnographies. Isolate and sequence clips from the 24 archived clips provided. Drag and drop your selected clips onto an open slot in the grid, then save and name your study. Now you're ready to finish by customizing your study under the *Custom Studies* button.

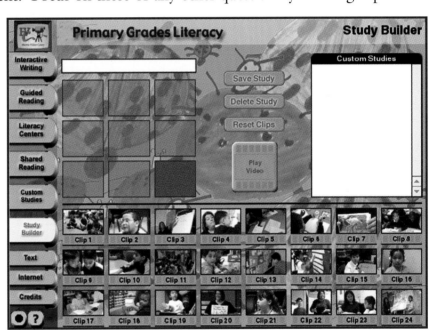

Step by Step

1. Decide on a question.
2. Select clips that focus on that query.
3. Drag and drop the clips into the 8 open slots.
4. Name the study.
5. Save the study.
6. Move on to the *Custom Studies* step.

For a more complete walk-through of this module, click on the *Help* button, then on *Using the Study Builder* under *Help Topics*.

Custom Study

Next, click on *Custom Studies*. Click on the name of your saved study in the Custom Studies field and add your own comments concerning each clip and the way it fits into your study in the Custom Studies commentary. Or add selected commentary from the researchers and participants by clicking on *Text* on the navigation bar, choosing a category, and scrolling through the categorized transcripts. When you find the appropriate comments, simply high-light the section, use the *Edit* button to copy the selection, and paste it into the commentary field on your custom study.

The *Using Custom Studies* link found on the Help screen provides a helpful reminder, should you need a bit of assistance creating your study.

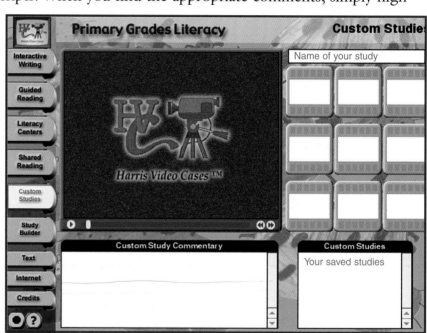

Step by Step
1. Open saved study.
2. Click on chosen clip.
3. Add comments of your own, or pull comments from the text button.
4. When you've added all your elements, save your study to your own hard drive or floppy disk.

Each custom study you create can be used to fulfill an assignment or become part of your electronic teaching portfolio. Create as many custom studies as you like and examine your own understanding of any number of teaching strategies, techniques, and concerns.

affect a child's ability to read (Adams, 1990). A more likely explanation for this relationship between letter knowledge and reading is that children who have been actively involved in reading and writing activities before entering first grade know the names of the letters, and they are more likely to begin reading quickly. Simply teaching the children to name the letters without accompanying reading and writing experiences does not have this effect.

Manuscript Handwriting

Children enter kindergarten with different backgrounds of handwriting experience. Some 5-year-olds have never held a pencil, but many others have written cursivelike scribbles or manuscript letterlike lines and circles. Some have learned to print their names and even a few other letters. Handwriting instruction in kindergarten typically includes developing children's ability to hold pencils, refining their fine motor control, and focusing on letter formation. Some people might argue that kindergartners are too young to learn handwriting skills, but young children should be encouraged to write from the first day of school. They write letters and words on labels, draw and write stories, keep journals, and write other types of messages. The more they write, the greater their need becomes for instruction in handwriting. Instruction is necessary so that students do not learn bad habits that later must be broken.

To teach children how to form letters, many kindergarten and first-grade teachers create brief directions for forming letters and sing the directions using a familiar tune. For example, to form a lowercase *a*, expand the direction "All around and make a tail" into a verse and sing it to the tune of "Mary Had a Little Lamb." As teachers sing the directions, they model the formation of the letter in the air on the chalkboard using large arm motions. Then children sing along and practice forming the letter in the air. Later, they practice writing letters using sponge paintbrushes dipped in water at the chalkboard or dry-erase pens on white boards.

Young children develop handwriting skills as they write at the writing center.

Handwriting research suggests that moving models are much more effective than still models in teaching children how to handwrite. Therefore, worksheets on the letters aren't very useful because children don't often form the letters correctly. Researchers recommend that children watch teachers form letters and then practice forming them themselves. Also, teachers supervise students as they write so that they can correct children who form letters incorrectly. It is important that students write circles counterclockwise, starting from 1:00, and form most lines from top to bottom and left to right across the page. When students follow these guidelines, they are less likely to tear the paper they are writing on, and they will have an easier transition to cursive handwriting.

YOUNG CHILDREN DEVELOP AS READERS AND WRITERS

Young children move through three broad stages as they learn to read and write (Juel, 1991). The stages are (1) emergent, (2) beginning, and (3) fluent. During the emergent stage, young children gain an understanding of the communicative purpose of print and they move from pretend reading to reading repetitive books and move from using scribbles to simulate writing to writing patterned sentences, such as *I see a bird. I see a tree. I see a car.* The focus of the second stage, beginning reading and writing, is to teach children to use phonics to "break the alphabetic code" in order to decode and spell words. In addition, children learn to read and write many high-frequency words. They also write several sentences to develop a story or other composition. In the fluent stage, children move from slow, word-by-word reading to become automatic, fluent readers, and in writing, they have good handwriting skills, spell many high-frequency words, and organize their writing into more than one paragraph.

The goal of reading and writing instruction in the primary grades is to ensure that all children reach the fluent stage by the end of third grade. Figure 2-5 summarizes children's accomplishments in reading and writing development at each of the three stages.

Four-year olds are usually emergent readers and writers who notice environmental print, play with sounds and rhyme through phonemic awareness activities, participate in shared reading, and experiment with writing.

Emergent Reading and Writing

Children gain an understanding of the communicative purpose of print and develop an interest in reading and writing during the emergent stage. They notice environmental print in the world around them and in the classroom. They develop concepts about print as teachers read and write with them. As children dictate stories for the teacher to record during language experience approach activities[C], for example, they learn that their speech can be written and they observe how teachers write from left to right and top to bottom.

Children make scribbles to represent writing. The scribbles may appear randomly on a page at first, but with experience, children line up the letters or scribbles from left to right and from top to bottom. Children also begin to "read," or tell what their writing says (Harste et al., 1984; Temple, Nathan, Burris, & Temple, 1988). At first, they can reread their writing only immediately after writing, but with experience, they learn to remember what their writing says, and as their writing becomes more conventional, they are able to read it more easily.

During the emergent stage, children accomplish the following:

- develop an interest in reading and writing
- acquire concepts about print

Figure 2-5   Young Children's Literacy Development

Stage	Reading	Writing
Emergent	Children: • notice environmental print • show interest in books • pretend to read • use picture cues and predictable patterns in books to retell the story • reread familiar books with predictable patterns • identify some letter names • recognize 5–10 familiar or high-frequency words • make text-to-self connections	Children: • distinguish between writing and drawing • write letters and letterlike forms or scribble randomly on the page • develop an understanding of directionality • show interest in writing • write their first and last names • write 5–10 familiar or high-frequency words • use sentence frames to write a sentence
Beginning	Children: • identify letter names and sounds • match spoken words to written words • recognize 20–100 high-frequency words • use beginning, middle, and ending sounds to decode words • apply knowledge of the cueing systems to monitor reading • self-correct while reading • read slowly, word by word • read orally • point to words when reading • make reasonable predictions • make text-to-self and text-to-world connections	Children: • write from left to right • print the upper- and lowercase letters • write one or more sentences • add a title • spell phonetically • spell 20–50 high-frequency words correctly • write single-draft compositions • use capital letters to begin sentences • use periods, question marks, and exclamation points to mark the end of sentences • can reread their writing
Fluent	Children: • identify most words automatically • read with expression • read at a rate of 100 words per minute or more • prefer to read silently • identify unfamiliar words using the cueing systems • recognize 100–300 high-frequency words • use a variety of strategies effectively • often read independently • use knowledge of text structure and genre to support comprehension • make text-to-self, text-to-world, and text-to-text connections • make inferences	Children: • use the writing process to write drafts and final copies • write compositions of one or more paragraphs in length • indent paragraphs • spell most of the 100 high-frequency words • use sophisticated and technical vocabulary • apply vowel patterns to spell words • add inflectional endings on words • apply capitalization rules • use commas, quotation marks, and other punctuation marks

• develop book-handling skills
• learn to identify the letters of the alphabet
• develop handwriting skills
• learn to read and write some familiar and high-frequency words

Children are usually emergent readers and writers in prekindergarten and kindergarten, but some children whose parents have read to them every day and provided a variety of literacy experiences do learn how to read before they come to school (Durkin, 1966). Caroline, a 5-year-old emergent reader and writer in Ms. McCloskey's classroom, is presented in the spotlight feature on pages 50–51.

Emergent readers and writers participate in a variety of literacy activities ranging from modeled and shared reading and writing, during which they watch as teachers read and write, to independent reading and writing that they do themselves. Ms. McCloskey's students, for example, listened to her read aloud books and read big books using shared reading, and they also participated in reading and writing workshop. When working with children at the emergent stage, however, teachers often use modeled and shared reading[C] and writing activities because they are demonstrating what readers and writers do and teaching concepts about print.

One shared literacy activity is morning messages. The teacher begins by talking about the day and upcoming events, and children share their news with the class. Then the children and teacher, working together, compose the morning message (Kawakami-Arakaki, Oshiro, & Farran, 1989). The message includes classroom news that is interesting to the children. Here is a morning message that Ms. McCloskey and her students wrote:

> Today is Thursday, March 10. Ms. McCloskey brought 3 frogs and 10 tadpoles for us to observe. They are in the pond.

The teacher writes the morning message on chart paper as children watch. While writing the message, the teacher demonstrates that writing is done from left to right and top to bottom and how to form letters. Then the teacher reads the message aloud, pointing to each word as it is read. The class talks about the meaning of the message, and the teacher uses the message to point out spelling, capitalization, or punctuation skills. Afterwards, children are encouraged to reread the message and pick out familiar letters and words. As the school year progresses, the morning message grows longer and children assume a greater role in reading and writing the message so that the activity becomes interactive writing.

Through the routine of writing morning messages, young children learn a variety of things about written language. Reading and writing are demonstrated as integrated processes, and children learn that written language is used to convey information. They learn about the direction of print, the alphabet, spelling, and other conventions used in writing. Children also learn about appropriate topics for messages and how to organize ideas into sentences.

To link to the *Center for the Improvement of Early Reading Achievement* for reports about innovative emergent literacy programs, visit our Companion Website at www.prenhall.com/tompkins

Beginning Reading and Writing

This stage marks children's growing awareness of the alphabetic principle. Children learn about phoneme-grapheme correspondences and phonics generalizations in *run, hand, this, make, day,* and *road,* and *r*-controlled vowel words, such as *girl* and *farm*. They also apply (and misapply) their developing phonics knowledge to spell words. For example, they spell *night* as NIT and *train* as TRANE. At the same time, they are learning to read and write high-frequency words, many of which can't be sounded out, such as *what, are, there,* and *get*.

Children usually read aloud slowly, in a word-by-word fashion, stopping often to sound out unfamiliar words. They point at each word as they read, but by the end of this stage, their reading becomes smoother and more fluent, and they point at words only when the text is especially challenging.

Although the emphasis in this stage is on decoding and recognizing words, children also learn that reading involves understanding what they are reading. They make predictions to guide their thinking about events in stories they read, and they make connections between what they are reading and their own lives and the world around them as they personalize the reading experience. They practice the cross-checking strategy so that they learn what to do when what they are reading doesn't make sense. They learn to consider phonological, semantic, syntactic, and pragmatic information in the text and make self-corrections (Fountas & Pinnell, 1996). They also learn about story structure, particularly that stories have a beginning, a middle, and an end, and they use this knowledge to guide their retelling of stories.

Children move from writing one or two sentences to developing longer compositions, with five, eight, or more sentences, organized into paragraphs by the end of this stage. Children's writing is better developed, too, because they are acquiring a sense of audience, and they want their classmates to like their writing. Children continue to write single-draft compositions but begin to make a few revisions and editing corrections as they learn about the writing process toward the end of the stage.

Children apply what they are learning about phonics in their spelling, and they correctly spell many of the high-frequency words that they have learned to read. They have learned to spell some of the high-frequency words, and they locate other words on word walls that are posted in the classroom. They learn to use capital letters to mark the beginnings of sentences and punctuation to mark the ends of sentences. Children are more adept at rereading their writing, both immediately after writing and days later because they are able to read many of the words they have written.

During the beginning stage of reading and writing development, children accomplish the following:

- learn phonics skills
- recognize 20–100 high-frequency words
- make reasonable predictions
- self-correct while reading
- write five or more sentences, sometimes organized into a paragraph
- spell phonetically
- spell 20–50 high-frequency words
- use capital letters to begin sentences
- use punctuation marks to mark the ends of sentences
- reread their writing

Most first and second graders are beginning readers and writers, and with instruction in reading and writing strategies and skills and daily opportunities to read and write, children move through this stage to reach the fluent stage. Anthony, a 6-year-old beginning reader and writer in Ms. McCloskey's classroom, is presented in the spotlight feature on pages 52–53.

Teachers plan activities for children at the beginning stage that range from modeled to independent reading and writing activities, but the emphasis in this stage is on interactive and guided activities. Through interactive writing, choral reading,[C] and guided reading, teachers scaffold children as they read and write and provide strategy and skill instruction. For example, Ms. McCloskey's students were divided into small, homogeneous groups for guided reading lessons. The children met together to read leveled books at their reading levels, and Ms. McCloskey introduced new vocabulary words, taught reading strategies, and monitored children's comprehension.

Children practice rereading familiar books and reading other books every day to apply phonics skills and read high-frequency words. One excellent source of books is

Spotlight on . . . *An Emergent*

F ive-year-old Caroline is a friendly, eager child who is learning to speak English as she learns to read and write. Caroline's grandparents emigrated from Thailand to the United States; her family speaks Hmong at home and she speaks English only at school. When her Hmong-speaking classmates start to talk in their native language, she admonishes them to speak English because "we learn English school."

When she came to kindergarten, Caroline didn't know any letters of the alphabet and had never held a pencil. She had not listened to stories read aloud and had no book-handling experience. She barely spoke a few words of English. The classroom culture and language were very different than those of her home, but Caroline was eager to learn. For the first few days, she stood back, observing her classmates; then she said "I do" and joined them.

Caroline has made remarkable growth in 5 months. She has been reading books with repetitive sentences on each page, but now at level 3, she is beginning to use phonics to sound out unfamiliar words. She knows the names of most letters and the sounds that the letters represent. She can read about 20 high-frequency words. She has developed good book-handling skills and follows the line of words on a page. She reads word by word and points at the text as she reads. She is learning consonant and vowel sounds, but because of her pronunciation of English sounds and lack of vocabulary, she has difficulty decoding words.

Caroline demonstrates that she understands the books she reads, and she makes text-to-self connections. Recently, she was reading a book about a child having a birthday, and she pointed to the picture of a young, blond mother wrapping a child's birthday present. She looked up at Ms. McCloskey and said, "She no mom, she sister. This wrong." The woman in the picture looks nothing like her mother.

Caroline began participating in writing workshop on the first day of school, and for several weeks, she scribbled. Within a month, she learned how to print some letters because she wanted her writing to look like her classmates'. Soon she wrote her own name, copied classmates' names, and wrote words she saw posted in the classroom.

A month ago, Ms. McCloskey gave Caroline a ring for key words. Every few days, Caroline chooses a new word to add

Emergent Reader and Writer Characteristics That Caroline Exemplifies

READING	WRITING
• shows great interest in reading	• shows great interest in writing
• has developed book-handling skills	• writes from left to right and top to bottom on a page
• identifies most of the letters of the alphabet	• prints most of the letters of the alphabet
• knows some letter sounds	• writes 20 high-frequency words
• sounds out a few CVC words	• leaves spaces between words
• reads 20 high-frequency words	• writes sentences
• uses predictable patterns in text to reread familiar books	• begins sentences with a capital letter
• makes text-to-self connections	• puts periods at the ends of sentences
	• rereads what she has written immediately after writing

Reader and Writer

to her ring. Ms. McCloskey writes the word on a word card that is added to Caroline's ring. Caroline has 31 words now, including *you* and *birthday*. She flips through the cards to practice reading and she uses the words when she writes sentences.

After 4 months of instruction, Caroline began writing sentences. Ms. McCloskey introduced the frame "I see a _____" and Caroline wrote sentences using familiar words, including some from her key words ring. Then, to make her writing longer, she wrote the same sentence over and over as shown in the "Apple" writing sample shown in the box that follows.

Next, she began reading and writing color words and she expanded her writing to two sentences. Her two-sentence writing sample, "Zebras," is also shown here. Most of the words that Caroline writes are spelled correctly because she uses key words and words she locates in a picture dictionary. Notice that Caroline puts a period at the end of each sentence, but recently she has noticed that some of her classmates put a period at the end of each line so she added periods at the end of each line in the "Zebra" sample, too. When she draws a picture to accompany a sentence, Caroline can usually read her writing immediately after she has written it, but by the next day, she often doesn't remember what she has written.

Caroline has one of the thickest writing folders in the classroom, and she's very proud of her writing. Nearly 100 pages of writing are stuffed into the folder, tracing her development as a writer over the 5 months she's been in school.

Over the 5 months she has been in kindergarten, Caroline has made excellent progress in learning to read and write. She is an emergent-stage reader and writer. She can read books with repetitive patterns and is learning phonics and high-frequency words. She can write words and craft sentences. A list of the emergent-stage characteristics that Caroline exemplifies is shown in the chart.

Spotlight on . . . A Beginning

Anthony, a first grader with a ready smile, is a beginning reader and writer. He's 6 years old and says that he likes to read and write. His best friend, Angel, is also in Ms. McCloskey's classroom, and they often sit together to read and write. (The photo shows Anthony, on the right, buddy-reading with his friend Angel.) The boys eat together in the lunchroom and always play together outside, too.

Anthony is a well-behaved child who is extremely competitive. He knows he's reading at level 12 now, and he announced to Ms. McCloskey that he wants to be reading at level 15. She explained that to do that, he needs to practice reading each night at home with his mom, and he's been taking several books home each night to practice. Ms. McCloskey predicts that Anthony will be reading at level 18 by the end of the year; level 18 is the school's benchmark for the end of first grade.

According to Ms. McCloskey's assessment of Anthony's reading at the end of the second quarter, he recognizes 80 of the 100 high-frequency words taught in first grade, and he can decode most one-syllable words with short- and long-vowel sounds, including words with consonant blends and digraphs, such as *shock, chest,* and *spike.* He is beginning to try to sound out some of the more complex vowel digraphs and diphthongs (e.g., *loud, boil, soon*) and *r*-controlled vowels (e.g., *chart, snore*), and in the past month, Ms. McCloskey has noticed that his ability to decode words is growing and that about two-thirds of the time he can identify these words with more complex vowel sounds in the context of a sentence. He is also decoding some two- and three-syllable words, such as *dinner, parents,* and *hospital,* successfully in books he is reading.

Anthony reads orally and points only when he reads challenging texts. He is beginning to chunk words into phrases as he reads, and he notices when something he is reading doesn't make sense. He uses the cross-checking strategy to make corrections and get back on track.

Anthony has read 17 books this month, according to his reading workshop log. He is increasingly choosing easy-to-read chapter books to read, including Arnold Lobel's *Mouse Soup* (1977) and *Owl at Home* (1975). After he reads, he often shares his books with his friend

Beginning Reader and Writer Characteristics That Anthony Exemplifies

READING	WRITING
• likes to read	• likes to write
• reads orally	• writes single-draft compositions
• points to words when he reads challenging texts	• adds a title
• reads 80 high-frequency words	• writes organized compositions on a single topic
• uses phonics skills to decode unfamiliar words	• writes more than five sentences in a composition
• makes good predictions	• has a beginning, middle, and end in his story
• uses the cross-checking strategy	• refers to the word wall to spell high-frequency words
• retells what he reads	• uses his knowledge of phonics to spell words
• makes text-to-self and text-to-world connections	• uses capital letters to mark the beginnings of sentences
	• uses periods to mark the ends of sentences
	• reads his writing to classmates

Reader and Writer

Angel and they reread them together and talk about their favorite parts. He regularly uses the connecting comprehension strategy and shares his text-to-self and text-to-world connections with Angel and Ms. McCloskey. When he reads two or more books by the same author, he shares text-to-text comparisons and can explain to his teacher how these comparisons make him a better reader: "Now I think and read at the same time," he explains.

Anthony likes to write during writing workshop. He identified his "Being Sick" story as the very best one he has written, and Ms. McCloskey agrees. Anthony tells an interesting and complete story with a beginning, middle, and end. And, you can hear his voice clearly in the story. Anthony's story is shown in the box, and here is a transcription of it:

Being Sick

Sometimes I go outside with no! jacket on and the air went in my ear. I went inside and stayed in the house. My ear started to hurt because I had pain. I went to see if Mom was there. I found her. I told her I have an ear ache. My mom put some ear ache stuff in my ear and it made it better.

Anthony's spelling errors are characteristic of phonetic spellers. He sounds out the spelling of many words such as *sum tims* (*sometimes*) and *hrt* (*hurt*), and he's experimenting with final *e* markers at the end of *tolde* and *pane,* but ignores them on other words. He uses the word wall in the classroom and spells many high-frequency words correctly (e.g., *with, went, have*).

Anthony writes single-draft compositions in paragraph form, and he creates a title for his stories. He writes in sentences and includes simple, compound, and complex sentences in his writing. He uses capital letters to mark the beginnings of sentences and periods to mark the ends of sentences well, but he continues to randomly use capital letters at the beginnings of words.

Anthony is at the beginning stage of reading and writing development. He reads word by word, uses his finger to track text while reading, and stops to decode unfamiliar words. He is applying what he is learning about phonics to decode words when reading and to spell words when writing. He writes multisentence compositions with good sentence structure, but his phonetic spelling makes his writing difficult to read.

Being Sick
Sum tims I go autsid
With No! Jakit on and the
err went in my ere. I
went insid and stad
in the house. My ere
Strdit to hrt becuase I had
pane. I went to see if
Mom Was ther. I fand
her. I tolde her I have A Eer
Fea. My Mom put Sum Ear
Fea Stuf in My Ear. And it Mad
it Betr.

interactive electronic books that are available on CD-ROM. Children can choose the level of support they want as they read. They can follow along as the computer reads the book aloud, read most of the text themselves but highlight unfamiliar words for the computer to identify, or read the book independently. Check the Technology Link below to learn more about these innovative texts.

Technology Link

Interactive Electronic Books

Beginning readers can read interactive electronic books available on CD-ROM. The text and illustrations are displayed page by page on the computer screen. The text can be read aloud with each word or phrase highlighted as it is read, children can read the book themselves and ask the computer to identify unfamiliar words, or children can read along with the computer to develop their reading fluency. Music and sound effects accompany each program. Many programs have reading logs[C], writing activities, word identification, and other interactive activities. Electronic books are available for Macintosh and IBM computers with color monitors and CD-ROM drives. Four companies that sell electronic books are Scholastic, Broderbund, Tom Snyder Productions, and Computer Curriculum Corporation.

Scholastic's "WiggleWorks: Beginning Literacy System" is a set of 24 electronic books, including Norman Bridwell's *Clifford the Big Red Dog* (1963), arranged into three levels of difficulty. The program includes paperback copies of books, audiocassettes, and teaching guides. For information, contact Scholastic at 800-325-6149.

Broderbund's electronic books for grades K–3 are called "The Living Books Framework." Mercer Mayer's *Just Grandma and Me* (1992) and Jack Prelutsky's *The New Kid on the Block* (1984) are presented in two sets, and some books are available in both English and Spanish. Paperback copies, teaching guides, and audiocassettes are included. For information, contact Broderbund at 800-474-8840.

"Reading Magic Library," from Tom Snyder Productions, presents five animated stories that let children choose what happens next. Two of the titles are retellings of folktales, and the others were created for this program. For information, contact Tom Snyder Productions at 800-342-0236.

Computer Curriculum Corporation has a wider range of electronic books, and some are designed for children learning English as a second language. Programs include Discover English (preschool and kindergarten), First Adventures (grades 1–3), Reading Adventures (grades 2–5), and Reading Investigations (grades 3–6). For information, contact Computer Curriculum Corporation at 800-455-7910.

Guidelines for selecting electronic books for classroom use include:

1. Choose electronic books that are high-quality children's literature and available as trade books.
2. Check to see that the software is compatible with your computer.
3. Preview the software before purchasing it.
4. Determine that the electronic book is interactive.
5. Examine the related activities, such as writing journal entries and creating new versions of the book.
6. Check that technical support is available from the manufacturer by telephone or on-line.

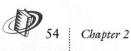

Teachers introduce the writing process to beginning-stage writers once they develop a sense of audience and want to make their writing better so that their classmates will like it. Children don't immediately begin writing rough drafts and final copies or doing both revising and editing. They often begin the writing process by rereading their compositions and adding a word or two, correcting a misspelled word, or changing a lowercase letter to a capital letter. These changes are usually cosmetic, but the idea that the writing process doesn't end after the first draft has been written is established. Next, children show interest in making a final copy that really looks good. They either recopy the composition by hand or use a computer and word process the composition and print out the final copy. Once the idea that writing involves a rough draft and a final copy is established, children are ready to learn more about revising and editing, and they usually reach this point at about the same time they become fluent writers.

Fluent Reading and Writing

The third stage is fluent reading and writing. Children are fluent readers. They can recognize hundreds and hundreds of words automatically, and they have the tools to identify unfamiliar words when reading. Children use the writing process to draft, revise, and publish their writing. They are familiar with a variety of genres and know how to organize their writing. They use conventional spelling and other elements of written language, including capital letters and punctuation marks. By the end of third grade, all students should be fluent readers and writers.

The distinguishing characteristic of fluent readers is that they read words accurately, rapidly, and automatically, and they read with expression. Their reading rate has increased to 100 words or more per minute. They automatically recognize many words and can identify unfamiliar words efficiently.

Most fluent readers prefer to read silently because they can read more quickly than when they read orally. No longer do they point at words as they read. Children actively make predictions as they read and monitor their understanding. They have a range of strategies available and use them to self-correct when the words they are reading do not make sense. Children can read most books independently.

Fluent readers' comprehension is stronger and they think more deeply about their reading than do readers in the previous stages. Researchers speculate that children's comprehension improves at this stage because they have more mental energy available for comprehension now that they recognize so many words automatically and can identify unfamiliar words more easily (LaBerge & Samuels, 1976; Perfitti, 1985; Stanovich, 1986). In contrast, beginning readers use much more mental energy in identifying words. So, as students become fluent readers, they use less energy for word identification and focus more energy on comprehending what they read.

When children talk about stories they are reading, they retell story events effectively, share details about the characters, and make connections between the stories and their own lives, between stories and the world, and between books or a book and a film. They also use background knowledge to make inferences. When they read informational books, children can distinguish between main ideas and details, notice information in illustrations and other graphics, and use technical vocabulary from the book.

Fluent readers read a variety of books in different genres. They read both picture books and chapter books, but generally prefer chapter books. They enjoy getting into a story. They can talk about books they have read recently, identify the genres of books they are reading, compare books and authors, explain why they liked a particular book, and make recommendations for classmates.

Children understand that writing is a process, and they use most of the writing process stages—prewriting, drafting, revising, editing, and publishing. They make plans for writing and write both rough drafts and final copies. They reread their rough draft compositions and make revisions and editing changes that reflect their understanding of writing forms and their purpose for writing. They increasingly share their rough drafts with classmates and turn to their classmates for advice on how to make their writing better.

Fluent writers get ideas for writing from books they have read and from television programs and movies they have viewed. They organize their writing into paragraphs, indent paragraphs, and focus on a single idea in each paragraph. They develop ideas more completely and use more sophisticated or technical vocabulary to express their ideas. They use figurative language, including similes and metaphors.

Children are aware of writing genres and organize their writing into stories, reports, letters, and poems. The stories they write have a beginning, middle, and end, and their reports are structured using sequence, comparison, or cause-and-effect structures. Their letters reflect an understanding of the parts of a letter and how the parts are arranged on a page. Their poems incorporate rhyme or other structures to create impressions.

Children's writing looks more conventional. They spell most of the 100 high-frequency words correctly and use phonics to spell other one-syllable words correctly. They add inflectional endings (e.g., *-s, -ed, -ing*) and experiment with two-syllable and longer words. They have learned to capitalize the first word in sentences and other names and to use punctuation marks correctly at the ends of sentences, although they are still experimenting with punctuation marks within sentences.

As fluent readers and writers, children accomplish the following:

- read fluently and with expression
- recognize most one-syllable words automatically and can decode other words efficiently
- use comprehension strategies effectively
- make text-to-self, text-to-world, and text-to-text connections
- write well-developed, multiparagraph compositions
- use the writing process to draft and refine their writing
- write stories, reports, letters, and other genres
- spell most high-frequency and other one-syllable words correctly
- use capital letters and punctuation marks correctly most of the time

Some second graders reach this stage, and all children should be fluent readers and writers by the end of third grade. Reaching this stage is an important milestone because it indicates that children are well prepared for the increased literacy demands of fourth grade. Fourth graders are expected to be able to read longer chapter book stories, use writing to respond to literature, read content-area textbooks, and write essays and reports. Jazmen, an 8-year-old fluent reader and writer in Ms. McCloskey's classroom, is profiled in the spotlight feature on pages 58–59.

During the fluent reading stage, children read longer, more sophisticated picture books and chapter books. They learn more about the genres of literature and literary devices, such as alliteration, personification, and symbolism. They participate in literature focus units that feature a single author, genre, or book, in small-group literature circles where children all read and discuss the same book, and in author studies where they read several books by the same author and examine that author's writing style.

Fluent readers learn more about comprehension. Through literature discussions and minilessons, they learn to make inferences and think more deeply about stories they are reading. Teachers encourage children to compare books they have read and make text-to-text connections.

A list of instructional recommendations for each of the three stages of reading and writing development is shown in Figure 2-6.

Stage	Reading	Writing
Emergent	• use environmental print • include literacy materials in play centers • read aloud to children • read poems on charts and big books using shared reading • introduce the title and author of books before reading • teach directionality and letter and word concepts using big books • encourage children to make predictions • encourage children to make text-to-self connections • have children retell and dramatize stories • have children respond to literature through talk and drawing • have children manipulate sounds using phonemic awareness activities • use alphabet-teaching routines • take children's dictation using the language experience approach • teach 20–24 high-frequency words • post words on a word wall	• have children use crayons for drawing and pencils for writing • encourage children to use scribble writing or write random letters if they cannot do more conventional writing • teach handwriting skills • use interactive writing for whole-class and small-group writing projects • have children write their names on sign-in sheets each day • write morning messages • have children write their own names and names of classmates • have children inventory words they know how to write • have children "write the classroom" and make lists of familiar words they find in the classroom • have children use frames such as "I like ____" and "I see a ____" to write sentences • encourage children to remember what they write so they can read it
Beginning	• read charts of poems and songs using choral reading • read leveled books using guided reading • provide daily opportunities to read and reread books independently • teach phonics skills • teach children to cross-check using the cueing systems • teach the 100 high-frequency words • point out whether texts are stories, informational books, or poems • model and teach predicting and other strategies • teach the elements of story structure, particularly beginning, middle, and end • have children write in reading logs and participate in grand conversations • have children make text-to-self and text-to-world connections • have children take books home to read with parents	• use interactive writing to teach concepts about print and spelling skills • provide daily opportunities to write for a variety of purposes and using different forms • introduce the writing process • teach children to develop a single idea in their compositions • teach children to proofread their compositions • teach children to spell the 100 high-frequency words • teach contractions • teach capitalization and punctuation skills • have children use computers to publish their writing • have children share their writing from the author's chair
Fluent	• have children participate in literature circles • have children participate in reading workshop • teach about genres and literary devices • involve children in author studies • teach children to make text-to-self, text-to-world, and text-to-text connections • respond to literature through talk and writing	• have children participate in writing workshop • teach children to use the writing process • teach children to revise and edit their writing • teach paragraphing skills • teach spelling generalizations • teach homophones • teach synonyms • teach root words and affixes • teach children to use a dictionary and thesaurus

Spotlight on . . . A Fluent

Jazmen is a confident and articulate African American third grader. She's 8 years old and celebrated her birthday last fall with a family trip to the Magic Mountain amusement park in Southern California. She smiles easily and likes to shake her head so that her braided, beaded hair swirls around her head. Jazmen is a pro at using computers, and she often provides assistance to her classmates. When asked about her favorite school activity, Jazmen says that she likes typing on the computer best of all. In fact, she is interested in learning more about careers that involve computers because she knows that she always wants to work with them.

Ms. McCloskey identified Jazmen as a fluent reader and writer for this feature because she has made such remarkable progress this year. This is the second year that Jazmen has been in Ms. McCloskey's class. Last year, she seemed stuck in the beginning stage of reading and writing development, not making too much progress, according to Ms. McCloskey, "but this year, it's like a lightbulb has been turned on!" She is now a fluent reader and writer.

Jazmen likes to read and reports that she has a lot of books at home. According to Accelerated Reader program, she is reading at 3.8 (third grade, eighth month) level, which means she is reading at or slightly above grade level. She enjoys reading the Marvin Redpost (e.g., *Marvin Redpost: Is He a Girl?* by Louis Sachar, 1994), Captain Underpants (e.g., *The Adventures of Captain Underpants* by Dav Pilkey, 1997), and Zack Files (e.g., *Never Trust a Cat Who Wears Earrings* by Dan Greenburg, 1997) series of easy-to-read paperback chapter books. She says that she enjoys these books because they're funny. Currently she is reading Paula Danziger's series of chapter-book stories about a third grader named Amber Brown who deals with the realities of contemporary life, including adjusting to her parents' divorce. The first book in the series is *Amber Brown Is Not a Crayon* (1994) about Amber and her best friend, Justin, who moves away at the end of the book; other chapter books in the series are *You Can't Eat Your Chicken Pox, Amber Brown* (1995b), *Amber Brown Goes Fourth* (1995a), *Amber Brown Is Feeling Blue* (1998), and *I, Amber Brown* (1999).

Jazmen reads well. She recognizes words automatically and

Fluent Reader and Writer Characteristics That Jazmen Exemplifies

READING	WRITING
• recognizes most words automatically	• uses the writing process
• reads with expression	• has a sense of audience and purpose
• reads more than 100 words per minute	• writes a complete story with a beginning, middle, and end
• reads independently	• writes in paragraphs
• uses a variety of strategies effectively	• indents paragraphs
• applies knowledge of story structure and genre when reading	• uses sophisticated language
• thinks inferentially	• spells most words correctly
• makes connections when reading	• uses capital letters and punctuation to mark sentence boundaries

Reader and Writer

reads with expression. She says that when you are reading to someone, you have to be interesting and that's why she reads the way she does. Her most outstanding achievement, according to Ms. McCloskey, is that she thinks inferentially about stories. She can juggle thinking about plot, characters, setting, and theme in order to make thoughtful connections and interpretations. She knows about various genres and literary elements, and she uses this knowledge as she reflects on her reading.

Jazmen likes to write. She gets her ideas for stories from television programs. She explains, "When I'm watching TV, I get these ideas and I draw pictures of them and that's how I think of a story." She's currently working on another story, entitled "Lucky and the Color Purple" about a princess named Lucky who possesses magical qualities. Why are her stories interesting? "Most important is that they are creative." She shares her stories with her classmates, and they agree that Jazmen is a good writer.

Jazmen is particularly pleased with her story "The Super Hero With the Long Hair," which is shown here. The story has a strong voice. Jazmen wanted her story to sound interesting, so she substituted *whined* and *grouched* for *said*. Ms. McCloskey explained that she likes the story because it is complete with a beginning, middle, and end, and because Jazmen uses dialogue (and quotation marks) effectively. The errors remaining on the final draft of the paper also suggest direction for future instruction. Jazmen spelled 95% of the words in her composition correctly. In particular, Jazmen appears ready to learn more about plurals and possessives and using commas within sentences.

During her third-grade year, Jazmen has become a fluent reader and writer, and she exemplifies the characteristics listed in the chart. In fact, her classmates look to her for leadership when they are working on reading and writing projects. They ask her assistance in choosing books and decoding difficult words. Jazmen's writing has become more polished this year, too. She now is a thoughtful writer, and she uses the writing process to draft and refine her writing. Her classmates ask her to respond to their writing, and they are eager to listen to her read her new stories from the author's chair.

The Super Hero With the Long Hair

One beutiful day Nancy woke up. When she realized her hair was more beutiful than ever. She started pumping n the bed.

After that she started brushing her hair. She kept on brushing and brushing and brushing. Then finally her sister's got so jealous they got mad.

Then they asked, "Can we brush you're hair and give you a little S...T...Y...L...E?" "Sure," said Nancy. They brushed and brushed.

All of a sudden they started cutting her hair. "What kind of S...T...Y...L...E are you doing?" "A pretty hair style." "Of course pretty. Is it really really pretty?"

"Yes yes it's really really pretty," Kelly said in a diskusting way. Then Kelly was done—Nancy went to go look in the bathroom mirror. She started to cry. Her sister's started to laugh.

Then the light started to glow on the phone. Niky answered it. It was the mayor. "Hello mayor yes we'll be right on our way. The mayor said townsvill's in trouble. There's a monster outside and he's distroying all of townsvill!" shouted Niky.

"Go whithout me," whined Nancy. "What?" "We ca'nt go without you. You're the leader." "Just go without me!" Grouched Nancy.

They left. She started to talk to her dad. She made up her mind about going. She also made up some joke's. She flew to the monster and told her joke's to him and he laghed so hard he flew all the way to Jupiter.

Her sister's said, "Are we even?" Then she lazorbeeded her sister's hair and said, "Now were even."

They lived happily everafter.

Review

Emergent literacy is the new way of looking at how children begin to read and write. Children's emergent literacy provides a foundation for their later literacy learning. Young children move through the emergent, beginning, and fluent stages as they learn to read and write in the primary grades. Effective teaching practices for working with young children are reviewed in the feature below.

How Effective Teachers . . .
Support Young Children's Literacy Development

Effective Practices

1. Teachers understand that young children can participate in reading and writing activities.
2. Teachers provide developmentally appropriate reading and writing activities for children beginning on the first day of school.
3. Teachers demonstrate the purposes of written language through a variety of literacy activities.
4. Teachers teach book-orientation concepts as they do shared reading and read aloud to children.
5. Teachers develop children's directionality concepts through shared reading and interactive writing.
6. Teachers help children develop letter and word concepts through minilessons and daily reading and writing experiences.
7. Teachers include literacy materials in play centers.
8. Teachers understand that children move through the emergent, beginning, and fluent stages of reading and writing.
9. Teachers monitor children's literacy development to see that they are moving through the three stages.
10. Teachers match instructional activities to children's stage of reading and writing development.

Professional References

Adams, M. J. (1990). *Beginning to read: Thinking and learning about print.* Cambridge, MA: MIT Press.

Baghban, M. J. M. (1984). *Our daughter learns to read and write: A case study from birth to three.* Newark, DE: International Reading Association.

Clay, M. M. (1967). The reading behaviour of five year old children. *New Zealand Journal of Educational Studies, 2,* 11–31.

Clay, M. M. (1989). Foreword. In D. S. Strickland & L. M. Morrow (Eds.), *Emerging literacy: Young children learn to read and write.* Newark, DE: International Reading Association.

Clay, M. M. (1991). *Becoming literate: The construction of inner control.* Portsmouth, NH: Heinemann.

Clay, M. M. (1993). *An observational survey of early literacy achievement.* Portsmouth, NH: Heinemann.

Downing, J. (1970). The development of linguistic concepts in children's thinking. *Research in the Teaching of English, 4,* 5–19.

Downing, J. (1971–1972). Children's developing concepts of spoken and written language. *Journal of Reading Behavior, 4,* 1–19.

Downing, J., & Oliver, P. (1973–1974). The child's conception of "a word." *Reading Research Quarterly, 9,* 568–582.

Durkin, D. (1966). *Children who read early.* New York: Teachers College Press.

Dyson, A. H. (1984). "N spell my Grandmama": Fostering early thinking about print. *The Reading Teacher, 38,* 262–271.

Fountas, I. C., & Pinnell, G. S. (1996). *Guided reading: Good first teaching for all children.* Portsmouth, NH: Heinemann.

Harste, J., Woodward, V., & Burke, C. (1984). *Language stories and literacy lessons.* Portsmouth, NH: Heinemann.

Heath, S. B. (1983). *Ways with words.* New York: Oxford University Press.

Herrell, A. L. (2000). *Fifty strategies for teaching English language learners.* Upper Saddle River, NJ: Merrill/Prentice Hall.

Holdaway, D. (1979). *The foundations of literacy.* Portsmouth, NH: Heinemann.

Juel, C. (1991). Beginning reading. In R. Barr, M. L. Kamil, P. Mosenthal, & P. D. Pearson (Eds.), *Handbook of reading research* (Vol. 2, pp. 759–788). New York: Longman.

Kawakami-Arakaki, A., Oshiro, M., & Farran, S. (1989). Research to practice: Integrating reading and writing in a kindergarten curriculum. In J. Mason (Ed.), *Reading and writing connections* (pp. 199–218). Boston: Allyn & Bacon.

LaBerge, D., & Samuels, S. J. (1976). Toward a theory of automatic information processing in reading. In H. Singer & R. Ruddell (Eds.), *Theoretical models and processes of reading* (pp. 548–579). Newark, DE: International Reading Association.

McGee, L. M., & Richgels, D. J. (2001). *Literacy's beginnings: Supporting young readers and writers* (3rd ed.). Boston: Allyn & Bacon.

Papandropoulou, I., & Sinclair, H. (1974). What is a word? Experimental study of children's ideas on grammar. *Human Development, 17,* 241–258.

Perfitti, C. A. (1985). *Reading ability.* New York: Oxford University Press.

Pinnell, G. S., & Fountas, I. C. (1998). *Word matters: Teaching phonics and spelling in the reading/writing classroom.* Portsmouth, NH: Heinemann.

Snow, C. E., Burns, M. S., & Griffin, P. (Eds.). (1998). *Preventing reading difficulties in young children.* Washington, DC: National Academy Press.

Stanovich, K. E. (1986). Matthew effects in reading: Some consequences of individual differences in the acquisition of literacy. *Reading Research Quarterly, 21,* 360–406.

Sulzby, E. (1985). Kindergartners as readers and writers. In M. Farr (Ed.), *Advances in writing research. Vol. 1: Children's early writing development* (pp. 127–199). Norwood, NJ: Ablex.

Taylor, D. (1983). *Family literacy: Young children learning to read and write.* Exeter, NH: Heinemann.

Taylor, D., & Dorsey-Gaines, C. (1987). *Growing up literate: Learning from inner-city families.* Portsmouth, NH: Heinemann.

Teale, W. H., & Sulzby, E. (1989). Emerging literacy: New perspectives. In D. S. Strickland & L. M. Morrow (Eds.), *Emerging literacy: Young children learn to read and write* (pp. 1–15). Newark, DE: International Reading Association.

Temple, C., Nathan, R., Burris, N., & Temple, F. (1988). *The beginnings of writing.* Boston: Allyn & Bacon.

Templeton, S. (1980). Young children invent words: Developing concepts of "word-ness." *The Reading Teacher, 33,* 454–459.

Children's Book References

Danziger, P. (1994). *Amber Brown is not a crayon.* New York: Scholastic.

Danziger, P. (1995a). *Amber Brown goes fourth.* New York: Scholastic.

Danziger, P. (1995b). *You can't eat your chicken pox, Amber Brown.* New York: Scholastic.

Danziger, P. (1998). *Amber Brown is feeling blue.* New York: Scholastic.

Danziger, P. (1999). *I, Amber Brown.* New York: Scholastic.

Greenburg, D. (1997). *Never trust a cat who wears earrings.* New York: Grosset & Dunlap.

Harper, C., & Randell, B. (1997). *Cats.* Crystal Lake, IL: Rigby.

Lobel, A. (1975). *Owl at home.* New York: HarperCollins.

Lobel, A. (1977). *Mouse soup.* New York: HarperCollins.

McCloskey, R. (1969). *Make way for ducklings.* New York: Viking.

Pilkey, D. (1997). *The adventures of Captain Underpants.* New York: Scholastic.

Prince, S. (1999). *Playing.* Littleton, MA: Sundance.

Sachar, L. (1994). *Marvin Redpost: Is he a girl?* New York: Random House.

Simont, M. (2001). *The stray dog.* New York: HarperCollins.

chapter 3

Assessing Young Children's Literacy Development

chapter
QUESTIONS

- Which assessment tools do teachers use to monitor students' learning in the classroom?

- How do teachers determine children's reading levels?

- How do teachers assign grades?

Mrs. McNeal Conducts Second-Quarter Assessments

The end of the second quarter is approaching, and Mrs. McNeal is assessing her first-grade students. She collects four types of assessment data about her students' reading, writing, and spelling development. Then she uses the data to document children's achievement, verify that children are meeting district standards, determine report card grades, write narratives to accompany the grades, and make instructional plans for the next quarter.

Today Mrs. McNeal assesses Seth, who is 6½ years old. He's a quiet, well-behaved child who regularly completes his work. She has a collection of Seth's writing and other papers he has done, but she wants to assess his current reading level. At the beginning of the school year, Mrs. McNeal considered him an average student but in the past month, his reading progress has accelerated. She is anxious to see how much progress he has made since the end of the first quarter.

Assessment 1: Determining Seth's Instructional Reading Level. Mrs. McNeal regularly takes running records[C] as she listens to children reread books they are familiar with in order to monitor their ability to recognize familiar and high frequency words, decode unfamiliar words, and use strategic reading behaviors. In addition, Mrs. McNeal assesses each child's instructional reading level at the beginning of the school year and at the end of each quarter. She uses the *Developmental Reading Assessment* (DRA) (Beaver, 1997), an assessment kit designed for kindergarten through third grade, which includes 44 small paperback books arranged from kindergarten to fifth-grade reading levels.

See the Compendium of Instructional Procedures, which follows Chapter 12, for more information on terms marked with the symbol [C].

To determine a child's instructional reading level, Mrs. McNeal chooses a book that the child has not read before and introduces it to the child by reading the title, examining the picture on the cover, and talking about the story. The child does a picture walk, looking through the book and talking about what is happening on each page, using the illustrations as clues. Next, the child reads the book aloud as Mrs. McNeal takes a running record, checking the words the child reads correctly and noting those read incorrectly. Then the child retells the story and the teacher prompts with questions if necessary to assess the child's understanding. Afterwards, Mrs. McNeal scores the running record to determine the child's instructional reading level.

At the beginning of the school year, most of Mrs. McNeal's first graders were reading at level 4; by midyear, they are reading at level 8; and by the end of the school year, they should be reading at levels 18 to 20. At the beginning of the school year, Seth was reading at level 4, like many of his classmates, and at the end of the first quarter, he was already reading at level 8. Mrs. McNeal decides to test him at level 16 because he is reading a level 16 book in his guided reading[C] group.

Seth reads *The Pot of Gold* (1997), a level 16 book in the DRA assessment kit. The book is an Irish folktale about a mean man named Grumble who makes an elf show him where his pot of gold is hidden. Grumble marks the spot by tying a scarf around a nearby tree branch while he goes to get a shovel with which to dig up the gold. Grumble admonishes the elf not to move the scarf, and he doesn't. Instead he ties many other scarves on nearby trees so that Grumble can't find the elf's gold. Mrs. McNeal takes a running record while Seth reads; it is shown in Figure 3-1.

As indicated on the running record sheet in Figure 3-1, there are 266 words in the book, and Seth makes 17 errors but self-corrects 5 of them. His accuracy rate is 95%. Mrs. McNeal analyzes Seth's errors and concludes that he overdepends on visual (or phonological)

Figure 3-1 — A Running Record Scoring Sheet

Name Seth **Date** Jan. 18

Level 16 **Title** The Pot of Gold   Easy (Instructional) Hard

Running Record		E	SC	E	SC
2	✓✓✓✓✓✓✓✓ ✓✓ ✓ grumply/Grumble |T ✓✓✓✓✓✓✓ ✓✓✓✓ always |A/T ✓✓✓✓✓ ✓✓✓✓✓✓✓	1 1	*Self correct*	m s (v) *vocabulary*	
3	✓✓✓✓✓✓ ✓✓✓✓✓✓ did not/didn't | ✓✓ ✓✓✓✓✓✓ ✓✓✓✓✓✓ ✓✓✓✓✓✓ ✓✓	1		(m)(s)v	
4	✓✓✓✓✓✓ ✓✓✓✓✓ ✓✓✓				
5	✓✓✓✓✓✓✓ ✓ ✓✓✓✓✓✓ I/I'll | make/move | ✓✓ ✓✓✓✓✓ safr/scarf | ✓✓✓✓✓ or/of | ✓✓	1 1 1 1		(m)(s)(v) (m)(s)(v) m s (v) m s (v)	
6	✓✓✓✓✓✓ ✓ me/my |sc self/scarf | ✓✓✓ ✓✓✓✓ ✓✓✓✓	1	1	m s (v) m s (v)	(m)(s)(v)
7	✓✓✓✓✓✓ ✓✓✓✓✓✓ ✓✓✓✓				
8	✓✓✓✓✓✓✓ ✓✓✓✓✓✓✓ ✓✓				
9	✓✓✓ take/taken | ✓ scafer/scarf | ✓✓✓ ✓✓✓✓✓✓✓	1 1		(m)s(v) m s (v)	
10	✓✓✓✓✓✓✓ ✓✓✓ they/that |sc ✓/R ✓✓✓✓✓✓ ✓✓✓✓ maybe/may | sit/still | ✓✓	1 1	1	m s (v) m s (v) m s (v)	(m)(s)(v)

Scoring 12/266 95% accuracy	Picture Walk Gets gist of story
Types of Errors: M S (V) overdependent on v cues	Oral Reading Reads fluently
Self-correction Rate 1:5	Retelling/Questions Tells BME but middle is brief

Assessment Tools

cues while ignoring semantic cues. Of the 12 errors, only one of the errors—*Grumply* for *Grumble*—makes reasonable sense in the sentence. When Seth retells the story, he shows that he understands the main idea, but his retelling is not especially strong. He retells the beginning and end of the story, but he leaves out the setting and important details in the middle; however, he does make interesting connections between the story and his own life. Mrs. McNeal concludes that level 16 is his instructional level and that his ability to read words is stronger than his comprehension.

Mrs. McNeal makes notes about Seth's instructional priorities for the next quarter. Comprehension will be her focus for Seth. She will teach Seth more about the structure of stories, including plot and setting, and help him use semantic cues to support his use of visual cues. She will encourage him to structure his oral and written retellings in three parts—beginning, middle, and end—and include more details in his retellings. She also decides to introduce Seth to easy chapter books, including Jane Yolen's Henry and Mudge series about a boy named Henry and the adventures he has with his dog, named Mudge (e.g., *Henry and Mudge and the Best Day of All,* 1995).

Assessment 2: Testing Seth's Knowledge of High-Frequency Words. Mrs. McNeal's goal is for her first graders to be able to read at least 75 of the 100 high-frequency words. At the beginning of the year, most children could read 12 or more of the words; Seth read 16 of the words correctly. Mrs. McNeal has a high-frequency word wall[C] posted in the classroom with more than 50 of the words displayed in alphabetical order. At the beginning of the year, she reviewed the 12 most common words introduced in kindergarten (e.g., *the, I, is*) and added them to the word wall, and she began adding 2 or 3 new words each week.

Today, Mrs. McNeal asks Seth to read the list of 100 high-frequency words again, which is arranged in order of difficulty. She expects that he will be able to read 50 or 60 of the words and when he misses 5 in a row, she will stop the test, but Seth surprises her and reads the entire list! He misses only these 6 words: *don't, how, there, very, were,* and *would*. Seth's high score on this assessment reinforces his results on the running record: He is a very good word reader.

Assessment 3: Checking Seth's Ability to Write and Spell Words. Several days ago, Mrs. McNeal administered the "Words I Know" Test to the whole class. She asked the children to write as many words as they could in 10 minutes without copying from charts posted in the classroom. At the beginning of the school year, most children can write and spell correctly 15 to 20 words, and Mrs. McNeal's goal is that they can write 50 words by the end of the school year. Seth wrote 22 words in August, and on the recent test he wrote 50 words that were spelled correctly. Seth's "Words I Know" test is shown in Figure 3-2.

Mrs. McNeal reviews the list of words that Seth wrote and notices that most of his words are one-syllable words with short vowels, such as *cat, pig,* and *fin,* but that he is beginning to write words with irregular or more complex spellings, such as *what, snow, come,* and *night,* words with inflectional endings, such as *trees* and *going,* and two-syllable words, such as *cowboys.* She concludes that Seth is making very good progress, both in terms of the number of words he is writing and the complexity of the spelling patterns he is using.

Assessment 4: Scoring Seth's Compositions. Mrs. McNeal looks through Seth's journal and chooses two representative samples written in the past 3 weeks to score. They are shown in Figure 3-3. The top one, which we'll call "Sleeping," is about a personal experience. The text (with conventional spelling and punctuation) reads:

> *Last night I kept waking up. My dad slept with me. Then I fell fast asleep. Then dad went to bed.*

Figure 3-2   Seth's "Words I Know" Test

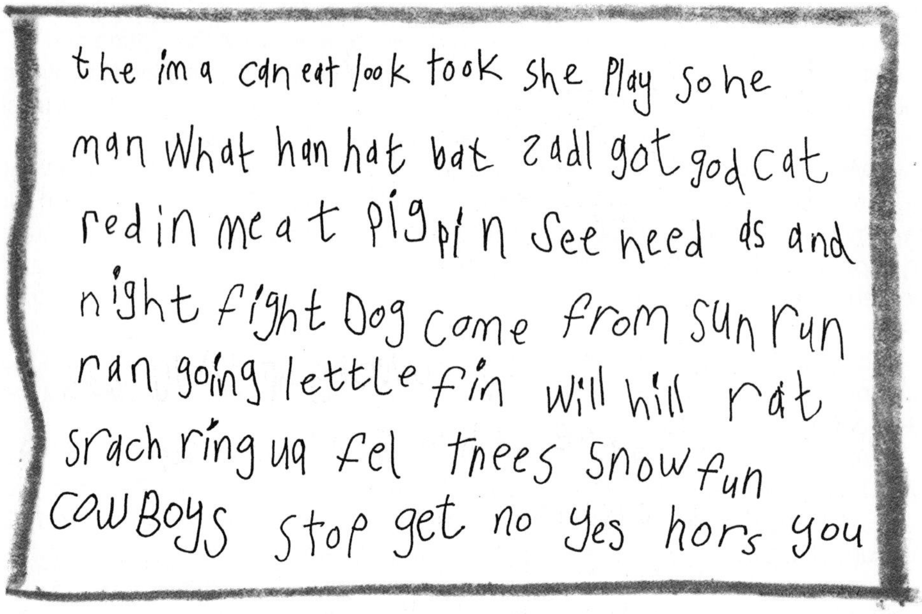

the im a can eat look took she play so he
man what han hat bat zadl got god cat
red in meat pig pi n see need ds and
night fight Dog come from sun run
ran going lettle fin will hill rat
srach ring ua fel tnees snow fun
cowboys stop get no yes hors you

The second entry is entitled "All About Planets" and demonstrates Seth's interest in the thematic unit. The text reads:

There are different planets in space like Jupiter and Saturn [and] Neptune. But the hottest one is the sun.

Using the school district's 6-point rubric, Mrs. McNeal scores the compositions as a 4. A score of 5 is considered grade-level at the end of the school year, and Mrs. McNeal feels that Seth will reach that level before then. Mrs. McNeal notes that Seth is writing two to four sentences in an entry, even though he often omits punctuation at the ends of sentences. He draws illustrations to support his compositions, and his sentences can be read. He is beginning to add titles to his entries, as shown in the "All About Planets" entry. Seth writes fluently but he sometimes omits a word or two. Mrs. McNeal plans to talk to Seth about the importance of rereading his writing to catch any omissions, add punctuation marks, and correct misspelled words.

Seth spells more than two-thirds of the words he writes correctly, and he uses invented spelling that usually represents beginning, middle, or ending sounds. In the "Sleeping" entry, Seth wrote 21 words, spelling 13 of them correctly. In the "Planets" entry, Seth again wrote 21 words, spelling 17 of them correctly. This means that Seth spelled 71% of the words in his compositions correctly. He reversed the order of letters in three words in the "Sleeping" entry (*lats* for *last*, *fli* for *fell*, *ot* for *to*) but did not make any letter-order reversals in the "All About Planets" entry. Mrs. McNeal recognizes that many first graders form letters backwards and make letter-order reversals; she isn't concerned about Seth's reversals because she thinks that with more writing practice, he'll outgrow them.

Assessment 5: Measuring Seth's Phonics and Spelling Knowledge. Each week, Mrs. McNeal and the first graders craft two sentences to use for a dictation test. On Monday, they create the sentences and write them on a piece of chart pa-

Figure 3-3   Seth's Journal Entries

Lat S mi I cap wachg up. My dad
Sept with me then I fli fast a sep
Then dad went ot bed.

All about Planis.

There are difer planis in space
like Juqiter and Saturn neptune
But the hots one is the sun.

per that is displayed in the classroom for the week. Often the sentences are about current events, books Mrs. McNeal reads aloud, or the thematic unit they are studying. During the week, the children practice writing the sentences on small white boards, and Mrs. McNeal uses the text for minilessons[c] during which she draws children's attention to high-frequency words they have studied, the phonetic features of various words, and capitalization and punctuation rules applied in the sentences. At the beginning of the school year, they wrote one sentence each week, but for the past 6 weeks, they have been writing two sentences. Last week's sentences focused on the class's thematic unit on the solar system and *The Magic School Bus Lost in the Solar System* (Cole, 1993), a book Mrs. McNeal read aloud to the class:

Their bus turned into a rocket ship. They wanted to visit all of the planets.

After practicing the sentences all week, Mrs. McNeal dictates the sentences for the students to write on Friday. She tells them to spell as many words correctly as they can and to write all the sounds they hear in the words they don't know how to spell. Seth wrote:

The bus turd into a rocket ship they wande to vist all of the planis.

Seth spelled 10 of the 15 words correctly and included 46 of 51 sounds in his writing. In addition, he omitted the period at the end of the first sentence and did not capitalize the first word in the second sentence.

Mrs. McNeal uses this test to check the students' phonics knowledge and ability to spell high-frequency words. Seth spelled most of the high-frequency words correctly, except that he wrote *the* for *their.* In the other four misspellings, Seth's errors involved the second syllable of the word or an inflectional ending. Mrs. McNeal concludes that Seth is making good progress in learning to spell high-frequency words and that he is ready to learn more about two-syllable words and inflectional endings.

Grading Seth's Reading, Writing, and Spelling Achievement. Having collected these data, Mrs. McNeal is ready to complete Seth's report card. Seth and his classmates receive separate number grades in reading, writing, and spelling. The grades range from 1, not meeting grade level standards, to 4, exceeding grade level standards. Seth will receive a 3 in reading, writing, and spelling. A score of 3 means that Seth is meeting grade level standards in all three areas. Even though his reading level is higher than average, his dependence on visual cues when decoding unfamiliar words and his weakness in comprehension keep him at level 3 in reading.

Mrs. McNeal writes narratives to explain each student's progress in reading and writing and to offer suggestions to parents about how they can help their students at home. She sends the narrative home along with the report card. Here is what Mrs. McNeal wrote about Seth's progress in reading and writing:

> <u>Reading progress</u>: *Seth is reading at level 16. He uses a variety of strategies and is a fluent reader. He is beginning to retell the beginning, middle, and end of stories, but he needs to use more details.*
> <u>Writing and spelling progress</u>: *Seth writes two to four sentences about a subject. He still uses a lot of invented spellings, especially in two-syllable words, although his sight word memory has grown from 26 to 50 words. He often forgets to put in ending punctuation marks.*

To link to *The Nation's Report Card,* which presents results of the National Assessment of Educational Programs (NAEP), visit our Companion Website at **www.prenhall.com/tompkins**

Assessment is an integral part of teaching and learning. The purpose of classroom assessment is to inform and influence instruction. Through assessment, teachers learn about their students, about themselves as teachers, and about the impact of the instructional program. Similarly, when students reflect on their learning and use self assessment, they learn about themselves as learners and also about their learning. Figure 3-4 presents guidelines for classroom assessment and describes how teachers can use assessment tools in their classrooms.

Figure 3-4 Guidelines for Classroom Assessment

1. Select Appropriate Assessment Tools
Teachers identify their purpose for assessment and choose an appropriate assessment tool. To gauge children's reading fluency, for example, teachers can do a running record, and to judge whether or not children are comprehending, they can examine children's reading logs and listen to their comments during a grand conversation.

2. Use a Variety of Assessment Tools
Teachers learn and then regularly use a variety of assessment tools that reflect current theories about how children learn and become literate, including running records, retellings, and reading logs.

3. Integrate Instruction and Assessment
Teachers use the results of assessment to inform their teaching. They observe and conference with children as they teach and supervise children during reading and writing activities. When children do not understand what teachers are trying to teach, teachers need to try other instructional procedures.

4. Focus on the Positive
Teachers focus on what children can do, not what they can't do. Too often, teachers want to diagnose children's problems and then remediate or "fix" these problems, but they should focus on how to facilitate children's development as readers and writers.

5. Examine Both Processes and Products
Teachers examine both the processes and the products of reading and writing. Teachers notice the strategies that children use as well as assess the products they produce through reading and writing.

6. Use Multiple Contexts
Teachers assess children's literacy development in a variety of contexts, including literature focus units, literature circles, reading and writing workshop, basal reader programs, and thematic units. Multiple contexts are important because children often do better in one type of activity than another.

7. Work With Individual Children
In addition to making whole-class assessments, teachers make time to observe, conference with, and do other assessment procedures with individual children in order to develop clear understandings of the child's development as a reader or writer.

8. Encourage Self-Assessment
Children's reflection on and self-assessment of their progress in reading and writing should be an integral part of assessment.

LITERACY ASSESSMENT TOOLS

Teachers use a variety of literacy assessment tools and procedures to monitor and document students' reading and writing development. These tools examine students' ability to identify words, read fluently, comprehend what they are reading, use the writing process, and spell words. Many of these tools are informal and created by teachers, but others have been developed, standardized, and published by researchers.

Teachers also use assessment tools to diagnose struggling students' reading and writing problems. Many of these assessments are used with individual students, and even though it takes time to administer individual assessments, the information the teacher gains is useful and valuable. Giving a paper-and-pencil test to the entire class rarely provides much useful information. Teachers learn much more about their students as they listen to individual students read, watch individual students write, and talk with individual students about their reading and writing.

Assessing Children's Concepts About Print

Teachers assess 4-year-olds' knowledge of book-orientation concepts, directionality concepts, and letter and word concepts by informally monitoring children's interactions with books and by administering Marie Clay's Concepts About Print Test as they read books individually with children.

Young children learn concepts about print as they observe written language in their environment, listen to parents and teachers read books aloud, and experiment with reading and writing themselves. They learn basic concepts about letters, words, writing, and reading, and they demonstrate this knowledge when they turn the pages in a book, participate in interactive writing[C] activities, and identify letters, words, and sentences on classroom charts.

Marie Clay (1985, 2000a) developed the Concepts About Print Test (CAP Test) to more formally assess young children's understanding of written language concepts. The test has 24 items, and it is administered individually in 10 minutes. As the teacher reads the story aloud, the child looks at a test booklet with a story that has a picture on one facing page and text on the other. The child is asked to open the book, turn pages, and point out particular features of the text, including letters, words, sentences, and punctuation marks, as the story is read.

Teachers can also create their own versions of the CAP Test to use with any story they are reading with a child. As with the CAP Test, teachers' adaptations examine children's understanding that print carries the meaning and their understanding of directionality of print, tracking of print, and letter, word, and sentence representation.

Assessment Resources

Concepts About Print

Marie Clay developed the Concepts About Print Test (CAP Test) to assess young children's understanding of concepts about print. These three types of concepts are assessed:

1. Book orientation concepts
2. Directionality concepts
3. Letter and word concepts

There are four forms of the CAP Test booklet available—*Sand* (Clay, 1972), *Stones* (Clay, 1979), *Follow Me, Moon* (Clay, 2000b), and *No Shoes* (Clay, 2000c)—as well as a Spanish version. Teachers use the CAP Test booklets or any big book or small book. They administer the test by reading a book to the child and asking the child to point to the first page of the story, show the direction of print, and point to letters, words, and punctuation marks. It is important that teachers carefully observe children as they respond and mark their responses on a scoring sheet. For more information, see *An Observational Survey of Early Literacy Assessment* (Clay, 1993) or *Concepts About Print: What Have Children Learned About the Way We Print Language?* (Clay, 2000a).

Figure 3-5 Concepts About Print Test Scoring Sheet

CAP Test Scoring Sheet

Name _____ Date _____

Title of Book _____

Check the items that the child demonstrates.

1. Book Orientation Concepts
☐ Shows the front of a book.
☐ Turns to the first page of the story.
☐ Shows where to start reading on a page.

2. Directionality Concepts
☐ Shows the direction of print across a line of text.
☐ Shows the direction of print on a page with more than one line of print.
☐ Points to track words as the teacher reads.

3. Letter and Word Concepts
☐ Points to any letter on a page.
☐ Points to a particular letter on a page.
☐ Puts fingers around any word on a page.
☐ Puts fingers around a particular word on a page.
☐ Puts fingers around any sentence on a page.
☐ Points to the first and last letters of a word.
☐ Points to a period or other punctuation mark.
☐ Points to a capital letter.

Summary Comments:

Assessment Tools

As they read any big book or small book with a child, teachers ask the child to show book-orientation concepts, directionality concepts, and letter and word concepts. Teachers can use the CAP Test scoring sheet shown in Figure 3–5 or develop one of their own to monitor children's growing understanding of these concepts.

Assessing Children's Phonemic Awareness and Phonics

Children learn about the alphabetic principle (that letters represent sounds) in the primary grades. Through phonemic awareness instruction, students learn strategies for segmenting, blending, and substituting sounds in words, and through phonics instruction, they learn about consonant and vowel sounds and phonics generalizations. Teachers often monitor students' learning as they participate in phonemic awareness and phonics activities in the classroom. When they sort picture cards according to beginning sounds or identify rhyming words in a familiar song, students are demonstrating their knowledge of phonemic awareness. Similarly, when students use magnetic letters to spell words ending in -*at,* such as *bat, cat, hat, mat, rat,* and *sat,* they are

Assessment Resources

Phonemic Awareness and Phonics

Teachers in kindergarten and first grade teach and monitor students' growing phonemic awareness by using a variety of classroom activities and these test instruments:

Phonemic Awareness in Young Children (Adams, Foorman, Lundberg & Beeler, 1997)

Test of Phonological Awareness (Torgesen & Bryant, 1994)

Yopp-Singer Test of Phonemic Segmentation (Yopp, 1995)

Primary teachers use these assessments from Clay's *Observational Survey* (1993) to assess young children's knowledge of letters of the alphabet, phonics, and words:

Letter Identification

Word Test

Dictation Task

   Teachers also check children's ability to read the 100 high-frequency words or other word lists of common words. Sometimes children read the words on flashcards, and at other times they read the words on word lists. Teachers mark which words students identify and keep track of how many words each child can read.

   Third- and fourth-grade teachers also use The Names Test (Cunningham, 1990; Duffelmeyer, Kruse, Merkley, & Fyfe, 1994) to assess their students' ability to use phonics to decode one-syllable and longer words.

demonstrating their phonics knowledge. To read more about phonemic awareness and phonics, turn to Chapter 4, "Breaking the Alphabetic Code."

Assessing Children's Fluency

During the primary grades, children become fluent readers as they learn to read words accurately, rapidly, and automatically. In addition, children chunk words into phrases and read with expression. Teachers monitor children's fluency as they listen to children read aloud. They check to see that children read with appropriate speed, chunking, expression, and pausing. They also notice if children demonstrate strategies for unlocking unfamiliar words. Fluency is important because children who read fluently are better able to comprehend what they read now that they have the mental energy to focus on what they are reading. To read more about fluency, turn to Chapter 6, "Developing Fluent Readers and Writers."

To link to the Reading Assessment Database for a list of reading assessment tools for kindergarten through third grade, visit our Companion Website at **www.prenhall.com/tompkins**

   Teachers often take running records of children's oral reading to assess their fluency (Clay, 1985, 2000d). Teachers, like Mrs. McNeal in the vignette at the beginning of the chapter, calculate the percentage of words the child reads correctly and then analyze the miscues or errors. Teachers make a series of check marks on a sheet of paper as the child reads each word correctly, and they use other marks to indicate words that the child substitutes, repeats, pronounces incorrectly, or doesn't know.

   After identifying the words that the child read incorrectly, teachers calculate the percentage of words read correctly. Teachers use this percentage to determine whether the book or other reading material is too easy, too difficult, or appropriate for the child

This teacher takes running records each week to monitor her first graders' reading progress.

at this time. If the student reads more than 95% of the words correctly with good comprehension, the book is "easy" or at the child's independent reading level. If the child reads 90–95% of the words correctly with adequate comprehension, the book is at the child's instructional level. If the child reads fewer than 90% of the words correctly or with poor comprehension, the book is hard; it is at the child's frustration level.

In addition to identifying children's errors, teachers consider why the child made the error; this type of analysis is called miscue analysis (K. S. Goodman, 1976). "Miscue" is another word for "error," and it suggests that children used the wrong cueing system to figure out the word. For example, if a child reads "Dad" for "Father," the error is meaning related because the child overrelied on the semantic system. If a child reads "Feather" for "Father," the error is more likely visual (or phonological), because the child overrelied on the letters and sounds in the word and didn't evaluate whether or not the word made sense semantically. The Dad/Father and Feather/Father miscues are both syntactically correct because a noun was substituted for a noun. Sometimes, however, children substitute words that don't make sense syntactically. For example, if a child reads "tomorrow" for "through" in the sentence "Father walked through the door," the error doesn't make sense either semantically or syntactically, even though both words are fairly long and begin with *t*.

Teachers categorize children's miscues as *meaning, visual,* or *syntactic errors,* as Mrs. McNeal did in the vignette at the beginning of the chapter, to examine what word identification strategies children are using. As they categorize children's miscues, teachers should ask themselves these questions:

Does the reader self-correct the miscue?
Does the miscue change the meaning of the sentence?
Is the miscue phonologically similar to the word in the text?
Is the miscue acceptable within the syntax (or structure) of the sentence?

The errors that interfere with meaning and those that are syntactically unacceptable are the most serious because the student doesn't realize that reading should make

Running records are especially useful for assessing second language learners' reading development and making instructional decisions because this assessment identifies what children can and can't do.

sense. Errors can be classified and charted, as shown in Figure 3-6. These errors were taken from first grader Seth's running record presented in Figure 3-1. Only words that children mispronounce or substitute can be analyzed. Repetitions and omissions are not calculated.

Determining Children's Instructional Reading Level

Thousands and thousands of books are available for elementary students, and effective teachers match students with books written at appropriate difficulty levels. Even though many books seem to be of similar difficulty because of the size of print, length of the book, or number of illustrations, they are not necessarily at the same reading level. Children need books written at an appropriate level of difficulty because they are more likely to be successful reading books that are neither too hard nor too easy, and research has shown that children who do the most reading make the greatest gains in reading (Gunning, 1998).

According to the Goldilocks Strategy (Ohlhausen & Jepsen, 1992), books can be classified as too easy, too difficult, or just right. This classification is individualistic, so what is too difficult for one child may be too easy for another. Teachers and researchers use other terms for the three levels. "Easy" books are at the independent level, and children read these books with 96–100% accuracy in word recognition and with strong comprehension (90% or higher). "Just right" books are those at the instructional level, where children read with 90–95% accuracy in word recognition and with good comprehension (75–89%). "Too difficult" books are at the frustration level, and children read them with less than 90% accuracy in word recognition and with poor comprehension (less than 75%).

Leveled Books. Basal readers and other texts have traditionally been leveled according to grade levels, but grade-level designations, especially in first grade, are too broad. Reading Recovery teachers have developed a text gradient to match children to books that are neither too hard nor too easy for them (Fountas & Pinnell, 1996). Barbara Peterson (2001) examined reading materials for young children to determine the characteristics of texts that support beginning readers. She identified five criteria:

Figure 3-6   Miscue Analysis of Seth's Errors

Child __Seth__   Date __Jan. 18__

Text __The Pot of Gold (Level 16)__

WORDS			MEANING	VISUAL	SYNTAX
Text	Child	Self-corrected?	Similar meaning?	Graphophonic similarity?	Grammatically acceptable?
Grumble	Grumply			✓	
always	–				
didn't	did not		✓	✓	✓
I'll	I		✓	✓	✓
move	make			✓	✓
scarf	safr			✓	
of	or			✓	
my	me	✓		✓	
scarf	self			✓	
taken	take		✓	✓	
scarf	scafer			✓	
that	they	✓		✓	
may	maybe			✓	
still	sit			✓	

Analysis: Seth overrelies on visual cues and rarely self-corrects errors.

1. *Placement of text.* Books with consistent placement of text on the page are easier for children to read than books with varied placement; and books with only one line of text on a page are easier to read than books with two or more lines of text.
2. *Repetition.* Text that is highly predictable, with one or two patterns and few word changes, is easier to read than less predictable text with varied sentence patterns.
3. *Language structures.* Books in which the text is similar to the children's oral language patterns are easier to read than text using written language or "book" structures.
4. *Content.* Books about familiar objects and experiences are easier to read than books about unfamiliar topics or those using unfamiliar, specialized vocabulary.

5. *Illustrations.* Pictures in which the meaning of the text is visually illustrated are more supportive than illustrations that are minimally related to the text.

Using these criteria, Reading Recovery teachers identified 26 levels for kindergarten through sixth grade. A sample trade book for each level is shown in Figure 3-7; 8,500 other leveled books are listed in *Matching Books to Readers: Using Leveled Books in Guided Reading, K–3* (Fountas & Pinnell, 1999) and *Guiding Readers and Writers Grades 3–6* (Fountas & Pinnell, 2001). Teachers are using the same criteria to level books for use in their classrooms. After they level the books, teachers code them with letters written on colored circles and place all books at the same level together in baskets or boxes.

Assessing Children's Writing

Teachers develop rubrics, or scoring guides, to assess children's growth as writers (Farr & Tone, 1994). Rubrics make the analysis of writing simpler and the assessment process more reliable and consistent. Rubrics may have 4, 5, or 6 levels, with descriptors related to ideas, organization, language, and mechanics at each level. Some

Figure 3-7

A List of Leveled Books According to Reading Recovery Levels

Level	Grade	Sample Book
A	K	Burningham, J. (1985). *Colors.* New York: Crown.
B	K–1	Carle, E. (1987). *Have you seen my cat?* New York: Scholastic.
C	K–1	Williams, S. (1989). *I went walking.* Orlando, FL: Harcourt Brace.
D	1	Peek, M. (1985). *Mary wore her red dress.* New York: Clarion.
E	1	Hill, E. (1980). *Where's Spot?* New York: Putnam.
F	1	Hutchins, P. (1968). *Rosie's walk.* New York: Macmillan.
G	1	Shaw, N. (1986). *Sheep in a jeep.* Boston: Houghton Mifflin.
H	1–2	Kraus, R. (1970). *Whose mouse are you?* New York: Macmillan.
I	1–2	Wood, A. (1984). *The napping house.* San Diego, CA: Harcourt Brace Jovanovich.
J	2	Rylant, C. (1991). *Henry and Mudge and the bedtime thumps.* New York: Simon & Schuster.
K	2	Stevens, J. (1992). *The three billy goats Gruff.* New York: Holiday House.
L	2–3	Allard, H. (1985). *Miss Nelson is missing!* Boston: Houghton Mifflin.
M	2–3	Park, B. (1992). *Junie B. Jones and the stupid smelly bus.* New York: Random House.
N	3	Danziger, P. (1994). *Amber Brown is not a crayon.* New York: Scholastic.
O	3–4	Cleary, B. (1981). *Ramona Quimby, age 8.* New York: HarperCollins.
P	3–4	Mathis, S. B. (1975). *The hundred penny box.* New York: Scholastic.
Q	4	Howe, D., & Howe, J. (1979). *Bunnicula: A rabbit-tale of mystery.* New York: Atheneum.
R	4	Paulsen, G. (1987). *Hatchet.* New York: Viking.
S	4–5	Paterson, K. (1984). *The great Gilly Hopkins.* New York: Crowell.
T	4–5	Curtis, C. P. (1999). *Bud, not Buddy.* New York: Delacorte.
U	5	Lowry, L. (1989). *Number the stars.* Boston: Houghton Mifflin.
V	5–6	Sachar, L. (1999). *Holes.* New York: Farrar, Straus & Giroux.
W	5–6	Choi, S. N. (1991). *Year of impossible goodbyes.* Boston: Houghton Mifflin.
X	6	Hesse, K. (1997). *Out of the dust.* New York: Scholastic.
Y	6	Lowry, L. (1993). *The giver.* Boston: Houghton Mifflin.
Z	6	Hinton, S. E. (1967). *The outsiders.* New York: Puffin/Penguin.

Fountas & Pinnell, 1999, 2001.

Assessment Resources

Kits With Leveled Books

Teachers use assessment kits with leveled books to monitor and assess children's reading development over time. These assessments identify children's instructional reading levels and document how well children use the cueing systems and demonstrate specific reading behaviors. Three popular assessment kits with collections of leveled texts ranging from kindergarten to fifth-grade reading levels are:

Beaver, J. (1997). *Developmental reading assessment.* Glenview, IL: Celebration Press/Addison-Wesley.

On-the-mark assessment of reading behavior. (2001). Bothell, WA: Wright Group/McGraw-Hill.

Nelley, E. & Smith, A. (2000). *Rigby PM benchmark kit: A reading assessment resource for grades K–5.* Crystal Lake, IL: Rigby.

These assessment kits have collections of leveled books ranging from kindergarten to fifth grade, scoring sheets, and a variety of other assessments including phonemic awareness and phonics tests, lists of high-frequency words, and other assessments.

Teachers work individually with children. The teacher selects a text for a child to read. After the teacher introduces the book, the child reads it and the teacher takes a running record of the child's reading. Then the child retells the text and answers comprehension questions. The teacher scores the reading and analyzes the results, and testing continues until the teacher determines the child's instructional level.

rubrics are general and appropriate for almost any writing assignment, whereas others are designed for a specific writing assignment. Figure 3-8 presents two rubrics. One is a general, 4-point kindergarten rubric, and the other is a 5-point second-grade rubric designed for a specific narrative writing project.

Children, too, can learn to create rubrics to assess the quality of their writing. To be successful, they need to examine examples of other children's writing and determine the qualities that demonstrate strong, average, and weak papers; teachers need to model how to address the qualities at each level in the rubric. Skillings and Ferrell (2000) taught second and third graders to develop the criteria for evaluating their writing, and the students moved from using the rubrics their teachers prepared to creating their own 3-point rubrics, which they labeled as the very best level, the okay level, and the not so good level. Perhaps the most important outcome of teaching children to develop rubrics, according to Skillings and Ferrell, is that children develop metacognitive strategies and the ability to think about themselves as writers.

Both children and teachers can use rubrics to assess writing. They read the composition and highlight words and phrases in the rubric that best describe the composition. The score is determined by examining the highlighted words and determining which level has the most highlighted words.

To link to the Northwest Regional Educational Laboratory's site and learn about the 6 + 1 Traits of Writing, visit our Companion Website at
www.prenhall.com/tompkins

Figure 3-8   Two Writing Rubrics

Kindergarten Writing Rubric

4   Exceptional Writer
- Writes several complete sentences or one more-sophisticated sentence.
- Spaces between words and sentences consistently.
- Spells some high-frequency words correctly.
- Spells some consonant-vowel-consonant words correctly.
- Uses capital letters to begin some sentences.
- Uses periods and other punctuation marks to end some sentences.

3   Developing Writer
- Writes a complete sentence.
- Spaces between some words.
- Spells one or more high-frequency words correctly.
- Spells beginning and ending sounds in most words.
- Uses both upper- and lowercase letters.

2   Beginning Writer
- Writes from left to right and top to bottom.
- Writes one or more words using one or more letters that represent beginning or other sounds in the word.
- Can reread the writing with one-to-one matching of words.

1   Emergent Writer
- Uses random letters that do not correspond to sounds.
- Uses scribbles to represent writing.
- Draws a picture instead of writing.
- Dictates words or sentences.

	Second-Grade Rubric for Stories
5	Writing has an original title.
	Story shows originality, sense of humor, or cleverness.
	Writer uses paragraphs to organize ideas.
	Writing contains few spelling, capitalization, or punctuation errors.
	Writer varies sentence structure and word choice.
	Writer shows a sense of audience.
4	Writing has an appropriate title.
	Beginning, middle, and end of the story are well developed.
	A problem or goal is identified in the story.
	Writing includes details that support plot, characters, and setting.
	Writing is organized into paragraphs.
	Writing contains few capitalization and punctuation errors.
	Writer spells most high-frequency words correctly and spells unfamiliar words phonetically.
3	Writing may have a title.
	Writing has at least two of the three parts of a story (beginning, middle, and end).
	Writing shows a sequence of events.
	Writing is not organized into paragraphs.
	Spelling, grammar, capitalization, or punctuation errors may interfere with meaning.
2	Writing has at least one of the three parts of a story (beginning, middle, and end).
	Writing may show a partial sequence of events.
	Writing is brief and underdeveloped.
	Writing has spelling, grammar, capitalization, and punctuation errors that interfere with meaning.
1	Writing lacks a sense of story.
	An illustration may suggest a story.
	Writing is brief and may support the illustration.
	Some words may be recognizable, but the writing is difficult to read.

Assessment Tools

Assessment Resources

Rubrics

Teachers use rubrics to assess the quality of children's compositions. Some rubrics are general and can be used for almost any writing assignment, whereas others are designed for a specific writing assignment. Sometimes teachers use rubrics developed by school districts; at other times, they develop their own rubrics to assess the specific components and qualities they have stressed in their classrooms. Rubrics should have 4 to 6 achievement levels and address ideas, organization, language, and mechanics. Search the Internet for other examples of writing rubrics. Many examples of rubrics are available that have been developed by teachers, school districts, state departments of education, and publishers of educational materials.

In addition, kindergarten and first-grade teachers often administer Clay's Writing Vocabulary Test, part of *An Observational Survey* (1993), to examine how many words young children can write in 10 minutes.

Assessing Children's Spelling

The choices children make as they spell words are important indicators of their knowledge of both phonics and spelling. For example, a child who spells phonetically might spell *money* as *mune,* and other students who are experimenting with long vowels might spell the word as *monye* or *monie.* No matter how they spell the word, children are demonstrating what they know about phonics and spelling. Teachers classify and analyze the words children misspell in their writing to gauge children's level of spelling development and to plan for instruction. For more information on children's spelling development, turn to Chapter 5, "Learning to Spell."

Assessment Resources

Spelling

Teachers monitor children's spelling development by examining misspelled words in the children's writing. They can classify misspelled words according to the five stages of spelling development and plan instruction on the basis of this analysis. Teachers also examine children's misspellings in weekly spelling tests and diagnostic tests, including the following:

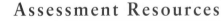

Developmental Spelling Analysis (Ganske, 2000)
Elementary Qualitative Spelling Inventory (Grades K–6) (Bear et al., 2000)
Qualitative Inventory of Spelling Development (Henderson, 1990)

After teachers mark spellings on the tests as correct or incorrect, they analyze children's errors to determine which skills they use correctly, which skills they are using but are confusing, and which skills they are not yet using. Then teachers plan instruction based on the test results.

The steps in determining a child's stage of spelling development are explained in Figure 3-9, and an analysis of a first grader's spelling development is shown in Figure 3-10.

Teachers can analyze the errors in children's writings or on weekly spelling tests or administer diagnostic tests, such as Bear's Elementary Qualitative Spelling Inventory for grades K–6 (Bear, Invernizzi, Templeton, & Johnston, 2000). These tests include 20–25 spelling words listed according to difficulty and can easily be administered to small groups or whole classes. Other spelling tests are available to provide grade-level scores.

Monitoring Children's Progress

Teachers monitor children's learning day by day, and they use the results of their monitoring to make instructional decisions (Baskwill & Whitman, 1988; Winograd & Arrington, 1999). As they monitor children's learning, teachers learn about their students, about themselves as teachers, and about the impact of the instructional program. Four ways to monitor children's progress are:

1. *Observe children as they participate in literacy activities.* Observation is the primary means of assessing children's learning before age 5, according to the National Educational Goals Panel (1998), and it continues to be a useful tool throughout the

Figure 3-9   How to Analyze Children's Spelling Errors

1. Choose Writing Samples
Teachers choose one or more writing samples written by a single child to analyze. In the primary grades, the samples should total at least 50 words, and in the middle grades at least 100 words. Teachers must be able to decipher most words in the sample in order to analyze it.

2. Identify Misspelled Words
Teachers read the writing samples and identify the misspelled words and the words the child was trying to spell. When necessary, teachers check with the child who wrote the composition to determine the intended word.

3. Make a Spelling Analysis Chart
Teachers draw a chart with five columns, one for each of the stages of spelling development, at the bottom of the child's writing sample or on another sheet of paper.

4. Categorize the Child's Misspelled Words
Teachers classify the child's spelling errors according to the stage of development. They list each spelling error in one of the stages, ignoring proper nouns, capitalization errors, and grammar errors. Teachers often ignore poorly formed letters or reversed letter forms in kindergarten and first grade, but these are significant errors when they are made by older children. They follow the child's spelling with the correct spelling in parentheses to make the analysis easier.

5. Tally the Errors
Teachers count the number of errors in each column to determine the stage with the most errors; this is the child's current stage of spelling development.

6. Identify Topics for Instruction
Teachers examine the misspelled words to identify spelling concepts for instruction, such as vowel patterns, possessives, homophones, syllabication, and cursive handwriting skills.

Assessment Tools

Figure 3-10   An Analysis of a First Grader's Spelling Errors

Writing Sample

To bay a perezun at home kob
uz anb seb that a bome wuz in
or skuwl anb mab uz go at zib
anb makbe uz wat a haf uf
a awr anb it mab uz wazt or
time on loren ee ing.

THE eNb

Translation

Today a person at home called us and said that a bomb was in our school and made us go outside and made us wait a half of an hour and it made us waste our time on learning. The end.

Spelling Analysis Chart

Emergent	Letter Name	Within-Word Patterns	Syllables and Affixes	Derivational Relations
	kod (called)	bome (bomb)	peresun (person)	
	sed (said)	or (our)	loreneeing (learning)	
	wus (was)	skuwl (school)		
	mad (made)	makde (made)		
	at (out)	uf (of)		
	sid (side)	awr (hour)		
	wat (wait)	or (our)		
	haf (half)			
	mad (made)			
	wazt (waste)			

Conclusion

Marc spelled 56% of the words correctly, and most of his spelling errors were in the Letter Name and Within-Word Patterns stages, which is typical of first graders' spelling.

Topics for Instruction

high-frequency words
CVCe vowel pattern
-ed inflectional ending

Teachers conference with students to monitor their progress.

elementary grades. Effective teachers are "kid watchers," a term Yetta Goodman (1978) coined. They understand how children learn to read and write and look for evidence of children's learning during the observation. Some observation times should be planned when the teacher focuses on particular children and makes anecdotal notes about the children's involvement in literacy events. The focus is on what children do as they read or write, not on whether or not they are behaving properly or working quietly. Of course, little learning can occur in disruptive situations, but during these observations, the focus is on literacy, not behavior.

2. *Take anecdotal notes of literacy events.* Teachers write brief notes as they observe children, and the most useful notes describe specific events, report rather than evaluate, and relate the events to other information about the child (Rhodes & Nathenson-Mejia, 1992). Teachers make notes about children's reading and writing activities, the questions children ask, and the strategies and skills they use fluently or indicate confusion about. These records document children's growth and pinpoint problem areas for future minilessons or conferences.

3. *Conference with children.* Teachers talk with children to monitor their progress in reading and writing activities as well as to set goals and help children solve problems. Figure 3-11 lists seven types of conferences that teachers have with students. Often these conferences are brief and impromptu, held at children's desks as the teacher moves around the classroom. At other times, the conferences are planned and children meet with the teacher at a designated conference table.

4. *Collect children's work samples.* Teachers have children collect their work in folders to document learning. Work samples might include reading logs^C, audiotapes of children's reading, photos of projects, videotapes of puppet shows and oral presentations, and books students have written. Often teachers send some of these work samples home with children along with their report cards or at the end of the school year, and they pass along some work samples to next year's teacher.

Figure 3-11   Seven Types of Conferences

1. On-the-Spot Conferences
The teacher visits briefly with children at their desks to monitor some aspect of the children's work or to check on progress. These conferences are brief; the teacher may spend less than a minute at each child's desk.

2. Prereading or Prewriting Conferences
The teacher and child make plans for reading or writing at the conference. At a prereading conference, they may talk about information related to the book, difficult concepts or vocabulary words related to the reading, or the reading log the child will keep. At a prewriting conference, they may discuss possible writing topics or how to narrow down a broad topic.

3. Revising Conferences
A small group of children meets with the teacher to get specific suggestions about revising their compositions. These conferences offer child writers an audience to provide feedback on how well they have communicated.

4. Book Discussion Conferences
Children meet with the teacher to discuss the book they have read. They may share reading log entries, discuss plot or characters, compare the story to others they have read, or make plans to extend their reading.

5. Editing Conferences
The teacher reviews children's proofread compositions and helps them correct spelling, punctuation, capitalization, and other mechanical errors.

6. Minilesson Conferences
The teacher meets with children to explain a procedure, strategy, or skill (e.g., writing a table of contents, using the visualization strategy when reading, capitalizing proper nouns).

7. Assessment Conferences
The teacher meets with children after they have completed an assignment or project to talk about their growth as readers or writers. Children reflect on their competencies and set goals.

ASSIGNING GRADES

Assigning grades is one of the most difficult responsibilities placed on teachers. "Grading is a fact of life," according to Donald Graves (1983, p. 93), but he adds that teachers should use grades to encourage children, not to hinder their achievement. The assessment procedures described in this chapter encourage children because they document what children can do as they read and write. Reviewing and translating this documentation into grades is the difficult part, but two effective techniques are unit assignment sheets and "show-me" tests.

Assignment Sheets

One way for teachers to monitor children's progress and grade their achievements is to use assignment sheets. Teachers create the assignment sheet as they plan the unit, and then they duplicate copies for each child and distribute them at the beginning of the unit. All assignments are listed on the sheet along with how they will be graded. These sheets can be developed for any type of unit—literature focus units, literature circles, reading and writing workshop, and thematic units. Teachers can also create assignment sheets to use with literacy centers.

An assignment sheet for a third-grade literature circles unit is shown in Figure 3-12. Children receive a copy of the assignment sheet at the beginning of the unit and keep it in their unit folders. They write notes each day in assignment boxes, so it is easy for the teacher to monitor children's progress periodically. At the end of the unit, the teacher collects the unit folders and grades the work.

Assignments can be graded as "done" or "not done," or they can be graded for quality. Some teachers assign points to each activity on the assignment sheet so that the total point value for the unit is 100 points; activities that involve more time and effort earn more points. The maximum number of points possible for each assignment is listed in parentheses.

A first-grade assignment sheet for centers is shown in Figure 3-13. Each week, the children receive a sheet and they monitor their progress during the week. The teacher has eight centers set up in the classroom, and children are required to complete at least four of them each week. Children must visit the three centers marked with a star on the assignment sheet, and they may choose among the other centers that they visit. As they complete each center, children use the stamp at that center to mark their completion on the sheet.

Checklists have the power to enhance children's learning and simplify assessment (Kuhs, Johnson, Agruso, & Monrad, 2001). Because children are more likely to be successful when they understand what is expected of them, teachers distribute the assignment sheets at the beginning of a unit so children will understand what they are to do. Later when teachers grade children's work, the grading is easier because teachers have already identified the criteria for grading. Grading is fairer, too, because teachers use the same criteria to grade all children's work.

"Show-Me" Tests

Children can use writing to demonstrate what they have learned during a unit. Third-grade teacher Whitney Donnelly developed an innovative approach that she calls "show-me" tests to document and grade her students' learning. Teachers begin by reviewing the key concepts in a thematic unit with students, and then they have students choose one of the concepts to write and draw about on the test. Students divide a piece of a paper into two parts. On one part, they draw pictures, diagrams, maps, or charts to describe the concept, and they label the drawings with key words and phrases. On the other part of the paper, they write about the concept. Then teachers grade the test according to the number of components related to the key concept students included in their drawings or writings.

A third grader's test on the skeletal system is presented in Figure 3-14. Students could choose to draw and write about one of three major systems in the human body: the skeletal, circulatory, or digestive system. In their tests, students were to draw at least three pieces of information and write three important things about the system. This student drew three pictures of the skeletal system, illustrating different kinds of bones, and he wrote about two functions of the skeleton—to give the body shape and to protect organs. He also points out that the bones, joints, and muscles work together to help a person move. Two other things that the class studied about the skeletal system that this child did not mention are that bone marrow helps keep blood healthy and that there are 206 bones in the body. In the middle of the written part, the child

Figure 3-12   An Assignment Sheet for Literature Circles

Name _____ Date _____

Book Title _____

Author _____

What is your book about?

What are you doing each day?

Monday	Tuesday	Wednesday	Thursday	Friday
☐ Log	☐ Log	☐ Log	☐ Log	☐ Log
☐ Log	☐ Log	☐ Log	☐ Log	☐ Log

What jobs are you doing?

Summarizer	Artist	Connector	Word Wizard

Remember to keep your reading log and other work in your literature circles folder. You will turn everything in at the end of the unit.

Figure 3-13   An Assignment Checklist for Centers

★ Center Jobs ★

Name _____ Week _____

Your job is to do 4 or more centers this week.
Put a stamp in the circle when you finish the center.

★ Book of the Week	◯	Listening	◯
★ Writing	◯	Word Wall	◯
★ Rereading	◯	Spelling	◯
Reading Charts	◯	Library	◯

Figure 3-14   A Third Grader's "Show-Me" Test

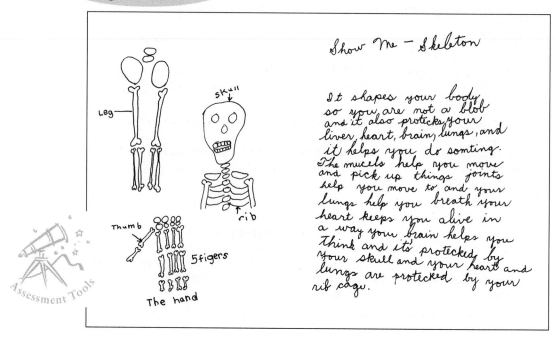

Show Me – Skeleton

It shapes your body
so you are not a blob
and it also protecks your
liver, heart, brain, lungs, and
it helps you do somting.
The mucels help you move
and pick up things joints
help you move to and your
lungs help you breath your
heart keeps you alive in
a way your brain helps you
think and it's protecked by
your skull and your heart and
lungs are protecked by your
rib cage.

included unrelated information about the functions of the heart, lungs, and brain. Out of a possible score of 6, the child received a 5. There are a few misspelled words and missing punctuation marks in the test, but they do not affect the grade because they do not interfere with the information presented.

Review

Assessment is more than testing; it is an essential part of teaching and learning. In classroom assessment, teachers use a variety of literacy assessment tools to assess children's phonemic awareness and phonics development, determine children's "easy," instructional, and "hard" reading levels, document their growth as writers, analyze children's spelling development, and monitor children's progress. Teachers use assignment sheets to monitor children's work during literature focus units, literature circles, reading and writing workshop, and thematic units, and to assign grades. Effective practices for assessing children's literacy learning are reviewed in the feature that follows.

How Effective Teachers . . .
Assess Children's Literacy Development

Effective Practices

1. Teachers use a variety of assessment tools to assess children's literacy development.
2. Teachers assess young children's understanding of written language using the Concepts About Print test.
3. Teachers check children's knowledge of phonemic awareness and phonics.
4. Teachers monitor children's ability to read high-frequency words and their reading fluency.
5. Teachers take running records to assess children's reading accuracy and comprehension.
6. Teachers use leveled books to determine children's instructional reading level.
7. Teachers use rubrics to assess the ideas, organization, vocabulary, style, and mechanics in children's compositions.
8. Teachers analyze children's spellings to determine their stage of development and to plan for instruction.
9. Teachers monitor children's learning using observation and anecdotal notes, conferences, checklists, and collections of children's work samples.
10. Teachers distribute assignment sheets during units so that children understand how they will be assessed and graded.

Professional References

Adams, M., Foorman, B., Lundberg, I., & Beeler, C. (1997). *Phonemic awareness in young children*. Baltimore: Paul H. Brookes.

Baskwill, J., & Whitman, P. (1988). *Evaluation: Whole language, whole child*. New York: Scholastic.

Bear, D. R., Invernizzi, M., Templeton, S., & Johnston, F. (2000). *Words their way: Word study for phonics, vocabulary, and spelling instruction* (2nd ed.). Upper Saddle River, NJ: Merrill/Prentice Hall.

Beaver, J. (1997). *Developmental reading assessment*. Glenview, IL: Celebration Press/Addison-Wesley.

Clay, M. M. (1972). *Sand–the Concepts About Print test*. Portsmouth, NH: Heinemann.

Clay, M. M. (1979). *Stones–the Concepts About Print test*. Portsmouth, NH: Heinemann.

Clay, M. M. (1985). *The early detection of reading difficulties: A diagnostic survey with recovery procedures*. Portsmouth, NH: Heinemann.

Clay, M. M. (1993). *An observational survey of early literacy assessment*. Portsmouth, NH: Heinemann.

Clay, M. M. (2000a). *Concepts about print: What have children learned about the way we print language?* Portsmouth, NH: Heinemann.

Clay, M. M. (2000b). *Follow me, moon*. Portsmouth, NH: Heinemann.

Clay, M. M. (2000c). *No shoes*. Portsmouth, NH: Heinemann.

Clay, M. M. (2000d). *Running records: For classroom teachers*. Portsmouth, NH: Heinemann.

Cunningham, P. (1990). The Names Test: A quick assessment of decoding ability. *The Reading Teacher, 44,* 124–129.

Duffelmeyer, F. A., Kruse, A. E., Merkley, D. J., & Fyfe, S. A. (1994). Further validation and enhancement of the Names Test. *The Reading Teacher, 48,* 118–128.

Farr, R., & Tone, B. (1994). *Portfolio and performance assessment*. Orlando: Harcourt Brace.

Fountas, I. C., & Pinnell, G. S. (1996). *Guided reading: Good first teaching for all children*. Portsmouth, NH: Heinemann.

Fountas, I. C., & Pinnell, G. S. (1999). *Matching books to readers: Using leveled books in guided reading, K–3*. Portsmouth, NH: Heinemann.

Fountas, I. C., & Pinnell, G. S. (2001). *Guiding readers and writers grades 3–6: Teaching comprehension, genre, and content literacy*. Portsmouth, NH: Heinemann.

Fry, E. B. (1980). The new instant word lists. *The Reading Teacher, 34,* 284–289.

Ganske, K. (2000). *Wordjourneys: Assessment-guided phonics, spelling and vocabulary instruction*. New York: Guildford Press.

Goodman, K. S. (1976). Behind the eye: What happens in reading. In H. Singer & R. B. Ruddell (Eds.), *Theoretical models and processes of reading* (2nd ed., pp. 470–496). Newark, DE: International Reading Association.

Goodman, Y. M. (1978). Kid watching: An alternative to testing. *National Elementary Principals Journal, 57,* 41–45.

Graves, D. H. (1983). *Writing: Teachers and students at work*. Portsmouth, NH: Heinemann.

Gunning, T. G. (1998). *Best books for beginning readers*. Boston: Allyn & Bacon.

Henderson, E. (1990). *Teaching spelling*. Boston: Houghton Mifflin.

Kuhs, T. M., Johnson, R. L., Agruso, S. A., & Monrad, D. M. (2001). *Put to the tests: Tools and techniques for classroom assessment*. Portsmouth, NH: Heinemann.

Ohlhausen, M. M., & Jepsen, M. (1992). Lessons from Goldilocks: "Somebody's been choosing my books but I can make my own choices now!" *The New Advocate, 5,* 31–46.

Peterson, B. (2001). *Literary pathways: Selecting books to support new readers*. Portsmouth, NH: Heinemann.

Rhodes, L. K., & Nathenson-Mejia, S. (1992). Anecdotal records: A powerful tool for ongoing literacy assessment. *The Reading Teacher, 45,* 502–511.

Skillings, M. J., & Ferrell, R. (2000). Student-generated rubrics: Bringing students into the assessment process. *The Reading Teacher, 53,* 452–455.

Torgesen, J. K., & Bryant, B. R. (1994). *Test of phonological awareness*. Austin, TX: Pro-Ed.

Winograd, P. & Arrington, H. J. (1999). Best practices in literacy assessment. In L. B. Gambrell, L. M. Morrow, S. B. Neuman, & M. Pressley (Eds.), *Best practices in literary instruction* (pp. 210–241). New York: Guilford Press.

Yopp, H. K. (1995). A test for assessing phonemic awareness in young children. *The Reading Teacher, 49,* 20–28.

Children's Book References

Cole, J. (1993). *The magic school bus lost in the solar system*. New York: Scholastic.

The pot of gold (an Irish folk tale). (1997). Glenview, IL: Celebration Press/Addison-Wesley.

Yolen, J. (1995). *Henry and Mudge and the best day of all*. New York: Scholastic.

chapter 4

Breaking the Alphabetic Code

chapter
QUESTIONS

- What is phonemic awareness?

- Why do children need to be phonemically aware in order to learn phonics?

- Which phonics concepts are most important for children to learn?

- How do teachers teach phonics?

Mrs. Hoddy Teaches Phonics

The first graders in Mrs. Hoddy's classroom are involved in an author study on Eric Carle. They are reading many of the books Carle has written and illustrated, including *The Very Hungry Caterpillar* (1969), *The Very Busy Spider* (1984), *The Very Quiet Cricket* (1990), and *The Very Lonely Firefly* (1995). Mrs. Hoddy has a class set of *The Very Hungry Caterpillar* and several copies of each of the other books that she places on a special shelf in the classroom library for the children to read and reread. She also has audiotapes of the books that she uses in the listening center.

For each book, Mrs. Hoddy begins by reading the book aloud to the children, and then children talk about the book, sharing their impressions and reactions. They make comparisons among the Eric Carle books they've read, pointing out the repetitive patterns, the themes, and Carle's unique illustration techniques. Children have watched *Eric Carle: Picture Writer* (Carle, 1993), a videotape of the author-illustrator demonstrating his illustration techniques, and they are creating their own books with bright tissue paper collage illustrations using the same techniques that Eric Carle does.

Children read and reread books in small groups, at the listening center, with buddies, and independently. They add important vocabulary words from each story to the word wall[C] and participate in phonics activities. Mrs. Hoddy reviews the letter-writing form, and children write letters to Eric Carle, telling him which of his books they like the best and about the books they are making with tissue paper collage illustrations.

See the Compendium of Instructional Procedures, which follows Chapter 12, for more information on terms marked with the symbol [C].

Mrs. Hoddy teaches minilessons[C] on phonics regularly during the author unit on Eric Carle. She uses a whole-part-whole approach. She begins by sharing the book with the children, giving them opportunities to read and respond to the book—the "whole." Then she focuses on skills and teaches minilessons on phonics using words from the story, and children practice the skills at the phonics center; the minilessons and practice activities are the "part." Afterwards, children apply the skills they are learning through reading and writing activities—the "whole" again. During this unit, children will continue reading Carle's books and write their own books.

After reading *The Very Hungry Caterpillar*, Carle's story about a caterpillar that eats through a large quantity of food before spinning a chrysalis, Mrs. Hoddy uses this book to teach a series of phonics minilessons. In one lesson with the whole class, she reviews the days of the week and focuses on the *-ay* rime using the days of the week and the words *bay, may, say, pay, ray, way, day, lay, play,* and *stay.* She begins by pointing out the days of the week on the calendar and reviewing with children what foods the caterpillar in the story ate each day. She writes the days of the week on the chalkboard and asks children to pronounce the words and note that they all rhyme. Then she asks one child to come to the chalkboard and circle the rime *-ay.* Next, she writes *say, may, play,* and several other *-ay* words on the chalkboard for children to decode. Then she gives a small magic slate to each child, and children each write their favorite day of the week at the top of their slates and circle the *-ay* rime. Then children take turns suggesting rhyming words to write on their slates. Mrs. Hoddy walks around the classroom, checking to see that children are sounding out the beginning sound and adding the rime correctly. For the last 2 minutes of the minilesson, she reviews the *-ill* rime that she taught last week, and children write *bill, still, will, mill, kill, gill, hill,* and *pill* on their magic slates.

Mrs. Hoddy alternates teaching minilessons to the whole class with teaching minilessons to small groups of first graders, often during guided reading^C groups. She introduces new concepts, skills, and generalizations to the whole class and then reinforces, reviews, and extends the lessons with small groups. These groups change often, and children are grouped together according to their reading levels and need to learn a specific skill.

One group of five children, for example, is still developing phonemic awareness—the ability to orally segment spoken words. Mrs. Hoddy meets with this group to orally segment words from the story, including *egg, moon, leaf, sun, food, pie, cheese, cupcake,* and *night.* When Mrs. Hoddy meets with the group, she brings along a copy of *The Very Hungry Caterpillar* and says to the group, "Let's find some interesting words in this book to break into sounds. How about *egg*?" The children respond, "e-g." Students break the words into sounds and say the sounds together as a group, and then children take turns segmenting the words individually.

Another group of 10 children reviews these six beginning sounds—/b/, /f/, /h/, /l/, /p/, and /s/—using words from the story. Mrs. Hoddy sets out six plastic baskets with a beginning sound written on the front of each one. Then she shows children these objects and pictures—a butterfly puppet, the number 4 cut out of cardboard, a photo of a house, a lollipop, a jar of pickles, and a drawing of the sun—and children place each object in front of the appropriate basket. Then Mrs. Hoddy reads these words, which she has written on word cards:

b: butterfly, better, beautiful, big
f: five, four, fat, food
h: house, hole, hungry, he
l: light, lay, little, leaf, lollipop, look
p: pushed, pop, pickle, piece, pears
s: Sunday, Saturday, sun, salami, sausage

Children identify the beginning sounds and place the cards in the appropriate baskets. Afterwards, children add pictures on the back of each word card. Then they think of other words beginning with each sound and draw pictures representing the words on cards. They write the word on the back of the card and add these cards to the appropriate baskets. Later, Mrs. Hoddy will place these materials in the phonics center.

Mrs. Hoddy passes out copies of *The Very Hungry Caterpillar* to another group of first graders, who look through the book to find examples of CVCe words (one-syllable words with a long vowel sound and ending with an e). Children locate these words and write them on cards that they place in the pocket chart: *came, ate, cake, ice, cone, slice, pie, ache, hole.* They also locate several words (e.g., *one, more*) that are exceptions to the rule. Mrs. Hoddy explains that *one* is a sight word and that the *r* in *more* overpowers the *o* and changes the sound, just like the *r* in *car* (a familiar word) is stronger than the *a.* The students reread the words several times, and all but two students are able to read the cards easily. Mrs. Hoddy excuses the rest of the group and continues to work with the remaining two children for several more minutes. She gives them magic slates and asks them to draw three lines and write an *e:* __ __ __ e. Then she dictates *came* for the two children to write. They carefully sound out the word and spell it correctly. Then Mrs. Hoddy repeats the process with *hole* and *cone.* She makes a note to give these students more practice later the next day with these CVCe words.

With another group of six children, Mrs. Hoddy uses a set of word cards with the words *caterpillar, little, morning, sun, ate, plum, Thursday, strawberries, chocolate, pickle, lollipop, cupcake, watermelon, stomachache, green, leaf, big, butterfly,* and *beautiful.* As she shows the cards, children read the words. Then she has them read the words a second time and break the words into syllables. Children clap as they say each syllable: *cat-er-pill-ar.* After children take turns saying each word, syllable by syllable, Mrs. Hoddy guides them as they sort the word cards into four piles: one-syllable words, two-syllable words, three syllable words, and four syllable words. Then Mrs. Hoddy explains that these cards will be placed in the phonics center for children to practice sorting by the number of syllables in the words.

Several days later, Mrs. Hoddy teaches the entire class a minilesson on making words[C]. She divides the class into groups of three and passes out packs of letter cards that together spell *caterpillar.* First, children arrange the letter cards to spell the words *cat, pat,* and *rat.* Then they spell *it, pit,* and *lit.* Next, *cap, lap, tap,* and *trap.* Then, *car, are, art, part,* and *cart.* Children volunteer some other words they can make: *eat, late, ape,* and *tape.* Finally, Mrs. Hoddy asks children to guess the big word that the letters spell all together. They know it is a word on the word wall. Quickly, Jonas guesses that the word is *caterpillar,* and all the children arrange the letters to spell the word. The next day, Mrs. Hoddy will repeat this activity in small groups, and she will take notes about the words that children in each group can make. Then she will put the materials in the spelling center.

Mrs. Hoddy could have chosen to teach other phonics skills through *The Very Hungry Caterpillar.* She could have focused on one consonant sound–the /v/ in *very,* the /h/ in *hungry,* the /k/ in *caterpillar,* or the /b/ in *beautiful butterfly,* for example. Or she could have used the words *green leaf* from the story to focus on two vowel patterns used to spell long *e.* To show children how phonics can help them when they read, Mrs. Hoddy uses words from the book they are reading for minilessons, whenever possible.

Mrs. Hoddy knows which phonics concepts, rules, and skills her first graders need to learn, and she develops minilessons and other activities using words drawn from the books she is reading during literature focus units. Together with the other first-grade teachers at her school, Mrs. Hoddy has developed a checklist of phonics skills that she is responsible for teaching. A copy of the checklist is shown in Figure 4-1. The skills on this checklist are phonemic awareness, consonants, consonant blends and digraphs, rimes, short and long vowels, and vowel rules. Mrs. Hoddy chooses topics for minilessons from this checklist, and she uses one copy of the checklist to keep track of the skills she has introduced, practiced, and reviewed. She also makes copies of the checklist for each child and uses them to document which skills children have learned. She uses the information on these checklists in putting together small groups for minilessons and related activities.

The alphabetic principle suggests a one-to-one correspondence between phonemes (or sounds) and graphemes (or letters), such that each letter consistently represents one sound. English, however, is not a purely phonetic language. The 26 letters represent approximately 44 phonemes, and three letters—*c, q,* and *x*—are superfluous because they do not represent unique phonemes. The letter *c,* for example, can represent either /k/ as in *cat* or /s/ as in *city,* and it can be joined

Figure 4-1　Mrs. Hoddy's Phonics Checklist

First Grade Phonics Skills

Name _____　Date _____

Phonemic Awareness

____ segmenting　　　　____ blending　　　　____ rhyming

Consonants

____ b	____ f	____ j	____ m	____ qu	____ t
____ c (k)	____ g	____ k	____ n	____ r	____ v
____ d	____ h	____ l	____ p	____ s	____ w

Blends

____ bl
____ dr
____ fl
____ st
____ tr

Digraphs

____ ch
____ sh
____ th
____ wh

Rimes

____ at
____ ill
____ op
____ ate
____ ike
____ ay

Short Vowels

____ a (fan)
____ e (web)
____ i (sit)
____ o (not)
____ u (cup)

Long Vowels

____ a (came, pail)
____ e (be, feet, eat)
____ i (ice, bite)
____ o (go, soap)
____ u (mule)

Rules

____ CVC
____ CVCe
____ *r*-controlled
____ syllables

Assessment Tools

---

with *h* for the digraph /ch/. To further complicate the situation, there are more than 500 spellings to represent the 44 phonemes. Consonants are more consistent and predictable than vowels. Long *e*, for instance, is spelled 14 ways in common words! Consider, for example, *me, seat, feet, people, yield, baby,* and *cookie.* How a word is spelled depends on several factors, including the location of the sound in the word and whether or not the word entered English from another language (Horn, 1957).

Researchers estimate that words are spelled phonetically approximately half the time (Hanna, Hanna, Hodges, & Rudorf, 1966), and the nonphonetic spelling of many words reflects morphological information. The word *sign,* for instance, is a shortened form of *signature,* and the spelling shows this relationship. Spelling the word phonetically (i.e., *sine*) might seem simpler, but the phonetic spelling lacks semantic information (Venezky, 1999).

Other reasons for this mismatch between phonemes, graphemes, and spellings can be found by examining events in the history of the English language (Tompkins & Yaden, 1986). The introduction of the printing press in England in 1476 helped to stabilize spelling. The word *said,* for example, continues to be spelled as it was pronounced in Shakespeare's time. Our pronunciation does not reflect the word's meaning as the past tense of *say* because pronunciations have continued to evolve in the last 500 years but few spellings have been "modernized." In addition, 75% of English words have been borrowed from other languages around the world, and many words—especially those acquired more recently—have retained their native spellings.

For example, *souvenir* was borrowed from French in the middle 1700s and retains its French spelling. Its literal meaning is "to remember."

The English spelling system can't be explained by the alphabetic principle alone because it is not merely a reflection of phoneme-grapheme correspondences. Our spelling system incorporates morphological, semantic, and syntactic elements, and it has been influenced by historical events.

PHONEMIC AWARENESS

Phonemic awareness is children's basic understanding that speech is composed of a series of individual sounds, and it provides the foundation for "breaking the code" (Yopp, 1992). When children can choose a duck as the animal whose name begins with /d/ from a collection of toy animals, identify *duck* and *luck* as rhyming words in a song, or blend the sounds /d/, /ŭ/, and /k/ to pronounce *duck*, they are phonemically aware. (Note that the emphasis is on the sounds of spoken words, not reading letters or pronouncing letter names.) Developing phonemic awareness enables children to use sound-symbol correspondences to read and spell words. Phonemic awareness is not sounding out words for reading, nor is it using spelling patterns to write words; rather, it is the foundation for phonics.

Phonemes are the smallest units of speech, and they are written as graphemes, or letters of the alphabet. In this book, phonemes are marked using diagonal lines (e.g., /d/) and graphemes are italicized (e.g., *d*). Sometimes phonemes (e.g., /k/ in *duck*) are spelled with two graphemes (*ck*).

Understanding that words are composed of smaller units—phonemes—is a significant achievement for young children because phonemes are abstract language units. Phonemes carry no meaning, and children think of words according to their meanings, not their linguistic characteristics (F. Griffith & Olson, 1992). When children think about ducks, for example, they think of feathered animals that swim in ponds, fly through the air, and make noises we describe as "quacks." They don't think of "duck" as a word with three phonemes or four graphemes, as a word beginning with /d/ and rhyming with *luck*. Phonemic awareness requires that children treat speech as an object and that they shift their attention away from the meaning of words to the linguistic features of speech. This focus on phonemes is even more complicated because phonemes are not discrete units in speech. Often they are slurred or clipped in speech. Think about the blended initial sound in *tree* and the ending sound in *eating*.

Components of Phonemic Awareness

Children develop phonemic awareness as they learn to segment, manipulate, and blend spoken language in these five ways:

1. *Match sounds to words.* Children learn to identify a word that begins or ends with a particular sound. For example, when shown a brush, a car, and a doll, they can identify *doll* as the word that ends with /l/.
2. *Isolate a sound in a word.* Children learn to isolate the sound at the beginning, middle, or end of a word. After the teacher says the word *hat*, for example, children identify /ă/ as the middle sound.
3. *Blend individual sounds in a word.* Children learn to blend two, three, or four individual sounds to form a word. The teacher says /b/, /ĭ/, /g/, for example, and the children repeat the sounds, blending them to form the word *big*.

4. **Substitute sounds in a word.** Children learn to remove a sound from a word and substitute a different sound. Sometimes they substitute the beginning sound, changing *bar* to *car,* for example. Or, children change the middle sound, making *tip* from *top,* or they substitute the ending sound, changing *gate* to *game.*

5. **Segment a word into its constituent sounds.** Children learn to break a word into its beginning, middle, and ending sounds. For example, children segment the word *feet* into /f/, /ē/, /t/ and *go* into /g/, /ō/ (Yopp, 1992).

These five components of phonemic awareness are strategies, rather than knowledge, that children use with phonics to decode and to encode words. When children use phonics to sound out a word they are trying to read, for example, they say the sounds represented by each letter, and then they blend them together to read the word. Blending is the phonemic awareness strategy that children use to decode the word. Similarly, when children want to spell a word, they say the word slowly to themselves, segmenting the sounds. Then they write the letters representing each sound to spell the word. Segmenting is the phonemic awareness strategy that children use to encode the word.

Teaching Phonemic Awareness

Teachers nurture children's phonemic awareness through the language-rich environment they create in the classroom. As they sing songs, chant rhymes, read aloud wordplay books, and play games, children have many opportunities to orally match, isolate, blend, and substitute sounds and to segment words into sounds (F. Griffith & Olson, 1992). Teachers often incorporate phonemic awareness components into other oral language and literacy activities, but it is also important to teach lessons that specifically focus on the components of phonemic awareness.

Phonemic awareness instruction should meet three criteria, according to Yopp and Yopp (2000). First, the activities should be appropriate for 4-, 5-, and 6-year-old children. Activities involving songs, nursery rhymes, riddles, and wordplay books are good choices because they are engaging and encourage children's playful experimentation with oral language. Second, the instruction should be planned and purposeful, not just incidental. When teachers have an objective in mind as they are teaching phonemic awareness, they are more likely to be effective in focusing children's attention on the sound structure of oral language. Third, phonemic awareness activities should be one part of a balanced literacy program and integrated with decoding, comprehension, writing, and spelling activities. It is important that children perceive the connection between oral and written language.

Teachers involve prekindergarten children in oral language play using nursery rhymes, songs, and wordplay books to develop their phonemic awareness.

Many wordplay books are available for young children. Books such as *Cock-a-doodle-moo!* (Most, 1996) and *The Baby Uggs Are Hatching* (Prelutsky, 1982) stimulate children to experiment with sounds and create nonsense words, and teachers focus children's attention on the smaller units of language when they read books with alliterative or assonant patterns, such as *Faint Frogs Feeling Feverish and Other Terrifically Tantalizing Tongue Twisters* (Obligado, 1983). A list of wordplay books for young children is shown in Figure 4-2. Teachers often read wordplay books aloud more than once. During the first reading, children usually focus on the characters and plot or what interests them in the book. During a second reading, however, children's attention shifts to the wordplay elements, and teachers help to focus children's attention on the way the author manipulated words and sounds by making comments and asking questions. Teachers make comments, such as "Did you notice how ____ and ____ rhyme?" and "This book is fun because of all the words

Figure 4-2   Wordplay Books to Enhance Children's Phonemic Awareness

Ahlberg, J., & Ahlberg, A. (1978). *Each peach pear plum.* New York: Scholastic.

Cameron, P. (1961). *"I can't," said the ant.* New York: Coward-McCann.

Degan, B. (1983). *Jamberry.* New York: Harper & Row.

Deming, A. G. (1994). *Who is tapping at my window?* New York: Penguin.

Downey, L. (2000). *The flea's sneeze.* New York: Henry Holt.

Ehlert, L. (1989). *Eating the alphabet: Fruits and vegetables from A to Z.* San Diego: Harcourt Brace Jovanovich.

Galdone, P. (1968). *Henny Penny.* New York: Scholastic.

Hague, K. (1984). *Alphabears.* New York: Henry Holt.

Hoberman, M. A. (1982). *A house is a house for me.* New York: Penguin.

Hutchins, P. (1976). *Don't forget the bacon!* New York: Mulberry Books.

Kuskin, K. (1990). *Roar and more.* New York: Harper & Row.

Lewiston, W. (1992). *"Buzz," said the bee.* New York: Scholastic.

Martin, B., Jr., & Archambault, J. (1987). *Chicka chicka boom boom.* New York: Simon & Schuster.

Most, B. (1990). *The cow that went oink.* San Diego, CA: Harcourt Brace.

Most, B. (1991). *A dinosaur named after me.* San Diego: Harcourt Brace Jovanovich.

Most, B. (1996). *Cock-a-doodle-moo!* San Diego: Harcourt Brace.

Obligado, L. (1983). *Faint frogs feeling feverish and other terrifically tantalizing tongue twisters.* New York: Puffin.

Prelutsky, J. (1982). *The baby uggs are hatching.* New York: Mulberry.

Prelutsky, J. (1989). *Poems of A. Nonny Mouse.* New York: Knopf. (See also the second volume in the series.)

Raffi. (1987). *Down by the bay.* New York: Crown.

Sendak, M. (1990). *Alligators all around: An alphabet.* New York: Harper & Row.

Seuss, Dr. (1963). *Hop on pop.* New York: Random House. (See also other books by the author.)

Shaw, N. (1986). *Sheep in a jeep.* Boston: Houghton Mifflin. (See also other books in this series.)

Showers, P. (1991). *The listening walk.* New York: Harper & Row.

Slate, J. (1996). *Miss Bindergarten gets ready for kindergarten.* New York: Dutton.

Slepian, J., & Seidler, A. (1967). *The hungry thing.* New York: Scholastic.

Sweet, M. (1992). *Fiddle-I-fee: A farmyard song for the very young.* Boston: Little, Brown.

Tallon, R. (1979). *Zoophabets.* New York: Scholastic.

Winthrop, E. (1986). *Shoes.* New York: Harper & Row.

Zemach, M. (1976). *Hush, little baby.* New York: Dutton.

beginning with the /m/ sound" and encourage children to make similar comments themselves (Yopp, 1995).

Teachers often incorporate wordplay books, songs, and games into the minilessons they teach. The feature on page 98 presents a kindergarten teacher's minilesson on blending sounds to make a word. The teacher reread Dr. Seuss's *Fox in Socks* (1965) and then asked children to identify words from the book that she pronounced sound by sound. This book is rich in wordplay and teaching opportunities. It could be used to teach rhyming (e.g., *do, you, goo, chew*), initial consonant substitutions (e.g., *trick, brick, chick, quick, slick*), vowel substitution (e.g., *blabber, blibber, blubber*), and alliteration (e.g., *Luke Luck likes lakes*).

Sound-Matching Activities. In sound matching, children choose one of several words beginning with a particular sound or say a word that begins with a particular sound (Yopp, 1992). For these games, teachers use familiar objects (e.g., feather, toothbrush, book) and toys (e.g., small plastic animals, toy trucks, artificial fruits and vegetables), as well as pictures of familiar objects.

Teachers can play a sound-matching guessing game (Lewkowicz, 1994). For this game, teachers collect two boxes and pairs of objects to place in the boxes (e.g., forks, mittens, erasers, combs, and books). One item from each pair is placed in each box.

Minilesson

Topic: Phonemic Awareness—Blending
Grade: Kindergarten
Time: One 20-minute period

Ms. Lewis regularly includes a 20-minute lesson on phonemic awareness in her literacy block. She usually rereads a familiar wordplay book and plays a phonemic awareness game with the kindergartners that emphasizes one of the components of phonemic awareness.

1. Introduce the Topic

Ms. Lewis brings her 19 kindergartners together on the rug and explains that she's going to reread Dr. Seuss's *Fox in Socks* (1965). It's one of their favorite books, and they clap their pleasure. She explains that after reading, they're going to play a word game.

2. Share Examples

Ms. Lewis reads aloud *Fox in Socks,* showing the pictures on each page as she reads. She encourages the children to read along. Sometimes she stops and invites the children to fill in the last rhyming word in a sentence or to echo read (repeating after her like an echo) the alliterative sentences. After they finish reading, she asks what they like best about the book. Pearl replies, "It's just a really funny book. That's why it is so good." "What makes it funny?" Ms. Lewis asks. "Everything," answers Pearl. Ms. Lewis asks the question again, and Teri explains, "The words are funny. They make my tongue laugh. You know—*fox–socks–box–Knox.* That's funny on my tongue!" "Oh," Ms. Lewis clarifies, "your tongue likes to say rhyming words. I like to say them, too." Other children recall other rhyming words in the book: *clocks–tocks–blocks–box, noodle–poodle,* and *new–do–blue–goo.*

3. Provide Information

"Let me tell you about our game," Ms. Lewis explains. I'm going to say some of the words from the book, but I'm going to say them sound by sound and I want you to blend the sounds together and guess the word." "Are they rhyming words?" Teri asks. "Sure," the teacher agrees. "I'll say two words that rhyme, sound by sound, for you to guess." She says the sounds /f/ /ŏ/ /x/ and /b/ /ŏ/ /x/ and the children correctly blend the sounds and say the words *fox* and *box.* She repeats procedure for *clock–tock, come–dumb, big–pig, new–blue, rose–hose, game–lame,* and *slow–crow.* Ms. Lewis stops and talks about how to "bump" or blend the sounds to figure out the words. She models how she blends the sounds together to form the word. "Make the words harder," several children say, and Ms. Lewis offers several more difficult pairs of rhyming words, including *chick–trick* and *beetle–tweedle.*

4. Guide Practice

Ms. Lewis continues playing the guessing game, but now she segments individual words rather than pairs of rhyming words for the children to guess. As each child correctly identifies a word, that child leaves the group and goes to work with the aide in another part of the classroom. Finally, six children remain who need additional practice blending sounds into words. They continue practicing *do, new* and other two-sound words and some of the easier three-sound words, including *box, come,* and *like.*

5. Assess Learning

Through the guided practice part of the lesson, Ms. Lewis checks to see which children need more practice blending sounds into words and provides additional practice for them.

After the teacher shows children the objects in the boxes and they name them together, two children play the game. One child selects an object, holds it, and pronounces the initial (or medial or final) sound. The second child chooses the same object from the second box and holds it up. Children check to see if the two players are holding the same object.

Children also identify rhyming words as part of sound-matching activities. They name a word that rhymes with a given word and identify rhyming words from familiar songs and stories. As children listen to parents and teachers read Dr. Seuss books, such as *Hop on Pop* (1963), and other wordplay books, they refine their understanding of rhyme.

Sound-Isolation Activities. Teachers say a word and then children identify the sounds at the beginning, middle, or end of the word, or teachers and children isolate sounds as they sing familiar songs. Yopp (1992) created new verses to the tune of "Old MacDonald Had a Farm":

> What's the sound that starts these words:
> Chicken, chin and cheek?
> (wait for response)
> /ch/ is the sound that starts these words:
> Chicken, chin, and cheek.
> With a /ch/, /ch/ here, and a /ch/, /ch/ there,
> Here a /ch/, there a /ch/, everywhere a /ch/, /ch/.
> /ch/ is the sound that starts these words:
> Chicken, chin, and cheek. (p. 700)

Teachers change the question at the beginning of the verse to focus on medial and final sounds. For example:

> What's the sound in the middle of these words?
> Whale, game, and rain. (p. 700)

And for final sounds:

> What's the sound at the end of these words?
> Leaf, cough, and beef. (p. 700)

Teachers also set out trays of objects and ask children to choose the one object that doesn't belong because it doesn't begin with the sound. For example, from a tray with a toy pig, a puppet, a teddy bear, and a pen, the teddy bear doesn't belong.

Sound-Blending Activities. Children blend sounds together in order to combine them to form a word. For example, children blend the sounds /d/, /ŭ/, and /k/ to form the word *duck*. Teachers play the "What am I thinking of?" guessing game with children by identifying several characteristics of the item and then saying the name of the item, articulating each of the sounds slowly and separately (Yopp, 1992). Then children blend the sounds together and identify the word, using the phonological and semantic information that the teacher provided. For example:

> I'm thinking of a small animal that lives in the pond when it is young. When it is an adult, it lives on land and it is called a /f/, /r/, /ŏ/, /g/. What is it?

The children blend the sounds together to pronounce the word *frog*. In this example, the teacher connects the game with a thematic unit, thereby making the game more meaningful for students.

Sound-Addition and Substitution Activities. Children play with words and create nonsense words as they add or substitute sounds in words in they sing or in books that are read aloud to them. Teachers read wordplay books such as Pat Hutchins's *Don't Forget the Bacon!* (1976), in which a boy leaves for the store with a mental list of four items to buy. As he walks, he repeats his list, substituting words each time. "A cake for tea" changes to "a cape for me" and then to "a rake for leaves." Children suggest other substitutions, such as "a game for a bee."

Children substitute sounds in refrains of songs (Yopp, 1992). For example, children can change the "Ee-igh, ee-igh, oh!" refrain in "Old MacDonald Had a Farm" to "Bee-bigh, bee-bigh, boh!" to focus on the initial /b/ sound. Teachers can choose one sound, such as /sh/, and have children substitute this sound for the beginning sound in their names and in words for items in the classroom. For example, *Jimmy* becomes *Shimmy, José* becomes *Shosé,* and *clock* becomes *shock.*

Sound-Segmentation Activities. One of the more difficult phonemic awareness activities is segmentation, in which children isolate the sounds in a spoken word (Yopp, 1988). An introductory segmentation activity is to draw out the beginning sound in words. Children enjoy exaggerating the initial sound in their own names and other familiar words. For example, a pet guinea pig named Popsicle lives in Mrs. Hoddy's classroom, and the children exaggerate the beginning sound of her name so that it is pronounced as "P-P-P-Popsicle." Children can also pick up objects or pictures of objects and identify the initial sound. A child who picks up a toy tiger says, "This is a tiger and it starts with /t/."

From that beginning, children move to identifying all the sounds in a word. Using a toy tiger again, the child would say, "This is a tiger, /t/, /ī/, /g/, /er/." Yopp (1992) suggests singing a song to the tune of "Twinkle, Twinkle, Little Star" in which children segment entire words. Here is one example:

> Listen, listen
> To my word
> Then tell me all the sounds you heard: coat
> (slowly)
> /k/ is one sound
> /ō/ is two
> /t/ is last in coat
> It's true. (p. 702)

After several repetitions of the verse segmenting other words, the song ends this way:

> Thanks for listening
> To my words
> And telling all the sounds you heard! (p. 702)

Teachers also use Elkonin boxes to teach children to segment words. This activity comes from the work of Russian psychologist D. B. Elkonin (Clay, 1985). As shown in Figure 4-3, the teacher shows an object or picture of an object and draws a series of boxes, with one box for each sound in the name of the object. Then the teacher or a child moves a marker into each box as the sound is pronounced. Children can move small markers onto cards on their desks, or the teacher can draw the boxes on the chalkboard and use tape or small magnets to hold the larger markers in place. Elkonin boxes can also be used for spelling activities. When a child is trying to spell a word, such as *duck,* the teacher can draw three boxes, do the segmentation activity, and then have the child write the letters representing each sound in the boxes. Spelling boxes for *duck* and other words with two, three, or four sounds are also shown in Figure 4-3.

Figure 4-3

How to Use Elkonin Boxes for Segmentation Activities

1. The teacher shows students an object or the picture of an object, such as a duck, a bed, a game, a bee, a cup, or a cat.

2. The teacher prepares a diagram with a series of boxes, corresponding to the number of sounds heard in the name of the object. For example, the teacher draws three boxes side by side to represent the three sounds heard in the word *duck*. The teacher can draw the boxes on the chalkboard or on small cards for each child to use. The teacher also prepares markers to place on the boxes.

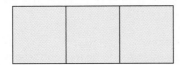

3. The teacher or students say the word slowly and move markers onto the boxes as each sound is pronounced.

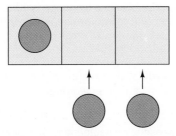

4. Elkonin boxes can also be used when spelling words. The teacher draws a series of boxes corresponding to the number of sounds heard in the words, and then the child and teacher pronounce the word, pointing to each box or sliding markers into each box. Then the child writes the letters representing each sound or spelling pattern in the boxes.

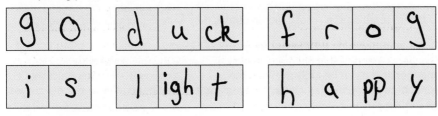

In these activities, children are experimenting with oral language. They do not usually read or write letters and words during phonemic awareness activities, because the focus is on speech. However, once children begin reading and writing, these activities reinforce the segmentation and blending activities they have learned. The phonemic awareness activities stimulate children's interest in language and provide valuable experiences with books and words. Effective teachers recognize the importance of building this foundation before children begin reading and writing. Guidelines for phonemic awareness activities are reviewed in Figure 4-4.

Why Is Phonemic Awareness Important?

The relationship between phonemic awareness and learning to read is extremely important, and researchers have concluded that at least some level of phonemic aware-

Figure 4-4 Guidelines for Phonemic Awareness Activities

---

1. Use Oral Activities
Phonemic awareness activities are oral activities. Objects and pictures are used instead of word cards, and children usually do not read or write letters and words during these activities. However, after children learn to identify the letters of the alphabet, reading and writing can be added.

2. Emphasize Experimentation
These language activities are intended to be fun, and teachers avoid drills and rote memorization activities. Children experiment with language as they sing songs, play word games, notice rhyming words, and create new words.

3. Plan Group Activities
Children do activities in a group, because language is a social activity. Teachers can read wordplay books and sing wordplay songs with the whole class, but for other activities, teachers usually work with small groups.

4. Read Wordplay Books
Teachers read and reread wordplay books and encourage students to experiment with rhyming words, alliteration, and other wordplay.

5. Teach Minilessons
Teachers teach explicit minilessons on segmenting, blending, and rhyming sounds in words. These lessons are a regular part of literature focus units. Teachers also teach phonemic awareness incidentally as children play with words and recite poems.

6. Connect to Reading and Writing
Phonemic awareness activities must be incorporated into the context of authentic reading and writing activities. After children gain some understanding of phonemes, the activities can be connected to big books children are reading and to the invented spelling that children use as they write in journals and make books.

7. Allow for Individual Differences
Teachers recognize that children develop phonemic awareness at different rates and therefore allow for individual differences. Some children will catch on to the concept of phonemes right away, whereas others may not understand the activities for a while.

Adapted from Griffith & Olson, 1992; Yopp, 1992.

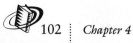

ness is a prerequisite for learning to read (Cunningham, 1999; Tunmer & Nesdale, 1985; Yopp, 1985). In fact, phonemic awareness seems to be both a prerequisite for and a consequence of learning to read (Liberman, Shankweiler, Fischer, & Carter, 1974; Perfitti, Beck, Bell, & Hughes, 1987; Stanovich, 1980). As they become phonemically aware, children recognize that speech can be segmented into smaller units, and this knowledge is very useful when children learn about sound symbol correspondences and spelling patterns.

Researchers have concluded that children can be explicitly taught to segment and manipulate speech, and that children who receive training in phonemic awareness do better in both reading and spelling (P. L. Griffith, 1991; Juel, Griffith, & Gough, 1986). Phonemic awareness can also be nurtured in spontaneous ways by providing children with language-rich environments and emphasizing wordplay as teachers read books aloud to children and engage them in singing songs, chanting poems, and telling riddles.

Moreover, phonemic awareness has been shown to be the most powerful predictor of later reading achievement (Juel et al., 1986; Lomax & McGee, 1987; Tunmer & Nesdale, 1985). In a study comparing children's progress in learning to read in whole-language and traditional reading instruction, Klesius, Griffith, and Zielonka (1991) found that children who began first grade with strong phonemic awareness did well regardless of the kind of reading instruction they received. And neither type of instruction was better for children who were low in phonemic awareness at the beginning of first grade.

To link to *Phonemic Awareness and the Teaching of Reading,* for the International Reading Association's position paper on the importance of phonemic awareness, visit our Companion Website at www.prenhall.com/tompkins

PHONICS

Phonics is the set of relationships between phonology (the sounds in speech) and orthography (the spelling patterns of written language). The emphasis is on spelling patterns, not individual letters, because there is not a one-to-one correspondence between phonemes and graphemes in English—sounds are spelled in different ways. There are several reasons for this variety. One reason is that the sounds, especially vowels, vary according to their location in a word (e.g., *go–got*). Adjacent letters often influence how letters are pronounced (e.g., *bed–bead*), as do vowel markers such as the final *e* (e.g., *bit–bite*) (Shefelbine, 1995).

Language origin, or etymology, of words also influences their pronunciation. For example, the *ch* digraph is pronounced in several ways. The three most common are /ch/ as in *chain* (English), /sh/ as in *chauffeur* (French), and /k/ as in *chaos* (Greek). Neither the location of the digraph within the word nor adjacent letters account for these pronunciation differences. In all three words, the *ch* digraph is at the beginning of the word and is followed by two vowels, the first of which is *a*. Some letters in words are not pronounced, either. In words such as *write,* the *w* isn't pronounced, even though it may have been at one time. The same is true in *knight, know,* and *knee.* "Silent" letters in words such as *sign* and *bomb* reflect their parent words *signature* and *bombard* and have been retained for semantic, not phonological, reasons (Venezky, 1999).

To link to research, updates, and resources about phonics from the National Right to Read Foundation, visit our Companion Website at www.prenhall.com/tompkins

Phonics Concepts, Skills, and Generalizations

Teachers teach sound-symbol correspondences, how to blend sounds together to decode words and segment sounds for spelling, and the most useful phonics generalizations or "rules." There is no simple way to explain all of the types of phonics information that students need to learn; nor can these concepts be listed in a clean, sequential order, because they are built on children's foundation of phonemic awareness. However, the most important are letters of the alphabet, consonants, vowels, blending, rimes and rhymes, and phonics generalizations. Most of these concepts are taught in the primary grades, but students continue to refine their knowledge of the phonological system during fourth grade and beyond.

Letters of the Alphabet. Children learn many things about the alphabet as preschoolers and during the kindergarten year (McGee & Richgels, 1989). They learn to name the letters, notice letter features, and form upper- and lowercase letters in handwriting. At first, they notice letters in environmental print, such as letters spelling the name of a familiar store or restaurant, and the letters in their own names. Kindergarten teachers help students focus on the letters in classmates' names, in familiar words, and in literature. For example, teachers might point out that two students in the class, Jesse and John, have names beginning with *J*, or that Miki's name starts like Max's in *Where the Wild Things Are* (Sendak, 1963).

One of the most useful ways to teach the alphabet is by singing the alphabet song. Once children know the song, they can use it as a strategy to figure out the names of unfamiliar letters. They locate the unfamiliar letter on an alphabet chart and then sing the song, pointing to each letter until they reach the unfamiliar letter. Learning and using this strategy gives young children a great deal of independence in using written language. They also use their knowledge of letter names as they invent spellings. As young children attempt to write "I love you," for example, they may spell it *I lv u,* with or without spaces between words. They recognize the letter *I* and write it for the word *I.* As they pronounce *love,* they focus on the initial consonant, *l,* or the two consonants *l* and *v,* which they can figure out by matching the sounds to the letter names as they say these letters. The last word, *you,* is easy to represent because they hear the name of the letter *u* clearly.

Kindergartners sing a song about the letters of the alphabet and stand up when the letter that begins their name is sung.

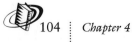

The concept that words are composed of letters and that these letters have names is abstract, but through many meaningful experiences with written language, young children learn about the letters and that letters are used in words that they read and write. To learn more about teaching the letters of the alphabet, turn back to Chapter 2, "Examining Children's Literacy Development."

Consonants. Phonemes are classified as either consonants or vowels. The consonants are *b, c, d, f, g, h, j, k, l, m, n, p, q, r, s, t, v, w, x, y,* and *z.* Most consonants represent a single sound consistently, but there are some exceptions. *C,* for example, does not represent a sound of its own. When it is followed by *a, o,* or *u,* it is pronounced /k/ (e.g., *castle, coffee, cut*), and when it is followed by *e, i,* or *y,* it is pronounced /s/ (e.g., *cell, city, cycle*). *G* represents two sounds, as the word *garbage* illustrates. It is usually pronounced /g/ (e.g., *glass, go, green, guppy*), but when *g* is followed by *e, i,* or *y,* it is pronounced /j/, as in *giant. X* is also pronounced differently according to its location in a word. At the beginning of a word, it is often pronounced /z/, as in *xylophone,* but sometimes the letter name is used, as in *X-ray.* At the end of a word, *x* is pronounced /ks/, as in *box.*

The letters *w* and *y* are particularly interesting. At the beginning of a word or syllable, they are consonants (e.g., *wind, yard*), but when they are in the middle or at the end, they are vowels (e.g., *saw, flown, day, by*).

Two kinds of combination consonants are blends and digraphs. Consonant blends occur when two or three consonants appear next to each other in words and their individual sounds are "blended" together, as in *grass, belt,* and *spring.* Consonant digraphs are letter combinations for single sounds that are not represented by either letter. The four most common are *ch* as in *chair* and *each, sh* as in *shell* and *wish, th* as in *father* and *both,* and *wh* as in *whale.* Another consonant digraph is *ph,* as in *graph* and *photo.*

Vowels. The remaining five letters—*a, e, i, o,* and *u*—represent vowels, and *w* and *y* are vowels when used in the middle and at the end of syllables and words. Vowels often represent several sounds. The two most common are short (marked with the symbol ˘, called a breve) and long sounds (marked with the symbol ‾, called a macron). The short-vowel sounds are /ă/ as in *cat,* /ĕ/ as in *bed,* /ĭ/ as in *win,* /ŏ/ as in *hot,* and /ŭ/ as in *cup.* The long-vowel sounds—/ā/, /ē/, /ī/, /ō/, and /ū/—are the same as the letter names, and they are illustrated in the words *make, feet, bike, coal,* and *mule.* Long-vowel sounds are usually spelled with two vowels, except when the long vowel is at the end of a one-syllable word (or a syllable), as in *be* or *belong* and *try* or *tribal.*

When *y* is a vowel at the end of a word, it is pronounced as long *e* or long *i,* depending on the length of the word. In one-syllable words such as *by* and *cry,* the *y* is pronounced as long *i,* but in longer words such as *baby* and *happy,* the *y* is usually pronounced as long *e.*

Vowel sounds are more complicated than consonant sounds, and there are many vowel combinations representing long vowels and other vowel sounds. Consider these combinations:

ai as in *nail*
au as in *laugh* and *caught*
aw as in *saw*
ea as in *peach* and *bread*
ew as in *sew* and *few*
ia as in *dial*
ie as in *cookie*

ELL

Vowels and their spellings are especially difficult for English-language learners because they are more complicated than consonants.

oa as in *soap*
oi as in *oil*
oo as in *cook* and *moon*
ou as in *house* and *through*
ow as in *now* and *snow*
oy as in *toy*

Most vowel combinations are vowel digraphs or diphthongs. When two vowels represent a single sound, the combination is a vowel digraph (e.g., *nail, snow*), and when the two vowels represent a glide from one sound to another, the combination is a diphthong. Two vowel combinations that are consistently diphthongs are *oi* and *oy*, but other combinations, such as *ou* as in *house* (but not in *through*) and *ow* as in *now* (but not in *snow*), are diphthongs when they represent a glided sound. In *through*, the *ou* represents the /o͞o/ sound as in *moon*, and in *snow* the *ow* represents the /ō/ sound.

When the letter *r* follows one or more vowels in a word, it influences the pronunciation of the vowel sound, as shown in the words *car, air, are, ear, bear, first, for, more, murder*, and *pure*. Students learn many of these words as sight words.

The vowels in the unaccented syllables of multisyllabic words are often softened and pronounced "uh," as in the first syllable of *about* and *machine*, and the final syllable of *pencil, tunnel, zebra*, and *selection*. This vowel sound is called schwa and is represented in dictionaries with an ə, which looks like an inverted *e*.

Blending Into Words. Readers "blend" or combine sounds in order to decode words. Even though children may identify each sound in a word, one by one, they must also be able to blend them together into a word. For example, in order to read the short-vowel word *best*, children identify /b/, /ĕ/, /s/, and /t/ and then combine them to form the word. For long-vowel words, children must identify the vowel pattern as well as the surrounding letters. In *pancake*, for example, children identify /p/, /ă/, /n/, /k/, /ā/, and /k/ and recognize that the *e* at the end of the word is silent and marks the preceding vowel as long. Shefelbine (1995) emphasizes the importance of blending and suggests that students who have difficulty decoding words usually know the sound-symbol correspondences but cannot blend the sounds together into recognizable words. The ability to blend sounds together into words is part of phonemic awareness, and children who have not had practice blending speech sounds into words are likely to have trouble blending sounds into words in order to decode unfamiliar words.

Rimes and Rhymes. One-syllable words and syllables in longer words can be divided into two parts, the onset and the rime. The onset is the consonant sound, if any, that precedes the vowel, and the rime is the vowel and any consonant sounds that follow it (Treiman, 1985). For example, in *show, sh* is the onset and *ow* is the rime, and in *ball*, *b* is the onset and *all* is the rime. For *at* and *up*, there is no onset; the entire word is the rime. Research has shown that children make more errors decoding and spelling final consonants than initial consonants and that they make more errors on vowels than on consonants (Treiman, 1985). These problem areas correspond to rimes, and educators now speculate that onsets and rimes could provide an important key to word identification.

The terms *onset* and *rime* are not usually introduced to children because they might confuse *rime* and *rhyme*. Instead, teachers call the rhyming words made from a rime "word families." Teachers can focus children's attention on a rime, such as *ay*, and create rhyming words, including *bay, day, lay, may, ray, say*, and *way*, as Mrs. Hoddy did in the vignette at the beginning of this chapter. These words can be read and spelled

ELL

ELL students learn to read and write many words using onsets and rimes. It's important, though, that second language learners understand the meaning of word-family words they are reading and writing (e.g., *bill, chill, dill, fill, gill, hill, mill, pill, quill, still, will*).

Figure 4-5   The 37 Rimes and Common Words
Using Them

-ack	black, pack, quack, stack	-ide	bride, hide, ride, side
-ail	mail, nail, sail, tail	-ight	bright, fight, light, might
-ain	brain, chain, plain, rain	-ill	fill, hill, kill, will
-ake	cake, shake, take, wake	-in	chin, grin, pin, win
-ale	male, sale, tale, whale	-ine	fine, line, mine, nine
-ame	came, flame, game, name	-ing	king, sing, thing, wing
-an	can, man, pan, than	-ink	pink, sink, think, wink
-ank	bank, drank, sank, thank	-ip	drip, hip, lip, ship
-ap	cap, clap, map, slap	-ir	birth, dirt, first, girl
-ash	cash, dash, flash, trash	-ock	block, clock, knock, sock
-at	bat, cat, rat, that	-oke	choke, joke, poke, woke
-ate	gate, hate, late, plate	-op	chop, drop, hop, shop
-aw	claw, draw, jaw, saw	-ore	chore, more, shore, store
-ay	day, play, say, way	-or	for, or, short, torn
-eat	beat, heat, meat, wheat	-uck	duck, luck, suck, truck
-ell	bell, sell, shell, well	-ug	bug, drug, hug, rug
-est	best, chest, nest, west	-ump	bump, dump, hump, lump
-ice	ice, mice, nice, rice	-unk	bunk, dunk, junk, sunk
-ick	brick, pick, sick, thick		

by analogy because the vowel sounds are consistent in rimes. Wylie and Durrell (1970) identified 37 rimes that can be used to produce nearly 500 common words. These rimes and some words made from them are presented in Figure 4-5.

Phonics Generalizations. Because English does not have a one-to-one correspondence between sounds and letters, linguists have created generalizations or rules to clarify English spelling patterns. One rule is that *q* is followed by *u* and pronounced /kw/, as in *queen, quick,* and *earthquake.* There are very few, if any, exceptions to this rule. Another generalization that has few exceptions relates to *r*-controlled vowels: *r* influences the preceding vowel so that the vowel is neither long nor short. Examples are *car, market, birth,* and *four.* There are exceptions, however, such as *fire.*

Many generalizations aren't very useful because there are more exceptions than words that conform to the rule (Clymer, 1963). A good example is this rule for long vowels: When there are two vowels side by side, the long vowel sound of the first one is pronounced and the second is silent. Teachers sometimes call this the "when two vowels go walking, the first one does the talking" rule. Examples of words conforming to this rule are *meat, soap,* and *each.* There are many more exceptions, however, including *food, said, head, chief, bread, look, soup, does, too, again,* and *believe.*

Only a few phonics generalizations have a high degree of utility for readers. The generalizations that work most of the time are the ones that students should learn because they are the most useful (Adams, 1990). Eight high-utility generalizations are listed in Figure 4-6. Even though these rules are fairly reliable, very few of them approach 100% utility. The rule about *r*-controlled vowels, for instance, has been calculated to be useful in 78% of words in which the letter *r* follows the vowel (Adams, 1990). Other commonly taught, useful rules have even lower percentages of utility. The CVC pattern rule—which says that when a one-syllable word has only one vowel and the vowel comes between two consonants, it is usually short, as in *bat, land,* and *cup*—is estimated to work only 62% of the time. Exceptions include *told, fall, fork,* and

Figure 4-6   The Most Useful Phonics Generalizations

Pattern	Description	Examples
Two sounds of *c*	The letter *c* can be pronounced as /k/ or /s/. When *c* is followed by *a, o,* or *u,* it is pronounced /k/—the hard *c* sound. When *c* is followed by *e, i,* or *y,* it is pronounced /s/—the soft *c* sound.	cat cough cut cent city cycle
Two sounds of *g*	The sound associated with the letter *g* depends on the letter following it. When *g* is followed by *a, o,* or *u,* it is pronounced as /g/—the hard *g* sound. When *g* is followed by *e, i,* or *y,* it is usually pronounced /j/—the soft *g* sound. Exceptions include *get* and *give.*	gate go guess gentle giant gypsy
CVC pattern	When a one-syllable word has only one vowel and the vowel comes between two consonants, it is usually short. One exception is *told.*	bat cup land
Final *e* or CVCe pattern	When there are two vowels in a one-syllable word and one of them is an *e* at the end of the word, the first vowel is long and the final *e* is silent. Three exceptions are *have, come,* and *love.*	home safe cute
CV pattern	When a vowel follows a consonant in a one-syllable word, the vowel is long. Exceptions include *the, to,* and *do.*	go be
R-controlled vowels	Vowels that are followed by the letter *r* are overpowered and are neither short nor long. One exception is *fire.*	car for birthday
-igh	When *gh* follows *i,* the *i* is long and the *gh* is silent. One exception is *neighbor.*	high night
Kn- and *wr-*	In words beginning with *kn-* and *wr-,* the first letter is not pronounced.	knee write

Adapted from Clymer, 1963.

birth. The CVCe pattern rule—which says that when there are two vowels in a one-syllable word and one vowel is an *e* at the end of the word, the first vowel is long and the final *e* is silent—is estimated to work in 63% of CVCe words. Examples of conforming words are *came, hole,* and *pipe;* but two very common words, *have* and *love,* are exceptions.

Teaching Phonics

Phonics instruction is an important part of reading and writing instruction during the primary grades, but it is crucial that children are involved in real reading and writing activities as they learn phonics. Without this meaningful application of what they are

The teacher presents a minilesson on /b/ as part of a literature focus unit on "The Three Bears."

learning, phonics instruction is often ineffective (Cunningham, 2000; Dahl, Scharer, Lawson, & Grogan, 2001; Freppon & Dahl, 1991). There is no consensus among researchers about the best way to teach phonics, but most agree that teachers should use a combination of direct and indirect methods for phonics instruction. They teach minilessons to introduce phonics concepts, skills, and generalizations in a systematic way, and they also take advantage of teachable moments during literacy activities to provide indirect instruction.

Explicit Instruction. Teachers present minilessons on specific high-utility phonics concepts, skills, and generalizations as part of a systematic program. According to Shefelbine (1995), the program should be "systematic and thorough enough to enable most students to become independent and fluent readers, yet still efficient and streamlined" (p. 2). Phonics instruction is always tied to reading and writing. Teachers emphasize that they are teaching phonics so that children can decode words fluently when reading and spell words conventionally when writing.

Teachers plan for the minilesson by identifying a phonics concept, skill, or generalization and choosing words from the story to introduce the lesson. Teachers clearly and explicitly present the phonics information and provide words to use in practicing the skill, as Mrs. Hoddy did in the vignette at the beginning of this chapter. During minilessons, teachers use the following activities to provide opportunities for children to read, write, and manipulate sounds, spelling patterns, and words:

Locate other examples of the sound or pattern in words in a book.
Sort objects and pictures by beginning sounds.
Cut words and pictures from newspapers and magazines for phonics posters.
Write words on magic slates or individual dry-erase boards.
Make a poster or book of words fitting a pattern.

Do a word sort[C] on the basis of spelling patterns.

Arrange a group of magnetic letters or letter cards to spell words.

Read books with many phonetically regular words, such as Dr. Seuss books and Nancy Shaw's "sheep" series (e.g., *Sheep in a Jeep*, 1986).

Write alphabet books and other books featuring phonetically regular words.

Make charts of words representing spelling patterns and other phonics generalizations, such as the two sounds of *g* and ways to spell long *o*.

Although a regular program of minilessons is important, it is essential that they do not overshadow reading and writing as meaning-making processes. Figure 4-7 reviews the guidelines for phonics instruction.

Teachers have to be knowledgeable about phonics in order to teach it well. They need to be able to draw words from children's reading materials, understand the phonics principles operating in these words, and cite additional examples. They also need to know about exceptions so that they can explain why some words don't fit par-

Figure 4-7   Guidelines for Phonics Instruction

1. Teach High-Utility Phonics
Teachers teach the phonics concepts, skills, and generalizations that are most useful for decoding and spelling unfamiliar words. Some phonics rules, such as the CVVC long-vowel rule, are not very useful (e.g., *said, soap, head*).

2. Follow a Developmental Continuum
Teachers follow a developmental continuum for systematic phonics instruction, beginning with rhyming and ending with phonics generalizations.

3. Use a Whole-Part-Whole Instructional Sequence
Teachers plan phonics instruction that grows out of reading using a whole-part-whole sequence. Reading the literature is the whole, phonics instruction is the part, and applying the phonics in additional literacy activities is the second whole.

4. Provide Explicit Instruction
Teachers use minilessons to clearly and directly present information about phonics skills and generalizations and provide examples from books students are reading and other common words. They also provide opportunities for children to read and write words applying the concepts they are teaching.

5. Apply Phonics Skills
Children apply what they are learning about phonics skills and generalizations through spelling, word sorts, making words, interactive writing, wordplay books such as Nancy Shaw's *Sheep in a Jeep* (1986), and other activities.

6. Use Teachable Moments
Teachers also take advantage of teachable moments when they can incorporate phonics information informally into reading and writing activities.

7. Reinforce Phonemic Awareness
Teachers reinforce phonemic awareness as children segment and blend written words through phonics and spelling instruction.

Adapted from Shefelbine, 1995; Stahl, 1992; Trachtenburg, 1990.

ticular generalizations. Too often, teachers want to purchase a packaged program, but it's preferable that they plan their phonics program themselves, as Mrs. Hoddy did at the beginning of the chapter. She decided on the organization of her program using the checklist shown in Figure 4-1, and then she developed activities using words from the books her students were reading during literature focus units.

Teachable Moments. Teachers often give impromptu phonics lessons as they engage children in authentic literacy activities using children's names, titles of books, and environmental print in the classroom. During these teachable moments, teachers answer children's questions about words, model how to use phonics knowledge to decode and spell words, and have children share the strategies they use for reading and writing (Mills, O'Keefe, & Stephens, 1992). For example, as she was introducing *The Very Hungry Caterpillar,* Mrs. Hoddy pointed out that *Very* begins with *v* and that not many words start with *v.* One child mentioned that *valentine* is another *v* word, and another said that her middle name is *Victoria.* Then a child who had been quietly looking at the cover of the book said, "I think *Very* is spelled wrong. The author made a mistake," and he pronounced the word *very,* emphasizing the final long *e* sound. "*Very* should have an *e* at the end, not a *y,*" he concluded. This comment gave Mrs. Hoddy an opportunity to explain that long *e* at the end of a two-syllable word is often spelled with a *y.*

Teachers also demonstrate how to apply phonics information as they read big books with the class and take children's dictation for language experience approach[C] charts. As they read and spell words, teachers break words apart into sounds and apply phonics rules and generalizations. For example, as Mrs. Hoddy talked about the life cycle of butterflies, the class created the chart shown in Figure 4-8. As she wrote,

Figure 4-8   **A Class Chart on Butterflies**

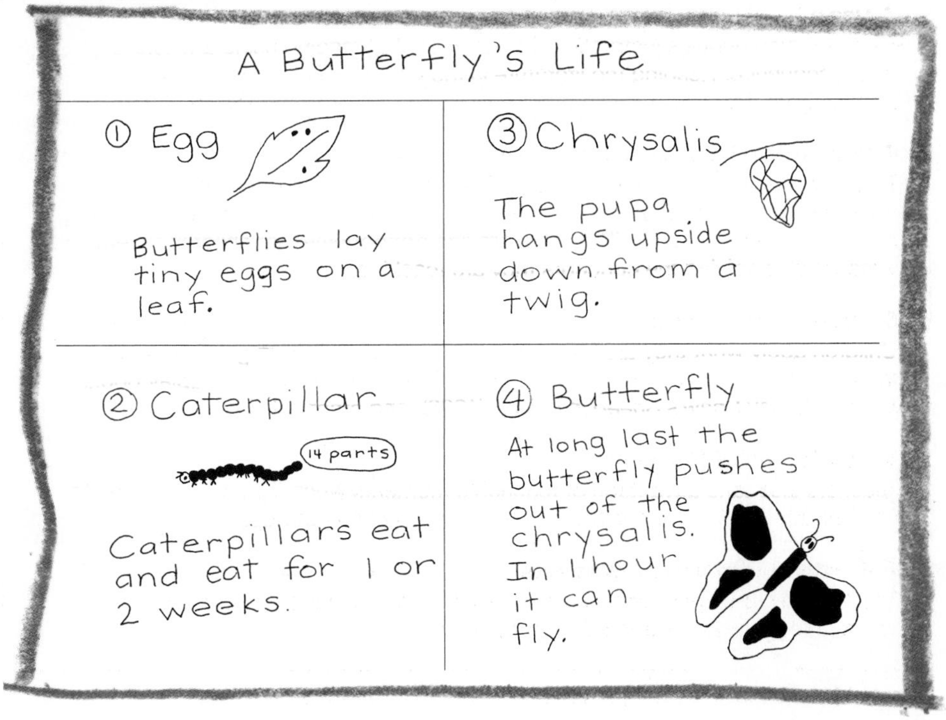

A Butterfly's Life

① Egg

Butterflies lay tiny eggs on a leaf.

② Caterpillar

(14 parts)

Caterpillars eat and eat for 1 or 2 weeks.

③ Chrysalis

The pupa hangs upside down from a twig.

④ Butterfly

At long last the butterfly pushes out of the chrysalis. In 1 hour it can fly.

she talked about plural -*s* marker on *eggs* and *caterpillars* and the interesting *tw-* blend at the beginning of *twig*. Also, each time she wrote *butterfly* and *caterpillar*, she spelled the words syllable by syllable. Then as children reread the completed chart, she prompts them on the word *pupa*, when they don't remember it, by sounding it out.

Teachers also use interactive writing[C] to support children's growing awareness of phonics (Collom, 1998; McCarrier, Pinnell, & Fountas, 2000). Interactive writing is similar to the language experience approach, except that children do as much of the writing themselves as they can. Children segment words into sounds and take turns writing letters and sometimes whole words on the chart. Teachers help children to correct any errors, and they take advantage of teachable moments to review consonant and vowel sounds and spelling patterns, as well as handwriting skills and rules for capitalization and punctuation.

What Is the Role of Phonics in a Balanced Literacy Program?

To link to *The Role of Phonics in Reading Instruction,* for the International Reading Association's position statement about this controversial topic, visit our Companion Website at www.prenhall.com/tompkins

Phonics is a controversial topic. Some parents and politicians, as well as even a few teachers, believe that most of our educational ills could be solved if children were taught to read using phonics. A few people still argue that phonics is a complete reading program, but that view ignores what we know about the interrelatedness of the four cueing systems. Reading is a complex process, and the phonological system works in conjunction with the semantic, syntactic, and pragmatic systems, not in isolation.

The controversy now centers on how to teach phonics. Marilyn Adams (1990), in her landmark review of the research on phonics instruction, recommends that phonics be taught within a balanced approach that integrates instruction in reading skills and strategies with meaningful opportunities for reading and writing. She emphasizes that phonics instruction should focus on the most useful information for identifying words and that it should be systematic, intensive, and completed by the third grade.

Phonics instruction looks different today than it did a generation ago (Strickland, 1998). At that time, phonics instruction often involved marking letters and words on worksheets. Today, however, students learn phonics through reading and writing as well as through minilessons and gamelike activities such as making words and word sorts.

Review

As they learn to read, children develop phonemic awareness and phonics concepts, skills, and strategies. Phonemic awareness is the ability to segment and blend spoken words, and it provides the foundation for phonics instruction. Phonics is the set of relationships between speech sounds and spelling patterns. During the primary grades, students learn phonics in order to decode words and invent spellings. To become fluent readers, students need to be able to decode unfamiliar words rapidly. The feature that follows reviews the recommended practices that effective reading teachers use in helping students to "break the code."

How Effective Teachers . . .
Assist Children in "Breaking the Code"

Effective Practices

1. Teachers develop students' phonemic awareness using songs, rhymes, and wordplay books.
2. Teachers teach five phonemic awareness strategies: matching sounds, isolating sounds, blending sounds, substituting sounds, and segmenting words into sounds.
3. Teachers teach minilessons on segmenting and blending sounds in words using familiar words drawn from books children are reading.
4. Teachers teach phonics using a whole-part-whole approach.
5. Teachers teach the high-utility phonics concepts, skills, and generalizations.
6. Teachers provide opportunities for children to read and write word families using onsets and rimes.
7. Teachers teach phonics systematically through minilessons.
8. Teachers take advantage of "teachable moments" to respond to children's questions and clarify misconceptions.
9. Teachers connect phonics instruction for decoding words to spelling words.
10. Teachers provide interventions for children who are not learning phonemic awareness strategies or phonics concepts, skills, and generalizations.

Professional References

Adams, M. J. (1990). *Beginning to read: Thinking and learning about print.* Cambridge, MA: MIT Press.

Carle, E. (1993). *Eric Carle: Picture writer* (videotape). New York: Philomel.

Clay, M. M. (1985). *The early detection of reading difficulties* (3rd ed.). Portsmouth, NH: Heinemann.

Clymer, T. (1963). The utility of phonic generalizations in the primary grades. *The Reading Teacher, 16,* 252–258.

Collom, S. (Ed.). (1998). *Sharing the pen: Interactive writing with young children.* Fresno: California State University, Fresno, and the San Joaquin Valley Writing Project.

Cunningham, P. M. (1999). *What should we do about phonics?* In L. B. Gambrell, L. M. Morrow, A. B. Neuman, and M. Pressley (Eds.), *Best practices in literacy instruction* (pp. 68–89). New York: Guilford Press.

Cunningham, P. M. (2000). *Phonics they use: Words for reading and writing* (3rd ed.). New York: Longman.

Dahl, K. L., Scharer, P. L., Lawson, L. L., & Grogan, P. R. (2001). *Rethinking phonics: Making the best teaching decisions.* Portsmouth, NH: Heinemann.

Freppon, P. A., & Dahl, K. L. (1991). Learning about phonics in a whole language classroom. *Language Arts, 68,* 190–197.

Griffith, F., & Olson, M. (1992). Phonemic awareness helps beginning readers break the code. *The Reading Teacher, 45,* 516–523.

Griffith, P. L. (1991). Phonemic awareness helps first graders invent spellings and third graders remember correct spellings. *Journal of Reading Behavior, 23,* 215–232.

Hanna, P. R., Hanna, J. S., Hodges, R. E., & Rudorf, E. H. (1966). *Phoneme-grapheme correspondences as cues to spelling improvement.* Washington, DC: U.S. Government Printing Office.

Horn, E. (1957). Phonetics and spelling. *Elementary School Journal, 57,* 233–235, 246.

Juel, C., Griffith, P. L., & Gough, P. B. (1986). Acquisition of literacy: A longitudinal study of children in first and second grade. *Journal of Educational Psychology, 78,* 243–255.

Klesius, J. P., Griffith, P. L., & Zielonka, P. (1991). A whole language and traditional instruction comparison: Overall effectiveness and development of the alphabetic principle. *Reading Research and Instruction, 30,* 47–61.

Lewkowicz, N. K. (1994). The bag game: An activity to heighten phonemic awareness. *The Reading Teacher, 47,* 508–509.

Liberman, I., Shankweiler, D., Fischer, F., & Carter, B. (1974). Explicit syllable and phoneme segmentation in the young child. *Journal of Experimental Child Psychology, 18,* 201–212.

Lomax, R. G., & McGee, L. M. (1987). Young children's concepts about print and meaning: Toward a model of word reading acquisition. *Reading Research Quarterly, 22,* 237–256.

McCarrier, A., Pinnell, G. S., & Fountas, I. C. (2000). *Interactive writing: How language and literacy come together, K–2.* Portsmouth, NH: Heinemann.

McGee, L. M., & Richgels, D. J. (1989). "K is Kristen's": Learning the alphabet from a child's perspective. *The Reading Teacher, 43,* 216–225.

Mills, H., O'Keefe, T., & Stephens, D. (1992). *Looking closely: Exploring the role of phonics in one whole language classroom.* Urbana, IL: National Council of Teachers of English.

Perfitti, C., Beck, I., Bell, L., & Hughes, C. (1987). Phonemic knowledge and learning to read are reciprocal: A longitudinal study of first grade children. *Merrill-Palmer Quarterly, 33,* 283–319.

Shefelbine, J. (1995). *Learning and using phonics in beginning reading* (Literacy research paper; volume 10). New York: Scholastic.

Stahl, S. A. (1992). Saying the "p" word: Nine guidelines for exemplary phonics instruction. *The Reading Teacher, 45,* 618–625.

Stanovich, K. (1980). Toward an interactive-compensatory model of individual differences in the development of reading fluency. *Reading Research Quarterly, 16,* 37–71.

Strickland, D. S. (1998). *Teaching phonics today: A primer for educators.* Newark, DE: International Reading Association.

Tompkins, G. E., & Yaden, D. B., Jr. (1986). *Answering students' questions about words.* Urbana, IL: ERIC Clearinghouse on Reading and Communication Skills and National Council of Teachers of English.

Trachtenburg, P. (1990). Using children's literature to enhance phonics instruction. *The Reading Teacher, 43,* 648–654.

Treiman, R. (1985). Onsets and rimes as units of spoken syllables: Evidence from children. *Journal of Experimental Child Psychology, 39,* 161–181.

Tunmer, W., & Nesdale, A. (1985). Phonemic segmentation skill and beginning reading. *Journal of Educational Psychology, 77,* 417–427.

Venezky, R. L. (1999). *The American way of spelling: The structure and origins of American English orthography.* New York: Guilford Press.

Wylie, R. E., & Durrell, D. D. (1970). Teaching vowels through phonograms. *Elementary English, 47,* 787–791.

Yopp, H. K. (1985). Phoneme segmentation ability: A prerequisite for phonics and sight word achievement in beginning reading? In J. Niles & R. Lalik (Eds.), *Issues in literacy: A research perspective* (pp. 330–336). Rochester, NY: National Reading Conference.

Yopp, H. K. (1988). The validity and reliability of phonemic awareness tests. *Reading Research Quarterly, 23,* 159–177.

Yopp, H. K. (1992). Developing phonemic awareness in young children. *The Reading Teacher, 45,* 696–703.

Yopp, H. K. (1995). Read-aloud books for developing phonemic awareness: An annotated bibliography. *The Reading Teacher, 48,* 538–542.

Yopp, H. K., & Yopp, R. H. (2000). Supporting phonemic awareness development in the classroom. *The Reading Teacher, 54,* 130–143.

Children's Book References

Carle, E. (1969). *The very hungry caterpillar.* New York: Philomel.

Carle, E. (1984). *The very busy spider.* New York: Philomel.

Carle, E. (1990). *The very quiet cricket.* New York: Philomel.

Carle, E. (1995). *The very lonely firefly.* New York: Philomel.

Hutchins, P. (1976). *Don't forget the bacon!* New York: Mulberry.

Most, B. (1996). *Cock-a-doodle-moo!* San Diego: Harcourt Brace.

Obligado, L. (1983). *Faint frogs feeling feverish and other terrifically tantalizing tongue twisters.* New York: Puffin.

Prelutsky, J. (1982). *The baby uggs are hatching.* New York: Mulberry.

Sendak, M. (1963). *Where the wild things are.* New York: Harper & Row.

Seuss, Dr. (1963). *Hop on pop.* New York: Random House.

Seuss, Dr. (1965). *Fox in socks.* New York: Random House.

Shaw, N. (1986). *Sheep in a jeep.* Boston: Houghton Mifflin.

chapter 5

Learning to Spell

- What are the stages of spelling development?

- Why do teachers analyze children's spelling errors?

- How do teachers teach spelling?

- Why are weekly spelling tests an incomplete spelling program?

Mrs. Zumwalt Matches Instruction to Children's Stage of Spelling Development

The 21 third graders in Mrs. Zumwalt's class have different spelling needs because they are working at varying levels of spelling development. During the first week of the school year, Mrs. Zumwalt collected writing samples from her students, analyzed their spelling errors, and determined each child's stage of spelling development, and she continues to analyze their spelling at the end of each quarter and regroup them for instruction. According to her most recent assessment, one group of 5 children are within-word pattern spellers: They are confusing more-complex consonant and vowel patterns. Nick spells *headache* as *hedakke, soap* as *sope,* and *heart* as *hart;* Jovana spells *wild* as *wilde, ears* as *erars,* and *found* as *foeund.* Another group of 13 children spell at the syllables and affixes stage: They spell most one-syllable words correctly, and their errors involve adding inflectional endings and spelling the schwa sound in unaccented syllables. Maribel spells *coming* as *comeing;* Raziel spells *uncle* as *unkol* and *believed* as *beeleved.* Three others are more sophisticated spellers; Aaron, for example, spells *actor* as *acter, collection* as *culection,* and *pneumonia* as *newmonia.* These children are beginning to move into the derivational relations stage of spelling development. At this stage, children investigate Latin and Greek root words and affixes and learn about etymologies of words.

Mrs. Zumwalt spends 30 minutes, from 11:15 to 11:45, every morning on spelling. On Monday, she administers the pretest for the textbook spelling program that her school uses, and on Friday, she administers the final test. On Tuesdays, Wednesdays, and Thursdays, while children practice the spelling words independently, she teaches minilessons[C] on spelling topics with small groups. The topics she chooses for the minilessons depend on the needs of her students and the standards set out for her district.

See the Compendium of Instructional Procedures, which follows Chapter 12, for more information on terms marked with the symbol [C].

One day, Mrs. Zumwalt teaches a minilesson to half of the class comparing plurals and possessives because the syllables-and-affixes-stage spellers are using apostrophes incorrectly in plurals. For example, one child writes: *The boy's rode their bike's up the biggest hill in town to reach Chavez Park.* Afterwards, the third graders review their writing notebooks, locate three interesting sentences using either plurals or possessives, and copy them on sentence strips. During a follow-up minilesson, the children share their sentences, identify the plurals or possessives, and correct any errors. Mrs. Zumwalt notices that several children are still confused about plurals and possessives, and she plans to continue to work with them.

One day as the children are making new science logs for a unit on astronomy, several ask Mrs. Zumwalt about the word *science* and why there is an unnecessary *c* following the *s.* She explains that *science* is a Latin word and that a few very special words that have come to English from Latin are spelled with both *s* and *c.* From that exchange, Mrs. Zumwalt decides to teach a minilesson about the ways to spell /s/. To begin, she asks students to collect as many words with the /s/ sound as they can from books they are reading, words posted in the classroom, and other words they know. After a day of collecting words, the children each write the five most interesting words they've found on small cards. Mrs. Zumwalt sorts the words and places them in rows on a pocket chart. Most of the words they have found are spelled with *s* or *ss,* and several children found words using *c* or *ce* to spell the /s/. Mrs. Zumwalt adds several additional word cards with *se* and *sc* spellings. The children examine the chart and draw some conclusions about how to spell the *s* sound. The chart they develop is shown in Figure 5-1.

Mrs. Zumwalt is teaching her third graders that good spellers think out the spellings of words; they don't just sound them out. Mrs. Zumwalt hung a "how to spell long words" chart in the classroom, and through a series of minilessons, the class developed these rules for spelling unfamiliar words:

1. Break the word into syllables.
2. Say each syllable to yourself.
3. Sound out the spelling of each syllable.
4. Think about rules for spelling vowels and endings.

Figure 5-1   **Third Graders' Chart of Ways to Spell /s/**

Spelling	Examples	Nonexamples	Rules
s	said monsters sister misbehave taste	shop wish	*S* is the most common spelling for the *s* sound, but *sh* does not make the *s* sound. *Sh* has a special sound.
c	cent bicycle city decide cereal mice circle face	cat chair cucumber	When *c* is followed by *e*, *i*, or *y*, it makes the *s* sound.
ce	office dance sentence prince science fence voice juice	cent cement	*Ce* is used only at the end of a word.
ss	class guessed kiss blossom fossil lesson		*Ss* is used in the middle and at the end of a word.
sc	scissors science scent	scare rascal	This spelling is unusual.
se	else house	sent	This spelling is used only at the end of a word.

5. Check to see that the word looks right.
6. Check the dictionary, if you're not sure.
7. Ask a friend for help.

At least once a month, Mrs. Zumwalt reviews the strategy chart with the group of children who are learning to spell two-syllable words. During the minilesson, she reads over the list of spelling strategies and models how to use them step-by-step with the word *welcome.* She breaks the word into two syllables, *wel·come,* and writes it on chart paper, spelling it this way: *wellcome.* Then she looks at the word and asks the children to look, too. She says, "I've written *well* and *come,* but the word doesn't look right, does it? It looks wrong in the middle. Maybe there is only one *l* in *welcome.*" She writes *welcome* under *wellcome* and asks the children if *welcome* looks better. They agree that it does, and Mrs. Hansen asks one child to check the spelling in the dictionary.

Then she chooses another word—*market*—and asks a child in the group to guide her through the steps. She divides *market* into two syllables—*mar·ket*—and writes the word on chart paper, spelling it *markket.* She looks at the word and tells the group that she thinks it looks correct, but they disagree. She looks at the word again and asks the children for help. They explain that only one *k* is needed, and she writes the word correctly on chart paper.

Then Mrs. Zumwalt passes out white boards and dry-erase markers for them to use to practice spelling some two-syllable words. The first word they practice the strategy with is *turkey.* They follow the same steps that Mrs. Zumwalt used, and she checks their spelling. Then they continue to practice the strategy using these words: *disturb, problem, number, garden, person,* and *orbit.* The group is very successful, so they ask Mrs. Zumwalt for more difficult words; they try these three-syllable words: *remember, hamburger, banana,* and *populate.*

The next day, Mrs. Zumwalt works with the group of students spelling at the within-word pattern stage. These children still confuse long- and short-vowel words, so Mrs. Zumwalt has prepared a sorting game with similar words, including *rid–ride, hop–hope, cub–cube, slid–slide, cut–cute, pet–Pete, hat–hate, not–note,* and *mad–made.* She passes out envelopes with cards on which the words have been printed. The children each sort their word cards, matching up the related long- and short-vowel words. Children practice reading the words and then write them on white boards. Finally, Mrs. Zumwalt asks the children to clarify the difference between the two groups of words. They have been asked this question before, but it's a hard question. The difference, they explain, is that the three-letter words have short vowels and the four-letter words have a final *e* and they are long-vowel words.

While Mrs. Zumwalt works with one group of students, other children are practicing their spelling words. They have a packet of practice sheets to write the words on. For each word, they spell the word in their minds, write the word, and check the spelling using the strategy that Mrs. Zumwalt taught the children at the beginning of the school year.

After they practice their spelling words, they can choose spelling games to play. Some children play the children's version of Boggle, and other children play computer spelling games, explore the Franklin Spelling Ace, or work at the spelling center in the classroom. The spelling center has three packets of activities. One packet has 15 plastic bags with magnetic letters, which children use to spell the 15 spelling words. The second packet has word cards with inflectional endings for children to sort and arrange on the pocket chart hanging next to the center. The word cards include *bunnies, walked, cars, running, hopped, foxes,* and *sleeping.* Several weeks

Figure 5-2   Words Made Using the Letters in the Word *Grandfather*

Making Words

This week's word is:

| g | r | a | n | d | f | a | t | h | e | r |

1	2	3	4	5	6	7	8
a	at he an	and the her are hat eat ate ear fat ran fan	hear hate date gate hare near tear gear then than hand	grand great after	father		

ago, children studied spelling words with inflectional endings in minilessons with Mrs. Zumwalt, so these cards have now been placed in the spelling center for extra practice and review. In the third packet are plastic letters for a making words[c] activity. This week's word is *grandfather*. Children work in small groups to spell as many words as possible: They manipulate the letters and arrange them to spell one-, two-, three-, four-, five-, and six-letter words. A completed sheet with 30 words made using the letters in *grandfather* is shown in Figure 5-2.

On Friday, Mrs. Zumwalt administers the weekly spelling test. She reads the 15 words aloud, and children write them on their papers. Then she asks them to go back and look at each of the words and put a check mark next to it if it looks right and circle the word if it doesn't. Some of her third-grade students—especially those at the within-word stage of spelling development—have not yet developed a visual sense of when words "look" right, and through this proofreading activity, Mrs. Zumwalt is trying to help them learn to identify misspelled words in their writing. She finds that her more advanced spellers can accurately predict whether or not their spellings "look" right, whereas the others cannot. As she grades their spelling tests, Mrs. Zumwalt gives extra credit to those students who can accurately predict whether or not their words are spelled correctly.

Young children apply what they are learning about phonemic awareness and phonics when they spell words. When beginning writers want to write a word, they say the word slowly, segmenting the sounds. Segmenting is a phonemic awareness strategy that writers use to spell words. Then they choose letters to represent the sounds they hear to spell the word. The letters children choose to represent sounds reflect what they have learned about phonics and spelling patterns. Many spellings are incorrect, of course: Sometimes the spellings are very abbreviated, sometimes they are strictly phonetic and ignore spelling patterns, and at other times letters are reversed. These incorrect spellings are clear demonstrations of children's phonological knowledge. As children's knowledge of English orthography, or the spelling system, grows, their spellings increasingly approximate conventional spelling.

Consider the ways young children might spell the word *fairy*. A 4-year-old might use scribbles or random letters to write the word or, perhaps, recognize the beginning sound of the word and use the letter *F* to represent the word. A kindergartner or first grader with well-developed phonemic awareness strategies could segment the word into its three sounds—/f/ /âr/ /ē/—and spell it FRE, using one letter to represent each sound. By second grade, a child with more knowledge of English spelling patterns might spell the word as FARIEY. This child also segments the word into its three sounds, hears the *r*-controlled vowel pattern, and correctly identifies the three letters used to spell the sound but reverses their order when writing them so that *air* is spelled *ari*. The letters *ey* are used to spell the /ē/ sound, perhaps by analogy to the word *money*. Through more experiences reading and writing the word *fairy* and other words with the same sounds, third and fourth graders will learn to spell the word conventionally.

During the primary grades, children move from spelling most words phonetically to spelling most words conventionally. In Mrs. Zumwalt's classroom, for instance, most of her third graders spell more than 90% of the words they write correctly. Their understanding of the alphabetic principle, that letters represent sounds, matures through a combination of many, many opportunities to read and write and explicit spelling instruction. In the past, weekly spelling tests were the main instructional strategy. Now, they are only one part of a comprehensive spelling program.

CHILDREN'S SPELLING DEVELOPMENT

As young children begin to write, they create unique spellings, called *invented spelling,* based on their knowledge of sound-symbol correspondences and spelling patterns. Charles Read (1971, 1975, 1986) found that young children use their knowledge of phonology to invent spellings. The children in Read's studies used letter names to spell words, such as U (*you*) and R (*are*), and they used consonant sounds rather consistently: GRL (*girl*), TIGR (*tiger*), and NIT (*night*). They used several unusual but phonetically based spelling patterns to represent affricates. For example, they replaced *tr* with *chr* (e.g., CHRIBLES for *troubles*) and *dr* with *jr* (e.g., JRAGIN for *dragon*). Words with long vowels were spelled using letter names: MI (*my*), LADE (*lady*), and FEL (*feel*). The children used several ingenious strategies to spell words with short vowels. The preschoolers selected letters to represent short vowels on the basis of place of articulation in the mouth. Short *i* was represented with *e,* as in FES (*fish*), short *e* with *a,* as in LAFFT (*left*), and short *o* with *i,* as in CLIK (*clock*). These spellings may seem odd to adults, but they are based on phonetic relationships.

Based on observations of children's spellings, researchers have identified five stages that children move through on their way to becoming conventional spellers. At each stage, they use different types of strategies and focus on different aspects of spelling. The stages are emergent spelling, letter-name spelling, within word pattern spelling, syllables and affixes spelling, and derivational relations spelling (Bear, Invernizzi, Templeton, & Johnston, 2000). The characteristics of the five stages of spelling development are summarized in Figure 5-3.

Figure 5-3   Stages of Spelling Development

Stage 1: Emergent Spelling

Children string scribbles, letters, and letterlike forms together, but they do not associate the marks they make with any specific phonemes. This stage is typical of 3- to 5-year-olds. Children learn:

- the distinction between drawing and writing
- how to make letters
- the direction of writing on a page
- some letter-sound matches

Stage 2: Letter-Name Spelling

Children learn to represent phonemes in words with letters. At first, their spellings are quite abbreviated, but they learn to use consonant blends and digraphs and short-vowel patterns to spell many short-vowel words. Spellers are 5- to 7-year-olds. Children learn:

- the alphabetic principle
- consonant sounds
- short-vowel sounds
- consonant blends and digraphs

Stage 3: Within-Word Pattern Spelling

Children learn long-vowel patterns and *r*-controlled vowels, but they may confuse spelling patterns and spell *meet* as *mete,* and they reverse the order of letters, such as *form* for *from* and *gril* for *girl.* Spellers are 7- to 9-year-olds, and they learn:

- long-vowel spelling patterns
- *r*-controlled vowels
- more complex consonant patterns
- diphthongs and other less common vowel patterns

Stage 4: Syllables and Affixes Spelling

Children apply what they have learned about one-syllable words to spell longer, multisyllabic words, and they learn to break words into syllables. They also learn to add inflectional endings (e.g., *-es, -ed, -ing*) and to differentiate between homophones, such as *your–you're.* Spellers are often 9- to 11-year-olds, and they learn:

- inflectional endings
- rules for adding inflectional endings
- syllabication
- homophones
- contractions
- possessives

Stage 5: Derivational Relations Spelling

Children explore the relationship between spelling and meaning and learn that words with related meanings are often related in spelling despite changes in sound (e.g., *wise–wisdom, sign–signal, nation–national*). They also learn about Latin and Greek root words and derivational affixes (e.g., *amphi-, pre-, -able, -tion*). Spellers are 11- to 14-year-olds. Students learn:

- consonant alternations
- vowel alternations
- Latin and Greek affixes and root words
- etymologies

Adapted from Bear, Invernizzi, Templeton, & Johnston, 2000.

Stage 1: Emergent Spelling

Young children string scribbles, letters, and letterlike forms together, but they do not associate the marks they make with any specific phonemes. Spelling at this stage represents a natural, early expression of the alphabet and other concepts about writing. Children may write from left to right, right to left, top to bottom, or randomly across the page, but by the end of the stage, they have an understanding of directionality. This stage is typical of 3- to 5-year-olds. Children who are emergent spellers are usually in the emergent stage of reading as well, and as they develop concepts of print and knowledge about the letters of the alphabet, they apply their new knowledge in spelling.

Most 4-year-olds are emergent spellers; they use pencils to make scribbles and letterlike forms to represent messages they are writing.

During the emergent stage, children learn:

- the distinction between drawing and writing
- how to form upper- and lowercase letters
- the direction of writing on a page
- some letter-sound matches

Some emergent spellers have a large repertoire of letter forms to use in writing, whereas others repeat a small number of letters over and over. They use both upper- and lowercase letters, but they show a distinct preference for uppercase letters. Toward the end of this stage, children are beginning to discover how spelling works and that letters represent sounds in words.

Stage 2: Letter-Name Spelling

Children enter the letter-name stage of spelling development when they learn to represent phonemes with letters. They develop an understanding of the alphabetic principle, that a link exists between letters and sounds. At first, the spellings are quite abbreviated and represent only the most prominent features in words. Children often use only several letters of the alphabet to represent an entire word. Examples of early Stage 2 spelling are D (*dog*) and KE (*cookie*), and children may still be writing mainly with capital letters. Children slowly pronounce the words they want to spell, listening for familiar letter names and sounds and ignoring the unfamiliar sounds.

In the middle of the letter-name stage, children use most beginning and ending consonants and often include a vowel in most syllables; they spell *like* as *lik* and *bed* as *bad*. By the end of the stage, children use consonant blends and digraphs and short vowel patterns to spell *hat, get,* and *win,* but some children still spell *ship* as *sep*. They can also spell some CVCe words such as *name* correctly.

Spellers at this stage are usually 5- to 7-year-olds, and they are in the beginning stage of reading and writing development. Their spellings demonstrate their phonemic awareness and phonics knowledge. During the letter-name stage, children learn:

- the alphabetic principle
- consonant sounds
- short vowel sounds
- consonant blends and digraphs

Stage 3: Within-Word Pattern Spelling

Children begin the within-word pattern stage when they can spell most one-syllable words with short-vowel sounds, and during this stage, they learn to spell more complex consonant and vowel sounds (Henderson, 1990). The focus remains on one-syllable words. More complex consonant sounds and spellings include *-ph* (*photo*), *-tch* (*match*), and *-dge* (*judge*).

Children experiment with long-vowel patterns and learn that words such as *come* and *bread* are exceptions that do not fit the vowel patterns. They often confuse spelling patterns and spell *meet* as *mete*, and learn to spell less common vowel patterns, such as *oi/oy* (*boy*), *au* (*caught*), *aw* (*saw*), *ew* (*sew, few*), *ou* (*house*), and *ow* (*cow*). Children also become aware of homophones and compare long- and short-vowel combinations (*hope-hop*) as they experiment with vowel patterns. They also reverse the order of letters, such as *form* for *from* and *gril* for *girl*, as they begin to view spelling as more than just sounding out words.

Children at this stage are usually 7- to 9-year-olds. Most of these children are still beginning readers and writers, but they are approaching the fluent stage. During the within-word stage, children learn:

- long-vowel spelling patterns
- *r*-controlled vowels
- more complex consonant patterns
- diphthongs and other less common vowel patterns

Stage 4: Syllables and Affixes Spelling

The focus is on syllables in this stage. Children apply what they have learned about one-syllable words to longer, two-syllable words, and they learn to break words into syllables. They have already learned to use *y* at the end of a one-syllable word, as in *cry* to spell /ī/, and in this stage, they learn that *y* at the end of a two-syllable word represents /ē/ as in *ready*. They also learn that sometimes *ey* is used to spell /ē/ in a two-syllable word (e.g., *honey, monkey*).

English-language learners' invented spellings reflect their pronunciation errors as well as their phonics knowledge.

Children practice spelling skills as they play educational games.

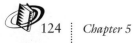

Children learn about inflectional endings (*-s, -es, -ed,* and *-ing*) and rules about consonant doubling, changing the final *y* to *i*, or dropping the final *e* before adding an inflectional suffix; for example, *run + ing = running, baby + s = babies,* and *have + ing = having.* They begin to notice some of the more common prefixes and suffixes and experiment with using them. A fourth grader, for example, proudly announced that her head was "thinkful," or full of thinking. She invented her new word by analogy—she knew that *beautiful* means full of beauty and *hopeful* means full of hope.

Children also learn several other sophisticated spelling concepts about one- and two-syllable words, including homophones, compound words, and contractions. At this stage, children become better able to think about words. They begin to consider homophone choices (e.g., *to, two,* or *too*), decide when words are compound and should be spelled as one word (e.g., *flashlight* but not *bright light*), and place apostrophes correctly in contractions and possessives. Although younger spellers often spell *don't* as *do'nt,* during this stage, children learn what the apostrophe represents and usually spell the word correctly.

Spellers in the syllables and affixes stage are generally 9- to 11-year-olds who have reached the fluent stage of reading and writing. In this stage, children learn:

- inflectional endings (*-s, -es, -ed, -ing*)
- rules for adding inflectional endings
- syllabication
- homophones
- compound words
- contractions
- possessives

Many ELL students omit inflectional endings on words when they write, and they benefit from minilessons drawing their attention to this linguistic feature when they're at the fourth stage of spelling development.

Stage 5: Derivational Relations Spelling

Older children explore the relationship between spelling and meaning during the derivational relations stage, and they learn that words with related meanings are often related in spelling despite changes in vowel and consonant sounds (e.g., *wise–wisdom, sign–signal, nation–national*) (Templeton, 1983). The focus in this stage is on morphemes, and children learn about Greek and Latin root words and affixes. They also begin to examine etymologies and the role of history in shaping how words are spelled. They learn about eponyms (words from people's names), such as *maverick* and *sandwich.*

Most spellers at this stage are 11- to 14-year-olds, but some third and fourth graders begin to make insights about the spelling patterns of related words that are characteristic of this stage. A third grader in Mrs. Zumwalt's classroom commented that he just noticed the word *sign* at the beginning of the word *signature* and now he understands why *sign* is spelled like it is. He continued to explain, "I used to think it should be spelled *sine* but now I think *s-i-g-n* is a better way to spell it." As children notice these relationships, they are entering the derivational relations stage. During this stage, children learn:

- consonant alternations (e.g., *soft–soften, magic–magician*)
- vowel alternations (e.g., *please–pleasant, define–definition, explain–explanation*)
- Greek and Latin affixes and root words
- etymologies

Children's spelling provides evidence of their growing understanding of English orthography, and as children move through the stages, the way they think about spelling matures. At the emergent stage, young children view spelling as making random marks on paper with no awareness of the alphabetic principle. Then during the letter-name and within-word pattern stages, children focus on applying phonics and spelling patterns to spelling words. By the time they enter the syllables and affixes stage, children are applying what they have learned about spelling one-syllable words to multisyllabic words. They understand that in addition to phonics, they need other spelling strategies. They visualize words and decide if they "look" right and apply spelling rules they have learned. Finally, children gain a historical perspective in the derivational relations stage as they learn to spell words with Latin and Greek roots and affixes.

Invented spelling is sometimes criticized because it may appear that children are learning bad habits by being allowed to misspell words, but researchers have confirmed that children grow more quickly in phonemic awareness, phonics, and spelling when they use invented spelling—as long as they are also receiving spelling instruction (Snow, Burns, & Griffin, 1998).

TEACHING SPELLING

Perhaps the most familiar way to teach spelling is through weekly spelling tests, but spelling tests alone are not a complete spelling program because children usually memorize spelling words. In order to become good spellers, children need to learn about the English orthographic system and move through the stages of spelling development. Children develop strategies to use in spelling unknown words and gain experience in using dictionaries and other resources. A complete spelling program:

- teaches spelling concepts, strategies, and skills
- matches instruction to children's stage of spelling development
- provides daily reading and writing opportunities
- requires children to learn to spell high-frequency words

When children are engaged in a spelling program that incorporates these components, there is evidence of children's learning in their writing. The number of errors that children make becomes progressively less, but more important, the types of spelling errors change; the errors become more sophisticated. Children move from spelling phonetically to using morphological information and spelling rules.

Spelling Concepts, Strategies, and Skills

Teachers choose the concepts, strategies, and skills to teach depending on children's stage of spelling development. Children at emergent stage, for example, learn the names of the letters of the alphabet and some of the sounds the letters represent, whereas children at the syllables and affixes stage learn how to add inflectional endings to words and how syllable boundaries influence spelling patterns. Figure 5-4 lists some of the concepts, strategies, and skills for each stage of spelling development. To learn how to assess a child's stage of spelling development, turn back to Chapter 3, "Assessing Young Children's Literacy Development," for step-by-step instructions.

Spelling Strategies. Children learn spelling strategies to figure out the spelling of unfamiliar words. As children move through the stages of spelling development, they be-

Figure 5-4

Spelling Concepts, Strategies, and Skills to Teach

Stage	Topics
Emergent	phonemic awareness naming the letters of the alphabet left-to-right progression of text printing the letters of the alphabet concepts of a letter and a word printing child's name and a few common words consonant sounds
Letter Name	initial and final consonant sounds blending and segmenting sounds initial and final consonant blends (e.g., *fl-, -nd*) short-vowel sounds (*a/cat, e/leg, i/hit, o/not, u/cut*) "sound-it-out" spelling strategy high-frequency words (e.g., *the, is, we, you*)
Within-Word Pattern	consonant digraphs (*ch, sh, th, wh, ph*) more complex consonant sounds (e.g., soft *c* and *g, -tch, -dge*) silent letters (e.g., *wr-, kn-, -ck, -lk*) more complex blends (e.g., *scr-, squ-*) long-vowel spelling patterns (e.g., CVCe, CVV) vowel digraphs (e.g., *ay, oa, oo, ea, aw*) vowel diphthongs (*ou, ow, oi, oy*) *r*-controlled vowels (*ar, er, ir, or, ur*) "think-it-out" spelling strategy high-frequency words (e.g., *your, house, there, should*)
Syllables and Affixes	syllables schwa sound inflectional endings (*-s, -ed, -ing*) common prefixes and suffixes (e.g., *re-, un-, -less, -ful, -y*) compound words contractions (e.g., *I'm, can't, he'll, you're*) homophones (e.g., *sea-see, there-their-they're*) dictionary use
Derivational Relations	Latin and Greek root words prefixes (e.g., *pre-, dis-, con-, trans-, mal-*) adjective suffixes (e.g., *-ous, -able/-ible, -al*) noun suffixes (e.g., *-tion, -ment, -ance/-ence*) etymologies

come increasingly more sophisticated in their use of phonological, semantic, and morphological knowledge to spell words; that is, they become more strategic. Strategies that children learn to use include:

- segmenting the word and spelling each sound
- predicting the spelling of a word by generating possible spellings and choosing the best alternative
- breaking the word into syllables and spelling each syllable
- applying affixes to root words

- spelling unknown words by analogy to known words
- using a letter or two as a placeholder for an unknown word
- proofreading to locate spelling errors
- locating the spelling of an unfamiliar word in a dictionary

Teachers often recommend that children "sound it out" when they don't know how to spell a word. This advice involves one strategy—segmenting the word and spelling each sound—that is useful to children in the second stage of spelling development. It is not useful to more advanced spellers, however. Instead of giving the traditional "sound it out" advice when children ask how to spell an unfamiliar word, teachers should suggest that children use a strategic "think it out" approach. This advice reminds children that spelling involves more than phonological information and encourages them to think about spelling patterns, root words and affixes, and even the shape of the word—what it looks like.

Spelling Options. In English, there are alternate spellings for many sounds because so many words have been borrowed from other languages and retain their native spellings. There are many more options for vowel sounds than for consonants. Even so, there are four spelling options for /f/ (*f, ff, ph, gh*). Spelling options sometimes vary according to the letter's position in the word. For example, *ff* and *gh* are used to represent /f/ in the middle or at the end of a word, as in *raffle* and *laugh*. Common spelling options for phonemes are listed in Figure 5-5.

Teachers point out spelling options as they write words on word walls[C] and when children ask about the spelling of a word. They also use minilessons to teach children about these options. During each lesson, children focus on one phoneme, such as /f/ or /ar/, and as a class or small group, they can develop a list of the various ways the sound is spelled in English and collect examples of each spelling. Then they examine how location in a word affects spelling and draw conclusions about the most common spelling patterns. A third grade chart on *r*-controlled vowels is presented in Figure 5-6.

Daily Reading and Writing Opportunities

Two of the most important ways that children learn to spell are through daily reading and writing opportunities (Smith, 1983). Children who read often are usually good readers, and good readers tend to be good spellers, too. As they read, children practice phonics skills and visualize words—the shape of the word and the configuration of letters within the word—and they use this knowledge to spell many words correctly and to recognize when a word they've written doesn't look right. Through writing, of course, children gain valuable practice using strategies they have learned to spell the words they are writing. And, as the teachers work with children to proofread and edit their writing, they learn more about spelling and other writing conventions.

Minilessons

Teachers teach lessons about the English orthographic system through minilessons on phonics, high-frequency words, spelling rules, and spelling strategies. The minilesson feature on page 131 shows how Mr. Cheng teaches his first graders to spell rhyming *-at* family words.

Figure 5-5 · Common Spelling Options

Sound	Spellings	Examples	Sound	Spellings	Examples
long a	a-e	date	short oo	oo	book
	a	angel		u	put
	ai	aid		ou	could
	ay	day		o	woman
ch	ch	church	ou	ou	out
	t(u)	picture		ow	cow
	tch	watch	s	s	sick
	ti	question		ce	office
long e	ea	each		c	city
	ee	feel		ss	class
	e	evil		se	else
	e-e	these	sh	ti	attention
	ea-e	breathe		sh	she
short e	e	end		ci	ancient
	ea	head		ssi	admission
f	f	feel	t	t	teacher
	ff	sheriff		te	definite
	ph	photograph		ed	furnished
j	ge	strange		tt	attend
	g	general	long u	u	union
	j	job		u-e	use
	dge	bridge		ue	value
k	c	call		ew	few
	k	keep	short u	u	ugly
	ck	black		o	company
l	l	last		ou	country
	ll	allow	z	s	present
	le	automobile		se	applause
m	m	man		ze	gauze
	me	come	syllabic l	le	able
	mm	comment		al	animal
n	n	no		el	cancel
	ne	done		il	civil
long o	o	go	syllabic n	en	written
	o-e	note		on	lesson
	ow	own		an	important
	oa	load		in	cousin
short o	o	office		contractions	didn't
	a	all		ain	certain
	au	author	r-controlled	er	her
	aw	saw		ur	church
oi	oi	oil		ir	first
	oy	boy		or	world
long oo	u	cruel		ear	heard
	oo	noon		our	courage
	u-e	rule			
	o-e	lose			
	ue	blue			
	o	to			
	ou	group			

Figure 5-6   A Third-Grade Chart of *r*-Controlled Vowels

ar	er	ir	or	ur
yarn	reader	birthday	morning	burn
card	perfect	whirl	born	furniture
farm	her	dirty	storm	turning
barnyard	longer	twirling	worms	fur
sharp	clerk	third	sword	nurse
market	germs	smirk	porch	curls
dark	nerve	mirror	short	blurry

Word Study Activities

Teachers plan a variety of activities for children to work on during centers or as a whole class to explore spelling concepts, strategies, and skills. These activities expand children's spelling knowledge and help them move through the stages of spelling development.

Posting Word Walls. Teachers use two types of word walls in their classrooms. One word wall features "important" words from books children are reading or social studies and science thematic units. Words may be written on a large sheet of paper hanging in the classroom or on word cards and placed in a large pocket chart. Then children refer to these word walls when they are writing. Seeing the words posted on word walls, clusters[C], and other charts in the classroom and using them in their writing help children learn to spell the words.

During a science unit on plants, for example, a first-grade teacher wrote these 11 words on word cards and placed them in a pocket chart word wall: *seed, root, stem, leaf, leaves, flower, plant, grow, soil, water,* and *sunshine.* The first graders practiced reading the words and used them when they drew diagrams about how plants grow and pictures of favorite flowers and wrote in their learning logs[C]. As a culminating activity, the children wrote books about plants to demonstrate what they had learned. Children drew a picture and wrote a sentence on each page, often referring to the word wall to check the spelling of plant-related words. A page from one child's book is shown in Figure 5-7. It reads: *Plants need three things to grow big and strong.* Notice that the child used conventional spelling for the science words and high-frequency words and invented spelling for other words.

The second type of word wall displays high-frequency words. Researchers have identified the most commonly used words and recommend that elementary students learn to spell 100 of these words because of their usefulness. The most frequently used words represent more than 50% of all the words children and adults write (Horn, 1926)! Figure 5-8 lists the 100 most frequently used words.

Teachers plan a variety of activities to teach students to read and spell high-frequency words; more information about teaching children to read these words is provided in Chapter 6, "Developing Fluent Readers and Writers." As children learn to read the words, they are also learning to spell them. Because most of the words are not spelled phonetically, children must memorize the spelling, and constant repetition as they read and write the words is useful. Also, children develop a visual representation of the word so that when they write it, they can recognize that their spelling is too short or long, or lacks a "tall" letter. For instance, *little* doesn't look right with only one *t*, does

Minilesson

Topic: -*at* Word Family
Grade: First Grade
Time: One 10-minute period

Mr. Cheng presents phonics concepts during guided reading lessons. He introduces, practices, and reviews phonics concepts using words from selections his first graders are reading. The children decode and spell words using letter and word cards, foam and magnetic letters, and white boards and dry-erase pens.

1. Introduce the Topic

Mr. Cheng holds up a copy of *At Home,* the small paperback level E book the children read yesterday, and asks them to reread the title. Then he asks the children to identify the first word, *at.* After they read the word, he hands a card with the word *at* written on it to each of the six children in the guided reading group. "Who can read this word?" he asks. Several children recognize it immediately and others carefully sound out the two-letter word.

2. Share Examples

Mr. Cheng asks the children to think about rhyming words: "Who knows what rhyming words are?" Mike answers that rhyming words sound alike at the end—for example, *Mike, bike,* and *like.* The teacher explains that there are many words in English that rhyme, and today they are going to read and write words that rhyme with *at.* "One rhyming word is *cat,*" he explains. Children name rhyming words, including *hat, fat,* and *bat.* Mr. Cheng helps each child in the guided reading group to name at least three rhyming words.

3. Provide Information

Mr. Cheng explains that the children can spell these *at* rhyming words by adding a consonant in front of *at.* For example, he places the foam letter *c* in front of his *at* card, and the children blend *c* to *at* to decode *cat.* Then he repeats the procedure by substituting other foam letters for the *c* to spell *bat, fat, hat, mat, pat, rat,* and *sat.* He continues the activity until all children in the group successfully decode one of the rhyming words.

4. Guide Practice

Mr. Cheng passes out small plastic trays with foam letters to each child and asks them to form each *at* rhyming word by adding one of the letters to their *at* cards to spell the *at* rhyming words as he pronounces them. He continues the activity until the children have had several opportunities to spell each of the rhyming words, and they can quickly choose the correct initial consonant to spell the word. Then Mr. Cheng collects the *at* cards and trays with foam letters.

5. Assess Learning

Mr. Cheng passes out small white boards and dry-erase pens to each child in the group. He asks them to write the rhyming words as he says each one: *cat, hat, mat, pat, rat, sat, bat, fat.* He carefully observes as each child segments the onset and rime to spell the word. The children hold up their white boards to show him their spellings. Afterwards, children erase the word and repeat the process, writing the next word. After children write all eight words, Mr. Cheng quickly jots a note about which children need additional practice with the -*at* word family before continuing with the guided reading lesson.

Figure 5-7   A Page From a First Grader's "All About Plants" Book

it? It's not long enough and there are not enough tall middle letters. Or, what about *houes*? Reversing the last two letters of *house* looks funny. Children learn to refer to the word wall to spell unfamiliar words when they are writing, and as children become more proficient writers, teachers should expect them to use the word wall and to spell high-frequency words correctly.

Collecting Words. Children investigate spelling patterns by collecting words from books they are reading and from their writing. Then they analyze the words to determine patterns. For example, Mrs. Zumwalt had her students collect words with *s* sounds to determine the different ways to spell the sound. They identified a number of ways to spell *s* and then determined that *s* was the most common choice. They also examined where in words particular spellings were used; the *sc* spelling was usually used at the beginning of a word, for example, and *ss* and *se* were used at the ends of words.

Making Words. Teachers choose a five- to eight-letter word (or longer words for older students) and prepare sets of letter cards for a making words activity (Cunningham & Cunningham, 1992; Gunning, 1995). Then children use letter cards to practice spelling words and review spelling patterns and rules. They arrange and rearrange the cards to spell one-letter words, two-letter words, three-letter words, and so forth, until they use all the letters to spell the original word. Second graders, for example, can create these words using the letters in *weather: a, at, we, he, the, are, art, ear, eat, hat, her, hear, here, hate, heart, wheat, there,* and *where.*

Sorting Words. Students use word sorts[C] to explore, compare, and contrast word features as they sort a pack of word cards. Teachers prepare word cards for students to sort into two or more categories according to their spelling patterns or other criteria (Bear et al., 2000). Sometimes teachers tell children what categories to use; this is a

To link to Making and Writing Words, where Timothy Rasinski explains his variation of the making words activity, visit our Companion Website at
www.prenhall.com/tompkins

Figure 5-8 — The 100 Most Frequently Used Words

A	B	C	D	E
a and about are after around all as am at an	back be because but by	came can could	day did didn't do don't down	
F for from	**G** get got	**H** had his have home he house her how him	**I** I into if is in it	**J** just
K know	**L** like little	**M** man me mother my	**N** no not now	**O** of our on out one over or
P people put	**QR**	**S** said saw school see she so some	**T** that think the this them time then to there too they two things	**U** up us
V very	**W** was when we who well will went with were would what	**X**	**Y** you your	**Z**

closed sort. At other times, students determine the categories themselves; this is an open sort. Children can sort word cards and then return them to an envelope for future use, or they can glue the cards onto a sheet of paper. Figure 5-9 shows a word sort for four vowel patterns using words with short and long *a*. In this sort, second graders worked with partners and sorted the words into five categories (CVC, CVCe, CVVC, and CVV).

Proofreading. Proofreading is a special kind of reading that children use to locate misspelled words and other mechanical errors in rough drafts. As children learn about the writing process, they are introduced to proofreading in the editing step. More in-depth instruction about how to use proofreading to locate spelling errors and then correct these misspelled words is part of spelling instruction (Cramer, 1998). Through a series of minilessons, children can learn to proofread sample student papers and mark misspelled words. Then, working in pairs, children can correct the misspelled words.

Figure 5-9   A Sort of Long- and Short-*a* Words

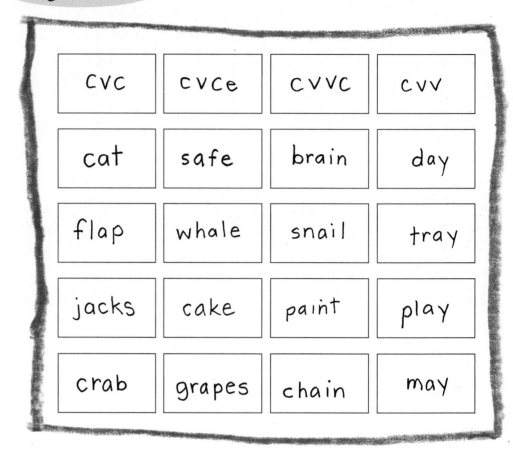

CVC	CVCe	CVVC	CVV
cat	safe	brain	day
flap	whale	snail	tray
jacks	cake	paint	play
crab	grapes	chain	may

Proofreading should be introduced in the primary grades. Young children and their teachers proofread their writings together, and through this experience, children view proofreading to identify and correct errors as a natural part of the writing process. For example, at the beginning of the school year, a first-grade teacher has her students use interactive writing[C] to share their daily news, but as the children learn to write more fluently and spell many words correctly, she changes the activity to a proofreading minilesson. The child chosen to share his or her news each day writes the news independently and brings it to a class meeting to share. One child's unedited sample is shown in the top part of Figure 5-10. The first grader wrote about her upcoming birthday and the party her father's boss was throwing for her. Her classmates were interested in this news and asked questions about her plans for the party. Then the teacher, the child-writer, and her classmates proofread the composition to identify errors and used interactive writing techniques to correct many of the errors, as shown in the bottom part of the figure. The teacher does not try to correct every single mistake, but corrects those that children notice and those that reflect concepts, skills, and strategies that have been taught. The rectangles represent correction tape that was used to cover misspelled words, and then correct spellings were written on top of the tape. The teacher took advantage of teachable moments to review spelling rules and high-frequency words.

Children practice proofreading skills as they read classmates' writings.

Using a Dictionary. Children need to learn to locate the spelling of unfamiliar words in the dictionary. Although it is relatively easy to find a "known" word in the diction-ary, it is hard to locate unfamiliar words, and children need to learn what to do when they do not know how to spell a word. One approach is to predict possible spellings for unknown words, then check the most probable ones in a dictionary.

During the primary grades, teachers introduce dictionaries and teach children how to locate words in the dictionary and read a dictionary entry. A number of excellent dictionaries for young children are currently available. These books are attractive, with lively illustrations, and the graphic design makes them easy for primary students to use. Figure 5-11 presents information about some recommended dictionaries.

Children should be encouraged to check the spellings of words in a dictionary as well as to use dictionaries to check multiple meanings of a word. Too often, children view consulting a dictionary as punishment; teachers must work to change this view of dictionary use. One way to do this is to appoint some children in the classroom as dictionary checkers. These children keep dictionaries on their desks, and they are con-sulted whenever questions about spelling arise.

Weekly Spelling Tests

Many teachers question the usefulness of spelling tests to teach spelling, because re-search on invented spelling suggests that spelling is best learned through reading and writing (Gentry & Gillet, 1993; Wilde, 1992). In addition, teachers complain that lists of spelling words are unrelated to the words children are reading and writing and that the 30 minutes of valuable instructional time spent each day in completing spelling textbook activities is excessive. Even so, parents and school board members value spelling tests as evidence that spelling is being taught.

The position in this text is that weekly spelling tests should be only one part of a comprehensive spelling program. Spelling instruction should reflect children's stage

Figure 5-10   A First Grader's Rough Draft and Edited Composition

My birthday is fabboWherey fith.
It is going to be a teyPrty
MY daddys bosse givs me my
birthday. She is Nighc.

My birthday is [February] fith.
It is going to be a [tea] [Party.]
MY daddys boss [gives] me my
birthday[Party.] She is [nice].

Figure 5-11 Recommended Dictionaries for Primary Students

Stage	Dictionary	Description
Emergent	Swanson, M. (1998). *The American Heritage picture dictionary.* Boston: Houghton Mifflin.	The 900 common words in this book designed for kindergartners are listed alphabetically and illustrated with lively color drawings. Nine thematic illustrations featuring related vocabulary are included at the back of the book.
Beginning	*The American Heritage first dictionary.* (1998). Boston: Houghton Mifflin.	More than 1,800 entries and 650 color photographs and graphics are included in this attractive reference book. A clearly stated definition and an easy-to-read sentence are provided for each entry.
	Levey, J. S. (1998). *Scholastic first dictionary.* New York: Scholastic.	More than 1,500 entries are in this visually appealing dictionary for beginning readers. Each entry word is highlighted, defined, and used in a sentence.
Fluent	*The American Heritage children's dictionary.* (1998). Boston: Houghton Mifflin.	This appealing hardcover dictionary contains 14,000 entries and more than 600 color photos and illustrations. Word history, language detective, synonym, and vocabulary-builder boxes provide additional interesting information. A 10-page phonics guide and a 6-page thesaurus are also included in this reference book. This dictionary is also available on CD-ROM.
	DK Merriam-Webster children's dictionary. (2000). London: Dorling Kindersley.	This stunning volume pairs the 32,000 entries from *Merriam-Webster's Elementary Dictionary* with the striking design and color illustrations that DK is famous for. This visually appealing book includes more than 3,000 photos and charts.
	Scholastic children's dictionary. (1996). New York: Scholastic.	More than 30,000 entries are presented with color illustrations and bright page decorations. Attractively designed boxes with information about synonyms, affixes, and word histories are featured throughout the book.

of spelling development and support what children are learning about phonemic awareness and phonics. It should focus on high-frequency words and the words that children need to be able to spell for their writing. To accomplish this, teachers need to personalize the way spelling textbooks are used.

Words to Study. Spelling textbooks usually list 10–20 words for children to study each week, and textbook developers assume that children are already familiar with the words—that they know the meanings of the words and can read them. Unfortunately, some struggling readers cannot read the words they are being asked to learn to spell, and many second language learners are not even familiar with the words in the spelling textbook because they do not use them in their oral language. Because it is not reasonable to expect children to learn to spell words they are not familiar with, primary-grade teachers need to have the flexibility to personalize spelling lists to meet individual children's needs.

Many of the words in spelling textbooks are high-frequency words that children need to be able to spell correctly in their writing, and sometimes the words are grouped by phonetic principles. For example, the words might have *r*-controlled vowels (e.g., *dark, first, curb*) or *-le* at the end of the second syllable (e.g., *circle, puzzle, handle*). The problem with lists of words that all have the same spelling pattern is that children rely on the pattern to write the words without really learning how to spell them, so it is often better to present several spelling patterns in a single list. For example, words with *r*-controlled vowels might be contrasted with words that have an *r* before the vowel, not after it (e.g., *from, rest*), or the *-le* words might be contrasted with *-el* words (e.g., *angel, travel*).

Teachers sometimes wonder about the number of words it is reasonable to expect their students to learn in a week. Children do not all learn at the same rate; more capable readers and writers can learn more words and learn them more quickly because they know more about English orthography and they get more practice with words. Even though spelling textbooks list 10 or more words for children to study each week, the textbook developers assume that children already know how to spell some of the words on the spelling list. If children do not know any of the words, teachers should personalize the list by reducing the number of words children are to study or by substituting other words that are more appropriate for those children based on their level of spelling development. For example, children who are struggling to spell one-syllable words such as *jump* and *rest* are wasting their time trying to spell two-syllable words such as *climate* and *promise*.

To link to publishers' websites to learn more about textbook spelling programs, visit our Companion Website at www.prenhall.com/tompkins

Weekly Schedule. Textbook spelling programs are organized into weekly units with three components: pretest, practice, and final test. On Monday, the teacher administers a pretest, and children spell as many of the words as they can. Researchers have found that the pretest is a critical component in learning to spell, because it eliminates words that children already know how to spell so that they can direct their study to the words that they don't know yet. As long ago as 1957, Ernest Horn recommended that the best way to improve children's spelling was for them to get immediate feedback by correcting their own pretests. His advice is still sound today.

On Tuesday, Wednesday, and Thursday, children spend approximately 10 minutes studying the words on their study lists. Research shows that instead of "busy work" activities such as using their spelling words in sentences or gluing yarn in the shape of the words, it is more effective for children to use this study strategy:

1. Look at the word and say it to yourself.
2. Say each letter in the word to yourself.
3. Close your eyes and spell the word to yourself.
4. Write the word, and check that you spelled it correctly.
5. Write the word again and check that you spelled it correctly.

This strategy focuses on the whole word. Teachers explain how to use the strategy during a minilesson at the beginning of the school year and then post a copy of it in the classroom. In addition to this study strategy, sometimes children trade word lists on Wednesday or Thursday or give each other a practice test.

The final test is administered on Friday. The teacher reads the list of words, and children write the words. When children's spelling lists are personalized, children write only those words they have practiced during the week. To make it easier to administer the test, children first list the numbers of the words they have practiced from their study lists on their test papers. Any words that children misspell should be included on their lists the following week.

What Is the Controversy About Spelling Instruction?

The press and concerned parent groups periodically raise questions about invented spelling and the importance of weekly spelling tests. There is a misplaced public perception that today's children cannot spell. Researchers who are examining the types of errors children make have noted that the number of misspellings increases in grades one through four, as children write longer compositions, but that the percentage of errors decreases. The percentage continues to decline in the upper grades (Taylor & Kidder, 1988).

Review

As young children begin writing, they use invented spelling to apply what they know about English spelling patterns. Their spelling changes to reflect the phonics skills and spelling patterns they are learning. The feature that follows reviews the recommended practices that effective teachers use in teaching spelling.

How Effective Teachers . . .
Assist Children in Learning to Spell

Effective Practices

1. Teachers encourage children to apply what they know about phonics through invented spelling.
2. Teachers analyze children's spelling errors as a measure of their understanding of phonics.
3. Teachers consider children's stage of spelling development in planning spelling instruction.
4. Teachers teach children to use spelling strategies and "think out" the spelling of unfamiliar words.
5. Teachers teach minilessons on spelling concepts, strategies, and skills using words from children's reading and writing.
6. Teachers provide children with daily reading and writing experiences because they understand that these activities contribute to children's spelling development.
7. Teachers use word walls, collecting words, making words, word sorts, and other activities as part of a complete spelling program.
8. Teachers teach children how to use dictionaries to locate unfamiliar spellings.
9. Teachers may use spelling textbooks, but only as part of a complete spelling program.
10. Teachers personalize spelling textbook programs to meet the needs of second language learners and struggling spellers.

Professional References

Bear, D. R., Invernizzi, M., Templeton, S., & Johnston, F. (2000). *Words their way: Word study for phonics, vocabulary, and spelling instruction.* Upper Saddle River, NJ: Merrill/Prentice Hall.

Cramer, R. L. (1998). *The spelling connection: Integrating reading, writing, and spelling instruction.* New York: Guilford Press.

Cunningham, P. M., & Cunningham, J. W. (1992). Making words: Enhancing the invented spelling-decoding connection. *The Reading Teacher, 46,* 106–115.

Gentry, J. R., & Gillet, J. W. (1993). *Teaching kids to spell.* Portsmouth, NH: Heinemann.

Gunning, T. G. (1995). Word building: A strategic approach to the teaching of phonics. *The Reading Teacher, 48,* 484–488.

Henderson, E. H. (1990). *Teaching spelling* (2nd ed.). Boston: Houghton Mifflin.

Horn, E. (1926). *A basic writing vocabulary.* Iowa City: University of Iowa Press.

Horn, E. (1957). Phonetics and spelling. *Elementary School Journal, 57,* 233–235, 246.

Read, C. (1971). Pre-school children's knowledge of English phonology. *Harvard Educational Review, 41,* 1–34.

Read, C. (1975). *Children's categorization of speech sounds in English* (NCTE Research Report No. 17). Urbana, IL: National Council of Teachers of English.

Read, C. (1986). *Children's creative spelling.* London: Routledge & Kegan Paul.

Smith, F. (1983). Reading like a writer. *Language Arts, 60,* 558–567.

Snow, C. E., Burns, M. S., & Griffin, P. (Eds.). (1998). *Preventing reading difficulties in young children.* Washington, DC: National Academy Press.

Taylor, K. K., & Kidder, E. B. (1988). The development of spelling skills: From first grade through eighth grade. *Written Communication, 5,* 222–244.

Templeton, S. (1983). Using the spelling/meaning connection to develop word knowledge in older students. *Journal of Reading, 27,* 8–14.

Wilde, S. (1992). *You kan red this! Spelling and punctuation for whole language classrooms, K–6.* Portsmouth, NH: Heinemann.

aders

en need to learn to read
า-frequency words?

es do children learn to
ize and spell unfamil-

dren become fluent

y important?

Developing Fluent Re
and Writers

Ms. Williams's Students Learn High-Frequency Words

Ms. Williams's second graders are studying hermit crabs and their tide pool environments. A plastic habitat box sits in the center of each grouping of desks, and a hermit crab is living in each box. As the children care for their crustaceans, they observe the crabs. They have examined hermit crabs up close using magnifying glasses and identified the body parts. Ms. Williams helped them draw a diagram of a hermit crab on a large chart and label the body parts. They have compared hermit crabs to true crabs and examined their exoskeletons. They have also learned how to feed hermit crabs, how to get them to come out of their shells, and how they molt. And, they've conducted experiments to determine whether hermit crabs prefer wet or dry environments.

These second graders use reading and writing as tools for learning. Eric Carle's *A House for Hermit Crab* (1987) is the featured book for this unit. Ms. Williams has read it aloud to the children several times, and they are rereading it at the listening center. *Moving Day* (Kaplan, 1996), *Pagoo* (Holling, 1990), and other stories and informational books, including *Hermit Crabs* (Pohl, 1987) and *Tide Pool* (Greenaway, 1992), are available on a special shelf in the classroom library. Ms. Williams has read some of the books aloud, and they listen to others at the listening center or read them independently or with buddies. Children make charts about hermit crabs that they post in the classroom, and they write about hermit crabs in learning logs[C]. One log entry is shown in Figure 6-1.

Ms. Williams and her students also write many interesting and important vocabulary words related to hermit crabs that they learn about on a word wall[C] made of a sheet of butcher paper. They write these words and add small drawings for some of the words on their word wall:

See the Compendium of Instructional Procedures, which follows Chapter 12, for more information on terms marked with the symbol [C].

coral	larvae	sea urchins
crustacean	molting	seaweed
eggs	pebbles	shells
enemies	pincers	shrimp
exoskeleton	regeneration	snails
lantern fish	scavenger	starfish
larva	sea anemone	tide pool

Then children refer to these words as they write about hermit crabs, and Ms. Williams uses them for various reading activities. This word wall will be displayed in the classroom only during the unit on hermit crabs.

Ms. Williams integrates many components of reading instruction, including word-recognition and fluency activities, into the unit on hermit crabs. To develop her second graders' ability to recognize many high-frequency words, she uses another word wall. This word wall is different from the hermit crab word wall, which contains only words related to these ocean animals. Her high-frequency word wall is a brightly colored alphabet quilt with 26 blocks, one for each letter of the alphabet. The most common words are written on small cards and displayed permanently on one wall of the classroom.

Figure 6-1   A Second Grader's Science Log Entry

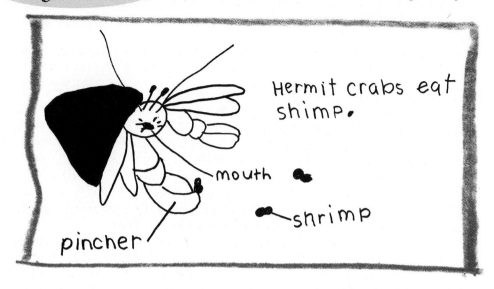

At the beginning of the school year, Ms. Williams and her students posted the 70 high-frequency words on the word wall that they were familiar with from first grade. Then each week, Ms. Williams adds 3 to 5 new words. At first, the words she chose were from her list of the 100 highest-frequency words, and after finishing that list, she has begun choosing words from a list of the second 100 high-frequency words. She doesn't introduce the words in the order that they are presented in the list, but rather chooses words from the list that she can connect to units and words that students misspell in their writing.

This week, Ms. Williams has chosen *soon, house, your,* and *you're* to add to the word wall. She chose *soon* and *house* because these words are used in *A House for Hermit Crab* and several children have recently asked her how to spell *house.* She chose the homophones *your* and *you're* because children are confusing and misspelling these two words. She also has noticed that some students are confused about contractions, and she plans to review contractions using *you're* as an example.

Ms. Williams has the children sit on the floor near the word wall to introduce the words and post them on the word wall. She uses a cookie sheet and large magnetic letters to introduce each new word. She explains that two of the new words—*house* and *soon*—are from *A House for Hermit Crab.* She scrambles the letters at the bottom of the cookie sheet and slowly builds the new word at the top of the sheet as students guess the word. She begins with *h,* adds the *ou,* and several children call out "house." Ms. Williams continues adding letters, and when they are all in place, a chorus of voices says, "house." Then Kari places the new word card in the *H* square of the word wall, and students chant and clap as they say the word and spell it. Ms. Williams begins, "House, house, h-o-u-s-e," and students echo her chant. Then she calls on Enrique to begin the chant, and students echo him. Then Ms. Williams repeats the procedure with the three remaining words.

The next day, Ms. Williams and her students use interactive writing[C] to compose sentences using each of the new words. They write:

The hermit crab has a good shell for a <u>house</u>. He likes it but <u>soon</u> he will move. "<u>You're</u> too small for me," he says. "I have to move, but I will always be <u>your</u> friend."

Children take turns writing these sentences on a chart, and after rereading the sentences, they underline the four new words. Each week, the children write sentences using the new word wall words on this chart. Ms. Williams and the children often reread the sentences they've written during previous weeks.

The next day, after the children practice the word wall words, Ms. Williams takes a few minutes to review contractions so that they understand that *you're* is a contraction of *you* and *are* and that the apostrophe indicates that a letter has been omitted. Then children volunteer other contractions. Michael identifies three: *I'm, can't,* and *don't.* The children use interactive writing to make a chart of contractions. They list the contractions and the two words that make up each one. Ms. Williams tells them that she'll put the chart in the word work center and that they can use the information to make books about contractions.

After this practice with high-frequency words, children participate in activities at literacy centers while Ms. Williams meets with guided reading[C] groups. Most of the center activities relate to the unit on hermit crabs and Eric Carle's book *A House for Hermit Crab,* but children also practice reading and writing high-frequency words at two of the centers. The eight literacy centers in Ms. Williams's classroom are described in Figure 6-2.

Each morning, a sixth-grade student aide comes to the classroom to monitor the children's work at the centers and provide assistance as needed. Ms. Williams worked with two sixth-grade teachers to train 10 students to serve as student aides, and these students come to the classroom once every week or two on a rotating basis.

The second graders keep track of their work in centers using small booklets with eight sheets of paper that Ms. Williams calls their "center passports." The student aide marks their passports with stickers or stamps at each center after they finish the assignment, and children leave their written work in a basket at the center.

As a culminating activity, Ms. Williams and her second graders write a retelling of *A House for Hermit Crab.* The children compose the text, and Ms. Williams uses the language experience approach[C] to write their rough draft on chart paper so that everyone can see it. Children learn revision strategies as they fine-tune their retelling, and then Ms. Williams types the text on five sheets of paper, duplicates copies, and compiles a booklet for each child. Children each receive a copy of the booklet to read. They also add illustrations. Later they will take their booklets home to read to their families.

Ms. Williams reads their retelling aloud as children follow along, and then they join in the reading. Children do choral reading[C] as they read in small groups, with classmates sitting at the same grouping of desks. The numbers on the left side indicate which group of students reads each sentence. As children read and reread the text aloud, they become increasingly fluent readers. Here is the last section of the class's retelling:

1   *<u>Soon</u> <u>it</u> <u>was</u> January.*
2   *Hermit Crab moved <u>out</u> <u>of</u> <u>his</u> <u>house</u> <u>and</u> <u>the</u> <u>little</u> crab moved in.*
3   *"Goodbye," <u>said</u> Hermit Crab. "<u>Be</u> good <u>to</u> <u>my</u> friends."*
4   *<u>Soon</u> Hermit Crab <u>saw</u> <u>the</u> perfect <u>house</u>.*
5   *<u>It</u> <u>was</u> <u>a</u> big, empty shell.*

Figure 6-2 Ms. Williams's Literacy Centers

1. Retelling Center
Children use pictures and labels with the month of the year to sequence the events in the book and retell the story.

2. Science Center
Children observe a hermit crab and make notes about its physical characteristics and eating habits in their learning logs.

3. Word Work Center
Children use magnetic letters to spell the four high-frequency words—*house, soon, your,* and *you're*—and the words from the last 2 weeks. They also make a book of contractions with picture and sentence examples.

4. Listening Center
Children use headphones to listen to an informational book on hermit crabs read aloud.

5. Word Wall Center
Children practice reading the word wall using the pointers. Then they take a clipboard and a sheet of paper divided into 10 sections; the letters spelling h-e-r-m-i-t c-r-a-b have been written in the sections. Then children choose two words from the word wall beginning with each letter to write in each section on their papers.

6. Writing Center
Children write "I am a Hermit Crab" poems following the model posted at the center. They also write and illustrate other books about hermit crabs.

7. Word Sort Center
Children sort vocabulary words from *A House for Hermit Crab* according to category. For example, months of the year are put in one category and ocean animals and plants in another.

8. Library Center
Children practice reading leveled books at their individual levels and other books about hermit crabs and the ocean that are placed on a special shelf in the classroom library. Ms. Williams includes *Moving Day* (Kaplan, 1996) (Level 7), *Hermit Crab* (Randell, 1994) (Level 8), and *Hermit's Shiny Shell* (Tuchman, 1997) (Level 10), three familiar books about hermit crabs, for students to reread.

1	*It looked a little plain but Hermit Crab didn't care.*
2	*He will decorate it*
3	*with sea urchins,*
4	*with sea anemones,*
5	*with coral,*
1	*with starfish,*
2	*with snails.*
ALL	*So many possibilities!*

The underlined words are high-frequency words that are posted on the word wall in Ms. Williams's classroom. Of the 68 words in this excerpt, 37 are high-frequency words! Also, two of the new words for this week, *soon* and *house,* are used twice.

As children learn to read, they move from word-by-word reading with little or no expression to fluent reading. Fluency is the ability to read smoothly and with expression, and to read fluently, children must be able to recognize many, many words automatically. By third grade, most children have moved from word-by-word reading into fluent reading, but 10–15% have difficulty learning to recognize words, and their learning to read is slowed (Allington, 1998).

Children become fluent readers through a combination of instruction and lots of reading experience. Through systematic phonics instruction, children learn how to identify unfamiliar words, and as they read and reread hundreds of books during the primary grades, these words become familiar and children learn to recognize them automatically. They also learn increasingly sophisticated strategies for identifying the unfamiliar words, including syllabic and morphemic analysis in which they break words into syllables and into root words and affixes.

At the same time children are becoming fluent readers, they are also becoming fluent writers. Through phonics instruction and lots of writing practice, children learn to spell many words automatically, apply capitalization and punctuation rules, and develop writing speed. They also develop strategies for spelling longer, multisyllabic words. Developing fluency is just as important for writers because both readers and writers must be able to focus on meaning, not on identifying and spelling words.

TEACHING CHILDREN TO READ AND WRITE WORDS

Teachers have two goals as they teach children to read and write words. The first is to teach children to instantly recognize a group of several hundred high-frequency words. They need to be able to read and write these words automatically, and they usually accomplish this goal by second or third grade. The second is to equip children with strategies, such as syllabic analysis, that they can use to identify unfamiliar words—often longer words they come across during reading and need to spell during writing.

Word Recognition

Children need to develop a large stock of words that they recognize instantly and automatically because it is impossible for them to analyze every word that they encounter when reading or want to spell when writing. These recognizable words are called sight words. Through repeated reading and writing experiences, children develop automaticity, the ability to quickly and accurately recognize words they read and to spell words they are writing (LaBerge & Samuels, 1976). The vital element in word recognition is learning each word's unique letter sequence. This knowledge about the sequence of letters is useful as children learn to spell. At the same time they are becoming fluent readers, children are also becoming fluent writers. They are learning to spell the words they write most often. Hitchcock (1989) found that by third grade, most children spell 90% of the words they use correctly.

High-Frequency Words. The most common words that readers and writers use again and again are high-frequency words. There have been numerous attempts to identify specific lists of these words and calculate their frequency in reading materials. Pinnell

To link to *High-Frequency Words* for ideas for teaching high-frequency words, visit our Companion Website at **www.prenhall.com/tompkins**

and Fountas (1998, p. 89) identified these 24 common words that kindergartners need to learn to recognize:

a	at	he	it	no	the
am	can	I	like	see	to
an	do	in	me	she	up
and	go	is	my	so	we

The 24 words are part of the 100 most commonly used words, and these 100 words account for more than half of the words children read and write. Children learn the rest of these 100 words in first grade. Eldredge (1995) has identified the 300 highest-frequency words used in first-grade basal readers and trade books found in first-grade classrooms; these 300 words account for 72% of the words that beginning readers read. Figure 6-3 presents Eldredge's list of 300 high-frequency words; the 100 most commonly used words are marked with an asterisk. (For a list of the 100 most commonly used words, turn to Chapter 5, "Learning to Spell." Children learn to both read and write these words during the primary grades.)

It is essential that children learn to read and write high-frequency words, but many of these words are difficult to learn because they cannot be easily decoded (Cunningham, 2000). Try sounding out *to, what,* and *could* and you will see why they are called "sight" words. Because these words can't be decoded easily, it is crucial that children learn to recognize them instantly and automatically. A further complication is that many of these words are function words in sentences and thus don't carry much meaning. Children find it much easier to learn to recognize *whale* than *what,* because *whale* conjures up the image of the aquatic mammal, whereas *what* is abstract. However, *what* is used much more frequently, and children need to learn to recognize it.

Children who recognize many high-frequency words are able to read more fluently than children who do not, and fluent readers are better able to understand what they are reading. Once children can read many of these words, they gain confidence in themselves as readers and begin reading books independently. Similarly, children who can spell these words are more successful writers.

Many of the high-frequency words are articles, prepositions, and other functions that are difficult for English-language learners. Make sure ELL students understand the meaning of high-frequency words they are learning to read.

Word Walls. Teachers create word walls in their classrooms to display high-frequency words that children are learning (Cunningham, 2000), as Ms. Williams did in the vignette at the beginning of the chapter. Some teachers use butcher paper or squares of construction paper for the word wall, and others use large pocket charts that they divide into sections for each letter of the alphabet. Word walls should be placed in a large, accessible location in the classroom so that new words can be added easily and all children can see the words.

Teachers prepare word walls at the beginning of the school year and then add words to them each week. Kindergarten teachers often begin the year by listing children's names on the word wall and then add the 24 highest-frequency words, 1 or 2 words per week, during the school year. First-grade teachers often begin with the 24 highest-frequency words already on the word wall at the beginning of the year, and then add 2 to 5 words to the word wall each week during the school year. Figure 6-4 presents a first-grade word wall with just over 100 words that were added during the school year. In second grade, teachers often begin the year with the easier half of the high-frequency words already on the word wall, and they add 50 to 75 more words during the school year. Third-grade teachers often test their students' knowledge of the 100 high-frequency words at the beginning of the year, add to the word wall those words that students cannot read and write, and then continue with words from the next 200 high-frequency words.

Figure 6-3 The 300 High-Frequency Words

*a	children	great	looking	ran	through
*about	city	green	made	read	*time
*after	come	grow	make	red	*to
again	*could	*had	*man	ride	toad
*all	couldn't	hand	many	right	together
along	cried	happy	may	road	told
always	dad	has	maybe	room	*too
*am	dark	hat	*me	run	took
*an	*day	*have	mom	*said	top
*and	*did	*he	more	sat	tree
animals	*didn't	head	morning	*saw	truck
another	*do	hear	*mother	say	try
any	does	heard	mouse	*school	*two
*are	dog	help	Mr.	sea	under
*around	*don't	hen	Mrs.	*see	until
*as	door	*her	much	*she	*up
asked	*down	here	must	show	*us
*at	each	hill	*my	sister	*very
ate	eat	*him	name	sky	wait
away	end	*his	need	sleep	walk
baby	even	*home	never	small	walked
*back	ever	*house	new	*so	want
bad	every	*how	next	*some	wanted
ball	everyone	*I	nice	something	*was
*be	eyes	I'll	night	soon	water
bear	far	I'm	*no	started	way
*because	fast	*if	*not	stay	*we
bed	father	*in	nothing	still	*well
been	find	inside	*now	stop	*went
before	fine	*into	*of	stories	*were
began	first	*is	off	story	*what
behind	fish	*it	oh	sun	*when
best	fly	it's	old	take	where
better	*for	its	*on	tell	while
big	found	jump	once	than	*who
bird	fox	jumped	*one	*that	why
birds	friend	*just	only	that's	*will
blue	friends	keep	*or	*the	wind
book	frog	king	other	their	witch
books	*from	*know	*our	*them	*with
box	fun	last	*out	*then	wizard
boy	garden	left	*over	*there	woman
brown	gave	let	*people	these	words
*but	*get	let's	picture	*they	work
*by	girl	*like	pig	thing	*would
called	give	*little	place	*things	write
*came	go	live	play	*think	yes
*can	going	long	pulled	*this	*you
can't	good	look	*put	thought	you're
cat	*got	looked	rabbit	three	*your

From *Teaching Decoding in Holistic Classrooms* by J. L. Eldredge, © 1995.
Adapted by permission of Prentice Hall, Inc., Upper Saddle River, NJ.
*The first 100 most frequently used words, as shown in Figure 5-8 on p. 133.

Figure 6-4 A First-Grade Word Wall

A	B	C	D
a are	be	call	did
about as	been	called	didn't
after at	boy	can	do
all	but	can't	does
am	by	come	don't
and		could	down

E	F	G	H
each	find	get	had him
eat	first	go	has his
	for	good	have how
	from		he
			her
			here

I	J	K	L
I	just	know	like
if			little
in			long
into			look
is			
it			

M	N	O	P
made must	no	of other	people
make my	not	on our	pretty
may	now	one out	
me		only over	
more		or	

QR	S	T	U
	said	than there	up
	saw	that these	us
	see	the they	
	she	their this	
	so	them to	
	some	then two	
	should		

V	W	XY	Z
very	was where	you	
	water which	your	
	way who		
	we will		
	were with		
	what words		
	when would		

Teachers carefully select the words they introduce each week. They choose words that children are familiar with and use in conversation. The selected words should have appeared in books children are reading or been introduced in guided reading lessons, or they should be words that they have misspelled in interactive writing or in other writing activities. Even though the words are listed alphabetically in Figure 6-4, they should not be taught in that order. In the vignette, Ms. Williams chose *soon* and *house*

Children practice reading high-frequency words using a pocket chart activity.

from A *House for Hermit Crab* and the homophones *your* and *you're* that her students were confusing in their writing.

Teaching high-frequency words is not easy because most of the words are functional words. Many words are abstract and have little or no meaning when they are read or written in isolation. Cunningham (2000) recommends this procedure for practicing the words being placed on the word wall:

1. *Introduce the word or words in context.* The words can be presented in the context of a book children are familiar with or by using pictures or objects. For example, to introduce the words *for* and *from*, teachers might bring a box wrapped with gift paper and tied with a bow, and an attached gift tag is labeled "for" and "from." Then teachers pass out extra gift tags they have made, and students read the words *for* and *from* and briefly talk about gifts they have given and received. Teachers also clarify that *for* is not the number *four* and show children where the number *four* is written on the number chart posted in the classroom.

2. *Have children chant and clap the spelling of the words.* Teachers introduce the new word cards that will be placed on the word wall and read the words. Then they begin a chant, "For, for, f-o-r," and clap their hands. Then children repeat the chant. After several repetitions, teachers begin a second chant, "From, from, f-r-o-m," and the children repeat the chant and clap their hands as they chant. Children practice chanting and clapping the words each day that week.

3. *Have children practice reading and spelling the words in a word work center.* Children use white boards and magnetic letters to practice spelling the words. For practice reading the words, they can also sort word cards. For example, the words *for, from, four, fun, fish, fast, free, from, for, four, free,* and *fun* are written on cards, and children sort them into three piles: one pile for *for,* a second pile for *from,* and a third pile for all other words.

4. *Have children apply the words they are learning in reading and writing activities.* Because these are high-frequency words, it is likely that children will read and

write them often. Teachers can also create writing opportunities through interactive writing activities.

Through this procedure, teachers make the high-frequency words more concrete, and easily confused words are clarified and practiced. Also, children have many opportunities to practice reading and writing the words.

Teaching and Assessing Word Recognition. Activities involving word walls are important ways that teachers teach word recognition; reading and writing practice are two other ways. Children develop rapid word recognition by reading words. They read words in the context of stories and other books, and they read them on word lists and on word cards. Practice makes children more fluent readers and even has an impact on their comprehension. Research is inconclusive about whether it is better to have children practice reading words in context or in isolation, but most teachers prefer to have children read words in the context of stories or other books because the activity is much more authentic (I. W. Gaskins, Ehri, Cress, O'Hara, & Donnelly, 1996/1997).

A minilesson[C] showing how a first-grade teacher focuses her students' attention on the high-frequency words they have placed on the word wall is presented in the feature on page 153. These first graders learn high-frequency words that come from big books they are reading. The teacher uses the whole-part-whole approach (Flood & Lapp, 1994; Trachtenburg, 1990). The children meet the words in their reading (the whole), and then they study three of the high-frequency words through word work activities (the part), and then they apply what they have learned in other reading and writing activities (the whole again). The value of the whole-part-whole approach is that children understand that what they are learning is useful in authentic literacy activities.

Children also practice word recognition through writing because they write high-frequency words again and again. For example, when a class of first graders were studying animals, they wrote riddle books. One first grader wrote this riddle book, entitled "What Is It?":

To link to *Teaching Word-Identification Strategies* to read about the word-identification strategies, the role of phonics, how to teach the strategies, and relating word identification to writing and spelling, visit our Companion Website at www.prenhall.com/tompkins

Page 1:   *It is a bird.*
Page 2:   *It can't fly but it can swim.*
Page 3:   *It is black and white.*
Page 4:   *It eats fish.*
Page 5:   *What is it?*
Page 6:   *A penguin.*

Of the words that the child wrote, more than half are among the 24 highest-frequency words listed on page 148. (These words are underlined.) Children learn to refer to the word wall when they are writing so that they can write fluently.

Because word recognition is so important in beginning reading, children's developing word recognition should be monitored and assessed on a regular basis (Snow, Burns, & Griffin, 1998). Teachers can ask children to individually read the words posted on the word wall or read high-frequency words on word cards. Kindergartners might be tested on the list of 24 words, first graders on the list of 100 words, and second and third graders on the list of 300 words. Teachers can also monitor children's spelling of the high-frequency words in their writing.

Word Identification

Beginning readers encounter many words that they don't recognize immediately, and more fluent readers also come upon words that they don't recognize at once. Children use word-identification strategies to identify these unfamiliar words. Young children of-

Minilesson

Topic: High-Frequency Words
Grade: First Grade
Time: One 15-minute period

Miss Shapiro teaches first grade, and her goal is for her first graders to be able to read at least 75 of the 100 highest frequency words. She has a large word wall on one wall of the classroom that is divided into sections for each letter of the alphabet. Each week, she introduces 3 new high-frequency words and adds them to the word wall. She chooses words from the big book she is using for shared reading. On Monday, she introduces the new words and over the next 4 days, she focuses on the new words and reviews those she has introduced previously. To make the word study more authentic, the children often hunt for the word in reading materials available in the classroom; sometimes they look in familiar big books, in small books they are rereading, on charts of familiar poems and songs, or on language experience and interactive writing charts. On other days, the children create sentences using the words, which she writes on sentence strips and displays in the classroom.

1. Introduce the Topic
"Let's read the D words on the word wall," Miss Shapiro says. As she points to the words, the class reads them aloud. "Which word is a new word this week?" she asks. The children respond, *"do."* Next they read the H words and identify *here* as a new word, and then the M words and identify *my* as a new word. She asks individual children to reread the D, H, and M words on the word wall.

2. Share Examples
"Who can come up and point to our three new words for this week?" Miss Shapiro asks. Aaron eagerly comes to the word wall to point out *do, here,* and *my.* As he points to each word, Miss Shapiro writes it on the chalkboard, pronounces it, and spells it aloud. She and Aaron lead the class as they chant and clap the spelling of the three words: "Do, do, d-o, do!" "Here, here, h-e-r-e, here!" "My, my, m-y, my!"

3. Provide Information
"Let's look for *do, here,* and *my* in these books," Miss Shapiro suggests as she passes out a familiar big book to the children at each table. In each group, the students reread the book, pointing out *do, here,* and *my* each time they occur. The teacher circulates around the classroom, checking that the children notice the words.

4. Guide Practice
Miss Shapiro asks Aaron to choose three classmates to come to the chalkboard to spell the words with large magnetic letters. Daniel, Elizabeth, and Wills spell the words and read them aloud. Then Aaron passes out plastic bags with small magnetic letters and word cards to each pair of students. They read the word cards and spell the three words at their desks.

5. Assess Learning
On Friday, Miss Shapiro works with the first graders in small groups, asking them to locate the words in sentences they have written and to read the words individually on word cards.

ten depend on phonics to identify unfamiliar words, but second through fourth graders develop a repertoire of strategies that use phonological information as well as semantic, syntactic, and pragmatic cues to identify words. Four word-identification strategies are:

> Phonic analysis
> By analogy
> Syllabic analysis
> Morphemic analysis

Writers use these same strategies to spell words as they write. As with reading, young children depend on phonics to spell many, many words, but as they learn more about words, they apply more of these strategies to spelling. The word-identification strategies are summarized in Figure 6-5.

Eldredge (1995) calls these strategies "interim strategies" because children use them only until they learn to recognize words automatically. For example, fourth graders may break the word *disruption* into syllables to identify the word the first time they encounter it, but with practice, they learn to recognize it automatically. Third graders writing reports during a science unit on the rocks and minerals may need to spell the word *geology*, and they learn to spell it using their knowledge of word parts. *Geo-* is a Greek word part meaning *earth*, and *-ology*, also a Greek word part, means *study of.* In time, children will write the word *geology* without breaking it into word parts or thinking about the meaning; they will write it automatically.

Figure 6-5   Word-Identification Strategies

Strategy	Description	Examples
Phonic Analysis	Children use their knowledge of sound-symbol correspondences and spelling patterns to decode words when reading and to spell words when writing.	*flat, peach, spring, blaze, chin*
By Analogy	Children use their knowledge of rhyming words to deduce the pronunciation or spelling of an unfamiliar word.	*creep* from *sheep, think* from *pink, include* from *dude*
Syllabic Analysis	Children break multisyllabic words into syllables and then use phonics and analogies to decode the word, syllable by syllable.	*cul-prit, tem-por-ary, vic-tor-y, neg-a-tive, sea-weed, bio-de-grad-able*
Morphemic Analysis	Children apply their knowledge of root words and affixes (prefixes at the beginning of the word and suffixes at the end) to identify an unfamiliar word. They "peel off" any prefixes or suffixes and identify the root word first. Then they add the affixes.	*trans-port, astro-naut, bi-cycle, centi-pede, pseudo-nym, tele-scope*

Phonic Analysis. Children use what they have learned about phoneme-grapheme correspondences, phonic generalizations, and spelling patterns to decode words when they are reading and to spell words when they are writing. Even though English is not a perfectly phonetic language, phonic analysis is a very useful strategy because almost every word has some phonetically regular parts. The words *have* and *come*, for example, are considered irregular words because the vowel sounds are not predictable; however, the initial and final consonant sounds in both words are regular.

Beginning readers often try to identify words based on a partial word analysis (Gough, Juel, & Griffith, 1992). They may guess at a word using the beginning sound or look at the overall shape of the word as a clue to word identification; however, these are not effective techniques. Through phonics instruction, students learn to focus on the letter sequences in words so that they examine the entire word as they identify it (Adams, 1990).

Researchers report that the primary difference between children who can identify words effectively and those who cannot is whether or not they survey the letters in the word and analyze the interior components (Stanovich, 1992; Vellutino & Scanlon, 1987). Capable readers notice all or almost all letters in a word, whereas less capable readers do not completely analyze the letter sequences of words. Struggling readers with limited phonics skills often try to decode words by sounding out the beginning sound and then making a wild guess at the word without using the cueing systems to verify their guesses (I. W. Gaskins et al., 1996/1997). And, as you might imagine, their guesses are usually wrong. Sometimes they don't even make sense in the context of the sentence.

Once children know some letter-sound sequences, the focus of phonics instruction should become using phonic analysis to decode and spell words. Here are the steps children follow in decoding an unfamiliar one-syllable word:

1. Determine the vowel sound in the word, and isolate that sound.
2. Blend all of the consonant sounds in front of the vowel sound with the vowel sound.
3. Isolate the consonant sound(s) after the vowel sound.
4. Blend the two parts of the word together so the word can be identified.
   (Eldredge, 1995, p. 108)

For children to use this strategy, they need to be able to identify vowels and vowel patterns in words. They also need to be able to blend sounds together to form recognizable words. For multisyllabic words, students break the word into syllables and then use the same procedure to decode each syllable. Because the location of stress in words varies, sometimes students have to try accenting different syllables to pronounce a recognizable word.

By Analogy. Students identify some words by associating them with words they already know. This procedure is known as decoding by analogy (Cunningham, 1975–1976; R. W. Gaskins, Gaskins, & Gaskins, 1991). For example, when readers come to an unfamiliar word such as *lend*, they might think of *send* and figure the word out by analogy; for *cart*, they might notice the word *art* and use that to figure the word out. Students use analogy to figure out the spelling of unfamiliar words as well. Students might use *cat* to help them spell *that*, for example. This strategy accounts for students' common misspelling of *they* as *thay*, because *they* rhymes with *day* and *say*.

This word-identification strategy is dependent on children's phonemic awareness and phonics knowledge. Children who can break words into onsets and rimes and substitute sounds in words are more successful than those who cannot. Moreover, researchers have found that only children who know many sight words can use this strategy because they must be able to identify patterns in familiar words to associate with those in unfamiliar words (Ehri & Robbins, 1992). Even though some first and second graders can use this strategy, older students are more likely to use it to decode and spell words.

Teachers introduce this strategy when they have students read and write "word families" or rimes. Using the *-ill* family, for example, children can read or write *bill, chill, fill, hill, kill, mill, pill, quill, spill, still,* and *will*. They can add inflectional endings to create even more words, including *filling, hills,* and *spilled*. Two-syllable words can also be created using these words: *killer, chilly,* and *hilltop*. Children read word cards, write the words using interactive writing, use magnetic letters to spell the words, and make rhyming word books during the primary grades to learn more about substituting beginning sounds, breaking words into parts, and spelling word parts. It is a big step, however, for children to move from these structured activities to using this strategy independently to identify unfamiliar words.

Syllabic Analysis. During second, third, and fourth grades, children learn to divide words into syllables in order to read and write multisyllabic words such as *biodegradable, admonition,* and *unforgettable*. Once a word is divided into syllables, children use phonic analysis and analogy to pronounce or spell the word. Identifying syllable boundaries is important, because these affect the pronunciation of the vowel sound. For example, compare the vowel sound in the first syllables of *cabin* and *cable*. For *cabin,* the syllable boundary is after the *b,* whereas for *cable,* the division is before the *b*. We can predict that the *a* in *cabin* will be short because the syllable follows the CVC pattern, and that the *a* in *cable* will be long because the syllable follows the CV pattern.

The most basic rule about syllabication is that there is one vowel sound in each syllable. Consider the words *bit* and *bite*. *Bit* is a one-syllable word because there is one vowel letter representing one vowel sound. *Bite* is a one-syllable word, too, because even though there are two vowels in the word, they represent one vowel sound. *Magic* and *curfew* are two-syllable words. There is one vowel letter and sound in each syllable in *magic,* but in the second syllable of *curfew,* the two vowels *ew* represent one vowel sound. Let's try a longer word: How many syllables are in *inconvenience?* There are six vowel letters representing four sounds in four syllables.

Syllabication rules are useful in teaching children how to divide words into syllables. Five of the most useful rules are listed in Figure 6-6. The following 12 two-syllable words are from *A House for Hermit Crab* (Carle, 1987), the book Ms. Williams read in the vignette at the beginning of the chapter, and they illustrate all but one of the rules:

a-round	prom-ise	her-mit
pret-ty	ur-chin	nee-dles
slow-ly	o-cean	ti-dy
with-out	cor-al	com-plain

The first two rules focus on consonants, and the last three focus on vowels. The first rule, to divide between two consonants, is the most common rule, and examples from the list are *her-mit* and *pret-ty*. The second rule deals with words where three consonants appear together in a word, such as *com-plain*. The word is divided between the *m* and the *p* in order to preserve the *pl* blend. The third and fourth rules involve the VCV pattern. Usually the syllable boundary comes after the first vowel, as in *ti-dy, o-cean,* and *a-round;* however, the division comes after the consonant in *cor-al* because dividing the word *co-ral* does not produce a recognizable word. The syllable boundary comes after the consonant in *without,* too, but this compound word has easily recognizable word parts. According to the fifth rule, words such as *qui-et* are divided between the two vowels because the vowels do not represent a vowel digraph or diphthong. This rule is the least common, and there were no examples of it in the story.

Figure 6-6 Syllabication Rules

Rules	Examples
1. When two consonants come between two vowels in a word, divide syllables between the consonants.	cof-fee bor-der hec-tic plas-tic jour-ney
2. When there are more than two consonants together in a word, divide syllables keeping the blends together.	em-ploy mon-ster lob-ster en-trance bank-rupt
3. When there is one consonant between two vowels in a word, divide syllables after the first vowel.	ca-jole bo-nus fau-cet plu-ral gla-cier
4. If following the third rule does not make a recognizable word, divide syllables after the consonant that comes between the vowels.	doz-en dam-age ech-o meth-od cour-age
5. When there are two vowels together that do not represent a . long-vowel sound or a diphthong, divide syllables between the vowels.	cli-ent du-et po-em cha-os li-on qui-et

Teachers use minilessons to introduce syllabication and teach the syllabication rules. During additional minilessons, children and teachers choose words from books students are reading and from thematic units for guided practice breaking words into syllables. After identifying syllable boundaries, children pronounce and spell the words, syllable by syllable. Teachers also mark syllable boundaries on multisyllabic words on word walls in the classroom and create center activities in which students practice dividing words into syllables and building words using word parts.

Morphemic Analysis. Children examine the root word and affixes of longer unfamiliar words in order to identify the words. A root word is a morpheme, the basic part of a word to which affixes are added. Many words are developed from a single root word. For example, the Latin words *portare* (to carry), *portus* (harbor), and *porta* (gate) are the sources of at least 12 words: *deport, export, exporter, import, port, portable, porter, report, reporter, support, transport,* and *transportation.* Latin is the most common source of English root words, and Greek and English are two other sources.

Some root words are whole words, and others are parts of words. Some root words have become free morphemes and can be used as separate words, but others cannot. For instance, the word *cent* comes from the Latin root word *cent,* meaning "hundred." English treats the word as a root word that can be used independently and in combination with affixes, as in *century* and *centipede*. The word *astronaut* comes from the Greek roots *astro,* meaning "stars," and *naut,* meaning "sailor"; they are not independent root words in English. English words such as *eye, tree,* and *water* are root words, too. New words are formed through compounding—for example, *eyelash, tree-top,* and *waterfall*—and other English root words, such as *read,* combine with affixes, as in *reader* and *unreadable.*

Affixes are bound morphemes that are added to words and root words. Prefixes are added to the beginning of words, as in *replay,* and suffixes are added to the end of words, as in *playing, playful,* and *player.* Like root words, some affixes are English and others come from Latin and Greek. Affixes often change a word's meaning, such as adding *un-* to *happy* to form *unhappy.* Sometimes they change the part of speech, too. For example, when *-tion* is added to *attract* to form *attraction,* the verb *attract* becomes a noun.

There are two types of suffixes: inflectional and derivational. Inflectional suffixes are endings that indicate verb tense and person, plurals, possession, and comparison, and these suffixes are English. They influence the syntax of sentences. Some examples are:

the *-ed* in *walked*	the *-es* in *beaches*
the *-ing* in *singing*	the *-'s* in *girl's*
the *-s* in *asks*	the *-er* in *faster*
the *-s* in *dogs*	the *-est* in *sunniest*

In contrast, derivational suffixes show the relationship of the word to its root word. Consider, for example, these words containing the root word *friend: friendly, friend-ship,* and *friendless.*

When a word's affix is "peeled off," the remaining word is usually a real word. For example, when the prefix *pre-* is removed from *preview* and the suffix *-er* is removed from *viewer,* the word *view* can stand alone. Some words contain letter sequences that might be affixes, but because the remaining word cannot stand alone, they are not affixes. For example, the *in-* at the beginning of *include* is not a prefix because *clude* is not a word. Similarly, the *-ic* at the end of *magic* is not a suffix because *mag* cannot stand alone as a word. Sometimes, however, Latin and Greek root words cannot stand alone. One example is *legible.* The *-ible* is a suffix, and *leg* is the root word even though it cannot stand alone. Of course, *leg*—meaning a part of the body—is a word, but the root word *leg-* from *legible* is not; it is a Latin root word, meaning "to read."

White, Sowell, and Yanagihara (1989) recommend that the most commonly used affixes be taught to third and fourth graders because of their usefulness in word identification, spelling, and vocabulary development. The recommended affixes include:

Prefixes	Inflectional Suffixes	Derivational Suffixes
over-	-ed	-ly
un-	-ing	-ness
dis-	-s/-es	-y
il-/im-/in-/ir-	-er	-er/-or/-ar
re-	-est	-tion
sub-	-'s	

Some of the most commonly used prefixes can be confusing because they have more than one meaning. The prefix *un-,* for example, can mean *not* (e.g., *unclear*) or it can reverse the meaning of a word (e.g., *tie-untie*).

After a series of minilessons on suffixes, a third-grade teacher developed the sorting game shown in Figure 6-7. Her students played the game as a center activity. They sorted the word cards according to suffix and placed them in columns as shown in the figure.

Figure 6-7   A Sorting Game Using Words With Suffixes

-ly	-est	-less	-y	-ful
loudly	biggest	helpless	windy	playful
badly	funniest	painless	dirty	careful
finally	coldest	spotless	stormy	wonderful
easily	laziest	homeless	noisy	beautiful
deadly	craziest	powerless	grouchy	helpful
honestly	quickest		stinky	

Teaching and Assessing Word Identification. Word-level learning is an essential part of a balanced literacy program (Hiebert, 1991), and teaching minilessons about analogies and phonic, syllabic, and morphemic analysis is a useful way to help students focus on words. Minilessons grow out of meaningful literature experiences or thematic units, and teachers choose words for minilessons from books children are reading, as Ms. Williams did in the vignette.

Delpit (1987) and Reyes (1991) have argued that learning words implicitly through reading and writing experiences assumes that children have existing literacy and language proficiencies and that the same sort of instruction works equally well for everyone. They point out that not all children have a rich background of literacy experiences before coming to school. Some children, especially those from nonmainstream cultural and linguistic groups, may not have been read to as preschoolers. They may not have recited nursery rhymes to develop phonemic awareness, or experimented with writing by writing letters to grandparents. Perhaps even more important, they may not be familiar with the routines of school—sitting quietly and listening while the teacher reads, working cooperatively on group projects, answering questions and talking about books, and imitating the teacher's literacy behaviors. Delpit and Reyes conclude that explicit instruction is crucial for nonmainstream children who do not have the same literacy background as middle-class students.

Fluent readers develop a large repertoire of sight words and use word-identification strategies to decode unfamiliar words. Less capable readers, in contrast, cannot read as many sight words and do not use as many strategies for decoding words. Researchers have concluded again and again that children who do not become fluent readers depend on explicit instruction to learn how to identify words (Calfee & Drum, 1986; R. W. Gaskins et al., 1991; Johnson & Baumann, 1984).

Many fourth-grade teachers notice that their students seem to stand still or even lose ground in their reading development. It has been assumed that the increased demands for reading informational books with unfamiliar, multisyllabic words caused this phenomenon. Now researchers are suggesting that lack of instruction in word-identification strategies might be the cause of the "fourth-grade slump" (Chall, Jacobs, & Baldwin, 1990). Perhaps more minilessons on identifying multisyllabic words will help eliminate this difficulty. The guidelines for teaching word identification are summarized in Figure 6-8.

Teachers informally assess children's ability to use word-identification strategies as they observe them reading and writing and monitor their use of the strategies. They can also assess children's use of word-identification strategies by asking them to read or write a list of grade-level-appropriate words or by asking them to think aloud and explain how they decoded or spelled a particular word. It is also important that teachers check to see that children use these strategies on an "interim basis" and that through practice they learn to read and write words automatically. Fourth graders, for example, may use syllabic analysis to read or write a word such as *important,* but with practice, they should learn to read and write the word automatically, without having to stop and analyze it.

What Is Fluency?

Fluency is the ability to read effectively, and it involves three components: reading rate, word recognition, and prosody (Rasinski, 2000; Richards, 2000). Reading rate refers to the speed at which children read; to read fluently, children need to read at least 100 words per minute. Most children reach this rate by third grade. Children's reading rate continues to grow, and by the time they are adults, they will read from 250 to 300 words per minute. Of course, both children and adults vary their reading speed depending on what they are reading, its difficulty level, and their purpose for reading, but excessively slow reading is often a characteristic of unsuccessful readers.

Word recognition is the second component of fluency. To read fluently, children need to instantly and automatically recognize most of the words they read. They need to know the 100 high-frequency words and other common words and have sounded out phonetically regular words so many times that these words, too, have become automatic. Usually, children encounter a few words that they do not know, but they use word-identification skills to quickly identify those words and continue reading. When children have to stop and decode words in every sentence, their reading will not be fluent.

The third component, prosody, is the ability to orally read sentences expressively, with appropriate phrasing and intonation. Dowhower (1991) describes prosody as "the ability to read in expressive, rhythmic, and melodic patterns" (p. 166). Children move from word-by-word reading with little or no expression to chunking words into phrases, attending to punctuation, and applying appropriate syntactic emphases. Fluent readers' oral reading approximates talking, and for their reading to be expressive, children have to read quickly and recognize automatically most of the words they are reading.

Fluent readers are better able to comprehend what they read because they can identify words easily (LaBerge & Samuels, 1976; Perfitti, 1985; Stanovich, 1986). Children who are not fluent readers often read hesitantly, in a word-by-word fashion and with great effort. These less successful readers spend too much mental energy in identifying words, leaving little energy to focus on comprehension. Readers do not have an unlimited amount of mental energy to use when they read, and they cannot focus on word recognition and comprehension at the same time. So, as children become fluent readers, they use less energy for word recognition and focus more energy on comprehending what they read.

Figure 6-8   Guidelines for Teaching Children to Identify Words

1. Teach as Part of a Balanced Program
Teachers present word-identification lessons as part of literature focus units and guided reading groups. A whole-part-whole approach for teaching word identification as well as other skills and strategies is recommended.

2. Teach High-Frequency Words
Teachers choose both high-frequency words and other interesting words from the reading selections for minilessons and other word-study activities. It is especially important that children learn high-frequency words in order to become fluent readers.

3. Select Words Carefully
Teachers consider the children, the text to be read, and the purpose for reading when deciding which words to focus on for word-study activities.

4. Introduce Key Words Before Reading
Introduce only a few key words before beginning to read, and teach other words during and after reading. Key words are meaningful words in the reading selection, such as characters' names, or words related to a key concept.

5. Use Shared Reading
Teachers often use shared reading to introduce trade books and selections in basal reader textbooks. As teachers read, they model word-identification strategies for children.

6. Highlight High-Frequency Words
Children and teachers highlight important and interesting words from the reading selection on word walls and make word banks of high-frequency words for children to refer to when reading and spelling.

7. Teach Word-Identification Strategies
Teachers present minilessons on the four word-identification strategies and related skills: phonic analysis, analogies, syllabic analysis, and morphemic analysis.

8. Use Reading Workshop
Children need daily opportunities to read self-selected books during reading workshop, and as they read and reread books appropriate to their reading levels, they apply word-identification strategies and related skills. Easy-to-read books written at the first-, second-, and third-grade levels are recommended for beginning readers.

9. Emphasize the Reading-Writing Connection
Integrated reading and writing instruction gives children many opportunities to write high-frequency words and other words related to reading selections in writing activities. Children write in reading logs, make story maps, and write innovations, or new versions of stories they are reading.

10. Focus on Fluency
The goal of word-recognition lessons is to help children become fluent readers. Fluent readers can identify most words automatically and use word-identification strategies to figure out unfamiliar words.

By third grade, most children have become fluent readers. They have acquired a large stock of high-frequency words that they can read automatically, and they have developed word-identification strategies, including phonic analysis and syllabic analysis, to use to figure out unfamiliar words. But some children continue to read slowly, in a halting manner and without expression. They do not read fluently, and they exemplify some of these characteristics:

- Children read slowly.
- Children cannot decode individual words.
- Children try to sound out phonetically irregular words.
- Children guess at words based on the beginning sound.
- Children do not remember a word the second or third time it is used in a passage.
- Children do not break multisyllabic words into syllables to decode them.
- Children do not break multisyllabic words into root words and affixes to decode them.
- Children point at words as they read.
- Children repeat words and phrases.
- Children read without expression.
- Children read word by word.
- Children ignore punctuation marks.
- Children do not remember or understand what they read.

Writing fluency is similar to reading fluency. Children need to be able to write quickly and easily so that their hands and arms do not hurt. Slow, laborious handwriting interferes with the expression of ideas. In addition, children must be able to spell words automatically so that they can take notes, write journal entries, and handle other writing assignments.

As children reread books, they increase reading speed and develop reading fluency.

Promoting Reading Fluency

Nonfluent readers can learn to read fluently (Allington, 1983). These readers may need to work on their reading speed or their phrasing or on both components of fluency.

Improving Reading Speed. The best approach to improve children's reading speed is repeated readings[C] (Samuels, 1979), in which children practice rereading a book or an excerpt from a book three to five times, striving to improve their reading rate and decrease the number of errors they make. Teachers often time children's reading and plot their speed on a graph so that improvements can be noted. Repeated readings also enhance children's ability to chunk words into meaningful phrases and read with more expression (Dowhower, 1987). Researchers have also found that through repeated readings, children deepen their comprehension of the books they reread (Yaden, 1988).

Teachers often incorporate repeated readings as part of guided reading when they want to assist children in rereading. Sometimes the teacher reads the passage aloud while children follow along or use echo reading, in which they repeat each phrase or sentence after the teacher reads it. Then children reread the passage using choral reading[C]. After several repetitions, children can reread the passage one more time, this time independently. Teachers can also set up rereading opportunities at a listening center. If children are timing their reading, then a stopwatch or other timing device can be added to the center. Teachers also use paired repeated readings in which children work together to read, reread, and evaluate their reading (P. A. Koskinen & Blum, 1986).

Teaching Phrasing. Schreider (1980) recommends teaching children how to phrase or chunk together parts of sentences in order to read. Fluent readers seem to understand how to chunk parts of sentences into meaningful units, perhaps because they have been read to or have had many reading experiences themselves, but many struggling readers do not have this ability. Consider this sentence from *Sarah, Plain and Tall* (MacLachlan, 1985): "A few raindrops came, gentle at first, then stronger and louder, so that Caleb and I covered our ears and stared at each other without speaking" (p. 47). This sentence comes from the chapter describing a terrible storm that the pioneer family endured, huddled with their animals in their sturdy barn. Three commas help children read the first part of this sentence, but then children must decide how to chunk the second part of the sentence.

Teachers can work with nonfluent readers to have them practice breaking sentences into chunks and then reading the sentences with expression. Teachers can make copies of a page from a book children are reading so that they can use a pencil to mark pauses in longer sentences. Or, teachers can choose a sentence to write on the chalkboard, chunking it into phrases like this:

> A few raindrops came,
> gentle at first,
> then stronger and louder,
> so that Caleb and I
> covered our ears
> and stared at each other
> without speaking.

After chunking, children practice reading the sentence in chunks with classmates and individually. After working with one sentence, children can choose another sentence to chunk and practice reading. Children who don't chunk words into phrases when they read aloud need many opportunities to practice chunking and rereading sentences.

ELL

English-language learners often benefit from practice with phrasing. Through choral reading and other oral language activities, they learn to chunk sentences and to read with more expression.

To link to *Lingualinks Library* for activities for developing fluent readers, including the neurological impress method, repeated readings, and reading along with audiotapes, visit our Companion Website at www.prenhall.com/tompkins

Reading activities such as choral reading also help children improve their phrasing. In choral reading, children and the teacher take turns reading the text, as Ms. Williams and her second graders did in the vignette at the beginning of the chapter. Students provide support for each other because they are reading in small groups, and they learn to phrase sentences as they read along with classmates. Choral reading also improves children's reading speed because they read along with classmates.

Reading Practice. To develop fluency, children need many opportunities to practice reading and rereading books. The best books for reading practice are ones that children are interested in reading and that are written at a level just below their instructional level. Books for fluency practice should be neither too easy nor too difficult. Children should automatically recognize most words in the book, but if the book is extremely easy, it provides no challenge to the reader. Similarly, when children read books that are too difficult, they read slowly because they stop again and again to identify unfamiliar words. This constant stopping reinforces nonfluent readers' already choppy reading style.

Figure 6-9 **Picture-Book and Chapter-Book Series for Developing Reading Fluency**

Series	Description	Sample Book	Reading Level
Amber Brown by Paula Danziger	Chapter-book stories about a spunky third grader.	*Amber Brown Is Not a Crayon*	Grades 3–4
Arthur by Marc Brown	Picture-book stories about Arthur the Aardvark.	*Arthur Meets the President*	Grades 1–2
The Bailey School Kids by Debbie Dadey and Marcia Thornton Jones	Chapter-book stories about the adventures of a diverse third-grade class at Bailey School.	*Vampires Don't Wear Polka Dots*	Grade 3
Amelia Bedelia by Peggy Parish	Comical stories about a housekeeper who takes instructions literally.	*Play Ball, Amelia Bedelia*	Grade 1
Black Lagoon by Mike Thaler	Picture-book series dealing with children's fears of the unknown.	*The Teacher From the Black Lagoon*	Grades 2–3
Cam Jansen by David A. Adler	Funny chapter books about Cam Jansen, girl detective.	*Cam Jansen and the Mystery of the Dinosaur Bones*	Grade 2
Captain Underpants by Dav Pilkey	Hilarious chapter-book series about the superhero Captain Underpants.	*The Adventures of Captain Underpants*	Grade 4
Clifford by Norman Bridwell	Picture-book stories about Clifford, the big red dog.	*Clifford Takes a Trip*	Grade 2
Curious George by Margaret and H. A. Rey	Picture-book stories about a mischief-making monkey.	*Curious George Rides a Bike*	Grade 2
Fox and Friends by Edward and James Marshall	Stories about Fox who likes to have everything his way.	*Fox in Love*	Grade 1
Franklin by Paulette Bourgeois	Picture-book stories featuring a gentle turtle-hero named Franklin.	*Franklin Has a Sleepover*	Grade 2

For reading practice, children often choose "pop" literature that is fun to read but rather ordinary. These series books are often more effective than some high-quality literature selections in helping children develop fluency because the vocabulary is more controlled and children can be more successful. Children like them because the stories are humorous or relate to their own lives. Series books, such as *Junie B. Jones and the Stupid Smelly Bus* (Park, 1992) and *Night of the Ninjas* (Osborne, 1995), are written at the first- and second-grade level, and *The Teacher From the Black Lagoon* (Thaler, 1989) and *The Adventures of Captain Underpants* (Pilkey, 1997) are written at the third- and fourth-grade level. A list of picture-book and chapter-book series written at first- through fourth-grade levels is presented in Figure 6-9. More and more easy-to-read picture books and chapter books that are suitable for first through fourth graders are becoming available each year, and many of these stories appeal to boys.

Teachers provide two types of daily opportunities for children to practice reading and rereading familiar stories and other books: Some activities provide assisted practice, and other activities provide students with opportunities to read independently, without assistance. In assisted practice, students have a model to follow as they read

To link to *Stories On Stage,* for scripts for readers theatre performances, how-to tips for scripting, staging, and performing, and links to related Internet sites, visit our Companion Website at www.prenhall.com/tompkins

Figure 6-9 *(Continued)*

Series	Description	Sample Book	Reading Level
George and Martha by James Marshall	Picture-book stories about two hippo friends named George and Martha.	*George and Martha Back in Town*	Grade 2
Henry and Mudge by Cynthia Rylant	Chapter-book stories about Henry and his lovable 180-pound dog, Mudge.	*Henry and Mudge Take the Big Test*	Grades 1–2
Horrible Harry by Suzy Kline	Hilarious chapter-book stories about a second-grade prankster named Harry.	*Horrible Harry and the Dungeon*	Grade 2
Junie B. Jones by Barbara Park	Chapter-book stories about a delightful kindgartner who is always getting in trouble.	*Junie B. Jones and the Stupid Smelly Bus*	Grades 1–2
The Kids in Ms. Colman's Class by Ann M. Martin	Chapter-book stories about the second graders in Ms. Colman's class.	*Summer School*	Grade 2
Magic Tree House by Mary Pope Osborne	Chapter-book stories about a magical tree house that transports children back in time.	*Night of the Ninjas*	Grades 1–2
Marvin Redpost by Louis Sachar	Funny chapter-book stories about third-grade Marvin Redpost.	*Alone in His Teacher's House*	Grades 2–3
Nate the Great by Marjorie W. Sharmat	Chapter-book stories about a boy-detective with outrageous rates.	*Nate the Great and the Fishy Prize*	Grade 2
Pee Wee Scouts by Judy Delton	A series of 35+ adventure stories about a group of Pee Wee Scouts.	*Greedy Groundhogs*	Grade 2
Pinky and Rex by James Howe	Very easy-to-read chapter books about two best friends, a boy named Pinky and a girl named Rex.	*Pinky and Rex and the Bully*	Grades 1–2
The Zack Files by Dan Greenburg	Time-travel stories featuring fifth-grade Zack.	*My Son, the Time Traveler*	Grades 2–3

or reread. Choral reading is one example, and readers theatre[C] is another. In readers theatre, students practice reading story scripts to develop fluency before reading the script to an audience of classmates. In a recent study, Martinez, Roser, and Strecker (1998/1999) found that practice reading using readers theatre scripts resulted in significant improvement in second graders' reading fluency. Other examples of assisted reading are echo reading, listening centers, shared reading[C], and buddy reading. Screen reading is another way to provide assisted reading practice. Check the Technology Link on page 167 for more information about how to use this underutilized technology.

In unassisted reading practice, children read independently. They do this type of reading during reading workshop and at reading centers. Another unassisted practice activity that is often used in primary-grade classrooms is reading the classroom, in which children walk around the classroom reading all the words and sentences that are posted. Sometimes children dress up for this activity. They can wear glasses from which the lenses have been removed and use pointers to track what they are reading as they walk around the classroom.

Older students often participate in read-arounds. In this activity, children choose a favorite sentence or paragraph from a book they have already read and practice reading the passage they have chosen several times. Then students take turns reading their passages aloud. They read in any order they want, and usually several children will read the same passage aloud. Teachers often plan this activity to bring closure to a literature focus unit.

Why Is Round-Robin Reading No Longer Recommended? Round-robin reading is an outmoded oral reading activity in which the teacher calls on children to read aloud, one after the other. Some teachers used round-robin reading in small groups and others used the procedure with the whole class, but neither version is advocated today. According to Opitz and Rasinski (1998), many problems are associated with round-robin reading. First of all, children may develop an inaccurate view of reading because they are expected to read aloud to the class without having opportunities to rehearse. In addition, they may develop inefficient reading habits because they slow their silent reading speed to match the various speeds of classmates when they read aloud. Children signal their inattention and boredom by misbehaving as classmates read aloud. In addition to these problems for children who are listening, round-robin reading causes problems for some children when they are called on to read. Struggling readers are often anxious or embarrassed when they read aloud.

Most teachers now agree that round-robin reading wastes valuable classroom time that could be spent on more meaningful reading activities. Instead of round-robin reading, children should read the text independently if it is at their reading level. If it is too difficult, children can read with buddies, participate in shared reading, or listen to the teacher or another fluent reader read aloud. Also, they might listen to the teacher read the material aloud and then try reading it with a buddy or independently.

Developing Writing Fluency

To become fluent writers, children must be able to form letters rapidly and spell words automatically. Just as nonfluent readers read word by word and have to stop to decode many words, nonfluent writers write slowly, word by word, and have to stop to check the spelling of many words. In fact, some nonfluent writers write so

Technology Link

Screen Reading: Using Captioned Television Programs to Develop Reading Fluency

Reading captioned television programs provides children with opportunities for reading practice that is entertaining and self-correcting. On captioned television programs, sentences corresponding to the words spoken on the video are printed on the screen, much like the subtitles on foreign films. All new televisions have the built-in circuitry to decode and display closed-captioned programming. TeleCaption decoders can be purchased for less than $200 and attached to older televisions without the capacity to display captions.

Captions were developed for hearing-impaired viewers, but now they have a valuable instructional purpose: screen reading (P. S. Koskinen, Wilson, Gambrell, & Neuman, 1993). Koskinen and her colleagues found that less fluent readers and bilingual students become more motivated readers when they use captioned television and video, and they proposed that the simultaneous multisensory processing enhances learning.

Teachers can use captioned television programs when they are broadcast, or they can videotape the programs to use later. One of the best uses is to videotape a program and use it as a prereading activity to build background knowledge and introduce vocabulary. Teachers might show a video related to the text children will read, or they might show the video version of the book children will read. Many fine videos, including the Reading Rainbow programs, which feature award-winning children's literature, are available. Children with reading difficulties can also practice rereading captioned videos, and they can view the videos as independent reading activities.

Guidelines for Using Captioned Television Programs

1. Choose programs related to literature and content-area instruction as a prereading activity.
2. Introduce the program and provide key vocabulary words.
3. Plan related activities to use after viewing the program.
4. Allow children learning English as a second language and students with reading difficulties to view the program several times.
5. Create a text set of books and other reading materials to use with the program.
6. Provide opportunities for children to review the program and read related texts.
7. Create a video library.

Some captioned videos, such as Reading Rainbow programs, can be purchased from video stores and from educational publishers. Captioned programs can be videotaped from television, but copyright laws restrict the length of time they can be saved and the number of times the tapes can be used.

For more information about captioned television programs and videos, contact The National Captioning Institute, 5203 Leesburg Pike, Falls Church, VA 22041; telephone 1-800-533-WORD.

slowly that they forget the sentence they are writing! Through varied, daily writing activities, children develop the muscular control to form letters quickly and legibly. They write high-frequency words again and again until they can spell them automatically. Being able to write fluently usually coincides with being able to read fluently because reading and writing practice are mutually beneficial (Shanahan, 1988; Tierney, 1983).

Children become fluent writers as they practice writing, and they need opportunities for both assisted and unassisted practice. Writing on white boards during interactive writing lessons is one example of assisted writing practice (Tompkins, 2000). The teacher and classmates provide support for students.

Quickwriting. Peter Elbow (1973, 1981) recommends using quickwriting[C] to develop writing fluency. In quickwriting, students write rapidly and without stopping as they explore an idea. As part of the unit on hermit crabs, Ms. Williams asked the second-grade students to do a quickwrite listing what they had learned about hermit crabs. Here is Arlette's quickwrite:

> *Hermit crabs live in tide pools. They have pincers and 10 legs in all. They can pinch you very hard. Ouch! They are crabs and they molt to grow and grow. They have to buro (borrow) shells to live in becus (because) other anmels (animals) will eat them. They like to eat fish and shrimp. Sea enomes (anemones) like to live on ther (their) shells.*

Arlette listed a great deal of information that she had learned about hermit crabs. She misspelled five words, and the correct spellings are given in parentheses. Arlette was able to write such a long quickwrite and to misspell very few words because she is already a fluent writer. While she was writing, she checked the hermit crab word wall and the high-frequency word wall in the classroom to spell *pincers, shrimp,* and *other.* The other words she knew how to spell and wrote them automatically.

In contrast, Jeremy is not yet a fluent writer. Here is his quickwrite:

> *The hermit crab liv (lives) in a hues (house)*
> *he eat (eats) shimp (shrimp).*

Jeremy writes slowly and laboriously. He stops to think of an idea before writing each sentence and starts each sentence on a new line. He rarely refers to the word walls in the classroom, and he spells most words phonetically. Even though Jeremy's writing is not as fluent as Arlette's, quickwriting is a useful activity for him because he will become more fluent through practice.

Ms. Williams has her second graders quickwrite several times each week. They quickwrite to respond to a story she has read aloud or to write about what they are learning in science or another content area. She reads and responds to the quickwrites, and she writes the correct form of misspelled words at the bottom of the page so that children will notice the correct spelling. Once in a while, she has children revise and edit their quickwrites and make a final, published copy, but her goal is to develop writing fluency, not to produce finished, polished compositions.

Why Is Copying From the Chalkboard No Longer Recommended? Some teachers write sentences and poems on the chalkboard for children to copy in hopes that this activity will develop writing fluency. Copying isn't a very effective instructional strategy, though, because children are merely passively copying letters, not actively creating sentences, breaking the sentences into words, and spelling the words. In fact, sometimes children are copying sentences they cannot read, so the activity becomes little more than handwriting practice. It is much more worthwhile for children to write sentences to express their own ideas and to practice spelling words.

Assessing Students' Reading and Writing Fluency

Primary grade teachers monitor students' developing reading and writing fluency by observing them as they read and write. Teachers assess children's reading fluency by listening to them read aloud. As they listen, teachers consider these four components of reading fluency:

1. *Speed.* Do children read hesitantly, or do they read quickly enough to understand what they are reading?
2. *Phrasing.* Do children read word by word, or do they chunk words into phrases?
3. *Prosody.* Do children read in a monotone, or do they read with expression in a manner that approximates talking?
4. *Automaticity.* Do children have to decode many words, or do they read most words automatically?

By third grade, children should be fluent readers. If children have difficulty with any of the four components, teachers provide instruction in that area in addition to reading practice to improve their fluency.

Teachers assess children's writing fluency in a similar manner. They observe children as they write and consider these four points:

1. *Ideas.* Do children have trouble thinking of something to write, or do they readily think of ideas for writing?
2. *Speed.* Do children write slowly, or do they write quickly enough to complete the writing task?
3. *Ease.* Do children write laboriously or easily?
4. *Automaticity.* Do children have to sound out or locate the spelling of most words, or do they spell most words automatically?

As with reading fluency, children should be fluent writers by third grade. If children have difficulty with any of the four components, teachers should provide instruction in that area plus lots of writing practice to improve their fluency.

Review

Children need to become fluent readers and writers by third grade. During the primary grades, children learn to recognize many high-frequency words in order to develop reading fluency. They also learn to spell these high-frequency words to become fluent writers. Teachers create word walls to call children's attention to the 100 to 300 highest-frequency words. In addition, children learn to use phonic analysis, analogies, syllabic analysis, and morphemic analysis to identify unfamiliar words when reading and to spell words when writing. The feature that follows presents a list of recommended practices that effective teachers use to promote reading and writing fluency.

Effective Practices

1. Teachers teach high-frequency words because they are the most useful for children.
2. Teachers post high-frequency words on word walls in the classroom and teach children to read and spell these words using chant and clap procedures.
3. Teachers provide daily opportunities for children to practice word recognition through word work centers and reading and writing practice.
4. Teachers teach four decoding strategies and related skills—phonic analysis, by analogy, syllabic analysis, and morphemic analysis.
5. Teachers encourage children to look at every letter in a word and to decode as much of the word as possible, not to just guess at the word.
6. Teachers involve children in choral reading, repeated reading, listening centers, and other reading activities to develop their reading fluency.
7. Teachers have children choose books written at levels just below their instructional level for fluency-building activities.
8. Teachers involve children in interactive writing, quickwriting, and other writing activities to develop their writing fluency.
9. Teachers observe children as they read and write to determine whether or not they are fluent.
10. Teachers ensure that children become fluent readers and writers by third grade.

Professional References

Adams, M. J. (1990). *Beginning to read: Thinking and learning about print*. Cambridge, MA: MIT Press.

Allington, R. L. (1983). Fluency: The neglected reading goal. *The Reading Teacher, 33*, 556–561.

Allington, R. L. (Ed.). (1998). *Teaching struggling readers*. Newark, DE: International Reading Association.

Calfee, R., & Drum, P. (1986). Research on teaching reading. In M. W. Wittrock (Ed.), *Handbook of research on teaching* (3rd ed., pp. 804–849). New York: Macmillan.

Chall, J. S., Jacobs, V. A., & Baldwin, L. E. (1990). *The reading crisis: Why poor children fall behind*. Cambridge, MA: Harvard University Press.

Cunningham, P. M. (1975–1976). Investigating a synthesized theory of mediated word identification. *Reading Research Quarterly, 11*, 127–143.

Cunningham, P. M. (2000). *Phonics they use: Words for reading and writing* (3rd ed.). New York: HarperCollins.

Delpit, L. (1987). The silenced dialogue: Power and pedagogy in educating other people's children. *Harvard Educational Review, 58*, 280–298.

Dowhower, S. L. (1987). Effects of repeated reading on second-grade transitional readers' fluency and comprehension. *Reading Research Quarterly, 22*, 389–406.

Dowhower, S. L. (1991). Speaking of prosody: Fluency's unattended bedfellow. *Theory Into Practice, 30*, 165–173.

Ehri, L. C., & Robbins, C. (1992). Beginners need some decoding skill to read words by analogy. *Reading Research Quarterly, 27*, 13–26.

Elbow, P. (1973). *Writing without teachers*. Oxford: Oxford University Press.

Elbow, P. (1981). *Writing with power*. Oxford: Oxford University Press.

Eldredge, J. L. (1995). *Teaching decoding in holistic classrooms*. Englewood Cliffs, NJ: Prentice Hall.

Flood, J., & Lapp, D. (1994). Developing literary appreciation and literacy skills: A blueprint for success. *The Reading Teacher, 48*, 76–79.

Gaskins, I. W., Ehri, L. C., Cress, C., O'Hara, C., & Donnelly, K. (1996/1997). Procedures for word learning:

Making discoveries about words. *The Reading Teacher, 50,* 312–326.

Gaskins, R. W., Gaskins, J. W., & Gaskins, I. W. (1991). A decoding program for poor readers—and the rest of the class, too! *Language Arts, 68,* 213–225.

Gough, P. B., Juel, C., & Griffith, P. L. (1992). Reading, spelling, and the orthographic cipher. In P. B. Gough, L. C. Ehri, & R. Treiman (Eds.), *Reading acquisition* (pp. 35–48). Hillsdale, NJ: Erlbaum.

Hiebert, E. H. (1991). The development of word-level strategies in authentic literacy tasks. *Language Arts, 68,* 234–240.

Hitchcock, M. E. (1989). *Elementary students' invented spellings at the correct stage of spelling development.* Unpublished doctoral dissertation, University of Oklahoma, Norman.

Johnson, D. D., & Baumann, J. F. (1984). Word identification. In P. D. Pearson (Ed.), *Handbook of reading research* (pp. 583–608). New York: Longman.

Koskinen, P. A., & Blum, I. H. (1986). Paired repeated reading: A classroom strategy for developing fluent reading. *The Reading Teacher, 40,* 70–75.

Koskinen, P. A., Wilson, R. M., Gambrell, L. B., & Neuman, S. B. (1993). Captioned video and vocabulary learning: An innovative practice in literacy instruction. *The Reading Teacher, 47,* 36–43.

LaBerge, D., & Samuels, S. J. (1976). Toward a theory of automatic information processing in reading. In H. Singer & R. Ruddell (Eds.), *Theoretical models and processes of reading* (pp. 548–579). Newark, DE: International Reading Association.

Martinez, M., Roser, N. L., & Strecker, S. (1998/1999). "I never thought I could be a star": A readers theatre ticket to fluency. *The Reading Teacher, 52,* 326–334.

Opitz, M. F., & Rasinski, T. V. (1998). *Good-bye round robin: Twenty-five effective oral reading strategies.* Portsmouth, NH: Heinemann.

Perfitti, C. A. (1985). *Reading ability.* New York: Oxford University Press.

Pinnell, G. S., & Fountas, I. C. (1998). *Word matters: Teaching phonics and spelling in the reading/writing classroom.* Portsmouth, NH: Heinemann.

Rasinski, T. V. (2000). Speed does matter in reading. *The Reading Teacher, 54,* 146–151.

Reyes, M. de la Luz. (1991). A process approach to literacy using dialogue journals and literature logs with second language learners. *Research in the Teaching of English, 25,* 291–313.

Richards, M. (2000). Be a good detective: Solve the case of oral reading fluency. *The Reading Teacher, 53,* 534–539.

Samuels, S. J. (1979). The method of repeated readings. *The Reading Teacher, 32,* 403–408.

Schreider, P. A. (1980). On the acquisition of reading fluency. *Journal of Reading Behavior, 12,* 177–186.

Shanahan, T. (1988). The reading-writing relationship: Seven instructional principles. *The Reading Teacher, 41,* 636–647.

Snow, C. E., Burns, M. S., & Griffin, P. (Eds.). (1998). *Preventing reading difficulties in young children.* Washington, DC: National Academy Press.

Stanovich, K. E. (1986). Matthew effects in reading: Some consequences of individual differences in the acquisition of literacy. *Reading Research Quarterly, 21,* 360–406.

Stanovich, K. E. (1992). Speculations on the causes and consequences of individual differences in early reading acquisition. In P. B. Gough, L. C. Ehri, & R. Treiman (Eds.), *Reading acquisition* (pp. 307–342). Hillsdale, NJ: Erlbaum.

Tierney, R. J. (1983). Writer-reader transactions: Defining the dimensions of negotiation. In P. L. Stock (Ed.), *Forum: Essays on theory and practice in the teaching of writing* (pp. 147–151). Upper Montclair, NJ: Boynton/Cook.

Tompkins, G. E. (2000). *Teaching writing: Balancing process and product* (3rd ed.). Upper Saddle River, NJ: Merrill/Prentice Hall.

Trachtenburg, P. (1990). Using children's literature to enhance phonics instruction. *The Reading Teacher, 43,* 648–654.

Vellutino, F. R., & Scanlon, D. M. (1987). Phonological coding, phonological awareness, and reading ability: Evidence from a longitudinal and experimental study. *Merrill-Palmer Quarterly, 33,* 321–363.

White, T. G., Sowell, J., & Yanagihara, A. (1989). Teaching elementary students to use word-part clues. *The Reading Teacher, 42,* 302–308.

Yaden, D. B., Jr. (1988). Understanding stories through repeated read-alouds: How many does it take? *The Reading Teacher, 41,* 556–560.

Children's Book References

Carle, E. (1987). *A house for hermit crab.* Saxonville, MA: Picture Book Studio.

Greenaway, F. (1992). *Tide pool.* New York: DK Publishing.

Holling, H. C. (1990). *Pagoo.* Boston: Houghton Mifflin.

Kaplan, R. (1996). *Moving day.* New York: Greenwillow.

MacLachlan, P. (1985). *Sarah, plain and tall.* New York: Harper & Row.

Osborne, M. P. (1995). *Night of the ninjas.* New York: Random House.

Park, B. (1992). *Junie B. Jones and the stupid smelly bus.* New York: Random House.

Pilkey, D. (1997). *The adventures of Captain Underpants.* New York: Scholastic.

Pohl, K. (1987). *Hermit crabs.* Milwaukee: Raintree.

Randell, B. (1994). *Hermit crab.* Crystal Lake, IL: Rigby Books.

Thaler, M. (1989). *The teacher from the black lagoon.* New York: Scholastic.

Tuchman, G. (1997). *Hermit's shiny shell.* New York: Macmillan/McGraw-Hill.

chapter 7

Expanding Children's Knowledge of Words

- How do children learn vocabulary words?

- What is the relationship between vocabulary knowledge and reading?

- How do teachers teach vocabulary?

- What are the components of word study?

Mrs. Dillon's Students Learn About Words

Before Mrs. Dillon's second graders read Kevin Henkes's *Chrysanthemum* (1991), a picture-book story about a mouse named Chrysanthemum who doesn't like her name, Mrs. Dillon brings a book box full of artificial flowers to the classroom. She talks about how she loves flowers, especially these flowers. She takes each flower out of the box as she names it: *rose, gladiola, daisy, chrysanthemum, pansy, delphinium, iris,* and *daffodil.* Children mention names of flowers they like or that grow in their gardens. Mrs. Dillon writes *Chrysanthemum* on the chalkboard, and the children are amazed by the size of the word. Dean notices the word *the* in the middle of the word. Mrs. Dillon tells the class that it is the name of one of the flowers she showed them and also the title of the book they are going to read. Mrs. Dillon's students pride themselves on being word detectives. Several of them guess the flower name right away!

Mrs. Dillon uses shared reading[C] to introduce the book to her students. She reads the book aloud as they follow in their own copies. Afterwards, children identify interesting and important words and phrases for the word wall[C]—a large sheet of butcher paper hanging on the wall—and list them in alphabetical order. Mrs. Dillon's word wall is shown in Figure 7-1. Many words are included in this list, such as *icing, sunniest,* and *absolutely,* that children know the meaning of but don't recognize in print. They are able to figure out how to pronounce other words, such as *wilted,* using their phonics knowledge,

See the Compendium of Instructional Procedures, which follows Chapter 12, for more information on terms marked with the symbol [C].

but they don't know the meaning of the words. In the story, Chrysanthemum "wilted" when someone hurt her feelings. "Does the word mean she cried?" Lizzie asks. Lizzie makes a good guess using the context clues in the story, but she isn't correct, so Mrs. Dillon dramatizes the word to clarify the meaning. They talk about how clever the author was to choose this word because flowers wilt, too. Other words, such as *scrawny, Parcheesi,* and *epilogue,* are new to them; children don't recognize the words or know what they mean.

Mrs. Dillon won't try to teach all of these words. The ones she chooses to focus on are those she thinks are important to the story and also common enough that her students will read them in other books. She chooses some fun words, too; *Parcheesi* is one such word. She brings in a Parcheesi game and teaches the children how to play.

Mrs. Dillon uses a variety of activities and lessons to draw children's attention to words on the word wall and deepen their understanding of individual words and vocabulary concepts. She teaches a minilesson[C] on comparatives and superlatives using *happy–happier–happiest* and *sunny–sunnier–sunniest* as examples, and students brainstorm a list of words that have comparative and superlative forms. Later, students work at the writing center to make pages for a class book on comparatives and superlatives. Children each choose a word from the brainstormed list and write the three forms of the word on a page. Then they draw pictures and write sentences using each word form to complete their page. Other word-study activities include:

- Teach a minilesson on syllables using words from the word wall; *Victoria, Chrysanthemum,* and *delphinium,* for example, all have four syllables.
- Introduce the concept of synonyms using words from the word wall, including *humorous, dainty, extremely, precious,* and *miserable.* Mrs. Dillon uses a children's thesaurus to locate some of the synonyms and shows the class how to

Figure 7-1   A Second-Grade Word Wall on
Chrysanthemum

ABC	DEF	GHI
absolutely	dainty	good luck
bathroom	daisy	happiest
beamed	delphinium	humorous
begrudging	discontented	icing
bloomed	dreadful	impressing
blushed	epilogue	indescribable
butterfly princess	extremely	
carnation	fairy queen	
chocolate cake	fascinating	
Chrysanthemum	frosting	
class musicale		
comfortable		
JKL	**MNO**	**PQR**
jealous	macaroni and cheese	Parcheesi
ketchup	marigold	parents
lily of the valley	messenger	perfect
longingly	mirror	pish
	miserably	pixie
	Mrs. Chud	precious
	Mrs. Twinkle	priceless
	nightmare	prized
		possessions
		route
ST	**UVW**	**XYZ**
scrawny	Victoria	
speechless	welcome	
sprouted	wildly	
success	wilted	
sunniest	winsome	
	wonder	
	worst	

use the book. Then she places the thesaurus in the word work center, and children locate words and synonyms in it and write them on cards that they place in a pocket chart.

- Read other books on flowers, such as *The Rose in My Garden* (Lobel, 1984), *The Flower Alphabet Book* (Pallotta, 1988), *The Reason for a Flower* (Heller, 1983), and *Alison's Zinnia* (Lobel, 1990), and locate examples of chrysanthemums and other flowers mentioned in the stories. Then children reread the books at the reading center or listen to them at the listening center.

- Teach a minilesson on capitalizing names. Children learn that *chrysanthemum* is a flower, but *Chrysanthemum* is a name.

- Have children make word posters illustrating a word from the word wall and using that word in a sentence at the vocabulary center.

- Make a Venn diagram comparing the characters Chrysanthemum and Victoria. The Venn diagram that Mrs. Dillon's class created is shown in Figure 7-2.

Figure 7-2   A Venn Diagram Comparing Two Characters

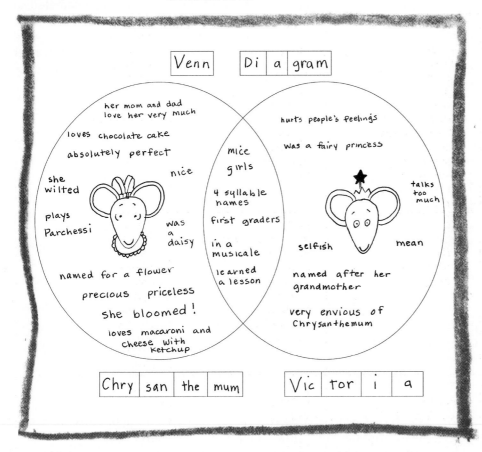

At the end of the unit, one of Mrs. Dillon's students, Lizzie, talks about the words in *Chrysanthemum:*

"I thought this book was going to be hard. Chrysanthemum is a big word and big words are hard sometimes. But this is a good book."

I ask whether she can read all the words in the book, and she is hesitant as she answers.

"Well, not all of them. I know *Chrysanthemum, absolutely perfect, wilted, Mrs. Chud, sunniest dress, delphinium, Mrs. Twinkle, good-luck charms, Parcheesi, . . .*" [she continues reading from the word wall].

"Can you pick out some words from the word wall that describe Chrysanthemum?"

"Yes I can. Chrysanthemum is wilted [and she dramatizes the word as Mrs. Dillon had done]. And Chrysanthemum is miserable because Victoria and Rita and the other kids hurt her feelings, and she is named after a flower, and at the end she bloomed because she likes her name now because Mrs. Twinkle named her baby Chrysanthemum. This book is love. It's good, you know."

My last question was, "How do you know these words?"

"I just do. We read and we talk about books every day. And we write lots of books. My teacher, Mrs. Dillon, says we are 'word detectives.' That means we know lots of words."

Mrs. Dillon incorporates word study throughout the reading process. She introduces a few key words before students read a book, but many other vocabulary activities come after reading, when children are especially interested in learning about the words in the book they have read. Mrs. Dillon creates and posts a word wall in the classroom, and her students choose the words and often write them on the word wall themselves. These words become their words. They refer to the list as they reread, write, and talk about the book, and Mrs. Dillon teaches vocabulary lessons focusing on some of the words.

Teachers use realia—real objects and pictures of objects—to teach vocabulary words to English-language learners because using language to explain words is often ineffective.

Children learn vocabulary by being immersed in words, and Mrs. Dillon engaged her second graders with words as they read and discussed *Chrysanthemum* (Henkes, 1991). Researchers have reported again and again that reading—both reading aloud to children and children reading books themselves—is the best way to expand children's vocabularies. Through reading, children learn many, many words incidentally, and teachers reinforce children's learning by directly teaching some difficult words that are significant to the story or important for general knowledge (Stahl, 1999).

Unfamiliar words are not equally hard or easy to learn; the degree of difficulty depends on what children already know about the word. Graves (1985) identifies four possible situations for unfamiliar words:

1. *Sight word.* Children recognize the word, know what it means when they hear someone say it, and can use it orally, but they don't recognize its written form.
2. *New word.* Children have a concept related to the word, but they are not familiar with the word, either orally or in written form.
3. *New concept.* Children have little or no background knowledge about the concept underlying the word, and they don't recognize the word itself.
4. *New meaning.* Children know the word, but they are unfamiliar with the way the word is used and its meaning in this situation.

The words in *Chrysanthemum* represented all four of these categories. Two sight words were *absolutely* and *sunniest*. As soon as Mrs. Dillon pronounced *absolutely*, the students recognized it as a familiar word that they used orally. She divided it into syllables—*ab-so-lute-ly*—so that children could decode it themselves. For *sunniest*, Mrs. Dillon explained that *sunny + est* is spelled as *sunniest*, and then the students recognized it easily. The flower words—*chrysanthemum, daisy, marigold, carnation,* and *delphinium*—were unfamiliar labels for flowers the children had seen in their neighborhood, but they knew them as "yellow flowers" or "pink flowers" or "blue flowers." Other label words that Mrs. Dillon's students learned were *wilted* and *blushed*. The children were familiar with the concepts, but they did not know the labels. They learned that *wilted* can mean that the flower "drooped" or became limp when it needed water, and that *blushed* means your face turned red because you were modest or embarrassed.

Mrs. Dillon taught two new concepts, and one was much easier to teach than the other. *Epilogue* was a new concept for the children, but because it is concrete, it was easy for them to learn. They understood that it is a short piece telling what happened to the characters after the story ended. *Jealousy* was a much more difficult concept because it is abstract. Mrs. Dillon talked about the concept, using as examples both Victoria's jealousy from the story and family and school experiences that children might be familiar with. Not all children understood the concept or the word, but many did.

Children learned that many words have more than one meaning, too. They learned that *chrysanthemum* is a flower and *Chrysanthemum* could be a girl's name. They knew that a *beam* can be a shaft of light as from a flashlight or a car's headlights, and they learned that the smile on a person's face can "beam," too. They learned the label *wilted* for what a flower does when it is thirsty, and they learned that a person can "wilt," too, when his or her feelings are hurt.

Of the four categories of word learning, the most difficult one for children is the one involving new concepts because they must first learn the concept and then attach a word label and learn the definition. Children often benefit from receiving direct instruction on unfamiliar concepts and the words to describe and explain them.

HOW DO CHILDREN LEARN WORDS?

Children's vocabularies grow at an astonishing rate—about 3,000 words a year, or roughly 7 to 10 new words every day (Nagy & Herman, 1985). By the time children graduate from high school, their vocabularies may reach 25,000 words or more. To learn words at such a prolific rate, it seems obvious that children learn words both in school and outside of school, and that children learn most words incidentally, not through explicit instruction. Reading has the greatest impact on children's vocabulary development, but other activities are important, too. Children learn words through family activities, hobbies, and trips. Television can also have a significant impact on children's vocabularies, especially when children view educational programs and limit the amount of time they spend watching television each day. Teachers often assume that children learn words primarily through the lessons they teach, but children actually learn many more words in other ways.

Levels of Word Knowledge

Children develop knowledge about a word slowly, through repeated exposure to the word. They move from not knowing the word at all, to recognizing that they have seen the word before, and then to a level of partial knowledge where they have a general sense of the word or know one meaning. Finally, children know the word fully; they know multiple meanings of the word and can use it in a variety of ways (Dale & O'Rourke, 1986; Nagy, 1988). The four levels or degrees of word knowledge are:

1. *Unknown word.* I don't know this word.
2. *Initial recognition.* I have seen or heard this word or I can pronounce it, but I don't know the meaning.
3. *Partial word knowledge.* I know one meaning of this word and can use it in a sentence.
4. *Full word knowledge.* I know more than one meaning or several ways to use this word. (Allen, 1999)

Once children reach the third level of word knowledge, they can usually understand the word in context and use it in their writing. Children do not reach the fourth level with all the words they learn. Stahl (1999) describes full word knowledge as "flexible": Children understand the core meaning of a word and how it changes in different contexts.

As children draw and write in response to literature, they practice new vocabulary words.

Incidental Word Learning

Children learn words incidentally, without explicit instruction, all the time, and because children learn so many words this way, teachers know that they do not have to teach the meaning of every unfamiliar word in a text. Three of the most important ways that children learn words incidentally are listening to the teacher read aloud[C] books, reading books independently, and participating in talk activities.

Reading Aloud to Children. The most valuable way that teachers encourage children's incidental learning of vocabulary in the primary grades is by reading aloud (Blachowicz & Fisher, 2002). Teachers read aloud stories to children every day, whether during "story time" or as part of literature focus units, or reading workshop. Interestingly, researchers report that children learn as many words incidentally while listening to teachers read aloud as they do by reading themselves (Stahl, Richek, & Vandevier, 1991).

Children's books are rich resources for word learning. *Hey, Al* (Yorinks, 1986), for example, is an award-winning picture-book story about a man named Al and his dog who leave their city apartment to find happiness on a tropical island paradise, only to learn that you make your own happiness and that things that sound too good to be true usually are. These words are included in the book:

aloft	ferried	plumed
beady	flitted	plunged
blissfully	fortunately	shimmering
cascaded	furiously	shrieked
cooed	gorgeous	sprouted
croaked	heartbroken	squawked
ecstasy	in a frenzy	struggling
exhausted	lush	talented
faithful	paradise	unbelievable

In addition to learning individual words as they listen to *Hey, Al* read aloud, children also hear language that is unique to stories, more complex sentence structures, and more mature linguistic expressions, such as:

Unbelievable! Lush trees, rolling hills, gorgeous grass. Birds flitted to and fro. Waterfalls cascaded into shimmering pools.

But ripe fruit soon spoils.

Eddie, in a frenzy, was flying in circles, higher and higher. (n.p.)

Well-written stories with rich vocabulary, figurative language, and word play are available for reading aloud to children at every grade level. Figure 7-3 lists 15 read-aloud stories recommended for each grade level, prekindergarten through fourth grade. As teachers read and reread these books and involve children in related talk and writing activities, children acquire many new vocabulary words.

Children learn words and concepts as they listen to informational books read aloud, too. They learn the names of animals, plants, and people, terms for physical phenomena and historical events, and other scientific concepts. For example, as kindergartners listen to *Hot and Cold* (Fowler, 1994), they expand their understanding of temperature and learn some of these words:

boil	high	steam
cold	hot	sun
contracts	ice	sweating
cook	low	temperature
cool	melt	thermometer
expand	North Pole	tropics
freeze	shivering	warm
heat	South Pole	weather

And as second or third graders listen to the teacher read aloud *The Magic School Bus Inside a Beehive* (Cole, 1996), they learn about bees and become familiar with these words:

adult	guard bees	pheromones
antennae	hexagon	pollen
beekeepers	hive	pollinate
bees	honey	pupa
buzz	honeycombs	queen bee
cells	insect	social
communicate	jobs	sting
dancing	larvae	swarming
drones	mate	wax
eggs	metamorphosis	wings
flower	nectar	worker bees
flying	nurse bees	

Children don't learn all of these words in a single reading, of course, but through repeated experiences with the words, their level of word knowledge deepens.

Independent Reading. A second way that children learn new words is through daily opportunities for independent reading. In fact, researchers report that the amount of time children spend reading independently is the best predictor of vocabulary growth after second grade (Beck & McKeown, 1991; Nagy, 1988). The books that children read independently should be appropriate for their reading levels. If children read books that are too easy or too hard, they will learn very few new words. Two ways to

Figure 7-3   Books to Read Aloud to Children

Prekindergarten

Bridwell, N. (1988). *Clifford, the big red dog.* New York: Scholastic.

Brown, M. W. (1991). *Goodnight moon.* New York: HarperCollins.

Carle, E. (2000). *Does a kangaroo have a mother, too?* New York: HarperCollins.

Christelow, E. (1991). *Five little monkeys jumping on the bed.* New York: Clarion.

Henkes, K. (2000). *Wemberly worried.* New York: Greenwillow.

Joosse, B. M. (1991). *Mama, do you love me?* San Francisco: Chronicle.

Keats, E. J. (1985). *Peter's chair.* New York: HarperCollins.

Marshall, J. (1996). *Goldilocks and the three bears.* New York: Dial.

Martin, B., Jr. (1996). *Brown bear, brown bear, what do you see?* New York: Holt.

Rathmann, P. (1994). *Goodnight gorilla.* New York: Putnam.

Rey, M., & Rey, H. A. (1974). *Curious George.* Boston: Houghton Mifflin.

Westcott, N. B. (1988). *I know an old lady who swallowed a fly.* Boston: Little, Brown.

Westcott, N. B. (1988). *The lady with the alligator purse.* Boston: Little, Brown.

Wood, A. (1983). *The napping house.* New York: Harcourt Brace.

Zelinsky, P. O. (1990). *The wheels on the bus.* New York: Dutton.

Kindergarten

Asch, F. (1982). *Happy birthday moon.* New York: Aladdin.

Brett, J. (1996). *The mitten.* New York: Putnam.

Brown, M. (1995). *Arthur's new puppy.* Boston: Little, Brown.

Carle, E. (1986). *The very hungry caterpillar.* New York: Putnam.

Eastman, P. D. (1988). *Are you my mother?* New York: Random House.

Galdone, P. (1975). *The gingerbread boy.* New York: Seabury.

Hutchins, P. (1983). *Rosie's walk.* New York: Aladdin.

Keats, E. J. (1981). *The snowy day.* New York: Viking.

Martin, B., Jr., & Archambault, J. (1989). *Chicka chicka boom boom.* New York: Simon & Schuster.

Most, B. (1996). *Cock-a-doodle-moo!* New York: Harcourt Brace.

Numeroff, L. (1987). *If you give a mouse a cookie.* New York: HarperCollins.

Potter, B. (1984). *Peter rabbit.* New York: Viking.

Sendak, M. (1988). *Where the wild things are.* New York: HarperCollins.

Seuss, Dr. (1957). *The cat in the hat.* New York: Random House.

Tafuri, N. (1996). *Have you seen my duckling?* New York: Greenwillow.

First Grade

Bayer, J. (1992). *A my name is Alice.* New York: Dutton.

dePaola, T. (1975). *Strega Nona.* Englewood Cliffs, NJ: Prentice Hall.

Freeman, D. (1976). *Corduroy.* New York: Viking.

Galdone, P. (1984). *Henny Penny.* Boston: Houghton Mifflin.

Henkes, K. (1995). *Chrysanthemum.* New York: Mulberry Books.

Kasza, K. (1996). *The wolf's chicken stew.* New York: Paper Star.

Martin, B. Jr., & Archambault, J. (1988). *Barn dance.* New York: Holt.

Mayer, M. (1992). *There's a nightmare in my closet.* New York: Dutton.

McDermott, G. (1987). *Anansi the spider: A tale from the Ashanti.* New York: Holt.

McGovern, A. (1992). *Too much noise.* Boston: Houghton Mifflin.

Rathmann, P. (1995). *Officer Buckle and Gloria.* New York: Putnam.

Ringgold, F. (1988). *Tar beach.* New York: Crown.

Waber. B. (1979). *Ira sleeps over.* Boston: Houghton Mifflin.

Williams, V. B. (1982). *A chair for my mother.* New York: Mulberry Books.

Yorinks, A. (1986). *Hey, Al.* New York: Farrar, Straus & Giroux.

---

provide opportunities for independent reading are reading workshop and literature circles. Through both of these activities, children have opportunities to read self-selected books that interest them and to learn words in context.

Talk Activities. A third way that children expand their vocabularies is through talk. As children participate in grand conversations[C] about stories and instructional con-

Figure 7-3 (Continued)

Second Grade

Allard, H. (1977). *Miss Nelson is missing!* Boston: Houghton Mifflin.

Baylor, B. (1986). *I'm in charge of celebrations.* New York: Atheneum.

Demi. (1996). *The empty pot.* New York: Holt.

Dorros, A. (1991). *Abuela.* New York: Dutton.

Henkes, K. (1996). *Lily's purple plastic purse.* New York: Greenwillow.

Lionni, L. (1969). *Alexander and the wind-up mouse.* New York: Knopf.

McKissack, P. (1986). *Flossie and the fox.* New York: Dutton.

McKissack, P., & McKissack, F. (1985). *Country mouse and city mouse.* Chicago: Children's Press.

Noble, T. H. (1980). *The day Jimmy's boa ate the wash.* New York: Dial.

Polacco, P. (1990). *Thunder cake.* New York: Philomel.

Rylant, C. (1985). *The relatives came.* New York: Bradbury.

Scieszka, J. (1989). *The true story of the 3 little pigs!* New York: Viking.

Soto, G. (1993). *Too many tamales.* New York: Putnam.

Wood, A. (1985). *King Bidgood's in the bathtub.* New York: Harcourt Brace.

Yolen, J. (1987). *Owl moon.* New York: Philomel.

Third Grade

Barrett, J. (1985). *Cloudy with a chance of meatballs.* New York: Aladdin.

Bunting, E. (1988). *How many days to America?* New York: Clarion.

Cleary, B. (1981). *Ramona Quimby, age 8.* New York: Morrow.

Coerr, E. (1988). *Chang's paper pony.* New York: HarperCollins.

Cohen, B. (1983). *Molly's pilgrim.* New York: Morrow.

Danziger, P. (1994). *Amber Brown is not a crayon.* New York: Putnam.

MacLachlan, P. (1985). *Sarah, plain and tall.* New York: HarperCollins.

McKissack, P. C. (1988). *Mirandy and brother wind.* New York: Knopf.

Pinkney, J. (1999). *The ugly duckling.* New York: Morrow.

Polacco, P. (1988). *Rechenka's eggs.* New York: Philomel.

Steig, W. (1969). *Sylvester and the magic pebble.* New York: Simon & Schuster.

Steptoe, J. (1984). *The story of jumping mouse.* New York: Mulberry.

Zelinsky, P. O. (1986). *Rumpelstiltskin.* New York: Dutton.

Fourth Grade

Blume, J. (1972). *Tales of a fourth grade nothing.* New York: Dutton.

Bunting, E. (1994). *Smoky night.* San Diego: Harcourt Brace.

Coville, B. (1991). *Jeremy Thatcher, dragon hatcher.* New York: Simon & Schuster.

Dahl, R. (1964). *Charlie and the chocolate factory.* New York: Bantam.

Gardiner, J. R. (1980). *Stone Fox.* New York: Crowell.

Howe, D., & Howe, J. (1979). *Bunnicula: A rabbit-tale of mystery.* New York: Atheneum.

Kellogg, S. (1984). *Paul Bunyan.* New York: Morrow.

King-Smith, D. (1995). *Babe: The gallant pig.* New York: Random House.

Naylor, P. R. (1991). *Shiloh.* New York: Atheneum.

Polacco, P. (1994). *Pink and Say.* New York: Philomel.

Rockwell, T. (1973). *How to eat fried worms.* New York: Franklin Watts.

Ruckman, I. (1984). *Night of the twisters.* New York: HarperCollins.

San Souci, R. D. (1989). *The talking eggs.* New York: Dial.

Van Allsburg, C. (1991). *The wretched stone.* Boston: Houghton Mifflin.

White, E. B. (1952). *Charlotte's web.* New York: HarperCollins.

Winter, J. (1988). *Follow the drinking gourd.* New York: Knopf.

versations[C] about informational books, they have many opportunities to use words from books in sentences and to listen to the words used by classmates and the teachers. Through these repeated exposures to words, children move through the levels of word knowledge. Teachers support children's developing word knowledge by using vocabulary from books themselves and encouraging children to pronounce new words and use them in sentences themselves.

Why Is Word Knowledge Important?

Word knowledge and reading achievement are closely related. Children with larger vocabularies are more capable readers because they develop word knowledge through reading (Nagy, 1988; Stahl, 1999). The idea that capable readers learn more vocabulary because they read more is an example of the Matthew effect (Stanovich, 1986). The Matthew effect suggests that "the rich get richer and the poor get poorer" in vocabulary development and other aspects of reading. Capable readers become better readers because they read more, and the books they read are more challenging and have sophisticated vocabulary words. The gulf between more capable and less capable readers grows larger because less capable readers read less and the books they do read are less challenging.

EXPLICIT TEACHING OF WORDS

Vocabulary instruction plays an important role in primary classrooms (Rupley, Logan, & Nichols, 1998/1999). Teachers highlight important vocabulary words related to literature focus units and thematic units and teach minilessons about compound words, synonyms and antonyms, multiple meanings of words, and other word-study skills. These lessons focus on words that children are reading and learning in thematic units (Blachowicz & Lee, 1991). The lessons are even more important to children who are English-language learners, because these children rely more heavily on explicit instruction than native speakers do. Figure 7-4 lists guidelines for teaching vocabulary.

Characteristics of Effective Instruction

During the primary grades, teachers' goals in teaching vocabulary are to expand children's word knowledge and to develop their awareness of words. According to Carr and Wixon (1986), Nagy (1988), and Allen (1999), effective vocabulary instruction exemplifies five characteristics:

1. *Connections to background knowledge.* For vocabulary instruction to be effective, children must relate new words to their background knowledge. Because learning words in isolation is rarely effective, teachers should teach words in concept clusters whenever possible.
2. *Repetition.* Children need to read, write, or say words 8 to 10 times or more before they recognize them automatically. Repetition helps children remember the words they are learning.
3. *Higher-level word knowledge.* The focus of instruction should be to help children develop higher-level word knowledge; just having children memorize definitions or learn synonyms will not lead to full word knowledge.
4. *Strategy learning.* Not only are children learning the meanings of particular words through vocabulary lessons, they are developing knowledge and strategies for learning new words independently.
5. *Meaningful use.* Children need to be actively involved in word-study activities and opportunities to use the words in projects related to literature focus units and thematic units.

Teachers apply these five characteristics when they teach minilessons about vocabulary. Too often, vocabulary instruction has emphasized looking up definitions of words in

Figure 7-4   Guidelines for Teaching Vocabulary

1. Choose Words to Study
Teachers and children choose words for vocabulary instruction from books they are reading and from thematic units. These words should be content-rich words, not high-frequency words, such as *what* and *because.* Vocabulary instruction grows out of words that *children* are reading and concepts they are learning about in the classroom.

2. Highlight Words on Word Walls
Children and teachers select important and interesting words to display on word walls during literature focus units and thematic units, and they use separate word walls for each unit. Teachers highlight a few key terms before reading, and then children and teachers choose other words to add during and after reading.

3. Develop Full Word Knowledge
Children need to learn more than just single definitions of words to develop full word knowledge. They need to learn multiple meanings of words, how root words and affixes combine to affect meaning, synonyms, antonyms, and homonyms, word histories, and figurative meanings.

4. Teach Minilessons
Teachers teach children the meanings of individual words, vocabulary concepts, and word-learning strategies through minilessons. In a minilesson, teachers introduce the topic, present information, provide a structured practice activity, review, and provide application activities.

5. Plan Word-Study Activities
Teachers plan word-study activities so that children can explore words after reading. Activities include word posters, word maps, dramatizing words, word sorts, word chains, and semantic feature analysis.

6. Read Aloud to Children Every Day
Teachers read aloud stories and informational books every day as part of literature focus units, reading workshop, and theme cycles. As they listen to these books and participate in discussions and word-study activities, children learn concepts and vocabulary words.

7. Promote Wide Reading
Children learn only a small percentage of the 3,000 or more words they learn each year through teacher-directed lessons and activities; wide reading is far more important in developing children's vocabularies. Teachers provide daily opportunities for children to read independently for at least 15 minutes in grades 1–3 and 30 minutes in grades 4–8. They also read aloud stories and informational books to children every day.

a dictionary, but this is not a particularly effective activity, at least not as it has been used in the past.

Minilessons. Teachers present minilessons to teach key words, vocabulary concepts, and strategies for unlocking word meanings. These lessons should focus on words that children are reading and writing and involve children in meaningful activities.

The minilesson on page 184 shows how a first-grade teacher teaches vocabulary as part of a thematic unit on the four seasons.

Minilesson

Topic: Word Sort
Grade: First Grade
Time: Two 30-minute periods

Mrs. Garcia's first graders are studying the four seasons. The teacher has read aloud several informational books about the seasons, and the children have added more than 25 words to the word wall that reflect the weather, holidays, clothes, plant and animal changes, and activities related to each season.

1. Introduce the Topic

Mrs. Garcia brings her 19 first graders together on the rug near their weather word wall. She asks children to take turns identifying familiar words. "Who can name a *spring* word?" she asks. Anthony points to *tadpoles* and reads the word aloud. Other children name *summer, autumn,* and *winter* words. Mrs. Garcia praises the children for including words representing all four seasons on their word wall.

2. Share Examples

Mrs. Garcia hangs up four narrow pocket charts (each with 10 pockets) and labels each pocket chart with the name of a season. She uses word cards to write the words the children have identified and asks other children to place these word cards in the appropriate pocket charts. The words *tadpoles* and *rain* are added to the *Spring* pocket chart, *swimming* and *crops* are added to the *Summer* pocket chart, *Halloween* and *Thanksgiving* to the *Autumn* pocket chart, and *snow* and *Christmas* to the *Winter* pocket chart. The children also identify several other words representing each season from the word wall to add to the pocket charts.

3. Provide Information

To locate additional words for each chart, the children suggest that they look in some of the books they have read or listened to Mrs. Garcia read aloud. Mrs. Garcia rereads an informational book about the seasons, and the children look through other familiar books. The teacher divides the children into four groups and asks each group to find words related to a different season. The children identify new words, and these are written on word cards and placed in the appropriate chart.

4. Guide Practice

During the second day of the lesson, Mrs. Garcia divides the class into groups of two or three children and gives each group a packet of small word cards and a large sheet of construction paper divided into four columns with the names of the seasons written at the top of the columns. The words on the small cards are the same as the words on the larger cards used the previous day in the large-group part of the lesson. The children practice reading the cards and sorting them according to season. Mrs. Garcia moves around the classroom, providing assistance as needed and monitoring the children's work.

5. Assess Learning

Mrs. Garcia puts several sets of the word cards and several construction paper diagrams in the word work center for the children to practice reading and sorting during center time. Later, she will have the children cut apart a list of the four seasons words and glue them in the appropriate columns on a construction paper diagram. She will assess these products.

Components of Word Study

Word knowledge involves more than learning definitions. Seven components of word study are:

1. Concepts and word meanings
2. Multiple meanings
3. Compound words
4. Synonyms
5. Antonyms
6. Homonyms
7. Figurative meanings

Children learn more than just the definition of a word; they learn one or more meanings for a word, how the word functions in the sentence, and synonyms and antonyms to compare and contrast meanings. Sometimes they confuse words they are learning with homonyms that sound or are spelled the same. And, children learn about idioms and figurative meanings of words.

Concepts and Word Meanings. Children use words to label concepts, and they learn words best when they are related to a concept. Consider the words *axle, groundwater, buffalo chips, wagon train, ford, fur trader, dysentery, outpost, guide, mountain men, oxen, Bowie knife, snag, cut-off, cholera, winch,* and *prairie dog:* They all relate to pioneers traveling west on the Oregon Trail. When fourth graders read a book about the Oregon Trail, for example, or during a social studies unit on the westward movement, children learn many of these words by connecting them to their Oregon Trail schema or concept. It is easier to learn a group of words relating to a concept than to learn a group of unrelated words.

Multiple Meanings of Words. Many words have more than one meaning. For some words, multiple meanings develop for the noun and verb forms of the word, but sometimes meanings develop in other ways. The word *bark,* for example, can mean the outside covering of a tree or the sound a dog makes. Young children assume that each word has one meaning, but they gradually acquire additional meanings for words during the primary grades. Children usually learn these new meanings through reading. When a familiar word is used in a new way, children often notice the new application and may be curious enough to ask a classmate or the teacher about the meaning or check the meaning in a dictionary.

Compound Words. Many English words are compound words, and the meaning is usually clear from the word parts and the context in which the word or phrase is used, as in the words *fingernail, birthday, footprint, earthquake,* and *anteater.*

Synonyms. Words that have nearly the same meaning as other words are synonyms. English has so many synonyms because many words have been borrowed from other languages. Synonyms are useful because they provide options, allowing writers to be more precise. Think of all the synonyms for the word *cold: cool, chilly, frigid, icy, frosty,* and *freezing.* Each word has a different shade of meaning: *Cool* means moderately cold; *chilly* is uncomfortably cold; *frigid* is intensely cold; *icy* means very cold; *frosty* means covered with frost; and *freezing* is so cold that water changes into ice. Our language would be limited if we had only the word *cold*.

Teachers should be careful to articulate the differences among synonyms. Nagy (1988) emphasizes that teachers should focus on teaching concepts and related words, not just provide single-word definitions using synonyms. For example, to tell a child that *frigid* means *cold* provides only limited information. And, when a child says, "I want my sweater because it's frigid in here," it shows that the child does not understand the different degrees of cold; there's a big difference between *chilly* and *frigid*. A list of synonyms that are appropriate for primary-grade students is presented in Figure 7-5.

Antonyms. Words that express opposite meanings are antonyms. Antonyms for the word *loud*, for example, are *soft, subdued, quiet, silent, inaudible, sedate, somber, dull,* and *colorless*. These words express shades of meaning just as synonyms do, and some opposites are more appropriate for one meaning of *loud* than for another. When loud means *gaudy*, for instance, opposites are *somber, dull,* and *colorless*; when loud means *noisy*, the opposites are *quiet, silent,* and *inaudible*. A list of antonyms for primary grade students is also included in Figure 7-5.

Students in third and fourth grades learn to use a thesaurus to locate both synonyms and antonyms. *A First Thesaurus* (Wittels & Greisman, 1985) is an excellent thesaurus designed for primary students. Children use this reference book to locate more effective words when revising their writing and for word-study activities.

Homonyms. Words that sound alike but are spelled differently, such as *right* and *write, to, too,* and *two,* and *there, their,* and *there,* are homonyms (also called homophones). A list of homophones is also presented in Figure 7-5. Sometimes children confuse the meanings of these words, but more often they confuse their spellings.

Many books of homonyms are available for children, including Gwynne's *The King Who Rained* (1970), *A Chocolate Moose for Dinner* (1976), *The Sixteen Hand Horse* (1980), and *A Little Pigeon Toad* (1988); Maestro's *What's a Frank Frank? Tasty Homograph Riddles* (1984); *What in the World Is a Homophone?* (Presson, 1996); and *Eight Ate: A Feast of Homonym Riddles* (Terban, 1982).

Teachers in the primary grades introduce the concept of homonyms and teach the easier pairs, including *see-sea, I-eye, right-write,* and *dear-deer*. In the upper grades, teachers focus on the homophones that children continue to confuse, such as *there-their-they're* and the more sophisticated pairs, such as *flare-flair*.

Intensive study is necessary because homonyms are confusing to many children. The words sound alike and the spellings are often very similar—sometimes only one letter differs or one letter is added: *pray-prey, hole-whole*. And sometimes the words have the same letters, but they vary in sequence: *bear-bare* and *great-grate*.

Teachers teach minilessons to explain the concept of homonyms and make charts of the homophone pairs and triplets. Calling children's attention to the spelling and meaning differences helps to clarify the words. Children can also make homophone posters, as shown in Figure 7-6. On the posters, children draw pictures and write sentences to contrast the homophones. Displaying these posters in the classroom reminds students of the differences between the words.

Figurative Meanings of Words. Many words have both literal and figurative meanings. Literal meanings are the explicit, dictionary meanings, and figurative meanings are metaphorical or use figures of speech. For example, consider the word *red*. Kindergartners know the literal meaning of the color red. They recognize the color word and

Figure 7-5 — Words for Word-Study Activities

Synonyms	Antonyms	Homonyms
angry-mad	add-subtract	ant-aunt
big-large	asleep-awake	ate-eight
boat-ship	back-front	bare-bear
build-construct	big-little	be-bee
cheap-inexpensive	black-white	blew-blue
close-shut	boy-girl	brake-break
correct-right	brother-sister	buy-by-bye
dirty-filthy	clean-dirty	cell-sell
earth-world	come-go	cent-scent-sent
fast-quick	dangerous-safe	close-clothes
few-several	daughter-son	dear-deer
finish-end	day-night	dew-do-due
foolish-silly	dog-cat	eye-I
forgive-excuse	early-late	flew-flu
funny-amusing	east-west	flour-flower
gift-present	fast-slow	hair-hare
good-fine	friend-enemy	hear-here
happy-glad	go-stop	hi-high
hard-difficult	good-bad	hoarse-horse
hurry-rush	happy-sad	hole-whole
joy-pleasure	hot-cold	hour-our
know-understand	in-out	knew-new
look-see	laugh-cry	knight-night
mistake-error	light-dark	knot-not
ocean-sea	love-hate	made-maid
often-frequently	man-woman	mail-male
pain-ache	many-few	meat-meet
quiet-silent	morning-evening	one-won
rich-wealthy	mother-father	pail-pale
rude-impolite	near-far	pair-pear
sad-unhappy	noisy-quiet	peace-piece
save-keep	north-south	plain-plane
scare-frighten	off-on	red-read
sick-ill	open-close	right-write
small-little	play-work	road-rode
smart-intelligent	remember-forget	sail-sale
smile-grin	rich-poor	sea-see
start-begin	same-different	sew-so
steal-rob	smooth-rough	son-sun
talk-speak	strong-weak	stake-steak
tasty-delicious	tight-loose	tail-tale
thin-slender	truth-lie	their-there-they're
trash-garbage	up-down	threw-through
woman-lady	wet-dry	to-too-two
wrong-incorrect	yes-no	wait-weight
yell-shout	young-old	wood-would

Figure 7-6   A Second Grader's Homophone Poster

can choose the red crayon from their crayon box, but when third graders read "When everyone started to laugh, he turned red," they may or may not understand that in this sentence, *red* is used figuratively to mean that he was embarrassed.

Two types of figurative language, similes and metaphors, both compare something to something else. A simile is a comparison signaled by the use of *like* or *as*. "The crowd was as rowdy as a bunch of marauding monkeys" and "My apartment was like an oven after the air conditioning broke" are two examples of similes. In contrast, a metaphor compares two things by implying that one is something else, without using *like* or *as*. "The children were frisky puppies playing in the yard" is an example. Metaphors are stronger comparisons, as these examples show:

Simile: She's as cool as a cucumber.
Metaphor: She's a cool cucumber.

Simile: The dead tree looked like a skeleton in the moonlight.
Metaphor: The dead tree was a skeleton in the moonlight.

Children learn traditional similes such as "happy as a clam" and "high as a kite," and later they notice and invent fresh, unexpected figurative expressions. To introduce figurative language to primary-grade students, kindergarten teachers often read Audrey Wood's *Quick as a Cricket* (1982). Teachers use these common (and somewhat trite) comparisons with young children so that they become familiar with them. Then teachers can encourage second and third graders to think of other ways to express the same idea. For example, instead of the traditional "quiet as a mouse," children can invent new expressions, such as "quiet as a whisper," "quiet as a stone," and "quiet as midnight." Of course, some children will suggest unusual comparisons, such as "quiet as a flower" and "quiet as a turtle." Teachers should encourage children to brainstorm as many comparisons as possible and then choose the most effective ones to use.

Once children begin to experiment with figurative language, they are also ready to begin changing similes to metaphors so that "The little girl was as quiet as a mouse" changes to "the little girl was a mouse" or "the little girl was a whisper." The "stone," "midnight," "flower," and "turtle" comparisons would not work as effectively in the sentence about the little girl. Children need to infer the "quiet" quality of a mouse or a whisper in order to understand these metaphors. Although it is true that a stone, midnight, a flower, and a turtle might all be quiet, they all better represent other qualities: A stone suggests a hard quality, midnight a dark and scary quality, a flower a colorful quality, and a turtle a slow and deliberate quality.

Children also learn some common idioms and sayings during the primary grade, including "easy as pie," "raining cats and dogs," "frog in your throat," "ants in your pants," and "when the cat's away, the mice will play." A handy resource for information about idioms and sayings is Marvin Terban's *Scholastic Dictionary of Idioms: More Than 600 Phrases, Sayings, and Expressions* (1996). Some sayings can be traced back to the Bible or to ancient Rome and Greece; others are from the Middle Ages or came into use more recently. "Put your John Hancock on the line," for example, originated in 1776. John Hancock, President of the Continental Congress, was the first to sign the Declaration of Independence, and he is reported to have explained to the other delegates that he was writing his name big enough so that King George III would have no trouble reading it. "John Hancock" means "name" in this saying, and the story behind the saying clarifies the meaning.

Parents and teachers often use idioms and other sayings as they talk with children, and children can often infer the figurative meaning from the saying itself or the context in which it is used. However, sometimes the meaning is less obvious and young children or English-language learners don't understand. When children look confused or don't respond, teachers need to clarify the meaning of the saying or ask other children to explain it.

Choosing Words to Study

To link to Merriam-Webster's Daily Buzzword to learn a new word each day, visit our Companion Website at www.prenhall.com/tompkins

Teachers choose the most important words from stories and informational books to teach. Important words include words that are essential to understanding the text, words that may confuse children, and general utility words that children will use as they read other books (Allen, 1999).

Teachers should avoid words that are unrelated to the central concept of the book or unit or words that are too conceptually difficult for children. As teachers choose words to highlight and for word-study activities, they consider their students, the book being read, and the instructional context. For example, a kindergarten teacher read aloud *The Three Bears* (Galdone, 1972) and *Somebody and the Three Blairs* (Tolhurst, 1990). Afterwards, she and the children chose these 10 key words and phrases to write on cards:

Papa Bear	porridge
Mama Bear	rocking chair
Baby Bear	bed
Goldilocks	just right
girl	home

Figure 7-7

A Kindergartner's Word Card for
Rocking Chair

The illustrated word card for *rocking chair* is shown in Figure 7-7. In addition to the child's drawing and the teacher's label, the child wrote "Baby Bear's rocking chair" from right to left using invented spelling. These words are vocabulary words—content-related words—not high-frequency words such as *who* and *this*. The kindergartners worked in pairs to illustrate the cards, and they displayed them on their pocket chart word wall. Over the next few days, they referred to the words as they drew and labeled a mural about the stories and made books about them. Having the words on the word wall helped the children to be more precise in the words they used to respond to the stories.

Spotlighting Words on Word Walls

Teachers post word walls in the classroom, made from large sheets of butcher paper and divided into sections for each letter of the alphabet, as Mrs. Dillon did in the vignette at the beginning of this chapter. Children and the teacher write interesting, confusing, and important words on the word wall. Usually children choose the words to write on the word wall and may even do the writing themselves. Teachers add other important words that children have not chosen. Words are added to the word wall as they come up in books children are reading or during a thematic unit, not in advance. Children use the word wall to locate a word they want to use during a grand conversation or to check the spelling of a word they are writing, and teachers use the words listed on the word wall for word-study activities.

Some teachers use pocket charts and word cards instead of butcher paper for their word walls. This way the word cards can easily be used for word-study activities, and they can be sorted and rearranged on the pocket chart. After the book or unit is completed, teachers punch holes in one end of the cards and hang them on a ring. Then

Figure 7-8   A Third Grader's Word Wall for
Molly's Pilgrim

A apartment	B	C clothespins	D dolls
E English Elizabeth	F freedom	G God	H homework hot as fire holiday
I	J Jewish	K	L
M Molly Miss Stickley Mama modern	N	O	PQ pilgrim Plymouth peace
R Russia religious freedom	S	T Thanksgiving Tabernacles	U
V	W Winter Hill	XY Yiddish	Z

the collection of word cards can be placed in the writing center for children to use in writing activities.

Word walls play an important role in vocabulary learning. The words are posted in the classroom so that they are visible to all children, and because they are so visible, children will read them more often and refer to the chart when writing. Their availability will also remind teachers to use the words for word-study activities.

Children also make individual word walls by dividing a sheet of paper into 24 boxes, labeling the boxes with the letters of the alphabet; they put P and Q together in one box and X and Y in another. Then children write important words and phrases in the boxes as they read and discuss the book. Figure 7-8 shows a third grader's word wall for *Molly's Pilgrim* (Cohen, 1983), a story about modern-day pilgrims.

Even though 25, 50, or more words may be added to the word wall, not all of them will be directly taught to students. As they plan, teachers create lists of words that will probably be written on word walls during the lesson. From this list, teachers choose the key words—the ones that are critical to understanding the book or the unit—and these are the words that they present in minilessons.

Activities for Exploring Words

Word-study activities provide opportunities for children to explore the meaning of words listed on word walls, other words related to books they are reading, and words they are learning during social studies and science units. Through these activities, children develop concepts, learn the meanings of words, and make associations among

Teachers use words from the word wall for minilessons and other vocabulary activities.

words. None of these activities require children to simply write words and their definitions or to use the words in sentences or in a contrived story.

Word Posters. Children choose a word from the word wall and write it on a small poster. Then they draw and color a picture to illustrate the word. They also use the word in a sentence on the poster. This is one way that children can visualize the meaning of a word.

Word Maps. Word maps are another way to visualize a word's meaning (Duffelmeyer & Banwart, 1992–1993; Schwartz & Raphael, 1985). Children draw a cluster^C on a small card or a sheet of paper and write a word from the word wall in the center circle. Then they draw rays from the center and write important information about the word to make connections between the word and what they are reading or studying. Three kinds of information are incorporated in a word map: a category for the word, examples, and characteristics or associations. Figure 7-9 shows a word map that first graders made on *fox,* after reading *Rosie's Walk* (Hutchins, 1968). For the examples section, they identified four stories about foxes that they had read.

Dramatizing Words. Children each choose a word from the word wall and dramatize it for classmates, who then try to guess the word. Sometimes an action is a more effective way to explain a word than a verbal definition; that's what Mrs. Dillon found when she dramatized the word *wilted* for her second graders. Dramatization is an especially effective activity for children who are learning English as a second language.

Figure 7-9 First Graders' Word Map on *Fox*

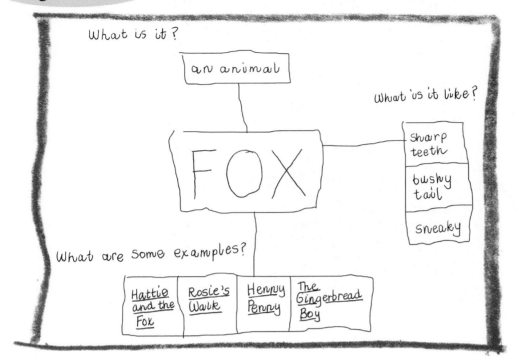

Word Sorts. Students sort a collection of words taken from the word wall into two or more categories in a word sort[C] (Bear, Invernizzi, Templeton, & Johnston, 2000). Usually children choose the categories they will use for the sort, but sometimes the teacher chooses them. For example, words from a story might be sorted by character, or words from a thematic unit on machines might be sorted according to type of machine. Figure 7-10 presents a word wall for *Paul Bunyan* (Kellogg, 1984) and a word sort using words from the word wall. The words can be written on cards, and then children sort a pack of word cards into piles. Or, children can cut apart a list of words, sort them into categories, and then paste the grouped words together.

Word Chains. Children choose a word from the word wall and then identify three or four words to sequence before or after the word to make a chain. For example, the word *tadpole* can be chained this way—*egg, tadpole, frog*—or words describing temperature can be chained this way—*freezing, cold, cool, warm, hot, boiling.* Children can draw and write their chains on a sheet of paper, or they can make a chain out of construction paper and write the words on each link.

Semantic Feature Analysis. Children select a group of related words and then make a chart to classify them according to distinguishing characteristics (Heimlich & Pittelman, 1986). A semantic feature analysis on the solar system is presented in Figure 7-11. Children completed the semantic feature analysis by placing a check mark, a circle, or a question mark under the characteristics.

Figure 7-10   A Word Wall and a Word Sort Using Words From *Paul Bunyan*

A	B	CD	EF
astonishing	backwoods	damage	extremely helpful
Appalachian Mountains	blue snow	deer	flip
ambushed	Babe	cradle	flapjacks
Arizona	beard	Creampuff Fatty	field of clover
ax	Big Tim Burr	camp buildings	exploded
Alaska	bunkhouses	colossal	extraordinary
	blizzard	den	
		depressed	
		discouraged	
		California	

G	HI	JKL	M
grizzlies	Hardjaw Murphy	largest	Maine
Gumberoos	Hackett brothers	logging	mountain ranges
griddle	hibernated	lumber wagon	
Great Lakes		legendary	
Great Plains		lumbermen	
Grand Canyon		longevity	

NO	PQ	R	S
Ox calf	Paul Bunyan	raced	strongest
Ole	pine tree	rescued	smartest
	pioneer	rough-and-tumble	sturdy
	popcorn	rumpus	Sourdough Slim
	Pacific Ocean	Rocky Mountains	St. Lawrence River
			sunglasses

T	UV	WX	YZ
tall tale	Underground ogres	wilderness	
thunderous note	Vermont maple syrup	wrestled	
Texas varmints	unusual size	weak	

Words Describing Paul Bunyan	Places Paul Bunyan Created	Places Paul Bunyan Visited	Words Describing Babe
strongest	St. Lawrence River	Maine	ox calf
smartest	Grand Canyon	Texas	blue
extremely helpful	Rocky Mountains	Arizona	depressed
colossal	Great Lakes	Great Plains	sturdy
legendary		California	unusual size
extraordinary		Pacific Ocean	
		Alaska	

Figure 7-11 A Semantic Feature Analysis on the Solar System

	is an inner planet	is an outer planet	has an atmosphere	supports life	made of rock and metal	made of gas	has moons	has rings
Mercury	✓	O	O	O	✓	O	O	O
Venus	✓	O	✓	O	✓	O	O	O
Earth	?	?	✓	✓	✓	O	✓	O
Mars	O	✓	✓	O	✓	O	✓	O
Jupiter	O	✓	O	O	O	✓	✓	✓
Saturn	O	✓	O	O	✓	O	✓	✓
Uranus	O	✓	O	O	✓	O	✓	✓
Neptune	O	✓	✓	O	✓	O	✓	O
Pluto	O	✓	O	O	✓	O	✓	O

Code: ✓ = yes

O = no

? = don't know

Review

Children add approximately **3,000 words** to their vocabularies every year. They learn some of the words through instruction that teachers provide, but they learn far more words incidentally through reading, writing, watching television, and other activities outside of school. Teachers have an important role in providing opportunities for incidental word learning through reading and teaching children how to unlock word meanings. Words should always be studied as part of meaningful reading and writing activities or content-area study. Teachers post vocabulary word walls in the classroom, teach minilessons using word wall words, and involve children in a variety of word-study activities, including word maps and word sorts. The feature that follows presents a list of recommended practices that effective teachers use in teaching vocabulary.

How Effective Teachers . . .

Expand Children's Knowledge of Words

Effective Practices

1. Teachers vary how they teach a word depending on what children already know about the word.
2. Teachers read aloud to children every day because children learn many new words incidentally as they listen to books read aloud.
3. Teachers provide daily opportunities for children to read stories and informational books because children learn many new words incidentally through reading.
4. Teachers involve children in grand conversations, instructional conversations, and other talk activities to provide practice using new words.
5. Teachers help children develop a repertoire of word-learning strategies in order to learn words incidentally.
6. Teachers choose the most useful words from the word wall for vocabulary activities.
7. Teachers explicitly teach minilessons on individual words, new concepts, and multiple meanings of words.
8. Teachers explicitly teach minilessons on vocabulary concepts, including antonyms, synonyms, compound words, and homophones.
9. Teachers explicitly teach minilessons on figurative language, including metaphors, similes, and idioms.
10. Teachers involve children in meaningful word-study activities, such as word maps, dramatizing words, word sorts, and semantic feature analysis, that are related to books children are reading and to thematic units.

Professional References

Allen, J. (1999). *Words, words, words.* Portsmouth, NH: Heinemann.

Bear, D. R., Invernizzi, M., Templeton, S., & Johnston, F. (2000). *Words their way: Word study for phonics, vocabulary, and spelling instruction.* Upper Saddle River, NJ: Merrill/Prentice Hall.

Beck, I., & McKeown, M. (1991). Conditions of vocabulary acquisition. In R. Barr, M. Kamil, P. Mosenthal, & P. D. Pearson (Eds.), *Handbook of reading research* (Vol. 2, pp. 789–814). White Plains, NY: Longman.

Blachowicz, C., & Fisher, P. J. (2002). Teaching vocabulary in all classrooms (2nd ed.). Upper Saddle River, NJ: Merrill/Prentice Hall.

Blachowicz, C. L. Z., & Lee, J. J. (1991). Vocabulary development in the whole literacy classroom. *The Reading Teacher, 45,* 188–195.

Carr, E., & Wixon, K. K. (1986). Guidelines for evaluating vocabulary instruction. *Journal of Reading, 29,* 588–595.

Dale, E., & O'Rourke, J. (1986). *Vocabulary building.* Columbus, OH: Zaner-Bloser.

Duffelmeyer, F. A., & Banwart, B. H. (1992–1993). Word maps for adjectives and verbs. *The Reading Teacher, 46,* 351–353.

Graves, M. (1985). *A word is a word . . . or is it?* Portsmouth, NH: Heinemann.

Heimlich, J. E., & Pittelman, S. D. (1986). *Semantic mapping: Classroom applications*. Newark, DE: International Reading Association.

Nagy, W. E. (1988). *Teaching vocabulary to improve reading comprehension*. Urbana, IL: ERIC Clearinghouse on Reading and Communication Skills and the National Council of Teachers of English and the International Reading Association.

Nagy, W. E., & Herman, P. (1985). Incidental vs. instructional approaches to increasing reading vocabulary. *Educational Perspectives, 23,* 16–21.

Rupley, W. H., Logan, J. W., & Nichols, W. D. (1998/1999). Vocabulary instruction in balanced reading programs. *The Reading Teacher, 52,* 336–346.

Schwartz, R., & Raphael, T. (1985). Concept of definition: A key to improving students' vocabulary. *The Reading Teacher, 39,* 198–205.

Stahl, S. A. (1999). *Vocabulary development*. Cambridge, MA: Brookline Books.

Stahl, S. A., Richek, M. G., & Vandevier, R. (1991). Learning word meanings through listening: A sixth grade replication. In J. Zutell & S. McCormick (Eds.), *Learning factors/teacher factors: Issues in literacy research. Fortieth yearbook of the National Reading Conference* (pp. 185–192). Chicago: National Reading Conference.

Stanovich, K. E. (1986). Matthew effects in reading: Some consequences of individual differences in the acquisition of literacy. *Reading Research Quarterly, 21,* 360–406.

Children's Book References

Cohen, B. (1983). *Molly's pilgrim*. New York: Morrow.

Cole, J. (1996). *The magic school bus inside a beehive*. New York: Scholastic.

Fowler, A. (1994). *Hot and cold*. Chicago: Childrens Press.

Galdone, P. (1972). *The three bears*. New York: Clarion Books.

Gwynne, F. (1970). *The king who rained*. New York: Windmill Books.

Gwynne, F. (1976). *A chocolate moose for dinner*. New York: Windmill Books.

Gwynne, F. (1980). *The sixteen hand horse*. New York: Prentice Hall.

Gwynne, F. (1988). *A little pigeon toad*. New York: Simon & Schuster.

Heller, R. (1983). *The reason for a flower*. New York: Grosset & Dunlap.

Henkes, K. (1991). *Chrysanthemum*. New York: Greenwillow.

Hutchins, P. (1968). *Rosie's walk*. New York: Macmillan.

Kellogg, S. (1984). *Paul Bunyan*. New York: Mulberry Books.

Lobel, A. (1984). *The rose in my garden*. New York: Morrow.

Lobel, A. (1990). *Alison's zinnia*. New York: Greenwillow.

Maestro, G. (1984). *What's a frank Frank? Tasty homograph riddles*. New York: Clarion Books.

Pallotta, J. (1988). *The flower alphabet book*. Watertown, MA: Charlesbridge.

Presson, L. (1996). *What in the world is a homophone?* New York: Barron's.

Terban, M. (1982). *Eight ate: A feast of homonym riddles*. New York: Clarion Books.

Terban, M. (1996). *Scholastic dictionary of idioms: More than 600 phrases, sayings, and expressions*. New York: Scholastic.

Tolhurst, M. (1990). *Somebody and the three Blairs*. New York: Orchard Books.

Wittels, H., & Greisman, J. (1985). *A first thesaurus*. New York: Golden Books.

Wood, A. (1982). *Quick as a cricket*. London: Child's Play.

Yorinks, A. (1986). *Hey, Al*. New York: Farrar, Straus & Giroux.

chapter 8

Guiding Children's Comprehension

chapter
QUESTIONS

- What is comprehension?

- How do teachers teach and assess comprehension?

- Which strategies and skills do readers and writers learn?

- How do teachers teach strategies and skills?

Mrs. Donnelly Focuses on Comprehension

As part of a unit on weather, Mrs. Donnelly's third-grade class reads *Cloudy With a Chance of Meatballs* (Barrett, 1978), a fantasy picture book about the town of Chewandswallow, where food and drink fall from the sky like rain three times each day. After Mrs. Donnelly introduces the book as an "absurd" fantasy, some children read it independently, others read it with a buddy, and seven children read it with the teacher. Those children reading the book with Mrs. Donnelly stop reading at predetermined points and use the say something strategy[C] to talk about the story (Hoyt, 1999). Children ask questions, connect events to their own lives, make predictions, and express how they are feeling about the book. When children stop reading after the page about the salt and pepper winds and the tomato tornado, they make these comments:

See the Compendium of Instructional Procedures, which follows Chapter 12, for more information on terms marked with the symbol [C].

Jared:	"It's real bad. I think they are going to die."
Sara:	"Yeah, at first it was fun to be in Chewandswallow but now it's not any fun at all."
Mike:	"I think they should move away."
Vanessa:	"Or turn off the weather."
Mike:	"They can't do that."
Annie:	"Well, maybe they can, like how you can turn a television on and off."
Perry:	"All I can say is that the weather is weird. It's out of control."
Lizzy:	"This story is like the *Wizard of Oz.* Dorothy and Toto were in a terrible tornado."
Jared:	"But it wasn't a tomato tornado."
Lizzy:	"No."
Mike:	"It makes me remember *The Night of the Twisters.* That's a good tornado story."

Mrs. Donnelly brings the group back to the story, and when they continue reading, they learn that Mike was right: The people from Chewandswallow sail away on a raft made from a stale slice of bread. Stopping periodically to talk about the story helps Mrs. Donnelly's students understand the story better.

After they finish reading the book, the children spend 25 minutes participating in a grand conversation[C] to talk more about their reactions to the book. They talk about a variety of topics:

- how much fun it would be to have the weather bring the food
- their favorite parts of the story
- why the people moved away from Chewandswallow
- why Grandpa told the story to the children
- whether or not the story was true
- the illustrator's use of black-and-white drawings at the beginning and end of the story and color drawings in the middle

The third graders also write in reading logs^C. Many of them continue thinking about topics and questions raised during the grand conversation as they write. Here is Molly's entry:

I don't think the story was real. It seems impossible to me. I think that the reason the colors were black and white sometimes and colors sometimes was because the only real true part was with Grandpa and the kids. That was the black and white part. The color part it was make believe. It was fantasy. I love that book. I want to read it to my Mom and Dad.

Later, in a minilesson^C, Mrs. Donnelly and her students examine how the author combined fantasy and reality in the book. The teacher also explains one of the center assignments—a sorting activity. Children draw a T-chart with two columns labeled *reality* and *fantasy.* Next, they read the sentences about the story and decide whether they represent reality or fantasy. Then they glue the sentences in the correct column on the chart. Figure 8-1 shows one child's sentence sort.

Josh, one of Mrs. Donnelly's students, talked to me about the book and what he does when he reads and writes. I ask, "What did you think about before you started reading this book?"

"I just looked at the cover, and I knew right away that it would be a weird book. This picture of this man getting a meatball like rain falling on his plate made me think it would be funny—like it would make me laugh. Mrs. Donnelly told us a little about this book, and I know our theme is weather, so I thought about all the stuff I know about rain, snow, clouds, and stuff. But then I read this little writing at the bottom of the page—'If food dropped like rain from the sky, wouldn't it be marvelous! Or would it?'—and I was thinking that something bad was going to happen. Maybe their rain would stop."

"What were you thinking about as you read the book?"

"Well, I wondered why the writing was in yellow boxes on some pages and in pink and orange boxes on other pages. I thought that maybe that was important, but it wasn't. And I couldn't read this word—*Chewandswallow*—at first. I didn't know it was the name of the town, but I just skipped over it and went on reading. It didn't seem important, and then I saw it way back in the book and my eyes saw that it was three words and it was easy to read."

"Mrs. Donnelly told you that *Cloudy With a Chance of Meatballs* was a fantasy, didn't she?"

"Yes, and that made me think that weird stuff would go on, and it did. I thought the weird stuff was going to start when Grandpa was making pancakes, but it didn't start until he told the story. That was sort of confusing, but I just kept reading and I figured it would make sense later on."

"After you finished reading, you wrote in your reading log, didn't you? Would you share it?"

"OK. This is my log: 'I would like to go to Chewandswallow. I want it to snow tacos and pizza and french fries and to rain Coke and hail chocolate chip cookies. I'd like all the free food, but I wouldn't like it when the weather got bad. Some of the weather was dangerous. I thought the book would have more information about weather but it didn't. It would have been more interesting if it did.' "

"That's very interesting. How do you decide what to write in your reading log?"

"Well, I write what's on my mind and the things I want to tell Mrs. Donnelly. I think about what I liked and I write that part and then I ask myself if there's anything that was bad for me and then I write that. I ask my brain what to write and it tells me and then I write it."

Figure 8-1   A Sentence Sort About *Cloudy With a Chance of Meatballs*

Realism	Fantasy
The children go sledding in the snow.	People carried plates, forks and napkins with them.
People buy food in supermarkets.	There was a tomato tornado.
One flying pancake lands on Henry.	Food got larger and larger.
Grandpa told the best bedtime story.	The people abandoned the town.
Grandpa flips pancakes.	The people watch the weather report on TV to find out the menu.
	There were storms of hamburgers and showers of orange juice.
	The Sanitation Department gave up trying to clean up the extra food.

"When you're reading, do you imagine that you're right there in the story?"

"I guess so. Sometimes when I'm reading, I sort of become the character that is most like me and then I think I'm there. But I didn't really do that in this book. It was too weird. I couldn't think of being there because it's something that would probably never happen."

"Was there anything that you learned when your class talked about the book after you finished reading it?"

Figure 8-2   Josh's Page From the Class Alphabet Book on Weather

What blows hot air and is full of rain?

NOSNOOW

M is for Monsoon

A monsoon is a kind of wind that begins in the Indian Ocean. It brings lots of rain to Asia. Some places get 240 inches of rain in a year becuse of monsoons.

HOT + COLD = MONSOON

"The colors. I was just reading the book and I didn't see that the pages, you know, were all colors during Grandpa's story and the pictures were plain at the beginning and at the end. That's what Molly said and she was right."

Mrs. Donnelly also involves the children in other activities to further their understanding of the story. She reads Judi Barrett's sequel, *Pickles to Pittsburgh* (1997), to the class, and they make a chart to compare it to *Cloudy With a Chance of Meatballs*.

The third graders also create their own fantastic weather reports and write a class alphabet book[C] about weather. Children use the writing process to draft and refine their book. Each student writes one page about a letter, and Josh writes about monsoons for the *M* page. His page is shown in Figure 8-2. He talks about his page and how he writes.

"How did you decide to write about monsoons?"

"Mrs. Donnelly read us this book called *Jumanji* [Van Allsburg, 1981], and it was about a monsoon. I didn't know about them but I thought it was a kind of weather. I wanted to learn about it so I did. I would like to be in a monsoon some-day if I went to places like India or Asia."

"What did you do when you were revising your page?"

"Well, monsoons are not easy to understand. Everybody knows about earth-quakes and tornadoes because they happen in California, but monsoons are very unusual. Mrs. Donnelly told me that I had to make sure that everyone could un-derstand my page. I read it to Mike and Perry and they said it was good but that I needed to make a chart about how a monsoon is made. So I did and my dad helped me do it. I made it like a math problem: Hot land plus cold water equals a monsoon wind. I want it to be good so everyone will like it. Everybody liked it when I read it when we sat in a circle for a read-around. Then I made a fancy *M* on my page so it would be special."

J osh is an effective reader and writer. He views reading and writing as meaning-making processes. He makes predictions before beginning to read, and he orga-nizes ideas before writing. Josh can talk about connecting what he is reading and writing to his own life and to books he has read. He also regulates or monitors what he does when he reads and writes. He has a sense of his audience when he writes. Josh tolerates confusion and ambiguity when he reads and writes, and he has confidence that he'll work through these problems.

Comprehension is the goal of reading instruction. Children must comprehend what they are reading to learn from the experience; they must make sense of their read-ing to maintain interest; and they must derive pleasure from reading to become life-long readers. Children who don't understand what they are reading don't find reading pleasurable and won't continue reading.

Comprehension is crucial for writers, too. As they write, children create composi-tions with clearly stated main ideas, relevant supporting details, effective transitions between ideas, and precise word choice. The reason why writers write is to share their ideas with readers, but compositions are unsuccessful when readers don't understand what writers have written.

THE COMPREHENSION PROCESS

Comprehension is a creative, multifaceted process in which students engage with the text (Tierney, 1990). Teachers often view comprehension as a mysterious process of making meaning or understanding what children read. It often seems mysterious be-cause it is invisible; some children read and understand what they read, and others seem to read just as well but don't understand what they read. Sometimes compre-hension problems relate to children's lack of fluency or limited vocabulary knowledge, but more often than not, children who don't comprehend seem no different from their classmates.

Three factors influence comprehension: the reader, the text, and the purpose (Irwin, 1991). The background knowledge that readers bring to the reading process influences how they understand the text as well as the strategies they know to use while reading. The text that is being read is the second factor: The author's ideas, the words the author uses to express those ideas, and how the ideas are organized and presented also affect comprehension. The purpose is the third factor: Readers vary the way they read according to their purpose. They read differently to cook a recipe, enjoy a letter from an old friend, understand the opinion expressed in an editorial, or read a novel.

Readers' comprehension varies because of these three factors. If you are a student learning how to teach reading, it seems obvious that your understanding will vary from your professor's. You and your professor have different levels of background knowledge and experience in teaching reading, and you and your professor are probably reading this chapter for different purposes. Perhaps you are focusing on the main ideas or reviewing before a test; in contrast, your professor may be preparing for class or writing a test. But even though comprehension varies from reader to reader, comprehension can always be supported with ideas from the text.

Judith Irwin (1991) defines comprehension as the reader's process of using prior experiences and the author's text to construct meaning that is useful to that reader for a specific purpose. Readers do many things as they read in order to comprehend what they are reading, and writers do similar things to create meaningful texts. Irwin (1991) has identified five subprocesses of comprehension:

1. Microprocesses
2. Integrative processes
3. Macroprocesses
4. Elaborative processes
5. Metacognitive processes

Figure 8-3 presents an overview of these subprocesses, and instructional and assessment techniques are suggested.

Microprocesses

The microprocesses focus on sentence-level comprehension. Readers chunk ideas into phrases and select what is important from the sentence to keep in short-term memory. Children who chunk ideas into phrases read fluently, not word by word, but those who do not chunk phrases meaningfully have difficulty understanding what they are reading. (To read more about fluency and chunking as a characteristic of fluent reading, turn to Chapter 6, "Developing Fluent Readers and Writers," pages 142–171.) For example, consider this sentence from *Cloudy With a Chance of Meatballs* (Barrett, 1978): "For lunch one day, frankfurters, already in their rolls, blew in from the northwest at about five miles an hour" (n.p.). How would you chunk the phrases? Here is one way:

> For lunch one day,
> frankfurters,
> already in their rolls,
> blew in
> from the northwest
> at about five miles an hour.

Figure 8-3   The Five Comprehension Subprocesses

Process	Instruction	Assessment
Microprocesses. Readers chunk ideas into phrases within a sentence to read fluently. Children who read word by word have difficulty understanding what they are reading. Similarly, writers must write fluently, chunking ideas into sentences.	Choral reading is a good way to help children chunk text appropriately because classmates and the teacher model appropriate chunking. Interactive writing and quickwrites are effective ways to develop writing fluency.	Teachers listen to children read aloud and check for appropriate chunking. For writing, they observe children as they write, checking for fluency.
Integrative processes. Readers infer connections and relationships between clauses and sentences by noticing pronoun substitutions, recognizing synonym substitutions, inferring cause and effect, and recognizing connectives such as *also, however,* and *unless.* In writing, children use these substitutions to clarify relationships.	Teachers ask questions to help children understand these connections by directing their attention to these relationships; for writing, teachers use sentence-combining activities.	Teachers ask questions to check children's ability to use connectives and understand relationships among words in a paragraph, and they examine the paragraphs children write for these connections.
Macroprocesses. Readers organize and summarize ideas as they read; that is, they look at the big picture of the entire text as well as the smaller units in the text. For writing, they use their knowledge of story structure, expository text structures, or poetic formulas to organize their compositions.	Children learn about structural patterns of different genres and draw graphic organizers to visually represent the main ideas. Children also do oral and written retellings and write summaries.	Teachers assess children's knowledge of macrostructures by examining children's graphic organizers, their retellings, and their compositions.
Elaborative processes. Readers elaborate on the author's message and use their background knowledge to make connections to their own lives and other literature. Children make predictions as they read and identify with characters. In writing, children use classmates' feedback when they revise and provide enough details so readers can make connections.	Children learn to make text-to-self, text-to-world, and text-to-text connections as they talk about stories in grand conversations and information books in instructional conversations and write in reading logs.	Teachers observe children as they participate in discussions and read their reading log entries to check that they are making corrections. And teachers monitor children's compositions, checking that they provide enough detail so readers can make connections.
Metacognitive processes. Readers monitor their comprehension and use problem-solving strategies to read and write effectively.	Teachers model reading strategies by "thinking aloud" as they read aloud and model writing strategies during writing lessons. They provide information about literacy strategies in minilessons. Then children apply the strategies when they read and write.	Teachers observe children as they read and write and ask them to "think aloud" about the strategies they are using. Teachers also ask children to reflect on their use of strategies during a reading or writing conference.

The commas help to chunk the text in this sentence. It is especially important that second language learners learn the ebb and flow of English phrases and sentences. Similarly, writers chunk the sentences they are writing into meaningful phrases. This chunking helps them to remember the sentence they are writing and to write fluently and with voice.

Children practice using the microprocesses whenever they read or reread sentences, paragraphs, and longer texts and chunk words into phrases as they read. Teachers listen to students read aloud to check that they are chunking words into phrases. Many beginning readers read slowly, word by word, and teachers can help these children chunk words into phrases with lots of reading and rereading practice. They can also provide assisted-practice activities using choral reading[C], buddy reading, and listening centers. As children read aloud with classmates or along with an audiotape at a listening center, they listen to how more fluent readers chunk words into phrases. Teachers can also write sentences from books children are reading on sentence strips and then cut the sentence apart into phrases. Then children arrange the phrase strips to complete the sentence.

Teachers can also adapt interactive writing[C] activities to give young children practice with chunking. Children and the teacher create a long sentence, break it into phrases, and write it phrase by phrase on chart paper and on white boards.

Integrative Processes

The integrative processes deal with the semantic and syntactic connections and relationships among sentences. Here are four sentences from the beginning of *Cloudy With a Chance of Meatballs* (Barrett, 1978): "In most ways, it was very much like any other tiny town. . . . But there were no food stores in the town of Chewandswallow. They didn't need any. The sky supplied all the food they could possibly want" (n.p.). In order to comprehend the story, children must understand that Chewandswallow is different from other towns. There were no food stores because food and drink came down from the sky, like rain or snow.

Readers infer these connections and relationships by noticing pronoun substitutions, recognizing synonym substitutions, inferring cause and effect, and recognizing connectives such as *also, however, because,* and *unless.* Similarly, writers include these connections and relationships in the paragraphs they write to clarify meaning.

Teachers facilitate children's understanding of integrative processes when they are reading with children and stop to ask clarifying questions. After reading the sentences from *Cloudy With a Chance of Meatballs,* teachers might ask one or more of these questions:

What is Chewandswallow?
How is Chewandswallow different from other towns?
Why didn't this town need any food stores?
Because they had no food stores, how did the people of Chewandswallow get food?
How does the sky supply food?

Teachers can stop to ask these questions as they are reading, or they can reread the sentences after reading and then ask the questions.

Teachers can also ask these clarifying questions to assess children's ability to use integrative processes. If children have difficulty answering the questions, teachers need to ask clarifying questions like these more often and model how they make connections and relationships among sentences.

Integrative processes are particularly difficult for many ELL students who don't recognize semantic and syntactic connections and relationships.

Teachers can also examine children's compositions to see if they make these connections and relationships in their writing. If children don't demonstrate knowledge of integrative processes, they can practice combining sentences. For example, combine these four sentences:

The weather came three times a day.
It came at breakfast.
It came at lunch.
It came at dinner.

These sentences might be combined this way: *The weather came three times a day, at breakfast, lunch, and dinner.* Now try combining this more complicated set of sentences:

The people lived in Chewandswallow.
The people woke up.
The people ate.
It was a shower of orange juice.
Then toast with butter and jelly blew in.
It drizzled milk.
The milk finished the meal.

Here's one combination: *The people of Chewandswallow woke up and drank a shower of orange juice. Then they ate the toast with the butter and jelly that blew in. It drizzled milk to finish the meal.* When children combine sentences, they realize the inferred connections and relationships among sentences.

Macroprocesses

Macroprocesses relate to the big picture—the entire text. The two components of the macroprocesses are recognizing the structure of text and selecting the most important information to remember (Irwin, 1991). Readers organize and summarize ideas as they read, and writers organize their ideas in order to write coherently. Both readers and writers use their knowledge of the overall structure of texts for macroprocessing. Stories, poems, and informational books have different organizations and structures. Even 4- and 5-year-olds recognize some of these differences, and during the primary grades, children learn more about different types of texts. Children use this knowledge about text structure to comprehend what they read. (You will learn more about the structure of stories, informational books, and poems in Chapter 9.)

To comprehend the story *Cloudy With a Chance of Meatballs,* children have to know about the fantasy genre and recognize, as Molly did in the vignette, that the use of color in the illustrations represents the fantasy part of the story. Similarly, when the third graders in Mrs. Donnelly's classroom wrote their alphabet book about weather, they used a sequence structure to organize it.

Learning to differentiate between the more and less important ideas is a part of macroprocessing. As children read, they choose the more important ideas to remember; when children write, they organize their compositions to focus on the more important ideas. If they are writing a story, they focus on the beginning, middle, and end; if they are writing a comparison, they explain the similarities and differences.

Teachers assess children's knowledge of macroprocesses through their oral and written retellings, the graphic organizers they draw, and the summaries they write. Teachers can also examine the overall structure of the compositions children write.

ELL

Researchers recommend that teachers explicitly teach ELL students about the structure of stories and informational books they are reading.

Elaborative Processes

Children use elaborative processes to activate their background knowledge and make connections with the book they are reading or listening to as it is read aloud. They make three types of connections: text-to-self, text-to-world, and text-to-text connections (Fountas & Pinnell, 2001). In text-to-self connections, children link the ideas they are reading about to their own life experiences; they are personal connections. A story event or character may remind them of something or someone in their own lives. For example, when preschool children or kindergartners listen to a parent or teacher read *Wemberly Worried* (Henkes, 2000), a story about a preschooler named Wemberly who worries about everything, including going to school for the first time, they might think about their own worries about going to school.

In text-to-world connections, children move beyond personal experience to relate what they are reading to world knowledge—information they have learned both in and out of school. If third graders are reading *Nature's Green Umbrella* (Gibbons, 1994), for example, they might connect the information they are reading about tropical rain forests with what they learned from a television documentary program about the Amazon.

When children make text-to-text connections, they link the text itself or an element of the text to another text they have read or movie they have viewed. Two of Mrs. Donnelly's students made literary connections in the vignette: Lizzy connected the tornado in *Cloudy With a Chance of Meatballs* to the one in *The Wizard of Oz* (Baum, 1970) and Mike connected it to *Night of the Twisters* (Ruckman, 1984).

Text-to-text connections are difficult for some children; however, Cairney's (1990, 1992) research indicates that children are aware of their past experiences with literature, and they use this literary knowledge as they read and write. Those children who have done more reading and who know more about literature are more likely to make text-to-text connections. It is not uncommon for preschoolers and kindergartners who have been read to every day to make text-to-text connections. Teachers can encourage children to make these connections and to share them with classmates. Through modeling, more children will think about connections between books. Children also make literary connections as they incorporate ideas, structures, and language from stories and other books they have read into their writing.

Teachers encourage children to make personal, world, and literary connections to books throughout the reading process. Teachers often ask children to brainstorm or cluster "world" information related to a book they are getting ready to read or to quickwrite[C] about a personal experience related to a book.

Teachers often model how to make the three types of connections. They stop reading periodically to share their connections or ask children to talk about connections they are thinking about. Teachers often make a chart with three columns labeled text-to-self, text-to-world, and text-to-text. Then the teacher or children write about their connections on small sticky notes that they place in the correct column of the chart. Figure 8-4 shows a first-grade class's connections chart that was made after they read *Officer Buckle and Gloria* (Rathmann, 1995), a story about a police officer and his dog.

Children also use the elaborative processes to go beyond literal comprehension to make inferences—connections that are not explicitly stated in the text (Keene & Zimmermann, 1997). Children must recognize clues in the text and use them to draw conclusions. In *Miss Nelson Is Missing!* (Allard, 1977), for example, children are not explicitly told that their teacher, Miss Nelson, is pretending to be the hated substitute teacher, Miss Viola Swamp, but there are enough clues that adults and some children realize that Miss Nelson and Miss Viola Swamp are one and the same. Other children think the two are different people, and they don't understand how their classmates inferred the connection.

Figure 8-4 A First-Grade Class's Connections Chart

Text-to-Self Connections	Text-to-World Connections	Text-to-Text Connections
Last year a lady police officer came to visit our kindergarten class. We got to sit in her police car but she didn't have a police dog.	I know that some police officers really do have police dogs, but they are usually German Shepherds.	This book is like *Martha Speaks*. They are both about smart dogs who help the police.
I want to be a police officer when I grow up.	I know that the police want everyone to be safe. That's why they give people tickets that cost a lot of money when they are speeding too fast on the freeway.	This book makes me think of a book called *Chrysanthemum* because it has a happy ending, too.
Some policemen came to our house after we got robbed.		I'm thinking about a book called *Hey, Al*. It's about a man named Al and his dog, Eddie. They are best friends, too.
My grandma is always telling me to be safe. She's like Officer Buckle!		

To help children reflect on their reading, Hoyt (1999) suggests the Two Words activity. Children choose two words to represent the book they have read. After they choose the words, they share their words, explain why they chose them, and say how the words relate to the book or their own lives. For example, after reading *Cloudy With a Chance of Meatballs*, Vanessa, one of Mrs. Donnelly's students, chose *impossible* and *delicious*. She explained her choices this way: "I know this story could never happen. It is *impossible*, but I think having food fall like the rain would be *delicious*. I would like going outside and opening my mouth to get a snack."

Teachers assess children's elaborative processes by checking to see that their predictions are reasonable, by listening to the comments that children make during grand conversations, and by reading their entries in reading logs. In particular, teachers should notice when children make inferences and intertextual comments during grand conversations and in their reading log entries.

Metacognitive Processes

Children's conscious awareness of their thinking is called *metacognition* (Baker & Brown, 1984). Both readers and writers use metacognitive strategies to monitor and evaluate their comprehension. Strategies such as predicting, visualizing, organizing, tapping prior knowledge, and self-questioning are conscious problem-solving behaviors that students use in order to read and write effectively. The strategies are metacognitive because students think about them as they read and write, applying and regulating their use.

Children's metacognitive knowledge grows as they learn about the reading and writing processes and the strategies that readers and writers use. As they gain experience, their attention in reading moves from decoding to comprehension. In writing,

To link to *Metacognition and Reading to Learn,* a publication of the ERIC Clearinghouse on Reading, English, and Communication (Digest #96), visit our Companion Website at www.prenhall.com/tompkins

their focus shifts from forming letters and spelling to communicating ideas. As novice readers and writers, children apply strategies when teachers guide and direct them to, but as they become more effective readers and writers, children regulate their use of strategies independently.

Teachers introduce the strategies to students in minilessons. They model how to use the strategies and provide opportunities during guided reading[C] and in other reading activities for students to practice using them. They also teach students to reflect on their use of strategies during think-alouds, in which students talk or write about thinking about reading and writing. In the vignette at the beginning of the chapter, Josh used the think-aloud procedure to reflect on his reading and writing.

The five comprehension subprocesses operate simultaneously during the reading and writing processes. It would be wrong to conclude that first students comprehend phrases in sentences, then sentences in paragraphs, and then the entire text. Instead, all five subprocesses work together throughout a variety of activities so that children refine their understanding. Figure 8-5 lists some ways that teachers can enhance children's comprehension.

Young children enhance their comprehension through talking about books in small groups, using puppets to retell stories, role-playing, and drawing pictures of characters and story events.

LITERACY STRATEGIES AND SKILLS

In the vignette at the beginning of the chapter, Josh applied a variety of literacy skills automatically and used problem-solving strategies in order to create meaning when he read and wrote. We all have skills we use automatically and self-regulated strategies we use thoughtfully for things we do well, such as driving defensively, playing volleyball, training a new pet, and maintaining classroom discipline. We apply skills that we have learned unconsciously and choose among skills as we think strategically. The strategies we use in these activities are problem-solving mechanisms that involve complex thinking processes.

When we are just learning how to drive a car, for example, we learn both skills and strategies. Some of the first skills we learn are how to start the engine, make left turns, and

Teachers guide children's use of comprehension strategies as they read books together.

Figure 8-5   Ways to Enhance Children's Comprehension

Before Reading
Develop background knowledge with books, videos, and hands-on materials.
Activate background knowledge with K-W-L charts, quickwrites, and discussions.
Make predictions.
Prepare graphic organizers.

During Reading
Use shared reading or read aloud to children.
Have children read with buddies.
Model reading strategies.
Use guided reading and monitor students' use of strategies.
Use "close reading" of short passages.
Use the "say something" activity.
Make additional predictions.

After Reading
Discuss the text in a grand conversation or instructional conversation.
Write in reading logs or do a quickwrite.
Use drama to reenact the story.
Reread the text.
Retell the text.
Use storyboards to sequence events in the text.
Complete graphic organizers.
Examine literary opposites.
Teach lessons on reading strategies and skills.
Teach lessons on the structure of texts (e.g., plot, cause and effect).
Teach lessons about the author or genre.
Make open-mind portraits.
Examine selected sentences in the text.
Complete the K-W-L chart.
Make projects to deepen understanding.
Read other books on the same topic.
Compare related books or book and film versions.
Write reports and other books on the same topic.

parallel park. With practice, these skills become automatic. Some of the first strategies we learn are how to pass another car and stay a safe distance behind other cars. At first, we have only a small repertoire of strategies, and we don't always use them effectively; that's one reason why we take driving lessons from a driving instructor and have a learner's permit that requires a more experienced driver to ride along with us. These more experienced drivers teach us defensive driving strategies. We learn strategies for driving on interstate highways, on slippery roads, and at night. With practice and guidance, we become more successful drivers, able to anticipate driving problems and take defensive actions.

The same is true for literacy: Strategic readers and writers control their own reading and writing and apply skills and strategies as they need them. They set purposes before they begin, revise their plans as they read and write, and deal with the difficulties they encounter while reading and writing. Strategies allow students to monitor understanding and solve problems as they read and write. Students use strategies deliberately with some understanding of their usefulness or effectiveness. To become expert readers and writers, children must become strategic.

Reading and Writing Strategies

Readers and writers are actively involved in creating meaning. They select and use appropriate strategies, monitor their understanding as they read, and refine their meaning as they write (Paris & Jacobs, 1984; Schmitt, 1990). This section focuses on 12 strategies that children learn to use for both reading and writing. These strategies are listed in Figure 8-6.

1. *Tapping prior knowledge.* Children think about what they already know about the topic about which they will read or write. This knowledge includes information and vocabulary about topics such as dinosaurs, as well as information about authors and literary genres such as folk tales and alphabet books. Children's knowledge is stored in schemata (or categories) and linked to other knowledge through a complex network of interrelationships. As children learn, they add the new information to their schemata.

2. *Predicting.* Children make predictions or thoughtful "guesses" about what will happen in the books they are reading. These guesses are based on what they already know about the topic and the literary genre, or on what they have read thus far. Children often make one prediction before beginning to read and several others at key points in the story or at the beginning of each chapter when reading chapter books

Figure 8-6   **Twelve Strategies That Readers and Writers Use**

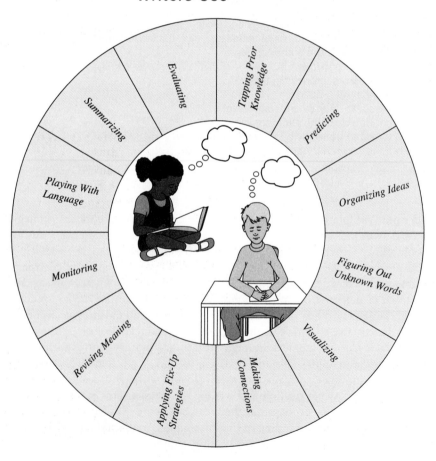

using the Directed Reading-Thinking Activity (DRTA)[C] (Stauffer, 1975). As they read, children either confirm or revise their predictions. When they are preparing to read informational books, for example, children often preview the text in order to make predictions. They also ask questions for which they would like to find answers as they read or set purposes for reading.

Children make plans and set purposes for writing, too. They make predictions about which ideas are important and which ones will interest their readers. They revise their plans as their writing moves in new or unexpected directions. Young children also make predictions about how long their writing will be when they count out the number of pages for their books.

3. *Organizing ideas.* Children organize ideas and sequence story events as they read, and they organize their ideas for writing using clusters[C] and other graphic organizers. The way children organize ideas varies depending on whether they are reading and writing stories, informational books, or poetry; each type of text has unique organizational patterns. When children read and write stories, they often organize the events into the beginning, middle, and end. When they read and write informational books, they often use sequence or another structure. When they read and write poetry, students use various poetic forms.

4. *Figuring out unknown words.* When children come across an unfamiliar word, they must decide what action to take. They might use phonic analysis, analogies, syllabic analysis, or morphemic analysis to identify an unfamiliar word, or they might decide to skip over the word and continue reading. Sometimes they ask the teacher or a classmate. When children are writing, they often need to write words that they don't know how to spell; again, they must decide what to do. They might write several letters to serve temporarily as a placeholder, and then check the spelling later by consulting a dictionary, a classmate, or the teacher. Or, they might sound out the word or "think it out." When thinking out the spelling, they consider spelling patterns and whether or not the word "looks right."

5. *Visualizing.* Children create mental pictures of what they are reading or writing. They often place themselves in the images they create, becoming a character in the story, traveling to that setting, or facing the conflict situations that the characters themselves face. Teachers sometimes ask children to close their eyes to help visualize the story or to draw pictures of the scenes and characters they visualize. How well children use visualization often becomes clear when they view film versions of books they have read. Children who use the visualization strategy are often disappointed with the film version, whereas children who don't visualize are often amazed by the film and prefer it to the book version.

When they are writing, children use description and sensory detail to make their writing more vivid and bring it to life for the people who will read their books. Sometimes teachers have children brainstorm lists of words related to each of the five senses and then incorporate some of the words in pieces they are writing. They also encourage children to use comparisons—metaphors and similes—to make their writing more vivid.

6. *Making connections.* Children personalize what they are reading by relating it to their own lives. They recall similar experiences or compare the characters to themselves or people they know. They connect the book they are reading to other literature they have read. Readers often make connections among several books written by one author or between two versions of the same story. Similarly, when they are writing, children make connections between what they are writing and books they have read or experiences they have had.

7. *Applying fix-up strategies.* When children are reading, they sometimes realize that something is not making sense; then they apply fix-up strategies. They may assume that things will make sense soon and continue reading, or they may reread, look at pictures, skip ahead, talk to a classmate about the book, or ask for help. Choosing an appropriate fix-up strategy is important so children can continue reading productively.

When writing, children sometimes realize that their writing isn't working the way they want it to; then they apply fix-up strategies. They might reread what they have written to get a jump start on their writing, do more prewriting to gather and organize ideas, read a book on the topic, talk about their ideas with a classmate, or ask a classmate or the teacher to read the piece and give some feedback. Sometimes they draw a picture.

8. *Revising meaning.* Reading and writing are processes of making meaning, and as children read and write, they are continually revising their understanding and the meaning they are creating. Children often reread for more information or because something doesn't make sense. They also study a book's illustrations, learn through the process of sharing, and get ideas from classmates during discussions. As they write in reading logs, children often gain new insights about a book.

Children often share their writing with classmates and get feedback from classmates and the teacher so that they can revise their writing and make it stronger. As they revise, children add words and sentences, make substitutions and deletions, and move their text around to communicate more effectively. They also add titles and illustrations to clarify meaning.

9. *Monitoring.* Children monitor their understanding as they read, though they may be aware of this monitoring only when comprehension breaks down. They also monitor their writing to see how well they are communicating. When they are reading and writing, children ask themselves questions to monitor their understanding, and they use fix-up strategies when they realize that understanding has broken down.

10. *Playing with language.* Children notice figurative and novel uses of language when they read, and they incorporate interesting language when they write. Some examples of playing with language are idioms, jokes, riddles, metaphors, similes, personification, sensory language, rhyme, alliteration, and invented words.

11. *Summarizing.* Readers choose important ideas to remember. Summarizing is important because big ideas are easier to remember than lots of details. As children write, they often state their big ideas at the beginning of a paragraph and then support them with facts. They want their readers to be able to pick out the important ideas. During revising, writers ask for feedback about how well their readers remember the important ideas.

12. *Evaluating.* Students make judgments about, reflect on, and value the books they are reading and writing. Readers think about what they have read, review the text, and evaluate their reading. They also value the books they read and what they do as readers. Writers do similar things: They ask themselves whether their own writing says what they want it to say—in other words, whether or not it is effective. They think about what they have experimented with in a particular piece of writing and reflect on the writing processes that they use. As a strategy, evaluation is not the teacher's judgment handed down to students, but rather students' own thinking about their goals and accomplishments.

Children don't use every one of these strategies every time they read or write, but effective readers and writers use most of them most of the time. Figure 8-7 shows how Mrs. Donnelly's students used these strategies in reading *Cloudy With a Chance of Meatballs* and in writing the class alphabet book about weather.

ELL

ELL students need to learn how and when to use reading and writing strategies through explicit instruction and guided practice.

Figure 8-7 How Third Graders Use Reading and Writing Strategies

Strategy	How Strategies Are Used When Reading *Cloudy With a Chance of Meatballs*	How Strategies Are Used When Writing an Alphabet Book About Weather
Tapping Prior Knowledge	The teacher tells children that the book is a fantasy about weather, and children think about what they know about weather books and fantasy stories.	Children brainstorm weather words beginning with each letter of the alphabet. They choose the word for each page of the alphabet book.
Predicting	Children identify a purpose or reason for reading. They make "guesses" about what will happen next as they read, and then they read to confirm their predictions.	Children conference with the teacher, sharing their clusters before beginning to draft their page.
Organizing Ideas	Children think about the sequence of events in the story and chunk the events into three parts: beginning, middle, and end.	Children make a cluster to organize information about the word before beginning to write.
Figuring Out Unknown Words	Children skip some unfamiliar words and ask the teacher and classmates about other words. They also write unfamiliar words in their journals.	Children use invented spelling for unfamiliar words while drafting. Later, during editing, they check the spellings on the word wall, in a dictionary, or in an informational book.
Visualizing	Children visualize the events in the story or put themselves into the story and imagine the events happening to themselves.	Children think about the audience that will read their informational book. They imagine what their page in the finished book will look like.
Making Connections	Children think about how they would feel if the story happened in their community. They think about other books they have read in which impossible events occur.	Children think about what information might be interesting to readers. They think about informational books they have read that they can use as models for their books.
Applying Fix-Up Strategies	Children are confused about the realistic event at the beginning of the story, but they decide to keep reading. They notice that the pictures at the beginning and end are black and white and the ones in the fantasy are in color. They reread to figure out why.	Children decide to add a comparison of lightning and thunder to make the section on thunderstorms clearer. They read more about fog to expand that part of the book.
Revising Meaning	Children turn back a page or two when something they read doesn't make sense. Children discuss the story after reading and elaborate their understanding as they talk and listen to classmates' comments.	Children stop drafting to reread what they have read and make revisions to communicate more effectively. Children meet in writing groups to share their drafts and get feedback to use in revising.

(continued)

Strategy	How Strategies Are Used When Reading *Cloudy With a Chance of Meatballs*	How Strategies Are Used When Writing an Alphabet Book About Weather
Monitoring	As they read, children ask themselves questions to be sure they understand what they are reading.	As they draft, children check the accuracy and completeness of the information they are writing.
	The teacher asks children to notice characteristics of fantasy in the story, and children look for characteristics as they reread it.	They put themselves in the place of their readers and ask themselves if they would find the page interesting.
Playing With Language	Children notice that the town's name—Chewandswallow—is an invented word.	Children decide to add a riddle to introduce each letter.
	They make up other invented words. *Lightning* becomes *flashandboom*.	
Summarizing	Children identify important ideas in the story.	Children focus on the big ideas about the word and add interesting details to explain the big ideas.
	They contrast the realism and fantasy in the story.	
Evaluating	In their journals or in conferences with the teacher, children give opinions about the story and say whether or not they liked it.	Children evaluate the effectiveness of each page and the accuracy of the information presented.

During the primary grades, children develop control of the reading and writing processes and learn to use strategies to construct meaning as they read and write (Baker & Brown, 1984). They acquire three types of knowledge about each strategy:

1. *Declarative knowledge.* Children know that readers and writers use strategies—or problem-solving behaviors—when they read and write. They understand that reading and writing are processes involving a variety of strategies and skills, and they can name the strategies that they know how to use.

2. *Procedural knowledge.* Children know how to use strategies to understand what they are reading and to develop compositions that communicate effectively. They have practiced the steps in the strategy and can use it independently.

3. *Conditional knowledge.* Children know when to use specific strategies. They learn how to choose strategies to avoid or solve reading and writing problems (Paris, Lipson, & Wixson, 1983).

As teachers explain strategies and model them for children, they emphasize all three types of knowledge because when children lack one or more types of knowledge about a strategy, they are unlikely to be able to use it effectively.

Why Is It Important That Children Become Strategic Readers and Writers? Being strategic is an important characteristic of learning. Readers and writers use strategies to generate, organize, and elaborate meaning more expertly than they could otherwise. During the primary grades, children learn all sorts of cognitive strategies, and the acquisition of reading and writing strategies coincides with this cognitive development. As children learn to reflect on their learning, for example, they learn to reflect on themselves as readers and writers; and as they learn to monitor their learning, they learn to monitor their reading and writing. Many of the cognitive strategies that children learn have direct application to reading and writing. In this way, children's growing awareness of their own processes and their knowledge of reading and writing are mutually supportive.

Strategies are cognitive tools that children learn to use selectively and flexibly as they become fluent readers and writers. For children to become fluent readers and writers, they need these thinking tools. These strategies are tools for learning across the curriculum, and strategic reading and writing enhance learning in math, social studies, science, and other content areas. Children's competence in reading and writing affects all areas of the curriculum.

Reading and Writing Skills

Skills are information-processing techniques that readers and writers use automatically and unconsciously as they construct meaning. Many skills focus at the word level, but some require readers and writers to attend to larger chunks of text. For example, readers use skills such as decoding unfamiliar words, noting details, and sequencing events; and writers employ skills such as forming contractions, using punctuation marks, and capitalizing people's names. Skills and strategies are not the same thing because strategies are problem-solving tactics selected deliberately to achieve particular goals (Paris, Wasik, & Turner, 1991). The important difference between skills and strategies is how they are used.

Children in prekindergarten through fourth grade learn five types of reading and writing skills:

1. *Comprehension skills.* Children use comprehension skills in conjunction with reading and writing strategies. For example, they recognize separate facts and opinions, compare and contrast, and recognize literary genres and structures.

2. *Decoding and spelling skills.* Children use decoding and spelling skills as they identify words when reading and spell words when writing. Examples of decoding and spelling skills include sounding out words, breaking words into syllables, using inflectional endings and other affixes to decode and spell words, and using abbreviations.

3. *Language skills.* Children use language skills to analyze words they are reading and to choose more precise words and phrases when they are writing. These skills include locating the meanings of words, noticing idioms, using figurative language, and choosing synonyms.

4. *Reference skills.* Children use reference skills to read newspaper articles, locate information in dictionaries and other informational books, and use library references. These skills include alphabetizing a list of words, comparing word meanings in a dictionary, using a table of contents and an index, and reading and making graphs.

5. *Study skills.* Children are introduced to study skills in third and fourth grades as they begin to read content-area textbooks and study for tests. Skimming and scanning, taking notes, making clusters, and previewing a book before reading are examples of study skills.

Examples of the five types of skills are presented in Figure 8-8.

Figure 8-8   Five Types of Skills That Readers and Writers Use

Type	Sample Skills	
Comprehension Skills Children use comprehension skills when they are reading in order to understand and summarize, and they use these skills when they are writing in order to make their writing easier to understand.	Sequence Categorize Classify Separate facts and opinions Note details Recognize literary genres	Identify cause and effect Compare and contrast Use context clues Notice organizational patterns of poetry, plays, business and friendly letters, stories, essays, and reports
Decoding and Spelling Skills Children use decoding skills to identify words when reading and many of the same skills to spell words when they are writing.	Sound out words using phonics Notice word families Decode by analogy Use classroom resources Consult a dictionary or glossary Use abbreviations	Apply spelling rules Recognize high-frequency words Divide words into syllables Capitalize proper nouns and adjectives
Language Skills Children use language skills when they focus on particular words during word study activities, and their knowledge of these types of words influences their reading and writing.	Use contractions Use possessives Use similes and metaphors Notice idioms and slang Choose synonyms Recognize antonyms Recognize parts of speech	Differentiate among homonyms Use root words and affixes Appreciate rhyme and other poetic devices Use punctuation marks Use simple, compound, and complex sentences
Reference Skills Children use reference skills when they read informational books, do research, and write reports and other types of expository writing.	Sort in alphabetical order Use a glossary or dictionary Use the pronunciation guide in the dictionary Locate information in books and on the Internet	Use a table of contents Use an index Use a card catalogue Read and make graphs, tables, and diagrams Use bibliographic forms Locate synonyms in a thesaurus
Study Skills Children use study skills when they review and prepare for tests.	Make clusters Take notes Paraphrase Follow directions	Skim Scan Preview

Teachers often wonder when they should teach the skills listed in Figure 8-8. School districts often prepare curriculum guides or frameworks that list the skills to be taught at each grade level, and they are usually listed on scope-and-sequence charts that accompany basal reader programs. On scope-and-sequence charts, textbook makers identify the grade level at which the skill should be introduced and the grade levels at which it is practiced. These resources provide guidelines, but teachers decide which skills to teach based on their children's level of literacy development and the reading and writing activities in which their students are involved.

Figure 8-9   How Third Graders Use Reading and Writing Skills

Skills	How Skills Are Used When Reading *Cloudy With a Chance of Meatballs*	How Skills Are Used When Writing an Alphabet Book About Weather
Comprehension Skills	Children separate realism and fantasy in the story. They sequence story events. They compare real weather to the "food" weather.	Children add at least three details on each page. They reread classmates' pages to check the accuracy of information.
Decoding and Spelling Skills	Children use picture clues to read food words, including *frankfurter* and *syrup*. They sound out words such as *prediction, Sanitation Department,* and *marvelous.*	During editing, children check the spelling of weather words in informational books. The teacher conferences with children about capitalization and punctuation marks.
Language Skills	Children notice weather-related words and phrases used in the story, such as "brief shower" and "gradual clearing."	Children use the "_____ is for _____" form on each page of their books. They write in complete sentences.
Reference Skills	Children check the card catalogue for other books by the same author. They compare "The Chewandswallow Digest" with their local newspaper. They read weather reports and examine weather maps in their local newspaper.	Children use the index in books to locate information for the pages they are writing. They make charts and diagrams for their pages. They sort their pages into alphabetical order.
Study Skills	Children scan the story looking for words for the word wall.	Children skim sections of informational books as they gather information for the alphabet book. They take notes as they read. They make clusters as they prepare to write their pages.

Mrs. Donnelly's third graders used a variety of reading skills as they read *Cloudy With a Chance of Meatballs,* and they used many writing skills as they wrote their class alphabet book on weather. For example, when Mrs. Donnelly's students were checking a weather book for information about thunderstorms, they didn't start in the front of the book and hunt page by page through the book; instead, they checked the index for the location of information about thunderstorms or whatever topic they were searching for and then read that section. Using an index is a reference skill. When the children wrote dialogue, they added quotation marks around the spoken words. They didn't make a conscious decision about whether or not to mark the dialogue; they automatically added the convention. Figure 8-9 provides other examples of the reading and writing skills that Mrs. Donnelly's students used.

Why Distinguish Between Skills and Strategies? Skills are more commonly associated with reading and writing instruction than strategies are, and for many years, teachers and parents equated teaching skills with teaching reading. They believed that the best way to help children learn to read was to teach them a set of discrete skills, using drill-and-practice worksheets and workbooks (Smith, 1965). But research during the last

35 or more years has shown that reading is a constructive process in which readers construct meaning by interacting with texts (Pearson, Roehler, Dole, & Duffy, 1990). Writing also is a constructive process, because writers construct meaning as they compose texts. Readers and writers use strategies differently than skills: They use strategies to orchestrate higher-order thinking skills when reading and writing, whereas they use skills automatically and unconsciously when reading and writing.

Although it continues to be important that children learn to use reading and writing skills automatically, of far greater importance is children's ability to use reading and writing strategies. When skills and strategies are lumped together, teachers tend to neglect reading and writing strategies because they are more familiar with skills.

Teaching Strategies and Skills

In balanced literacy classrooms, teachers use two approaches—direct instruction and teachable moments—to teach strategies and skills (Spiegel, 1992). Teachers plan and teach minilessons on skills and strategies on a regular basis. These direct-instruction lessons are systematic and planned in conjunction with books or other selections children are reading or books that teachers are reading aloud. Children learn other strategies and skills incidentally through teachable moments as they observe and work collaboratively with teachers and classmates. In both kinds of instruction, teachers support children's learning, and children apply what they are learning in authentic literacy activities. Guidelines for skill and strategy instruction are presented in Figure 8-10.

Minilessons. Minilessons (Atwell, 1998) are 15- to 30-minute direct-instruction lessons designed to help students learn literacy skills and become more strategic readers and writers. Sometimes these lessons continue for several days as children and the teacher focus on a single goal. The children are aware of why it is important to learn the skill or strategy, and they are explicitly taught how to use a particular skill or strategy through modeling, explanation, and practice. Then independent application takes place using authentic literacy materials, and responsibility is transferred from the teacher to students (Bergman, 1992; Duffy & Roehler, 1987; Pearson & Gallagher, 1983).

Many researchers recommend using a whole-part-whole organization for teaching skills and strategies (Flood & Lapp, 1994; Trachtenburg, 1990). Children read and respond to a text—this is the whole; then teachers focus on a skill or strategy and teach a minilesson using examples from the text whenever possible—this is the part. Finally, children return to the text or to another text to apply what they have learned by doing more reading or writing or by doing a project—this is the whole again. The skills approach to reading is described as part-to-whole, and the holistic approach is described as whole-to-part. This approach takes both into account. Instead of isolated drill-and-practice activities that are often meaningless to students, this approach encourages teachers to clearly connect what children are learning in minilessons to authentic literacy activities.

The minilesson feature on page 222 shows how Mrs. Donnelly taught her third graders about literary opposites (Temple, 1992) during a literature focus unit on *Amos and Boris* (Steig, 1971). In the story, a whale named Amos rescues a shipwrecked mouse named Boris, and later Boris saves Amos when he becomes beached near Boris's home. Literary opposites are any opposites in a story—two very different settings, characters, events, and emotions in the story, for example—and most stories have more than one pair of opposites. One of the opposites in *Amos and Boris* is that the two animals, who are so different, become friends. Not only are they different in size, but one is a land animal and the other lives in the ocean.

To link to *Explicit Instruction in Comprehension Strategies* to read more about strategy instruction and other comprehension issues, visit our Companion Website at www.prenhall.com/tompkins

Figure 8-10   Guidelines for Skill and Strategy
Instruction

1. Teach Minilessons

Teachers present minilessons to teach skills and strategies. During the lesson, teachers explain and model the procedure. Then children practice the skill or strategy and later apply it in reading and writing activities.

2. Differentiate Between Skills and Strategies

Teachers understand that skills are automatic behaviors that readers and writers use, whereas strategies are problem-solving tactics, and they differentiate between skills and strategies as they teach minilessons and model how they use strategies. They are also careful to use the terms "skills" and "strategies" correctly when they talk to children.

3. Provide Step-by-Step Explanations

Teachers describe the skill or strategy step by step so that it is sensible and meaningful to children. For strategies, they can use think-aloud procedures to demonstrate how the strategy is used. Teachers also explain to children why they should learn the skill or strategy, how it will make reading and writing easier, and when to use it.

4. Use Modeling

Teachers model using strategies for children in the context of authentic reading and writing activities, rather than in isolation. Children are also encouraged to model using strategies for classmates.

5. Provide Practice Opportunities

Children have opportunities to practice the skill or strategy in meaningful reading and writing activities. Teachers need to ensure that all children are successful using the skill or strategy so that they will be motivated to use it independently.

6. Apply in Content Areas

Teachers provide opportunities for children to use the skill or strategy in reading and writing activities related to social studies, science, and other content areas. The more opportunities children have to use the skill or strategy, the more likely they are to learn it.

7. Use Reflection

Teachers ask children to reflect on their use of the skill or strategy after they have had the opportunity to practice it and apply it in meaningful reading and writing activities.

8. Hang Charts of Skills and Strategies

Teachers often hang lists of skills and strategies children are learning in the classroom and encourage children to refer to them when reading and writing. Separate charts should be used for skills and strategies so that children can remember which are which.

Adapted from Winograd & Hare, 1988; Pressley & Harris, 1990.

Minilesson

Topic: Literary Opposites
Grade: Third Grade
Time: One 45-minute period

During a literature focus on *Amos and Boris* (Steig, 1971), a story of an unlikely friendship between a mouse and a whale, Mrs. Donnelly teaches this minilesson on literary opposites. Her goal is to help her third-grade students think more deeply about the theme of the story. Mrs. Donnelly describes her students as good literal comprehenders; they can identify the characters and retell the story, but they have difficulty with inferential comprehension.

1. Introduce the Topic

"Let's talk about opposites," Mrs. Donnelly explains to her third graders. "One way to understand a story better is to think of opposites. There are many opposites in stories—kind and mean characters, stories in different settings, and happy and sad events. If you think about the opposites, it will often help you identify a theme."

2. Share Examples

Mrs. Donnelly reviews Jan Brett's *Town Mouse, Country Mouse* (1994), a story the students have read before, and uses the think-aloud technique to point out these opposites: town-country, plain-fancy, mouse-cat, dark-light, mouse-owl, and quiet-noisy. She writes the list on the chalkboard and stands back to reflect on it.

3. Provide Information

Then Mrs. Donnelly circles *plain-fancy* and thinks aloud:

> Yes, I think *plain* and *fancy* are important opposites. I can think of lots of examples: plain and fancy clothes, plain and fancy food, and plain and fancy houses. These two mice are really different. The country mouse likes plain things and the city mouse likes fancy things. So, I think that one of the author's messages was that it is good to be different or unique.

"You can talk to a friend the way I talked to you or write a quickwrite to figure out a theme," Mrs. Donnelly points out. She also explains that some opposites may not be so useful, *mouse-owl* or *dark-light,* for example.

4. Guide Practice

Mrs. Donnelly asks the children to reread *Amos and Boris* with partners and look for opposites. After reading, Mrs. Donnelly's students list these opposites:

big-little	helping-being helped	life-death
hope-hopeless	forgetting-remembering	in the water-on land

Then Mrs. Donnelly asks the third graders each to choose one of the pairs of opposites and quickwrite about it in order to discover a theme of the story. One child writes:

> I think big-little is the most important opposite. The mouse is the little animal and of course the big animal is the whale. A theme is a little animal can help a big animal. This story is like "The Lion and the Mouse." I think the same for people. Kids can help their parents.

Children share their quickwrites with partners and then some children read aloud to the class.

5. Assess Learning

Mrs. Donnelly reviews the children's quickwrites to gauge their understanding of literary opposites. She also encourages them to think about opposites in the stories they are reading during reading workshop and asks children about the opposites as she conferences with them.

Teachable Moments. Teachers often use informal techniques called "teachable moments" to share their knowledge as expert readers and writers. These give students opportunities to apply what they are learning in authentic reading and writing activities (Staab, 1990). Sometimes teachers take advantage of teachable moments to explain or demonstrate something with the whole class, and at other times they are used with small groups of students.

Modeling is an instructional technique that teachers use to show children how to perform an unfamiliar reading or writing skill or strategy (Bergman, 1992). Teachers are expert readers and writers, and through modeling, they show children—novice readers and writers—how to perform a strategy or skill so that they can build their own understanding of the activity. Classmates also serve as models for each other.

Teachers informally model reading and writing strategies for children whenever they participate in literacy activities. Young children learn concepts about books, for example, as they watch teachers hold books, turn pages, and read from left to right and top to bottom. As children work with teachers and observe them, they develop the understanding that readers and writers do some things automatically but at other times have to take risks, think out solutions to problems, and deal with ambiguities.

Teachers use think-alouds to model for children the thought processes they go through as they use reading and writing strategies (Baumann & Schmitt, 1986; Davey, 1983; Wade, 1990). Through this modeling, children become more aware of what fluent readers and writers do and learn to think aloud about their own use of strategies. Kindergarten and first-grade teachers, for example, introduce thinking aloud as they make predictions and explain the predictions as they read a book aloud. In the vignette at the beginning of this chapter, Mrs. Donnelly used a think-aloud as she introduced alphabet books to her third-grade class. She talked about how she looked at an alphabet book and what she noticed about the pattern of one letter per page with a picture and a sentence. She described the steps she used to examine an alphabet book, and then she passed out copies of various alphabet books for the students to examine. Here is an excerpt from Mrs. Donnelly's think-aloud:

As I'm looking at *The Furry Alphabet Book* by Jerry Pallotta [1991], I am thinking about all the interesting information the author and illustrator included in this book about mammals. Here is the "A" page. I notice that there is an illustration and a paragraph of text. The text has lots of information about a rare African animal called an aye-aye. The illustration was very useful, and I think it will help me remember the information I am reading. I think this mammal looks a lot like a bat and I am thinking about it eating insects, just like bats do.

Now I'm reading the "B" page, the "C" page, the "D" page, and the "E" page, and I am noticing how much these pages are alike even though they are about different animals. Look, they all have the upper- and lowercase letters written in a corner, a paragraph of text with lots of information, and a good illustration to show the animal and make the information easier to understand.

I always like to look to see what the author found for the hard letters, such as "Q," "X," and "Z." I think Jerry Pallotta was very smart to find animals for these letters. For "Q," he chose quokka, a kind of small kangaroo from Australia. Then for "X," he used xukazi, the Zulu word for a female lamb, and for "Z," he described the zorilla, which is the smelliest skunk. I am thinking that these three are very unusual. I'd like to ask him how he ever found out about them.

Look here, after the "Z" page. I see another special page about the naked mole rat, which the author says doesn't deserve to be in this book because it doesn't have any fur. I like this; it's kind of like a secret between me and the author.

Then Mrs. Donnelly asked her third graders to look through alphabet books, to notice the format of the pages and the interesting words chosen for the "hard" letters, and to look for any special pages. Using this think-aloud, she articulated the procedure her students were to use to investigate alphabet books in preparation for writing their own class alphabet book about weather.

Teachers also take advantage of teachable moments to share information about strategies and skills with students. They introduce, review, or extend a skill or strategy in these very brief lessons. As teachers listen to children read aloud or talk about the processes they use during reading, they often have an opportunity to teach a particular strategy or skill (Atwell, 1998). Similarly, as teachers conference with children about their writing or work with them to revise or edit their writing, teachers share information about writing skills and strategies. Children also ask questions about skills and strategies or volunteer information about how they handled a reading or writing problem. Teachers who are careful observers and listen closely to their students don't miss these teachable moments.

Why Teach Skills and Strategies? Some teachers argue about whether to teach strategies and skills directly or implicitly. The position in this book is that teachers have the responsibility to teach students how to read and write, and part of that responsibility is teaching students the skills and strategies that fluent readers and writers use. Although it is true that children learn many things inductively through meaningful literacy experiences, direct instruction is important, too. Effective teachers do teach skills and strategies.

Researchers have compared classrooms in which teachers focused on teaching skills directly with other programs in which skills and strategies were taught inductively, and they concluded that traditional skills programs were no more effective according to students' performance on standardized reading texts. Moreover, researchers suggest that traditional skills programs may be less effective when we take into account that students in the balanced reading programs also think of themselves as readers and writers and have more knowledge about written language.

Freppon (1991) compared the reading achievement of first graders in traditional and balanced reading classrooms and found that the balanced group was more successful. Similarly, Reutzel and Hollingsworth (1991) compared children who were taught skills with children who spent an equal amount of time reading books, and they found that neither group did better on skill tests. This research suggests that children who do not already know skills and strategies do benefit from instruction, but the instruction must stress application to authentic reading and writing activities.

Carefully planned instruction, however, may be especially important for minority students. Lisa Delpit (1987) cautions that many children who grow up outside the dominant culture are disadvantaged when certain knowledge, strategies, and skills expected by teachers are not made explicit in their classrooms. Explicitness is crucial because people from different cultures have different sets of understandings. When they teach children from other cultures, teachers often find it difficult to get their meaning across unless they are very explicit (Delpit, 1991). Delpit's writing has created a stir because she claims that African American children and nonmainstream children frequently are not given access to the codes of power unless literacy instruction is explicit. Too often, teachers assume that children make the connection between the strategies and skills they are teaching and the future use of those strategies and skills in reading and writing, but Delpit claims that many don't.

On the other hand, several studies suggest that both mainstream and nonmainstream students learn best with balanced reading instruction. Morrow (1992) and Dahl and Freppon (1995) found that minority students in balanced reading classrooms do as well as students in skill-based classrooms, plus they develop a greater sense of the purposes of literacy and see themselves as readers and writers.

Review

Comprehension is a creative, multifaceted process that children use for reading and writing. For reading, it is the reader's process of using prior experiences and the author's text to construct meaning that is useful to that reader for a specific purpose. The five subprocesses are microprocesses, integrative processes, macroprocesses, elaborative processes, and metacognitive processes. Children learn to use both strategies and skills for reading and writing. Strategies are problem-solving behaviors, and skills are information-processing techniques that children use automatically and unconsciously. Teachers use both direct instruction and teachable moments to teach strategies and skills in balanced reading classrooms. Ways that effective teachers facilitate children's comprehension are reviewed in the feature below.

How Effective Teachers . . .
Facilitate Children's Comprehension

Effective Practices

1. Teachers view comprehension as a multifaceted process involving five subprocesses.
2. Teachers teach the five comprehension subprocesses: microprocesses, integrative processes, macroprocesses, elaborative processes, and metacognitive processes.
3. Teachers incorporate comprehension activities representing all five subprocesses into the reading process.
4. Teachers monitor and assess children's ability to use all five subprocesses.
5. Teachers teach 12 strategies: tapping prior knowledge, predicting, organizing ideas, figuring out unknown words, visualizing, making connections, applying fix-up strategies, revising meaning, monitoring, playing with language, summarizing, and evaluating.
6. Teachers teach five types of skills: comprehension skills, decoding and spelling skills, language skills, reference skills, and study skills.
7. Teachers understand the difference between strategies and skills.
8. Teachers teach minilessons on skills and strategies to the whole class or to small groups, depending on children's needs.
9. Teachers take advantage of teachable moments to answer children's questions and clarify misconceptions.
10. Teachers use think-alouds to model their use of strategies and skills for children.

Professional References

Atwell, N. (1998). *In the middle: New understandings about writing, reading, and learning* (2nd ed.). Portsmouth, NH: Heinemann.

Baker, L., & Brown, A. L. (1984). Metacognitive skills and reading. In P. D. Pearson, R. Barr, M. Kamil, & P. Mosenthal (Eds.), *Handbook of reading research* (Vol. 1, pp. 353–394). New York: Longman.

Baumann, J. F., & Schmitt, M. C. (1986). The what, why, how, and when of comprehension instruction. *The Reading Teacher, 39,* 640–647.

Bergman, J. L. (1992). SAIL—A way to success and independence for low-achieving readers. *The Reading Teacher, 45,* 598–602.

Cairney, T. (1990). Intertextuality: Infectious echoes from the past. *The Reading Teacher, 43,* 478–484.

Cairney, T. (1992). Fostering and building students' intertextual histories. *Language Arts, 69,* 502–507.

Dahl, K. L., & Freppon, P. A. (1995). A comparison of inner-city children's interpretations of reading and writing instruction in the early grades in skills-based and whole language classrooms. *Reading Research Quarterly, 30,* 50–74.

Davey, B. (1983). Think-aloud—Modeling the cognitive processes of reading comprehension. *Journal of Reading, 27,* 44–47.

Delpit, L. (1987). The silenced dialogue: Power and pedagogy in educating other people's children. *Harvard Educational Review, 58,* 280–298.

Delpit, L. (1991). A conversation with Lisa Delpit. *Language Arts, 68,* 541–547.

Duffy, G. G., & Roehler, L. R. (1987). Improving reading instruction through the use of responsible elaboration. *The Reading Teacher, 20,* 548–554.

Flood, J., & Lapp, D. (1994). Developing literary appreciation and literacy skills: A blueprint for success. *The Reading Teacher, 48,* 76–79.

Fountas, I. C., & Pinnell, G. S. (2001). *Guiding readers and writers, grades 3–6.* Portsmouth, NH: Heinemann.

Freppon, P. A. (1991). Children's concepts of the nature and purpose of reading in different instructional settings. *Journal of Reading Behavior, 23,* 139–163.

Hoyt, L. (1999). *Revisit, reflect, retell: Strategies for improving reading comprehension.* Portsmouth, NH: Heinemann.

Irwin, J. W. (1991). *Teaching reading comprehension processes* (2nd ed). Boston: Allyn & Bacon.

Keene, E. O., & Zimmermann, S. (1997). *Mosaic of thought: Teaching comprehension in a reader's workshop.* Portsmouth, NH: Heinemann.

Morrow, L. M. (1992). The impact of a literature-based program on literacy achievement, use of literature, and attitudes of children from minority backgrounds. *Reading Research Quarterly, 27,* 251–275.

Paris, S. G., & Jacobs, J. E. (1984). The benefits of informed instruction for children's reading awareness and comprehension skills. *Child Development, 55,* 2083–2093.

Paris, S. G., Lipson, M. Y., & Wixson, K. (1983). Becoming a strategic reader. *Contemporary Educational Psychology, 8,* 293–316.

Paris, S. G., Wasik, B. A., & Turner, J. C. (1991). The development of strategic readers. In R. Barr, M. L. Kamil, P. B. Mosenthal, & P. D. Pearson (Eds.), *Handbook of reading research* (Vol. 2, pp. 609–640). New York: Longman.

Pearson, P. D., & Gallagher, M. C. (1983). The instruction of reading comprehension. *Contemporary Educational Psychology, 8,* 317–344.

Pearson, P. D., Roehler, L. R., Dole, J. A., & Duffy, G. G. (1990). *Developing expertise in reading comprehension: What should be taught? How should it be taught?* (Technical Report No. 512). Champaign, IL: University of Illinois, Center for the Study of Reading.

Pressley, M., & Harris, K. R. (1990). What we really know about strategy instruction. *Educational Leadership, 48,* 31–34.

Reutzel, D. R., & Hollingsworth, P. M. (1991). Reading comprehension skills: Testing the skills distinctiveness hypothesis. *Reading Research and Instruction, 30,* 32–46.

Schmitt, M. C. (1990). A questionnaire to measure children's awareness of strategic reading processes. *The Reading Teacher, 43,* 454–461.

Smith, N. B. (1965). *American reading instruction.* Newark, DE: International Reading Association.

Spiegel, D. L. (1992). Blending whole language and systematic direct instruction. *The Reading Teacher, 46,* 38–46.

Staab, C. F. (1990). Teacher mediation in one whole literacy classroom. *The Reading Teacher, 43,* 548–552.

Stauffer, R. G. (1975). *Directing the reading-thinking process.* New York: Harper & Row.

Temple, C. (1992). Lots of plots: Patterns, meanings, and children's literature. In C. Temple & P. Collings (Eds.), *Stories and readers: New perspectives on literature in the elementary classroom* (pp. 3–13). Norwood, MA: Christopher-Gordon.

Tierney, R. J. (1990). Redefining reading comprehension. *Educational Leadership, 47,* 37–42.

Trachtenburg, P. (1990). Using children's literature to enhance phonics instruction. *The Reading Teacher, 43,* 648–654.

Wade, S. E. (1990). Using think alouds to assess comprehension. *The Reading Teacher, 43,* 442–453.

Winograd, P., & Hare, V. C. (1988). Direct instruction of reading comprehension strategies: The nature of teacher explanation. In C. Weinstein, E. Goetz, & P. Alexander (Eds.), *Learning and study strategies: Issues in assessment, instruction, and evaluation* (pp. 121–139). San Diego, CA: Academic Press.

Children's Book References

Allard, H. (1977). *Miss Nelson is missing!* Boston: Houghton Mifflin.

Barrett, J. (1978). *Cloudy with a chance of meatballs.* New York: Macmillan.

Barrett, J. (1997). *Pickles to Pittsburgh.* New York: Atheneum.

Baum, L. F. (1970). *The wizard of Oz.* New York: Macmillan.

Brett, J. (1994). *Town mouse, country mouse.* New York: Putnam.

Gibbons, G. (1994). *Nature's green umbrella: Tropical rain forests.* New York: Mulberry.

Henkes, K. (2000). *Wemberly worried.* New York: Greenwillow.

Pallotta, J. (1991). *The furry alphabet book.* Watertown, MA: Charlesbridge.

Rathmann, P. (1995). *Officer Buckle and Gloria.* New York: Putnam.

Ruckman, I. (1984). *Night of the twisters.* New York: HarperCollins.

Steig, W. (1971). *Amos and Boris.* New York: Farrar, Straus & Giroux.

Van Allsburg, C. (1981). *Jumanji.* Boston: Houghton Mifflin.

chapter 9

Becoming Familiar With the Structure of Text

- How are stories organized?
- How are informational books organized?
- How are poems organized?
- How does the structure of text affect children's reading and writing?

Mrs. Mast's Students Read "The Three Bears"

The kindergartners in Mrs. Mast's classroom listen as their teacher reads Paul Galdone's *The Three Bears* (1972) at the beginning of a weeklong focus unit on this familiar folktale. After Mrs. Mast reads *The Three Bears* aloud, the children talk about the story in a grand conversation[C]. "You shouldn't leave your front door unlocked," Angela reminds her class-mates. Kayleen adds, "Goldilocks was bad. You shouldn't go into some-one else's house like that. You could get shot and killed." Other students mention the repetition of threes in the story and ask questions about how dangerous bears are and whether or not the bears in the story might have killed Goldilocks in real life. Mrs. Mast assures the class that they will learn more about bears during the week.

See the Compendium of In-structional Procedures, which follows Chapter 12, for more information on terms marked with the symbol [C].

Mrs. Mast puts pictures of Papa Bear, Mama Bear, Baby Bear, and Goldilocks in a pocket chart and sets out word cards with the bears' names. She also sets out letter cards for each name so that children can build the names of the characters. These word cards for the key words in the book constitute a word wall[C] for kindergartners. During center time, children often sort the word cards, matching them to the pictures of the characters, and use the letter cards to spell the characters' names, matching the letters to the word cards.

The next day, Mrs. Mast passes out a set of 12 story boards[C], pictures of the events in the story made by cutting apart two old copies of the book, backing the illustrations with cardboard and colored paper, and laminating them. The illustrations taken from the beginning of the story are backed with green paper, the illustrations from the middle with yellow paper, and the illustrations from the end with red paper. The children look at the story board they receive and figure out where it fits in the story, using the colored paper backings to guide their thinking. Then the children line up in sequence along one wall in the classroom. The children not holding story boards join Mrs. Mast in retelling the story using the story boards to guide them.

During the week, Mrs. Mast reads two other versions of the folktale, both entitled *Goldilocks and the Three Bears* (Brett, 1987; Cauley, 1981), and a related book, *Deep in the Forest* (Turkle, 1976), a wordless picture book about a small bear who has an ad-venture similar to Goldilocks's. After Mrs. Mast has read all three versions of the folk-tale, the children compare them and decide that they like Cauley's version the best. They feel that her version is more satisfying than Galdone's or Brett's because at the end of Cauley's, Goldilocks is home with her mother, being scolded for what she did and warned not to go into other people's houses.

Mrs. Mast sets up five literacy centers that are related to the literature focus unit. During the week, the children work at each center, either on their own or with the as-sistance of an adult. The five centers are:

1. **Listening center.** Children listen to a tape recording of Galdone's version of *The Three Bears,* following along in copies of the book.
2. **Literacy play center.** Children use puppets of the three bears and Goldilocks in retelling the story. A flannel board with pictures related to the story is also available in the center.

3. ***Reading center.*** Children reread Galdone's version as a small group with a fifth grader or a parent volunteer. Mrs. Mast also has "bear" books in the center for students to look at.
4. ***Writing center.*** Children write in reading logs[C] with the assistance of the aide and work on their pages for the class "Book of Threes."
5. ***Skills center.*** Mrs. Mast works with small groups of students on literacy skills.

Her topics at the skills center this week are phonemic awareness, letter sounds, and making words[C]. She asks children to break these spoken words from the story into sounds: *bowl, chair, bed, house, sleep, my,* and *bear.* Next, she asks children to notice the *G* in *Goldilocks* and *B* in *bear* as she writes the words on a small chalkboard. She has a collection of small objects and pictures, many beginning with *G* and *B,* in a tub. Objects include a *book, ghost, zebra, bear, green crayon, letter, button, girl, banana, gold ring,* and *gate.* Children sort the objects into three categories: *B, G,* and "other." Mrs. Mast varies the amount of time she spends on each of these activities according to which children are in the group and what skills they already know.

Later in the week, Mrs. Mast shares the wordless book *Deep in the Forest* (Turkle, 1976) with the class. First she shows each illustration in the book without saying very much. Then she goes through the book a second time, and she and the kindergartners create the story to accompany the illustrations. The children quickly notice the twist on this story: Goldilocks has become a bear cub, and he causes a ruckus in a home belonging to a human family. The children dramatize the story using props such as bowls, chairs, and towels laid on the floor for beds.

Mrs. Mast focuses on the repetition of threes in this folktale and in others with which the children are familiar, such as "The Three Little Pigs" and "The Three Billy Goats Gruff." The children in Mrs. Mast's class usually make a collaborative book[C] as a project in each literature focus unit, and for this unit, they decide to make a "Book of Threes." Each child chooses something related to bears or the story—three chairs, three bears, three jars of honey, three bear caves, three polar bears, three bowls of porridge, and so on. They draw pictures of the objects and add a title for their page. Figure 9-1 shows one page from the book. On this page, Mario has drawn the three bears from the story and labeled them *MB* for Mama Bear, *BB* for Baby Bear, and *PB* for Papa Bear. He has also numbered the bears 1, 2, and 3. Like many young children, Mario often reverses *B,* as he did in the title and started to do on *MB* and *PB.* Mrs. Mast usually ignores reversed letters because she understands that as children have more experience with reading and writing, they begin using the correct forms. However, as Mario was writing his page, the child sitting next to him pointed out the reversed letter and encouraged him to cross out the backward *B* and write the correct form above it. After children complete their pages, they get into a circle to share them with classmates. Then Mrs. Mast helps the children compile the pages into a book. One child creates the cover page, and the book is bound together. Mrs. Mast adds the book to the classroom library, and children look at it often.

At the writing center, children make their own "Book of Threes." They take three sheets of paper and write pages as they did for the class book. Then they add a construction paper cover and compile the pages. The aide at the center helps the children bind the books together using yarn, brads, or staples, depending on the child's choice.

Because the children ask so many questions about bears—What do they eat? Are the bears in the story grizzly bears? What about polar bears?—Mrs. Mast reads an informational book, *Alaska's Three Bears* (Gill, 1990), which is about

brown or grizzly bears, black bears, and polar bears. The 5-year-olds are fascinated by the three kinds—another three—and they make three charts of information. Mrs. Mast uses the language experience approach[C] to take the children's dictation as they make charts with information about each of the three types of bears. Here is their chart about polar bears:

> *Polar bears are big and white.*
> *Polar bears are taller than people.*
> *Polar bears weigh more than 1,000 pounds.*
> *Polar bears live in ice and snow.*
> *Polar bears have good noses. They can smell a seal 20 miles away.*
> *Polar bears eat meat—seals, walruses, and foxes.*

Mrs. Mast laminates the charts, and the children read and reread them each day. Soon the children have memorized most of the sentences. After they reread the charts, children pick out and circle particular letters and words such as *polar bears* with a pen for writing on laminated charts.

Mrs. Mast notices a note to Goldilocks on the classroom message board, and she takes the note and jots an answer in childlike handwriting. Soon more children are writing notes to Goldilocks from the perspective of a bear. Most of the children realize that Mrs. Mast is pretending to be Goldilocks, and they are anxious for her to write notes back to them. One note written by an emergent writer reads:

GOOOOS	Goldilocks,
D YOU NO	Don't you know (that it is)
DDZTO GOTO	dangerous to go to
A BearH?	a bear's house?
BS.	Be safe.
FMBear	From Mother Bear

Mrs. Mast writes back:

Dear Mother Bear,
I have learned a good lesson.
I will never go into a bear's house again.
Love, Goldilocks

The children have been writing notes and sending pictures back and forth to class-mates for several months, but this is the first time they assume the role of a character in a book they are reading.

At the end of the unit, Mrs. Mast places one copy of each of "The Three Bears" books, the story boards for Galdone's version of the book, and three small teddy bears—one brown, one black, and one white—in a small "traveling" bag. Children will take turns taking the traveling bag home to share with their parents.

Mrs. Mast's language arts block is fast-paced, taking into account young children's short attention spans, their need for active involvement, and their desire to manipulate materials. Her schedule is:

8:30–8:45 Morning Message
Mrs. Mast talks briefly with the children about their news and compiles important news and daily activities in a paragraph-length message that she writes using interactive writing.[C] Afterwards, Mrs. Mast reads the message aloud twice and children join in to read familiar words.

8:45–9:15 Shared Reading
Mrs. Mast uses shared reading[C] to read the focus book or related books. After reading, children participate in a grand conversation or other whole-class activity.

9:15–10:00 Guided Reading and Centers
During guided reading[C] groups, children read leveled books and Mrs. Mast teaches phonics lessons with small groups of children while the rest of the class works at the centers related to the focus book set up in the classroom. Children rotate through the literacy centers so that each week they work at all five centers. Other centers, including blocks, a water and sand tray, and a restaurant center, are available for children to use as time permits.

10:00–10:25 Recess and Snack

10:25–10:55 Other Focus Book Activities

Children work in groups or together as a class in other reading and writing activities or related drama and art activities. One day each week, fifth graders come to Mrs. Mast's class to read books to the kindergartners.

10:55–11:00 Songs, Poems, and Fingerplays

Mrs. Mast leads the class in songs, poems, fingerplays, and other oral language activities. Whenever possible, she relates the wordplay activities to the featured book.

Mrs. Mast's lesson plan for the weeklong literature focus unit on "The Three Bears" is shown in Figure 9-2.

Young children read and listen to all three types of literature—stories, informational books, and poems—just as the students in Mrs. Mast's classroom do. These "real" books are called trade books. Many children also use reading textbooks (often called basal readers) that contain stories, informational articles, and poetry, too. In recent years, there has been a great deal of controversy about whether trade books or textbooks should be used to teach reading. Lapp, Flood, and Farnan (1992) believe that textbooks and trade books are compatible and that children should read both types.

Stories, informational books, and poems have unique structures or organizations; stories are organized differently from poems and informational books. Sometimes teachers call all literature that children read and write "stories," but stories are unique: They have specific structure elements, including plot, characters, and setting. Teachers need to introduce the three types of literature and use the labels for each type correctly.

Books for young children are available in picture-book and chapter-book formats. Picture books have brief texts, usually spread over 32 pages, in which text and illustrations combine to tell a story, provide information, or paint word pictures. The text is often minimal, and the illustrations supplement the sparse text. The illustrations in many picture books are striking. Chapter books are longer texts written in a chapter format. Many are written for older students, but some chapter-book stories, such as Dan Greenburg's series of humorous time-warp adventures featuring a boy named Zack, including *My Son, the Time Traveler* (1997a) and *Never Trust a Cat Who Wears Earrings* (1997b), are for children reading at the second-grade level.

The stories that children write reflect the stories they have read. De Ford (1981) and Eckhoff (1983) found that when primary-grade students read basal reading textbooks, the stories they write reflect the short, choppy linguistic style of the readers published at that time. In contrast, when children read stories published as picture books and chapter books, their writing reflects the more sophisticated language structures and literary style of these books. Similarly, when children learn about the structure of informational books, both their reading comprehension and their nonfiction writing improve (Flood, Lapp, & Farnan, 1986; McGee & Richgels, 1985; Piccolo, 1987).

STORIES

When preschoolers listen to family members tell stories and read them aloud, they develop an understanding or concept about stories by the time they come to school.

Figure 9-2   Mrs. Mast's Unit Plan for "The Three Bears"

	Activity	Monday	Tuesday	Wednesday	Thursday	Friday
8:30–8:45	Morning Message	———————————————————————→				
8:45–9:15	Shared Reading/Reading Aloud	Read Galdone's *The Three Bears* using a big book Grand conversation	Read Cauley's *Goldilocks and the Three Bears* Grand conversation	Read *Alaska's Three Bears* Grand conversation	Make charts on three kinds of bears: Grizzly bears Black bears Polar bears	Read *Deep in the Forest* Retell story Grand conversation
9:15–10:00	Guided Reading/Centers	Meet with guided reading groups while students work at literacy centers ——→				
10:00–10:25	Recess and Snack	———————————————————————→				
10:25–10:55	Other Focus Book Activities	Begin word wall Sequence *The Three Bears* story boards Talk about threes in story	Read Brett's *Goldilocks and the Three Bears* Compare three versions	Talk about threes in folktales Make a class "Book of Threes" Compile the book	Fifth-grade reading buddies read "bear" books	Dramatize *Deep in the Woods* Sequence story boards Graph favorite story
10:55–11:00	Songs, Poems, and Fingerplays	———————————————————————→				

Children use and refine this knowledge as they read and write stories during the primary grades. Many educators, including Jerome Bruner (1986) and Don Holdaway (1979), recommend using stories as a way into literacy.

Prekindergarten teachers often begin the day by reading a story aloud, and then the story becomes the focus for the day's activities.

Genres of Stories

Stories can be categorized in different ways, and one way is according to genres or types of stories (Buss & Karnowski, 2000). Three broad categories are folklore, fantasies, and realistic fiction.

To link to *The Children's Literature Web Guide* for Internet resources related to books for children, visit our Companion Website at www.prenhall.com/tompkins

Folklore. Stories that began hundreds of years ago and were passed down from generation to generation by storytellers before being written down are folk literature. These stories, including fables, folktales, and myths, are an important part of our cultural heritage. Fables are brief narratives designed to teach a moral. A story format is used to make the lesson easier to understand, and the moral is usually stated at the end. The characteristics of fables are:

1. They are short, often less than a page long.
2. The characters are usually animals.
3. The characters are one-dimensional, strong or weak, wise or foolish.
4. The setting is barely sketched; the stories could take place anywhere.
5. The theme is usually stated as a moral at the end of the story.

Our best-known fables, including "The Hare and the Tortoise" and "The Ant and the Grasshopper," are believed to have been written by a Greek slave named Aesop in the 6th century B.C. Collections of Aesop's fables are available for primary students, including *Aesop's Fables* (Hague, 1985) and *Doctor Coyote: A Native American Aesop's Fables* (Bierhorst, 1987). Individual fables are also available as picture-book stories, including *The Hare and the Tortoise* (Ward, 1999), *The Lion and the Rat* (Jones, 1997), and *Town Mouse, Country Mouse* (Brett, 1994).

Folktales began as oral stories, told and retold by medieval storytellers as they traveled from town to town. The problem in a folktale usually revolves around one of four situations: a journey from home to perform a task, a journey to confront a monster, the miraculous change from a harsh home to a secure home, or a confrontation between a wise beast and a foolish beast. Other characteristics are:

1. The story often begins with the phrase "Once upon a time . . .".
2. The setting is generalized and could be located anywhere.
3. The plot structure is simple and straightforward.
4. Characters are one dimensional, good or bad, stupid or clever, industrious or lazy.
5. The end is happy, and everyone lives "happily ever after."

Some folktales are cumulative tales, such as *Henny Penny* (Galdone, 1968) and *The Gingerbread Boy* (Galdone, 1975). These stories are built around the repetition of words and events. Others are talking animal stories. In these stories, such as *The Three Little Pigs* (Zemach, 1988), animals act and talk like humans. The best-known folktales, however, are fairy tales. These stories have motifs or small recurring elements, including magical powers, transformations, enchantments, magical objects, trickery, and wishes that are granted, and they feature witches, giants, fairy godmothers, and other fantastic characters. Well-known examples are *Cinderella* (Ehrlich, 1985), *The Sleeping Beauty* (Yolen, 1986), and *Jack and the Beanstalk* (Howe, 1989).

Today, some of the best-known folktales have three, four, or even more variations. Some versions came about as storytellers personalized the stories, and other variations reflect geographic and cultural diversity. Well-known folktales with different versions include "The Three Little Pigs," "Cinderella," "Goldilocks and the Three Bears," and "The Gingerbread Boy." For example, in one version of "The Gingerbread Boy" titled *The Runaway Tortilla* (Kimmel, 2000), the main character is a tortilla and it is eventually eaten by a coyote, not a fox. Folktale variations are listed in Figure 9-3.

Figure 9-3   Variations of Familiar Folktales

"Cinderella"

Climo, S. (1989). *The Egyptian Cinderella.* New York: Crowell.

Climo, S. (1993). *The Korean Cinderella.* New York: HarperCollins.

Coburn, J. R. (1996). *Jouanah: A Hmong Cinderella.* Arcadia, CA: Shen's Books.

Cole, B. (1987). *Prince Cinders.* New York: Putnam.

Compton, J. (1994). *Ashpet: An Appalachian tale.* New York: Holiday.

Ehrlich, A. (1985). *Cinderella.* New York: Dial.

Galdone, P. (1978). *Cinderella.* New York: McGraw-Hill.

Hickox, R. (1998). *The golden sandal: A Middle Eastern Cinderella story.* New York: Holiday House.

Hooks, W. H. (1987). *Moss gown.* New York: Clarion.

Huck, C. (1989). *Princess Furball.* New York: Greenwillow.

Jaffe, N. (1998). *The way meat loves salt: A Cinderella tale from the Jewish tradition.* New York: Henry Holt.

Louie, A. L. (1982). *Yeh-Shen: A Cinderella story from China.* New York: Philomel.

Martin, R. (1992). *The rough-face girl.* New York: Putnam.

Munsch, R. N. (1980). *The paper bag princess.* Toronto, Canada: Annick Press.

Pollock, P. (1996). *The turkey girl: A Zuni Cinderella story.* Boston: Little, Brown.

San Souci, R. D. (1998). *Cendrillon: A Caribbean Cinderella.* New York: Aladdin Books.

Schroeder, A. (1997). *Smoky Mountain Rose: An Appalachian Cinderella.* New York: Puffin Books.

Steptoe, J. (1987). *Mufaro's beautiful daughters: An African tale.* New York: Lothrop.

"The Gingerbread Boy"

Amoss, B. (1994). *The Cajun gingerbread boy.* New Orleans: MTC Press.

Asbjorsen, P. C., & Moe, J. (1980). *The runaway pancake.* New York: Larousse.

Brown, M. (1972). *The bun: A tale from Russia.* New York: Harcourt Brace Jovanovich.

Cauley, L. B. (1988). *The pancake boy: An old Norwegian folk tale.* New York: Putnam.

Galdone, P. (1975). *The gingerbread boy.* New York: Seabury.

Jarrell, R. (1964). *The gingerbread rabbit.* New York: Collier.

Kimmel, E. A. (2000). *The runaway tortilla.* Delray Beach, FL: Winslow Press.

Oppenheim, J. (1986). *You can't catch me!* Boston: Houghton Mifflin.

Sawyer, R. (1953). *Journey cake, ho!* New York: Viking.

Ziefert, H. (1995). *The gingerbread boy.* New York: Viking.

"Goldilocks and the Three Bears"

Cauley, L. B. (1981). *Goldilocks and the three bears.* New York: Putnam.

Ernst, L. C. (2000). *Goldilocks returns.* New York: Simon & Schuster.

Galdone, P. (1972). *The three bears.* New York: Clarion.

Petach, H. (1995). *Goldilocks and the three hares.* New York: Putnam.

Tolhurst, M. (1990). *Somebody and the three Blairs.* New York: Orchard.

Turkle, B. (1976). *Deep in the forest.* New York: Dutton.

"The Three Little Pigs"

Bishop, G. (1989). *The three little pigs.* New York: Scholastic.

Galdone, P. (1970). *The three little pigs.* New York: Seabury.

Lowell, S. (1992). *The three little javelinas.* Flagstaff, AZ: Northland.

Marshall, J. (1989). *The three little pigs.* New York: Dial.

Scieszka, J. (1989). *The true story of the three little pigs!* New York: Viking.

Trivizas, E. (1993). *The three little wolves and the big bad pig.* New York: McElderry Books.

Wiesner, D. (2001). *The three pigs.* New York: Clarion.

Zemach, M. (1988). *The three little pigs.* New York: Farrar, Straus & Giroux.

People around the world have created myths to explain natural phenomena. Some myths explain the origin of the world and how human beings were brought into existence; some explain the seasons, the sun and moon, and the constellations; and others explain the mountains and other physical features of the earth. Ancient peoples used myths to explain many things that have more recently been explained by scientific theories and investigations. Characteristics of myths are:

1. Myths explain creations.
2. Characters are often heroes with supernatural powers.
3. The setting is barely sketched.
4. Magical powers are required.

Picture-book retellings of myths from various cultures are available for children. The Greek myth *Persephone* (Hutton, 1994) tells how spring originated, and the Native American myth *The Legend of the Bluebonnet* (de Paola, 1983) recounts how these flowers came to beautify the countryside. Other myths tell how animals came to be or why they look the way they do, including *Iktomi and the Boulder* (Goble, 1988) and *The Story of Jumping Mouse* (Steptoe, 1984).

Legends are myths about heroes and heroines who have done something important enough to be remembered in story; they are thought to have some basis in history but are not verifiable. Stories about Robin Hood and King Arthur, for example, are legends. American legends are tall tales, and three of the best known are available as picture books written and illustrated by Steven Kellogg: *Paul Bunyan* (1984), *Johnny Appleseed* (1988), and *Pecos Bill* (1986).

Fantasies. Fantasies are stories that could not really take place. Authors create new worlds for their characters, but these worlds must be based in reality so that readers will believe they exist. Two well-known examples are *Charlotte's Web* (White, 1952) and *Harry Potter and the Sorcerer's Stone* (Rowling, 1997). Four types of fantasies are modern literary tales, fantastic stories, science fiction, and high fantasy.

Modern literary tales are related to folktales and fairy tales because they often incorporate many characteristics and conventions of traditional literature, but they have been written more recently and have identifiable authors. The best-known author of modern literary tales is Hans Christian Andersen, a Danish writer of the 1800s who wrote *The Emperor's New Clothes* (Westcott, 1984) and *The Ugly Duckling* (Pinkney, 1999). Other examples of modern literary tales include *Alexander and the Wind-up Mouse* (Lionni, 1969), *The Wolf's Chicken Stew* (Kasza, 1987), and *The Principal's New Clothes* (Calmenson, 1989).

Fantastic stories are realistic in most details, but some events require readers to suspend disbelief. The characteristics of fantasies are:

1. The events in the story are extraordinary; things that could not happen in today's world.
2. The setting is realistic.
3. Main characters are people or personified animals.
4. Themes often deal with the conflict between good and evil.

Through character and theme, readers are drawn to suspend their disbelief (Lukens, 1999). In *Where the Wild Things Are* (Sendak, 1962), for example, after Max is sent to his bedroom for misbehaving, his bedroom is transformed into a different world and he travels to the land of the wild things and then back home again. Children find it believable that a forest grows in Max's room and a boat arrives to take Max to the land of the wild things, but adults recognize that Max's trip is a dream. The theme—that there's no place like home—also seems reasonable to both adults and children.

Some fantastic stories are animal fantasies, such as *A Toad for Tuesday* (Erickson, 1974) and *Charlotte's Web* (White, 1952). In these stories, the main characters are animals that are endowed with human traits. Third and fourth graders often realize that the animals symbolize human beings, and these stories explore human relationships. Other fantasies are toy fantasies, such as *Winnie-the-Pooh* (Milne, 1961). Toy fantasies are similar to animal fantasies except that the main characters are talking toys, usually stuffed animals or dolls. Other fantasies involve enchanted journeys during which wondrous things happen. The journey must have a purpose, but it is usually overshadowed by the thrill and delight of the fantastic world. Examples include *Peter Pan* (Barrie, 1950), *Alice's Adventures in Wonderland* (Carroll, 1984), and *Charlie and the Chocolate Factory* (Dahl, 1964).

In science fiction stories, authors create a world in which science interacts with every area of society (Norton, 2003). Many stories involve traveling through space to distant galaxies or meeting alien societies. Authors hypothesize scientific advancements and imagine technology of the future to create the plot. Characteristics of science fiction are:

1. The story is set in the future.
2. Conflict is usually between the characters and natural or mechanical forces, such as robots.
3. The characters believe in the advanced technology.
4. A detailed description of scientific facts is provided.

Most science fiction stories are written for older students, but Jane Yolen has written an entertaining series of Commander Toad easy-to-read chapter books for second graders; for example, *Commander Toad in Space* (Yolen, 1980). Time-warp stories in which the characters move forward and back in time are also classified as science fiction. Jon Scieszka's Time Warp Trio stories, including *Knights of the Kitchen Table* (1991), are popular with third and fourth graders.

In high fantasy, heroes and heroines confront evil for the good of humanity. The primary characteristic is the focus on the conflict between good and evil, as in C. S. Lewis's *The Lion, the Witch and the Wardrobe* (1994). High fantasy is related to folk literature in that it is characterized by motifs and themes. Most stories include magical kingdoms, quests, tests of courage, magical powers, and fantastic characters. These stories are usually written for older students.

Realistic Fiction. These stories are lifelike and believable, without magic or supernatural powers. The outcome is reasonable and the story is a representation of action that seems truthful. Realistic fiction helps children discover that their problems and desires are not unique and that they are not alone in experiencing certain feelings and situations. Realistic fiction also broadens children's horizons and allows them to experience new adventures. Two types of realistic fiction are contemporary stories and historical stories.

When children read contemporary stories, they identify with characters who are their own age and have similar interests and problems. In *Ramona Quimby, Age 8* (Cleary, 1981), for example, children read about Ramona and her typical family tensions. Characteristics of contemporary fiction are:

1. Characters act like real people or like real animals.
2. The setting is in the world as we know it today.
3. Stories deal with everyday occurrences or "relevant subjects."

Other contemporary stories include *Ira Sleeps Over* (Waber, 1972), *How Many Days to America* (Bunting, 1988), and *Tales of a Fourth Grade Nothing* (Blume, 1972).

To link to sites that present interviews with many children's authors, including Lois Ehlert, Patricia MacLachlan, and Eric Carle, visit our Companion Website at www.prenhall.com/tompkins

Historical stories are set in the past. Details about food, clothing, and transportation must be typical of the era in which the story is set because the setting influences the plot. Characteristics of this genre are:

1. The setting is historically accurate.
2. Conflict is often between characters or between a character and society.
3. The language is appropriate to the setting.
4. Themes are universal, both to the historical period of the book and for today.

Examples of historical fiction include *Sarah, Plain and Tall* (MacLachlan, 1985) and *Molly's Pilgrim* (Cohen, 1983). Through historical fiction, children are immersed in historical events, appreciate the contributions of people who have lived before them, and understand human relationships.

Figure 9-4 reviews the folklore, fantasy, and realistic fiction genres, and lists additional examples of stories for primary-grade students.

Elements of Story Structure

Stories have unique structural elements that distinguish them from other types of literature. Four story elements are plot, characters, setting, and theme. These elements work together to structure a story, and authors manipulate them to make their stories hold readers' attention.

Plot. The sequence of events involving characters in conflict situations is plot. A story's plot is based on the goals of one or more characters and the processes they go through to attain these goals (Lukens, 1999). The main characters want to achieve a goal, and other characters are introduced to oppose the main characters or prevent them from being successful. The story events are set in motion by characters as they attempt to overcome conflict, reach their goals, and solve their problems.

The most basic aspect of plot is the division of the main events of a story into three parts: beginning, middle, and end. In *The Tale of Peter Rabbit* (Potter, 1902), for instance, the three story parts are easy to pick out. As the story begins, Mrs. Rabbit sends her children out to play after warning them not to go into Mr. McGregor's garden. In the middle, Peter goes into Mr. McGregor's garden and is almost caught. Finally, Peter finds his way out of the garden and gets home safely—the end of the story. Children can make a story map of the beginning-middle-end of the story using words and pictures, as the chart in Figure 9-5 shows.

Specific information is presented in each of the three story parts. In the beginning, the author introduces the characters, describes the setting, and presents a problem. Together the characters, setting, and events develop the plot and sustain the theme through the story. In the middle, the plot unfolds, with each event preparing readers for what will follow. Conflict heightens as the characters face roadblocks that keep them from solving their problems. How the characters tackle these problems adds suspense to keep readers interested. In the end, all is reconciled and readers learn whether or not the characters' struggles are successful.

Attempting to solve the problem introduced at the beginning of the story is what drives the plot. In the middle, characters meet roadblocks or other obstacles to solving the problem, and then the problem is finally resolved at the end. Plot development involves four components:

1. *A problem.* A problem is presented at the beginning of the story. The middle of the story usually begins soon after the problem is introduced.

Figure 9-4   The Story Genres

Category	Genre	Description and Examples
Folklore	Fables	Brief tales told to point out a moral. For example: *Town Mouse, Country Mouse* (Brett, 1994), *Seven Blind Mice* (Young, 1992), and *The Hare and the Tortoise* (Ward, 1999).
	Folktales	Stories in which heroes and heroines demonstrate virtues to triumph over adversity. For example: *Rumpelstiltskin* (Zelinsky, 1986) and *The Three Billy Goats Gruff* (Stevens, 1987).
	Myths	Stories created by ancient peoples to explain natural phenomena. For example: *Why Mosquitoes Buzz in People's Ears* (Aardema, 1975) and *Iktomi and the Boulder* (Goble, 1988).
	Legends	Hero tales that recount the courageous deeds of people as they struggled against each other or against gods and monsters. For example: *Paul Bunyan: A Tall Tale* (Kellogg, 1984).
Fantasy	Modern Literary Tales	Stories written by modern authors that exemplify the characteristics of folktales. For example: *The Ugly Duckling* (Pinkney, 1999) and *The Wolf's Chicken Stew* (Kasza, 1987).
	Fantastic Stories	Imaginative stories that explore alternate realities and contain one or more elements not found in the natural world. For example: *Charlie and the Chocolate Factory* (Dahl, 1964), *The Mouse and the Motorcycle* (Cleary, 1965), and *Charlotte's Web* (White, 1952).
	Science Fiction	Stories that explore scientific possibilities. For example: *Commander Toad in Space* (Yolen, 1980) and *Knights of the Kitchen Table* (Scieszka, 1991).
	High Fantasy	Stories that focus on the conflict between good and evil and often involve quests. For example: *The Lion, the Witch and the Wardrobe* (Lewis, 1994) and *Harry Potter and the Sorcerer's Stone* (Rowling, 1997).
Realistic Fiction	Contemporary Stories	Stories that portray the real world and contemporary society. For example: *Ira Sleeps Over* (Waber, 1972), *Ramona and Her Father* (Cleary, 1990), and *Tales of a Fourth Grade Nothing* (Blume, 1972).
	Historical Stories	Realistic stories set in the past. For example: *The Watsons Go to Birmingham—1963* (Curtis, 1995) and *Sarah, Plain and Tall* (MacLachlan, 1985).

2. ***Roadblocks.*** Characters face roadblocks as they attempt unsuccessfully to solve the problem in the middle of the story.
3. ***The high point.*** The high point in the action (or the climax) occurs when the problem is about to be solved. This high point marks the division of the middle and end of the story.
4. ***The solution.*** The problem is solved and the roadblocks are overcome at the end of the story.

Figure 9-6 presents a plot diagram shaped like a mountain that incorporates these four components.

After introducing the problem, authors throw roadblocks in the way of an easy solution. As characters remove one roadblock, authors devise another to further thwart the characters. Stories may contain any number of roadblocks, but many stories for young children contain three. In *Hog-eye* (Meddaugh, 1995), for example, a young pig taking a shortcut through the woods is caught by a hungry wolf and is about to become pig soup. To avoid being eaten, the pig outwits the wolf by sending him off three times—the three roadblocks—to get ingredients for the soup. First he goes to get some vegetables from Mr. Gray's garden and gets caught in a trap; next he goes to get more vegetables at Devil's Cliff and falls off the cliff; and third, he goes to get

Second graders learn about the structure of stories as they dramatize a familiar story.

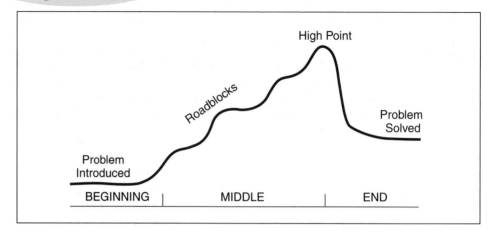

Figure 9-6 A Plot Diagram

High Point

Roadblocks

Problem
Solved

Problem
Introduced

| BEGINNING | MIDDLE | END |

water at Torrential Falls and nearly drowns when he falls in the water. While the wolf is gone each time, the pig tries to escape but the wolf returns before she gets away.

The high point of the action occurs when the solution of the problem hangs in the balance. Tension is high, and readers continue reading to learn whether or not the main characters solve the problem. The young pig is desperate, so she sends the wolf for one more ingredient—poison ivy, which she calls Green Threeleaf. She tells the wolf to roll in a patch of it to crush the leaves first and then to put the leaves inside his shirt as he picks them to keep them warm. When the wolf returns, he begins to make the soup, but the pig threatens to cast an evil spell—the hog-eye—on him so he will itch all over, if he doesn't let her go. He refuses so she casts the spell, and, of course, he soon begins to itch. That's when the wolf agrees to let the young pig go, and she goes home safely. As the story ends, the problem is solved and the goal achieved.

Figure 9-7 lists books illustrating plot and the other elements of story structure that are appropriate for young children.

Characters. Characters are the people or personified animals who are involved in the story. Characters are often the most important structural element because the story is centered on them. Usually, one or two fully rounded characters and several supporting characters are involved in a story. Fully developed main characters have many character traits, both good and bad; that is to say, they have all the characteristics of real people. Inferring a character's traits is an important part of reading. Through character traits, we get to know a character well, and the character seems to come to life. A list of stories with fully developed main characters is also included in Figure 9-7.

Characters are developed in four ways: through appearance, action, dialogue, and monologue. Some description of the characters' physical appearance is usually included when they are introduced. Readers learn about characters by the description of their facial features, body shapes, habits of dress, mannerisms, and gestures. On the first page of *Tacky the Penguin* (Lester, 1988), the illustration of Tacky wearing a bright floral shirt and a purple-and-white tie suggests to readers that Tacky is an "odd bird"! Lester confirms this impression as she describes how Tacky behaves.

The second way—and often the best way—to learn about characters is through their actions. In Van Allsburg's *The Stranger* (1986), readers deduce that the stranger is Jack Frost because of what he does: He watches geese flying south for the winter,

Figure 9-7 Stories Illustrating the Elements of Story Structure

Elements	Books
Plot	Bauer, M. D. (1986). *On my honor.* Boston: Houghton Mifflin. (Grade 4)
	Brett, J. (1989). *The mitten.* New York: Putnam. (preK–1)
	Edwards, P. D., & Cole, H. (1996). *Livingston Mouse.* New York: HarperCollins. (K–2)
	Galdone, P. (1975). *The gingerbread boy.* New York: Seabury. (preK–1)
	Polacco, P. (1988). *Rechenka's eggs.* New York: Philomel. (K–2)
	Potter, B. (1902). *The tale of Peter Rabbit.* New York: Warne. (preK–1)
	Sendak, M. (1962). *Where the wild things are.* New York: Harper & Row. (preK–1)
	Steig, W. (1969). *Sylvester and the magic pebble.* New York: Simon & Schuster. (1–3)
Characters	Blume, J. (1972). *Tales of a fourth grade nothing.* New York: Dutton. (3–4)
	Brett, J. (1994). *Town mouse, country mouse.* New York: Putnam. (1–3)
	Cleary, B. (1981). *Ramona Quimby, age 8.* New York: Morrow. (2–3)
	Henkes, K. (1991). *Chrysanthemum.* New York: Greenwillow. (1–2)
	Lester, H. (1988). *Tacky the penguin.* Boston: Houghton Mifflin. (1–2)
	Meddaugh, S. (1995). *Hog-eye.* Boston: Houghton Mifflin. (K–2)
	Naylor, P. R. (1991). *Shiloh.* New York: Atheneum. (4)
	Steig, W. (1971). *Amos and Boris.* New York: Farrar, Straus & Giroux. (2–4)
	Waber, B. (1972). *Ira sleeps over.* Boston: Houghton Mifflin. (K–1)
	Zelinsky, P. O. (1986). *Rumpelstiltskin.* New York: Dutton. (K–2)
Setting	Bunting, E. (1994). *Smoky night.* San Diego: Harcourt Brace. (3–4)
	Curtis, C. P. (1995). *The Watsons go to Birmingham—1963.* New York: Delacorte. (4)
	McCloskey, R. (1969). *Make way for ducklings.* New York: Viking. (preK–1)
	Ryan, P. M. (1998). *Riding Freedom.* New York: Scholastic. (3–4)
	Steig, W. (1987). *Brave Irene.* New York: Farrar, Straus & Giroux. (2–3)
Theme	Bunting, E. (1994). *A day's work.* New York: Clarion. (2–4)
	Cohen, B. (1983). *Molly's pilgrim.* New York: Lothrop, Lee & Shepard. (3–4)
	Lionni, L. (1969). *Alexander and the wind-up mouse.* New York: Pantheon. (K–3)
	Polacco, P. (1990). *Thundercake.* New York: Philomel. (K–3)
	Soto, G. (1993). *Too many tamales.* New York: Putnam. (K–3)
	Speare, E. (1983). *The sign of the beaver.* Boston: Houghton Mifflin. (4)
	White, E. B. (1952). *Charlotte's web.* New York: Harper & Row. (3–4)

blows a cold wind, labors long hours without becoming tired, has an unusual rapport with wild animals, and is unfamiliar with modern conveniences.

Dialogue is the third way characters are developed. For example, in *Martha Speaks* (Meddaugh, 1992), the story of a talking dog, it is the dog's dialogue that both gets her in trouble and saves the day. Authors also provide insight into characters by revealing their thoughts, or internal monologue. In *Sylvester and the Magic Pebble* (Steig, 1969), thoughts and wishes are central to the story. Sylvester, a donkey, foolishly wishes to become a rock, and he spends a miserable winter that way. Steig shares the donkey's thinking with us. He thinks about his parents, who are frantic with worry, and we learn how Sylvester feels in the spring when his parents picnic on the rock he has become.

Children often make open-mind portraits[C] to examine these four dimensions of characters. Figure 9-8 shows a third grader's open-mind portrait of Sarah, the mail-order bride who travels from Maine to make a new home on the prairie in the award-winning book *Sarah, Plain and Tall* (MacLachlan, 1985). The portrait of Sarah shown on the left side of the figure is placed on top, and the picture on the right showing Sarah's thoughts is placed underneath. This open-mind portrait focuses on the things that Sarah loves—the Maine coast, her cat named Seal, sand dunes and hay dunes, and her new prairie family.

Setting. In some stories, the setting is barely sketched; these are called backdrop settings. The setting in many folktales, for example, is relatively unimportant, and the convention "Once upon a time . . ." is enough to set the stage. In other stories, the setting

Figure 9-8   **An Open-Mind Portrait of Sarah of *Sarah, Plain and Tall***

is elaborate and essential to the story's effectiveness; these settings are called integral settings (Lukens, 1999). A list of stories with integral settings is also presented in Figure 9-7. The setting in these stories is specific, and authors take care to ensure the authenticity of the historical period or geographic location in which the story is set.

Four dimensions of setting are location, weather, time period, and time. Location is an important dimension in many stories. For example, the Boston Commons in *Make Way for Ducklings* (McCloskey, 1969) is integral to that story's effectiveness. The setting is artfully described and adds something unique to the story. In contrast, many stories take place in predictable settings that do not contribute to the story's effectiveness.

Weather is a second dimension of setting and, like location, is crucial in some stories, but in other books, weather is not mentioned because it does not affect the outcome of the story. Many stories take place on warm, sunny days, such as *Hog-eye* (Meddaugh, 1995), in which the weather is unimportant.

The third dimension of setting is the time period, an important element in stories set in the past. Many stories set in the American past are available for primary students. For example, *The Josefina Story Quilt* (Coerr, 1986), a story about a girl and her family going to California in a covered wagon, realistically depicts how the pioneers traveled west 150 years ago, and *The Bracelet* (Uchida, 1993), a story of a Japanese American family's relocation to an internment camp in 1942, illustrates the unfairness of the government's treatment of Americans of Japanese descent during World War II.

The fourth dimension, time, involves both time of day and the passage of time. Most stories ignore time of day, except for scary stories that take place after dark. In stories such as *The Ghost-Eye Tree* (Martin & Archambault, 1985), in which two children must walk past a scary tree at night to get a pail of milk, time is a more important dimension than in stories that take place during the day, because night makes things more scary.

Many short stories span a brief period of time—often less than a day, and sometimes less than an hour. In *Jumanji* (Van Allsburg, 1981), Peter and Judy's bizarre adventure, during which their house is overtaken by exotic jungle creatures, lasts only several hours. Other stories, such as *The Ugly Duckling* (Pinkney, 1999), span a long enough period for the main character to grow to maturity.

Children can draw maps to show the setting of a story. These maps might show the path a character traveled or the passage of time in a story. Figure 9-9 shows a map for *Tulip Sees America* (Rylant, 1998). In this story, a man and his dog, named Tulip, take a trip across the United States and decide to stay in Oregon where they can see the Pacific Ocean.

Theme. The underlying meaning of a story is the theme, and it embodies general truths about human nature (Lehr, 1991; Lukens, 1999). Theme usually deals with the characters' emotions and values. Themes can be stated either explicitly or implicitly; explicit themes are stated openly and clearly in the story, whereas implicit themes must be inferred from the story. Themes are developed as the characters attempt to overcome the obstacles that prevent them from reaching their goals. A list of stories with themes that are appropriate for young children is presented in Figure 9-7.

In a fable, the theme is often stated explicitly at the end, but in most stories, the theme emerges through the thoughts, speech, and actions of the characters as they seek to resolve their conflicts. In *A Chair for My Mother* (Williams, 1982), for example, a young girl demonstrates the importance of sacrificing personal wants for her family's welfare as she and her mother collect money to buy a new chair after they lose all of their belongings in a fire.

Stories usually have more than one theme, and their themes usually cannot be articulated with a single word. *Charlotte's Web* (White, 1952) has several "friendship"

Figure 9-9 A Second Grader's Story Map for *Tulip Sees America*

themes, one explicitly stated and others inferred from the text. Friendship is a multi-dimensional theme—qualities of a good friend, unlikely friends, and sacrificing for a friend, for instance. Teachers can probe students' thinking as they work to construct a theme and move beyond one-word labels (Au, 1992).

Why Do Teachers Need to Know About Story Elements?

Most teachers are familiar with story terms such as *character, plot,* and *setting,* but to plan for reading instruction, teachers need to understand how authors combine the story elements to craft stories. Teachers cannot assume that teacher's manuals or other guides will be available for every story they read with their students, or that these guides provide the necessary information about story structure. Teachers must be prepared to think about the structure of stories they will use in their classrooms.

For example, after reading *Sarah, Plain and Tall* (MacLachlan, 1985), teachers might think about how the story would be different if Sarah, not Anna, were telling the story. They might wonder if the author meant to send a message of promise of future happiness for the family by setting the story in the springtime. They also might speculate that the storm was the turning point in the story or wonder about the role of colors. This kind of thoughtful reflection allows teachers to know the story better, prepare themselves to guide their students through the story, and plan activities to help students explore the story's meaning.

Teachers teach minilessons[C] about story elements so that students can use this knowledge to enhance their comprehension. The minilesson feature on page 248 shows how Ms. Tomas teaches her first graders about the beginning, middle, and end of stories. According to Irwin (1991), when children recognize the author's organizational pattern, they are better able to comprehend what they are reading or listening to being read aloud. During grand conversations, teachers often direct students' attention to how the setting or a character's dialogue has influenced a story. Primary-grade students also use this knowledge to organize their retellings of favorite fairy tales into beginning-middle-end parts or to compare versions of a story, as Mrs. Mast's students did in the vignette at the beginning of the chapter. Similarly, when teachers conference with children about stories they are writing, knowledge about story structure and related terminology, such as *beginning, middle, end, characters,* and *theme,* enrich the conversation.

English-language learners are better able to use macroprocesses to comprehend stories they are reading when they know about the elements of story structure.

INFORMATIONAL BOOKS

Stories have been the primary genre for reading and writing instruction in the elementary grades because it has been assumed that constructing stories in the mind is a fundamental way of learning (Wells, 1986). Recent research, however, suggests that children may prefer to read informational or nonfiction books and are able to understand them as well as they do stories (Pappas, 1993). Certainly, children are interested in learning about their world—how lions and tigers hunt for food, how a road is built, how the Native Americans lived, or about Abraham Lincoln's childhood—and informational books provide this knowledge. Even preschool children listen to informational books read aloud to learn about the world around them.

Russell Freedman, who won the 1988 Newbery Award for *Lincoln: A Photobiography* (1987), talks about the purpose of informational books and explains that it is not enough for an informational book to provide information: "[An informational book] must create a vivid and believable world that the reader will enter willingly and leave only with reluctance. . . . It should be just as compelling as a good story" (1992, p. 3). High-quality informational books like Freedman's engage readers and tap their curiosity. A new wave of engaging and artistic informational books is being published today, and these books show increased respect for children. Peter Roop (1992) explains that for years, informational books were the "ugly duckling" of children's literature, but now they have grown into a beautiful swan.

Four qualities of informational books are accuracy, organization, design, and style (Vardell, 1991). First and foremost, the facts must be current and complete. They must be well researched, and, when appropriate, varying points of view should be presented. Stereotypes are to be avoided, and details in both the text and the illustrations

Minilesson

Topic: The Middle of a Story
Grade: First Grade
Time: One 30-minute period

Ms. Tomas is teaching a series of minilessons to her first-grade class about the characteristics of the beginning, middle, and end of stories. Several days ago, she taught a lesson about story beginnings, and the children analyzed the beginnings of several familiar stories. In this minilesson, Ms. Tomas uses the same stories to analyze the characteristics of story middles.

1. Introduce the Topic
Ms. Tomas begins by asking her first graders to name the three parts of a story, and they respond "beginning, middle, and end" in unison. She invites Kevin to read aloud the chart about the characteristics of story beginnings that they made previously. Then Ms. Tomas explains that in today's minilesson, they will examine the middle part of a story.

2. Share Examples
Ms. Tomas shows the children three familiar books: *Hey, Al* (Yorinks, 1986), *The Wolf's Chicken Stew* (Kasza, 1987), and *Tacky the Penguin* (Lester, 1988). She reminds them that several days ago, she read aloud the beginnings of these stories and explains that today she will read aloud the middle parts. She briefly summarizes *Hey, Al* and then reads the middle part aloud. She repeats the procedure with the other two stories.

3. Provide Information
The teacher asks the children to think about the middle of the stories. Alexi replies that the problem is getting worse in the middle of each story: "It looks like the hunters will get the penguins in *Tacky the Penguin,* and the wolf looks like he is getting ready to eat the little chicks in *The Wolf's Chicken Stew,* and something bad is happening to Al and Eddie in *Hey, Al.*" Ms. Tomas explains that authors add roadblocks to keep characters from solving their problems too quickly. The first graders identify the roadblocks in each story. Jack mentions another characteristic of story middles: "You meet other characters." Clara offers another characteristic: "I think it's important that you get a little hint about how the story is going to end. I mean, Mr. Wolf is beginning to like the little chicks—you can tell." The teacher also points out that the middle is the longest part of the story, and children count the pages to assure themselves that she is right.

4. Guide Practice
Ms. Tomas uses interactive writing with her students to develop a chart about the middle of stories. Their chart lists these characteristics:

1. The problem gets worse.
2. There are roadblocks.
3. You meet new characters.
4. You get a hint about the ending.
5. It is the longest part.

5. Assess Learning
After Ms. Tomas teaches a minilesson on the end of stories, she will read *Martha Speaks* (Meddaugh, 1992). Afterwards, the children will make flip booklets and will retell the beginning on the first page, the middle on the second page, and the end on the third page. Ms. Tomas will monitor their understanding of beginning, middle, and end through their retellings.

must be authentic. Second, information should be presented clearly and logically, using organizational patterns to increase the book's readability. Third, the book's design should be eye-catching and enhance its usability. Illustrations should complement the text, and explanations should accompany each illustration. Last, the style should be lively and stimulating so as to engage readers' curiosity and wonder.

Genres of Informational Books

Informational books are available today on topics ranging from biological sciences, physical sciences, and social sciences to arts and biographies. *Cactus Hotel* (Guiberson, 1991) is a fine informational book about the desert ecosystem; the author discusses the life cycle of a giant saguaro cactus and describes its role as a home for desert creatures. Other books, such as *Whales* (Simon, 1989), illustrated with striking full-page color photos, and *Antarctica* (Cowcher, 1990), illustrated with dramatic double-page paintings, are socially responsible and emphasize the threats people pose to animals and the earth.

Books About Letters and Numbers. Some informational books focus on letters and numbers. Although many alphabet and counting books with pictures of familiar objects are designed for young children, others provide a wealth of information on various topics. In his alphabet book *Illuminations* (1989), Jonathan Hunt presents detailed information about medieval life, and in *The Underwater Alphabet Book* (1991), Jerry Pallotta provides information about 26 types of fish and other sea creatures. Muriel and Tom Feelings present information about Africa in *Moja Means One: Swahili Counting Book* (1971), and Ann Herbert Scott presents information about cowboys in *One Good Horse: A Cowpuncher's Counting Book* (1990). In some of these books, new terms are introduced and illustrated, and in others, the term is explained in a sentence or a paragraph.

Other informational books focus on mathematical concepts (Whitin & Wilde, 1992). Tana Hoban's *26 Letters and 99 Cents* (1987) presents concepts about money, *What Comes in 2's, 3's and 4's?* (Aker, 1990) introduces multiplication, and *If You Made a Million* (Schwartz, 1989) focuses on big numbers.

Biographies. Biographies also are informational books. Those being written today are more realistic than in the past, presenting well-known personalities warts and all. Jean Fritz's portraits of Revolutionary War figures, such as *Will You Sign Here, John Hancock?* (1976), are among the best known, but she has also written comprehensive biographies, including *The Great Little Madison* (1989). Fritz and other authors often include notes in the back of books to explain how the details were researched and to provide additional information. Only a few autobiographies are available to students, but more are being published each year. Autobiographies about authors and illustrators, such as Cynthia Rylant's *Best Wishes* (1992), are also popular.

Combination Books. Other books present information within a story context; authors of these books devise innovative strategies for combining information with a story. Margy Burns Knight's *Who Belongs Here? An American Story* (1993), a two-part book, is a good example. One part is the story of Nary, a young Cambodian refugee who escapes to the United States after his parents are killed by the Khmer Rouge. This story is told in a picture-book format, with the story text accompanying each picture. The second part of the book is information about refugees, immigration laws, and cultural diversity in the United States. The text for this second part is printed in a different typeface and appears below the story text on each page. Additional information about the United States as a nation of immigrants is presented at the back of the book. The two parts work together to create a very powerful book.

To link to *Carol Hurst's Children's Literature Site* for reviews of informational books for social studies and science units, visit our Companion Website at www.prenhall.com/tompkins

Some combination informational/story books are imaginative fantasies. The Magic School Bus series is perhaps the best known of this type. In *The Magic School Bus Inside a Beehive* (Cole, 1996), for example, Ms. Frizzle and her class study bees and take a field trip on the magic school bus into a beehive to learn about the life cycle of honeybees, how honey is made, and bee society. The page layout is innovative, with charts and reports containing factual information presented at the outside edges of most pages.

Expository Text Structures

Informational books are organized in particular ways called expository text structures. Five of the most common organizational patterns are description, sequence, comparison, cause and effect, and problem and solution (Meyer & Freedle, 1984; Niles, 1974).

Figure 9-10   The Five Expository Text Structures

Pattern	Description	Graphic Organizer	Sample Passage
Description	The author describes a topic by listing characteristics, features, and examples. Cue words include *for example* and *characteristics are*.		The Olympic symbol consists of five interlocking rings. The rings represent the five continents from which athletes come to compete in the games. The rings are colored black, blue, green, red, and yellow. At least one of these colors is found in the flag of every country sending athletes to compete in the Olympic games.
Sequence	The author lists items or events in numerical or chronological order. Cue words include *first, second, third, next, then*, and *finally*.	1. _____ 2. _____ 3. _____ 4. _____ 5. _____	The Olympic games began as athletic festivals to honor the Greek gods. The most important festival was held in the valley of Olympia to honor Zeus, the king of the gods. This festival became the Olympic games in 776 B.C. They were ended in A.D. 394. No Olympic games were held for more than 1,500 years. Then the modern Olympics began in 1896. Almost 300 male athletes competed in the first modern Olympics. In the 1900 games, female athletes were allowed to compete. The games have continued every four years since 1896 except during World War II.
Comparison	The author explains how two or more things are alike and/or how they are different. Cue words include *different, in contrast, alike, same as*, and *on the other hand*.	Alike / Different	The modern Olympics is very unlike the ancient Olympic games. While there were no swimming races in the ancient games, for example, there were chariot races. There were no female contestants, and all athletes competed in the nude. Of course, the ancient and modern Olympics are also alike in many ways. Some events, such as the javelin and discus throws, are the same. Some people say that cheating, professionalism, and nationalism in the modern games are a disgrace to the Olympic tradition. But according to the ancient Greek writers, there were many cases of cheating, nationalism, and professionalism in their Olympics, too.

Figure 9-10 *(Continued)*

Pattern	Description	Graphic Organizer	Sample Passage
Cause and Effect	The author lists one or more causes and the resulting effect or effects. Cue words include *reasons why, if . . . then, as a result, therefore,* and *because.*	Cause → Effect #1 / Effect #2 / Effect #3	There are several reasons why so many people attend the Olympic games or watch them on television. One reason is tradition. The name *Olympics* and the torch and flame remind people of the ancient games. People can escape the ordinariness of daily life by attending or watching the Olympics. They like to identify with someone else's individual sacrifice and accomplishment. National pride is another reason, and an athlete's or a team's hard-earned victory becomes a nation's victory. There are national medal counts, and people keep track of how many medals their country's athletes have won.
Problem and Solution	The author states a problem and lists one or more solutions for the problem. A variation of this pattern is the question-and-answer format in which the author poses a question and then answers it. Cue words include *problem is, dilemma is, puzzle is, solved,* and *question . . . answer.*	Problem → Solution	One problem with the modern Olympics is that it has become very expensive to operate. A stadium, pools, and playing fields must be built for the athletic events, and housing is needed for the athletes who come from around the world. And these facilities are used for only 2 weeks! In 1984, Los Angeles solved these problems by charging a fee for companies who wanted to be official sponsors. Many buildings that were already built in the Los Angeles area were also used. The Coliseum where the 1932 games were held was used again, and many colleges in the area became playing and living sites.

Figure 9-10 describes these patterns and presents sample passages and cue words that signal use of each pattern. When readers are aware of these patterns, they understand better what they are reading, and when writers use these structures to organize their writing, it is more easily understood by readers. Sometimes the pattern is signaled clearly by means of titles, topic sentences, and cue words, and sometimes it is not.

Description. In this organizational pattern, a topic is described by listing characteristics, features, and examples. Phrases such as *for example* and *characteristics are* cue this structure. Examples of books using description are *Spiders* (Gibbons, 1992) and *Mercury* (Simon, 1993), in which the authors describe many facets of their topic. When students delineate any topic, such as the Mississippi River, eagles, or Alaska, they use description.

Sequence. In this pattern, items or events are listed or explained in numerical or chronological order. Cue words for sequence include *first, second, third, next, then,* and *finally.* Caroline Arnold describes the steps in creating a museum display in *Dinosaurs All Around: An Artist's View of the Prehistoric World* (1993). Children use the sequence pattern to write directions for a science experiment or to identify the stages in an animal's life cycle.

Comparison. In the comparison structure, two or more things are compared. *Different, in contrast, alike,* and *on the other hand* are cue words and phrases that signal this structure. In *Horns, Antlers, Fangs, and Tusks* (Rauzon, 1993), for example, the author compares animals with distinctive types of headgear. When students compare and contrast book and movie versions of a story, reptiles and amphibians, or life in ancient Greece with life in ancient Egypt, they use this organizational pattern.

Cause and Effect. The writer explains one or more causes and the resulting effect or effects. *Reasons why, if . . . then, as a result, therefore,* and *because* are words and phrases that cue this structure. Explanations of why dinosaurs became extinct, the effects of pollution on the environment, and the causes of the Civil War are written using this pattern. *How Do Apples Grow?* (Maestro, 1992) and *What Happens to a Hamburger?* (Showers, 1985) are two books that exemplify this structure.

Problem and Solution. In this expository structure, the writer states a problem and offers one or more solutions. In *Man and Mustang* (Ancona, 1992), for example, the author describes the problem of wild mustangs and explains how they are rescued. A variation is the question-and-answer format, in which the writer poses a question and then answers it. One question-and-answer book is . . . *If You Traveled West in a Covered Wagon* (Levine, 1986). Cue words and phrases include *the problem is, the puzzle is, solve,* and *question . . . answer.* Students use this structure when they write about why money was invented, why endangered animals should be saved, or why dams are needed to ensure a permanent water supply. They often use the problem-solution pattern in writing advertisements and other persuasive writing.

Figure 9-11 lists other books that illustrate each of the five expository text structures.

When English-language learners are aware of expository text structures, they organize, summarize, and recall what they have read more effectively.

Why Do Teachers Need to Know About Expository Text Structures?

When teachers use informational books as instructional materials, they should consider how the books are organized as they prepare for instruction. Often teachers give children a purpose for reading and develop graphic organizers to record information after reading. Researchers have confirmed that when children use the five expository text structures to organize their reading and writing, they are more effective readers and writers. Most of the research on expository text structures has focused on older students' use of these patterns in reading; however, primary students also use the patterns and cue words in their writing (Langer, 1986; Raphael, Englert, & Kirschner, 1989; Tompkins, 2000).

POETRY

Poetry "brings sound and sense together in words and lines," according to Donald Graves, "ordering them on the page in such a way that both the writer and reader get a different view of life" (1992, p. 3). Poetry surrounds us; children chant jump-rope rhymes on the playground and dance in response to songs and their lyrics. Larrick (1991) believes that we enjoy poetry because of the physical involvement that the words evoke. Also, people play with language as they invent rhymes and ditties, create new words, and craft powerful comparisons.

Today, more poets are writing for children, and more books of poems for children are being published than ever before. No longer is poetry confined to rhyming verse about daffodils, clouds, and love. Recently published poems about dinosaurs, Halloween, chocolate, baseball, and insects are very popular. Children choose to read poetry and share favorite poems with classmates. They read and respond to poems containing beautiful language and written on topics that are meaningful to them.

Figure 9-11
Informational Books Representing the Expository Text Structures

Description

Balestrino, P. (1971). *The skeleton inside you.* New York: Crowell.

Branley, F. M. (1986). *What the moon is like.* New York: Harper & Row.

Fowler, A. (1990). *It could still be a bird.* Chicago: Childrens Press.

Hansen, R., & Bell, R. A. (1985). *My first book of space.* New York: Simon & Schuster.

Horvatic, A. (1989). *Simple machines.* New York: Dutton.

Morris, A. (1989). *Hats, hats, hats.* New York: Mulberry Books.

Sequence

Aliki. (1992). *Milk from cow to carton.* New York: HarperCollins.

Cole, J. (1991). *My puppy is born.* New York: Morrow.

Gibbons, G. (1993). *Pirates.* Boston: Little, Brown.

Comparison

Gibbons, G. (1984). *Fire! Fire!* New York: Harper & Row.

Markle, S. (1993). *Outside and inside trees.* New York: Bradbury Press.

Rauzon, M. J. (1993). *Horns, antlers, fangs, and tusks.* New York: Lothrop, Lee & Shepard.

Cause and Effect

Branley, F. M. (1985a). *Flash, crash, rumble, and roll.* New York: Harper & Row.

Branley, F. M. (1985b). *Volcanoes.* New York: Harper & Row.

Branley, F. M. (1986). *What makes day and night?* New York: Harper & Row.

Heller, R. (1983). *The reason for a flower.* New York: Grosset & Dunlap.

Selsam, M. E. (1981). *Where do they go? Insects in winter.* New York: Scholastic.

Showers, P. (1985). *What happens to a hamburger?* New York: Harper & Row.

Problem and Solution

Cole, J. (1983). *Cars and how they go.* New York: Harper & Row.

Heller, R. (1986). *How to hide a whippoorwill and other birds.* New York: Grosset & Dunlap.

Lauber, P. (1990). *How we learned the earth is round.* New York: Crowell.

Combination

Aliki. (1981). *Digging up dinosaurs.* New York: Harper & Row.

Carrick, C. (1993). *Whaling days.* New York: Clarion.

Guiberson, B. Z. (1991). *Cactus hotel.* New York: Henry Holt.

Hoyt-Goldsmith, D. (1992). *Hoang Anh: A Vietnamese-American boy.* New York: Holiday House.

Types of Poetry Books

Three types of poetry books are published for children. A number of picture-book versions of single poems or songs in which each line or stanza is illustrated on a page are available, such as *The Owl and the Pussycat* (Lear, 1998), a narrative poem about the Owl and his unlikely love who travel around the world, and *Casey at the Bat: A Ballad of the Republic Sung in the Year 1888* (Thayer, 2000), a narrative poem about baseball that is authentically illustrated with a collage of baseball memorabilia. Other books are specialized collections of poems, either written by a single poet or related to a single theme, such as Lee Bennett Hopkins's *Sports! Sports! Sports! A Poetry Collection* (1999). Comprehensive anthologies are the third type of poetry books for children, and they feature 50 to 500 or more poems arranged by category. One of the best anthologies is Jack Prelutsky's *The Random House Book of Poetry for Children* (2001). A list of poetry books with examples of each of the three types is presented in Figure 9-12.

Poetic Forms

Poems for children assume many different forms, including rhymed verse, narratives, haiku, and free verse. Children don't read poems in order to identify the poetic form, but teachers should be aware of the differences so that they know what to point out

Figure 9-12   Collections of Poetry Written for Children

Picture Book Versions of Single Poems

Lear, E. (1998). *The owl and the pussycat.* New York: HarperCollins.

Moore, C. (1980). *The night before Christmas.* New York: Holiday House.

Sandburg, C. (1993). *Arithmetic.* New York: Harcourt Brace.

Thayer, E. L. (2000). *Casey at the bat: A ballad of the republic sung in the year 1888.* New York: Handprint.

Westcott, N. B. (1988). *The lady with the alligator purse.* Boston: Little, Brown.

Specialized Collections

Adoff, A. (2000). *Touch the poem.* New York: Scholastic.

George, K. O. (1998). *Old elm speaks: Tree poems.* New York: Clarion Books.

Graham, J. B. (1999). *Flicker flash.* Boston: Houghton Mifflin.

Greenfield, E. (1988). *Under the Sunday tree.* New York: Harper & Row.

Hoberman, M. A. (1998). *The llama who had no pajama: 100 favorite poems.* New York: Browndeer.

Hopkins, L. B. (1987). *Click, rumble, roar: Poems about machines.* New York: Crowell.

Hopkins, L. B. (1998). *Climb into my lap: First poems to read together.* New York: Simon & Schuster.

James, S. (Compiler). (2000). *Days like this: A collection of small poems.* New York: Candlewick.

Lewis, J. P. (1998). *The little buggers: Insect and spider poems.* New York: Dial.

Prelutsky, J. (1984). *The new kid on the block.* New York: Greenwillow.

Prelutsky, J. (1989). *Poems of A. Nonny Mouse.* New York: Knopf.

Prelutsky, J. (1996). *A pizza the size of the sun.* New York: Greenwillow.

Prelutsky, J. (1997). *Read-aloud rhymes for the very young.* New York: Knopf.

Prelutsky, J. (2000). *It's raining pigs and noodles.* New York: Greenwillow.

Schertle, A. (1999). *I am the cat.* New York: Lothrop.

Shannon, G. (2000). *Frog legs: A picture book of action verse.* New York: Greenwillow.

Siebert, D. (1984). *Truck song.* New York: Harper & Row.

Sierra, J. (1998). *Antarctic antics: A book of penguin poems.* San Diego: Gulliver.

Stevenson, J. (2000). *Cornflakes.* New York: Greenwillow.

Stevenson, R. L. (1999). *A child's garden of verses.* New York: Simon & Schuster.

Comprehensive Anthologies

de Paola, T. (Compiler). (1988). *Tomie de Paola's book of poems.* New York: Putnam.

de Regniers, B. S., Moore, E., White, M. M., & Carr, J. (Compilers). (1988). *Sing a song of popcorn: Every child's book of poems.* New York: Scholastic.

Prelutsky, J. (Compiler). (1999). *The 20th century children's poetry treasury.* New York: Knopf.

Prelutsky, J. (Compiler). (2001). *The Random House book of poetry for children.* New York: Random House.

to children. For example, when the poem is a rhyme, teachers often point out the rhyming words and emphasize how much fun it is to read or recite the poem. Or, when the story is free verse, teachers often point out the image or emotion that the poem evokes.

When children write poems, they use many of the same forms, and the quality of their poems often reflects their experiences reading poems and listening to poems read aloud. It's important for writers to know about poetic forms so that they can organize their poem in a familiar format.

Rhymed Verse. The most common type of poetry is rhymed verse, as in *Hailstones and Halibut Bones* (O'Neill, 1989), *My Parents Think I'm Sleeping* (Prelutsky, 1985), and *Take Me Out of the Bathtub and Other Silly Dilly Songs* (Katz, 2001). Poets use various rhyme schemes, and the effect of the rhyming words is a poem that is pleasurable to read and listen to when it is read aloud. Children should savor the rhyming words but not be expected to pick out the rhyme scheme.

Rhyme is the sticking point for many would-be poets. In searching for a rhyming word, children often create inane verse; for example:

I see a funny little goat
Wearing a blue sailor's coat
Sitting in an old motorboat.

Certainly children should not be forbidden to write rhyming poetry, but rhyme should never be imposed as a criterion for acceptable poetry. Children may use rhyme when it fits naturally into their writing. When children write poetry, they are searching for their own voices, and they need freedom to do that. Freed from the pressure to write rhyming poetry and from other constraints, children create sensitive word pictures, vivid images, and unique comparisons.

Narrative Poems. Poems that tell a story are narrative poems. Perhaps our best-known narrative poem is Clement Moore's classic, "The Night Before Christmas." Other narrative poems include Longfellow's *The Midnight Ride of Paul Revere* (2000), illustrated by Jeffrey Thompson; and Jeanette Winter's *Follow the Drinking Gourd* (1988), which is about the Underground Railroad.

Haiku and Related Forms. Haiku is a Japanese poetic form that contains just 17 syllables arranged in three lines of 5, 7, and 5 syllables. Haiku poems deal with nature and present a single clear image. Haiku is a concise form, much like a telegram. Because of its brevity, it has been considered an appropriate form of poetry for children to read and write. A fourth grader wrote this haiku about a spider web she saw one morning:

Spider web shining
Tangled on the grass with dew
Waiting quietly.

Books of haiku to share with students include *Shadow Play: Night Haiku* (Harter, 1994) and *Cool Melons—Turn to Frogs! The Life and Poems of Issa* (Gollub, 1998). The artwork in these picture books may give students ideas for illustrating their haiku poems.

Children read books of poetry written by Jack Prelutsky during an author study.

A poetic form similar to haiku is the cinquain, a five-line poem containing 22 syllables in a 2-4-6-8-2 syllable pattern. Cinquains often describe something, but they may also tell a story. Have students ask themselves what their subject looks like, smells like, sounds like, and tastes like, and record their ideas using a five-senses cluster. The formula is as follows.

Line 1: a one-word subject with two syllables
Line 2: four syllables describing the subject
Line 3: six syllables showing action
Line 4: eight syllables expressing a feeling or observation about the subject
Line 5: two syllables describing or renaming the subject

Children in a fourth-grade class wrote cinquains as part of a thematic unit on westward movement. One child wrote this cinquain about the transcontinental railroad:

Railroads
One crazy guy's
Transcontinental dream . . .
With a golden spike it came true.
Iron horse

Another child wrote about the gold rush:

Gold rush
Forty-niners
were sure to strike it rich
Homesickness, pork and beans, so tired.
Panning

Another related form is the diamante (Tiedt, 1970), a seven-line contrast poem written in the shape of a diamond. This poetic form helps students apply their knowledge of opposites and parts of speech. The formula is:

Line 1: one noun as the subject
Line 2: two adjectives describing the subject
Line 3: three participles (ending in -*ing*) telling about the subject
Line 4: four nouns (the first two related to the subject and the last two related to the opposite)
Line 5: three participles telling about the opposite
Line 6: two adjectives describing the opposite
Line 7: one noun that is the opposite of the subject

A third-grade class wrote this diamante poem about the stages of life:

Baby
wrinkled tiny
crying wetting sleeping
rattles diapers money house
caring working loving
smart helpful
Adult

Notice that the children created a contrast between *baby*, the subject represented by the noun in the first line, and *adult*, the opposite in the last line. This contrast gives children the opportunity to play with words and apply their understanding of opposites. The third word in the fourth line, *money*, begins the transition from *baby* to its opposite, *adult*.

Free Verse. Free verse is unrhymed poetry. Rhythm is less important in free verse than in other types of poetry; word choice and visual images take on greater importance. *Nathaniel Talking* (Greenfield, 1988) and *Neighborhood Odes* (Soto, 1992) are two collections of free verse. In *Nathaniel Talking,* Eloise Greenfield writes from the viewpoint of a young African American child who has lost his mother but not his spirit. Most of the poems are free verse, but one is a rap and several others rhyme. Greenfield uses few capital letters or punctuation marks. In *Neighborhood Odes,* Gary Soto writes about his childhood as a Mexican American child living in Fresno, California. Soto adds a few Spanish words to his poems to sharpen the pictures the poems paint of life in his neighborhood.

In free verse, children choose words to describe something and put them together to express a thought or tell a story, without concern for rhyme or other arrangements. The number of words per line and use of punctuation vary.

Children can use several methods for writing free verse. They can select words and phrases from brainstormed lists and clusters[C] to create the poem, or they can write a paragraph and then "unwrite" it to create the poem by deleting unnecessary words. They arrange the remaining words to look like a poem. During a literature focus unit on MacLachlan's *Sarah, Plain and Tall* (1985), a third-grade class wrote this free-form poem after discussing the two kinds of dunes in the story:

> Dunes of sand
> on the beach.
> Sarah walks on them
> and watches the ocean.
> Dunes of hay
> beside the barn.
> Papa makes them for Sarah
> because she misses Maine.

Found Poems. Children create found poems by culling words from various sources, such as newspaper articles, stories, and informational books. Found poems give students the opportunity to manipulate words and sentence structures they don't write themselves. A small group of third graders composed the following found poem, "This Is My Day," after reading *Sarah Morton's Day: A Day in the Life of a Pilgrim Girl* (Waters, 1989):

> Good day.
> I must get up and be about my chores.
> The fire is mine to tend.
> I lay the table.
> I muck the garden.
> I pound the spices.
> I draw vinegar to polish the brass.
> I practice my lessons.
> I feed the fire again.
> I milk the goats.
> I eat dinner.

I say the verses I am learning.
My father is pleased with my learning.
I fetch the water for tomorrow.
I bid my parents good night.
I say my prayers.
Fare thee well.
God be with thee.

To compose the found poem, the children collected their favorite words and sentences from the book and organized them sequentially to describe the pilgrim girl's day.

Other Poetic Forms. Children use a variety of other forms when they write poems, even though few adults use them. These forms provide a scaffold or skeleton for children's poems. After collecting words, images, and comparisons, children craft their poems, choosing words and arranging them to create a message. Meaning is always most important, and form follows the search for meaning. Poet Kenneth Koch (1970), working with children in the elementary grades, developed some simple formulas that make it easy for nearly every child to become a successful poet. These formulas call for children to begin every line the same way or to insert a particular kind of word in every line. The formulas use repetition, a stylistic device that is more effective for young poets than rhyme. Some forms may seem more like sentences than poems, but the dividing line between poetry and prose is a blurry one, and these poetry experiences help children move toward poetic expression.

1. *"I Wish . . ." Poems.* Children begin each line of their poems with the words "I wish" and complete the line with a wish (Koch, 1970). In this second-grade class collaboration poem, children simply listed their wishes:

Our Wishes
I wish I had all the money in the world.
I wish I was a star fallen down from Mars.
I wish I were a butterfly.
I wish I were a teddy bear.
I wish I had a cat.
I wish I were a pink rose.
I wish it wouldn't rain today.
I wish I didn't have to wash a dish.
I wish I had a flying carpet.
I wish I could go to Disney World.
I wish school was out.
I wish I could go outside and play.

After this experience, children choose one of their wishes and expand on the idea in another poem. One child expanded her wish this way:

I wish I were a teddy bear
Who sat on a beautiful bed
Who got a hug every night
By a little girl or boy
Maybe tonight I'll get my wish
And wake up on a little girl's bed
And then I'll be as happy as can be.

2. ***Color Poems.*** Children begin each line of their poems with a color. They can re-peat the color in each line or choose a different color (Koch, 1970). As part of a unit on weather, kindergartners wrote this color poem, "The Rainbow's Colors," using interactive writing:

> *Red is a heart*
> *and it says "I love you."*
> *Orange is the juice we drink*
> *because we want to be healthy.*
> *Yellow is the sun*
> *that shines down on us.*
> *Green is growing things*
> *like trees and grass and bushes.*
> *Blue is the ocean*
> *where the whales swim and play.*
> *Purple is our teacher's favorite color*
> *and we like it, too!*

The class wrote the poem over 6 days, one couplet each day.

A useful book of brief, four-line color poems for kindergartners and first graders is *Red Are the Apples* (Harshman & Ryan, 2001); *Hailstones and Halibut Bones* (O'Neill, 1989) is another source of color poems. However, both books use rhyme as a poetic device, and it is important to emphasize that children's poems need not rhyme.

3. ***Five-Senses Poems.*** Children write about a topic using each of the five senses. Sense poems are usually five lines long, with one line for each sense, but sometimes an extra line is added, as this poem written by a first grader demonstrates:

> *Popcorn*
> *Sounds like thunder when it's popping.*
> *Sounds like crunch when you eat it.*
> *Looks like a little white cloud puff,*
> *Tastes like a salty treat.*
> *Feels like a surprise in my hand.*
> *Smells like delicious.*
> *Can I have some more?*

It is often helpful to have children develop a five-senses data chart[C] and collect ideas for each sense. Children select from the chart the most vivid or strongest idea for each sense to use in a line of the poem.

4. ***"If I Were . . ." Poems.*** Children write about how they would feel and what they would do if they were something else—a dinosaur, a hamburger, sunshine (Koch, 1970). They begin each poem with "If I were" and tell what it would be like to be that thing. In this example, a first grader writes about what he would do if he were a dinosaur:

> *If I were a Tyrannosaurus Rex*
> *I would terrorize other dinosaurs*
> *And eat them up for supper.*

In composing "If I were . . ." poems, children use personification, explore ideas and feelings, and consider the world from a different vantage point.

Why Do Teachers Need to Know About Poetic Forms?

When children in the primary grades read and recite poetry, the emphasis is on introducing them to poetry so that they have a pleasurable experience. Children need to have fun as they do choral readings^C of poems, pick out favorite lines, and respond to poems. Teachers need to be aware of poetic forms so that they can point out the form when it is appropriate or provide information about a poetic form when children ask. For example, sometimes when children read free verse, they say it isn't poetry because it doesn't rhyme. At this time, it's appropriate to point out that poetry doesn't have to rhyme and that this poem is a poem—that this type of poetry is called free verse. Teachers might also explain that in free verse, creating an image or projecting a voice is more important than the rhyme scheme. It is not appropriate for children to analyze the rhyme scheme or search out the meaning of the poem. Instead, children should focus on what the poem means to them. Teachers introduce poetic forms when children are writing poetry. When children use poetic formulas such as color poems and haiku, they are often more successful than when they attempt to create rhyming verse, because the formulas provide a framework for their writing.

Review

Three broad types of literature are stories, informational books, and poetry, and they are included in basal readers and published as trade books. Each type of text has a unique structure or organization. Story elements are plot, characters, setting, and theme. Informational books are organized into expository text structures, of which the five most common patterns are description, sequence, comparison, cause and effect, and problem and solution. The most common poetic forms for children are rhymed verse, narrative poems, haiku, and free verse. Teachers need to be aware of the structure of text so that they can help students become more successful readers and writers. Guidelines for effectively teaching students about the structure of text are summarized in the feature that follows.

How Effective Teachers . . .
Teach the Structure of Text

Effective Practices

1. Teachers use the terms "story," "informational books" and "poems" correctly, and they don't call all books "stories."
2. Teachers point out differences among stories, informational books, and poems.
3. Teachers read aloud all three types of literature—stories, informational books, and poems.
4. Teachers choose high-quality literature because they understand that children's writing reflects what they are reading.
5. Teachers teach minilessons about story elements, expository text structures, and poetic forms.
6. Teachers have children examine story elements in stories they are reading as part of literature focus units.

7. Teachers have children examine expository text structure in informational books as part of thematic units.
8. Teachers emphasize that not all poems rhyme.
9. Teachers point out the patterns authors use to write poems and have children write poems using some of the same patterns.
10. Teachers have children use their knowledge of text structure when writing stories, informational books, and poems.

Professional References

Au, K. H. (1992). Constructing the theme of a story. *Language Arts, 69,* 106–111.

Bruner, J. (1986). *Actual minds, possible worlds.* Cambridge, MA: Harvard University Press.

Buss, K., & Karnowski, L. (2000). *Reading and writing literary genres.* Newark, DE: International Reading Association.

De Ford, D. (1981). Literacy: Reading, writing, and other essentials. *Language Arts, 58,* 652–658.

Eckhoff, B. (1983). How reading affects children's writing. *Language Arts, 60,* 607–616.

Flood, J., Lapp, D., & Farnan, N. (1986). A reading-writing procedure that teaches expository paragraph structure. *The Reading Teacher, 39,* 556–562.

Freedman, R. (1992). Fact or fiction? In E. B. Freeman & D. G. Person (Eds.), *Using nonfiction tradebooks in the elementary classroom: From ants to zeppelins* (pp. 2–10). Urbana, IL: National Council of Teachers of English.

Graves, D. H. (1992). *Explore poetry.* Portsmouth, NH: Heinemann.

Holdaway, D. (1979). *The foundations of literacy.* Portsmouth, NH: Heinemann.

Irwin, J. W. (1991). *Teaching reading comprehension processes* (2nd ed.). Boston: Allyn & Bacon.

Koch, K. (1970). *Wishes, lies, and dreams.* New York: Vintage.

Langer, J. A. (1986). *Children reading and writing: Structures and strategies.* Norwood, NJ: Ablex.

Lapp, D., Flood, J., & Farnan, N. (1992). Basal readers and literature: A tight fit or a mismatch? In K. D. Wood & A. Moss (Eds.), *Exploring literature in the classroom: Contents and methods* (pp. 35–57). Norwood, MA: Christopher-Gordon.

Larrick, N. (1991). *Let's do a poem! Introducing poetry to children.* New York: Delacorte.

Lehr, S. S. (1991). *The child's developing sense of theme: Responses to literature.* New York: Teachers College Press.

Lukens, R. J. (1999). *A critical handbook of children's literature* (6th ed.). New York: Longman.

McGee, L. M., & Richgels, D. J. (1985). Teaching expository text structures to elementary students. *The Reading Teacher, 38,* 739–745.

Meyer, B. J., & Freedle, R. O. (1984). Effects of discourse type on recall. *American Educational Research Journal, 21,* 121–143.

Niles, O. S. (1974). Organization perceived. In H. L. Herber (Ed.), *Perspectives in reading: Developing study skills in secondary schools.* Newark, DE: International Reading Association.

Norton, D. E. (2003). *Through the eyes of a child* (6th ed.). Upper Saddle River, NJ: Merrill/Prentice Hall.

Pappas, C. (1993). Is narrative "primary"? Some insights from kindergartners' pretend readings of stories and information books. *Journal of Reading Behavior, 25,* 97–129.

Piccolo, J. A. (1987). Expository text structures: Teaching and learning strategies. *The Reading Teacher, 40,* 838–847.

Raphael, T. E., Englert, C. S., & Kirschner, B. W. (1989). Acquisition of expository writing skills. In J. M. Mason (Ed.), *Reading and writing connections* (pp. 261–290). Boston: Allyn & Bacon.

Roop, P. (1992). Nonfiction books in the primary classroom: Soaring with the swans. In E. B. Freeman & D. G. Person (Eds.), *Using nonfiction tradebooks in the elementary classroom: From ants to zeppelins* (pp. 106–112). Urbana, IL: National Council of Teachers of English.

Tiedt, I. (1970). Exploring poetry patterns. *Elementary English, 45,* 1082–1084.

Tompkins, G. E. (2000). *Teaching writing: Balancing process and product* (3rd ed.). Upper Saddle River, NJ: Merrill/Prentice Hall.

Vardell, S. (1991). A new "picture of the world": The NCTE Orbis Pictus Award for outstanding nonfiction for children. *Language Arts, 68,* 474–479.

Wells, G. (1986). *The meaning makers: Children learning language and using language to learn.* Portsmouth, NH: Heinemann.

Whitin, D. J., & Wilde, S. (1992). *Read any good math lately? Children's books for mathematical learning, K–6.* Portsmouth, NH: Heinemann.

Aardema, V. (1975). *Why mosquitoes buzz in people's ears.* New York: Dial.

Aker, S. (1990). *What comes in 2's, 3's, and 4's?* New York: Simon & Schuster.

Ancona, G. (1992). *Man and mustang.* New York: Macmillan.

Arnold, C. (1993). *Dinosaurs all around: An artist's view of the prehistoric world.* New York: Clarion.

Barrie, J. M. (1950). *Peter Pan.* New York: Scribner.

Bierhorst, J. (1987). *Doctor Coyote: A Native American Aesop's fables.* New York: Macmillan.

Blume, J. (1972). *Tales of a fourth grade nothing.* New York: Dutton.

Brett, J. (1987). *Goldilocks and the three bears.* New York: Dodd, Mead.

Brett, J. (1994). *Town mouse, country mouse.* New York: Putnam.

Bunting, E. (1988). *How many days to America? A Thanksgiving story.* New York: Clarion.

Calmenson, S. (1989). *The principal's new clothes.* New York: Scholastic.

Carroll, L. (1984). *Alice's adventures in Wonderland.* New York: Knopf.

Cauley, L. B. (1981). *Goldilocks and the three bears.* New York: Putnam.

Cauley, L. B. (1984). *The town mouse and the country mouse.* New York: Putnam.

Cleary, B. (1965). *The mouse and the motorcycle.* New York: HarperCollins.

Cleary, B. (1981). *Ramona Quimby, age 8.* New York: Morrow.

Cleary, B. (1990). *Ramona and her father.* New York: HarperCollins.

Coerr, E. (1986). *The Josefina story quilt.* New York: HarperCollins.

Cohen, B. (1983). *Molly's pilgrim.* New York: Lothrop, Lee & Shepard.

Cole, J. (1996). *The magic school bus inside a beehive.* New York: Scholastic.

Cowcher, H. (1990). *Antarctica.* New York: Farrar, Straus & Giroux.

Curtis, C. P. (1995). *The Watsons go to Birmingham—1963.* New York: Delacorte.

Dahl, R. (1964). *Charlie and the chocolate factory.* New York: Knopf.

de Paola, T. (1983). *The legend of the bluebonnet.* New York: Putnam.

Ehrlich, A. (1985). *Cinderella.* New York: Dial.

Erickson, R. E. (1974). *A toad for Tuesday.* New York: Lothrop, Lee & Shepard.

Feelings, M., & Feelings, T. (1971). *Moja means one: Swahili counting book.* New York: Dial.

Freedman, R. (1987). *Lincoln: A photobiography.* New York: Clarion.

Fritz, J. (1976). *Will you sign here, John Hancock?* New York: Coward-McCann.

Fritz, J. (1989). *The great little Madison.* New York: Putnam.

Galdone, P. (1968). *Henny Penny.* New York: Seabury.

Galdone, P. (1972). *The three bears.* New York: Seabury.

Galdone, P. (1975). *The gingerbread boy.* New York: Seabury.

Gibbons, G. (1992). *Spiders.* New York: Holiday House.

Gill, S. (1990). *Alaska's three bears.* Homer, AK: Paws IV.

Goble, P. (1988). *Iktomi and the boulder: A Plains Indian story.* New York: Orchard.

Gollub, M. (1998). *Cool melons—turn to frogs! The life and poems of Issa.* New York: Lee & Low.

Greenburg. D. (1997a). *My son, the time traveler.* New York: Grosset & Dunlap.

Greenburg, D. (1997b). *Never trust a cat who wears earrings.* New York: Grosset & Dunlap.

Greenfield, E. (1988). *Nathaniel talking.* New York: Black Butterfly Children's Books.

Guiberson, B. Z. (1991). *Cactus hotel.* New York: Henry Holt.

Hague, M. (1985). *Aesop's fables.* New York: Holt, Rinehart and Winston.

Harshman, M., & Ryan, C. (2001). *Red are the apples.* San Diego: Harcourt.

Harter, P. (1994). *Shadow play: Night haiku.* New York: Simon & Schuster.

Hoban, T. (1987). *26 letters and 99 cents.* New York: Greenwillow.

Hopkins, L. B. (1999). *Sports! Sports! Sports! A poetry collection.* New York: HarperCollins.

Howe, J. (1989). *Jack and the beanstalk.* Boston: Little, Brown.

Hunt, J. (1989). *Illuminations.* New York: Bradbury.

Hutton, W. (1994). *Persephone.* New York: McElderry Books.

Jones, C. (1997). *The lion and the rat.* Boston: Houghton Mifflin.

Kasza, K. (1987). *The wolf's chicken stew.* New York: Putnam.

Katz, A. (2001). *Take me out of the bathtub and other silly dilly songs.* New York: McElderry Books.

Kellogg, S. (1984). *Paul Bunyan: A tall tale.* New York: Morrow.

Kellogg, S. (1986). *Pecos Bill: A tall tale.* New York: Morrow.

Kellogg, S. (1988). *Johnny Appleseed: A tall tale.* New York: Morrow.

Kimmel, E. A. (2000). *The runaway tortilla.* Delray Beach, FL: Winslow Press.

Knight, M. B. (1993). *Who belongs here? An American story.* Gardiner, ME: Tulbury House.

Lear, E. (1998). *The owl and the pussycat.* New York: HarperCollins.

Lester, H. (1988). *Tacky the penguin.* Boston: Houghton Mifflin.

Levine, E. (1986). *. . . . If you traveled west in a covered wagon.* New York: Scholastic.

Lewis, C. S. (1994). *The lion, the witch and the wardrobe.* New York: HarperCollins.

Lionni, L. (1969). *Alexander and the wind-up mouse.* New York: Pantheon.

Longfellow, H. W. (2000). *The midnight ride of Paul Revere*. Washington, DC: National Geographic Society.

MacLachlan, P. (1985). *Sarah, plain and tall*. New York: Harper & Row.

Maestro, B. (1992). *How do apples grow?* New York: HarperCollins.

Martin, B., Jr., & Archambault, J. (1985). *The ghost-eye tree*. New York: Holt, Rinehart and Winston.

McCloskey, R. (1969). *Make way for ducklings*. New York: Viking.

Meddaugh, S. (1992). *Martha speaks*. Boston: Houghton Mifflin.

Meddaugh, S. (1995). *Hog-eye*. Boston: Houghton Mifflin.

Milne, A. A. (1961). *Winnie-the-Pooh*. New York: Dutton.

O'Neill, M. (1989). *Hailstones and halibut bones*. New York: Doubleday.

Pallotta, J. (1991). *The underwater alphabet book*. Watertown, MA: Charlesbridge.

Pinkney, J. (1999). *The ugly duckling*. New York: Morrow.

Potter, B. (1902). *The tale of Peter Rabbit*. New York: Warne.

Prelutsky, J. (1985). *My parents think I'm sleeping*. New York: Greenwillow.

Prelutsky, J. (2001). *The Random House book of poetry for children*. New York: Random House.

Rauzon, M. J. (1993). *Horns, antlers, fangs, and tusks*. New York: Lothrop, Lee & Shepard.

Rowling, J. K. (1997). *Harry Potter and the sorcerer's stone*. New York: Levine.

Rylant, C. (1992). *Best wishes*. Katonah, NY: Richard C. Owen.

Rylant, C. (1998). *Tulip sees America*. New York: Blue Sky.

Schwartz, D. (1989). *If you made a million*. New York: Lothrop, Lee & Shepard.

Scieszka, J. (1989). *The true story of the three little pigs!* New York: Viking.

Scieszka, J. (1991). *Knights of the kitchen table*. New York: Viking.

Scott, A. H. (1990). *One good horse: A cowpuncher's counting book*. New York: Greenwillow.

Sendak, M. (1962). *Where the wild things are*. New York: Harper & Row.

Showers, P. (1985). *What happens to a hamburger?* New York: Harper & Row.

Simon, S. (1989). *Whales*. New York: Crowell.

Simon, S. (1993). *Mercury*. New York: Morrow.

Soto, G. (1992). *Neighborhood odes*. San Diego: Harcourt Brace Jovanovich.

Steig, W. (1969). *Sylvester and the magic pebble*. New York: Simon & Schuster.

Steptoe, J. (1984). *The story of Jumping Mouse: A native American legend*. New York: Lothrop, Lee & Shepard.

Stevens, J. (1987). *The three billy goats Gruff*. San Diego, CA: Harcourt Brace.

Thayer, E. L. (2000). *Casey at the bat: A ballad of the republic sung in the year 1888*. New York: Handprint.

Turkle, B. (1976). *Deep in the forest*. New York: Dutton.

Uchida, Y. (1993). *The bracelet*. New York: Philomel.

Van Allsburg, C. (1981). *Jumanji*. Boston: Houghton Mifflin.

Van Allsburg, C. (1986). *The stranger*. Boston: Houghton Mifflin.

Waber, B. (1972). *Ira sleeps over*. Boston: Houghton Mifflin.

Ward, C. (1999). *The hare and the tortoise*. New York: Millbrook.

Waters, K. (1989). *Sarah Morton's day: A day in the life of a pilgrim girl*. New York: Scholastic.

Westcott, N. B. (1984). *The emperor's new clothes*. Boston: Little, Brown.

White, E. B. (1952). *Charlotte's web*. New York: Harper & Row.

Williams, V. B. (1982). *A chair for my mother*. New York: Mulberry.

Winter, J. (1988). *Follow the drinking gourd*. New York: Knopf.

Yolen, J. (1980). *Commander Toad in space*. New York: Coward-McCann.

Yolen, J. (1986). *The sleeping beauty*. New York: Random House.

Yorinks, A. (1986). *Hey, Al*. New York: Farrar, Straus & Giroux.

Young, E. (1992). *Seven blind mice*. New York: Philomel.

Zelinsky, P. O. (1986). *Rumpelstiltskin*. New York: Dutton.

Zemach, M. (1988). *The three little pigs*. New York: Farrar, Straus & Giroux.

chapter 10

Scaffolding Children's Reading Development

- What are the stages in the reading process?

- What is shared reading?

- What is guided reading?

- How do teachers use the reading process in preparing literature focus units, literature circles, reading workshop, and basal reader programs?

Mrs. Ohashi Uses the Reading Process

Mrs. Ohashi's third graders are reading "The Great Kapok Tree," a selection in their *Spotlight on Literacy* basal reader program (Aoki et al., 1997). This story, which is set in the Amazon rain forest, was originally published as a trade book for children by Lynne Cherry in 1990. In the basal reader version, the text is unabridged from the original book, but because text from several pages has been printed on a single page, some illustrations from the original book version have been deleted.

The children spend one week reading "The Great Kapok Tree" and participating in a variety of related literacy activities. Mrs. Ohashi's language arts block lasts 2½ hours each morning. During the first hour, she works with reading groups while other children work independently at centers. During the second hour, she teaches spelling, grammar, and writing. The last half hour is independent reading time when children read self-selected books from the classroom library or the reading center.

The skills that Mrs. Ohashi teaches each week are set by the basal reading program. She will focus on cause and effect as children read and think about the selection. The vocabulary words she will highlight in the selection are *community, depend, environment, generations, hesitated, ruins, silent,* and *squawking.* The third graders will learn about persuasive writing, and they will write a persuasive letter to their parents. Mrs. Ohashi will teach minilessons[C] on irregular past-tense verbs, and children will study the list of spelling words provided by the basal reading program.

See the Compendium of Instructional Procedures, which follows Chapter 12, for more information on terms marked with the symbol [C].

Mrs. Ohashi's class is divided into four reading groups, and the children in all of the groups, except one group reading at the first-grade level, can read the basal reader with her support. Her district's policy is that in addition to reading books at their instructional level, all children should be exposed to the grade-level textbooks. Mrs. Ohashi involves all children in most instructional activities, but she reads the story to the children in the lowest group and then these children read leveled books at their level.

To choose names for the groups at the beginning of the school year, Mrs. Ohashi put crayons into a basket. A child from each group chose a crayon, and the crayon's name became the name of the group. The children who read at or almost at grade level are heterogeneously grouped into the Wild Watermelon, Electric Lime, and Blizzard Blue groups. The six remaining children form the Atomic Tangerine group.

Today, Mrs. Ohashi begins the reading process with the first stage, prereading. She builds the students' background knowledge about the rain forest by reading aloud *Nature's Green Umbrella* (Gibbons, 1994). Children talk about rain forests and together compile a list of information they have learned, including the fact that each year, over 200 inches of rain fall in the rain forest. Next she introduces the selection of the week, and children "picture walk" through the story, looking at the illustrations, connecting with what they already know about rain forests, and predicting events in the story.

The second stage is reading. Most of the third graders read the story with buddies, but the Atomic Tangerine group reads the selection with Mrs. Ohashi. These children join Mrs. Ohashi at the reading group table, and she uses shared reading[C] to read the story. She reads the story aloud while they follow along in their books. She stops periodically to explain a word, make predictions, clarify any confusions, and think aloud about the story.

Responding is the third stage. After everyone finishes reading the selection, children come together to talk about the story in a grand conversation[C]. Children respond to the story, talking about why the rain forests must be preserved. Ashley explains, "I know why the author wrote the story. On page 71, it tells about her. Her name is Lynne Cherry and it says that she wants to 'try to make the world a better place.' That's the message of this story." Then Katrina compares this story to *Miss Rumphius* (Cooney, 1982), the selection they read the previous week: "I think this story is just like the one we read before. It was about making the world more beautiful with flowers and that's almost the same."

Then Mrs. Ohashi asks what would happen if there were no more rain forests. Children mention that animals in the rain forest might become extinct because they wouldn't have homes and that there would be more air pollution because the trees wouldn't be able to clean the air. Then Mrs. Ohashi introduces a basket of foods, spices, and other products that come from the rain forest, including chocolate, coffee, tea, bananas, cashews, cinnamon, ginger, vanilla, bamboo, and rubber. Her students are amazed at the variety of things they and their parents use every day that come from the rain forest.

Next, Mrs. Ohashi moves on to the fourth stage, exploring. She introduces the grammar skill of the week: the past tense of irregular verbs. She has prepared a series of 10 sentence strips with sentences about "The Great Kapok Tree," leaving blanks for the past-tense verbs, as suggested in the teacher's guide for the basal reading program. On separate cards, she has written correct and incorrect verb forms on each side, for example: *The birds comed/came down from their trees.* She puts the sentence strips and verb cards in a pocket chart. She begins by talking about the past-tense form of regular verbs. The children understand that -ed marks the past tense of many verbs, as in this sentence: *The man walked into the rain forest.* Other verbs, she explains, have different forms for present and past tense. For example, *The man sleeps/slept in the rain forest.* Then children read the sentences in the pocket chart and choose the correct form of the irregular verb.

Next she explains that many irregular verbs have three forms—present tense, past tense, and past tense using *have, has,* or *had*—as in *sing–sang–sung.* She puts word cards with these 10 present-tense forms in another pocket chart: *go, give, come, begin, run, do, eat, grow, see,* and *sing.* Then she passes out additional word cards listing the two past-tense forms of each verb. As they talk about each verb, children holding word cards with the past-tense forms come and add them to the pocket chart.

During the week, children will continue to practice these irregular verbs at centers, using worksheets from the Grammar Practice Book that is part of the basal reading program, and through other minilessons.

During the last 20 minutes of the language arts block, Mrs. Ohashi introduces the 10 centers where children will work during the week. These centers are described in Figure 10-1. The centers are arranged next to bulletin boards, at tables, or in corners of the classroom, and children follow Mrs. Ohashi as she explains each one.

During the rest of the week, Mrs. Ohashi meets with reading groups during the first hour of the language arts block while other children work independently at centers. She meets with each group two to four times during the week and uses guided reading strategies as children reread the selection and supplemental or other leveled books. She also teaches vocabulary and comprehension as directed in the teacher's guide.

Mrs. Ohashi likes to begin with the Atomic Tangerine group each morning because she feels that it gets them off to a more successful start. She uses guided

Figure 10-1   The Literacy Centers in Mrs. Ohashi's Classroom

Center	Description
Vocabulary	Children sort rain forest word cards into several categories. Also, children make word maps for three of these words from the story: *community, depend, environment, generations, hesitated, ruins, silent, squawking.* They use the glossaries in the anthologies to check the definitions.
Comprehension	Children examine the cause-and-effect relationships using two activities. Children match a set of pictures of the animals from the story to their reasons why the kapok tree should not be cut down. For example, the monkey's reason was that if the kapok tree is cut down, the roots will die and the soil will wash away. Mrs. Ohashi has also placed a poster in the center with the question "What do you think would have happened if the man had chopped down the tree?" and children are encouraged to write their predictions. In addition, they complete the worksheet on page 108 in the Practice Book by answering eight comprehension questions.
Sentences	Children choose a favorite sentence from the story, write it on a sentence strip, and post it on the bulletin board near the center.
Reading and Rereading	Children read books from the text set on rain forests and supplemental books from the *Spotlight on Literacy* basal reading program. Mrs. Ohashi also has a 1-minute timer at the center and children practice rereading copies of page 68 from "The Great Kapok Tree" to see how many words they can read in a minute. They read the page once for practice, then read the page and mark how many words they read in a minute. Then they read the page again and mark how many words they read this time. Children work to improve their reading speed because all third graders are expected to reach a reading speed of at least 100 words per minute.
Grammar	Children practice irregular past-tense verbs through several activities. Children read sentences about the story written on sentence strips and paper clip word cards with the correct form of verb to the sentence strip. Children also sort verb cards and put present, past, and past participle forms of the same verb together, such as *go–went–gone.* Children also complete page 71 of the Grammar Practice Book.
Listening	Children listen to audiotapes of "The Great Kapok Tree" or "The Mahogany Tree," and afterwards they write and/or draw a response in listening logs that are kept at the center.
Spelling	Children participate in a variety of activities to practice their spelling words. Lists of words are available at the center, and children build the words using linking letters. They sort spelling word cards according to spelling patterns. They complete Spelling Activity Book page 86 by identifying the correct spelling of each word. And, they write each spelling word three times in their spelling notebooks that are kept at the center.
Writing	Children write a rain forest book with information about plants and animals in the rain forest and the products we use that come from the rain forest.
Chart	Children mark the rain forest on world maps using information from pages 72–73 of their basal readers. They also add labels with names of the countries, rivers, and continents.
Computers	Children use a phonics program to review *r*-controlled vowels and word processing for writing activities.

reading[C] with these children. They begin by rereading several familiar leveled books, and Mrs. Ohashi listens to the children as they read. Next, she reviews one- and two-syllable words with *ar,* and they decode these words: *car, carpet, mark, bookmark, sharp, sharpest,* and *sharks.* Mrs. Ohashi introduces their new book, *Hungry, Hungry Sharks* (Cole, 1986). Children text walk through the first 11 pages, looking at illustrations and making predictions. They put a bookmark at page 11 to remember where to stop reading. Mrs. Ohashi asks children to read to find out if sharks are dinosaurs, and they eagerly begin. Children mumble-read so that Mrs. Ohashi can hear them as they read. When children don't know a word (such as *creatures, dragons,* and *hundred*), Mrs. Ohashi helps them sound it out or, if necessary, pronounces it for them. She writes the words on word cards to review after children finish reading. As soon as they finish reading, children discuss possible answers to her question. Several believe that sharks were dinosaurs, but others disagree. So, Mrs. Ohashi rereads page 10, which says, "There are no more dinosaurs left on earth. But there are plenty of sharks." After they agree that sharks are not dinosaurs, they practice reading the word cards that Mrs. Ohashi prepared while children were reading.

Next, the children compose this sentence about sharks using interactive writing[C]: *There are more than three hundred kinds of sharks today.* Children write on individual white boards as they take turns writing on chart paper. Then they reread the five sentences they wrote last week. During the rest of the week, children in the Atomic Tangerine group will continue reading *Hungry, Hungry Sharks* and participating in phonics, spelling, vocabulary, and writing activities with Mrs. Ohashi.

Next, Mrs. Ohashi meets with the Wild Watermelon group to reread "The Great Kapok Tree." The children read silently, but Mrs. Ohashi asks individual children to read a page aloud so that she can conduct running records[C] to check their fluency. After they finish reading, Mrs. Ohashi asks the children to talk about what the man might have been thinking as he walked away from the kapok tree on the last page of the story.

Next, she focuses on the cause and effect in the story. She asks the children what is causing a problem in the story, and they respond that cutting down the rain forest is the problem. When she asks what the effects of cutting down the trees might be, children mention several, including air pollution and destroying animal habitats. Then she passes out cards, each with a picture of an animal from the story, and asks children to scan the story to find the effect that that animal mentioned to the sleeping man. Children reread and then share what they found.

Then Mrs. Ohashi repeats these activities with the other two reading groups. On the fourth and fifth days, she meets with the three reading groups that are on grade level to focus on vocabulary words from the selection.

In the second hour, Mrs. Ohashi begins a persuasive writing project. She explains that people read and write for three purposes—to entertain, to inform, and to persuade. "Which purpose," she asks, "do you think Lynne Cherry had for writing 'The Great Kapok Tree'?" The students respond that she had all three purposes, but that perhaps the most important purpose was to persuade. Then Mrs. Ohashi explains that in persuasive writing, authors use cause and effect. They explain a problem and then tell how to solve it. They also give reasons why it must be solved and tell what will happen if it isn't solved.

The fifth stage is applying, and in this stage, children create projects to extend their learning. The children talk about environmental problems in their com-

Figure 10-2   A Third Grader's Persuasive Letter

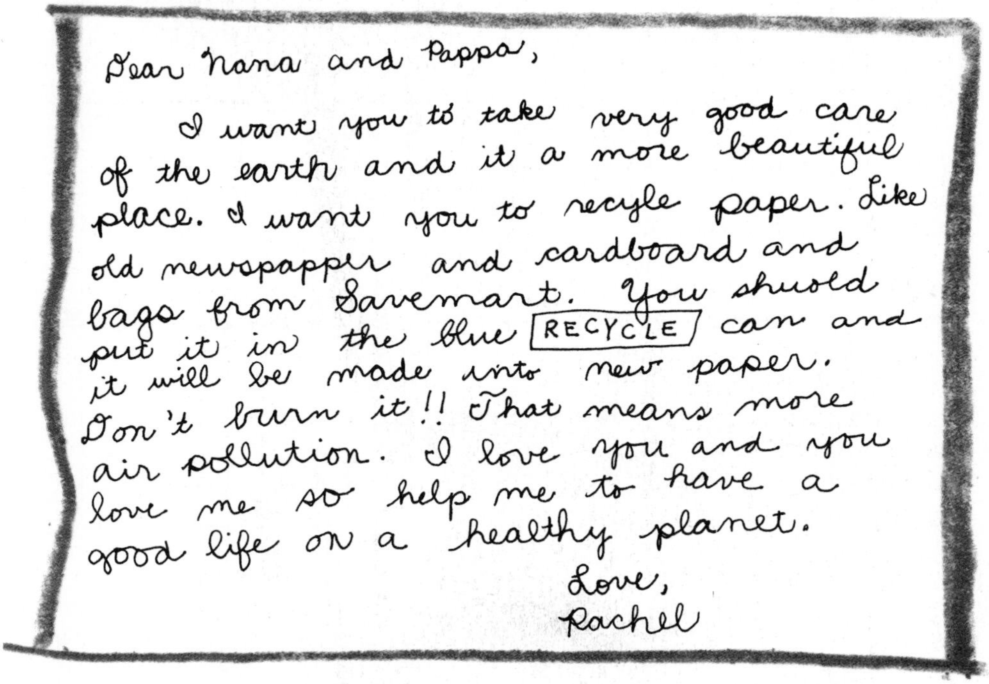

> Dear Nana and Pappa,
>
> I want you to take very good care of the earth and it a more beautiful place. I want you to recycle paper. Like old newspapper and cardboard and bags from Savemart. You shuold put it in the blue [RECYCLE] can and it will be made into new paper. Don't burn it!! That means more air pollution. I love you and you love me so help me to have a good life on a healthy planet.
>
> Love,
> Rachel

munity and decide to write letters to their parents and grandparents urging them to recycle and take good care of the environment. The format they will use is:

Sentence 1: Urge their parents to conserve and recycle.
Sentence 2: Tell how to conserve and recycle.
Sentence 3: Tell another way.
Sentence 4: Tell why it is important.
Sentence 5: Urge their parents to conserve and recycle.

Mrs. Ohashi and the third graders brainstorm many ideas and words on the chalkboard before they begin writing their rough drafts. Then on Wednesday and Thursday, they revise and edit their letters, and Mrs. Ohashi meets with children to work on their letters. By Friday, most children are writing their final copies and addressing envelopes so their letters can be mailed. Before they begin recopying, Mrs. Ohashi reviews the friendly letter form so children will be sure to format the letter correctly. Rachel's letter to her grandparents is shown in Figure 10-2.

Mrs. Ohashi ends the language arts block on Friday by showing the video version of "The Great Kapok Tree," which appeared on PBS's Reading Rainbow series, and having her students read their favorite sentences from the story in a read-around[C].

Figure 10-3 shows Mrs. Ohashi's block schedule for teaching "The Great Kapok Tree" using basal reading textbooks. She follows the reading process and includes reading groups, literacy center activities, grammar minilessons, and writing activities in the schedule.

Figure 10-3 Mrs. Ohashi's Block Schedule

	Monday	Tuesday	Wednesday	Thursday	Friday
8:30–9:30	Build background knowledge about the rain forest. Read aloud *Nature's Green Umbrella.* Read "The Great Kapok Tree" pp. 50–71 with buddies and Atomic Tangerines read with Mrs. O. Grand conversation	Atomic Tangerines read *Hungry, Hungry Sharks,* pp. 1–11. ML on *ar* words. Interactive writing Wild Watermelon Electric Lime Blizzard Blue Students not in reading groups work at centers	pp. 12–23 Reread selection Take running records Focus on cause-effects using pictures of animals	pp. 24–35 Wild Watermelon Electric Lime Blizzard Blue	pp. 36–47 Review vocabulary Locate sentences Check meanings in the glossary
9:30–10:30	Minilesson on irregular past-tense verbs Pretest on spelling words Introduce centers	Review irregular past-tense verbs Introduce persuasive writing assignment Brainstorm ideas Discuss format	Spelling Practice Test Draft and revise letters Remind students to get addresses	Grammar check using Grammar Practice Book p. 73 Revise and edit letters Review friendly letter format Begin final copies	Spelling Test Finish letters Address envelopes and prepare to mail
10:30–11:00	Independent Reading				Show video "The Great Kapok Tree" Read-around

The reading process that Mrs. Ohashi uses represents a significant shift in thinking about what people do as they read. Mrs. Ohashi understands that readers construct meaning as they negotiate the texts they are reading, and that they use their life and literature experiences and knowledge of written language as they read. She knows that meaning does not exist on the pages of the book readers are reading; instead, comprehension is created through the interaction between readers and the texts they are reading.

The reading process involves a series of stages during which readers construct interpretations as they read and respond to the text. The term *text* refers to all reading materials—stories, maps, newspapers, cereal boxes, textbooks, and so on; it is not limited to basal reader textbooks.

To link to several publishers' websites to learn about a variety of commercial reading programs, visit our Companion Website at www.prenhall.com/tompkins

THE READING PROCESS

Reading is a process in which readers comprehend and construct meaning. During reading, the meaning does not go from the page to readers. Instead, reading is a complex negotiation among the text, readers, and their purpose for reading that is shaped by many factors:

- Readers' knowledge about the topic
- Readers' knowledge about reading and about written language
- The language community to which readers belong
- The match between readers' language and the language used in the text
- Readers' culturally based expectations about reading
- Readers' expectations about reading based on their previous experiences (Weaver, 1988)

The reading process involves five stages: prereading, reading, responding, exploring, and applying. Figure 10-4 presents an overview of these stages.

Stage 1: Prereading

The reading process does not begin as readers open a book and read the first sentence; rather, the first stage is preparing to read. In the vignette, Mrs. Ohashi developed her students' background knowledge and stimulated their interest in "The Great Kapok Tree" as they learned about the rain forest. As readers prepare to read, they activate background knowledge, set purposes, and plan for reading.

Activating Background Knowledge. Readers activate their background knowledge, or schemata, about the text they plan to read. They make connections to personal experiences, to literary experiences, or to thematic units in the classroom. The topic of the book, the title, the author, the genre, an illustration, a comment someone makes about the text, or something else may trigger this activation, but for readers to make meaning with the text, schemata must be activated. For instance, first and second graders who enjoy reading the Junie B. Jones series (e.g., *Junie B. Jones and Her Big Fat Mouth*, 1993) often choose other series books to read, and others who like Eric Carle's illustrations often choose books he has written to read and reread.

Sometimes teachers collect objects related to the book and create a book box[C] to use in introducing the book to the class. In the vignette at the beginning of this chapter, Mrs. Ohashi collected a variety of rain forest products to share with her third graders.

English learners benefit from direct experience, concrete objects, and social interaction with classmates as they activate and develop background knowledge.

Figure 10-4   Key Features of the Reading Process

Stage 1: Prereading
- Set purposes.
- Connect to prior personal experiences.
- Connect to prior literary experiences.
- Connect to thematic units or special interests.
- Make predictions.
- Do a picture walk or text walk to preview the text.
- Consult the index to locate information.

Stage 2: Reading
- Make predictions.
- Apply skills and strategies.
- Read independently, with a partner, or using shared reading or guided reading; or listen to the text read aloud.
- Read the illustrations, charts, and diagrams.
- Read the entire text from beginning to end.
- Read one or more sections of text to learn specific information.
- Take notes.

Stage 3: Responding
- Write in a reading log.
- Participate in a grand conversation or instructional conversation.

Stage 4: Exploring
- Reread and think more deeply about the text.
- Make connections with personal experiences.
- Make connections with other literary experiences.
- Examine the author's craft.
- Identify memorable quotes.
- Learn new vocabulary words.
- Participate in minilessons on reading procedures, concepts, strategies, and skills.

Stage 5: Applying
- Construct projects.
- Use information in thematic units.
- Connect with related books.
- Reflect on their interpretation.
- Value the reading experience.

Setting Purposes. The two overarching purposes for reading (and listening to the teacher read aloud) are pleasure and information. When children read for pleasure or enjoyment, they read aesthetically, to be carried into the world of the text; when they read to locate information or for directions about how to do something, they read efferently (Rosenblatt, 1978). Often readers use elements of both purposes as they read, but usually one purpose is more important to the reading experience than the other.

Purpose setting is usually directed by the teacher during literature focus units, but in reading workshop, children set their own purposes because everyone is reading different self-selected books. For teacher-directed purpose setting, teachers explain how children are expected to read and what they will do after reading. The goal of teacher-directed purpose setting is to help children learn how to set personally relevant purposes when they are reading independently (Blanton, Wood, & Moorman, 1990). Children should always have a purpose for reading, whether they are reading aesthetically or efferently, whether reading a text for the first time or the tenth. Readers are more successful when they have a single purpose for reading the entire selection. A single purpose is more effective than multiple purposes, and sustaining a single purpose is more effective than presenting children with a series of purposes as they read.

When readers have purposes for reading (or listening to the teacher read aloud), their comprehension of the selection is enhanced in three ways, whether teachers provide the purpose or children set their own purpose (Blanton et al., 1990). First of all, the purpose guides the reading process that children use. Having a purpose provides motivation and direction for reading, as well as a mechanism that children use for monitoring their reading. As they monitor their reading, children ask themselves whether or not they are fulfilling their purpose.

Second, setting a purpose activates a plan for readers to use while reading. Purpose setting causes children to draw on background knowledge, consider strategies they might use as they read, and think about the structure of the text they are reading. Children are better able to sort out important from unimportant information as they read when they have a purpose for reading. Teachers direct children's attention to relevant concepts as they set purposes for reading and show them how to connect the concepts they are reading about to their prior knowledge about a topic.

Children read differently depending on their purpose for reading, and the instructional procedures that teachers use also vary according to the purpose for reading. When children are reading stories, teachers might use the Directed Reading-Thinking Activity[C] (DRTA) to help children predict and then read to confirm or reject their predictions, or have children create story maps[C] to focus their attention on plot, characters, or another element of story structure. When children are reading informational books, teachers might use a cluster[C] to activate prior knowledge, or use a data chart[C] to explore a concept from different viewpoints.

In contrast to teacher-directed purpose setting, children set their own purposes for reading during literature circles, reading workshop, and at other times when they choose their own books to read. Often they choose materials that are intrinsically interesting or that describe something they want to learn more about. As children gain experience in reading, identify favorite authors and illustrators, and learn about genres, they acquire other criteria to use in choosing books and setting purposes for reading. When teachers conference with children, they often ask them about their purposes for reading and why they choose particular books to read.

Planning for Reading. Children preview the reading selection during the prereading stage. The preview is called a *picture walk* when children are examining a picture book and a *text walk* when they are examining a chapter book. Often the teacher guides children through the previewing activity. In a picture walk, teachers read the title and author of the book as children look at the cover. They talk about the title and cover illustration and make predictions about the text, if enough information is provided; otherwise, they postpone making predictions until they have examined the illustrations on several more pages. Teachers and children continue to look at each page of the text, talking about the illustrations, and teachers highlight specific vocabulary or concepts that children need to be familiar with before reading. Text walks are similar to picture walks; teachers and children read the title and author and examine the cover illustration. They look through the book and read chapter titles and make predictions about the story.

Children also take picture walks and text walks when they are preparing to read independently during reading workshop and literature circles. As they look through the selection, children make predictions, examine the illustrations, and read the title and perhaps the first page of text. They also consider the reading difficulty in order to judge the general suitability of the selection for them as readers.

Previewing serves an important function as children connect their prior knowledge, identify their purpose for reading, and take their first look at the selection. Teachers set the guidelines for the reading experience, explain how the book will be read—independently, in small groups, or as a class—and set the schedule for reading. Setting the schedule is especially important when children are reading a chapter book. Often teachers and children work together to create a 1- or 2-week schedule for reading and responding and then write the schedule on a calendar to which children can refer.

When children are preparing to read informational books, they preview the selection by flipping through the pages and noting section headings, illustrations, diagrams, and other charts. Sometimes they examine the table of contents to see how the book is organized, or consult the index to locate specific information they want to read. They may also notice unfamiliar terminology and other words they can check in the glossary, ask a classmate or the teacher about, or look up in a dictionary.

Children often draw pictures and make notes in learning logs^C as they explore informational books. These notes take several different forms. Sometimes children write quickwrites^C to activate prior knowledge and explore the concepts to be presented in the selection, or write down important terminology. Or children draw clusters, data charts, and other diagrams they will complete as they read. As they move through the remaining stages in the reading process, children add other information to their learning logs. Figure 10-5 shows two entries from a first grader's learning log written during a unit on the sun and the moon. The first entry is a quickwrite written before the teacher read *The Moon Book* (Gibbons, 1997). Notice that the child is confused about the sun and the moon. The second entry was written after the child listened to the book read aloud and participated in an instructional conversation^C about the book. In the second entry, the child clarifies that the moon and the sun are not the same and writes about the phases of the moon and other new information. Before children began each of the entries, the teacher brainstormed lists of words that they might want to use in their entries. That explains why the child spelled several technical terms correctly or almost correctly.

Stage 2: Reading

Children read the book or other selection in the reading stage. They use their knowledge of decoding and word identification, sight words, strategies, skills, and vocabulary while they read. Fluent readers are better able to understand what they are reading because they identify most words automatically and use decoding skills when necessary. They also apply their knowledge of the structure of text as they create meaning. They continue reading as long as what they are reading fits the meaning they are constructing. When something doesn't make sense, readers slow down, back up, and reread until they are making meaning again.

Children usually read the entire text from beginning to end in one sitting, unless they are reading a longer chapter book. Children may decide, however, to put a book down if it does not capture their interest or if it is too difficult to read. It is unrealistic to assume that children will always read entire texts or finish reading every book they begin.

In the classroom, teachers involve children in five types of reading activities: shared reading, guided reading, independent reading, buddy reading, and listening while the teacher reads aloud. Teachers choose the type of reading experience according to the purpose for reading, children's reading levels, and the number of copies available.

To view shared reading and guided reading in action, play the CD-ROM titled *Primary Grades Literacy: A K–3 Unit on Insects* that accompanies this text.

Shared Reading. Teachers use shared reading to read aloud books and other texts that are appropriate for children's interest level but too difficult for children to read on their own (Holdaway, 1979; Parkes, 2000). Often primary-grade teachers use big

Figure 10-5 A First Grader's Quickwrites About the Moon

The Moon

The moon is white,
I see it at night.
The moon is the suh at night.
I think the meon is cool,

A Satelite

The moon goes aroud the earth.

The moon is hot the suh!

The moon looks like it changes shape but it does hot.

The moon reflects the suns light.

Did you know that astronauts have walked on the moon?

books or texts written on charts so that both small groups and whole-class groups can see the text and read along with the teacher. Teachers model what fluent readers do as they involve students in enjoyable reading activities (Fountas & Pinnell, 1996). After the text is read several times, teachers use it to teach phonics concepts and high-frequency words. Children can also read small versions of the book independently or with partners, and the pattern or structure used in the text can be used for writing activities (Slaughter, 1993).

Shared reading is part of a balanced literacy program for emergent and beginning readers in the primary grades. Teachers read aloud books that are appropriate for children's interest level but too difficult for them to read for themselves. The books chosen for shared reading are available in both big-book and small-book formats and are close to children's reading level, but still beyond their ability to read independently. As an instructional strategy, shared reading differs from reading aloud to children because children see the text as the teacher reads. Also, children often join in the reading of predictable refrains and rhyming words, and after listening to the teacher read the text several times, children often remember enough of the text to read along with the teacher. The steps in a shared reading lesson are listed in Figure 10-6.

Big books are greatly enlarged picture books that teachers use in shared reading, most commonly with primary-grade students. In this technique, developed in New Zealand, teachers place an enlarged picture book on an easel or chart stand where all children can see it. Then they read it with small groups of children or with the whole

Teachers regularly use shared reading to read big books to prekindergartners. Through their reading, teachers model reading strategies and teach concepts about print.

Figure 10-6   A Shared Reading Lesson

1. Prereading

Teachers use poems or other texts that they have copied on chart paper, or they select quality books that are available in big-book format with text that is large enough for children to see. It is also important that the books are interesting so that children will want to listen to them read aloud several times and later read them themselves. Teachers talk about the book or other text by activating or building background knowledge and by reading the title and the author's name aloud. Children usually make predictions before beginning to read.

2. Reading

Teachers read aloud the book or other text using a pointer (a dowel rod with a pencil eraser on the end) to track as they read. They read with good expression and highlight key vocabulary words and repetitive patterns. They invite children to join in reading the repetitive refrains, rhymes, and other familiar words. During the first reading, teachers make very few stops, but they do stop once or twice for children to make more predictions. Depending on children's interest, teachers may stop after the first reading to talk about the book, or they may reread the book once or twice and encourage children to join in the reading.

3. Responding

Children and the teacher talk about the book in a grand conversation, and children share their responses to the book. Teachers clarify misconceptions, expand on children's comments, and ask higher-level questions, such as "What would happen if . . .?" and "What did this book make you think of?" After the grand conversation, children draw or write in reading logs or share the pen to write a sentence or two interactively about the book.

4. Exploring

Teachers and children reread the book or other text over a period of several days. Children take turns turning the pages and using the pointer to track the reading. Teachers invite children to join in reading familiar and predictable words, and children increasingly read more and more of the words. Teachers also take advantage of opportunities to teach capitalization and punctuation marks, use graphophonic cues, and model reading. As children gain experience reading the text, they often reread the book using individual books, too.

Also during the exploring stage, children add important words to the word wall, and teachers present minilessons on phonics concepts, skills and strategies, and high-frequency words. Teachers also present more information about the author and illustrator and introduce a text set with other books by the same people.

5. Applying

Children often create "innovations," or their own versions of the poem or book using the pattern found in the text. Sometimes children collaborate to write a class book, and at other times they write individual books. Also, children read small books if they haven't already read them. Many times, children create art projects related to the text.

class. Trachtenburg and Ferruggia (1989) used big books with their class of transitional first graders and found that making and reading big books dramatically improved children's reading scores on standardized achievement tests. The teachers reported that children's self-concepts as readers were decidedly improved as well.

With the big book on a chart stand or easel, the teacher reads it aloud, pointing to every word. Before long, children join in the reading. Then the teacher rereads the book, inviting children to help with the reading. The next time the book is read, the teacher reads to the point that the text becomes predictable, such as the beginning of a refrain, and the children supply the missing text. Having children supply the missing words is important because it leads to independent reading. When children have become familiar with the text, they are invited to read the big book independently (Parkes, 2000).

The stories and other books that teachers use for shared reading with young children often have repeated words and sentences, rhyme, or other patterns. Books that use these patterns are known as predictable books. These books are a valuable tool for emergent readers because the repeated words and sentences, patterns, and sequences enable children to predict the next sentence or episode in the text (Bridge, 1979; Tompkins & Webeler, 1983). Four types of predictable books are:

1. *Repetitive sentences.* Phrases and sentences are repeated over and over in some books. Sometimes each episode or section of the text ends with the same words or a refrain, and in other books, the same statement or question is repeated. In *The Little Red Hen* (Galdone, 1973), the animals repeat "Not I" when the Little Red Hen asks them to help her plant the seeds, harvest the wheat, and bake the bread; after their refusals to help, the hen says, "Then I will."

2. *Repetitive sentences in a cumulative structure.* The phrases or sentences are repeated and expanded in each episode in some books. In *The Gingerbread Boy* (Galdone, 1975), for instance, the Gingerbread Boy repeats and expands his boast as he meets each character on his run away from the Little Old Man and the Little Old Woman.

3. *Rhyme and rhythm.* Rhyme and rhythm are important devices in some books. The sentences have a strong beat, and rhyme is used at the end of each line or in another poetic scheme. Also, some books have an internal rhyme within lines rather than at the end of rhymes. One example is Dr. Seuss's *Hop on Pop* (1963).

4. *Sequential patterns.* Some books use a familiar sequence, such as months of the year, days of the week, numbers 1 to 10, and letters of the alphabet, to structure the text. For example, *The Very Hungry Caterpillar* (Carle, 1969) combines number and day-of-the-week sequences as the caterpillar eats through an amazing array of foods during the week.

A list of predictable books illustrating each of these patterns is presented in Figure 10-7.

Guided Reading. Teachers use guided reading to work with groups of four or five students who are reading at the same level (Clay, 1991). They select a book that children can read at their instructional level, with approximately 90–94% accuracy. Teachers support children's reading and their use of reading strategies during guided reading (Depree & Iversen, 1996; Fountas & Pinnell, 1996). Children do the actual reading themselves, although the teacher may read aloud with children to get them started on the first page or two. Beginning readers often murmur the words softly as they read, and this helps the teacher keep track of children's reading and the strategies they are using. Older students who are more fluent readers usually read silently during guided reading.

Guided reading lessons usually last 25 to 30 minutes. When the children arrive for the small-group lesson, they often reread, either individually or with a buddy, familiar books used in previous guided reading lessons. For the new guided reading lesson,

Figure 10-7   Predictable Books

Repetitive Sentences

Asch, F. (1981). *Just like Daddy.* New York: Simon & Schuster.

Bennett, J. (1985). *Teeny tiny.* New York: Putnam.

Brown, R. (1981). *A dark, dark tale.* New York: Dial.

Carle, E. (1973). *Have you seen my cat?* New York: Philomel.

Carle, E. (1984). *The very busy spider.* New York: Philomel.

Carle, E. (1990). *The very quiet cricket.* New York: Philomel.

Gág, W. (1956). *Millions of cats.* New York: Coward-McCann.

Galdone, P. (1973). *The little red hen.* New York: Seabury.

Guarino, D. (1989). *Is your mama a llama?* New York: Scholastic.

Hill, E. (1980). *Where's Spot?* New York: Putnam.

Hutchins, P. (1972). *Good-night, owl!* New York: Macmillan.

Hutchins, P. (1986). *The doorbell rang.* New York: Morrow.

Martin, B., Jr. (1983). *Brown bear, brown bear, what do you see?* New York: Holt, Rinehart and Winston.

Martin, B., Jr. (1992). *Polar bear, polar bear, what do you hear?* New York: Holt, Rinehart and Winston.

Peek, M. (1981). *Roll over!* Boston: Houghton Mifflin.

Peek, M. (1985). *Mary wore her red dress.* New York: Clarion.

Rosen, M. (1989). *We're going on a bear hunt.* New York: Macmillan.

Weiss, N. (1987). *If you're happy and you know it.* New York: Greenwillow.

Weiss, N. (1989). *Where does the brown bear go?* New York: Viking.

Westcott, N. B. (1988). *The lady with the alligator purse.* Boston: Little, Brown.

Wickstrom, S. K. (1988). *Wheels on the bus.* New York: Crown.

Williams, S. (1989). *I went walking.* San Diego: Harcourt Brace Jovanovich.

Repetitive Sentences in a Cumulative Structure

Brett, J. (1989). *The mitten.* New York: Putnam.

Flack, M. (1932). *Ask Mr. Bear.* New York: Macmillan.

Fox, M. (1986). *Hattie and the fox.* New York: Bradbury.

Galdone, P. (1975). *The gingerbread boy.* New York: Seabury.

Kellogg, S. (1974). *There was an old woman.* New York: Parents.

Kraus, R. (1970). *Whose mouse are you?* New York: Macmillan.

Tolstoi, A. (1968). *The great big enormous turnip.* New York: Watts.

Westcott, N. B. (1980). *I know an old lady who swallowed a fly.* Boston: Little, Brown.

Zemach, H. (1969). *The judge.* New York: Farrar, Straus & Giroux.

Zemach, M. (1983). *The little red hen.* New York: Farrar, Straus & Giroux.

Rhyme and Rhythm

Brown, M. (1987). *Play rhymes.* New York: Dutton.

de Paola, T. (1985). *Hey diddle diddle and other Mother Goose rhymes.* New York: Putnam.

Messenger, J. (1986). *Twinkle, twinkle, little star.* New York: Macmillan.

Sendak, M. (1962). *Chicken soup with rice.* New York: Harper & Row.

Seuss, Dr. (1963). *Hop on Pop.* New York: Random House.

Seuss, Dr. (1988). *Green eggs and ham.* New York: Random House.

Sequential Patterns

Alain. (1964). *One, two, three, going to sea.* New York: Scholastic.

Carle, E. (1969). *The very hungry caterpillar.* Cleveland: Collins-World.

Carle, E. (1977). *The grouchy ladybug.* New York: Crowell.

Carle, E. (1987). *A house for hermit crab.* Saxonville, MA: Picture Book Studio.

Domanska, J. (1985). *Busy Monday morning.* New York: Greenwillow.

Keats, E. J. (1973). *Over in the meadow.* New York: Scholastic.

Mack, S. (1974). *10 bears in my bed.* New York: Pantheon.

Numeroff, L. J. (1985). *If you give a mouse a cookie.* New York: HarperCollins.

Numeroff, L. J. (1991). *If you give a moose a muffin.* New York: HarperCollins.

Wood, A. (1984). *The napping house.* San Diego: Harcourt Brace Jovanovich.

First graders build sentences using word cards during a guided reading lesson.

children read books that they have not read before. Beginning readers usually read small picture books at one sitting, but fluent readers who are reading easy chapter books take several days to read their books. The steps in a guided reading lesson are listed in Figure 10-8.

Teachers observe children as they read during guided reading lessons. They spend a few minutes observing each child, either sitting in front of or beside the child. Teachers observe the child's behaviors for evidence of strategy use and confirm the child's attempts to identify words and solve reading problems. The strategies and problem-solving behaviors that teachers look for include:

- self-monitoring
- checking predictions
- decoding unfamiliar words
- determining if the word makes sense
- checking that a word is appropriate in the syntax of the sentence
- using all sources of information
- chunking phrases to read more fluently

Teachers take notes about their observations and use the information in deciding what minilessons to teach and what books to choose for children to read.

Teachers also take running records of one or two children during each guided reading lesson and use this information as part of their assessment. Teachers check to see that the books children are reading are at their instructional level and that they are making expected progress toward increasingly more difficult levels of books.

Independent Reading. When children read independently, they read by themselves, for their own purposes, and at their own pace (Hornsby, Sukarna, & Parry, 1986). Fluent readers often read silently during independent reading, but emergent and beginning

Figure 10-8   A Guided Reading Lesson

1. Prereading

Teachers introduce the new reading selection and prepare children to read. Teachers begin by activating or building background knowledge of a topic related to the selection or the genre. Then they show the cover of the book, say the title and the author's name, and talk about the problem in the story or one or two main ideas in an informational book. They set the purpose for reading, and children often make predictions. They continue with a book walk to give an overview of the selection, but they do not read it aloud to children. Teachers introduce vocabulary words that are essential to the meaning of the text and teach or review a strategy that children should use while reading.

2. Reading

Teachers guide children through one or more readings of the selection. During the first reading, children and the teacher may read the first page or two together. Then children read the rest of the selection independently, reading aloud softly to themselves or silently, depending on their reading level. Teachers prompt for strategies and word identification as needed, and they move from child to child, listening in as the child reads. Teachers usually do a running record as children read aloud. After young children finish reading the selection, teachers often invite them to reread it. Older children often have a brief writing assignment to do after they finish reading and while they wait for classmates to finish.

3. Responding

Children discuss the selection, making text-to-self, text-to-world, and text-to-text connections. Teachers ask inferential and critical-level questions, such as "What would happen if . . .?" "Why did . . .?" and "If . . . , what might have happened next?" Children also reread to locate evidence for their answers. After talking about the selection, teachers often work with young children to write a summary sentence interactively, whereas older students usually write in reading logs or share what they wrote earlier.

4. Exploring

Teachers involve children in three types of activities:

- *Strategy instruction.* Teachers review and reinforce the reading strategy that children used in reading the selection. Sometimes teachers model how they used the strategy or ask children to reread a portion of the selection and think aloud about their strategy use.
- *Literary analysis.* Teachers explain genres, present information about story elements or other text structures, and locate examples of literary devices in the selection. Sometimes children create story maps or other graphic organizers.
- *Word work.* Teachers focus children's attention on words from the selection. Primary-grade teachers review high-frequency words and have children practice writing several words from the story using magnetic letters and small white boards. Teachers also write sentences from the book on sentence strips and cut the strips apart; then students sequence the words to re-create the sentence. Middle-grade teachers review vocabulary words from the selection and teach children to identify words by breaking them into syllables or using inflectional endings.

5. Applying

Children apply the strategies they are learning in independent reading activities such as reading workshop and Sustained Silent Reading.

readers usually read aloud softly to themselves. For young children to read independently, the selections must be at their reading level. Children often reread books they have already read with the teacher during shared reading and guided reading. Rereading books is worthwhile for many reasons. For example, children develop confidence in themselves as readers because they are successful. They enjoy books and view reading as a pleasurable activity. As they reread, children recognize words more automatically and become more fluent because they are familiar with the selection and better able to chunk words into phrases.

Reading workshop provides opportunities for independent reading. Children read independently in books they have chosen themselves. Children think of themselves as readers when they choose their own books. Even children in kindergarten and prekindergarten do a variation of reading workshop when they look at picture books that interest them, creating their own text to accompany the illustrations. They also look at picture books the teacher has read aloud and retell the story to themselves as they look at the illustrations.

Children need to learn how to choose appropriate books for independent reading. These books should be interesting to children and should be at their reading level. Ohlhausen and Jepsen (1992) developed a strategy for choosing books that they called the "Goldilocks Strategy." These teachers created three categories of books—"Too Easy" books, "Too Hard" books, and "Just Right" books—using "The Three Bears" folktale as their model. The books in the "Too Easy" category were books children had read before or that had no unfamiliar words. Books in the "Too Hard" category were unfamiliar and confusing, and books in the "Just Right" category were interesting and had just a few unfamiliar words. Figure 10-9 presents a chart made by a third-grade class about choosing books using the Goldilocks Strategy. Emergent, beginning, and fluent readers can use this strategy for choosing books to read independently. The books in each category vary according to the child's reading level; books that are too hard for one child may be just right or too easy for another.

Another format for independent reading is Sustained Silent Reading (SSR). This is a special time set aside during the school day for children in one class or the entire school to silently read self-selected books. In some schools, everyone—students, teachers, principals, secretaries, and custodians—stops to read, usually for 15 to 30 minutes. SSR is a popular reading activity that is known by a variety of names, including Drop Everything and Read Time (DEAR Time), Sustained Quiet Reading Time (SQUIRT), and Our Time to Enjoy Reading (OTTER).

Teachers use SSR to increase the amount of reading children do every day (Hunt, 1967; McCracken & McCracken, 1978). A number of studies have shown that SSR is beneficial in developing children's reading ability (Krashen, 1993; Pilgreen, 2000). In addition, SSR promotes a positive attitude toward reading and encourages children to develop the habit of daily reading.

Buddy Reading. In buddy reading, children read or reread a selection with a classmate. Sometimes children read with buddies because it is an enjoyable social activity, and sometimes they read together to help each other. Often children can read selections together that neither child could read individually. Buddy reading is a good alternative to independent reading because children can choose books they want to read and then read at their own pace. By working together, they are often able to figure out unfamiliar words and talk out comprehension problems.

As teachers introduce buddy reading, they show children how to read with buddies and how to support each other as they read. Children take turns reading aloud to each other or read in unison. They often stop and help each other identify an unfamiliar word or take a minute or two at the end of each page to talk about what they

Figure 10-9 A Third-Grade Chart Applying the Goldilocks Strategy

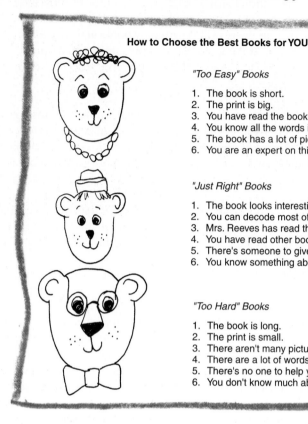

How to Choose the Best Books for YOU

"Too Easy" Books

1. The book is short.
2. The print is big.
3. You have read the book before.
4. You know all the words in the book.
5. The book has a lot of pictures.
6. You are an expert on this topic.

"Just Right" Books

1. The book looks interesting.
2. You can decode most of the words in the book.
3. Mrs. Reeves has read this book aloud to you.
4. You have read other books by this author.
5. There's someone to give you help if you need it.
6. You know something about this topic.

"Too Hard" Books

1. The book is long.
2. The print is small.
3. There aren't many pictures in the book.
4. There are a lot of words that you can't decode.
5. There's no one to help you read this book.
6. You don't know much about this topic.

have read. Buddy reading is a valuable way of providing the practice that beginning readers need to become fluent readers; it is also an effective way to work with children with special learning needs and students who are learning English. However, unless the teacher has explained the approach and taught children how to work collaboratively, buddy reading often deteriorates into the stronger of the two buddies reading aloud to the other child, and that is not the intention of this type of reading.

One approach to buddy reading is to use a class of upper-grade students in a cross-age reading buddies program with primary-grade children. Older students read books aloud to younger children, and they also listen to the younger children read aloud. The effectiveness of cross-age tutoring is supported by research (Cohen, Kulik, & Kulik, 1982), and teachers report that both older and younger students' reading fluency and attitudes toward school and learning improve (Labbo & Teale, 1990; Morrice & Simmons, 1991).

Teachers arranging a buddy-reading program decide when children will get together, how long each session will last, and what the schedule will be. Primary-grade teachers explain the program to their students and talk about activities the buddies will be doing together, and upper-grade teachers explain to their students how to work with young children. In particular, they should teach students how to read aloud and encourage younger children to make predictions, how to select books to appeal to younger children, and how to help them respond to books. Then older students choose books to read aloud and practice reading them until they can read the books fluently. At the first meeting, students pair off, get acquainted, and read together.

Children take turns reading with classmates during buddy reading.

They also talk about the books they read and perhaps write in special reading logs[C]. Buddies also may want to go to the library and choose the books they will read at the next session.

Cross-age tutoring programs offer significant social benefits, too. Children get acquainted with other children they might otherwise not meet, and they learn how to work with older or younger children. As they talk about books they have read, students share personal experiences and interpretations. They also talk about reading strategies, how to choose books, and their favorite authors or illustration styles. Sometimes reading buddies write notes back and forth, or the two classrooms plan holiday celebrations together. These activities strengthen the social connections between the children.

A second way to encourage more buddy reading is to involve parents in the program by using traveling bags of books. Teachers collect text sets of four or five books on various topics for children to take home and read with their parents (Reutzel & Fawson, 1990). For example, teachers might collect copies of *Hattie and the Fox* (Fox, 1986), *The Gingerbread Boy* (Galdone, 1975), *Flossie and the Fox* (McKissack, 1986), and *Rosie's Walk* (Hutchins, 1968) for a traveling bag of fox stories. Then children and their parents buddy read one or more of the books and draw or write a response to the books they have read in the reading log that accompanies the books in the traveling bag. Children keep the bag at home for several days, often rereading the books each day with their parents, and then return it to school so that another child can borrow it. Text sets for 10 traveling bags are listed in Figure 10-10. Many of these text sets combine stories, informational books, and poems. Teachers can also add small toys, stuffed animals, audiotapes of one or more of the books, or other related objects to the bags.

Teachers often introduce traveling bags at a special parents' meeting or openhouse get-together at which they explain to parents how to read with their children, modeling how to have children make predictions, figure out unfamiliar words, and talk about the book after reading. It is important that parents understand that their children may not be familiar with the books and that children are not expected to be able to read them independently. Teachers also talk about the responses children and parents write in the reading log and show sample entries from the previous year.

Figure 10-10   Text Sets for Traveling Bags

Books About Airplanes

Barton, R. (1982). *Airport.* New York: Harper & Row.
McPhail, D. (1987). *First flight.* Boston: Little, Brown.
Petersen, D. (1981). *Airplanes* (A new true book). Chicago: Childrens Press.
Ziegler, S. (1988). *A visit to the airport.* Chicago: Childrens Press.

Books About Dogs

Barracca, D., & Barracca, S. (1990). *The adventures of taxi dog.* New York: Dial.
Bridwell, N. (1963). *Clifford the big red dog.* New York: Greenwillow.
Cole, J. (1991). *My puppy is born.* New York: Morrow.
Reiser, L. (1992). *Any kind of dog.* New York: Greenwillow.

Books by Ezra Jack Keats

Keats, E. J. (1962). *The snowy day.* New York: Viking.
Keats, E. J. (1964). *Whistle for Willie.* New York: Viking.
Keats, E. J. (1967). *Peter's chair.* New York: Harper & Row.
Keats, E. J. (1969). *Goggles.* New York: Macmillan.
Keats, E. J. (1970). *Hi cat!* New York: Macmillan.

Books About Frogs and Toads

Lobel, A. (1970). *Frog and Toad are friends.* New York: Harper & Row.
Mayer, M. (1974). *Frog goes to dinner.* New York: Dial.
Pallotta, J. (1990). *The frog alphabet book: And other awesome amphibians.* Watertown, MA: Charlesbridge.
Watts, B. (1991). *Frog.* New York: Lodestar.
Yolen, J. (1980). *Commander Toad in space.* New York: Coward-McCann.

Books About Mice

Cauley, L. B. (1984). *The town mouse and the country mouse.* New York: Putnam.
Henkes, K. (1991). *Chrysanthemum.* New York: Greenwillow.
Lionni, L. (1969). *Alexander and the wind-up mouse.* New York: Pantheon.
Lobel, A. (1977). *Mouse soup.* New York: Harper & Row.
Numeroff, L. J. (1985). *If you give a mouse a cookie.* New York: Harper & Row.

Books About Numbers

Aker, S. (1990). *What comes in 2's, 3's, & 4's?* New York: Simon & Schuster.
Bang, M. (1983). *Ten, nine, eight.* New York: Greenwillow.
Giganti, P., Jr. (1992). *Each orange had 8 slices: A counting book.* New York: Greenwillow.
Tafuri, N. (1986). *Who's counting?* New York: Greenwillow.

Books About Plants

Ehlert, L. (1991). *Red leaf, yellow leaf.* San Diego: Harcourt Brace Jovanovich.
Fowler, A. (1990). *It could still be a tree.* Chicago: Childrens Press.
Gibbons, G. (1984). *The seasons of Arnold's apple tree.* San Diego: Harcourt Brace Jovanovich.
King, E. (1990). *The pumpkin patch.* New York: Dutton.
Lobel, A. (1990). *Alison's zinnia.* New York: Greenwillow.

Books About Rain

Branley, F. M. (1985). *Flash, crash, rumble, and roll.* New York: Harper & Row.
Polacco, P. (1990). *Thunder cake.* New York: Philomel.
Shulevitz, U. (1969). *Rain rain rivers.* New York: Farrar, Straus & Giroux.
Spier, P. (1982). *Rain.* New York: Doubleday.

Books About the Three Bears

Cauley, L. B. (1981). *Goldilocks and the three bears.* New York: Putnam.
Galdone, P. (1972). *The three bears.* New York: Clarion Books.
Tolhurst, M. (1990). *Somebody and the three Blairs.* New York: Orchard Books.
Turkle, B. (1976). *Deep in the forest.* New York: Dutton.

Books About Trucks

Crews, D. (1980). *Truck.* New York: Greenwillow.
Owen, A. (1990). *Bumper to bumper.* New York: Knopf.
Rockwell, A. (1984). *Trucks.* New York: Dutton.
Rockwell, A. (1986). *Big wheels.* New York: Dutton.
Siebert, D. (1984). *Truck song.* New York: Harper & Row.

Reading Aloud to Children. In prekindergarten through fourth grade, teachers read aloud to children for a variety of purposes each day. During literature focus units, for example, teachers read aloud featured selections that are appropriate for children's interest level but too difficult for them to read themselves. Sometimes it is also appropriate to read the featured selection aloud before distributing copies of it for children to read with buddies or independently. When they read aloud, teachers model what good readers do and how good readers use reading strategies. Reading aloud also provides an opportunity for teachers to think aloud about their use of reading strategies.

The advantages and drawbacks for each type of reading are outlined in Figure 10-11. Teachers should incorporate all five types of reading activities in their instructional programs.

Stage 3: Responding

During the third stage, readers respond to their reading and continue to negotiate meaning. Two ways that children make tentative and exploratory comments immediately after reading are by writing in reading logs and participating in grand conversations.

English learners comprehend better when they connect talk with dramatizing episodes or drawing pictures about what they are reading.

Writing in Reading Logs. Children write and draw their thoughts and feelings about what they have read in reading logs[C]. Rosenblatt (1978) explains that as children write about what they have read, they unravel their thinking and, at the same time, elaborate on and clarify their responses. When children read informational books, they sometimes write in reading logs, as they do after reading stories and poems, but at other times they make notes of important information or draw charts and diagrams to use in thematic units.

Children usually make reading logs by stapling together 5 to 10 sheets of paper at the beginning of a literature focus unit or reading workshop. At the beginning of a thematic unit, children make learning logs to draw and write in during the unit. They decorate the covers, keeping with the theme of the unit, write entries related to their reading, and make notes related to what they are learning in minilessons. Teachers monitor children's entries during the unit, reading and often responding to their entries. They focus their responses on the children's ideas, but they expect children to spell the title of the book and the names of characters accurately. At the end of the unit, teachers review children's work and often grade the journals based on whether children completed all the entries and on the quality of the ideas in their entries.

Participating in Discussions. Children also talk about stories with classmates in grand conversations. Peterson and Eeds (1990) explain that in this type of discussion, children share their personal responses and tell what they liked about the text. After sharing personal reactions, they shift the focus to "puzzle over what the author has written and . . . share what it is they find revealed" (p. 61). Often children make connections between the text and their own lives or between the text and other literature they have read. If they are reading a chapter book, they also make predictions about what will happen in the next chapter.

Teachers often share their ideas in grand conversations, but they act as interested participants, not leaders. The talk is primarily among the children, but teachers ask questions regarding things they are genuinely interested in learning more about and share information in response to questions that children ask or to clarify misconceptions. In the past, many discussions have been "gentle inquisitions" during which children recited answers to factual questions teachers asked about books that children were reading (Eeds & Wells, 1989). Teachers asked these questions to determine

Figure *10-11*

Advantages and Disadvantages of the Five Types
of Reading

Type	Advantages	Drawbacks
Shared Reading Teacher reads aloud while children follow along using individual copies of the book, a class chart, or a big book.	• Access to books children could not read themselves. • Teacher models fluent reading. • Opportunities to model reading strategies. • Children practice fluent reading. • Develops a community of readers.	• Multiple copies, a class chart, or a big book needed. • Text may not be appropriate for all children. • Children may not be interested in the text.
Guided Reading Teacher supports children as they apply reading strategies and skills to read a text.	• Teach skills and strategies. • Teacher provides direction and scaffolding. • Opportunities to model reading strategies. • Use with unfamiliar texts.	• Multiple copies of text needed. • Teacher controls the reading experience. • Some children may not be interested in the text.
Independent Reading Children read a text on their own.	• Develops responsibility and ownership. • Self-selection of texts. • Experience is more authentic.	• Children may need assistance to read the text. • Little teacher involvement and control.
Buddy Reading Two children read or reread a text together.	• Collaboration between children. • Children assist each other. • Use to reread familiar texts. • Develops reading fluency. • Children talk and share interpretations.	• Limited teacher involvement. • Less teacher control.
Reading Aloud to Children Teacher or other fluent reader reads aloud to children.	• Access to books children could not read themselves. • Reader models fluent reading. • Opportunities to model reading strategies. • Develops a community of readers. • Use when only one copy of text is available.	• No opportunity for children themselves to read. • Text may not be appropriate for all children. • Children may not be interested in the text.

whether or not children understood what they read. Although teachers can still judge children's comprehension, the focus in grand conversations is on clarifying and deepening children's understanding of the story they have read.

Teachers and children have similar discussions, called *instructional conversations,* after reading informational books. Children talk about what interested them in the book and what they learned about the topic, but teachers also focus children's attention on key concepts, ask clarifying questions, share information, and reread brief sections to clarify a concept.

These discussions can be held with the whole class or with small groups. Young children usually meet as a class, whereas third and fourth graders often prefer to talk with classmates in small groups. When children meet as a class, there is a feeling of community, and the teacher can be part of the group. When children meet in small groups, they have more opportunities to participate in the discussion and share their interpretations, but fewer viewpoints are expressed in each group and teachers must move around, spending only a few minutes with each group. Some teachers compromise and have children begin their discussions in small groups and then come together as a class and have each group share what their group discussed.

Stage 4: Exploring

Children go back into the text to examine it more analytically in the exploring stage. They reread the selection, examine the author's craft, and focus on words from the selection. Teachers also present minilessons on procedures, concepts, strategies, and skills, as Mrs. Ohashi did in the vignette at the beginning of the chapter.

Rereading the Selection. As children reread the selection, they think again about what they have read. Each time they reread a selection, children benefit in specific ways (Yaden, 1988). They deepen their comprehension and make further connections between the selection and their own lives or between the selection and other books they have read. Children often reread a basal reader story, a picture book, or excerpts from a chapter book several times. If the teacher used shared reading to read the selection with children in the reading stage, children might reread it with a buddy once or twice, read it with their parents, and, after these experiences, read it independently.

Examining the Author's Craft. Teachers plan exploring activities to focus children's attention on the structure of text and the literary language that authors use. Children notice opposites in the story, use story boards[C] to sequence the events in the story, and make story maps to highlight the plot, characters, and other elements of story structure. Another way children learn about the structure of stories is by writing books based on the selection they have read. Children often write innovations, or new versions, for the selection, in which they follow the same sentence pattern but use their own ideas. First graders often write innovations for Bill Martin, Jr.'s *Brown Bear, Brown Bear, What Do You See?* (1983) and *Polar Bear, Polar Bear, What Do You Hear?* (1991), and third graders write innovations for *Alexander and the Terrible, Horrible, No Good, Very Bad Day* (Viorst, 1977).

Teachers share information about the author of the featured selection and introduce other books by the same author. Sometimes teachers help children make comparisons among several books written by a particular author. They also provide information about the illustrator and the illustration techniques used in the book. To focus on literary language, children often reread favorite excerpts in read-arounds and write memorable quotes on quilts[C] that they create.

Focusing on Words and Sentences. Teachers and children add "important" words to word walls[C] after reading and post these word walls in the classroom. Children refer to the word walls when they write, using these words for a variety of activities during the exploring stage. Children make word posters and word clusters to highlight particular words. They also make word chains, do word sorts[C], create semantic feature analysis charts to analyze related words, and play word games.

Teachers choose words from word walls to use in minilessons, too. Words can be used to teach phonics skills, such as beginning sounds, rhyming words, vowel patterns, *r*-controlled vowels, and syllabication. Other concepts, such as compound words, contractions, and metaphors, can also be taught using examples from word walls. Teachers may decide to teach a minilesson on a particular concept, such as forming plurals by changing the *y* to *i* and adding *es*, because five or six words representing the concept are listed on the word wall.

Children also locate "important" sentences in books they read. These sentences might be important because of figurative language, because they express the theme or illustrate a character trait, or simply because children like them. Children often copy the sentences on sentence strips to display in the classroom and use in other exploring activities. Also, children can copy the sentences in their reading logs.

Teaching Minilessons. Teachers present minilessons on reading procedures, concepts, strategies, and skills during the exploring stage. In a minilesson, teachers introduce the topic and make connections between the topic and examples in the featured selection students have read. In this way, children are better able to connect the information teachers are presenting with their own reading process. In the vignette, Mrs. Ohashi presented a minilesson on irregular verbs and then placed the materials in a center for children to practice.

Figure 10-12   **Projects Children Develop During the Applying Stage**

Art Projects

1. Experiment with the illustration techniques (e.g., collage, watercolor, line drawing) used in a favorite book. Examine other books illustrated with the same technique.
2. Create a collage to represent the theme of a book.
3. Design a book jacket for a book, laminate it, and place it on the book.
4. Decorate a coffee can or a potato chip can using scenes from a book. Fill the can with quotes from characters in the story.
5. Construct a shoebox or other miniature scene of an episode from a favorite book (or use a larger box to construct a diorama).
6. Make illustrations for each important event in a book.
7. Make a map of a book's setting or something related to the book.
8. Construct the setting of the book in the block center, or use other construction toys such as Lego's.
9. Construct a mobile illustrating a book.
10. Make a comic strip to illustrate the sequence of events in a book.
11. Prepare bookmarks for a book and distribute them to classmates.
12. Prepare flannel board pictures to use in retelling the story.
13. Use or prepare illustrations of characters for pocket props to use in retelling the story.
14. Use or prepare illustrations of the events in the story for clothesline props to use in retelling the story.
15. Make a mural of the book.
16. Make a book box and decorate it with scenes from a book. Collect objects, poems, and illustrations that represent characters, events, or images from the book to add to the box.

Writing Projects

17. Write a letter about a book to a classmate, friend, or pen pal.
18. Dictate or write another episode or sequel for a book.
19. Write a simulated letter from one book character to another.
20. Copy five "quotable quotes" from a book and list them on a poster.
21. Make a scrapbook about the book and label all items in the scrapbook.
22. Write a poem related to the book. Some types of poems to choose from are acrostic, concrete poem, color poem, "I wish" poem, "If I were" poem, or haiku.

Stage 5: Applying

During the applying stage, readers extend their comprehension, reflect on their understanding, and value the reading experience. Building on the initial and exploratory responses they made immediately after reading, children create projects. These projects can involve reading, writing, talk and drama, art, or research and can take many forms, including creating murals, writing readers theatre[C] scripts, and reading other books by the same author. Usually children choose which projects they will do instead of the entire class doing the same project. Sometimes, however, the class decides to work together on a project. A list of projects is presented in Figure 10-12. The purpose of these activities is for children to expand the ideas they read about, create a personal interpretation, and value the reading experience.

Have children work in small groups to create projects because English learners benefit from social interaction, gain content knowledge, and refine their English skills through collaboration.

USING THE READING PROCESS TO ORGANIZE FOR INSTRUCTION

Teachers use the five-stage reading process to plan a comprehensive and balanced instructional program. They provide opportunities for children to participate in shared

---

Figure 10-12 *(Continued)*

23. Write a lifeline related to the book, the era, the character, or the author.
24. Write a business letter to a company or organization requesting information on a topic related to the book.
25. Write the story from another point of view (e.g., write the story of *The Little Red Hen* from the perspective of the lazy characters).
26. Make a class collaboration book. Each child dictates or writes one page.

Reading Projects
27. Read another book by the same author.
28. Read another book by the same illustrator.
29. Read another book on the same theme.
30. Read another book in the same genre.
31. Read another book about the same character.
32. Read and compare another version of the same story.
33. Listen to and compare a tape, filmstrip, film, or video version of the same story.

Drama and Talk Projects
34. Give a readers theatre presentation of a book.
35. Dramatize a book.
36. Make puppets and use them in retelling a book.
37. Dress as a character from the book and answer questions from classmates.

Literary Analysis Projects
38. Make a chart to compare the story with another version or with the film version of the story.
39. Make an open-mind portrait to probe the thoughts of one character.
40. Make a Venn diagram to compare two characters.

Research Projects
41. Research the author of the book on the Internet and compile information on a poster or in a book.
42. Research a topic related to the book using book and Internet resources. Present the information on a poster or in a book.

and guided reading, read independently or with a buddy, and listen to the teacher read aloud. Teachers also plan minilessons on decoding, vocabulary, and comprehension skills and strategies and opportunities for children to apply what they are learning. The four types of programs are literature focus units, literature circles, reading workshop, and basal reader programs. Figure 10-13 shows how each of these programs incorporates the reading process.

Literature Focus Units

Teachers focus on a trade book and involve students in a variety of responding, exploring, and applying activities using that book in a literature focus unit. To read about a literature focus unit, check these vignettes: The vignette in Chapter 7, "Expanding Children's Knowledge of Words," features Mrs. Dillon's literature focus unit on *Chrysanthemum*; the vignette in Chapter 8, "Guiding Children's Comprehension," features Mrs. Donnelly's literature focus unit on *Cloudy With a Chance of Meatballs*; and the vignette in Chapter 9, "Becoming Familiar With the Structure of Text," features Mrs. Mast's literature focus unit on "The Three Bears" stories.

Teachers develop a literature focus unit through a seven-step series of activities:

Step 1: Select the Book. Teachers select the reading materials for the unit and collect supplemental materials, including puppets, stuffed animals, and toys; charts and diagrams; book boxes of materials to use in introducing the book; and information about the author and illustrator.

Step 2: Develop a Unit Plan. Teachers read or reread the selected book and choose a focus for the unit. Then they identify the activities they will use at each of the five stages of the reading process.

Step 3: Introduce the Book. Teachers involve children in an activity to interest them in the book, activate or build background knowledge, and introduce key vocabulary.

Step 4: Read and Respond to the Book. Children read the book, participate in grand conversations to talk about the book, and write in reading logs[C]. Teachers use shared reading, reading aloud to children, or another type of reading, depending on children's reading level.

Step 5: Provide Instruction. Teachers highlight important words on a word wall, teach minilessons on reading skills and strategies, and present information about story structure, genres, and authors.

Step 6: Develop Projects. Children develop reading, writing, oral language, and art projects to extend their reading experiences. Sometimes children make individual projects, and at other times, they work in small groups or together as a class to develop a project. Afterwards, children share their projects with classmates or another audience.

Step 7: Manage Record Keeping and Assessment. Teachers plan ways to document children's learning and assign grades. They use assignment checklists to help children keep track of assignments and monitor children's learning through observations and conferences.

Literature Circles

One of the best ways to nurture children's love of reading is through literature circles— small, child-led book discussion groups (Daniels, 1994; Day, Spiegel, McLellan, &

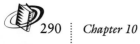

Figure 10-13 How the Four Instructional Programs Use the Reading Process

Stage	Literature Focus Units	Literature Circles	Reading Workshop	Basal Reader Programs
Prereading	Teachers introduce the featured selection by building and/or activating background knowledge and introducing key vocabulary.	Children select books to read and then form literature circles. They set a schedule for reading and responding to the book with the teacher's assistance.	Children select books that they can read independently from the classroom or school library or from collections of leveled books.	Teachers introduce the selection by building and/or activating background knowledge, introducing key vocabulary, and previewing the selection.
Reading	Children read the selection in one of these ways: independently, with a buddy, through shared reading, through guided reading, or by listening to the teacher read it aloud.	Children read independently or with a partner, depending on the difficulty level of the book. They prepare for the grand conversation by listing unfamiliar words, favorite quotes, or questions to ask during the discussion. Or, if they have assumed roles, they complete their assignments.	Children read independently for 15–30 minutes. Often teachers also read books during this period, but some teachers conference with individual children while the rest of the class is reading.	Teachers use guided reading procedures to support children as they read and reread the selection.
Responding	Children and the teacher discuss the selection in a grand conversation, sharing their reactions, asking questions, and making connections to their own lives, the world around them, and other literature. They also write in reading logs.	Children participate in a grand conversation to talk about the book. They share their reactions, ask questions, and make text-to-self, text-to-world, and text-to-text connections. Children also write in reading logs	Sometimes children keep reading logs in which they write responses to books they are reading, and at other times they simply list the title and author of the book they have read in their reading logs. They conference with the teacher to talk about their reading.	Children talk about the story, often in response to questions listed in the teacher's manual that the teacher asks. Sometimes children also write responses in workbooks.
Exploring	Teachers post vocabulary on a word wall and involve children in vocabulary activities. They teach minilessons on skills and strategies and story structure, and they share information about the author and illustrator.	Teachers teach minilessons on an element of story structure, provide information about the author or the genre, or teach a literacy skill or strategy.	Teachers often teach minilessons on procedures for choosing books, elements of story structure, reading strategies, and other topics that children need in order to be successful.	Teachers teach minilessons on skills and strategies and children apply what they have learned in practice activities in workbooks and teacher-directed activities.
Applying	Children develop individual or small-group projects and share them with their classmates.	Groups share their books with the class, or they may develop a more extensive project related to the book and share it with the class.	Children give book talks to share their books with classmates.	Children apply strategies and skills they have learned in reading and writing activities.

Brown, 2002). The three key features are choice, literature, and response. Although many teachers think of literature circles as more appropriate for older children, first and second graders can get together to read and discuss books with more teacher support (Frank, Dixon, & Brandts, 2001; Martinez-Roldan & Lopez-Robertson, 1999/2000).

Teachers organize and manage literature circles using a six-step series of activities:

Step 1: Select the Books. Teachers present brief book talks[C] to introduce six or seven books (with multiple copies available), and then children choose the books they want to read.

Step 2: Form Literature Circles. The children form literature circles to read each book. The group begins by setting a schedule for reading and discussing the book within the time limits that the teacher has set. Sometimes children also choose roles or jobs so that they can prepare for the discussion after reading. Figure 10-14 lists the roles children assume in literature circles.

Step 3: Read the Book. Children read part or all of the book independently or with a partner, depending on the difficulty level of the book. Young children can also listen to the teacher read the book aloud, or participate in a shared reading activity. After reading, children prepare for the discussion by drawing and writing in their reading logs, or, if they have assumed roles, they complete their assignments to prepare for the discussion.

Step 4: Participate in a Discussion. Children meet with the teacher to talk about a book; these grand conversations usually last about 30 minutes. The teacher guides the discussion at first and models how to share ideas and to participate in a grand conversation. Just as in any other grand conversation, the talk is meaningful because children share what interests them in the book, make text-to-self, text-to-world, and text-to-text connections, point out illustrations and other book features, ask questions, and discuss social issues and other themes.

Step 5: Share With the Class. Children in each literature circle share the book they have read with their classmates through a book talk or other presentation, and then choose new books to read.

Step 6: Monitor and Assess Learning. Teachers observe children as they read and as they collaborate with classmates. They also monitor children's progress as they check their reading log entries and assessments that they complete. A second-grade assessment checklist is shown in Figure 10-15. Children complete this form at the end of a literature circle and then meet with the teacher to discuss their learning.

Reading Workshop

Nancie Atwell introduced reading workshop in 1987 as an alternative to traditional reading instruction. The three components of reading workshop are children reading and responding to books, teachers presenting minilessons, and children sharing the books they have read with classmates (Atwell, 1998). To see how one teacher implements reading workshop, check the vignette in Chapter 2, "Examining Children's Literacy Development," featuring Ms. McCloskey and her multigrade primary class.

Teachers organize for reading workshop through a six-step series of activities:

Step 1: Select the Books. Children choose the books that they read during reading workshop from the classroom or school library or from sets of leveled books available in the classroom.

Figure 10-14 Roles Children Play in Literature Circles

Role	Responsibilities
Discussion Director	The discussion director guides the group's discussion and keeps the group on task. To get the discussion started or to redirect the discussion, the discussion director may ask: • What did the reading make you think of? • What questions do you have about the reading? • What do you predict will happen next?
Passage Master	The passage master focuses on the literary merits of the book. This child chooses several memorable passages to share with the group and tells why he or she chose each one.
Word Wizard	The word wizard is responsible for vocabulary. This child identifies four to six important, unfamiliar words from the reading and looks them up in the dictionary. The word wizard selects the most appropriate meaning and other interesting information about the word to share with the group.
Connector	The connector makes connections between the book and the children's lives. These connections might include happenings at school or in the community, current events or historical events from around the world, or something from the connector's own life. Or the connector can make comparisons with other books by the same author or on the same topic.
Summarizer	The summarizer prepares a brief summary of the reading to convey the main ideas to share with the group. This child often begins the discussion by reading the summary aloud to the group.
Illustrator	The illustrator draws a picture or diagram related to the reading. The illustration might relate to a character, an exciting event, or a prediction. The child shares the illustration with the group, and the group talks about it before the illustrator explains it.
Investigator	The investigator locates some information about the book, the author, or a related topic to share with the group. This child may search the Internet, check an encyclopedia or library book, or interview a person with special expertise on the topic.

Adapted from Daniels, 1994; Daniels & Bizar, 1998.

Step 2: Read the Books. Children spend 15 to 30 minutes or more independently reading books. Teachers often read books, magazines, or the newspaper during reading workshop to emphasize the importance of reading. They also conference with children about the books they are reading during this time.

Step 3: Respond to Books. Children usually keep reading logs in which they write and draw their responses to the books they are reading. Sometimes, however, children only

Figure 10-15 A Second-Grade Evaluation Form for Literature Circles

---

Literature Circles Report Card

Name _____ Book _____

1. How did you help your group?

2. What did you think of your book?

3. What did you say in the conversation?

4. What did you learn about your book?

5. What grade does the book get?

✷	✷✷	✷✷✷

6. What grade do you get?

✷	✷✷	✷✷✷

Assessment Tools

---

keep a list of books they are reading because teachers want them to spend more time actually reading.

Step 4: Teach Minilessons. Teachers present brief minilessons on reading workshop procedures and reading strategies and skills. Topics for minilessons are usually drawn from children's observed needs, comments children make during conferences, and procedures that children need to know how to do for reading workshop.

Step 5: Share With the Class. To end reading workshop, the class gathers together and children talk about the books they have finished reading and why they liked them. Afterwards, children often trade books with classmates because the sharing activity has interested children in reading the book.

Step 6: Monitor and Assess Learning. Teachers use a "state of the class" report to monitor children's work each day (Atwell, 1998). At the beginning of each session, children briefly tell whether they are browsing in the classroom library to select a book, reading a book, responding in a reading log, or waiting to conference with the teacher. Teachers also conference with children about the books they are reading. They often ask children to read a brief passage aloud to gauge fluency and to talk about the story to assess comprehension.

Basal Reader Programs

Commercial reading programs, which are commonly called basal readers, have been a staple in reading instruction for at least 50 years. In the past 20 years, however, basal readers have been criticized for their controlled vocabulary, for their emphasis on iso-lated skills, and for stories that lack conflict or authentic situations. Educators have de-manded more authentic texts—selections that have not been edited or abridged—and publishers of commercial reading programs have redesigned their programs to bring them more in line with the balanced reading movement. Now many basal readers, like the series Mrs. Ohashi used in the vignette at the beginning of this chapter, include authentic, unabridged literature in their programs.

At the center of a basal reader program is the student textbook. These basal read-ers are colorful and inviting books, often featuring pictures of children and animals on the covers of primary-level books. The selections in each textbook are grouped into units, and each unit includes stories, poems, and informational articles. Many multi-cultural selections have been added, and illustrations usually feature ethnically diverse people. Information about authors and illustrators is provided for many selections.

Commercial reading programs provide a wide variety of materials to support stu-dent learning. Consumable workbooks are probably the best-known support material; children write letters, words, and sentences in these books to practice phonics, com-prehension, and vocabulary skills. In addition, transparencies and blackline masters of additional worksheets are available for teachers to use in teaching skills and strategies. Big books and kits with letter and word cards, wall charts, and manipulatives are avail-able for kindergarten and first-grade programs. Blackline masters of parent letters are also available. Multimedia materials, including CD-ROMs, are included with the pro-grams. Collections of trade books are available for each grade level to provide supple-mental reading materials. Many kindergarten and first-grade books have decodable text to provide practice on phonics skills and high-frequency words.

A teacher's instructional guidebook is provided at each grade level. This oversize handbook provides comprehensive information about how to plan lessons, teach the selections, and assess children's progress. The selections are shown in reduced size in the guidebook, and each page includes background information about the selection, instructions for reading the selections, and coordinating skill and strategy instruction. In addition, information is presented about which supplemental books to use with each selection and how to assess children's learning. Figure 10-16 summarizes the ma-terials provided in most basal reader programs.

Teachers prepare to teach basal reader lessons through a seven-step series of activities:

Step 1: Choose the Reading Selection. Teachers choose a selection that reflects the chil-dren's instructional level.

Step 2: Prepare to Teach the Reading Selection. Teachers read the selection and plan how they will teach it. They consider how to develop children's background knowl-edge and which main ideas to develop before reading. They choose a reading strategy to teach, prepare for word work activities, and plan other after-reading activities. Many teachers use little sticky notes to mark teaching points in the textbook.

Step 3: Introduce the Selection. Teachers activate and build background knowledge on a topic related to the selection. They read the title of the selection and the author's name, and then talk about the problem in the story or the main ideas in an informa-tional selection. They set the purpose for reading, and children make predictions. They present an overview of the selection using a picture walk and introduce key vo-cabulary words. They teach or review a strategy for children to practice while reading.

Step 4: Read the Selection. Teachers use guided reading procedures as children read. The children do the actual reading themselves, although the teacher may read aloud

Figure 10-16   Materials in Basal Reader Programs

Materials	Description
Textbook or Anthology	The child's book of reading selections. The selections are organized thematically and include literature from trade books. Often the textbook is available in a series of softcover books or a single hardcover book.
Big Books	Enlarged copies of books for shared reading. These books are used in kindergarten and first grade.
Supplemental Books	Collections of trade books for each grade level. Kindergarten-level books often feature familiar songs and wordless stories. First- and second-grade books often include patterned language for practicing phonics skills and high-frequency words. In grades 3 to 6, books are often related to unit themes.
Workbooks	Consumable books of phonics, comprehension, and vocabulary worksheets.
Transparencies	Color transparencies to use in teaching skills and strategies.
Blackline Masters	Worksheets that teachers duplicate and use to teach skills and provide additional practice.
Kits	Alphabet cards, letter cards, word cards, and other instructional materials.These kits are used in kindergarten through second grade.
Teacher's Guide	An oversize book that presents comprehensive information about how to teach reading using the basal reader program. The selections are shown in reduced size, and background information about the selection, instructions for teaching the selections, and instructions on coordinating skill and strategy instruction are given on each page. In addition, information is presented about which supplemental books to use with each selection and how to assess students' learning.
Parent Materials	Blackline masters that teachers can duplicate and send home to parents. Information about the reading program and lists of ways parents can work with their children at home are included. Often these materials are available in English and Spanish.
Assessment Materials	A variety of assessments, including selection assessments, running records, placement evaluations, and phonics inventories, are available along with teacher's guides.
Multimedia	Audiocassettes of some selections, CD-ROMs of some selections that include interactive components, related videos, and website connections are provided.

with children to get them started on the first page or two. Beginning readers often mumble the words softly as they read, and this practice helps the teacher keep track of children's reading and the strategies they are using. Older students who are more fluent readers usually read silently.

Step 5: Respond to the Selection. Children discuss the selection, and teachers ask questions to guide their discussion. Teachers move from literal questions to higher-level questions to lead children to think more deeply about the selection.

Step 6: Provide Instruction. Teachers provide three types of instruction. First, they teach and review reading strategies. Second, they present information on genres, story elements and other text structures, and authors. Third, they teach vocabulary and involve children in word work activities.

Step 7: Monitor and Assess Learning. Teachers monitor children as they read, spending a few minutes observing each child, sitting either in front of or right beside the child. Teachers observe the child's behaviors for evidence of strategy use and confirm the child's attempts to identify words and solve reading problems. Teachers also take running records to monitor children's reading progress.

Review

Teachers incorporate the five stages of the reading process—prereading, reading, responding, exploring, and applying—in planning for instruction. Teachers include shared reading, guided reading, independent reading, buddy reading, and reading aloud to children in their instructional programs. To provide additional opportunities for buddy reading, teachers organize cross-age reading buddies and have parents read with their children. The feature that follows presents guidelines for effectively teaching the reading process to children.

How Effective Teachers . . .
Teach the Reading Process

Effective Practices

1. Teachers use the five-stage reading process to plan an integrated, balanced instructional program.
2. Teachers and children set purposes for reading.
3. Children preview the selection by doing a picture walk or a text walk before reading.
4. Teachers incorporate different types of reading into their instructional program: shared reading, guided reading, independent reading, buddy reading, and reading aloud to children.
5. Teachers use shared reading to read big books with emergent and beginning readers.
6. Teachers use guided reading to read leveled books with beginning and fluent readers.
7. Children respond to their reading as they participate in grand conversations and instructional conversations and write in reading logs.
8. Children reread the selection, examine the author's craft, and focus on words during the exploring stage.
9. Teachers teach skills and strategies during the exploring stage.
10. Teachers provide opportunities for children to complete application projects.

Professional References

Aoki, E., Flood, J., Lapp, D., Martinez, M., Priestley, M., & Smith, C. B. (1997). *Spotlight on literacy (grade 3)*. New York: Macmillan/McGraw-Hill.

Atwell, N. (1998). *In the middle: New understandings about reading and writing with adolescents* (2nd ed.). Upper Montclair, NJ: Boynton/Cook.

Blanton, W. E., Wood, K. D., & Moorman, G. B. (1990). The role of purpose in reading instruction. *The Reading Teacher, 43,* 486–493.

Bridge, C. A. (1979). Predictable materials for beginning readers. *Language Arts, 56,* 503–507.

Clay, M. M. (1991). *Becoming literate: The construction of inner control.* Portsmouth, NH: Heinemann.

Cohen, P., Kulik, J. A., & Kulik, C. (1982). Educational outcomes of tutoring: A meta-analysis of findings. *American Educational Research Journal, 19,* 237–248.

Daniels, H. (1994). *Literature circles: Voice and choice in the student-centered classroom.* York, ME: Stenhouse.

Daniels, H., & Bizar, M. (1998). *Methods that matter: Six structures for best practice classrooms.* York, ME: Stenhouse.

Day, J. P., Spiegel, D. L., McLellan, J. & Brown, V. B. (2002). *Moving forward with literature circles.* New York: Scholastic.

Depree, H., & Iversen, S. (1996). *Early literacy in the classroom: A new standard for young readers.* Bothell, WA: Wright Group.

Eeds, M., & Wells, D. (1989). Grand conversations: An exploration of meaning construction in literature study groups. *Research in the Teaching of English, 23,* 4–29.

Fountas, I. C., & Pinnell, G. S. (1996). *Guided reading: Good first teaching for all children.* Portsmouth, NH: Heinemann.

Frank, C. R., Dixon, C. N., & Brandts, L. R. (2001). Bears, trolls, and pagemasters: Learning about learners in book clubs. *The Reading Teacher, 54,* 448–462.

Holdaway, D. (1979). *The foundations of literacy.* Portsmouth, NH: Heinemann.

Hornsby, D., Sukarna, D., & Parry, J. (1986). *Read on: A conference approach to reading.* Portsmouth, NH: Heinemann.

Hunt, L. (1967). Evaluation through teacher-pupil conferences. In T. C. Barrett (Ed.), *The evaluation of children's reading achievement* (pp. 111–126). Newark, DE: International Reading Association.

Krashen, S. (1993). *The power of reading.* Englewood, CO: Libraries Unlimited.

Labbo, L. D., & Teale, W. H. (1990). Cross-age reading: A strategy for helping poor readers. *The Reading Teacher, 43,* 362–369.

Martinez-Roldan, C. M., & Lopez-Robertson, J. M. (1999/2000). Initiating literature circles in a first grade bilingual classroom. *The Reading Teacher, 53,* 270–281.

McCracken, R., & McCracken, M. (1978). Modeling is the key to sustained silent reading. *The Reading Teacher, 31,* 406–408.

Morrice, C., & Simmons, M. (1991). Beyond reading buddies: A whole language cross-age program. *The Reading Teacher, 44,* 572–577.

Ohlhausen, M. M., & Jepsen, M. (1992). Lessons from Goldilocks: "Somebody's been choosing my books but I can make my own choices now!" *The New Advocate, 5,* 31–46.

Parkes, B. (2000). *Read it again! Revisiting shared reading.* Portland, ME: Stenhouse.

Peterson, R., & Eeds, M. (1990). *Grand conversations: Literature groups in action.* New York: Scholastic.

Pilgreen, J. L. (2000). *The SSR handbook: How to organize and manage a sustained silent reading program.* Portsmouth, NH: Boynton/Cook/Heinemann.

Reutzel, D. R., & Fawson, P. C. (1990). Traveling tales: Connecting parents and children in writing. *The Reading Teacher, 44,* 222–227.

Rosenblatt, L. (1978). *The reader, the text, the poem: The transactional theory of the literary work.* Carbondale: Southern Illinois University Press.

Slaughter, J. P. (1993). *Beyond storybooks: Young children and the shared book experience.* Newark, DE: International Reading Association.

Tompkins, G. E., & Webeler, M. (1983). What will happen next? Using predictable books with young children. *The Reading Teacher, 36,* 498–502.

Trachtenburg, R., & Ferruggia, A. (1989). Big books from little voices: Reaching high risk beginning readers. *The Reading Teacher, 42,* 284–289.

Weaver, C. (1988). *Reading process and practice: From sociopsycholinguistics to whole language.* Portsmouth, NH: Heinemann.

Yaden, D. B., Jr. (1988). Understanding stories through repeated read-alouds: How many does it take? *The Reading Teacher, 41,* 556–560.

Children's Book References

Carle, E. (1969). *The very hungry caterpillar.* Cleveland: Collins World.

Cole, J. (1986). *Hungry, hungry sharks.* New York: Random House.

Cooney, B. (1982). *Miss Rumphius.* New York: Viking.

Fox, M. (1986). *Hattie and the fox.* New York: Bradbury Press.

Galdone, P. (1973). *The little red hen.* New York: Seabury.

Galdone, P. (1975). *The gingerbread boy.* New York: Seabury.

Gibbons, G. (1994). *Nature's green umbrella.* New York: Morrow.

Gibbons, G. (1997). *The moon book.* New York: Scholastic.

Hutchins, P. (1968). *Rosie's walk.* New York: Macmillan.

Martin, B., Jr. (1983). *Brown bear, brown bear, what do you see?* New York: Holt, Rinehart and Winston.

Martin, B., Jr. (1991). *Polar bear, polar bear, what do you hear?* New York: Holt, Rinehart and Winston.

McKissack, P. C. (1986). *Flossie and the fox.* New York: Dial.

Park, B. (1993). *Junie B. Jones and her big fat mouth.* New York: Scholastic.

Seuss, Dr. (1963). *Hop on pop.* New York: Random House.

Viorst, J. (1977). *Alexander and the terrible, horrible, no good, very bad day.* New York: Atheneum.

chapter 11

Scaffolding Children's Writing Development

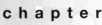

chapter
QUESTIONS

- What are the stages in the writing process?

- How are the reading and writing processes alike?

- What is interactive writing?

- How do teachers use the writing process to organize instruction?

First Graders Participate in Writing Workshop

The 20 first graders in Mrs. Ockey's class participate in writing workshop from 10:20 to 11:30. The schedule for writing workshop is:

10:20–10:40 Shared reading/minilesson
10:40–11:15 Writing and conferencing with Mrs. Ockey
11:15–11:30 Author's chair

Mrs. Ockey devotes more than an hour each morning to writing workshop because she wants her students to have time to talk about their experiences, extend their vocabulary, and manipulate basic English syntactic patterns through writing and talking. Many of these 5- and 6-year-olds are English learners whose parents or grandparents immigrated to the United States from southeast Asia and speak Hmong, Khmer, or Lao at home. They are learning to speak English as they learn to read and write in English.

The writing workshop begins with a 20-minute whole-class meeting. Mrs. Ockey either reads a big book using shared reading[C] procedures or teaches a minilesson[C], often using something from the big book she has read previously as an example. Yesterday, Mrs. Ockey read *An Egg Is an Egg* (Weiss, 1990), an informational book about egg-laying animals. After reading the big book twice, Mrs. Ockey and the children participated in an instructional conversation[C] and talked about animals that lay eggs and those that don't.

See the Compendium of Instructional Procedures, which follows Chapter 12, for more information on terms marked with the symbol [C].

Today, Mrs. Ockey rereads *An Egg Is an Egg,* and the children join in to read familiar words. Afterwards, she reads the book again, asking the children to look for words on each page with *ou* and *ow* spellings. In a previous minilesson, Mrs. Ockey explained that usually these spellings are pronounced /ou/ as in *ouch,* but sometimes *ow* is pronounced /ō/ as in *snow,* and they began a chart of words with each spelling or pronunciation. The first graders locate several more words to add to their chart. After adding the new words from the big book, Shaqualle suggests *hour* and Leticia suggests *found,* words they noticed in books they were reading. The children practice reading the lists of words together, and Der reads the lists by himself. He smiles proudly as his classmates clap. Now the chart looks like this:

ou	ow	ow (long o)
loud	clown	low
sound	brown	blowing
cloud	down	tow
outside	town	slowly
flour	flower	sown
around	tower	snows
shout	now	
hour		
found		

Mrs. Ockey quickly reviews the class's rules for writing because two children have recently joined the class, and she has noticed that some of the other children aren't on task during the writing and conferencing period. The class's rules for writing are posted on a chart that the children wrote using interactive writing[C] earlier in the school year. Mrs. Ockey rereads each rule and then asks a child to explain the rule in his or her own words. The rules are:

1. Think about your story.
2. Draw pictures on a storyboard.
3. Write words by the pictures.
4. Tell your story to 1 editor.
5. Write your story.
6. Read your story to 2 editors.
7. Illustrate your story.
8. Publish your story.

The second part of writing workshop is writing and conferencing. The children use a process approach to write personal narratives, stories about their families, pets, and events in their lives. To begin, the children plan their stories using storyboards, sheets of paper divided into four, six, or eight blocks. (Note these are different from story boards[C], which are described in the Compendium.) They sketch a drawing in each numbered block and then add a word or two to describe the picture. Next they use their storyboards to tell their stories to one of five first graders who are serving as editors that day; today's editors are Pauline, Lily, Mai, Destiny, and Khammala. You can tell the editors in Mrs. Ockey's classroom because they are wearing neon-colored plastic visors with the word "Editor" printed on them.

After this rehearsal, the children write their stories using one sheet of paper for each block on their planning sheets. Next they read their writing to two editors, who often ask the child to add more detail or to add a word or phrase that has been omitted. Then the children draw and color a picture to complement and extend the words on each page. Sometimes the children add a cover and title page and staple their stories together, and at other times, they turn in their drafts for the bilingual aide in the classroom to word process.

Children complete an editing sheet when they share their writing with the two classmates who are serving as editors. A copy of the editing sheet that they complete is shown in Figure 11-1. The author writes his or her name and the title of the story at the top of the sheet and then the editors check off each box as they read their classmate's story. They sign their names at the bottom of the page. Mrs. Ockey often calls herself their third editor, and the children know that they must complete this editing sheet with two classmates before they ask Mrs. Ockey to edit their writing.

Mrs. Ockey has divided the class into five conference groups, and she meets with one group each day while the other children are working on their stories. The children bring their writing folders to the conference table and talk with Mrs. Ockey about their work. They are working at different stages of the writing process.

Mrs. Ockey begins by asking the children to each explain what they are writing about and where they are in the writing process. Then, she examines each child's storyboard or writing and offers compliments, asks questions, and provides feedback about their work. She also makes notes about each child's progress.

Today, she is meeting with Lily, Der, Dalany, and Matthew. Lily begins by showing Mrs. Ockey her storyboard for a story about her cousin's birthday. She has developed eight blocks for her story, and she talks about each one, working to

Figure 11-1   **Mrs. Ockey's Editing Sheet**

Name _____

Title of your story _____

Check Your Work!

Does the story make sense?	☐ ☐
Punctuation marks	☐ ☐
Capital letters	☐ ☐
Spelling	☐ ☐

My editors are:

_____   _____

express her ideas in a sentence or two. Mrs. Ockey praises Lily for tackling such a long story and for including a beginning, middle, and end in her story. She encourages Lily to begin writing, and a week later, Lily completes her book and shares it with her classmates. Here is Lily's published story, "My Cousin's Birthday":

Page 1   This is my cousin's birthday.

Page 2   I bought her a present.

Page 3   I have clothes for her present.

Page 4   She makes a wish on her birthday cake.

Page 5   We eat cake.

Page 6   We play games.

Page 7   My cousin is happy.

Page 8   We went to sleep.

Next, Mrs. Ockey turns to Der, who thinks that he is working on a storyboard for a story about his grandmother's cat, but he can't find it. Mrs. Ockey checks her notes and recalls that Der couldn't find his storyboard for the same story last week, so she asks him to get a new storyboard and start again. They talk out the story together. Der wants to describe what his grandmother's cat looks like and then tell all the things that she can do. He begins drawing a picture in the first block while Mrs. Ockey watches. After he draws the picture, Mrs. Ockey will help him add one or two key words in the block. Then she'll help him do a second block.

Once Der is working hard, Mrs. Ockey turns her attention to Matthew, who is finishing his ninth book, "The Soccer Game." He reads it to Mrs. Ockey:

Page 1	Me and my friends play soccer.
Page 2	I won a trophy.
Page 3	I won another point.
Page 4	I played at the soccer field.
Page 5	I won again.
Page 6	I went home.

Then they read it over again, and Mrs. Ockey helps him correct the spelling of *trophy* and *soccer* and correct several letters that were printed backwards. He also shows her his editing sheet, which indicates that he had already edited his story with Pauline and Sammy serving as his editors. Matthew tells Mrs. Ockey that he wants to finish the book today so that he can share it at the author's chair. Mrs. Ockey sends him over to write his name on the sharing list posted beside the author's chair.

Dalany is next. She reminds Mrs. Ockey that she finished her book, "The Apple Tree," last week, and she is waiting for it to be word processed. Mrs. Ockey tells her that it is done and gives her the word-processed copy. They read it over together and Dalany returns to her desk to draw the illustrations. Here is Dalany's book, "The Apple Tree":

Page 1	I see the apple tree.
Page 2	I picked the apple up.
Page 3	I ate the apple.
Page 4	I see another girl pick up the apple.
Page 5	The girl ate the apple.
Page 6	We are friends.

Figure 11-2 shows page 5 from Dalany's word-processed book with hand-drawn illustrations.

After the children write their stories, an aide types them on the computer and prints them out along with a title page, a dedication page, and a "Readers' Comments" page. The child draws an illustration on each page. Then Mrs. Ockey laminates the title page and adds a back cover and the child staples the book together. The author shares the book at that day's author's chair and then the book is placed in the classroom library. Children take turns reading each other's books and adding comments on the back page. Children take great pride in reading their classmates' comments in their books. Mrs. Ockey and the first graders have written these comments in Matthew's book about playing soccer:

Figure 11-2

A Page From a First Grader's Story About "The Apple Tree"

The girl ate the apple.

I have a trophy. Der
I like Matthew play soccer. Pauline
You are a good soccer player! Mrs. Ockey
Nice story. Rosemary
You good soccer play. Jesse
Do you win and win? Lily
I like play soccer. Michael

Although not all of the comments are grammatically correct, Matthew can read them all, and he has walked around and thanked each person for his or her comment. It is important to him that lots of people read his book and write comments.

The third part of writing workshop is author's chair. Each day, three children sit in a special chair called "the author's chair" and share their published stories. After children read their stories, their classmates offer comments and ask clarifying questions. Then they clap for the author, and the published book is ceremoniously placed in a special section of the classroom library for everyone to read and reread.

The writing process, like the reading process, involves a series of five recursive stages. Children participate in a variety of activities as they gather and organize ideas, draft their compositions, revise and edit their drafts, and finally, publish their writings. During the primary grades, children, like Mrs. Ockey's first graders, learn about the writing process and move beyond writing single-draft compositions.

Reading and writing have been thought of as the flip sides of a coin—as opposites; readers decoded or deciphered written language, and writers encoded or produced written language. Then researchers began to notice similarities between reading and writing and talked of both of them as processes. Now reading and writing are viewed as parallel processes of meaning construction, and we understand that readers and writers use similar strategies for making meaning with text.

THE WRITING PROCESS

The focus in the writing process is on what children think and do as they write. The five stages are prewriting, drafting, revising, editing, and publishing. The labeling and numbering of the stages do not mean that the writing process is a linear series of neatly packaged categories. Rather, research has shown that the process involves recurring cycles, and labeling is simply an aid for identifying and discussing writing activities. In the classroom, the stages merge and recur as children write. The key features of each stage in the writing process are shown in Figure 11-3.

Stage 1: Prewriting

Prewriting is the "getting ready to write" stage. The traditional notion that writers have a topic completely thought out and ready to flow onto the page is ridiculous. If writers wait for ideas to fully develop, they may wait forever. Instead, writers begin tentatively—talking, reading, writing—to see what they know and in what direction they want to go. Prewriting has probably been the most neglected stage in the writing process; however, it is as crucial to writers as a warm-up is to athletes. Murray (1982) believes that at least 70% of writing time should be spent in prewriting. During the prewriting stage, children choose a topic, consider purpose, audience, and form, and gather and organize ideas for writing.

Choosing a Topic. Choosing a topic for writing can be a stumbling block for children who have become dependent on teachers to supply topics. For years, teachers have supplied topics by suggesting gimmicky story starters and relieving children of the "burden" of topic selection. These "creative" topics often stymied children, who were forced to write on topics they knew little about or were not interested in. Graves (1976) calls this situation "writing welfare." Instead, children need to choose their own writing topics.

Some children complain that they don't know what to write about, but teachers can help them brainstorm a list of three, four, or five topics and then identify the one topic they are most interested in and know the most about. Children who feel they cannot generate any writing topics are often surprised that they have so many options available. Then, through prewriting activities, children talk, draw, read, and even write to develop information about their topics.

Asking children to choose their own topics for writing does not mean that teachers never give writing assignments; teachers do provide general guidelines. They may specify the writing form, and at other times they may establish the function, but children should choose their own content.

Figure 11-3   Key Features of the Writing Process

Stage 1: Prewriting
- Write on topics based on personal experiences.
- Engage in rehearsal activities before writing.
- Identify the audience who will read the composition.
- Identify the function of the writing activity.
- Choose an appropriate form for the composition based on audience and function.

Stage 2: Drafting
- Write a rough draft.
- Emphasize content rather than mechanics.

Stage 3: Revising
- Reread the composition.
- Share writing in writing groups.
- Participate constructively in discussions about classmates' writing.
- Make changes in the composition to reflect the reactions and comments of both teacher and classmates.
- Between the first and final drafts, make substantive rather than only minor changes.

Stage 4: Editing
- Proofread the composition.
- Help proofread classmates' compositions.
- Identify and correct mechanical errors.
- Meet with the teacher for a final editing.

Stage 5: Publishing
- Publish writing in an appropriate form.
- Share the finished writing with an appropriate audience.

Considering Purpose. As children prepare to write, they need to think about the purpose of their writing. Are they writing to entertain? to inform? to persuade? Setting the purpose for writing is just as important as setting the purpose for reading, because purpose influences decisions children make about audience and form.

Considering Audience. Children may write primarily for themselves—to express and clarify their own ideas and feelings—or they may write for others. Possible audiences include classmates, younger children, parents, foster grandparents, and pen pals. Other audiences are more distant and less well known. For example, children write letters to businesses to request information, articles for the local newspaper, or stories and poems for publication in literary magazines.

   Children's writing is influenced by their sense of audience. Britton and his colleagues (1975) define audience awareness as "the manner in which the writer expresses a relationship with the reader in respect to the writer's understanding" (pp. 65–66). Children adapt their writing to fit their audience, just as they vary their speech to meet the needs of the people who are listening to them.

Considering Form. One of the most important considerations is the form the writing will take: a story? a letter? a poem? a journal entry? A writing activity could be handled in any one of these ways. As part of a science unit on hermit crabs, for instance, children could write a story or poem about a hermit crab, write a report on hermit crabs with information about how they obtain shells to live in, or write a description of the pet hermit crabs in the classroom. There is a wide variety of writing forms or genres that children learn to use during the elementary grades. A list of six genres is presented in Figure 11-4. Children need to experiment with a wide variety of writing forms and explore the potential of these functions and formats.

Through reading and writing, children develop a strong sense of these genres and how they are structured. Langer (1985) found that by third grade, children responded in distinctly different ways to story- and report-writing assignments; they organized the writing differently and included varied kinds of information and elaboration. Similarly, Hidi and Hildyard (1983) found that elementary children could differentiate between stories and persuasive essays. Because children are clarifying the distinctions between various writing genres during the primary grades, it is important that teachers use the correct terminology and not label all children's writing "stories."

Decisions about function, audience, and form influence each other. For example, if the function is to entertain, an appropriate form might be a story, script, or poem—and these three forms look very different on a piece of paper. Whereas a story is written in the traditional block format, scripts and poems have unique page arrangements. Scripts are written with the character's name and a colon, and the dialogue is set off. Action and dialogue, rather than description, carry the story line in a script. In contrast, poems have unique formatting considerations, and words are used judiciously. Each word and phrase is chosen to convey a maximum amount of information.

Gathering and Organizing Ideas. Children engage in activities to gather and organize ideas for writing. Graves (1983) calls what writers do to prepare for writing "rehearsal" activities. Rehearsal activities take many forms, including:

Drawing. Drawing is the way young children gather and organize ideas for writing. Primary-grade teachers often notice that children draw before they write and, thinking that they are eating dessert before the meat and vegetables, insist that they write first. But many young children cannot write first because they don't know what to write until they see what they draw (Dyson, 1982, 1986).

Clustering. Children make clusters[C] (weblike diagrams) in which they write the topic in a center circle and then draw rays from the circle for each main idea. Then they add details and other information on the rays. Through clustering, children organize their ideas for writing. Clustering is a better prewriting strategy than outlining because it is nonlinear.

Talking. Children talk with their classmates to share ideas about possible writing topics, try out ways to express an idea, and ask questions.

Reading. Children gather ideas for writing and investigate the structure of various written forms through reading. They may retell a favorite story in writing, write new adventures for favorite story characters, or experiment with repetition, onomatopoeia, or another poetic device used in a poem they have read. Informational books also provide raw material for writing. For example, if children are studying polar bears, they read to gather information about the animal—its habitat and predators, for example—that they may use in writing a report.

Role-playing Children discover and shape ideas they will use in their writing through role-playing. Children can role-play the beginning, middle, and end of a story they have read before writing a retelling or rewriting a story from a different point of view.

Figure 11-4   Writing Genres

Genre	Purpose	Activities
Descriptive Writing	Children become careful observers and choose precise language when they use description. They take notice of sensory details and learn to make comparisons (metaphors and similes) in order to make their writing more powerful.	Character sketches Comparisons Descriptive paragraphs Descriptive sentences Five-senses poems Found poems Observations
Informational Writing	Children collect and synthesize information for informative writing. This writing is objective, and reports are the most common type of informative writing. Children use informational writing to give directions, sequence steps, compare one thing to another, explain causes and effects, or describe problems and solutions.	Alphabet books Autobiographies Biographies Data charts Dictionaries Directions Interviews Posters Reports Summaries
Journals and Letters	Children write to themselves and to specific, known audiences in journals and letters. Their writing is personal and often less formal than other genres. They share news, explore new ideas, and record notes. Letters and envelopes require special formatting, and children learn these formats during the primary grades.	Business letters Courtesy letters E-mail messages Friendly letters Learning logs Personal journals Postcards Reading logs
Narrative Writing	Children retell familiar stories, develop sequels for stories they have read, write stories called personal narratives about events in their own lives, and create original stories. They include a beginning, middle, and end in the narratives they write. In the beginning, they introduce the characters, identify a problem, and interest readers in the story. In the middle, the problem becomes worse or additional roadblocks are set up to thwart the main character as he/she attempts to solve the problem. In the end, the problem is resolved.	Original short stories Personal narratives Retellings of stories Sequels to stories Scripts of stories
Persuasive Writing	Persuasion is winning someone to your viewpoint or cause. The three ways people are persuaded are by appeals to (1) logic, (2) moral character, and (3) emotion. Children present their position clearly and then support it with examples and evidence.	Advertisements Book and movie reviews Persuasive letters Persuasive posters
Poetry Writing	Children create word pictures and play with rhyme and other stylistic devices as they create poems. As children experiment with poetry, they learn that poetic language is vivid and powerful but concise, and they learn that poems can be arranged in different ways on a page.	Acrostic poems Cinquain poems Color poems Diamante poems Five-senses poems Found poems Free verse Haiku "I am" poems "If I were . . ." poems "I wish . . ." poems Riddles

Stage 2: Drafting

Children write and refine their compositions through a series of drafts. During the drafting stage, they focus on getting their ideas down on paper. Because writers don't begin writing with their pieces already composed in their minds, children begin with tentative ideas developed through prewriting activities. The drafting stage is the time to pour out ideas, with little concern about spelling, punctuation, and other mechanical errors.

Children skip every other line when they write rough drafts to leave space for revisions. They use arrows to move sections of text, cross-outs to delete sections, and scissors and tape to cut apart and rearrange text, just as adult writers do. They write only on one side of a sheet of paper so it can be cut apart and rearranged. Because computers are increasingly available in elementary classrooms, revising, with all its moving, adding, and deleting of text, is becoming much easier. However, for children who handwrite their compositions, the wide spacing is crucial. Teachers might make small x's on every other line of children's papers as a reminder to skip lines as they draft their compositions.

Children label their drafts by writing *Rough Draft* in ink at the top or by using a ROUGH DRAFT stamp. This label indicates to the writer, other children, parents, and administrators that the composition is a draft in which the emphasis is on content, not mechanics. It also explains why the teacher has not graded the paper or marked mechanical errors.

Instead of writing drafts by hand, children can use computers to compose rough drafts, polish their writing, and print out final copies. There are many benefits of using computers for word processing. For example, children are often more motivated to write, and they tend to write longer pieces. Their writing looks neater, and they can use spellcheck programs to identify and correct misspelled words. Even young children can word-process their compositions using Magic Slate and other programs designed for beginning writers. To learn more about word-processing and other writing-related computer programs for primary children, check the Technology Link on pages 312–313.

During drafting, children may need to modify their earlier decisions about purpose, audience, and, especially, the form their writing will take. For example, a composition that began as a story may be transformed into a report, letter, or poem. The new format allows children to communicate more effectively. The process of modifying earlier decisions continues into the revising stage.

As children write rough drafts, it is important for teachers not to emphasize correct spelling and neatness. Children are encouraged to check word walls[C] and spell as many words as they can correctly, but this is not the time to check spellings in the dictionary. Pointing out mechanical errors during the drafting stage sends children a false message that mechanical correctness is more important than content (Sommers, 1982). Later, during editing, children clean up mechanical errors and put their composition into a neat final form.

Stage 3: Revising

Writers refine ideas in their compositions when they revise. Children often break the writing process cycle as soon as they complete a rough draft, believing that once they have jotted down their ideas, the writing task is complete. Experienced writers, however, know they must turn to others for reactions and revise on the basis of these comments. Revision is not just polishing; it is meeting the needs of readers by adding, substituting, deleting, and rearranging material. *Revision* means "seeing again," and in this stage, writers see their compositions again with the help of classmates and the

Children share their rough drafts and get feedback from classmates and the teacher during writing groups.

teacher. The revising stage consists of three activities: rereading the rough draft, sharing the rough draft in a writing group, and revising on the basis of feedback.

Rereading the Rough Draft. After finishing the rough draft, writers need to distance themselves from it for a day or two, then reread it from a fresh perspective, as a reader might. As they reread, children make changes—adding, substituting, deleting, and moving—and place question marks by sections that need work. It is these trouble spots that children ask for help with in their writing groups.

Sharing in Writing Groups. Children meet in writing groups[C] to share their compositions with classmates. They respond to the writer's rough draft and suggest possible revisions. Writing groups provide a scaffold in which teachers and classmates talk about plans and strategies for writing and revising (Applebee & Langer, 1983; Calkins, 1983).

Writing groups can form spontaneously when several children have completed drafts and are ready to share their compositions, or they can be formal groupings with identified leaders. In some classrooms, writing groups form when four or five children finish writing their rough drafts. Children gather around a conference table or in a corner of the classroom and take turns reading their rough drafts aloud. Classmates in the group listen and respond, offering compliments and suggestions for revision. Sometimes the teacher joins the writing group, but if the teacher is involved in something else, children work independently.

In other classrooms, the writing groups are assigned. Children get together when all children in the group have completed their rough drafts and are ready to share their writing. Sometimes the teacher participates in these groups, providing feedback along with the children. Or, the writing groups can function independently. For these assigned groups, each cluster is made up of four or five children, and a list of groups and their members is posted in the classroom. The teacher puts a star by one child's name, and that student serves as a group leader. The leader changes every quarter.

Technology Link

Computer Programs for Writers

A variety of word-processing programs, desktop publishing programs, and graphics packages support children who use the process approach to writing (Cochran-Smith, 1991; DeGroff, 1990). Children revise and edit their rough drafts more easily when they use word processors, and they print out neat and "clean" final copies without the drudgery of recopying their compositions (Strickland, 1997). They use digital cameras, graphics packages, and drawing and painting programs to create illustrations. And, with desktop publishing programs, children create professional-looking newspapers, brochures, and books. Here's a list of writing-related computer programs:

Type of Program	Title
Integrated packages	Claris Works
	Microsoft Works
	The Writing Center
Word-processing programs	Amazing Writing Machine
	Kid Works II
	Kidwriter Gold
	Mac Write Pro
	Microsoft Word
	Magic Slate
	Talking Text Writer
	Writer's Helper
Desktop publishing programs	Big Book Maker
	The Children's Writing and Publishing Center
	Make-a-Book
	Newspaper Maker

Making Revisions. Children make four types of changes to their rough drafts: additions, substitutions, deletions, and moves (Faigley & Witte, 1981). As they revise, children might add words, substitute sentences, delete paragraphs, and move phrases. Children often use a blue or red pen to cross out, draw arrows, and write in the space left between the double-spaced lines of their rough drafts so that revisions will show clearly. That way teachers can see the types of revisions children make by examining their revised rough drafts. Revisions are another gauge of children's growth as writers.

Stage 4: Editing

Editing is putting the piece of writing into its final form. Until this stage, the focus has been primarily on the content of children's writing. Once the focus changes to mechanics, children polish their writing by correcting spelling mistakes and other mechanical errors. The goal here is to make the writing "optimally readable" (Smith, 1982, p. 127). Writers who write for readers understand that if their compositions are not readable, they have written in vain because their ideas will never be read.

	Pagemaker
	Print Shop
	Publish It!
	Ready, Set, Go!
	Super Print
	Toucan Press
Graphics packages	Bannermania
	PrintShop Deluxe
	SuperPrint
Drawing and painting programs	DazzleDraw
	Freehand
	Kid Pix Studio Deluxe
	Kid Works Deluxe
Presentation software	Kid Pix Slide Show
Digital cameras	QuickTake
	XapShot
Keyboarding programs	Kid Keys
	Kids on Keys
	Microtype: The Wonderful World
	of Paws
	Type to Learn

It's a good idea to make the first writing project a class collaboration so children can review word-processing procedures. The next several writing projects should be short so that children can concentrate on working through the word-processing procedures. Often one or two children will assume an important new status as "computer expert" because of special interest or expertise. These experts help other children with word-processing tasks and using the printer.

Mechanics are the commonly accepted conventions of written Standard English. They consist of capitalization, punctuation, spelling, sentence structure, usage, and formatting considerations specific to poems, scripts, letters, and other writing forms. The use of these commonly accepted conventions is a courtesy to those who will read the composition.

Children learn mechanical skills best through hands-on editing of their own compositions, not through workbook exercises. When they edit a composition that will be shared with a genuine audience, children are more interested in using mechanical skills correctly so they can communicate effectively. Calkins (1980) compared how teachers in two third-grade classrooms taught punctuation skills. She found that the children in the class who learned punctuation marks as a part of editing could define or explain more marks than the children in the other class, who were taught punctuation skills in a traditional manner, with instruction and practice exercises on each punctuation mark. The results of this research, as well as other studies (Bissex, 1980; Elley, Barham, Lamb, & Wyllie, 1976; Graves, 1983), suggest that it is more effective to teach mechanical skills as part of the writing process than through practice exercises.

Children move through three activities in the editing stage: getting distance from the composition, proofreading to locate errors, and correcting errors.

Getting Distance. Children are more efficient editors if they set the composition aside for a few days before beginning to edit. After working so closely with a piece of writing during drafting and revising, they are too familiar with it to notice many mechanical errors. With the distance gained by waiting a few days, children are better able to approach editing with a fresh perspective and gather the enthusiasm necessary to finish the writing process by making the paper optimally readable.

Proofreading. Children proofread their compositions to locate and mark possible errors. Proofreading is a unique type of reading in which children read slowly, word by word, hunting for errors rather than reading quickly for meaning (King, 1985). Concentrating on mechanics is difficult because of our natural inclination to read for meaning. Even experienced proofreaders often find themselves reading for meaning and thus overlooking errors that do not inhibit meaning. It is important, therefore, to take time to explain proofreading to children and to demonstrate how it differs from regular reading.

To demonstrate proofreading, teachers copy a piece of writing on the chalkboard or display it on an overhead projector. The teacher reads it several times, each time hunting for a particular type of error. During each reading, the teacher reads the composition slowly, softly pronouncing each word and touching the word with a pencil or pen to focus attention on it. The teacher marks possible errors as they are located.

Errors are marked or corrected with special proofreaders' marks. Children enjoy using these marks, the same ones that adult authors and editors use. Proofreaders' marks that elementary children can learn to use in editing their writing are presented in Figure 11-5.

Figure 11-5   Proofreaders' Marks

Delete	℮	Most whales are ~~big and~~ huge creatures.
Insert	∧	A baby whale is a calf. *(called inserted above)*
Indent paragraph	¶	¶Whales look a lot like fish, but the two are quite different.
Capitalize	≡	In the United states it is illegal to hunt whales.
Change to lower case	/	Why do beached Whales die?
Add period	⊙	Baleen whales do not have any teeth ⊙
Add comma	∧	Some baleen whales are blue whales gray whales and humpback whales.
Add apostrophe	∨	People are the whale's only enemy.

Editing checklists help children focus on particular types of errors. Teachers can develop checklists with two to six items appropriate for the grade level. A first-grade checklist, for example, might have only two items—perhaps one about capital letters at the beginning of sentences and a second about periods at the end of sentences. In contrast, a middle-grade checklist might contain items such as using commas in a series, indenting paragraphs, capitalizing proper nouns and adjectives, and spelling homonyms correctly. Teachers revise the checklist during the school year to focus attention on skills that have recently been taught. A sample third-grade editing checklist is presented in Figure 11-6.

The writer and a classmate work as partners to edit their compositions. First, children proofread their own compositions, searching for errors in each category on the checklist, and, after proofreading, check off each item. After completing the checklist, children sign their names and trade checklists and compositions. Now they become editors and complete each other's checklists. Having writer and editor sign the checklist helps them to take the activity seriously.

Correcting Errors. After children proofread their compositions and locate as many errors as they can, they use red pens to correct the errors individually or with an editor's assistance. Some errors are easy to correct, some require use of a dictionary, and others involve instruction from the teacher. It is unrealistic to expect children to locate and correct every mechanical error in their compositions. Not even published books are always error free! Once in a while, children may change a correct spelling or punctuation mark and make it incorrect, but they correct far more errors than they create.

Editing can end after children and their editors correct as many mechanical errors as possible, or after children meet with the teacher in a conference for a final editing.

Figure 11-6   A Third-Grade Editing Checklist

EDITING CHECKLIST

Author   Editor

1. I have circled the words that might be misspelled.

2. I have checked that all sentences begin with capital letters.

3. I have checked that all sentences end with punctuation marks.

4. I have checked that all proper nouns begin with a capital letter.

Signatures:

Author: _____   Editor: _____

Assessment Tools

When mechanical correctness is crucial, this conference is important. Teachers proofread the composition with the student, and they identify and make the remaining corrections together, or the teacher makes check marks in the margin to note errors for the student to correct independently.

Stage 5: Publishing

Children bring their compositions to life in the publishing stage by writing final copies and by sharing them orally with an appropriate audience. When they share their writing with real audiences of classmates, other children, parents, and the community, children come to think of themselves as authors.

Making Books. One of the most popular ways for children to publish their writing is by making books. Simple booklets can be made by folding a sheet of paper into quarters, like a greeting card. Children write the title on the front and use the three remaining sides for their composition. They can also construct booklets by stapling sheets of writing paper together and adding covers made out of construction paper. Sheets of wallpaper cut from old sample books also make sturdy covers. These stapled booklets can be cut into various shapes, too. Children can make more sophisticated books by covering cardboard covers with contact paper, wallpaper samples, or cloth. Pages are sewn or stapled together, and the first and last pages (endpapers) are glued to the cardboard covers to hold the book together. Directions for making one type of hardcover book are shown in Figure 11-7.

To link to *Cyberkids,* an on-line magazine written by children for children ages 7 to 11, visit our Companion Website at www.prenhall.com/tompkins

Sharing Writing. Children read their writing to classmates or share it with larger audiences through hardcover books placed in the class or school library, plays performed for classmates, or letters sent to authors, businesses, and other correspondents. Here are some other ways to share children's writing:

- Submit the piece to writing contests
- Display the writing as a mobile
- Contribute to a class anthology
- Contribute to the local newspaper
- Make a shape book
- Record the writing on a cassette tape
- Submit it to a literary magazine
- Read it at a school assembly
- Share it at a read-aloud party
- Share it with parents and siblings
- Display poetry on a "poet-tree"
- Send it to a pen pal
- Display it on a bulletin board
- Make a big book
- Design a poster about the writing
- Read it to foster grandparents
- Share it as a puppet show
- Display it at a public event
- Read it to children in other classes

Figure 11-7 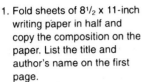 Directions for Making Hardcover Books

1. Fold sheets of 8½ x 11-inch writing paper in half and copy the composition on the paper. List the title and author's name on the first page.

2. Put an additional sheet of writing paper, construction paper, or other colorful paper on the outside of the folded sheets of writing paper to be the book's endpaper.

Add tape along fold.

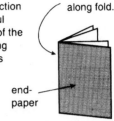

end-paper

3. Staple the folded papers together with two or three staples on the fold. Use a long-arm stapler to reach the fold more easily.

stapler

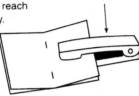

4. Cut a sheet of contact paper, 11 x 15 inches, for the outside covering.

5. Cut two pieces of cardboard, 6 x 9 inches, for the front and back covers.

6. Peel the backing from the contact paper and place the two pieces of cardboard on the contact paper, centering them and leaving ¼ inch between the two pieces.

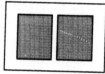

7. Cut off the four corners of the contact paper and place them on the adjacent corners of the cardboard pieces.

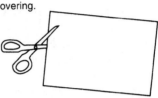

8. Fold the edges of contact paper back onto the cardboard pieces.

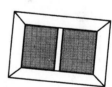

9. Set the stapled booklet inside the contact paper cover so that the stapled edge fits into the space between the two cardboard pieces.

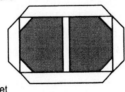

10. Glue the outside of the endpaper to the cardboard pieces. First glue one side, making sure to keep the stapled edge in the space between the two cardboard pieces Then glue the other side of the paper to the second cardboard piece.

glue →

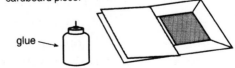

Through this sharing, children communicate with genuine audiences who respond to their writing in meaningful ways. Sharing writing is a social activity that helps children develop sensitivity to audiences and confidence in themselves as authors. Dyson (1985) advises that teachers consider the social interpretations of sharing—the children's behavior, the teacher's behavior, and the interaction between children and teacher—within the classroom context. Individual children interpret sharing differently. Beyond just providing the opportunity for children to share writing, teachers need to teach children how to respond to their classmates. Teachers themselves serve as a model for responding to children's writing without dominating the sharing.

Introducing Young Children to Writing

Children are introduced to writing as they watch their parents and teachers write and as they experiment with drawing and writing. Teachers help children emerge into writing as they show them how to use invented spelling, teach minilessons[C] about written language, and involve children in writing activities.

Through a variety of literacy activities, teachers demonstrate to children that people use written language to represent their thoughts and model the writing process. However, adult models can be very intimidating to young children who feel at a loss to produce adult writing that is neatly written and spelled conventionally. Teachers can contrast their writing—adult writing—with the "kid" writing that children can do. Young children's writing takes many different forms. During the emergent writing stage, children make scribbles or a collection of random marks on paper. Sometimes children are imitating adults' cursive writing as they scribble. Children may string together letters that have no phoneme-grapheme correspondences, or they may use one or two letters to represent entire words. Children with more experience with written language are at the beginning stage of writing, and they invent spellings that represent more sound features of words and apply spelling rules. Their handwriting develops, too, as children learn to form letters and differentiate between upper- and lowercase letters. A child's writings of "Abbie is my dog. I love her very much" over a year and a half are presented in Figure 11-8. The child's "kid" writing moves from the emergent stage where she uses scribbles and then single letters to represent words to the beginning stage where she uses invented spelling, and to the fluent stage where she uses mostly conventional spellings.

Invented spelling is an important concept for young children because it gives them permission to experiment with written language when they write. Too often, children assume they should spell like adults do, but they cannot. Without this confidence, children do not want to write, or they ask teachers to spell every word or copy text out of books or from charts. Invented spelling teaches students several strategies for writing, and it allows them to invent spellings that reflect their knowledge of phonics and spelling.

Young children's writing grows out of talk and drawing. As children begin to write, their writing is literally their talk written down, and they can usually express in writing the ideas they talk about. At the same time, children's letterlike marks develop from their drawing. With experience, children differentiate between drawing and writing. Some kindergarten teachers explain to children that they should use crayons when they draw and use pencils when they write. Teachers can also differentiate where on a page children write and draw: The writing might go at the top or bottom of a page, or children can use paper with space for drawing at the top and lines for writing at the bottom.

Figure 11-8 **Stages of Development in a Child's "Kid" Writing**

Emergent Writing	Scribble Writing
	One-Letter Writing
	Invented Spelling Without Spacing AZMIDDOQiLRETS
Beginning Writing	Invented Spelling With Spacing ABe.isMi. doG.I.(uv hr. vre ms.
	Invented Spelling With Application of Rules Abie is my dog. I love hur vrey mus.
Fluent Writing	Nearly Conventional Spelling 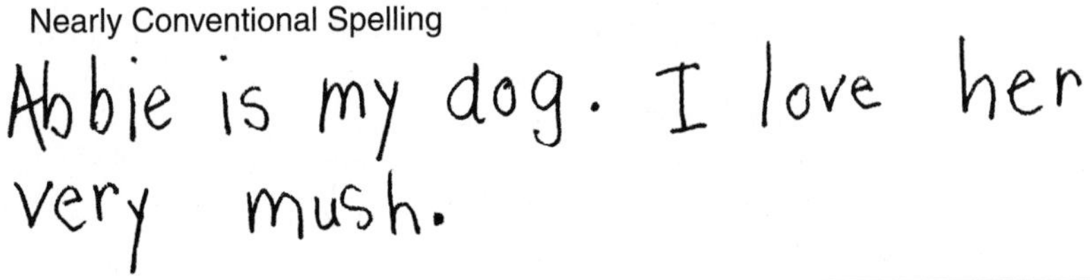 Abbie is my dog. I love her very mush.

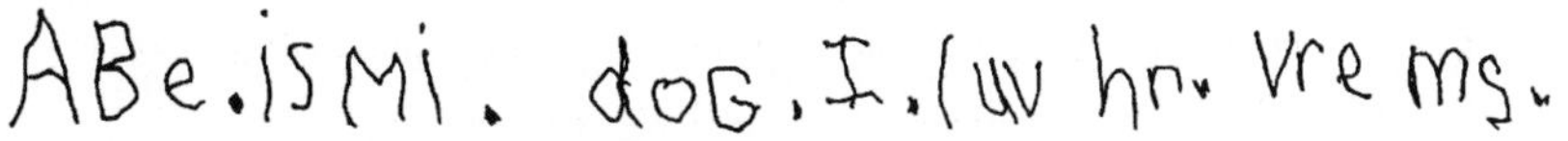

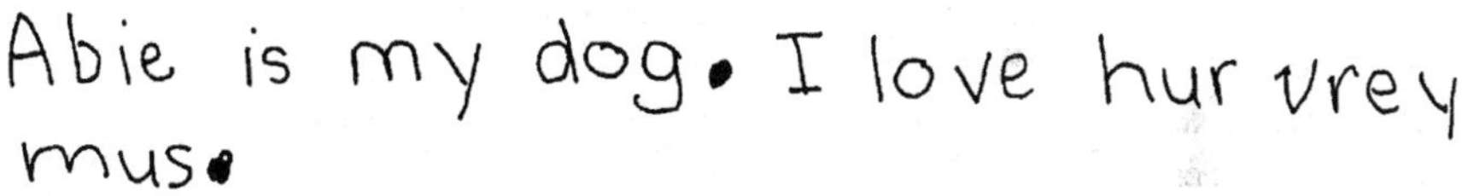

Adapting the Writing Process for Young Children

Teachers often simplify the writing process for young children by abbreviating the revising and editing steps. At first, children's revising is limited to reading the text to themselves or to the teacher to check that they have written all that they want to say. Revising becomes more elaborate as children learn about audience and decide they want to "add more" or "fix" their writing to make it appeal to their classmates. Some emergent and beginning writers ignore editing altogether—as soon as they have dashed off their drafts, they are ready to publish or share their writing. However, others change a spelling, fix a poorly written letter, or add a period to the end of the text as they read over their writings. When children begin writing, teachers accept their writing as it is written and focus on the message. As children gain experience with writing, teachers encourage them to "fix" more and more of their errors. Guidelines for adapting the writing process for emergent and beginning writers are presented in Figure 11-9.

Interactive Writing

Children and the teacher create a text together in interactive writing[C] and "share the pen" as they write the text on chart paper (Button, Johnson, & Furgerson, 1996; Mc-Carrier, Pinnell, & Fountas, 2000). The text is composed by the group, and the

Figure 11-9 **Guidelines for Adapting the Writing Process for Emergent Writers**

1. Prewriting
Prewriting is as important to young children as it is to other writers. Children write about topics they know well and for which they have the necessary vocabulary. Topics include personal experiences, classroom activities, stories students have heard read aloud or have read independently, and thematic unit topics. Children use drawing to gather and organize ideas before writing. Children often talk about the topic or dramatize it before beginning to write.

2. Drafting
Young children usually write single-draft compositions. They add words to accompany drawings they have already made. The emphasis is on expressing ideas, not on handwriting skills or conventional spelling. Often children write in small booklets of paper, and they write equally well on lined or unlined paper.

3. Revising
Teachers downplay this stage until children have learned the importance of revising to meet the needs of their readers. At first, children reread their writings to see that they have included everything they wanted to say, and they make very few changes. As they gain experience, they begin to make changes to make their writing clearer and add more information to make their writing complete.

4. Editing
Like revising, this stage is deemphasized until children have learned conventional spellings for some words and have gained control over rules for capitalizing words and adding punctuation marks. To introduce editing, teachers help children make one or two corrections by erasing the error and writing the correction in pencil on the child's writing. Teachers do not circle errors on a child's paper with a red pen. As children become more fluent writers, teachers help them make more corrections.

5. Publishing
Children read their writings to their classmates and share their drawings. Through sharing, children develop a concept of audience and learn new ways of writing from their classmates. Kindergartners and first graders usually do not recopy their writings, but sometimes the teacher or an aide types the final copy, changing the child's writing into conventional form. Unless there is a good reason for converting the kid writing to adult writing, adults should refrain from recopying young children's writing because they send a message that the children's writing is inadequate.

teacher guides children as they write the text word by word on chart paper. Children take turns writing known letters and familiar words, adding punctuation marks, and marking spaces between words. All children participate in creating and writing the text on chart paper, and they also write the text on small white boards, on small chalkboards, or on paper as it is written on the chart paper. After writing, children read and reread the text using shared reading[C] and independent reading.

Children use interactive writing to write class news, predictions before reading, retellings of stories, thank-you letters, reports, math story problems, and many other types of group writings (Collom, 1998). Two interactive writing samples are shown in Figure 11-10. The one at the top of the page was written by a kindergarten class during a health unit, and the second sample is a first-grade class's interactive writing of a math story problem. After writing this story problem, children wrote other subtraction problems individually. The boxes drawn around some of the letters and words represent correction tape that was used to correct misspellings or poorly

To view interactive writing in action, play the CD-ROM titled *Primary Grades Literacy: A K–3 Unit on Insects* that accompanies this text.

Figure 11-10   **Two Samples of Interactive Writing**

Wash your hands with soap to kill germs.

Luis had 5 pieces of candy but he ate 3 of them. Then he gave 1 to his friend Mario. How many does he have now?

formed letters. In the kindergarten sample, children took turns writing individual letters; in the first-grade sample, children took turns writing entire words.

Through interactive writing, children learn concepts about print, letter-sound relationships and spelling patterns, handwriting concepts, and capitalization and punctuation skills. Teachers model conventional spelling and use of conventions of print, and children practice segmenting the sounds in words and spelling familiar words. Children use the skills they learn through interactive writing when they write independently.

During interactive writing, teachers help children spell all words conventionally. They teach high-frequency words such as *the* and *of,* assist children in segmenting sounds and syllables in other words, point out unusual spelling patterns such as *pieces* and *germs,* and teach other conventions of print. Whenever children misspell a word or form a letter incorrectly, teachers use correction tape to cover the mistake and help children make the correction. For example, when a child wrote the numeral *8* to spell *ate* in the second sample in Figure 11-10, the teacher explained the *eight–ate* homophone, covered the numeral with correction tape, and helped the child "think out" the spelling of the word, including the silent *e.* Teachers emphasize the importance of using conventional spelling as a courtesy to readers, not that a child made a mistake. In contrast to the emphasis on conventional spelling in interactive writing, children are encouraged to use invented spelling and other spelling strategies when writing independently. They learn to look for familiar words posted on classroom word walls or in books they have read, think about spelling patterns and rimes, or ask a classmate for help. Teachers also talk about purpose and explain that in personal writing and rough drafts, children do use invented spelling. Increasingly, however, children want to use conventional spelling and even ask to use the correction tape to fix errors they make as they write.

Teachers model and teach conventional spelling, capitalization, and punctuation to ELL students through interactive writing.

Writing Centers

Writing centers can be set up in prekindergarten and kindergarten classrooms so that children have a special place where they can go to write. The center should be located at a table with chairs, and a box of supplies, including pencils, crayons, a date stamp, different kinds of paper, journal notebooks, a stapler, blank books, notepaper, and envelopes, should be stored nearby. The alphabet, printed in upper- and lowercase letters, should be available on the table for children to refer to as they write. In addition, there should be a crate where children can file their work. They can also share their completed writings by sending them to classmates or while sitting in a special chair called the "author's chair."

When children come to the writing center, they draw and write in journals, compile books, and write messages to classmates. At first, they write single-draft compositions, but the social interaction that is part of life at a center encourages children to consider their audience and make revisions and editorial changes. Teachers should be available to encourage and assist children at the center. They can observe children as they invent spellings and can provide information about letters, words, and sentences as needed. If the teacher cannot be at the writing center, perhaps an aide, a parent volunteer, or an upper-grade student can assist.

Figure 11-11 presents two reading log[C] entries created by young children at the writing center. The top sample shows an emergent-stage kindergartner's response to *If You Give a Mouse a Cookie* (Numeroff, 1985). The child's kid writing says, "I love chocolate chip cookies." The bottom sample was written by a beginning-stage first grader after reading *Are You My Mother?* (Eastman, 1960). The child wrote, "The bird said, 'Are you my mother, you big ole Snort?'" After the child shared his log entry during a grand conversation, he added, "The mommy said, 'Here is a worm. I am

Children participate in writing activities at the writing center.

here. I'm here.'" Notice that the part the mother says is written as though it were coming out of the bird's mouth and going up into the air.

Young children also make books at the writing center based on the books they have read. For example, they can use the same patterns as in *Polar Bear, Polar Bear, What Do You Hear?* (Martin, 1991), *If You Give a Mouse a Cookie* (Numeroff, 1985), and *If the Dinosaurs Came Back* (Most, 1978) to create innovations, or new versions of familiar stories. A first grader's four-page book about a mouse named Jerry, written after reading *If You Give a Mouse a Cookie,* is shown in Figure 11-12. In these writing projects, beginning writers often use invented spelling, but they are encouraged to spell familiar words correctly. They also learn to use the books they are reading to check the spelling of characters' names and other words from the stories.

READING AND WRITING ARE SIMILAR PROCESSES

Reading and writing are both meaning-making processes, and readers and writers are involved in many similar activities. It is important that teachers plan literacy activities so that children can connect reading and writing.

Comparing the Two Processes

The reading and writing processes have comparable activities at each stage (Butler & Turbill, 1984). In both reading and writing, the goal is to construct meaning, and, as shown in Figure 11-13 (p. 326), reading and writing activities at each stage are similar. For example, notice the similarities between the activities listed for the third stage of reading and writing—responding and revising, respectively. Fitzgerald (1989) analyzed these two activities and concluded that they draw on similar processes of author-reader-text interactions. Similar analyses can be made for other activities as well.

Figure 11-11   Two Young Children's Reading Log
Entries

Tierney (1983) explains that reading and writing are multidimensional and involve
concurrent, complex transactions between writers, between writers as readers, between readers, and between readers as writers. Writers participate in several types of
reading activities. They read other authors' works to obtain ideas and to learn about
the structure of stories, but they also read and reread their own work in order to problem solve, discover, monitor, and clarify. The quality of these reading experiences

Figure 11-12
A First Grader's Innovation for *If You Give a Mouse a Cookie*

seems closely tied to success in writing. Readers as writers is a newer idea, but readers participate in many of the same activities that writers use—generating ideas, organizing, monitoring, problem solving, and revising.

Classroom Connections

Teachers can help children appreciate the similarities between reading and writing in many ways. Tierney explains: "What we need are reading teachers who act as if their children were developing writers and writing teachers who act as if their children were readers" (1983, p. 151). Here are some ways to point out the relationships between reading and writing:

- Help writers assume alternative points of view as potential readers.
- Help readers consider the writer's purpose and viewpoint.
- Point out that reading is much like composing, so that children will view reading as a process, much like the writing process.
- Talk with children about the similarities between the reading and writing processes.
- Talk with children about reading and writing strategies.

Figure 11-13   A Comparison of the Reading and Writing Processes

	What Readers Do	What Writers Do
Stage 1	*Prereading*	*Prewriting*
	Readers use knowledge about • the topic • reading • literature • language systems Readers' expectations are cued by • previous reading/writing experiences • format of the text • purpose for reading • audience for reading Readers make predictions.	Writers use knowledge about • the topic • writing • literature • language systems Writers' expectations are cued by • previous reading/writing experiences • format of the text • purpose for writing • audience for writing Writers gather and organize ideas.
Stage 2	*Reading*	*Drafting*
	Readers • use word-identification strategies • use comprehension strategies • monitor reading • create meaning	Writers • use transcription strategies • use meaning-making strategies • monitor writing • create meaning
Stage 3	*Responding*	*Revising*
	Readers • respond to the text • interpret meaning • clarify misunderstandings • expand ideas	Writers • respond to the text • interpret meaning • clarify misunderstandings • expand ideas
Stage 4	*Exploring*	*Editing*
	Readers • examine the impact of words and literary language • explore structural elements • compare the text to others	Writers • identify and correct mechanical errors • review paragraph and sentence structure
Stage 5	*Applying*	*Publishing*
	Readers • go beyond the text to extend their interpretations • share projects with classmates • reflect on the reading process • make connections to life and literature • value the piece of literature • feel success • want to read again	Writers • produce the finished copy of their compositions • share their compositions with genuine audiences • reflect on the writing process • value the composition • feel success • want to write again

Adapted from Butler & Turbill, 1984.

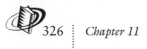

Readers and writers use similar strategies for constructing meaning as they interact with print. As readers, we use a variety of problem-solving strategies to make decisions about an author's meaning and to construct meaning for ourselves. As writers, we also use problem-solving strategies to decide what our readers need as we construct meaning for them and for ourselves. Comparing reading to writing, Tierney and Pearson (1983) described reading as a composing process because readers compose and refine meaning through reading much as writers do through writing.

There are practical benefits of connecting reading and writing: Reading contributes to children's writing development, and writing contributes to children's reading development. Shanahan (1988) has outlined seven instructional principles for relating reading and writing so that children develop a clear concept of literacy:

1. Involve children in reading and writing experiences every day.
2. Introduce the reading and writing processes in kindergarten.
3. Plan instruction that reflects the developmental nature of reading and writing.
4. Make the reading-writing connection explicit to children.
5. Emphasize both the processes and the products of reading and writing.
6. Emphasize the purposes for which children use reading and writing.
7. Teach reading and writing through authentic literacy experiences.

These principles are incorporated into a balanced literacy program in which children read and write books and learn to view themselves as readers and writers.

Review

Teachers introduce the five stages of the writing process—prewriting, drafting, revising, editing, and publishing—and teach children how to write and refine their compositions. For young children, teachers adapt the writing process and focus on the prewriting, drafting, and publishing stages. The goal of both reading and writing is to construct meaning, and the two processes involve similar activities in each stage. Researchers recommend that teachers connect reading and writing because they are mutually supportive processes. The feature that follows presents guidelines for effectively teaching the writing process to children.

How Effective Teachers . . .
Teach the Writing Process

Effective Practices

1. Teachers teach children during the primary grades how to use each of the five stages in the writing process.
2. Teachers teach children to gather and organize ideas during prewriting.
3. Teachers teach children to work in writing groups to revise their writing.
4. Teachers teach children to edit their writing.
5. Teachers have children share their finished writing from the author's chair.
6. Teachers adapt the writing process for young children and emphasize the prewriting, drafting, and publishing stages.

7. Teachers introduce "kid" writing and encourage children to use invented spelling.
8. Teachers use interactive writing to teach concepts about print, letters of the alphabet, high-frequency words, and other skills and strategies.
9. Teachers have young children write at a writing center so that they can interact with classmates and share their writing.
10. Teachers emphasize the connections between the reading and writing processes.

Professional References

Applebee, A. N., & Langer, J. A. (1983). Instructional scaffolding: Reading and writing and natural language activities. *Language Arts, 60,* 168–175.

Bissex, G. L. (1980). *Gyns at wrk: A child learns to write and read.* Cambridge: Harvard University Press.

Britton, J., Burgess, T., Martin, N., McLeod, A., & Rosen, H. (1975). *The development of writing abilities (11–18).* London: Schools Council Publications.

Butler, A., & Turbill, J. (1984). *Towards a reading-writing classroom.* Portsmouth, NH: Heinemann.

Button, K., Johnson, M. J., & Furgerson, P. (1996). Interactive writing in a primary classroom. *The Reading Teacher, 49,* 446–454.

Calkins, L. M. (1980). When children want to punctuate: Basic skills belong in context. *Language Arts, 57,* 567–573.

Calkins, L. M. (1983). *Lessons from a child: On the teaching and learning of writing.* Portsmouth, NH: Heinemann.

Cochran-Smith, M. (1991). Word processing and writing in elementary classrooms: A critical review of related literature. *Review of Educational Research, 61,* 107–155.

Collom, S. (Ed.). (1998). *Sharing the pen: Interactive writing with young children.* Fresno: California State University, Fresno, and the San Joaquin Valley Writing Project.

DeGroff, L. (1990). Is there a place for computers in whole language classrooms? *The Reading Teacher, 43,* 568–572.

Dyson, A. H. (1982). The emergence of visible language: Interrelationships between drawing and early writing. *Visible Language, 6,* 360–381.

Dyson, A. H. (1985). Second graders sharing writing: The multiple social realities of a literacy event. *Written Communication, 2,* 189–215.

Dyson, A. H. (1986). The imaginary worlds of childhood: A multimedia presentation. *Language Arts, 63,* 799–808.

Elley, W. B., Barham, I. H., Lamb, H., & Wyllie, M. (1976). The role of grammar in a secondary school English curriculum. *Research in the Teaching of English, 10,* 5–21.

Faigley, L., & Witte, S. (1981). Analyzing revision. *College Composition and Communication, 32,* 400–410.

Fitzgerald, J. (1989). Enhancing two related thought processes: Revision in writing and critical thinking. *The Reading Teacher, 43,* 42–48.

Graves, D. H. (1976). Let's get rid of the welfare mess in the teaching of writing. *Language Arts, 53,* 645–651.

Graves, D. H. (1983). *Writing: Teachers and children at work.* Exeter, NH: Heinemann.

Hidi, S., & Hildyard, A. (1983). The comparison of oral and written productions in two discourse modes. *Discourse Processes, 6,* 91–105.

King, M. (1985). Proofreading is not reading. *Teaching English in the Two-Year College, 12,* 108–112.

Langer, J. A. (1985). Children's sense of genre. *Written Communication, 2,* 157–187.

McCarrier, A., Pinnell, G. S., & Fountas, I. C. (2000). *Interactive writing: How language and literacy come together, K–2.* Portsmouth, NH: Heinemann.

Murray, D. H. (1982). *Learning by teaching.* Montclair, NJ: Boynton/Cook.

Shanahan, T. (1988). The reading-writing relationship: Seven instructional principles. *The Reading Teacher, 41,* 636–647.

Smith, F. (1982). *Writing and the writer.* New York: Holt, Rinehart and Winston.

Sommers, N. (1982). Responding to student writing. *College Composition and Communication, 33,* 148–156.

Strickland, J. (1997). *From disk to hard copy: Teaching writing with computers.* Portsmouth, NH: Boynton/Cook.

Tierney, R. J. (1983). Writer-reader transactions: Defining the dimensions of negotiation. In P. L. Stock (Ed.), *Forum: Essays on theory and practice in the teaching of writing* (pp. 147–151). Upper Montclair, NJ: Boynton/Cook.

Tierney, R. J., & Pearson, P. D. (1983). Toward a composing model of reading. *Language Arts, 60,* 568–580.

Children's Book References

Eastman, P. D. (1960). *Are you my mother?* New York: Random House.

Martin, B., Jr. (1991). *Polar bear, polar bear, what do you hear?* New York: Holt, Rinehart and Winston.

Most, B. (1978). *If the dinosaurs came back.* San Diego: Harcourt Brace.

Numeroff, L. J. (1985). *If you give a mouse a cookie.* New York: Harper & Row.

Weiss, N. (1990). *An egg is an egg.* New York: Putnam.

chapter 12

Integrating Reading and Writing Into Thematic Units

- How do teachers use informational books, stories, and poems to teach science and social studies?

- How do children use reading and writing as tools for learning?

- How do children demonstrate what they have learned?

- How do teachers develop a thematic unit?

Mrs. Roberts's Class Learns About Penguins

Mrs. Roberts's first and second graders begin their 2-week unit on penguins by starting a K-W-L chart[C] (Ogle, 1986). Mrs. Roberts asks the children what they already know about penguins and records their information in the "K: What We Know" column. Children mention that penguins live at the South Pole, that they eat fish, and that they can swim. Paula asks if penguins can fly, and Mrs. Roberts writes this question as the first entry in the "W: What We Want to Learn" column. As the discussion continues, more information and questions are added to the chart. The third column, "L: What We Learned," is still empty, but later in the unit, Mrs. Roberts and her students will add entries in that column.

See the Compendium of Instructional Procedures, which follows Chapter 12, for more information on terms marked with the symbol [C].

Children read stories, poems, and informational books about penguins during their language arts block, and they continue learning about penguins during science. During the first week of the 2-week thematic unit, they read *Tacky the Penguin* (Lester, 1988), the story of an oddball penguin who saves the penguins from some hunters, and they examine the beginning, middle, and end of the story. They make posters with story maps[C] to diagram the three parts. Children also make a circle quilt[C] to celebrate the story. Children write their favorite quotes from the story around the outside of the circles, and in the middle of the circles, they draw pictures of Tacky. One piece of the quilt is shown in Figure 12-1.

Mrs. Roberts has collected a text set of stories, poetry, and informational books about penguins for this thematic unit. She reads some of the books aloud, including sequels about Tacky and informational books, and children read other books during reading workshop or at the listening center. Still others she saves for children to read in literature circles during the second week of the unit. She copies several poems from *Antarctic Antics: A Book of Penguin Poems* (Sierra, 1998) on chart paper for the children to read using shared reading[C], and she also writes the lines of the poems on sentence strips so that children can arrange them to re-create the poem or make a new poem using a pocket chart. Mrs. Roberts's text set of penguin books is shown in Figure 12-2.

Mrs. Roberts's class has guided reading/reading workshop for an hour each day. For guided reading groups, Mrs. Roberts uses leveled books at children's reading levels, and the books are usually not related to penguins. It is more important that children are reading books at their reading levels and receiving appropriate instruction during guided reading, but for the reading workshop, she encourages all children to read books related to penguins. Because some of her students are emergent and beginning readers, Mrs. Roberts creates patterned books and other easy-to-read books about penguins to supplement the books in the text set. Each year, she and her emergent readers write a book about penguins. One book they created was based on *Brown Bear, Brown Bear, What Do You See*? (Martin, 1983). The book begins this way:

Page 1: Little penguin, little penguin, what do you see?

Page 2: I see a leopard seal looking at me.

Page 3: Leopard seal, leopard seal, what do you see?

Page 4: I see two gulls looking at me.

Page 5: Two gulls, two gulls, what do you see?

Figure 12-1

A Square from the Class's Penguin Quilt

Another year, Mrs. Roberts and her students created a number book with pictures of penguins and related objects. It begins this way:

Page 1: One fish for a hungry penguin.

Page 2: Two penguins standing by a nest.

Page 3: Three seals hunting for a penguin.

This year, the small group of emergent readers decides to make a "What Can Penguins Do?" book. Children decide on these sentences:

Page 1: Penguins can swim.

Page 2: Penguins can dive.

Page 3: Penguins can eat fish.

Page 4: Penguins can waddle.

Page 5: Penguins can sit on nests.

Page 6: Penguins can lay eggs.

Page 7: Penguins can feed babies.

Page 8: But, penguins cannot fly!

Figure 12-2   A Text Set of Penguin Books

Stories
Geraghty, P. (1996). *Solo.* New York: Crown.
Lester, H. (1991). *Three cheers for Tacky.* Boston: Houghton Mifflin.
Lester, H. (1998). *Tacky in trouble.* Boston: Houghton Mifflin.
Lester, H. (2000). *Tacky and the emperor.* Boston: Houghton Mifflin.
Wood, A. (1989). *Little penguin's tale.* San Diego: Harcourt Brace Jovanovich.

Informational Books
Crewe, S. (1997). *The penguin.* Austin, TX: Raintree.
Gibbons, G. (1998). *Penguins!* New York: Holiday House.
Guiberson, B. Z. (2001). *The emperor lays an egg.* New York: Holt.
Jenkins, M. (1999). *The emperor's egg.* Cambridge, MA: Candlewick.
Kalmen, V. (1995). *Penguins.* New York: Crabtree.
Reid, K. (2000). *Penguin.* Austin, TX: Raintree.
Webb, S. (2000). *My season with penguins: An Antarctic journal.* Boston: Houghton
   Mifflin.

Poems
Sierra, J. (1998). *Antarctic antics: A book of penguin poems.* Boston: Houghton
   Mifflin.

Together, Mrs. Roberts and the children draw and color the pictures, add the sentences, and compile the book. Then they share it with the other children in the class.

During the second week of the unit, children form literature circles. Mrs. Roberts does a book talk[C] about these four informational books, and children choose one of them to read:

- *It Could Still Be a Bird* (Fowler, 1990), a book that describes the characteristics of birds, using the predictable pattern "It could still be a bird."
- *Penguin* (Fletcher, 1993), a book that describes the first 2 ½ years of a penguin's life.
- *Antarctica* (Cowcher, 1990), a vividly illustrated book about penguins and other animals living in Antarctica.
- *A Penguin Year* (Bonners, 1981), a book showing what penguins do during each season.

Children read the informational book they have chosen and talk about the big ideas in an instructional conversation[C] with Mrs. Roberts or the student teacher. Later during the week, children reread the book as scientists, hunting for information about penguins to share with classmates. Children take notes on chart paper and then share what they have learned.

At the beginning of the unit, Mrs. Roberts posts an alphabetized word wall[C], and the children add "science" words to it during the unit. At the end of the unit, they have added 22 words and phrases. Their completed word wall is shown in Figure 12-3.

Children use the words from the word wall as they write and talk about penguins, the books they are reading, and science they are learning. Children draw pictures of Antarctica in their learning logs[C] and label at least eight things in their pictures using words from the word wall.

Mrs. Roberts uses words from the word wall as she teaches minilessons[C] on phonemic awareness (segmenting and blending sounds in words), building words that rhyme with *chick* and with *coat,* and comparing *e* sounds in *egg, nests, feet,*

Figure 12-3   A Word Wall of Penguin Words

AB Adelie penguins Antarctica birds	*CD* chicks crests crop in throat divers	*EF* emperor penguins feathers flippers
GHI hatch from eggs	*JKL* krill leopard seals	*MNO* nursery
PQR penguins rookery	*STU* skua gulls stand upright swimmers	*VWXYZ* waddle waterproof coat webbed feet

and *seal*. She also teaches minilessons on *r*-controlled vowels, using *birds, leopard seals, nursery,* and *Antarctica* for the more fluent readers in her class.

The first and second graders develop multigenre poster projects with at least three writings and/or drawings to illustrate the "repetend" or idea that penguins are unique animals. The children develop drawings and writings that they then attach to a poster and decorate. For single-page drawings and writings, they glue the paper onto the poster, but they put longer pieces, such as books, into envelopes or plastic bags that they attach to the poster.

All of Mrs. Roberts's students write "All About Penguins" books as one of the writings for their projects. They use a modified version of the writing process as they write their books. To begin, children brainstorm facts that they have learned about penguins, such as:

Penguins are black and white birds.
Penguins are covered with feathers.
Penguins are good swimmers, but they can't fly.
Mother penguins lay eggs.
Father penguins hold the eggs on their feet to keep them warm.
Penguin chicks stay together in the rookery.
Penguins look funny when they waddle on land.
Penguins eat fish and krill.
Leopard seals are a dangerous enemy, but people are an even worse enemy.

Mrs. Roberts writes these facts on sentence strips and places them in pocket charts. Children read and reread these facts and think about the facts they want to include in their "All About Penguins" books.

Next, children collect five or six sheets of white paper for the inside of their books. They draw a picture and write a fact on each page. Most children think of the sentences they want to write and write them using invented spelling, but a few need more support; they locate the sentence strips and dutifully copy the fact so that their book will be written in "adult" spelling. As children write and draw,

Mrs. Roberts circulates around the classroom, helping children choose facts, correcting their misconceptions about life in Antarctica, showing them how to draw penguins and other animals, and encouraging them to invent spellings. Mrs. Roberts insists that children spell *penguin* correctly, so she places word cards with the word at each table. All children are encouraged to check their spellings with words on the word wall, but Mrs. Roberts is more insistent that the more fluent writers check their spelling.

After children finish drawing and writing the pages for their books, they meet with Mrs. Roberts to review their work. Some children make revisions to add more information or correct misinformation. Some children add a second or third sentence on a page to clarify or expand the information they have provided. Mrs. Roberts also helps children to use capital letters and punctuation marks correctly and to correct spelling errors. Mrs. Roberts doesn't try to correct every error; instead she considers each child's stage of writing development and helps each child to make some appropriate changes. For example, a child who is using one letter to represent a word can be helped to use two or three letters to represent a word. Or, a child who is a safe writer and writes a single nearly perfect four-word sentence on each page can be helped to write longer sentences or several sentences on a page. Mrs. Roberts's goal is to move the first and second graders forward in their understanding of how written language works.

Pages from two children's penguin books are shown in Figure 12-4. The page about laying eggs was written by a second grader, who is a beginning writer, and it says, "Penguins lay eggs and keep them warm with their feet and their stomachs." The page about seals eating penguins was written by a first grader who is learning English as a second language. The page says, "The seal likes to

Figure 12-4   EXCERPTS FROM TWO STUDENTS' BOOKS
ABOUT PENGUINS

eat penguins." This child, who is an emergent writer, is experimenting with word boundaries, and he adds a dot between words. As he says the sentence, "to eat" sounds like one word to him. He also makes two word cards beside his picture because his teacher had made the word cards for him.

After the children finish drawing and writing facts, they compile their pages and add black and white covers—penguin colors. Before children make their covers, Mrs. Roberts teaches a brief minilesson on choosing titles and explains how to capitalize all the important words in a title. Most children title their books "The Penguin Book" or "All About Penguins," but several children experiment with other titles; one child chooses "Penguins in Antarctica," and another selects "The Adventures of Penguins." Children also add their names as the authors.

The children also complete two or more additional writings and drawings for their multigenre posters. Their other genres include:

- draw a picture of a penguin and label all body parts
- make a circle chart showing the life cycle of a penguin
- write a riddle about a penguin or another animal living in Antarctica
- write a shape poem about a penguin
- write a story about a penguin

Then students arrange their drawings and writings on a sheet of posterboard. They attach the pieces, add a title, and more illustrations if space allows.

To emphasize the repetend during the thematic unit, Mrs. Roberts often remarks how unique penguins are. To complete their multigenre posters, Mrs. Roberts asks each child to complete this sentence on a sentence strip: *Penguins are unique because* _____. Here are four children's responses:

Penguins are unique because they live in Antarctica and they don't freeze up.
Penguins are unique because they are birds but they can't fly.
Penguins are unique because the father takes care of the babies.
Penguins are unique because they are birds but they don't have feathers.

The children add these sentence strips to complete their posters.

Prekindergarten through fourth-grade students read and write all through the day as they learn science, social studies, and other content areas. Just as Mrs. Roberts's first and second graders learned about penguins by reading and writing, young children read and write to learn about insects, the solar system, rain forests, Native Americans, and their town or state.

The goal of content-area instruction is to help children construct their own understanding of big ideas. Children are naturally curious about the world, and they learn as they investigate new ideas. Children learn labels for concepts and develop new ways of expressing ideas. Reading and writing are useful learning tools, and through talking, reading, and writing, children explore concepts and make connections between what they are learning and what they already know.

Teachers organize content-area study into thematic units, and together with children, they identify big ideas to investigate. Units are time-consuming because student-constructed learning takes time. Teachers can't try to cover every topic; if they do, their students will probably learn very little. Teachers must make careful choices as they plan units, because only a relatively few topics can be presented in depth during a school year. During thematic units, children need opportunities to question, discuss, explore, and apply what they are learning (Harvey, 1998). It takes time for children to become deeply involved in learning so that they can apply what they are learning in their own lives. The only way children acquire a depth of knowledge is by focusing on key concepts. Even the first and second graders in Mrs. Roberts's class learned key concepts about penguins. They learned (1) about the ecosystem in Antarctica, (2) how penguins have adapted to their environment, (3) about the life cycle of a penguin, and (4) that people pose a threat to the environment of Antarctica.

TOOLS FOR LEARNING

Reading, writing, and talking are tools for learning about social studies and science (Bamford & Kristo, 1998; Winograd & Higgins, 1994–1995). Children acquire information and new vocabulary as they read books, and as they write about what they are learning, that knowledge is reinforced and connections are made. Through talking, too, children use new vocabulary words as they explore concepts they are learning and clarify misconceptions. Teachers plan opportunities for children to use these three learning tools during thematic units, as Mrs. Roberts did in the vignette on penguins at the beginning of this chapter.

Reading Informational Books

Children are curious, and they read informational books to find out about the world around them. Stephanie Harvey (1998, p. 70) lists these reasons why children enjoy reading informational books:

- to acquire information
- to understand the world more fully
- to understand new concepts and expand vocabulary
- to make connections to our lives and learning
- to write good nonfiction
- to have fun

They learn about whales in *Going on a Whale Watch* (McMillan, 1992), the Revolutionary War in . . . *If You Lived at the Time of the American Revolution* (Moore, 1997), bees in *The Magic School Bus Inside a Beehive* (Cole, 1996), and levers, inclined planes, and other simple machines and how they work in *Simple Machines* (Horvatic, 1989). In fact, high-quality informational books are available on almost any topic that interests children, and reading informational books is fun.

According to Horowitz and Freeman (1995), high-quality trade books play a significant role in science and other across-the-curriculum thematic units. Doiron (1994) argues that nonfiction books also have aesthetic qualities that make them very attractive and motivating for young readers.

Informational books are different from stories, and they place different demands on readers. They differ from stories in three basic ways:

1. *Organizational patterns.* Informational books are organized using expository text structures.

To link to *Carol Hurst's Children's Literature Site* for reviews of informational books and teaching ideas, visit our Companion Website at **www.prenhall.com/tompkins**

2. *Vocabulary.* Informational books include technical vocabulary related to concepts presented in the book.
3. *Special features.* Informational books have special features, such as a table of contents, an index, a glossary, photo illustrations, and charts, graphs, maps, and other diagrams.

When teachers introduce informational books to children, they point out these differences and show children how they can take advantage of the special features to enhance their comprehension. Teachers also take these differences into account as they read informational books with children as part of thematic units.

Teachers help children read expository text by teaching them about expository text structures. They teach children to recognize the organizational patterns and to adjust their purposes for reading to fit the structure. Children also learn about the cue words that authors use to signal structures and how to recognize them.

The four informational books about penguins that Mrs. Roberts used in the vignette at the beginning of this chapter illustrate three expository text structures. For example, *It Could Still Be a Bird* (Fowler, 1990) is organized using a description structure. The book points out these characteristics of birds:

1. All birds have feathers.
2. Birds have wings.
3. Birds usually can fly.
4. Birds lay eggs.
5. Some birds can swim.
6. Birds can be big or little.
7. Birds can be many different colors.
8. Birds can live almost anywhere.

Children learn about the world around them as teachers read informational books to them.

Both *Penguin* (Fletcher, 1993) and *A Penguin Year* (Bonners, 1981) employ a sequence structure. *Penguin* focuses on a penguin's development from hatching to age 2½, and on the last page of the book, a series of photographs reviews the sequence. *A Penguin Year* shows how penguins live from the dark winter through spring, summer, and fall. The author emphasizes that in the spring, penguins return to the rookery where they were hatched in order to lay eggs, and she explains how penguin parents hatch and care for their chicks season by season. In *Antarctica* (1990), Helen Cowcher uses a problem-solution structure to identify three of the penguins' enemies—leopard seals, skua gulls, and people—and to make a plea that people not destroy the penguins' environment. Figure 12-5 shows a chart that Mrs. Roberts's children made to emphasize the information they learned about penguins' enemies. The children shared this information with other children during a book talk.

Teachers consider the structure of text as they decide how to introduce an informational book, what type of graphic organizer or diagram to make to help emphasize the key points, and what points to emphasize in discussions. When teachers provide this type of structure, children are better able to focus on key concepts in each book rather than trying to remember a number of unrelated or unorganized facts.

Integrating Stories and Poetry

Stories bring content-area studies to life by providing a window through which children view yesterday's world and today's (Nelson, 1994; Smith & Johnson, 1994). Facts and content-area concepts are imbedded in fiction (Doiron, 1994). The settings of many stories provide historical and geographic information, and the conflict situations the characters face provide a glimpse into cultural, economic, and political issues. For example, children learn about penguins in *Tacky the Penguin* (Lester, 1988),

To link to *The Children's Literature Web Guide* for recommended books, author biographies, links to other websites, and teaching suggestions, visit our Companion Website at
www.prenhall.com/tompkins

Figure 12-5   **A Problem-Solving Chart**

understand the discrimination that immigrants face in *Molly's Pilgrim* (Cohen, 1983), and think about the consequences of pollution in *Ben's Dream* (Van Allsburg, 1990).

Whether children are reading stories as part of literature focus units, literature circles, reading workshop, or content-area units, they read aesthetically, for the lived-through literary experience. Even though children aren't reading efferently to pick out information, they learn information and develop concepts as they read. As they develop their understanding of a story, children often ask questions during grand conversations[C] about historical settings and unfamiliar cultural traditions. Stories are an important way of learning social studies and science.

Poetry is also used as part of content-area learning. Many books of poetry written for children can be used in teaching social studies and science units. Figure 12-6 presents a list of some of these poetry books. For example, *Desert Voices* (Baylor, 1981), a collection of poems written in the first person from the viewpoint of desert animals, and *Mojave* (Siebert, 1988), a book-length poem written from the viewpoint of the desert and illustrated with striking full-page illustrations, can be used in a unit on the desert.

Writing to Learn

When children write, they brainstorm ideas, make connections among ideas, and explore their comprehension. Writing is more than a school activity; it becomes a tool for learning.

Children use writing as a learning tool during thematic units. They take notes, make diagrams, and organize information through writing. Mrs. Roberts's students, for example, learned about penguins as they dictated facts for the K-W-L chart and wrote sentences on sentence strips. The focus in these activities is on using writing as a tool for learning, not on writing for publication (Tompkins, 2000). Nevertheless, children should use classroom resources, such as word walls, to spell many words correctly and write as neatly as possible so that they can reread their writing. Three types of writing activities are learning logs, quickwrites[C], and graphic organizers.

Learning Logs. Children draw and write entries in learning logs to record and react to what they are learning in science and social studies. Toby Fulwiler (1987) explains, "When people write about something they learn it better" (p. 9). As children write in these journals, they make notes of important concepts, reinforce the vocabulary words they are learning, reflect on their learning, discover gaps in their knowledge, and explore relationships between what they are learning and their past experiences.

Science-related learning logs can take several forms. One type of learning log is an observation log, in which children make daily entries to track the growth of plants or animals. For instance, a class of second graders took a walk in the woods wearing old socks over their shoes to collect seeds, in much the same way that animals pick up seeds on their fur coats and transport them. To simulate winter, the teacher placed the children's socks in the freezer for several weeks. Then they "planted" one student's sock in the class terrarium and observed it each day as they waited for the seeds to sprout. Children kept science logs with daily entries. Two pages from a second grader's log documenting the experiment are presented in Figure 12-7. In the top entry, the child wrote "No plants so far and still dirt!" In the second entry, he wrote "I see a leaf with a point on it!"

Another type of learning log is one in which children make entries during a thematic unit. Children may take notes during presentations by the teacher, after reading a book, or after viewing a video. Sometimes children make entries in list form, sometimes in clusters[C], charts, or maps, and at other times in sentences and paragraphs. Mrs. Roberts's first and second graders kept learning logs during their thematic unit on penguins, and they made these eight entries in their journals:

Figure 12-6　Books of Poetry That Can Be Used in Thematic Units

Amon, A. (Sel.). (1981). *The earth is sore: Native Americans on nature.* New York: Atheneum.

Asch, F. (1998). *Cactus poems.* San Diego: Gulliver.

Baird, A. B. (2001). *Storm coming!* Honesdale, PA: Boyds/Wordsong. (Poems about weather)

Baylor, B. (1981). *Desert voices.* New York: Scribner.

Fisher, A. (1983). *Rabbits, rabbits.* New York: Harper & Row.

Fisher, A. (1988). *The house of a mouse.* New York: Harper & Row. (Poems about mice)

Florian, D. (1999). *Winter eyes.* New York: Greenwillow.

Florian, D. (2001). *Lizards, frogs, and polliwogs.* San Diego: Harcourt Brace. (Poems about reptiles)

Goldstein, B. S. (Sel.). (1992). *What's on the menu?* New York: Viking. (Poems about food)

Graham, J. B. (1999). *Flicker flash.* Boston: Houghton Mifflin. (Poems about light)

Hopkins, L. B. (Sel.). (1976). *Good morning to you, valentine.* New York: Harcourt Brace Jovanovich. (See other collections of holiday poems by the same selector.)

Hopkins, L. B. (Sel.). (1983). *The sky is full of song.* New York: Harper & Row. (Poems about the seasons)

Hopkins, L. B. (Sel.). (1985). *Munching: Poems about eating.* Boston: Little, Brown.

Hopkins, L. B. (Sel.). (1987a). *Click, rumble, roar: Poems about machines.* New York: Crowell.

Hopkins, L. B. (Sel.). (1987b). *Dinosaurs.* San Diego: Harcourt Brace Jovanovich.

Hopkins, L. B. (Sel.). (1991). *On the farm.* Boston: Little, Brown.

Hopkins, L. B. (Sel.). (1992). *To the zoo: Animal poems.* Boston: Little, Brown.

Hopkins, L. B. (Sel.). (1999a). *Spectacular science: A book of poems.* New York: Simon & Schuster.

Hopkins, L. B. (1999b). *Sports! Sports! Sports!: A poetry collection.* New York: HarperCollins.

Hopkins, L. B. (Sel.). (2000). *Yummy! Eating through a day.* New York: Simon & Schuster.

Johnston, T. (2000). *It's about dogs.* San Diego: Harcourt Brace.

Larrick, N. (Sel.). (1988). *Cats are cats.* New York: Philomel.

Larrick, N. (Sel.). (1990). *Mice are nice.* New York: Philomel.

Lewis, J. P. (1998). *The little buggers: Insect and spider poems.* New York: Dial.

Livingston, M. C. (1985). *Celebrations.* New York: Holiday House. (Poems about holidays)

Livingston, M. C. (Sel.). (1987). *Cat poems.* New York: Holiday House.

Livingston, M. C. (Sel.). (1988). *Space songs.* New York: Holiday House.

Livingston, M. C. (Sel.). (1990). *Dog poems.* New York: Holiday House.

Livingston, M. C. (Sel.). (1992). *If you ever meet a whale.* New York: Holiday House.

Prelutsky, J. (1977). *It's Halloween.* New York: Greenwillow. (See other books of holiday poems by the same author.)

Prelutsky, J. (1983). *Zoo doings: Animal poems.* New York: Greenwillow.

Prelutsky, J. (1984). *It's snowing! It's snowing!* New York: Greenwillow.

Prelutsky, J. (1988). *Tyrannosaurus was a beast: Dinosaur poems.* New York: Greenwillow.

Siebert, D. (1988). *Mojave.* New York: Harper & Row.

Siebert, D. (1991). *Sierra.* New York: HarperCollins.

Sierra, J. (1998). *Antarctic antics: A book of penguin poems.* San Diego: Gulliver.

Wise, W. (2000). *Dinosaurs forever.* New York: Dial.

Yolen, J. (1990a). *Bird watch: A book of poetry.* New York: Philomel.

Yolen, J. (1990b). *Dinosaur dances.* New York: Putnam.

Yolen, J. (1993). *Weather report.* Honesdale, PA: Wordsong.

Yolen, J. (1995). *Water music.* Honesdale, PA: Wordsong.

Yolen, J. (1998). *Snow, snow! Winter poems for children.* Honesdale, PA: Wordsong.

- a drawing of a penguin with body parts labeled
- a brainstormed list of three facts about penguins written after listening to the teacher read aloud *Penguins!* (Gibbons, 1998)
- a circle diagram showing the life cycle of a penguin
- a drawing of Antarctica with labels
- a list of the penguin's enemies
- a Venn diagram comparing penguins with other birds

Figure 12-7   Two Pages From a Second Grader's
Science Log

- a world map with the United States and Antarctica marked
- a question from the "W" section of the KWL chart with an answer to the question

Sometimes teachers compile blank learning logs before giving them to students, and at other times, children collect the papers they do in a folder and compile the learning log at the end of the unit.

Quickwriting and Quickdrawing. After teachers read books aloud to children, show videos, or demonstrate experiments, they often ask children to write a sentence or a paragraph about something they learned or to draw a picture and label it. When children are writing, the activity is called *quickwriting,* and when children are drawing pictures, it is called *quickdrawing.* The activity is quick, as the name implies; children write or draw for 5 to 10 minutes, exploring the topic and using new vocabulary without worrying about mechanics or revisions. Afterwards, children share their writings or drawings with classmates and their learning is reinforced, clarified, and expanded.

During a thematic unit on the solar system, for example, fourth graders each chose a word from the word wall to quickwrite about. This is one child's quickwrite on *Mars:*

> Mars is known as the red planet. Mars is Earth's neighbor. Mars is a lot like Earth. On Mars one day lasts 24 hours. It is the fourth planet in the solar system. Mars may have life forms. Two Viking ships landed on Mars. Mars has a dusty and rocky surface. The Viking ships found no life forms. Mars' surface shows signs of water long ago. Mars has no water now. Mars has no rings.

Another child chose the word *sun* to write about:

> The sun is an important star. It gives the planets light. The sun is a hot ball of gas. Even though it appears large, it really isn't. It's pretty small. The sun's light takes time to travel to the planets so when you see light it's really from a different time. The closer the planet is to the sun the quicker the light reaches it. The sun has spots where gas has cooled. These are called sun spots. Sun spots look like black dots. The sun is the center of the universe.

These quickwrites, which took 10 minutes for children to draft, provide a good way of checking on what children are learning and an opportunity to clarify misconceptions.

Graphic Organizers. Teachers and students make charts called graphic organizers to arrange information in meaningful ways. These charts take many forms: When children show the life cycle of a penguin, they make a circle flowchart, for example; when they compare a penguin with other birds, they make a Venn diagram; when they describe a penguin's body parts, they draw and label a diagram; when they brainstorm what makes a penguin unique, they make a cluster; and when they research penguins and other animals that live in Antarctica, they use a data chart[C]. Two of these charts are shown in Figure 12-8; the top chart is a first grader's Venn diagram comparing penguins and other birds, and the bottom chart is a second grader's cluster about what makes a penguin a unique animal.

When they make graphic organizers, children and teachers write words, phrases, and sentences and arrange them in charts and diagrams to emphasize relationships and connections. Sometimes children make the graphic organizers in their learning logs, and sometimes teachers make them on posters and display them in the classroom. After making the graphic organizer with students, teachers can prepare a second chart and write the words and phrases on cards so that children can practice arranging the cards to complete the chart as a center activity.

Figure 12-8   Two Graphic Organizers

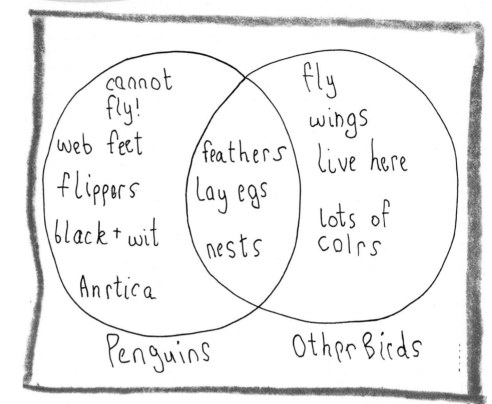

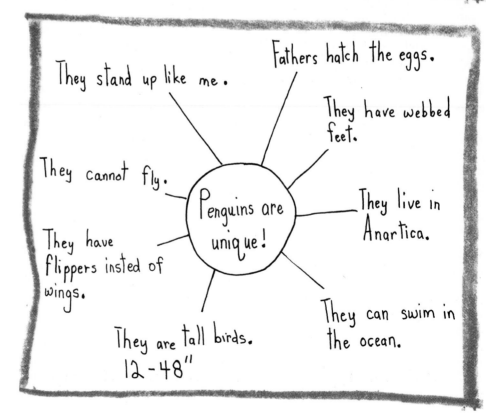

Instructional Conversations

Children talk about content area learning in instructional conversations (Goldenberg, 1992/1993). They talk about concepts or big ideas they are learning in thematic units—the interdependence of people in a community, the water cycle, the difference between reptiles and amphibians, or the impact of weather on our lives—and use the technical vocabulary they are learning in the conversations, as Mrs. Roberts's students did in the vignette at the beginning of this chapter.

Instructional conversations provide opportunities for children to enhance their conceptual learning and their linguistic abilities, according to Goldenberg. Like grand conversations, these discussions are interesting and engaging, and students are active participants, building on classmates' ideas with their own comments. Teachers are participants in the conversation, too, making comments much as the children do, but they also assume the teacher role to clarify misconceptions, ask questions, and provide instruction. Goldenberg has identified these content and linguistic elements of an instructional conversation:

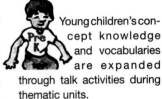 Young children's concept knowledge and vocabularies are expanded through talk activities during thematic units.

- The conversation focuses on a content-area topic.
- Students activate or build knowledge about the topic during the instructional conversation.
- Teachers provide information and directly teach concepts when necessary.
- Teachers promote students' use of more complex and technical vocabulary and language to express the ideas being discussed.
- Teachers encourage children to provide support for the ideas they present using information found in informational books and other resources in the classroom.
- Students and teachers ask higher-level questions, often questions with more than one answer, during instructional conversations.
- Students participate actively in the instructional conversation and make comments that build on and expand classmates' comments.
- The classroom is a community of learners where both children's and teachers' comments are respected and encouraged.

Researchers have compared the effectiveness of discussions with other instructional approaches and found that children's learning is enhanced when they relate what they are learning to their own experiences—especially when they do so in their own words (Wittrock & Alesandrini, 1990). Similarly, Pressley (1992) reported that children's learning was promoted when they had opportunities to elaborate ideas through talk activities.

DEMONSTRATING LEARNING

Children use writing and talking to demonstrate their learning when they prepare written reports and other projects and make oral presentations to their classmates. Through these demonstrations, they synthesize their knowledge and apply their knowledge in new ways. In addition, children also celebrate and bring closure to their study during a thematic unit.

Writing Projects

Children often use writing to demonstrate their learning. This type of writing is more formal, and children use the writing process to revise and edit their writing before making a final copy. Reports are the best-known type of writing to demonstrate learning. Children in the primary grades write many types of reports, ranging from posters, riddles, and alphabet books[C] to the "All About . . ." books that Mrs. Roberts's students made. Too often, children are not exposed to report writing until they are faced with writing a term paper in high school, and then they are overwhelmed with learning how to take notes on note cards, how to organize and write the paper, and how to compile a bibliography. There is no reason to postpone report writing until children reach high school; early, successful experiences with informative writing teach children about content-area topics as well as how to write reports (Harvey, 1998; Krogness, 1987; Tompkins, 2000).

"All About . . ." Books. The first reports that young children write are "All About . . ." books, in which they provide information about familiar topics, such as "Signs of Fall" and "Sea Creatures" (Bonin, 1988; Sowers, 1985). Young children write an entire booklet on a single topic. Usually one piece of information and an illustration appear on each page. Mrs. Roberts's first and second graders wrote "All About Penguins" books in the vignette at the beginning of this chapter.

Collaborative Reports. Children work together to write collaborative reports[C]. Sometimes children each write one page for the report, or they can work together in small groups to write chapters for the report. Alphabet books are one kind of collab-

Technology Link

Researching on the Internet

Children can use the vast information resources available on the World Wide Web as they study content-area topics (Harvey, 1998). Displays at websites include text information, pictures, sound, video, and animated graphics, and they also provide connections to related information using hypertext links. Although most websites have been developed by adults, some have been created by elementary children as part of thematic units, and children especially enjoy visiting these sites. Children can keep abreast of current news events and weather reports at certain websites, investigate scientific discoveries and delve into history at other sites, or visit on-line museums and art galleries (Heide & Stilborne, 1999).

The World Wide Web is easy to navigate. Children locate websites with information related to their topics using search engine software. One of the best search engines for elementary children is Yahoo for Kids (*www.yahooligans.com*). On the search engine's homepage, children type in the topic for the search and the software program searches for websites related to the topic. A list of websites with their URL addresses and brief annotations then appears on the homepage.

Children review the list and then click on an address to connect to that website. Children look over the site, and if it seems useful, they "bookmark" it or add it to their list of "favorites" so that they can return to it easily. Then children connect to other websites and read the information available there, take notes, and bookmark the sites if they want to return to them. Children can print out copies of all of the information available in the websites to read or collect, but they are usually most interested in printing photographs, diagrams, maps, and other graphics to incorporate into reports or multigenre projects. Using the World Wide Web not only enhances children's content-area learning, it also increases their computer literacy (Leu & Leu, 1998).

orative report in which children each write a page representing one letter of the alphabet. Then the pages are compiled in alphabetical order and bound into a book. Children also create collaborative reports on almost any science or social studies topic.

Primary-grade children might make collaborative books about weather: Each student develops a page by writing one interesting fact about weather and drawing a picture illustrating the fact, and then the pages are compiled into a book. Children can also write collaborative biographies: Each student or small group writes about one event or accomplishment in the person's life, and then the pages are assembled in chronological order. Or, children work in small groups to write chapters for a collaborative report on the planets in the solar system or life on the Oregon Trail.

Children benefit from writing a collaborative report before tackling individual reports because they learn how to write a report with the group as a scaffold or support system. Also, working in groups lets them share the laborious parts of the work.

Individual Reports. Children also write individual reports[C] as projects during thematic units. Toby Fulwiler (1985) recommends that children do "authentic" research, in which they explore topics that interest them or hunt for answers to questions that puzzle them. When children become immersed in content-area study, questions arise that they want to explore. In addition, increasingly children are turning to the Internet to research topics. For more information about using the Internet, check the Technology Link on these two pages.

Possible Pitfalls

The World Wide Web is unregulated, and some websites are not appropriate for young children because of pornographic, racist, and other offensive content. All schools should use Internet filtering software to block children's access to inappropriate websites. Although some children may be actively searching for these sites, many others stumble into them accidentally when they mistype a URL address.

A possibility exists that information presented in websites is inaccurate or misleading because there is no editorial review or other regulation of sites as there is in publishing books, magazines, and newspapers. Children should be aware that some information may be incorrect, and teachers should preview websites if possible, or at least review sites whenever children raise questions.

In addition, when children freely browse the Internet, they may waste valuable instructional time as they explore websites and hypertext links. Also, some children become frustrated when they end up at sites that are "under construction" or not available.

The Teacher's Role

Because of the possible problems with websites and Internet access, teachers should preview sites before children use the Internet to investigate content-area topics. Many teachers prefer to prepare a list for children of appropriate websites related to the topic rather than giving them free access to the World Wide Web. They can mark these sites with bookmarks or develop a handout for children listing the URL addresses. Teachers can also create their own web pages that incorporate the appropriate hypertext links. Many teachers compile a list of on-line resources in a card file or computer database for each thematic unit to simplify their previewing.

The World Wide Web is an important complement to books, and it links children to the world of information technology. For more information, check *The Teacher's Complete and Easy Guide to the Internet* (Heide & Stilborne, 1999) and *Teaching With the Internet: Lessons From the Classroom* (Leu & Leu, 1998).

Multigenre Projects

A new approach to demonstrating learning is the multigenre project (Allen, 2001; Romano, 1995, 2000) in which children explore a topic and demonstrate their learning using different genres, such as:

"all about . . ." books	K-W-L charts
alphabet books	letters
books	maps
charts	poems
clusters	quotations
collaborative reports	riddles
collection of objects	sentences
data charts	stories
diagrams	time lines
drawings	Venn diagrams
individual reports	word walls
journals	

Tom Romano (1995) explains, "Each genre offers me ways of seeing and understanding that others do not" (p. 109). After studying a content-area topic, children write several pieces, make drawings and charts, collect photos and other visual representations, and compile them on a poster or in a booklet for a multigenre project.

Children develop a repetend, a controlling idea or common thread, in the multigenre project through their writings and drawings. The repetend for Mrs. Roberts's students' penguin projects described in the vignette at the beginning of the chapter was that penguins are unique animals. A repetend for a weather unit might be that weather affects our lives in many ways, or for a community unit, the repetend might be that people work together in a community for the good of all.

Figure 12-9 presents one of Mrs. Roberts's students' multigenre projects on penguins. The second grader included four genres in her project—a diagram of a penguin's body, a poem about penguin chicks, a life cycle chart, and a report. The report "All About Penguins" is a six-page booklet, which is presented in a plastic envelope so that it can be removed and read. The repetend, "penguins are unique animals," is specifically stated in the "Important Idea" box presented on the lower left of the chart.

Oral Presentations

Children need a variety of daily opportunities to talk in classrooms during the primary grades. They use talk to socialize with classmates, to play with language, to ask questions and participate in discussions, to share information, and for many other purposes (Pinnell, 1996). Beginning in prekindergarten and kindergarten, children give oral presentations. Show and tell is probably the best-known oral presentation, but other types of oral presentations are usually more interesting and more educationally valid. During thematic units, for example, children can share pictures they have drawn, information they have learned, and books they have read. When children begin standing up and speaking in front of their classmates as soon as they enter school, they view the experience as a natural part of school life, and they develop a sense of audience, which carries over to their writing, too.

As part of thematic units, teachers often have children in the primary grades develop and give brief oral presentations. A good first oral presentation is a picture report. Children's presentations are as simple as sharing a picture they have drawn to illustrate an important fact. As they talk about the picture, teachers encourage children to use content-related vocabulary and to articulate the important facts. During

Figure 12-9 **A Second Grader's Multigenre Project on Penguins**

The life of a Penguin

1. ◯ egg
2. chick
3. adult

Penguins

All About Penguins

Penguin Chick

Little penguin chick
You are always hungry.
"More! More!" you say.
Mommy will feed you fish.

Little penguin chick
You sit on Daddy's feet.
See the snow and ice?
It's all around you!

A Penguin's Body

head
black feathers
flipper
stomach
white feathers
webbed feet

Important Idea

Penguins are unique animals because they are swimers not flyers!

a unit on the solar system, for example, children can draw a picture of a planet and then share their pictures with the class, pointing out several features of the planet that they included in their drawings.

A second quick and easy oral presentation is the question-and-answer report. Teachers and children generate a list of questions related to a unit, and then children

Even young children can give effective oral presentations as part of thematic units.

develop very brief reports to answer the questions. For example, a child might prepare a report to answer one of these questions about the solar system: Is the sun a planet? What are the inner planets? Are there people on other planets? A variation of the question-and-answer report is the true-false report: A child prepares a statement that could be either true or false, shares it with the class, tells whether it is true or false, and then gives a couple of reasons for his or her answer.

A third type of beginning presentation is the three-things-I-know report. Children choose a topic and develop a brief presentation to share three things that they know about it. For example, a child might share these three things about the moon:

1. The moon is the earth's satellite.
2. The moon reflects the sun's light.
3. The astronauts have walked on the moon.

When children give a three-things report, they often hold up three fingers and point to a finger as they talk about each thing.

As they gain more experience, children develop the poise and confidence to give longer, more sophisticated oral reports. For these presentations, children follow several steps that are similar to the stages of the writing process. First, they focus their topic. For example, a presentation on the solar system is too broad, but one on whether or not life is possible on each planet is more specific and more interesting. Next, children identify several main ideas, gather information about each idea, and decide how to organize the presentation. Third, children create a visual to support their presentation; they might create a poster listing their main ideas, a chart with a diagram to help listeners visualize some information, or an illustration about their topic. Sometimes they also collect artifacts or make a costume to wear. Fourth, they rehearse their presentation, thinking about how they will share the information they have gathered about each main idea succinctly and incorporate important vocabulary words. Finally, they give the presentation to their classmates.

Sometimes children do individual oral presentations, and at other times, they work in small groups and share the presentation. In a group presentation, each child gives one part. For a presentation on whether or not life is possible on each planet, for instance, one child could delineate the qualities necessary for life and other children could explain whether or not each planet exhibits these qualities. In this way, children can tackle complex topics because they are sharing the responsibility.

Classmates who are the listeners also play an important role in successful oral presentations. Children should be attentive, listen to the speaker, ask questions, and applaud the speaker. Young children are better listeners when they understand what is expected of them, when the presentations are brief and supported by visuals, and when only one or two are presented at a time.

THEMATIC UNITS

Thematic units are interdisciplinary units that integrate reading and writing with social studies, science, and other curricular areas. Children are involved in planning the thematic units and identifying questions they want to explore and the activities that interest them. Children are involved in authentic and meaningful learning activities. They explore topics that interest them and research answers to questions they have posed and are genuinely interested in answering. Children share their learning at the end of the unit and are assessed on what they have learned as well as on the processes they used in learning and working in the classroom.

Children learning English develop in-depth background knowledge through thematic units because they study concepts in authentic and meaningful ways.

How to Develop a Thematic Unit

To begin planning a thematic unit, teachers choose the general topic and then identify three or four key concepts that they want to develop through the unit. The goal of a unit is not to teach a collection of facts but to help children grapple with several big understandings (Tunnell & Ammon, 1993). Next, teachers identify the resources that they have available for the unit and develop their teaching plan. Eight important considerations in developing a thematic unit are:

To link to databases of lesson plans and thematic units, visit our Companion Website at www.prenhall.com/tompkins

1. *Collect a text set of stories, informational books, and poems.* Teachers collect books and other reading materials for the text set related to the unit. The text set is placed in the special area in the classroom library for materials related to the unit. Teachers plan to read some of these books aloud to children (or tape-record them for the listening center), some will be read independently, and others will be read together by children as shared or guided readings. These materials can also be used for minilessons—to teach children, for example, about reading strategies and expository text structure. Other books can be used as models or patterns for writing projects. Teachers also write the poems on charts to share with children.

2. *Set up a listening center.* Teachers select audiotapes to accompany stories or informational books, or the tapes can be used to provide additional reading experiences for children who listen to a tape when they read or reread a story or informational book.

3. *Locate multimedia materials.* Teachers locate videos, websites, computer programs, maps, models, and other materials to be used in connection with the unit. Some materials are used to develop children's background knowledge about the unit, and others are used in teaching the key concepts. Teachers use some multimedia materials for lessons and set up other materials in centers. And, children make other materials during the unit to display in the classroom.

4. ***Identify potential words for the word wall.*** Teachers preview books in the text set and identify potential words for the word wall. This list is useful in planning vocabulary activities, but teachers do not simply use their word lists for the classroom word wall. Children and the teacher develop the classroom word wall together as they read and discuss the key concepts and other information related to the unit.

5. ***Identify literacy skills and strategies to teach during the unit.*** Teachers plan minilessons to teach literacy skills and strategies, such as using an index, writing an alphabet book, and conducting an interview. Children have opportunities to apply what they learn in minilessons in reading and writing activities.

6. ***Design centers to support content-area and literacy learning.*** Teachers plan centers for children to work at independently or in small groups to practice strategies and skills that were presented to the whole class and to explore topics and materials related to the unit. Possible centers include a computer center, a reading center, a listening center, a writing center, a word work center, a chart-making center, a learning log center, and a project center.

7. ***Brainstorm possible projects children may create to extend their learning.*** Teachers think about projects children may choose to develop to extend and personalize their learning during the unit. This planning makes it possible for teachers to collect needed supplies and to have suggestions ready to offer to children who need assistance in choosing a project. Children work on the project independently or in small groups and then share it with the class at the end of the theme. Projects involve writing, talk, art, music, or drama. Some suggestions are:

- Create a poster to illustrate a key concept.
- Make a quilt about the unit.
- Write and mail a letter to get information related to the unit.
- Write a story related to the unit.
- Perform a readers theatre^C production, puppet show, or other dramatization related to the unit.
- Write a poem or song related to the unit.
- Write an "All About . . ." book or report about one of the key concepts.

8. ***Plan for the assessment of the unit.*** Teachers consider how they will assess children's learning as they make plans for activities and assignments. In this way, teachers can explain to children how they will be assessed at the beginning of the unit and check to see that their assessment will emphasize children's learning of the main ideas.

Teachers consider the resources they have available, brainstorm possible activities, and then develop clusters to guide their planning. The goal in developing plans for a thematic unit is to consider a wide variety of resources that integrate listening, talking, reading, and writing with the content of the theme (Pappas, Kiefer, & Levstik, 1990).

PreK teachers link thematic units and literacy through play centers that include literacy materials and charts and signs the children have made.

Topics for Thematic Units

During the primary grades, teachers develop thematic units on a variety of social studies and science topics. Figure 12-10 lists possible topics for thematic units at each grade level. Topics listed at the beginning of each list focus on science and those at the end are social studies–related.

The units that teachers develop are organized to meet the curriculum standards and guidelines set by their school districts and to provide opportunities for children to apply their reading, writing, and oral language skills. The spotlight feature on pages 354–355 describes Ms. Jones's 2-week unit on houses for prekindergartners. The children learn about houses as they observe one being built across the street from their school and participate in literacy and play activities in the classroom.

A second spotlight feature on pages 356–357 presents Mr. Morris's third-grade unit on desert life. The third graders integrate reading, writing, and science as they read desert-related books in literature circles, do an author study of Byrd Baylor, and read other books about desert life in reading workshop. They also work in small groups to study the desert ecosystem and develop multigenre projects.

 To view a primary-grade unit on insects, play the CD-ROM titled *Primary Grades Literacy: A K–3 Unit on Insects* that accompanies this text.

Figure 12-10   Topics for Thematic Units

Prekindergarten	Kindergarten	First Grade
Caring for Pets	Zoo Animals	Animals Around the World
Comparing Animals and Plants	Plants	How Plants Grow
Farm Animals	Water	Solids, Liquids, and Gases
Floating and Sinking	Being a Scientist	Energy
All About Me	Five Senses	Weather
My Family	Being Healthy	Seasons
Celebrations and Traditions	My School	My Neighborhood
	We Are Americans	Traditions
	Foods Around the World	Homes Around the World

Second Grade	Third Grade	Fourth Grade
Animal Life Cycles	Eco-systems (Deserts, Ponds, Oceans, Rainforests)	Food Chains
Motion		Electricity
Sound	Types of Animals (Mammals, Birds, Fish, Reptiles, Amphibians, Insects)	Light
Water Cycle		Solar System
The Earth's Surface		Rocks and Minerals
People Grow and Change	Properties of Matter	Ecology
Nutrition	My County	Archeology
My Town or City	American Indians	My State
Inventors and Inventions	Pioneers	Immigrants
Patriotism		Famous Americans

Spotlight on . . . A PreK Unit

In this 2-week unit, the 4- and 5-year-olds in Ms. Jones's prekindergarten class learn that people live in different sorts of houses depending on where they live and what their needs are. They also learn about how houses are built in their community and the types of building materials that are used. Through field trips to a site where a house is being built across the street from the school, children watch as the house is built.

When they visit the house, the children interview cement layers, electricians, carpenters, plumbers, and other people who are building the house, and they learn the names of some of the tools and building supplies.

On each visit, Ms. Jones takes snapshots of the progress on the house and of the construction workers the children talk to. When they get back to the classroom, Ms. Jones and the children write about their visit on chart paper using the language experience approach^C. After the photos are developed, Ms. Jones adds them to the chart along with pictures that the children draw and label.

Ms. Jones features two big books during the unit. During the first week, she uses shared reading to read Ann Morris's *Houses and Homes* (1992), an informational book with photographs of homes around the world, and the class makes their own big book of homes by drawing pictures and adding captions. During the second week, Ms. Jones reads *A House Is a House for Me* (Hoberman, 1978), a story written in verse about the houses that people and animals live in. She also reads aloud a variety of other stories, informational books, and poems that are available as small books. The children also look at these books at the library center after Ms. Jones has read them aloud.

on Houses

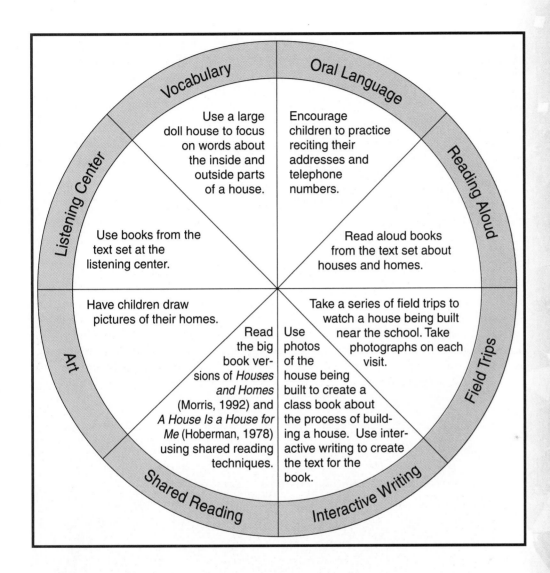

A planning cluster for a unit on houses is shown above.

Vocabulary
Use a large doll house to focus on words about the inside and outside parts of a house.

Oral Language
Encourage children to practice reciting their addresses and telephone numbers.

Listening Center
Use books from the text set at the listening center.

Reading Aloud
Read aloud books from the text set about houses and homes.

Art
Have children draw pictures of their homes.

Shared Reading
Read the big book versions of *Houses and Homes* (Morris, 1992) and *A House Is a House for Me* (Hoberman, 1978) using shared reading techniques.

Interactive Writing
Use photos of the house being built to create a class book about the process of building a house. Use interactive writing to create the text for the book.

Field Trips
Take a series of field trips to watch a house being built near the school. Take photographs on each visit.

A large doll house sits on a table in the classroom, and Ms. Jones and the children use it to talk about the outside and inside parts of a house. Mrs. Jones meets with the children in small groups to talk about the rooms in the house, names of furniture, and what families do in each room. Afterwards, the doll house becomes the children's favorite center activity, and they enjoy moving the furniture and the dolls that fit in the house from room to room.

Many of the children live in single-family homes, but some live in apartments, so these children work with Ms. Jones to draw a large picture of an apartment building. They share their picture with the class and talk about the ways their homes are like and different from single-family houses.

Even after the unit ends, Ms. Jones and the children will continue to visit the house under construction, take photographs, and record their visits by writing charts. Once the house is finished, Ms. Jones plans to compile the charts to make a big book.

A planning cluster for a unit on houses is shown above.

Spotlight on . . . A Third-Grade

Mr. Morris's third graders are studying desert life for 3 weeks; the thematic unit involves both language arts time in the morning and social studies/science time in the afternoon.

During the language arts period, they read and respond to literature about the desert. During the first week, the children work in literature circles to read and respond to self-selected books about the desert. During the second week, children participate in an author study of Byrd Baylor, a woman who lives in the desert and writes about desert life, and they read many of her books. During the third week, children participate in a reading workshop in which they read other desert books and reread favorite books.

During the afternoon period, the children divide into three groups to investigate the people, plants, and animals that live in the desert. The children learn about desert ecosystems, how deserts form, and how they change, and as they read books, participate in discussions, and do writings about the desert, they have a specific purpose—to focus on their group's topic.

Mr. Morris also posts a desert word wall on one side of the classroom, and children contribute words about the desert that they find in the books they are reading. These words are posted in alphabetical order, and Mr. Morris uses some of the words for minilessons.

Unit on Desert Life

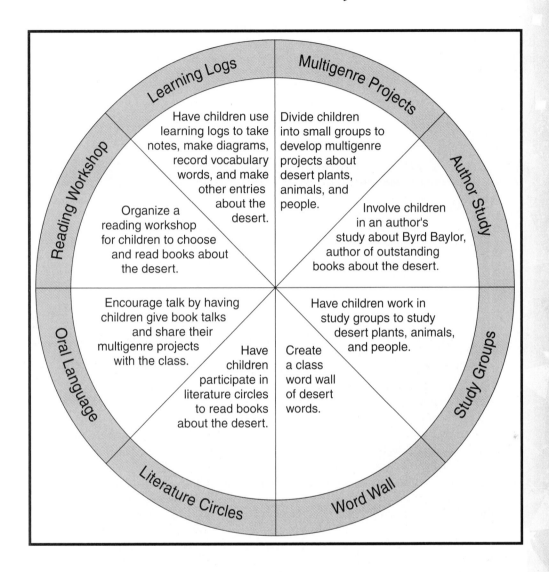

Learning Logs
Have children use learning logs to take notes, make diagrams, record vocabulary words, and make other entries about the desert.

Multigenre Projects
Divide children into small groups to develop multigenre projects about desert plants, animals, and people.

Author Study
Involve children in an author's study about Byrd Baylor, author of outstanding books about the desert.

Reading Workshop
Organize a reading workshop for children to choose and read books about the desert.

Study Groups
Have children work in study groups to study desert plants, animals, and people.

Oral Language
Encourage talk by having children give book talks and share their multigenre projects with the class.

Literature Circles
Have children participate in literature circles to read books about the desert.

Word Wall
Create a class word wall of desert words.

At the end of the unit, the groups each create a multigenre project to share what they have learned. They choose a repetend or theme to emphasize in their project, and they choose five or more genres to illustrate the repetend. The children use the writing process to draft and refine their compositions and lay out their projects on large boards, which they display in the classroom. The children in each group also give brief oral reports to share their project boards and read their compositions aloud to their classmates.

A planning cluster for a unit on the desert is shown above.

Review

Children use reading, writing, and talking as tools for learning in the content areas. Children read informational books, stories, poems, and other materials as they learn about social studies and science. They also use writing activities, such as learning logs, and talking activities, such as instructional conversations, to explore what they are learning. Children also develop writing projects and present oral reports to document their learning. Many of the ways that effective teachers use reading and writing in thematic units are reviewed in the feature that follows.

How Effective Teachers . . .
Teach Literacy in Thematic Units

Effective Practices

1. Teachers use informational books, stories, and poems for thematic units.
2. Teachers teach children how to read informational books, and explain the expository text structures.
3. Teachers encourage children to use reading, writing, and talking as tools for learning.
4. Teachers teach children to use learning logs, quickwrites, and graphic organizers as learning tools.
5. Teachers have children participate in instructional conversations to talk about the big ideas in informational books.
6. Teachers have children write reports and multigenre projects to demonstrate learning.
7. Teachers encourage children to demonstrate their learning through oral presentations to classmates and other audiences.
8. Teachers focus on big ideas in thematic units.
9. Teachers list important words on word walls and use a variety of activities to teach vocabulary.
10. Teachers have children create projects to extend their learning.

Professional References

Allen, C. A. (2001). *The multigenre research paper: Voice, passion, and discovery in grades 4–6.* Portsmouth, NH: Heinemann.

Bamford, R. A., & Kristo, J. V. (Eds.). (1998). *Making facts come alive: Choosing quality nonfiction literature K–8.* Norwood, MA: Christopher-Gordon.

Bonin, S. (1988). Beyond storyland: Young writers can tell it other ways. In T. Newkirk & N. Atwell (Eds.), *Under-* *standing writing* (2nd ed., pp. 47–51). Portsmouth, NH: Heinemann.

Doiron, R. (1994). Using nonfiction in a read-aloud program: Letting the facts speak for themselves. *The Reading Teacher, 47,* 616–624.

Fulwiler, T. (1985). Research writing. In M. Schwartz (Ed.), *Writing for many roles* (pp. 207–230). Upper Montclair, NJ: Boynton/Cook.

Fulwiler, T. (1987). *The journal book*. Portsmouth, NH: Heinemann/Boynton-Cook.

Goldenberg, C. (1992/1993). Instructional conversations: Promoting comprehension through discussion. *The Reading Teacher, 46*, 316–326.

Harvey, S. (1998). *Nonfiction matters: Reading, writing, and research in grades 3–8*. York, ME: Stenhouse.

Heide, A., & Stilborne, L. (1999). *The teacher's complete and easy guide to the Internet*. New York: Teachers College Press.

Horowitz, R., & Freeman, S. H. (1995). Robots versus spaceships: The role of discussion in kindergartners' and second graders' preferences for science text. *The Reading Teacher, 49*, 30–40.

Krogness, M. M. (1987). Folklore: A matter of the heart and the heart of the matter. *Language Arts, 64*, 808–818.

Leu, D. J., & Leu, D. D. (1998). *Teaching with the Internet: Lessons from the classroom* (2nd ed.). Norwood, MA: Christopher-Gordon.

Nelson, C. S. (1994). Historical literacy: A journey of discovery. *The Reading Teacher, 47*, 552–556.

Ogle, D. M. (1986). K-W-L: A teaching model that develops active reading of expository text. *The Reading Teacher, 39*, 564–570.

Pappas, C. C., Kiefer, B. Z., & Levstik, L. S. (1990). *An integrated language perspective in the elementary school: Theory into action*. New York: Longman.

Pinnell, G. S. (1996). Ways to look at the functions of children's language. In B. M. Power & R. S. Hubbard (Eds.), *Language development: A reader for teachers* (pp. 146–154). Upper Saddle River, NJ: Merrill/Prentice Hall.

Pressley, M. (1992). Encouraging mindful use of prior knowledge: Attempting to construct explanatory answers facilitates learning. *Educational Psychologist, 27*, 91–109.

Romano, T. (1995). *Writing with passion: Life stories, multiple genres*. Portsmouth, NH: Heinemann/Boynton Cook.

Romano, T. (2000). *Blending genre, altering style*. Portsmouth, NH: Heinemann/Boynton Cook.

Smith, L. J., & Johnson, H. (1994). Models for implementing literature in content studies. *The Reading Teacher, 48*, 198–209.

Sowers, S. (1985). The story and the "all about" book. In J. Hansen, T. Newkirk, & D. Graves (Eds.), *Breaking ground: Teachers relate reading and writing in the elementary school* (pp. 73–82). Portsmouth, NH: Heinemann.

Tompkins, G. E. (2000). *Teaching writing: Balancing process and product* (3rd ed.). Upper Saddle River, NJ: Merrill/Prentice Hall.

Tunnell, M. O., & Ammon, R. (Eds.). (1993). *The story of ourselves: Teaching history through children's literature*. Portsmouth, NH: Heinemann.

Winograd, K., & Higgins, K. M. (1994–1995). Writing, reading, and talking mathematics: One interdisciplinary possibility. *The Reading Teacher, 48*, 310–317.

Wittrock, M. C., & Alesandrini, K. (1990). Generation of summaries and analogies and analytic and holistic abilities. *American Educational Research Journal, 27*, 489–502.

Children's Book References

Baylor, B. (1981). *Desert voices*. New York: Scribner.

Bonners, S. (1981). *A penguin year*. New York: Delacorte.

Cohen, B. (1983). *Molly's pilgrim*. New York: Lothrop, Lee & Shepard.

Cole, J. (1996). *The magic school bus inside a beehive*. New York: Scholastic.

Cowcher, H. (1990). *Antarctica*. New York: Farrar, Straus & Giroux.

Fletcher, N. (1993). *Penguin*. London: Dorling Kindersley.

Fowler, A. (1990). *It could still be a bird*. Chicago: Childrens Press.

Gibbons, G. (1998). *Penguins!* New York: Holiday House.

Hoberman, M. A. (1978). *A house is a house for me*. New York: Puffin Books.

Horvatic, A. (1989). *Simple machines*. New York: Dutton.

Lester, H. (1988). *Tacky the penguin*. Boston: Houghton Mifflin.

Martin, B., Jr. (1983). *Brown bear, brown bear, what do you see?* New York: Holt.

McMillan, B. (1992). *Going on a whale watch*. New York: Scholastic.

Moore, K. (1997). *. . . If you lived at the time of the American Revolution*. New York: Scholastic.

Morris, A. (1992). *Houses and homes*. New York: Mulberry Books.

Siebert, D. (1988). *Mojave*. New York: Harper & Row.

Sierra, J. (1998). *Antarctic antics: A book of penguin poems*. San Diego: Harcourt Brace.

Van Allsburg, C. (1990). *Ben's dream*. Boston: Houghton Mifflin.

Compendium of
Instructional Procedures

This Compendium presents 35 instructional procedures used in balanced reading classrooms with step-by-step directions and student samples. You have read about story maps, grand conversations, word sorts, minilessons, word walls, reading logs, and other procedures in the 12 chapters of the text; they were highlighted with a ^{C} in the text to cue you to consult the Compendium for more detailed information. The Compendium is a handy resource to consult as you develop lesson plans and teach in early elementary classrooms. A list of the procedures follows.

Alphabet books

Anticipation guides

Book boxes

Book talks

Choral reading

Clusters, maps, and webs

Collaborative books and reports

Data charts

Directed reading-thinking activity

Grand conversations

Guided reading

Individual books and reports

Instructional conversations

Interactive writing

K-W-L charts

Language experience approach (LEA)

Learning logs

Making words

Minilessons

Open-mind portraits

Quickwriting

Quilts

Read-arounds

Readers theatre

Reading aloud to children

Reading logs

Repeated readings

Running records

Say something

Shared reading

Story boards

Story maps

Word sorts

Word walls

Writing groups

ALPHABET BOOKS

Children construct alphabet books much like the alphabet trade books published for children (Tompkins, 2000). These child-made books are useful reading materials for beginning readers, and children often make alphabet books as part of literature focus units and content-area units. Children can make alphabet books collaboratively as a class or in a small group. Interested children can make individual alphabet books, but with 26 pages to complete, it is an arduous task. The steps in constructing an alphabet book with a group of children are:

1. Examine alphabet trade books. Children examine alphabet trade books published for children to learn how the books are designed and how the authors use titles, text, and illustrations to lay out their pages. Good examples include *Eating the Alphabet: Fruits and Vegetables From A to Z* (Ehlert, 1989) and *A for Antarctica* (Chester, 1995). Or, children can examine student-made alphabet books made by other classes.

2. Make an alphabet list. Children write the letters of the alphabet in a column on a long sheet of butcher paper for the group to use for brainstorming words for the book.

3. Have children brainstorm words. Children identify words beginning with each letter of the alphabet related to the literature focus unit or content-area unit, and they write these words on the sheet of butcher paper. Children often consult the word wall[c] and books in the text set as they try to think of related words.

4. Have children choose letters. Children each choose the letter for the page they will create.

5. Design the format of the page. As a class or small group, children decide where the letter, the illustration, and the text will be placed.

6. Write the pages. Children use the writing process to draft, revise, and edit their pages. Then children make final copies of their pages, and one child makes the cover.

7. Compile the pages. Children and the teacher compile the pages in alphabetical order and bind the book.

Alphabet books are often used as projects at the end of a unit of study, such as the oceans, the desert, or California missions. The "U" page from a fourth-grade class's alphabet book on the California missions is shown in Figure 1.

ANTICIPATION GUIDES

Anticipation guides (Head & Readence, 1986) are lists of statements about a topic that children discuss before reading stories and informational books. Teachers prepare a list of statements about the topic; some of the statements should be true and accurate, and others incorrect or based on misconceptions. Before reading, children discuss each statement and agree or disagree with it. Then they discuss the statements again after reading. The purpose of this activity is to stimulate children's interest in the topic and to activate prior knowledge before reading. A third-grade anticipation guide about pilgrims used with *Molly's Pilgrim* (Cohen, 1983), the story of a modern-day pilgrim, is shown in Figure 2.

The steps in developing an anticipation guide are:

1. Identify several major concepts. Teachers consider their children's knowledge about the topic and any misconceptions they might have as they identify concepts related to the reading assignment or unit.

2. Develop a list of three to six statements. Teachers write a statement about each major concept they identified. These statements should be general enough to stimu-

Figure 1   The "U" Page From a Fourth-Grade
Class's Alphabet Book

Some of the Indians thought life was
UNBEARABLE at the missions. They thought
this because they couldn't hunt or do the
things they were used to. Once they were
at the missions they couldn't leave.
They were sometimes beaten if they did.

late discussion and useful for clarifying misconceptions. The list can be written on a chart, or individual copies can be duplicated for each student.

3. *Discuss the statements on the anticipation guide.* Teachers introduce the anticipation guide and have children respond to the statements. Children think about the statements and decide whether they agree or disagree with each one.

4. *Read the text.* Children read the text and compare their responses to what the reading material states.

5. *Discuss the statements again.* After reading, children reconsider their earlier responses to each statement and locate information in the text that supports or refutes the statement.

BOOK BOXES

Teachers and children collect three or more objects or pictures related to a story, informational book, or poem and put them in a box along with the book or other reading

Figure 2   Anticipation Guide on *Molly's Pilgrim*

Before Reading		Statements	After Reading	
Yes	No		Yes	No
		Parents should help with homework.		
		Getting teased hurts.		
		It is difficult to be a new student in the class.		
		Teachers help children understand.		
		Holidays are celebrated in different ways.		

material. For example, a book box for *Sarah, Plain and Tall* (MacLachlan, 1985) might include seashells, a train ticket, a yellow bonnet, colored pencils, a map of Sarah's trip from Maine to the prairie, and letters. Or, for *Eating the Alphabet: Fruits and Vegetables From A to Z* (Ehlert, 1989), teachers can collect plastic fruits and vegetables. The steps in preparing a book box are:

1. *Read the book.* While reading the book, teachers notice important objects that are mentioned and think about how they might collect these objects or replicas of them.

2. *Choose a book box.* Teachers choose a box, basket, or plastic tub to hold the objects, and decorate it with the name of the book, pictures, and words.

3. *Fill the book box.* Teachers place three or more objects and pictures in the box to represent the book. When children are making book boxes, they may place an inventory sheet in the box with all the items listed and an explanation of why the items were selected.

4. *Share the completed book box.* When teachers make book boxes, they use them to introduce the book and provide background information before reading. In contrast, children often make book boxes as a project during the applying stage of the reading process and share them with classmates at the end of a unit.

Book boxes are especially useful for children learning English as a second language and for nonverbal children who have small vocabularies and difficulty developing sentences to express ideas.

Book talks are brief teasers that teachers present to interest children in particular books. Teachers use book talks to introduce children to books in the classroom library, books for literature circles, or a text set of books for a unit or books written by a particular author. Children also give book talks to share books they have read during reading workshop. The steps are:

1. Select one or more books to share. When teachers share more than one book, the books are usually related in some way; they may be part of a text set, written by the same author, or on a related topic.

2. Plan a brief presentation for each book. During the 1- or 2-minute presentation, teachers tell the title and author of the book and give a brief summary. They also explain why they liked the book and why children might be interested in it. The teacher may also read a short excerpt and show an illustration.

3. Display the books. Teachers show the book during the book talk and then display it on a chalk tray or shelf to encourage children's interest.

The same steps are used when children give book talks. If children have prepared a project related to the book, they also share it during the book talk.

A good way to develop children's reading fluency is through choral reading. Poems are usually the texts chosen for choral reading, but other texts can also be used. As children read aloud, they practice chunking words together, varying their reading speed, and reading more expressively. Children take turns reading lines or sentences of the text as they read together as a class or in small groups. Four possible arrangements for choral reading are:

- **Echo reading.** The leader reads each line, and the group repeats it.
- **Leader and chorus reading.** The leader reads the main part of the poem, and the group reads the refrain or chorus in unison.
- **Small-group reading.** The class divides into two or more groups, and each group reads one part of the poem.
- **Cumulative reading.** One student or one group reads the first line or stanza, and another student or group joins in as each line or stanza is read so that a cumulative effect is created.

The steps in choral reading are:

1. Select a poem for choral reading. Teachers select a poem or other text to use for choral reading and copy it onto a chart or make multiple copies for children to read.

2. Arrange the text for choral reading. Teachers work with children to decide how to arrange the text for reading. They add marks to the chart or have children mark individual copies so that they can follow the arrangement.

3. Do the choral reading. Children read the poem or other text several times, and teachers emphasize that children should pronounce words clearly and read with expression. Teachers may want to tape-record children's reading so that they can hear themselves.

Choral reading makes children active participants in the poetry experience, and it helps them learn to appreciate the sounds, feelings, and magic of poetry. Many poems

ELL

Choral reading is recommended for English learners because it is an enjoyable, low-anxiety activity that helps children learn English intonation patterns and improve their reading fluency.

can be used for choral reading; try, for example, Shel Silverstein's "Boa Constrictor," Karla Kuskin's "Full of the Moon," Laura E. Richards's "Eletelephony," and Eve Merriam's "Catch a Little Rhyme."

CLUSTERS, MAPS, AND WEBS

Clusters are weblike diagrams with the topic written in a circle centered on a sheet of paper. Main ideas are written on rays drawn out from the circle, and branches with details and examples are added to complete each main idea (Rico, 1983). Clusters are used to organize information children are learning and to organize ideas before beginning to write a composition. A third-grade class's cluster about the four layers of the rain forest is shown in Figure 3. Teachers and children can work together to make a cluster, or children can work in small groups or make clusters individually. The steps are:

1. *Draw the center of the cluster.* Teachers or children select a topic and write the word in the center of a circle drawn on a chart or sheet of paper.

2. *Brainstorm a list of words.* Children brainstorm as many words and phrases as they can that are related to the topic, and then they organize the words into categories. The teacher may prompt children for additional words or suggest categories.

Figure 3 **A Third-Grade Class's Cluster About the Four Layers of the Rain Forest**

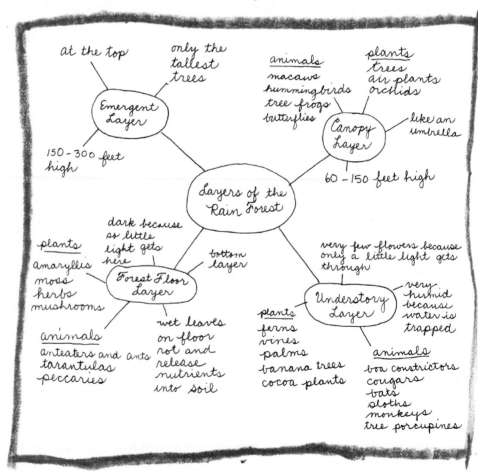

3. *Add main ideas and details.* Children determine the main ideas and details from the brainstormed list of words. The main ideas are written on rays drawn out from the circled topic, and details are written on rays drawn out from the main ideas.

Clusters are sometimes called maps and webs, and they are similar to story maps[C]. In this book, the diagrams are called clusters when used for writing, and they are called maps when used for reading.

Children divide the work of writing an informational book or report when they work collaboratively. Children each contribute one page for a class book or work with partners or in small groups to research and write sections of the report. Then the children's work is compiled, and the book or report is complete (Tompkins, 2000). Children use a process approach as they research their topics and compose their sections of the report or book. The steps are:

1. *Choose the topic.* Children choose specific topics related to the general topic of the unit for their pages or sections. Children work in small groups, with partners, or individually to research and write their sections of the informational book or report.

2. *Plan the organization.* If children are each contributing one page for a class informational book, they might draw a picture and add a fact or other piece of information. Children working on chapters for a longer report will need to design research questions. These questions emerge as children study a topic and brainstorm a list of questions on a chart posted in the classroom. If they are planning a report on the human body, for example, the small groups that are studying each organ may decide to research the same three questions: "What does the organ look like?" "What job does the organ do?" and "Where is the organ located in the human body?"

3. *Rehearse the procedure.* Teachers and children write one section of the report or book together as a class before children begin working on their section of the report.

4. *Gather and organize ideas.* Children gather and organize information for their sections. Children writing pages for informational books often draw pictures as prewriting. Those working in small groups or with partners search for answers to the research questions. Children can use clusters[C] or data charts[C] to record the information they gather. The research questions are the same for each data-collection instrument. On a cluster, children add information as details to each main-idea ray; if they are working with data charts, they record information from the first source in the first row under the appropriate question, from the second source in the second row, and so on.

5. *Draft the sections of the report.* Children write rough drafts of their sections. When children are working in small groups, one child is the scribe and writes the draft while the other children dictate sentences, using information from a cluster or data chart. Next, they share their drafts with the class and make revisions on the basis of feedback they receive. Last, children proofread and correct mechanical errors.

6. *Compile the pages or sections.* Children compile their completed pages or sections, and then the entire book or report is read aloud so children can catch inconsistencies or redundant passages. Children also add front and back pages. For an informational book, children add a title page and covers. For reports, children also write a table of contents, an introduction, and a conclusion and add a bibliography at the end.

7. *Publish the informational book or report.* Children make a final copy with all the parts of the book or report in the correct sequence. For longer reports, it is much

COLLABORATIVE BOOKS AND REPORTS

easier to print out the final copy if the sections have been drafted and revised on a computer. To make the book sturdier, teachers often laminate the covers (or all pages in the book) and bind everything together using yarn, brads, or metal rings.

8. *Make copies for children.* Teachers often make copies of the informational book or report for each child, whereas the special bound copy is often placed in the class or school library.

DATA CHARTS

Data charts are grids that children make and use as a tool for organizing information about a topic (McKenzie, 1979). In literature focus units, children use data charts to record information about versions of folktales and fairy tales, such as "Cinderella" stories, or a collection of books by an author, such as Eric Carle and Eve Bunting. In content-area units, data charts are used to record information about the solar system, Native American tribes, or modes of transportation. Children also use data charts to gather and organize information before writing reports. A data chart for a report on the human body is shown in Figure 4. The steps in making a data chart are:

1. *Design the data chart.* Teachers or children choose a topic and decide how to set up the data chart with characteristics of the topic listed across the top of the chart and examples or resources listed in the left column.

2. *Draw the chart.* Teachers or children create a skeleton chart on butcher paper for a class project or on a sheet of unlined paper for an individual project. Then they write the characteristics across the top of the chart and the examples or resources down the left column.

3. *Complete the chart.* Children complete the chart by adding words, pictures, sentences, or paragraphs in each cell.

Figure 4   A Data Chart for a Report on the Human Body

Human Body Report Data Chart

Organ _____   Researchers _____
_____

Source of information	What does it look like?	Where is it located?	What job does it do?	Other important information

Children use data charts in a variety of ways. They can make a chart in their reading logs[C], contribute to a class chart during a content-area unit, make a data chart with a classmate as a project after reading a book, or make a data chart as part of a writing project.

Children are actively involved in reading stories or listening to stories read aloud in the Directed Reading-Thinking Activity (DRTA) because they make predictions and then read or listen to confirm their predictions (Stauffer, 1975). DRTA is a useful approach for teaching children how to use the predicting strategy. It helps children think about the structure of stories, and it can be used with both picture-book and chapter-book stories. However, DRTA should not be used with informational books and content-area textbooks, because with nonfiction texts, children do not predict what the book will be about, but rather read to locate main ideas and details. The steps in DRTA are:

1. *Introduce the story.* Before beginning to read, teachers might discuss the topic or show objects and pictures related to the story to draw on prior knowledge or create new experiences. They also show children the cover of the book and ask them to make a prediction about the story using one or more of these questions:

- What do you think a story with a title like this might be about?
- What do you think might happen in this story?
- Does this picture give you any ideas about what might happen in this story?

If necessary, the teacher reads the first paragraph or two to provide more information for children to use in making their predictions. After a brief discussion in which all children commit themselves to one or another of the alternatives presented, the teacher asks these questions:

- Which of these ideas do you think would be the likely one?
- Why do you think that idea is a good one?

2. *Read the beginning of the story.* Teachers have children read the beginning of the story or listen to the beginning of the story read aloud. Then the teacher asks children to confirm or reject their predictions by responding to questions such as:

- What do you think now?
- What do you think will happen next?
- What do you think would happen if . . . ?
- Why do you think that idea is a good one?

Children continue reading or the teacher continues reading aloud, stopping at several key points to repeat this step.

3. *Have children reflect on their predictions.* Children talk about the story, expressing their feelings and making connections to their own lives and experiences with literature. Then children reflect on the predictions they made as they read or listened to the story read aloud, and they provide reasons to support their predictions. Teachers ask these questions to help children think about their predictions:

- What predictions did you make?
- What in the story made you think of that prediction?
- What in the story supports that idea?

DIRECTED READING-THINKING ACTIVITY

The Directed Reading-Thinking Activity is useful only when children are reading or listening to an unfamiliar story so that they can be actively involved in the prediction-confirmation cycle.

GRAND CONVERSATIONS

A grand conversation is a book discussion in which children deepen their comprehension and reflect on their feelings during the responding stage of the reading process (Eeds & Wells, 1989; Peterson & Eeds, 1990). These discussions often last 10 to 30 minutes, and children sit in a circle so that they can see each other. The teacher serves as a facilitator, but the talk is primarily among the children. Traditionally, literature discussions have been "gentle inquisitions"; here the talk changes to dialoguing among children. The steps are:

1. *Read the book.* Children prepare for the grand conversation by reading the book or a part of the book, or by listening to the teacher read it aloud.

2. *Prepare for the grand conversation.* Children may respond to the book in a quickwrite[C] or in a reading log[C] to begin reflecting on the story. This step is optional.

3. *Discuss the book.* Children come together as a class or in a smaller group to discuss the book. The children take turns sharing their ideas about the events in the story, the literary language and favorite quotes, the author's craft, and the illustrations. To start the grand conversation, the teacher asks children to share their personal responses. Possible openers are "What did you think?" and "Who would like to share?" Children may read from their quickwrites or reading log entries. They all participate, and may build on classmates' comments and ask for clarifications. So that everyone gets to participate, many teachers ask children to make no more than two or three comments until everyone has spoken once. Children may refer to the book or read a short piece to make a point, but there is no round-robin reading. Teachers can also participate in the discussion, offering comments and clarifying confusions.

4. *Ask questions.* After children have had a chance to share their reflections, teachers ask questions to focus children's attention on one or two aspects of the story that have been missed. Teachers might focus on illustrations, authors, or an element of story structure. Or, they may ask children to compare this book with a similar book, the film version of the story, or other books by the same author. Pauses may occur, and when children indicate that they have run out of things to say, the grand conversation ends. If children are reading a chapter book, teachers may ask children to make predictions before continuing to read the book.

5. *Write in reading logs.* Teachers may have children write (or write again) in a reading log. This step is optional, but children often have many ideas for reading log entries after participating in the discussion. Also, children may record their predictions before continuing to read chapter books.

Grand conversations are discussions about stories; discussions about informational books and content-area textbooks are called instructional conversations[C], and their focus is slightly different.

GUIDED READING

Teachers use guided reading to read leveled books with a small group of children who read at approximately the same reading level (Clay, 1991). They select a book that children can read at their instructional level, with approximately 90–95% accuracy. Teachers use the reading process and support children's reading and their use of comprehension strategies during guided reading (Depree & Iversen, 1996; Fountas & Pinnell, 1996). The steps in guided reading are:

1. *Choose a book.* Teachers choose an appropriate book, often a leveled book, for the guided reading group. They choose selections that children can read with 90–95% accuracy. Teachers collect copies of the book for each child in the group.

2. *Introduce the book.* Teachers introduce the selection to the small group by showing the cover, reading the title and author's name, and activating children's prior knowledge on a topic related to the book. Teachers often use key vocabulary as they talk about the book, but they don't use vocabulary flash cards to drill children on the new words before reading. They set the purpose for reading and guide children on a "picture walk" through the book, looking at illustrations and talking about them. If children are preparing to read a story, they also make predictions.

3. *Have children read the book.* Teachers often read the first page along with children, and then children continue reading on their own. Teachers provide support with decoding and reading strategies, as needed, to children as they read. Young children mumble-read softly, whereas older children read silently. Teachers take turns listening to individual children as they read and assessing their use of word-identification and comprehension strategies. They help individual children decode unfamiliar words, deal with unfamiliar sentence structures, and comprehend ideas presented in the text whenever assistance is required. Teachers invite children to read short texts a second or third time while they wait for other children in the group to finish reading.

4. *Provide opportunities for children to respond to the book.* Teachers encourage children to talk about the book in a grand conversation[C], and children make comments, ask questions, and make connections between the book and their own lives, the world around them, and other books they have read.

5. *Involve children in exploring activities.* Teachers use the book as the basis for minilessons[C] and other exploring activities, including:

- teaching a phonics skill or a comprehension strategy
- examining a genre or an element of story structure
- reviewing vocabulary words

6. *Provide additional opportunities for independent reading.* Teachers place the book in a book basket or in the classroom library so that children can reread the book independently during reading workshop or Sustained Silent Reading.

Guided reading is a valuable instructional procedure because children have opportunities to read books at their instructional level and to receive explicit instruction on decoding skills and comprehension strategies in a small-group setting.

INDIVIDUAL BOOKS AND REPORTS

Children write individual reports and informational books much like they write collaborative books and reports[C]: They design research questions, gather information to answer the questions, and compile what they have learned in a report. Writing individual reports demands two significant changes: First, children narrow their topics, and second, they assume the entire responsibility for writing the report (Tompkins, 2000). The steps are:

1. *Choose and narrow topics.* Children choose topics for informational books and reports from a content area, hobbies, or other interests. After choosing a general topic, such as cats or the solar system, they need to narrow the topic so that it is manageable.

The broad topic of cats might be narrowed to pet cats or tigers, and the solar system to one planet.

2. *Design research questions.* Children design research questions by brainstorming a list of questions in a learning log[C]. They review the list, combine some questions, delete others, and finally arrive at four to six questions that are worthy of answering. Once they begin their research, they may add new questions and delete others if they reach a dead end.

3. *Gather and organize information.* During the prewriting step, children use clusters[C] or data charts[C] to gather and organize information. Data charts, with their rectangular spaces for writing information, serve as a transition for upper-grade children between clusters and note cards.

4. *Write the reports.* Children use the writing process to write their reports. They write a rough draft from the information they have gathered. Each research question can provide the basis for a paragraph, a page, or a chapter in the report. Teachers work with children to revise and edit their books or reports. Children meet in writing groups to share their rough drafts and make revisions based on the feedback they receive from their classmates. After they revise, children use an editing checklist to proofread their reports and identify and correct mechanical errors.

5. *Publish the books.* Children recopy their reports in book form and add covers, a title page, a table of contents, and bibliographic information. Research reports can also be published in several other ways; for example, as a video presentation, a series of illustrated charts or dioramas, or a dramatization.

Children often write informational books and reports as projects during literature focus units, writing workshop, and content-area units. Through these activities, children have opportunities to extend and personalize their learning and to use the writing process.

INSTRUCTIONAL CONVERSATIONS

Instructional conversations are like grand conversations[C] except that they are about nonfiction topics, not about literature. These conversations provide opportunities for children to talk about the main ideas they are learning in content-area units and enhance both children's conceptual learning and their linguistic abilities (Goldenberg, 1992/1993). Like grand conversations, these discussions are interesting and engaging, and children are active participants, building on classmates' ideas with their own comments. Teachers are participants in the conversation, making comments much like the children do, but they also assume the teacher role to clarify misconceptions, ask questions, and provide instruction. The steps in an instructional conversation are:

1. *Choose a focus.* Teachers choose a focus for the instructional conversation that is related to the goals of a content-area unit or the main ideas presented in an informational book.

2. *Prepare for the instructional conversation.* Teachers present background knowledge in preparation for the discussion, or children may read an informational book to learn about the topic.

3. *Begin the conversation.* Children come together as a class or in a smaller group for the instructional conversation. Teachers begin with the focus they have identified. They make a statement or ask a question, and then children respond, sharing information they have learned, asking questions, and offering opinions. Teachers assist children as they make comments, helping them extend their ideas and use appropriate vocabulary. In addition, teachers write children's comments in a list or on a cluster[C] or other graphic organizer.

4. *Expand the conversation.* After children have discussed the teacher's focus, the conversation continues and moves in other directions. Children may share other interesting information, make personal connections to information they are learning, or ask questions. Teachers may also want to have children do a read-around[C] and share important ideas from their reading.

5. *Write in learning logs.* Children write and draw in learning logs[C] and record the important ideas discussed during the instructional conversation. Children may refer to the brainstormed list or cluster that the teacher made during the first part of the discussion.

Instructional conversations are useful for helping children grapple with important ideas they are learning in social studies, science, and other content areas. When children are discussing literature, they should use grand conversations.

INTERACTIVE WRITING

Children and the teacher create a message and "share the pen" as they write the message on chart paper in interactive writing (Button, Johnson, & Furgerson, 1996). This instructional strategy is designed for emergent and beginning writers. The message is composed by the group, and the teacher guides children as they write the message word by word on chart paper. Children take turns writing known letters and familiar words, adding punctuation marks, and marking spaces between words. All children participate in creating and writing the message—usually a sentence in length—on chart paper, and they also write the message on small white boards. Figure 5 shows a first-grade class's prediction about what will happen to Rosie written before reading *Rosie's Walk* (Hutchins, 1968). The dotted letters represent letters that the teacher wrote, and the rectangles indicate that correction tape was used to correct an error. Interactive writing is used to show children how writing works and how to construct words using their knowledge of sound-symbol correspondences and spelling patterns (Fountas & Pinnell, 1996). The steps are:

1. *Collect materials.* Teachers collect chart paper, colored marking pens, white correction tape, an alphabet chart, magnetic letters, and a pointer. For individual children's writing, they also collect small white boards, dry-erase pens, and erasers.

Figure 5 **First Graders' Prediction About *Rosie's Walk* Written Interactively**

> We think the fox will catch. Rosie the hen.

2. *Set a purpose for the activity.* Teachers present a stimulus activity or set a purpose for the interactive writing activity. Often they read or reread a trade book as a stimulus, but children also write daily news, compose a letter, or brainstorm information they are learning in a social studies or science unit.

3. *Choose a sentence to write.* Teachers negotiate the message—often a sentence or two—with children. Children repeat the sentence several times and segment it into words. They also count the number of words in the sentence. The teacher also helps the children remember the message as it is written.

4. *Pass out writing supplies.* Teachers pass out the individual white boards, dry-erase pens, and erasers for children to use to write the text individually as it is written on chart paper. Teachers periodically ask children to hold up their white boards so they can see what the children are writing.

5. *Write the message.* Children and the teacher write the first sentence word by word. Before writing the first word, the teacher and children slowly pronounce the word, "pulling" it from their mouths or "stretching" it out. Then children take turns writing the letters in the first word. The teacher chooses children to write each sound or the entire word, depending on children's knowledge of phonics and spelling. Teachers often have children use a pen of one color for the letters they write, and they use another color to write the parts of words that children don't know how to spell. In that way, teachers can keep track of how much writing children are able to do. Teachers keep a poster with the upper- and lowercase letters of the alphabet to refer to when children are unsure how to form a letter, and they use white correction tape when children write a letter incorrectly or write the wrong letter. After writing each word, one student serves as the "spacer"; this student uses his or her hand to mark the space between words and sentences. Teachers have children reread the sentence from the beginning each time a new word is completed. When appropriate, teachers call children's attention to capital letters, punctuation marks, and other conventions of print. This procedure is repeated to write additional sentences to complete the message. When teachers use interactive writing to write a class book, this activity can take several days or a week or longer to complete.

6. *Display the interactive writing.* After the writing is completed, teachers display it in the classroom and have children reread the text using shared reading[C] or independent reading. Children often reread interactive charts when they "read the room." They may also add artwork to "finish" the chart.

When children begin interactive writing in kindergarten, they write letters to represent the beginning sounds in words and write familiar words such as *the, a,* and *is.* The first letters that children write are often the letters in their own names. As children learn more about sound-symbol correspondences and spelling patterns, they do more of the writing. Once children are writing words fluently, they can continue to do interactive writing as they work in small groups. Each student in the group uses a particular color pen and takes turns writing letters, letter clusters, and words. They also get used to using the white correction tape to correct poorly formed letters and misspelled words.

K-W-L CHARTS

Teachers use K-W-L charts during content-area units (Ogle, 1986, 1989). The letters *K, W,* and *L* stand for What We Know, What We Want to Learn (What We Wonder), and What We Learned. The format of a K-W-L chart is shown in Figure 6. Teachers introduce a K-W-L chart at the beginning of a content-area unit and use the chart to activate children's background knowledge and identify interesting questions. The

Figure 6 A K-W-L Chart

K What We Know	W What We Want to Learn	L What We Learned

questions often stimulate children's interest in the topic. At the end of the unit, children complete the last section of the chart, listing what they have learned. This instructional procedure helps children to combine new information with prior knowledge and develop their vocabularies. The steps are:

1. *Post a K-W-L chart.* Teachers post a large sheet of butcher paper on a classroom wall, dividing it into three columns and labeling the columns K (What We Know), W (What We Want to Learn or What We Wonder), and L (What We Learned).

2. *Complete the K column.* At the beginning of the unit, teachers ask children to brainstorm what they know about the topic. Teachers write this information in phrases or complete sentences in the K (What We Know) column. Children also suggest questions they would like to explore during the unit.

3. Complete the W column. Teachers write the questions that children suggest in the W (What We Want to Learn or What We Wonder) column. Teachers continue to add questions to the W column throughout the unit.

4. Complete the L column. At the end of the unit, children brainstorm a list of information they have learned to complete the L column of the chart. It is important to note that children do not try to answer each question listed in the W column, although the questions in that column may trigger some information that they have learned. Teachers write the information that children suggest in the L column.

LANGUAGE EXPERIENCE APPROACH

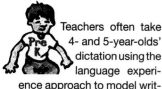

Teachers often take 4- and 5-year-olds' dictation using the language experience approach to model writing and emphasize that speech can be written down.

Children dictate words and sentences about their experiences in the language experience approach (LEA), and teachers write the dictation for the children (Ashton-Warner, 1965; Lee & Allen, 1963; Stauffer, 1970). The text they develop together becomes the reading material. Because the language comes from the children themselves and because the content is based on their experiences, children are usually able to read the text easily. A kindergartner's LEA writing is shown in Figure 7. The child drew this picture of the Gingerbread Baby and dictated the sentence after listening to the teacher read Jan Brett's *Gingerbread Baby* (1999), a new version of "The Gingerbread Man" story. LEA is a type of shared writing, and reading and writing are integrated because children are actively involved in reading what they have written. The steps are:

1. Provide an experience. The experience serves as the stimulus for the writing. For group writing, it can be an experience shared in school, a book read aloud, a field trip, or some other experience that all children are familiar with, such as having a pet

Figure 7   **A Kindergartner's LEA Writing Sample About *Gingerbread Baby***

The Gingerbread Baby runs and runs into the gingerbread house.

or playing in the snow. For individual writing, the stimulus can be any experience that is important for the particular child.

2. *Talk about the experience.* The teacher and children talk about the experience to generate words, and they review the experience so that the children's dictation will be more interesting and complete. Teachers often begin with an open-ended question, such as "What are you going to write about?" As children talk about their experiences, they clarify and organize ideas, use more specific vocabulary, and extend their understanding.

3. *Record the child's dictation.* Texts for individual children are written on sheets of writing paper or in small booklets, and group texts are written on chart paper. Teachers print neatly, spell words correctly, and preserve children's language as much as possible. It is a great temptation to change the child's language to the teacher's own, in either word choice or grammar, but editing should be kept to a minimum so that children do not get the impression that their language is inferior or inadequate. For individual texts, teachers continue to take the child's dictation and write until the child finishes or hesitates. If the child hesitates, the teacher rereads what has been written and encourages the child to continue. For group texts, children take turns dictating sentences, and the teacher rereads each sentence after writing it down.

4. *Read the text aloud, pointing to each word.* This reading reminds children of the content of the text and demonstrates how to read it aloud with appropriate intonation. Then children join in the reading. After reading group texts together, individual children can take turns rereading. Group texts can also be duplicated so each child has a copy to read independently.

5. *Extend the experience.* Teachers encourage children to extend the experience through one or more of these activities:

- Add illustrations to their writing.
- Read their texts to classmates from the author's chair.
- Take their texts home to share with family members.
- Add this text to a collection of their writings.
- Pick out words from their texts that they would like to learn to read.

The language experience approach is an effective way to help children emerge into reading. Even children who have not been successful with other types of reading activities can read what they have dictated. There is a drawback, however: Teachers provide a "perfect" model when they take children's dictation—they write neatly and spell words correctly. After language experience activities, some young children are not eager to do their own writing, because they prefer their teacher's "perfect" writing to their own childlike writing. To avoid this problem, young children should be doing their own writing in personal journals, at the writing center, and through other writing activities as well as participating in language experience activities. In this way, they will learn that sometimes they do their own writing, but at other times, the teacher takes their dictation.

LEARNING LOGS

Children write in learning logs as part of content-area units. Learning logs, like other types of journals, are booklets of paper in which children record information they are learning, write questions and reflections about their learning, and make charts, diagrams, and clusters[C] (Tompkins, 2000). The steps are:

1. *Prepare learning logs.* Children make learning logs at the beginning of a unit. They typically staple together sheets of lined writing paper and plain paper for drawing diagrams and add construction paper covers.

2. Write entries. Children make entries in their learning logs as part of content-area unit activities. They take notes, draw diagrams, do quickwrites[C], and make clusters.

3. Monitor children's entries. Teachers read children's entries, and in their responses they answer children's questions and clarify confusions.

Children's writing is impromptu in learning logs, and the emphasis is on using writing as a learning tool rather than creating polished products. Even so, children should work carefully and spell words found on the word wall[C] correctly.

MAKING WORDS

Making words is an activity in which children arrange letter cards to spell words. As they make words using the letter cards, they review and practice phonics and spelling concepts (Cunningham & Cunningham, 1992; Gunning, 1995). Teachers choose key words that exemplify particular phonics or spelling patterns for children to practice from books children are reading or from a content-area unit. Then they prepare a set of letter cards that small groups of children or individual children can use to spell words. The teacher leads children as they create a number of smaller words using the letters. A making words activity that two first graders completed using the letters in the word *sandwich* is shown in Figure 8. The steps in making words are:

1. Make letter cards. Teachers make a set of small letter cards (1- to 2-inch-square cards) for children to use in word-making activities. For high-frequency letters (vowels, *s*, *t*, and *r*) make three or four times as many letter cards as there are children in the class. For less frequently used letters, make one or two times as many letter cards as there are children in the class. Print the lowercase letter form on one side of the letter cards and the uppercase form on the other side. Package cards with each letter separately in small boxes, plastic trays, or plastic bags. Teachers may also want to make a set of large letter cards (3- to 6-inch-square cards) to display in a pocket chart or on the chalkboard during the activity.

2. Choose a word for the activity. Teachers choose a word to use in the word-making activity, but they do not tell children what the word is. The word is often taken from a word wall[C] in the classroom and relates to a book children are reading or to a content-area unit. The word should be long enough and have enough vowels that children can easily make at least 8 or 10 words using the letters.

3. Distribute letter cards. A child distributes the needed letter cards to individual children or to small groups of children, and children arrange the letter cards on one side of their desks. It is crucial that children have letter cards to manipulate; it is not sufficient to write the letters on the chalkboard, because children can spell more words using the cards, and some children need the tactile activity to be able to spell the words.

4. Make words using the cards. Children manipulate the letter cards to spell words that the teacher pronounces. For younger children, the teacher can identify the letters needed to spell the word and then the children arrange the letters in the right order. As children spell words, the teacher makes a chart and records the words that children spell correctly using the letter cards on the chart. Teachers can also use the large letter cards to spell words along with the children or to help children correctly spell a tricky word.

5. Repeat the activity at a center. After completing the word-making activity, teachers put the chart the class created and several sets of letter cards in a literacy center so that children can repeat the activity. As children make words, they write them on a chart. Children can refer to the chart, if needed.

Figure 8 First Graders' Making Words Activity
Using the Word *Sandwich*

Making Words Activity

Name __Jesse + Sammy__

Letters: a c d h i n s w

1	2	3
is his	as has	an can
4	5	6
a an and	hand sand	in win chin
7	8	9
dish wish	dash wash	was saw

The big word is:

sandwich

Children can also use letter cards to practice spelling rimes. For example, to practice the *-ake* rime, children use the *b, c, f, h, l, m, r, s, t,* and *w* letter cards and the *-ake* rime card. Using the cards, children make these words: *bake, shake, cake, make, flake, rake, lake, take,* and *wake.* Teachers often add several other letter cards, such as *d, p,* and *v,* to make the activity more challenging.

MINILESSONS

Teachers teach minilessons on literacy procedures, concepts, strategies, and skills (Atwell, 1987). These lessons are brief, often lasting only 15 to 30 minutes. Minilessons are usually taught as part of the reading process during the exploring stage, or as part of the writing process during the editing stage. The steps in conducting a minilesson are:

1. *Introduce the topic.* Teachers begin the minilesson by introducing the procedure, concept, strategy, or skill. They name the topic and provide essential information about it.

2. *Share examples of the topic.* Teachers share examples taken from books children are reading or children's own writing projects.

3. *Provide information about the topic.* Teachers provide additional information about the procedure, concept, strategy, or skill and make connections to children's reading or writing.

4. *Provide opportunities for guided practice.* Teachers involve children in guided practice activities so that children can bring together the information and the examples introduced earlier.

5. *Assess children's learning.* Teachers check that children understand the procedure, concept, strategy, or skill well enough to apply it independently. They often monitor children during guided practice or review children's work, but sometimes teachers administer a quiz or other more formal assessment.

Teachers present minilessons to the whole class or to small groups to introduce or review a topic. The best time to teach a minilesson is when children will have immediate opportunities to apply what they are learning. Afterwards, it is crucial that teachers provide additional opportunities for children to use the procedures, concepts, strategies, or skills they are learning in meaningful ways and in authentic literacy activities.

OPEN-MIND PORTRAITS

To help children think more deeply about a character and reflect on story events from the character's viewpoint, children draw an open-mind portrait of the character. These portraits have two parts: The face of the character is on one page, and the mind of the character is on the second page. A second grader's open-mind portrait of the little piggy in *Hog-eye* (Meddaugh, 1995), is shown in Figure 9. The steps are:

1. *Make a portrait of a character.* Children draw and color a large portrait of the head and neck of a character in a book they are reading.

2. *Cut out the portrait and open-mind pages.* Children cut out the character's portrait and trace around the character's head on one or more sheets of paper. Children may make open-mind portraits with one "mind" page or with several pages to show what the character is thinking at important points in the story or in each chapter of a chapter book. Then they cut out the mind pages and attach the portrait and mind pages with a brad or staple to a sheet of heavy construction paper or cardboard. The portrait goes on top. It is important that children place the brad or staple at the top of the portrait so that there will be space to write and draw on the mind pages.

Figure 9   An Open-Mind Portrait of the Little Piggy in *Hog-eye*

3. *Design the mind pages.* Have children lift the portrait and draw and write about the character, from the character's viewpoint, on the mind pages. Children focus on what the character is thinking and doing at various points in the story.

4. *Share completed open-mind portraits.* Have children share their portraits with classmates and talk about the words and pictures they chose to include in the mind of the character.

QUICKWRITING

Children use quickwriting as they write in response to literature and for other types of impromptu writing. Quickwriting, originally called "freewriting" and popularized by Peter Elbow (1973), is a way to help children focus on content rather than on mechanics. Children reflect on what they know about a topic, ramble on paper, generate words and ideas, and make connections among the ideas. Young children often do quickwrites in which they draw pictures and add labels. Some children do a mixture of writing and drawing. Figure 10 presents a first grader's quickwrite made after reading *Sam, Bangs, and Moonshine* (Ness, 1966). In this Caldecott Medal story, a girl named Sam tells "moonshine" about a make-believe baby kangaroo to her friend

If you lying you wel git inBig Chruvol And you wel hrt yor frins.

Thomas; the results are almost disastrous. In the quickwrite, the child writes, "If you lie, you will get in big trouble and you will hurt your friends." The steps are:

1. *Choose a topic.* Children identify a topic for their quickwrite and write it at the top of the paper.

2. *Write or draw about the topic.* Children write sentences or paragraphs and/or draw a picture related to the topic. Children should focus on interesting ideas, make connections between the topic and their own lives, and reflect on their reading or learning.

3. *Share quickwrites.* After children write, they usually share their quickwrites in small groups or during grand conversations[C], and then one student in each group shares with the class.

Children do quickwrites for a variety of purposes in several of the stages of the reading process, including:

- to activate background knowledge before reading
- as an entry for reading logs[C]
- to define or explain a word on the word wall[C]
- to analyze the theme of a story
- to describe a favorite character
- to compare book and film versions of a story
- to discuss a favorite book during an author study
- to discuss the project the student is creating

Children also do similar quickwrites during content-area units.

QUILTS

Children make squares out of construction paper and arrange them to make a quilt to respond to a book they have read or to present information they have learned in a content-

area unit. Quilts about stories are designed to highlight the theme, reinforce symbolism, and recall favorite sentences in a book children have read. A square from a quilt about *Fly Away Home* (Bunting, 1991), a story about a homeless boy and his dad who live at an airport, is shown in Figure 11. The third graders created a modified "wedding ring" quilt pattern for their quilt. The steps in making a quilt are:

1. *Design the quilt square.* Teachers and children choose a design for the quilt square that is appropriate for the story—its theme, characters, or setting—or reflects the topic of the content-area unit. Children can choose a quilt design or create their own design that captures an important dimension of the story or unit. They also choose colors for each shape in the quilt square.

2. *Make the squares.* Children each make a square and add an important piece of information from the unit or a favorite sentence from the story around the outside of the quilt square or in a designated section of the square.

3. *Assemble the quilt.* Teachers tape the squares together and back the quilt with butcher paper, or staple the squares side by side on a large bulletin board.

Quilts can be made of cloth, too. As an end-of-the-year project or to celebrate Book Week, teachers cut out squares of light-colored cloth and have children use fabric markers to draw pictures of their favorite stories and add the titles and authors. Then teachers or other adults sew the squares together, add a border, and complete the quilt.

READ-AROUNDS

Read-arounds are celebrations of stories and other books, usually performed at the end of literature focus units or literature circles. Children choose favorite passages from a book to read aloud. Read-arounds are sometimes called "Quaker readings" because of their "unprogrammed" format. The steps are:

1. *Choose a favorite passage.* Children skim a book they have already read to locate one or more favorite passages (a sentence or paragraph) and mark the passages with bookmarks.

2. *Practice reading the passage.* Children rehearse reading the passages so that they can read them fluently.

3. *Read the passages.* Teachers begin the read-around by asking a student to read a favorite passage aloud to the class. Then there is a pause and another student begins to read. Teachers don't call on children; any student may begin reading when no one else is reading. The passages can be read in any order, and more than one student can read the same passage. Teachers, too, read their favorite passages. The read-around continues until everyone who wants to has read.

Children like participating in read-arounds because the featured book is like a good friend. They enjoy listening to classmates read favorite passages and noticing literary language. They seem to move back and forth through the story, remembering events and reliving the story.

READERS THEATRE

Readers theatre is a dramatic production of a script by a group of readers (Martinez, Roser, & Strecker, 1998/1999). Each child assumes a role and reads the character's lines in the script. Readers interpret a story without using much action. They may stand or sit, but they must carry the whole communication of the plot, characterization, mood, and theme by using their voices, gestures, and facial expressions. Readers theatre avoids many of the restrictions inherent in theatrical productions: Children do not memorize their parts; elaborate props, costumes, and backdrops are not needed; and long, tedious hours are not spent rehearsing. For readers theatre presentations, children can read scripts in trade books and textbooks, or they can create their own scripts. The steps are:

1. *Select a script.* Children and the teacher select a script and then read and discuss it as they would any story.

2. *Choose parts.* Children volunteer to read each part and mark their lines on the script. They also decide how to use their voice, gestures, and facial expressions to interpret the character they are reading.

3. *Rehearse the production.* They read the script several times, striving for accurate pronunciation, voice projection, and appropriate inflections. Less rehearsal is needed for an informal, in-class presentation than for a more formal production; nevertheless, interpretations should always be developed as fully as possible.

4. *Stage the production.* Readers theatre can be presented on a stage or in a corner of the classroom. Children stand or sit in a row and read their lines in the script. They stay in position through the production or enter and leave according to the characters' appearances "onstage." If readers are sitting, they may stand to read their lines; if they are standing, they may step forward to read. The emphasis is not on production quality; rather, it is on the interpretive quality of the readers' voices and expressions. Costumes and props are unnecessary; however, adding a few small props enhances interest and enjoyment as long as they do not interfere with the interpretive quality of the reading.

Children in the primary grades should listen to the teacher read several books aloud every day. So many excellent picture books are available for children today that it is easy to choose award-winning stories to share as part of literature focus units and stories, poems, and informational books to read in connection with thematic units. Teachers do more than just pick up a book and begin reading; to make the most of the experience, teachers use the reading process and incorporate before-, during-, and after-reading activities into their reading aloud experience. The steps in reading aloud to children are:

1. *Introduce the book.* Teachers introduce the book by showing the cover and reading the title and author's name. They activate or build background knowledge on a topic related to the book often by sharing an experience, asking questions, or showing realia. When reading a story, teachers ask children to make predictions.

2. *Do a picture walk.* Whenever they are preparing to read a picture book aloud, teachers do a picture walk, looking at the illustrations on each page and talking about the book.

3. *Read the book.* Teachers read the book aloud, showing the pictures on each page as they read. They read with expression to maintain children's interest in the story. They judge their pacing of reading and showing pictures to satisfy children's interest, and they answer children's questions without unnecessarily prolonging the experience.

4. *Have children respond to the book.* If the book is a story or a poem, children participate in a grand conversation[C] to talk about the book, and if the book is an informational book, children participate in an instructional conversation[C]. They also draw pictures, make interactive writing[C] charts, and write in reading logs[C] to respond to the book.

Sometimes teachers end the reading aloud experience after the fourth step, but at other times, they use the book for exploring and applying activities as part of a literature focus unit or thematic unit. The children can listen to the teacher read the book again or read the book themselves. Or, the teacher might use the book to teach children about genre or story structure or for another minilesson[C]. Children can also use the book for writing activities, too.

READING LOGS

Children keep reading logs to write their reactions and opinions about books they are reading or listening to the teacher read aloud. Children also add lists of words from the word wall[C], diagrams about story elements, and information about authors and genres (Tompkins, 2000). For a chapter book, children write after reading every chapter or two. The steps are:

1. *Prepare the reading logs.* Children make reading logs by stapling paper into booklets. They write the title of the book on the cover and add an appropriate illustration.

2. *Write entries.* Children write their reactions and reflections about the book or chapter they have read or listened to the teacher read aloud. Instead of summarizing the book, children relate the book to their own lives or to other literature they have read. Children may also list interesting or unfamiliar words, jot down quotable quotes, and take notes about characters, plot, or other story elements. The primary purpose of reading logs, though, is for children to think about the book, deepen their understanding of it, and connect literature to their lives.

3. *Read and respond to the entries.* Teachers read children's entries and write comments back to children about their interpretations and reflections. Some teachers read

and respond to all entries, and other teachers, because of time limitations, read and respond selectively. Because children's writing in reading logs is informal, teachers do not expect them to spell every word correctly, but it is not unreasonable to expect children to spell characters' names and other words on the word wall correctly.

REPEATED READINGS

Teachers often encourage children to reread the featured book several times during literature focus units and to reread favorite books during reading workshop. Children become more fluent readers when they reread books, and each time they reread a book, their comprehension deepens. Jay Samuels (1979) has developed an instructional procedure to help children increase their reading fluency and accuracy through rereading. The steps in the individualized procedure are:

1. *Conduct a pretest.* The child chooses a textbook or trade book and reads a passage from it aloud while the teacher records the reading time and any miscues. The teacher clarifies any miscues so that the child won't practice reading the error and reinforce a problem.

2. *Practice rereading the passage.* The child practices rereading the passage orally or silently several times.

3. *Conduct a posttest.* The child rereads the passage while the teacher again records the reading time and notes any miscues.

4. *Compare pre- and posttest results.* The child compares his or her reading time and accuracy between the first and last readings. Then the child prepares a graph to document his or her growth between the first and last readings.

This procedure is useful for children who are slow and inaccurate readers. When teachers monitor children's readings on a regular basis, they become more careful readers. Making a graph to document growth is an important component of the procedure, because the graph provides concrete evidence of the child's growth.

The repeated readings activity is recommended for English learners who need additional practice to develop reading fluency.

RUNNING RECORDS

Teachers observe individual children as they read aloud and take running records of children's reading to assess their reading fluency (Clay, 1985). Through a running record, teachers calculate the percentage of words the child reads correctly and then analyze the miscues or errors. Running records are easy to take, although teachers need some practice before they are comfortable with the procedure. Teachers make a check mark on a sheet of paper as the child reads each word correctly. They use other marks to indicate words that the child doesn't know or pronounces incorrectly. The steps in conducting a reading record are:

1. *Choose a book.* Teachers have the child choose an excerpt 100 to 200 words in length from a book he or she is reading. For beginning readers, the text may be shorter.

2. *Take the running record.* As the child reads the excerpt aloud, the teacher makes a record of the words read correctly as well as those read incorrectly. The teacher makes check marks on a sheet of blank paper for each word read correctly. Errors are marked in these ways:

- If the child reads a word incorrectly, the teacher writes the incorrect word and the correct word under it:

  <u>gentle</u>
  generally

- If the child self-corrects an error, the teacher writes *SC* (for self-correction) following the incorrect word:

  bathSC
  ———
  bathe

- If the child attempts to pronounce a word, the teacher records each attempt and adds the correct text underneath:

  com-com-company
  ——————————
      companion

- If the child skips a word, the teacher marks the error with a dash:

    —
  ———
  own

- If the child says words that are not in the text, the teacher writes an insertion symbol ^ (caret) and records the inserted words:

  where he
  ————
     ^

- If the child can't identify a word and the teacher pronounces the word for him or her, the teacher writes *T:*

    T
  ———
  routine

- If the child repeats a word or phrase, the repetition is not scored as an error, but the teacher notes the repetition by drawing a line under the word or phrase (marked in the running record with check marks) that was repeated:

    √ √ √
  ————

A sample running record is shown in Chapter 3.

3. *Calculate the percentage of miscues.* Teachers calculate the percentage of miscues or oral reading errors. When the child makes 5% or fewer errors, the book is considered to be at the independent level for that child. When there are 6–10% errors, the book is at the instructional level, and when there are more than 10% errors, the book is too difficult—the frustration level.

4. *Analyze the miscues.* Teachers look for patterns in the miscues to determine how the child is growing as a reader and what skills and strategies the student should be taught. A miscue analysis of a running record is also shown in Chapter 3.

Many teachers conduct running records with all their children at the beginning of the school year and at the end of grading periods. In addition, teachers do running records more often during guided reading groups and with children who are not making expected progress in reading in order to track their growth as readers and make instructional decisions.

When children are reading with a buddy, they can use the say something strategy to stop and talk about their reading. By sharing their responses, they will improve their comprehension (Harste, Woodward, & Burke, 1984). Children of all ages enjoy reading

SAY
SOMETHING

with a buddy and using the say something strategy to clarify misconceptions, make predictions, and share reactions. The steps are:

1. *Divide children into pairs for reading.* Teachers divide children into pairs for buddy reading. Children can read stories, informational books, or basal reader selections.

2. *Read one page.* Children read a page of text before stopping to talk. They can read silently or mumble-read, or one student can read to the other. The type of reading depends on the level of the book and the children participating in the activity.

3. *Briefly talk about the page.* After they finish reading the page, children stop to talk. They each make a comment or ask a question before continuing to read. Sometimes the discussion continues longer because of a special interest or a question, but after a brief discussion, children read the next page and then stop to talk again. For content-area textbooks, children often stop after reading a single paragraph to talk about their reading because the text is often densely written and needs clarification.

Teachers often use a book they are reading aloud to the class to model the procedure. After they read a page, they make a comment to the class and one student is chosen to make a response. With this practice, children are better able to use the say something strategy independently.

SHARED READING

Teachers use shared reading to read books and other texts with children who could not read them independently (Holdaway, 1979). Teachers use enlarged texts, including big books, poems written on charts, language experience[C] stories, and interactive writing[C] charts, so that both small groups and whole-class groups can see the text and read along with the teacher. Teachers focus on concepts about print, including left-to-right direction of print, words, letters, and punctuation marks. Teachers model what fluent readers do as they involve children in enjoyable reading activities (Depree & Iversen, 1996; Fountas & Pinnell, 1996). The steps in shared reading are:

1. *Introduce the text.* Teachers talk about the book or other text by activating or building background knowledge on a topic related to the book, and by reading the title and the author's name aloud. When children are preparing to read a story, they usually make predictions about what might happen.

2. *Read the text aloud.* Teachers use a pointer (a dowel rod with a pencil eraser on the end) to track the text as they read, and they invite children to join in the reading if the text is predictable or repetitive. During this first reading, teachers usually stop several times at key points in the text to have children make more predictions or to highlight key vocabulary, but they are careful not to draw the experience out so long that children lose interest.

3. *Have a grand conversation*[C]. Teachers and children talk about the text after reading. They make comments, ask questions to clarify understanding, make connections, and extend their understanding.

4. *Have children write about the text.* Sometimes teachers work with children to write a response on chart paper using interactive writing, or children write individually in reading logs[C].

5. *Reread the text.* As teachers reread the text, children take turns using the pointer to track the reading and join in reading familiar and predictable words. During each rereading, children should be able to read more of the text. Also, teachers take advantage of opportunities to teach and practice phonics skills and comprehension strategies as they reread the text.

6. *Have children read independently.* After children become familiar with the text, teachers distribute individual copies of the book or other text for children to read independently.

Third- and fourth-grade teachers also use shared reading when reading chapter books with older students who could not read the books independently, but they read the book only once. The teacher reads aloud and children follow along in individual copies of the book using the steps listed here. Children who are fluent readers can also take turns doing the reading.

STORY BOARDS

Story boards are cards to which the illustrations and text (or only the illustrations) from a picture book have been attached. Teachers make story boards by cutting apart two copies of a picture book. Children use story boards to sequence the events of a story, to examine a picture book's illustrations, and for other exploring activities. The steps in making story boards are:

1. *Collect two copies of a book.* It is preferable to use paperback copies of the books because they are less expensive to purchase. In a few picture books, all the illustrations are on either the right-hand or left-hand pages, so only one copy of these books is needed for illustration-only story boards. In Chris Van Allsburg's *The Mysteries of Harris Burdick* (1984), for example, all illustrations are on the right-hand pages.

2. *Cut the books apart.* Teachers remove the covers and separate the pages. Next, they trim the edges of the cut-apart sides.

3. *Attach the pages to pieces of cardboard.* Teachers glue each page or double-page spread to a piece of cardboard, making sure that each page in the story is included.

4. *Laminate the cards.* Teachers laminate the cards so that they can withstand use by children.

5. *Use the cards in sequencing activities.* Teachers pass out the cards in random order to children. Children read their pages, think about the sequence of events in the story, and arrange themselves in a line around the classroom to sequence the story events.

Story boards can also be used when there are only a few copies of a picture book so that children can identify words for the word wall[C], notice literary language, and examine the illustrations.

STORY MAPS

Teachers and children make a variety of diagrams and charts to examine the structure of stories they are reading (Bromley, 1991; Claggett, 1992; Macon, Bewell, & Vogt, 1991). Six types of story maps are:

- Beginning-middle-end diagrams to examine the plot of a story
- Character clusters to examine the traits of a main character (Macon et al., 1991)
- Venn diagrams to compare book and film versions of a story or for other comparisons
- Plot profiles to chart the tension in each chapter of a chapter book (Johnson & Louis, 1987)

- Sociograms to explore the relationships among characters (Johnson & Louis, 1987)
- Clusters[C] to probe the theme, setting, genre, author's style, or other dimensions of the story

"Skeleton" diagrams for these six types of story maps are presented in Figure 12. Children use information from the story they are reading and add words, sentences, and illustrations to complete the story maps.

The steps in using story maps are:

1. *Choose a story map.* Teachers choose the type of story map that is appropriate for the story and the purpose of the lesson.

Figure 12   Six Types of Story Maps

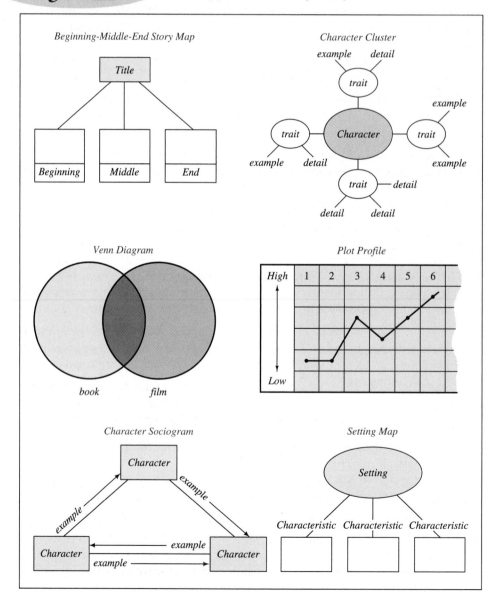

2. *Draw the diagram.* Teachers make a "skeleton" diagram on the chalkboard or on a chart.

3. *Complete the diagram.* Teachers work with children to complete the diagram. Children usually work together as a class the first time they do a story map. The next few times they do the story map, they work in small groups. After this experience, children make maps individually. For most story maps, children use a combination of words and pictures.

Children often make story maps as an exploring activity, but they can also choose to make a story map as a project. There are many other types of story maps children can make, and teachers can invent their own maps to help children visualize other structures and relationships in stories.

WORD SORTS

Children examine words and their meanings, sound-symbol correspondences, or spelling patterns by using word sorts (Morris, 1982; Schlagal & Schlagal, 1992). Children sort a group of words (or objects or pictures) according to one of these characteristics:

- Conceptual relationships, such as words related to one of several characters in a story or words related to the inner or outer planets in the solar system
- Rhyming words, such as words that rhyme with *ball, hit,* or *flake*
- Consonant sounds, such as pictures and objects of words beginning with *r* or *l*
- Sound-symbol relationships, such as words in which the final *y* sounds like long *i* (*cry*) and words in which the final *y* sounds like long *e* (*baby*)
- Spelling patterns and rules, such as long-*e* words with various spelling patterns (*sea, greet, be, Pete*)
- Number of syllables, such as *pig, happy, afternoon,* and *television*
- Syllable division rules, using words such as *mag-net, can-dle, ti-ger, stor-y,* and *po-et*

Sometimes teachers determine the categories for the sort and at other times children choose the categories. When teachers determine the categories, it is a closed word sort, and when children choose them, it is an open word sort (Bear, Invernizzi, Templeton, & Johnston, 2000). The steps in this instructional strategy are:

1. *Compile a list of words.* Teachers compile a list of 10 to 20 words that exemplify a particular pattern and write the words on small cards. With younger children, small objects or picture cards can be used.

2. *Determine the categories for the sort.* Teachers determine the categories for the sort and tell children, or children read the words and determine the categories themselves. They may work individually or together in small groups or as a class.

3. *Sort the cards.* Children sort the words into two or more categories and write the sorted words on a chart or glue the sorted word cards onto a piece of chart paper.

4. *Share the completed sorts.* Children share their word sort with classmates, emphasizing the categories they used for their sort.

Many of the words chosen for word sorts should come from high-frequency word walls[C], books children are reading, or content-area units. Figure 13 shows a first-grade word sort using words from Nancy Shaw's books *Sheep in a Jeep* (1986), *Sheep on a Ship* (1989), and *Sheep in a Shop* (1991). Children sorted the words according to three rimes—*eep, ip,* and *op.*

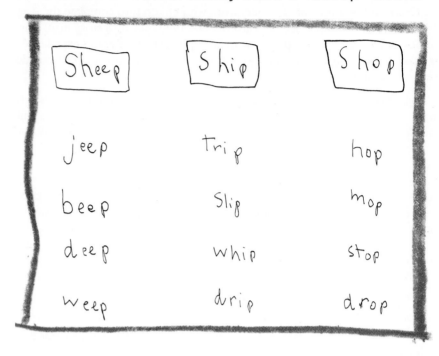

WORD WALLS

Word walls are alphabetized collections of words posted in the classroom that children can refer to when they are reading and writing and for word-study activities. Words for the word wall can be written on large sheets of butcher paper or on cards displayed in pocket charts, and they are often written in alphabetical order so that children can locate the words more easily.

Teachers have developed three types of word walls. One type is a high-frequency word wall, where primary teachers post the 100 highest-frequency words (Cunningham, 2000). A second type of word wall is a content-area word wall, on which teachers and children write important words related to the unit. A third type of word wall is a literature word wall, where teachers and children write interesting, confusing, and important words from the story they are reading. A literature word wall for *Sarah, Plain and Tall* (MacLachlan, 1985) is shown in Figure 14. The three types of word walls should be posted separately in the classroom because if the words are mixed, children will have difficulty categorizing them.

The steps in using a literature word wall are:

1. *Prepare the word wall.* Teachers hang a long sheet of butcher paper on a blank wall in the classroom and divide it into alphabetical categories. Or, teachers can display a large pocket chart on a classroom wall and prepare a stack of cards on which to write the words. Then they add the title of the book children are reading at the top of the word wall.

2. *Introduce the word wall.* Teachers introduce the word wall and add character names and several other key words during preparing activities before reading.

3. *Add words to the word wall.* After reading a picture book or after reading each chapter of a chapter book, children suggest additional "important" words for the

Figure 14   A Literature Word Wall for *Sarah, Plain and Tall*

AB	C	D	E
Anna	Caleb	dough	eagerly
biscuits	coarse	dunes	energetic
bonnet	carpenter		
ayuh	cruel		
	chores		
	collapsed		

FG	H	IJ	KL
gophers	hearthstones	Indian paintbrush	longing
feisty	homely		
fogbound	hollow		
	harshly		
	housekeeper		

M	NO	P	QR
mild mannered	nip	Papa	rascal
Maine	oyster	prairie	roamer
	offshore	paddock	
		pesky	
		preacher	
		pitchfork	

S	T	UVW	XYZ
sing	troublesome	widened	
Sarah	tumbleweed	woodchuck	
shovel	treaded (water)	wooly ragwort	
slippery		wild-eyed	
squall		windbreak	
suspenders		wretched	
shuffling			

word wall. Children and the teacher write the words in alphabetical categories on the butcher paper or on word cards, making sure to write large enough so that most children can see the words. Or, if a pocket chart is being used, children arrange the word cards in alphabetical order.

4. Use the word wall for exploring activities. Children use the word wall words for a variety of vocabulary activities, such as word sorts[C] and story maps[C]. Children also refer to the word wall when they are writing in reading logs[C] or working on projects.

For other types of word walls, teachers follow a similar approach to post words on the word walls and highlight the words through various activities.

WRITING GROUPS

During the revising stage of the writing process, children meet in writing groups to share their rough drafts and get feedback on how well they are communicating (Tompkins, 2000). Revising is probably the most difficult part of the writing process because it is difficult for children to evaluate their writing objectively. Children need to learn how to work together in writing groups and provide useful feedback to classmates. The steps are:

1. *Read drafts aloud.* Children take turns reading their rough drafts aloud to the group. Everyone listens politely, thinking about compliments and suggestions they will make after the writer finishes reading. Only the writer looks at the composition, because when classmates and teacher look at it they quickly notice and comment on mechanical errors, even though the emphasis during revising is on content. Listening as the writing is read aloud keeps the focus on content.

2. *Offer compliments.* After listening to the rough draft read aloud, classmates in the writing group offer compliments, telling the writer what they liked about the composition. These positive comments should be specific, focusing on strengths, rather than the often-heard "I liked it" or "It was good"; even though these are positive comments, they do not provide effective feedback. When teachers introduce revision, they should model appropriate responses because children may not know how to offer specific and meaningful comments. Teachers and children can brainstorm a list of appropriate comments and post it in the classroom for children to refer to. Comments may focus on organization, introductions, word choice, voice, sequence, dialogue, theme, and so on. Possible comments are:

> I like the part where . . .
> I'd like to know more about . . .
> I like the way you described . . .
> Your writing made me feel . . .
> I like the order you used in your writing because . . .

3. *Ask clarifying questions.* After a round of positive comments, writers ask for assistance with trouble spots they identified earlier when rereading their writing, or they may ask questions that reflect more general concerns about how well they are communicating. Admitting the need for help from one's classmates is a major step in learning to revise. Possible questions to ask classmates are:

> What do you want to know more about?
> Is there a part I should throw out?
> What details can I add?
> What do you think is the best part of my writing?
> Are there some words I need to change?

4. *Offer other revision suggestions.* Members of the writing group ask questions about things that were unclear to them and make suggestions about how to revise the composition. Almost any writer resists constructive criticism, and it is especially difficult for elementary children to appreciate suggestions. It is important to teach children what kinds of comments and suggestions are acceptable so that they will word what they say in helpful rather than hurtful ways. Possible comments and suggestions that children can offer are:

> I got confused in the part about . . .
> Do you need a closing?
> Could you add more about . . . ?
> I wonder if your paragraphs are in the right order because . . .
> Could you combine some sentences?

5. *Repeat the process.* The writing group members repeat the process so that all children have an opportunity to share their rough drafts. The first four steps are repeated for each child's composition. This is the appropriate time for teachers to provide input as well.

6. _Make plans for revision._ At the end of the writing group session, each child makes a commitment to revise his or her writing based on the comments and suggestions of the group members. The final decision on what to revise always rests with the writers themselves, but with the understanding that their rough drafts are not perfect comes the realization that some revision will be necessary. When children verbalize their planned revisions, they are more likely to complete the revision stage. Some children also make notes for themselves about their revision plans. After the group disbands, children make the revisions.

Professional References

Ashton-Warner, S. (1965). _Teacher._ New York: Simon & Schuster.

Atwell, N. (1987). _In the middle: Writing, reading, and learning with adolescents._ Portsmouth, NH: Heinemann.

Bear, D. R., Invernizzi, M., Templeton, S., & Johnston, F. (2000). _Words their way: Word study for phonics, vocabulary, and spelling instruction._ Upper Saddle River, NJ: Merrill/Prentice Hall.

Bromley, K. D. (1991). _Webbing with literature: Creating story maps with children's books._ Boston: Allyn & Bacon.

Button, K., Johnson, M. J., & Furgerson, P. (1996). Interactive writing in a primary classroom. _The Reading Teacher, 49,_ 446–454.

Claggett, F. (1992). _Drawing your own conclusions: Graphic strategies for reading, writing, and thinking._ Portsmouth, NH: Heinemann.

Clay, M. M. (1985). _The early detection of reading difficulties_ (3rd ed.). Portsmouth, NH: Heinemann.

Clay, M. M. (1991). _Becoming literate: The construction of inner control._ Portsmouth, NH: Heinemann.

Cunningham, P. M. (2000). _Phonics they use: Words for reading and writing_ (3rd ed.). New York: HarperCollins.

Cunningham, P. M., & Cunningham, J. W. (1992). Making words: Enhancing the invented spelling-decoding connection. _The Reading Teacher, 46,_ 106–115.

Depree, H., & Iversen, S. (1996). _Early literacy in the classroom: A new standard for young readers._ Bothell, WA: Wright Group.

Eeds, M., & Wells, D. (1989). Grand conversations: An exploration of meaning construction in literature study groups. _Research in the Teaching of English, 23,_ 4–29.

Elbow, P. (1973). _Writing without teachers._ London: Oxford University Press.

Fountas, I. C., & Pinnell, G. S. (1996). _Guided reading: Good first teaching for all children._ Portsmouth, NH: Heinemann.

Goldenberg, C. (1992/1993). Instructional conversations: Promoting comprehension through discussion. _The Reading Teacher, 46,_ 316–326.

Gunning, T. G. (1995). Word building: A strategic approach to the teaching of phonics. _The Reading Teacher, 48,_ 484–488.

Harste, J. C., Woodward, V. A., & Burke, C. L. (1984). _Language stories and literacy lessons._ Portsmouth, NH: Heinemann.

Head, M. H., & Readence, J. E. (1986). Anticipation guides: Meaning through prediction. In E. K. Dishner, T. W. Bean, J. E. Readence, & D. W. Moore (Eds.), _Reading in the content areas_ (2nd ed., pp. 229–234). Dubuque, IA: Kendall/Hunt.

Holdaway, D. (1979). _Foundations of literacy._ Aukland, NZ: Ashton Scholastic.

Johnson, T. D., & Louis, D. R. (1987). _Literacy through literature._ Portsmouth, NH: Heinemann.

Lee, D. M., & Allen, R. V. (1963). _Learning to read through experience_ (2nd ed.). New York: Meredith.

Macon, J. M., Bewell, D., & Vogt, M. E. (1991). _Responses to literature, grades K–8._ Newark, DE: International Reading Association.

Martinez, M., Roser, N. L., & Strecker, S. (1998/1999). "I never thought I could be a star": A readers theatre ticket to fluency. _The Reading Teacher, 52,_ 326–334.

McKenzie, G. R. (1979). Data charts: A crutch for helping pupils organize reports. _Language Arts, 56,_ 784–788.

Morris, D. (1982). "Word sort": A categorization strategy for improving word recognition. _Reading Psychology, 3,_ 247–259.

Ogle, D. M. (1986). K-W-L: A teaching model that develops active reading of expository text. _The Reading Teacher, 39,_ 564–570.

Ogle, D. M. (1989). The know, want to know, learn strategy. In K. D. Muth (Ed.), _Children's comprehension of text: Research into practice_ (pp. 205–223). Newark, DE: International Reading Association.

Peterson, R., & Eeds, M. (1990). _Grand conversations: Literature groups in action._ New York: Scholastic.

Rico, G. L. (1983). _Writing the natural way._ Los Angeles: Tarcher.

Samuels, S. J. (1979). The method of repeated readings. _The Reading Teacher, 32,_ 403–408.

Schlagal, R. C., & Schlagal, J. H. (1992). The integral character of spelling: Teaching strategies for multiple purposes. _Language Arts, 69,_ 418–424.

Stauffer, R. G. (1970). *The language experience approach to the teaching of reading.* New York: Harper & Row.

Stauffer, R. G. (1975). *Directing the reading-thinking process.* New York: Harper & Row.

Tompkins, G. E. (2000). *Teaching writing: Balancing process and product* (3rd ed.). Upper Saddle River, NJ: Merrill/Prentice Hall.

Children's Book References

Brett, J. (1999). *Gingerbread baby.* New York: Putnam.

Bunting, E. (1991). *Fly away home.* New York: Clarion.

Chester, J. (1995). *A for Antarctica.* New York: Tricycle.

Cohen, B. (1983). *Molly's pilgrim.* New York: Lothrop, Lee & Shepard.

Ehlert, L. (1989). *Eating the alphabet: Fruits and vegetables from A to Z.* Orlando, FL: Harcourt Brace Jovanovich.

Hutchins, P. (1968). *Rosie's walk.* New York: Macmillan.

MacLachlan, P. (1985). *Sarah, plain and tall.* New York: Harper & Row.

Meddaugh, S. (1995). *Hog-eye.* Boston: Houghton Mifflin.

Ness, E. (1966). *Sam, Bangs, and moonshine.* New York: Holt, Rinehart and Winston.

Shaw, N. (1986). *Sheep in a jeep.* Boston: Houghton Mifflin.

Shaw, N. (1989). *Sheep on a ship.* Boston: Houghton Mifflin.

Shaw, N. (1991). *Sheep in a shop.* Boston: Houghton Mifflin.

Van Allsburg, C. (1984). *The mysteries of Harris Burdick.* Boston: Houghton Mifflin.

GLOSSARY

Aesthetic reading   Reading for pleasure.

Affix   A morpheme added to the beginning (prefix) or end (suffix) of a word to change the word's meaning (e.g., *il-* in *illiterate* and *-al* in *national*).

Alphabetic principle   The assumption underlying alphabetical language systems that each sound has a corresponding graphic representation (or letter).

Antonyms   Words that mean the opposite (e.g., *good–bad*).

Applying   The fifth stage of the reading process, in which readers go beyond the text to use what they have learned in another literacy experience, often by making a project or reading another book.

Background knowledge   A child's knowledge or previous experiences about a topic.

Basal readers   Reading textbooks that are leveled according to grade.

Basal reader program   A collection of student textbooks, workbooks, teacher's manuals, and other materials and resources for reading instruction used in kindergarten through sixth grade.

Big books   Enlarged versions of picture books that teachers read with children, usually in the primary grades.

Blend   To combine the sounds represented by letters to pronounce a word.

Bound morpheme   A morpheme that is not a word and cannot stand alone (e.g., *-s, tri-*).

Closed syllable   A syllable ending in a consonant sound (e.g., *make, duck*).

Cloze procedure   An informal assessment activity in which words are strategically omitted from a text; readers use context to supply the missing words.

Cluster   A spiderlike diagram used to collect and organize ideas after reading or before writing; also called a map or a web.

Comprehension   The process of constructing meaning using both the author's text and the reader's background knowledge for a specific purpose.

Concepts about print   Basic understandings about the way print works, including the direction of print, spacing, punctuation, letters, and words.

Consonant digraph   Two adjacent consonants that represent a sound not represented by either consonant alone (e.g., *th–this, ch–chin, sh–wash, ph–telephone*).

Content area reading   Reading in social studies, science, and other areas of the curriculum.

Cueing systems   The phonological, semantic, syntactic, and pragmatic cues that students rely on as they read.

Decoding   Using word-identification strategies to pronounce and attach meaning to an unfamiliar word.

Diphthong   A sound produced when the tongue glides from one sound to another; it is represented by two vowels (e.g., *oy–boy, ou–house, ow–how*).

Drafting   The second stage of the writing process, in which writers pour out ideas in a rough draft.

Echo reading   The teacher or other reader reads a sentence and a group of students reread or "echo" what was read.

Editing   The fourth stage of the writing process, in which writers proofread to identify and correct spelling, capitalization, punctuation, and grammatical errors.

Efferent reading   Reading for information.

Elaborative processes   The component of comprehension that focuses on activating prior knowledge, making inferences, and connecting to the text being read.

Elkonin boxes   A strategy for segmenting sounds in a word that involves drawing a box to represent each sound in a word.

Emergent literacy   Children's early reading and writing development before conventional reading and writing.

Environmental print   Signs, labels, and other print found in the community.

Explicit instruction   Systematic instruction of concepts, strategies, and skills that builds from simple to complex.

Exploring   The fourth stage of the reading process, in which readers reread the text, study vocabulary words, and learn strategies and skills.

Expository text   Nonfiction writing.

Fluency   Reading smoothly, quickly, and with expression.

Free morpheme   A morpheme that can stand alone as a word (e.g., *book, cycle*).

Frustration level   The level of reading material that is too difficult for a child to read successfully.

Genre   A category of literature such as folklore, science fiction, biography, and historical fiction.

Goldilocks Strategy   A tool for choosing "just right" books.

Grand conversation   A small-group or whole-class discussion about literature.

Grapheme   A written representation of a sound using one or more letters.

Graphic organizers   Diagrams that provide organized, visual representations of information from texts.

Guided reading   Children work in small groups to read as independently as possible a text selected and introduced by the teacher.

High-frequency word   A common English word, usually a word among the 100 or 300 most common words.

Homographic homophones   Words that sound alike and are spelled alike but have different meanings (e.g., baseball *bat* and the animal *bat*).

Homographs   Words that are spelled alike but are pronounced differently (e.g., a *present* and to *present*).

Homonyms   Words that sound alike but are spelled differently (e.g., *sea–see, there–their–they're*); also called homophones.

Hyperbole   A stylistic device involving obvious exaggerations.

Imagery   The use of words and figurative language to create an impression.

Independent reading level   The level of reading material that a student can read independently with high comprehension and an accuracy level of 95–100%.

Inferential comprehension   Using background knowledge and determining relationships between objects and events in a text to draw conclusions not explicitly stated in the text.

Inflectional endings   Suffixes that express plurality or possession when added to a noun (e.g., *girls, girl's*), tense when added to a verb (e.g., *walked, walking*), or comparison when added to an adjective (e.g., *happier, happiest*).

Informal Reading Inventory (IRI)   An individually administered reading test composed of word lists and graded passages that is used to determine children's independent, instructional, and frustration levels and listening capacity levels.

Instructional reading level   The level of reading material that a child can read with teacher support and instruction with 90–94% accuracy.

Integrative processes   The component of comprehension that focuses on recognizing pronoun substitutions, synonyms, and cohesive ties between sentences in a paragraph.

Interactive writing   A writing activity in which children and the teacher write a text together, with the students taking turns to do most of the writing themselves.

Invented spelling   Children's attempts to spell words that reflect their developing knowledge about the spelling system.

K-W-L   An activity to activate background knowledge and set purposes for reading an informational text and to bring closure after reading. The letters stand for What I (we) K̲now, What I (we) W̲onder (or W̲ant to Learn), and What I (we) L̲earned.

Language Experience Approach (LEA)   A child's oral composition is written by the teacher and used as a text for reading instruction; it is usually used with beginning readers.

Leveling books   A method of estimating the difficulty level of a text.

Listening comprehension level   The highest level of graded passage that can be comprehended well when read aloud to the student.

Literacy   The ability to read and write.

Literal comprehension   The understanding of what is explicitly stated in a text.

Literature circle   An instructional approach in which children meet in small groups to read and respond to a book.

Literature focus unit   An approach to reading instruction in which the whole class reads and responds to a piece of literature.

Long vowels   The vowel sounds that are also names of the alphabet letters: $/\bar{a}/$ as in *make*, $/\bar{e}/$ as in *feet*, $/\bar{\imath}/$ as in *ice*, $/\bar{o}/$ as in *coat*, and $/\bar{u}/$ as in *flute*.

Lowercase letters   The letters in manuscript and cursive handwriting that are smaller and usually different from uppercase letters.

Macroprocesses   The component of comprehension that focuses on the big ideas in the text.

Metacognition   Children's thinking about their own thought and learning processes.

Metacognitive processes   The component of comprehension that focuses on children's use of strategies.

Metaphor   A comparison expressed directly, without using *like* or *as*.

Microprocesses   The component of comprehension that focuses on fluency and chunking words into idea units when reading.

Minilesson   Explicit instruction about literacy procedures, concepts, strategies, and skills that are taught to individual students, small groups, or the whole class, depending on students' needs.

Miscue analysis   A strategy for categorizing and analyzing a child's oral reading errors.

Morpheme   The smallest meaningful part of a word; sometimes it is a word (e.g., *cup, hope*), and sometimes it is not a whole word (e.g., *-ly, bi-*).

Narrative   A story.

Onset   The part of a syllable (or one-syllable word) that comes before the vowel (e.g., *str* in *string*).

Open syllable   A syllable ending in a vowel sound (e.g., *sea*).

Orthography   The spelling system.

Phoneme   A sound; it is represented in print with slashes (e.g., /s/ and /th/).

Phoneme-grapheme correspondence   The relationship between a sound and the letter that represents it.

Phonemic awareness   The ability to manipulate the sounds in words orally.

Phonics   Instruction about phoneme-grapheme correspondences and spelling rules.

Phonology   The sound system of language.

Polysyllabic   Words containing more than one syllable.

Pragmatics   The social use system of language.

Prediction   A strategy in which children state what they think will happen in a story and then read to verify their guesses.

Prefix   A morpheme added to the beginning of a word to change the word's meaning (e.g., *re-* in *reread*).

Prereading   The first stage of the reading process, in which readers activate background knowledge, set purposes, and make plans for reading.

Prewriting   The first stage of the writing process, in which writers gather and organize ideas for writing.

Proofreading   Reading a composition to identify and correct spelling and other mechanical errors.

Publishing   The fifth stage of the writing process, in which writers make the final copy of their writing and share it with an audience.

Quickwrite   A writing activity in which children write on a topic for 5–10 minutes without stopping.

Readability formula   A method of estimating the difficulty level of a text.

Reading   The second stage of the reading process, in which readers read the text for the first time using independent reading, shared reading, or guided reading, or by listening to it read aloud.

Reading workshop   An approach in which children read self-selected texts independently.

Responding   The third stage of the reading process, in which readers respond to the text, often through grand conversations and by writing in reading logs.

Revising   The third stage of the writing process, in which writers clarify meaning in the writing.

Rhyming   Words with the same rime sound (e.g., *white, bright*).

Rime   The part of a syllable (or one-syllable word) that begins with the vowel (e.g., *ing* in *string*).

Scaffolding   The support a teacher provides to children as they read and write.

Segment   To pronounce a word slowly, saying each sound distinctly.

Semantics   The meaning system of language.

Shared reading   The teacher reads a book aloud with a group of children as they follow along in the text, often using a big book.

Short vowels   The vowel sounds represented by /ă/ as in *cat*, /ĕ/ as in *bed*, /ĭ/ as in *big*, /ŏ/ as in *hop*, and /ŭ/ as in *cut*.

Simile   A comparison expressed using *like* or *as*.

Strategy   Problem-solving behaviors that children use in reading and writing, such as predicting, monitoring, visualizing, and summarizing.

Suffix   A morpheme added to the end of a word to change the word's meaning (e.g., *-y* in *hairy*, *-ful* in *careful*).

Sustained Silent Reading (SSR)   Independent reading practice for 20–30 minutes in which everyone in the class or in the school stops and spends time reading a self-selected book.

Syllable   The written representation of an uninterrupted segment of speech that includes a vowel sound (e.g., *get, a-bout, but-ter-fly, con-sti-tu-tion*).

Symbol   The author's use of an object to represent something else.

Synonyms   Words that mean nearly the same thing (e.g., *road–street*).

Syntax   The structural system of language or grammar.

Trade book   A published book that is not a textbook; the type of books in bookstores and libraries.

Uppercase letters   The letters in manuscript and cursive handwriting that are larger and are used as first letters in a name or at the beginning of a sentence.

Vowel   A voiced speech sound made without friction or stoppage of the airflow as it passes through the vocal tract.

Vowel digraph   Two or more adjacent vowels in a syllable that represent a single sound (e.g., *bread, eight, pain, saw*).

Whole-part-whole   An instructional sequence that begins with reading or writing authentic texts (the first whole), continues with teaching concepts, strategies, or skills using examples drawn from the texts (the part), and ends with applying the newly learned information in more reading or writing activities (the second whole).

Word families Groups of words that rhyme (e.g., *ball, call, fall, hall, mall, tall,* and *wall*).

Word identification Strategies that children use to decode words, such as phonic analysis, analogies, syllabic analysis, and morphemic analysis.

Word sort A word study activity in which children group words into categories.

Word wall An alphabetized chart posted in the classroom listing words students are learning.

Writing process The process in which children use prewriting, drafting, revising, editing, and publishing to develop and refine a composition.

Writing workshop An approach in which children use the writing process to write books and other compositions on self-selected topics.

Zone of proximal development The distance between a child's actual developmental level and his or her potential developmental level that can be reached with scaffolding by the teacher or classmates.

AUTHOR AND TITLE INDEX

SUBJECT INDEX

Purposes
  of reading, 6, 272, 273
  of writing, 268, 307
Purpose setting, 272–273

"Quaker readings," 384
Qualitative Inventory of Spelling
  Development, 80
Questions
  clarifying, 206
  in grand conversation, 370
  for writing groups, 394
Quickdrawing, 343
Quickwriting, 168, 274, 275, 343,
  381–382
  on text-to-self connections, 208
Quilts, 382–383
  in classroom vignette, 331, 332

Rate of reading, 160
Read-arounds, 166, 384
Reader response learning theories, 4, 6
Readers theatre, 17, 166, 384
Readiness activities, 38
Reading. *See also* Beginning reading and
  writing; Emergent reading and
  writing; Fluent reading and writing
  stage; Guided reading; Prereading;
  Shared reading; Literacy
  buddy, 166, 281–283, 286
  choral, 17, 145, 163, 164, 166, 260,
    365–366
  echo, 166, 365
  independent, 16, 19–20, 179–180,
    277, 279, 281, 286, 389
  in instructional programs, 291
  interactive, 16, 17–18
  and interactive learning theories, 5
  modeled, 16–17
  purposes of, 6, 272, 273
  repeated, 163, 386
  round-robin, 166
  screen, 166, 167
  small-group, 365
  and spelling, 128, 135
  and vocabulary development, 176,
    177, 179–180, 182
  and writing, 168, 306, 308, 327
Reading aloud to children, 178–179,
  180–181, 183, 285, 286, 385
  in thematic unit, 355
Reading center, in classroom
  vignette, 230
Reading development. *See also*
  Beginning reading and writing;
  Emergent reading and writing;

Fluent reading and writing stage;
  Literacy development
  "fourth-grade slump" in, 159–160
  and letter knowledge, 43, 45
  Mathew effect in, 182
  stages of, 46–49, 55–57
  and writing, 327
Reading fluency, 147, 160, 162
  assessment of, 169
  effective practices for, 170
  promoting of, 163–166
  and word identification, 152,
    154–160, 161
  and word recognition, 147–152, 160
Reading instruction
  on comprehension, 205
  as organized through reading
    process, 289–297
  promoting fluency, 163–166
  on strategies and skills, 220–224
Reading Is Fundamental (RIF), 29
Reading level, determination of,
  74–76, 77
Reading logs, 12, 23, 25, 285,
  385–386
  in classroom vignette, 200
  in grand conversation, 370
  in interactive electronic books, 54
  as work samples, 82
  in writing center, 322, 324
Reading practice, 164–165, 166
Reading process, 271
  classroom vignette on (Mrs. Ohashi),
    265–270, 271, 288
  effective practices in teaching of, 297
  instruction organized through,
    289–297
  stage 1 of (prereading), 167, 265,
    271–274, 276, 280, 291, 326
  stage 2 of (reading), 265, 272,
    274–285, 326
  stage 3 of (responding), 266, 272,
    276, 280, 285–287, 291,
    326, 385
  stage 4 of (exploring), 266, 272,
    276, 280, 287–288, 291, 326
  stage 5 of (applying), 272, 276, 280,
    288–289, 291, 326
  writing process as similar to, 323–327
Reading projects, 289
Reading Rainbow programs, 167
Reading rate, 160
Reading Recovery teachers, 74, 76
Reading and rereading literacy
  center, 267
Reading the Room literacy center, 37

Reading skills. *See* Skills
Reading speed, improvement of, 163
Reading stage of reading process, 272,
  274–285
  in classroom vignette, 265
  in comparison with writing, 326
  in guided reading lesson, 280
  in shared reading lesson, 276
Reading strategies. *See* Strategies
Reading workshop, 20, 23, 161, 281,
  291, 292–294, 331
  in thematic unit, 357
Reading-writing connection, 161
Realistic fiction, 238–239, 240
Reflection, on skill or strategy, 221
Repeated readings, 163, 386
Repetend, 348
Repetition
  and beginning readers, 75
  in cumulative tales, 235
  in writing poems, 258
Repetitive sentences, in predictable
  books, 277, 278
Reports
  collaborative, 346, 367–368
  individual, 347, 371–372
Rereading, 281, 287
Researching
  designing questions for, 372
  on Internet, 346–347
Research literacy center, 37
Research projects, 289
Responding stage, 272, 285–287
  in classroom vignette, 266
  in comparison of reading and
    writing, 326
  in guided reading lesson, 280
  in instructional programs, 291
  in reading aloud, 385
  in shared reading lesson, 276
Response, in community of learners,
  12, 13
Responsibility, in community of
  learners, 11–12
Restaurant center, 42
Retelling center, 146
Reversed letters, 230
Revising conferences, 83
Revising stage, 307, 310–312
  and adaptation of writing
    process, 319
  in comparison of reading and
    writing, 326
  for emergent writers, 320
  and writing group, 393–395
Revisions, types of, 312